위아텝스
실전모의고사
3

위아텝스 실전모의고사 3 Intermediate

지은이 EMD MEDIA

펴낸곳 (주)위아북스
펴낸이 전수용·조상현
기획책임 최상호
편집팀 권수아
영업마케팅 신철호, 김민아

등록번호 제300-2007-164호
주소 서울특별시 마포구 합정동 359-1 정촌빌딩 1층
전화 02-725-9988 ● **팩스** 02-725-9863
홈페이지 www.wearebooks.co.kr

디자인 나인플럭스
제작 정민문화사
출력 우성 C&P

ISBN 978-89-93258-55-4 18740

위아텝스
실전모의고사

700+ **3** Intermediate

EMD MEDIA 지음

We're
위아북스

TEPS는 Test of English Proficiency developed by Seoul National University의 약자로 서울대학교에서 개발한 한국형 영어능력 측정시험입니다. 1999년 처음 시행된 이래로 많은 기업체는 물론 대학 및 대학원 심지어는 특목고 입시에까지 적용됨으로써 그 활용도가 갈수록 높아지고 있습니다.

텝스는 기존의 영어 시험들과는 달리 일상생활에서 누구나 쉽게 접할 수 있는 상황에 바탕을 둔 실용 영어에 중점을 두고 있을 뿐만 아니라 내용면에서도 다양한 주제를 바탕으로 수준 높은 내용을 다루고 있기 때문에 체계적으로 학습하지 않으면 고득점을 얻기 어려운 시험이라고 할 수 있습니다.

무릇 성적을 매기는 영어시험을 치르는 사람들은 누구나 고득점을 얻고자 합니다. 그러나 노력하지 않고는 누구나 고득점을 얻지 못합니다. 그렇다면 고득점이라는 목표에 도달하기 위해서 가장 먼저 무엇을 준비해야 할까요? 그것은 바로 그 시험에 대해 '제대로 아는 것' 입니다. '제대로 아는 것' 다음에는 '친숙해지는 것' 이 필요합니다.

다시 말하자면, 텝스가 무엇을 평가하는 시험인지 먼저 살펴본 다음, 실제 시험 유형에 자꾸 부딪쳐 보면서 실전 감각을 키우는 것이 중요하다는 이야기입니다.

이 책은 텝스 시험을 치러야 하는 학습자들이 매번 전과정을 소화하는 데 무려 3시간씩이나 투여해야 하는 번거로움을 덜어주면서 짧은 시간에 반복시행을 통해 텝스에 쉽게 적응할 수 있도록 개발한 것입니다.

12회분으로 구성된 Actual Test는 실제 텝스 시험을 본다는 느낌으로 매회 풀어나갈 수 있도록 학습시간과 문항수를 고려하여 학습용으로 축소해 놓은 것입니다. Actual Test는 각각 40문항으로 구성되어 있는데, 어느 부분이든 5회분의 모의고사를 모으면 하나의 완전한 텝스 세트가 됩니다. 적은 분량이지만 12회분의 모의고사를 푸는 동안 실전 감각을 익힐 수 있습니다.

그런 다음 그래도 염려스러워서 마지막으로 100문항으로 구성된 Half Test를 연습함으로써 장시간 긴장감을 유지하는 훈련을 거치도록 배려했습니다.

또 한 가지 이 책을 활용하려면 Actual Test 1회당 200점 만점으로 계산하는데, 청해 12문항×7점=84점, 문법 10문항×2=20점, 어휘 10문항×2=20점, 독해 8문항×9점 =72점을 모두 더한 점수(196점)에 4점을 첨가하면 됩니다. 이것을 5회분 모으면 1,000점 으로서 실제 텝스 채점과 매우 가까운 점수 계산법이 됩니다.

텝스는 결코 만만하게 볼 시험이 아닙니다. 막연하게 열심히 공부하는 것만으로는 원하는 목표를 달성할 수 없습니다. 평소에 텝스에서 제시되는 영어 상황에 스스로를 노출시켜야 함은 물론 반드시 실제 텝스 시험과 같은 환경을 반복해서 경험해봄으로써 시험장에서 당황하지 않고 시험에 임할 수 있는 것입니다.

잘 모르는 길을 혼자서 빠른 시간 안에 가기는 쉽지 않습니다. 이 때에 지도가 있거나 그 길을 먼저 가본 사람들의 조언을 들어보면 혼자일 때보다는 훨씬 그 길이 수월해지겠지요. 그렇게 몇 번을 가다 보면 어느새 그 길이 친숙해져서 더 빠른 시간에 갈 수 있게 되고, 그런 반복이 계속되는 어느 순간에는 눈 감고도 찾아갈 수 있을 정도가 될 것입니다.

텝스를 준비하는 모든 분들에게 이 책이 흥미로운 지도가 되고, 따스한 조언자가 될 수 있기를 간절히 바랍니다. 또한 독자 여러분은 이 책을 이용하여 자신이 바라는 만큼의 성과를 반드시 얻을 수 있게 되기를 기원합니다.

EMD MEDIA

Contents 차례

TEPS란 Test of English Proficiency developed by Seoul National University의 약자로 서울대학교 언어교육원에서 개발하고 TEPS관리위원회에서 주관·시행하는 국가 공인 영어시험입니다.

▶ TEPS는 서울대학교 언어교육원이 다년간의 연구를 통해 개발한 영어 능력 평가시험입니다.

▶ 서울대학교 언어교육원은 대한민국 정부가 공인하는 외국어 능력 측정기관으로 32년간 정부기관, 각급 단체 및 기업체를 대상으로 어학 능력을 측정해 왔습니다.

▶ TEPS는 국내외 유수한 대학에 종사하는 최고 수준의 영어 관련 전문가 100여 명이 참여해 문제를 출제하고 세계적인 권위자로 구성된 자문위원회에서 검토하는 시험입니다.

▶ TEPS는 청해·문법·어휘·독해에 걸쳐 총 200문항, 990점 만점의 시험입니다.

▶ TEPS는 언어 테스팅 분야의 세계적인 권위자 Bachman 교수(미국 UCLA)와 Oller 교수(미국 뉴멕시코대)에게서 타당성을 검증받았으며, 여러 번의 시험적 평가에서 이미 그 신뢰도와 타당도가 입증된 시험입니다.

▶ TEPS는 우리나라 사람들의 살아 있는 영어 실력, 즉 의사소통 능력을 가장 효과적이고 정확하게 측정해 주는 시험이라고 할 수 있습니다. TEPS는 진정한 실력자와 비실력자를 확실히 구분할 수 있도록 구성된 시험으로서 변별력에 있어서 본인의 정확한 실력 파악에 실제적인 도움이 됩니다. 또한 TEPS 성적표는 수험생의 영어 능력을 영역별로 세분화한 평가를 해 주기 때문에 수험자가 어느 영역에서 탁월한지 잘 알 수 있을 뿐만 아니라 효과적인 영어 공부 방향을 제시해 주기도 합니다.

▶ TEPS는 다양하고 일반적인 영어 능력을 평가하는 시험으로 대학교, 기업체, 각종 기관 및 단체, 개인이 다양한 목적을 위해 응시할 수 있는 시험입니다.

TEPS의 구성

TEPS는 청해·문법·어휘·독해 4개 영역에 걸쳐 총 200문항으로 구성되어 있으며 시험 시간은 약 2시간 20분입니다. 만점은 문항반응이론에 따라 채점하기 때문에 990점입니다.

영역	Part별 내용		문항 수	시간 / 배점
청해 Listening Comprehension	Part I	문장 하나를 듣고 이어질 대화 고르기	15	55분 / 396점
	Part II	3 문장의 대화를 듣고 이어질 대화 고르기	15	
	Part III	6-8 문장의 대화를 듣고 이어질 대화 고르기	15	
	Part IV	담화문의 내용을 듣고 질문에 해당하는 답 고르기	15	
문법 Grammar	Part I	대화문의 빈칸에 적절한 표현 고르기	20	25분 / 99점
	Part II	문장의 빈칸에 적절한 표현 고르기	20	
	Part III	대화에서 어법상 틀리거나 어색한 부분 고르기	5	
	Part IV	단문에서 문법상 틀리거나 어색한 부분 고르기	5	
어휘 Vocabulary	Part I	대화문의 빈칸에 적절한 단어 고르기	25	15분 / 99점
	Part II	단문의 빈칸에 적절한 단어 고르기	25	
독해 Reading Comprehension	Part I	지문을 읽고 질문의 빈칸에 들어갈 내용 고르기	16	45분 / 396점
	Part II	지문을 읽고 질문에 가장 적절한 내용 고르기	21	
	Part III	지문을 읽고 문맥상 어색한 내용 고르기	3	

TEPS 등급표

등급	점수	영역	능력검정기준
1+급 Level 1+	901 – 990	전반	**외국인으로서 최상급 수준의 의사소통 능력:** 교양 있는 원어민에 버금가는 정도로 의사소통이 가능하고 전문 분야 업무에 대처할 수 있음 (Native Level of Communicative Competence)
	361 – 400	청해	교양 있는 원어민에 버금가는 수준의 청해력
		독해	교양 있는 원어민에 버금가는 수준의 독해력
	91 – 100	문법	교양 있는 원어민에 버금가는 수준으로 내재화된 문법능력
		어휘	교양 있는 원어민에 버금가는 수준으로 내재화된 어휘력
1급 Level 1	801 – 900	전반	**외국인으로서 거의 최상급 수준의 의사소통 능력:** 단기간 집중 교육을 받으면 대부분의 의사소통이 가능하고 전문 분야 업무에 별 무리 없이 대처할 수 있음 (Near-Native Level of Communicative Competence)
	321 – 360	청해	다양한 상황의 수준 높은 내용을 별 무리 없이 이해할 수 있는 정도의 청해력
		독해	다양한 소재의 수준 높은 내용을 별 무리 없이 이해할 수 있는 정도의 독해력
	81 – 90	문법	다양한 구문을 별 무리 없이 신속하게 이해할 수 있을 정도로 내재화된 문법 능력
		어휘	다양한 표현을 별 무리 없이 신속하게 이해할 수 있을 정도로 내재화된 어휘력
2+급 Level 2+	701 – 800	전반	**외국인으로서 최상급 수준의 의사소통 능력:** 교양 있는 원어민에 버금가는 정도로 의사소통이 가능하고 전문 분야 업무에 대처할 수 있음 (Native Level of Communicative Competence)
	281 – 320	청해	일반적 상황에 보통 수준의 내용을 별 무리 없이 이해하는 정도의 청해력
		독해	일반적 소재에 보통수준의 내용을 별 무리 없이 이해하는 정도의 독해력
	71 – 80	문법	일반적인 구문을 별 무리 없이 이해하는 정도의 문법 능력
		어휘	일반적인 표현을 별 무리 없이 이해하는 정도의 어휘력
2급 Level 2	601 – 700	전반	**외국인으로서 중상급 수준의 의사소통 능력:** 중장기간 집중 교육을 받으면 일반 분야 업무를 큰 어려움 없이 수행할 수 있음 (High Intermediate Level of Communicative Competence)
	241 – 280	청해	일반적 상황에 보통 수준의 내용을 대체로 이해하는 정도의 청해력
		독해	일반적 소재에 보통수준의 내용을 대체로 이해하는 정도의 독해력
	61 – 70	문법	일반적인 구문을 대체로 이해하는 정도의 문법 능력
		어휘	일반적인 표현을 대체로 이해하는 정도의 어휘력

등급	점수	영역	능력검정기준
3⁺급 Level 3+	501 – 600	전반	**외국인으로서 중급 수준의 의사소통 능력:** 중장기간 집중 교육을 받으면 한정된 분야의 업무를 큰 어려움 없이 수행할 수 있음 (Mid Intermediate Level of Communicative Competence)
	201 – 240	청해	일반적 상황에 보통 수준의 내용을 다소 이해하는 정도의 청해력
		독해	일반적 소재에 보통 수준의 내용을 다소 이해하는 정도의 독해력
	51 – 60	문법	일반적인 구문에 대한 의미파악이 어느 정도 가능한 문법 능력
		어휘	일반적인 표현에 대한 의미파악이 어느 정도 가능한 어휘력
3급 Level 3	401 – 500	전반	**외국인으로서 중하급 수준의 의사소통 능력:** 중장기간 집중 교육을 받으면 한정된 분야의 업무를 다소 미흡하지만 큰 지장은 없이 수행할 수 있음 (Low Intermediate Level of Communicative Competence)
	161 – 200	청해	일반적 상황에 보통수준의 내용을 이해하기 다소 어려운 정도의 청해력
		독해	일반적 소재에 보통수준의 내용을 이해하기 다소 어려운 정도의 독해력
	41 – 50	문법	일반적 구문에 대한 신속한 의미 파악이 다소 어려운 정도의 문법 능력
		어휘	일반적인 표현에 대한 신속한 의미 파악이 다소 어려운 정도의 어휘력
4⁺급 Level 4+	301 – 400 201 – 300	전반	**외국인으로서 하급 수준의 의사소통 능력:** 장기간의 집중 교육을 받으면 한정된 분야의 업무를 대체로 어렵게 수행할 수 있음 (Novice Level of Communicative Competence)
5⁺급 Level 4+	101 – 200 10 – 100	전반	**외국인으로서 최하급 수준의 의사소통 능력:** 단편적인 지식만을 갖추고 있어 의사소통이 거의 불가능함 (Near–Zero Level of Communicative Competence)

이 책의 구성과 특징

TEPS TIPS • 문법

문법에 관한 Tip은 여러 가지가 있겠으나 여기서는 현장, 즉 시험장에서 반드시 알고 있어야만 하는 필수 문법사항을 12회에 걸쳐서 제시한다. 이미 기본적인 문법사항은 알고 있기 때문에 혼동하기 쉽거나 자주 착각하는 사항을 간단한 설명과 짧은 예문 또는 짧은 문제로 구성해서 제시하고 있다.

TEPS TIPS • 어휘·표현 정리

청해는 물론 어휘, 문법, 독해에 반드시 필요한 어휘와 표현을 주제별 또는 영역별로 정리하여 제시하고 있다. 자주 나오는 표현과 그에 대한 답변, 2어 동사와 구동사, Collocations와 함께 꼭 알아두어야 할 Idoms까지 소개하고, 정치, 경제, 사회, 과학 등 주요 영역별 단어를 소개함으로써 텝스에 대비하는 미니단어장 역할을 한다.

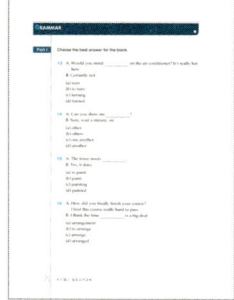

Actual Test • 1〜12회

텝스는 한번 시험보기에 3시간가량의 시간과 공간적 환경을 필요로 하기에 실제 시험보기 전에는 적응하기가 매우 어렵다. 따라서 여기서는 학습시간과 문항수를 고려하여 텝스의 최소단위를 반복적으로 제시함으로써 텝스에 익숙해지도록 만들어준다. Actual Test 1회당 200점 만점으로 계산하는데, 청해 12문항×7점=84점, 문법 10문항×2=20점, 어휘 10문항×2=20점, 독해 8문항×9점=72점을 모두 더한 점수(196점)에 4점을 첨가하면 된다. 이것을 5회분 모으면 1,000점으로서 실제 텝스 채점과 매우 가까운 점수 계산법이 된다.

Answer Key • 적절한 번역, 탄탄한 해설, 상세한 어휘풀이

청해, 문법, 어휘, 독해 각각의 영역마다 그에 꼭 알맞은 해설을 제시한다. 영어의 특성과 우리말의 차별성을 뛰어넘는 적절한 해석과 꼭 필요한 부분을 속 시원하게 풀어주는 탄탄한 해설 그리고 풍부한 어휘풀이를 통해 문제를 풀면서, 채점하면서, 복습하면서도 공부가 되도록 만든다. 그리고 부피를 줄이기 위해서 불필요한 군더더기 부분을 과감히 삭제하고, 해설집으로서 꼭 필요한 요소만으로 해설집을 구성했다.

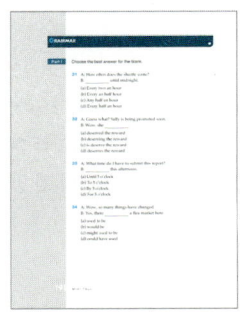

Actual Test 100 • 실제 문제와 더 가까워진 최종 확인

최소단위 Actual Test를 통해 텝스의 모든 것을 쉽게 알 수 있었지만, 실제 시험장에서 3시간 가까이 집중력을 유지하는 것도 쉬운 일은 아니다. 따라서 실제의 절반 정도의 시간을 투자해봄으로써 시험장 감각을 익혀 두도록 한다. 또한 요즘 일어나고 있는 현실적 이슈들을 문제화하여 제시함으로써 나중에 실제 시험에서 나올 법한 유망한 예상문제를 제공한다. Actual Test 100은 말 그대로 100문항으로 구성되는데, 청해 30문항×13점=390점, 문법 25문항×4=100점, 어휘 25문항×4=100점, 독해 20문항×20점=400점을 모두 더하면 990점으로 실제 텝스의 점수와 유사하게 된다. 그러나 이것은 편의상의 계산이므로 계산된 점수는 참고용으로 이용하기 바란다.

MP3 CD • 청해용

실제 텝스 시험과 똑같은 구성으로 청해용 CD를 제공한다. 외국인의 어조, 말하는 속도까지 실제 시험과 같은 청해 환경을 제공한다.

TEPS 파트별 공략법

청해는 총 60문제로 대화와 담화를 중심으로 이루어진다. 빠른 시간 안에 의미를 파악할 수 있으려면 상황별, 기능별로 많이 등장하는 어휘와 표현들을 충분히 익혀두어야 한다. 또한 어휘나 표현들을 학습할 때에는 서로 연관되는 것들을 함께 학습하고, 뉘앙스나 문맥도 고려하여 학습하는 것이 고득점을 얻기 위한 중요한 기초가 된다.

Part 1 (15문항)

A-B 형태의 대화에서 B에 들어갈 문장을 고르는 문제로 순발력을 요구하는 문제이다. 주로 Yes-No Questions, 의문사를 이용한 의문문, 평서문에 이어지는 응답을 고르는 문제들이 출제되는데 함정에 주의해야 한다. 예를 들면 Yes-No Questions라고 해서 꼭 Yes나 No로 정답이 정해져 있다는 것은 아니며, when으로 물어보았다고 해서 시점에 해당하는 응답이 나오는 것만은 아니라는 뜻이다. 따라서 집중력을 가지고 전체 문장을 듣고 뜻을 파악하려고 노력하는 것이 중요한데, 만약 그것이 쉽지 않을 경우 문장의 첫 부분이라도 기억해 두면 의외로 답을 쉽게 고를 수 있는 경우도 있다.

Part 2 (15문항)

A-B-A-B 형태의 대화에서 마지막 B에 들어갈 문장을 고르는 문제이다. Part 1과 유형은 같으나 길이가 길어진 형태라고 볼 수 있다. 대화의 전반적인 내용을 파악하는 것도 중요하지만 그것이 부담이 된다면 마지막 화자의 대사는 반드시 놓치지 않도록 집중해서 들어야 한다. 또한 대화에서 나온 단어가 보기에서 반복이 될 경우 정답으로 고르기 쉬운데, 함정일 경우가 많으므로 주의해야 한다.

Part 3 (15문항)

Part 1, 2와는 달리 긴 대화를 들려주고 질문을 들려준 뒤 질문에 대한 답을 고르는 문제이다. 대화의 길이는 2.5 turn에서 4 turn까지 다양하다. 대화뿐만 아니라 질문도 집중해서 들어야 정답을 고를 수 있다. Part 1, 2와는 달리 대화를 두 번 들려주기 때문에 처음 들으면서 전반적인 내용을 파악하고 질문을 들은 다음 어느 부분에 초점을 맞추어야 하는지 파악한 뒤 두 번째로 들을 때 정답을 찾아낼 수 있도록 한다. 질문의 경우 전반적인 내용을 파악하는 문제, 세부 내용을 파악하는 문제, 추론문제가 나온다.

Part 4 (15문항)

담화문을 들려주고 질문을 들려준 뒤 질문에 대한 답을 고르는 문제이다. Part 3과 마찬가지로 두 번씩 들려준다. 담화는 안내방송, 강의, 뉴스, 광고, TV 프로그램, 인터뷰 등 다양하다. 문제 유형은 Part 3과 마찬가지로 전반적인 내용을 묻는 문제, 세부 사항을 파악하는 문제, 추론 문제가 나온다. 특히 세부 사항을 파악하는 문제의 경우 담화를 듣는 중간 중간 필요한 내용을 메모하는 것이 좋다.

문법은 총 50문항으로 구성되어 있으며 25분에 풀어야 한다. 쉬운 문제는 의도적으로 문법 규칙을 적용하기보다는 평소에 많이 접해서 입에 붙어있는 수준을 묻는 중1 수준의 문제에서부터 동사의 특징을 생각하고 문장의 구조와 어순을 생각해야 하는 고난도 문제까지 다양하다. 출제 비중은 문법별로 동사에 관련된 문제가 가장 많고 명사, 관사에 관련된 것도 빠지지 않고 출제되고 있다. 전반적으로 다양한 문법을 다루고 있어서 파트별 공략법이 크게 달라지는 것은 아니지만 세부적으로 관찰해 보면 출제자의 의도를 읽을 수 있는 부분이 있다. 자주 나오는 문법 목록으로는 시제를 포함한 동사관련 문제가 50% 이상이며, 다음으로 명사, 형용사, 접속사, 전치사순으로 출제되고 있다.

Part 1 (20문항)

구어체 문장 표현을 묻기 때문에 평소에 자주 쓰이는 간단한 회화체 표현을 많이 알아두는 것이 좋다.

Part 2 (20문항)

본격적인 난이도로 문어체 표현을 통해 다양한 문법요소를 묻기 때문에 빈칸이 있는 문제와 선택지를 동시에 보면서 거꾸로 대입시키며 문법규칙을 적용시켜가는 것이 시간을 줄이는 방법이다.

Part 3 (5문항)

대화체 표현 중에서 흔히 나오는 문법적 오류를 찾는 문제로 대화를 읽고 난 후 동사의 태나 시제, 수일치 정도에서 크게 눈에 띄는 오류를 찾지 못했을 경우엔 명사의 가산성과 관사에 초점을 맞춰 볼 것을 권한다.

Part 4 (5문항)

4문장으로 구성된 문어체 문장에서 오류를 찾아내는 문제로 역시 Part 3을 공략했던 방법과 같은 방식으로 마지막 명사와 관사, 시제까지 확인 할 필요가 있다.

어휘 문제는 총 50문제로 구어체에서 많이 쓰이는 어휘, 연어, 구동사(동사+전치사 or 부사), 관용어, 형태·의미가 혼동되는 어휘, 이디엄, 문어체에서 많이 쓰이는 어휘 등을 중심으로 출제가 되고 있다. 따라서 어휘를 단편적으로 학습하는 것은 별로 도움이 되지 않고 문맥을 통한 학습이 이루어져야 문제를 정확하게 풀 수 있다.

Part 1 (25문항)

A-B 형태로 된 대화 가운데 빈 칸에 가장 알맞은 단어를 고르는 문제이다. 주로 구어체에 많이 등장하는 어휘들을 묻는 형태로서 청해 파트에서 다루는 대화 상황과 크게 다르지 않으므로 청해 파트에서 자주 등장하는 단어와 문장들을 학습해두면 어휘 Part 1에도 큰 도움이 될 것이다.

Part 2 (25문항)

하나 또는 두 개의 서술문 가운데 빈 칸에 가장 적절한 단어를 넣는 문제이다. Part 1과는 달리 문어체 문제가 주로 출제된다. 문맥을 통해 빈 칸에 들어갈 어휘를 추론하는 능력이 중요하므로 어휘를 학습할 때에는 함께 쓰이는 어휘와 그 어휘가 사용된 예문들을 같이 살펴보는 방식의 학습이 중요하다.

독해

Part 1 (빈칸 넣기, 16문항)

빈 칸 채우기 문제는 16문제로 구성되어 있으며, 학습자들이 가장 어렵게 느끼는 부분일 것이다. 대부분의 빈 칸은 주제문이나 정리하는 문장에 해당되는 앞이나, 뒤에 있고 드물게 중간에 오는 경우가 있다. 앞에 오는 경우도 15% 이하로 출제 되면서 비중이 낮다. 앞에 나오는 빈칸은 보통 빈칸 이후 2~3줄 정도만 읽어서 답을 유추해낼 수 있어야 한다. 물론 빈칸 이후 예를 들어 자세히 설명하는 부분은 건너뛰는 것이 시간을 줄이는 요령일 것이다. 실제로 Part 1의 16문항 중 접속사나 접속부사를 넣는 연결어 문제 15번, 16번 두 문항을 제외하고는 15분내에 문제의 답을 찾지 않으면 남은 문제에 대해 강한 압박감으로 고득점을 얻기 어려워진다. 빈 칸의 위치에 따른 출제 빈도는 앞에 빈칸이 오는 경우는 15% 정도, 중간이 20% 정도이며 끝에 오는 경우가 거의 대부분이다.

Part 2 (세부 사항과 내용 이해, 21문항)

지문의 main idea, title을 묻는 것을 시작으로 없는 내용을 발전시켜 추론까지 해야 하는 infer문제까지 다뤄지며, 총 21문항이 출제된다. 여기에서도 문제를 푸는 시간을 줄이는 요령은 문제와 선택지를 먼저 읽고서 지문을 읽기를 권한다. 특히 correct문제의 경우엔 더욱 그렇다. 이 경우는 정답이 나오는 시점에 지문을 그만 읽어도 되기 때문에 시간을 절약할 수 있다. 그 부분에서는 항상 조심할 것이 선택지에 매력적으로 유혹하는 오답이 있다는 것이다. 주어진 시간 안에 모두 풀었고, 거기다 쉽게 풀었다고 생각하는데 점수가 오르지 않는다면 이 매력적인 오답에 빠졌을 가능성이 많다. 그러나 출제자의 입장에서는 오답이 오답이고, 정답이 정답인 명백한 이유가 있기 때문에 평소에 틀린 문제를 꼼꼼하게 챙기고 갈 것을 권한다. 출제 유형은 주로 17~22번은 main idea, what about?, the purpose of the passage, best title, best summary를 묻는 문제이고, 23~37번은 특정 세부사항 묻는 문제와 correct/true, not true문제로 구성되어 있다.

Part 3 (흐름 파악, 3문항)

첫 문장을 주고 그 내용과 글이 자연스럽게 연결되지 않는 부분을 찾는 3문제가 출제되며 아주 내용이 멀리 떨어져 있는 것을 찾는 것이 아니라 다른 문장들과 소재와 내용은 같은 것이나 약간 일관성이 떨어지거나 초점이 벗어난 부분이 정답이다. 많이 권하는 요령은 어색한 문장이라고 생각해서 제외한 문장을 빼고 앞과 뒤 문장이 자연스럽게 연결되는지 확인하는 것도 좋은 방법이다. TEPS 독해는 45분 안에 40문제를 푸는 속도 시험이다. 문제 당 1분 정도를 할애해야 하므로 집중해서 정답이 나올 때까지만 지문을 읽어야 하며, 비교적 쉽고 득점에 유리한 Part 2, 3부터 푸는 것도 좋은 방법이다. 참고로 Part 3은 문항 수는 적으나 배점이 가장 높은 부분이므로 시간문제로 포기할 수 없는 부분이다.

TEPS

ACTUAL TEST

TEPS TIPS • 꼭꼭 숨어 있는 주어 찾기

주부가 주절주절 길 때는 우선 주부가 어디까지인지 찾은 다음, 숨어 있는 한 단어 주어를 찾아서 동사와의 수 일치를 확인하는 것이 중요하다.

The methods of transportation to and from the authorized service center // (is, are) the responsibility of the customer.

---

1 **단수로 취급하는 경우**: 주어가 동명사, to부정사, 명사절인 경우, 과목, the number of +명사

The article says the number of children missing // (jump, jumps) to 35 percent every year.

2 **복수로 취급하는 경우**: a number of +복수명사, and로 연결된 각각 독립된 명사 또는 각 관사가 붙은 명사가 주어일 때

A number of people // (are, is) gathering to watch the marathon held near the park.

3 **주어가 여러 개인 경우**: not only A but also B /neither A nor B: 동사는 가까운 주어에 일치한다.(근접성의 원리) 그러나 B as well as A 만은 예외로 B를 강조한 표현이기 때문에 명사 B가 동사와 거리가 멀다 해도 B에 일치한다.

Not only he but also I // (am, is) interested in traveling the space.

I as well as he // (is, am) interested in traveling the space.

4 **분수, 퍼센트**: 부분을 나타내는 표현들은 뒤에 오는 명사에 따라 단수로 취급하거나 복수로 취급한다.

About 90 percent of body fat // (was, were) not a significant correlation of lean body mass.

About 90 percent of movie stars // (is, are) driving the car.

안부 묻기(어떻게 지내세요? 잘 지내요? 별일 없죠?)

How are you?
How are you doing?
How's everything going?
How's everything with you?
How are things going?
How are you getting along?
How have you been doing?
How's it going?
Is everything okay with you?
What's new?
What's up?

인사에 대한 답변

Not much. 별일 없어.
= Nothing special.
= Nothing new.
= Nothing to speak of.
= Same as usual. 늘 똑같지 뭐.
= Same old same old. 항상 그렇지 뭐.
= So so. 그저 그래.
Couldn't be better. 매우 좋아.
Could be better. 좋아지겠지.
I'm doing OK. I'm fine. 괜찮아.
So far, so good. 지금까지는 좋아.

우연히 만났을 때

What a surprise to meet(see) you here!
   여기서 만나다니 뜻밖이야!
What brings you here? 여기는 웬일이야?
What are you doing here? 여기는 웬일이야?
I didn't expect to see you here.
   여기서 만날 줄 몰랐어.

Phrasal verbs

bump into 우연히 만나다
come across 우연히 만나다
run across 우연히 만나다
run into 우연히 만나다
call at + 장소 방문하다
call on + 사람 방문하다
drop in (예정에 없이) 방문하다
fix sb up 만남을 주선하다
fit in ~와 조화하다, 잘 어울리다
fool around 장난치다

Collocations

a bed of roses 안락한 환경
a fish out of water 주위 환경에 익숙지 않은 사람
as fit as a fiddle/flea 매우 건강한
a skeleton in the cupboard 집안의 비밀
a smack in the eye 거절
farewell party 송별회
man in the street 평범한 사람
slip of the tongue 실언
the talk of the town 장안의 화제
white lie 선의의 거짓말

Idioms

a long face 우울한, 시무룩한
down in the dumps 침체된, 우울한
a slap in the face 퇴짜 놓기, 거절
a wet blanket 흥을 깨는 사람
all in a day's work 일상적이고 평이한
Break a leg! 잘 되길 빌게! 잘 해봐!
break the ice 서먹서먹한 분위기를 극복하다
feel under the weather 몸이 아프다
from out of the blue 예기치 않게, 느닷없이
keep one's fingers crossed 잘 되기를 빌다

Part I   Choose the most appropriate response to the statement.

1   (a)   (b)   (c)   (d)

2   (a)   (b)   (c)   (d)

3   (a)   (b)   (c)   (d)

Part II   Choose the most appropriate response to complete the conversation.

4   (a)   (b)   (c)   (d)

5   (a)   (b)   (c)   (d)

6   (a)   (b)   (c)   (d)

Choose the option that best answers the question.

7 (a)   (b)   (c)   (d)

8 (a)   (b)   (c)   (d)

9 (a)   (b)   (c)   (d)

Part IV Choose the option that best answers the question.

10 (a)   (b)   (c)   (d)

11 (a)   (b)   (c)   (d)

12 (a)   (b)   (c)   (d)

Part I Choose the best answer for the blank.

13 A: Would you mind _____ on the air conditioner?
It's really hot here.
B: Certainly not.

(a) turn
(b) to turn
(c) turning
(d) turned

14 A: Can you show me _____ ?
B: Sure, wait a minute, sir.

(a) other
(b) others
(c) one another
(d) another

15 A: The fence needs _____ .
B: Yes, it does.

(a) to paint
(b) paint
(c) painting
(d) painted

16 A: How did you finally finish your course?
I find this course really hard to pass.
B: I think the time _____ is a big deal.

(a) arrangement
(b) to arrange
(c) arrange
(d) arranged

Choose the best answer for the blank.

17 Give the presents to _____ takes good care of children.

(a) whom
(b) whomever
(c) whoever
(d) whatever

18 The UN urged North Korea to _____ disclose its nuclear weapon programs and proliferation activities within 24 hours.

(a) complete
(b) completed
(c) completely
(d) completion

19 Once, people would buy _____ bread for a whole family.

(a) a loaf of
(b) a liter of
(c) a pair of
(d) an amount of

20 _____ the bottom of the castle when her colleague gave her a great push.

(a) Hardly she had reached
(b) She hardly had reached
(c) Had she hardly reached
(d) Hardly had she reached

Identify the option that contains an awkward expression or an error in grammar.

21 (a) A: What's the hurry, Michael?
    (b) B: I have doctor's appointment, but it totally slipped my mind.
    (c) A: Take your time.
    (d) B: Sorry, I don't have enough, I'm supposed to be there by five.

Identify the option that contains an awkward expression or an error in grammar.

22 (a) There are many reasons to visit Scotland any time of the year. (b) Especially Edinburgh boasts great architecture which it is blending the old and the new. (c) Other Victorian buildings help you visualize that you are in the dramatic and historical period. (d) It is recommended that visitors had better make arrangements at the places where they want to go ahead of time.

Choose the best answer for the blank.

23 A: Hey, Richard. Well, I was wondering if...
B: Don't _____ around the bush. Just tell me.

(a) hit
(b) beat
(c) hang
(d) tap

24 A: When is your baby due?
B: It was last week. My baby is one week _____.

(a) expired
(b) overdue
(c) hold
(d) overlaid

25 A: I kept calling you last night. But I couldn't _____.
B: I was very busy all day.

(a) get in
(b) get on
(c) get through
(d) get over

26 A: Thanks for dinner. Next time lunch is on me.
B: All right. Next time you'll _____.

(a) treat
(b) take
(c) hold
(d) welcome

27 A: Let's _____ it a day!

B: Are you leaving already? I've got tons of work to do.

(a) finish

(b) end

(c) say

(d) call

Part II Choose the best answer for the blank.

28 He was in his first term in _____ when the scandal broke.

(a) official

(b) years

(c) office

(d) position

29 For low-income parents, getting child care _____ are inevitable.

(a) scholarship

(b) subsidies

(c) investment

(d) sponsorship

30 Compared to young people, old people are rather _____ to the flu.

(a) vulnerable

(b) worse

(c) harmed

(d) allergic

31 Within 15 business days from the date you _____ the complaint, you will be known whether action will be taken.

(a) formed
(b) received
(c) sued
(d) filed

32 The president had been under investigation for _____ but he cleared himself of all charges within a week.

(a) embezzlement
(b) embodiment
(c) robbery
(d) burglary

Part I Read the passage. Then choose the option that best completes the passage.

33 Many people who are not attracted to traditional team sports think that traditional team sports have lots of rules, competition, and coaching. For this reason, more and more people—especially young people—tend to be more excited with _____ extreme sports. There are no such things like winning or losing, and little organizations like teams or leagues in extreme sports. Each person who really loves adventure and seeks it out competes against himself and pushes himself to his own limits.

(a) personal and traditional
(b) competitive and stressful
(c) independent and conventional
(d) individual and unconventional

34 When a non-native English speaking student writes an essay for English speaking readers, organization of ideas is problematical because different cultural backgrounds call for different organizational patterns. Typical readers of English expect the development of ideas to be in a straight line which includes introductions, main ideas, topic sentences, supporting details, conclusions, etc. An Asian writer, however, will often develop ideas in a spiral pattern which means using a variety of facts related to a topic before arriving at the conclusion. It is such an indirect pattern that native English readers often fail to get his or her main point. Although it is not an easy task, it is essential to _____ especially if one wants to be read.

(a) adapt to Asian culture
(b) develop ideas in order of time
(c) meet those cultural expectations
(d) stick to his or her own writing pattern

35 Michael Phelps, who won eight gold medals in the 2008 Olympics, is known for struggling with ADHD (Attention Deficit Hyperactivity Disorder) as a child. His mother, Deborah Phelps, recalls that he never sat still, was always asking zillions of questions and jumping from one thing to another. Finally, his doctor, Charles Wax, diagnosed his case as ADHD and prescribed a stimulant medication for Phelps when he was 9 years old. Although the medication was somewhat helpful at school, swimming was what truly helped him cope with ADHD. It played an important role in helping him _____ .

(a) win the gold medals
(b) focus and calm down
(c) overact and exaggerate
(d) hide his medical history

Part II Read the passage and the question. Then choose the option that best answers the question.

36 Although it is based on the underlying principle of minimizing adverse affects on the environment and local communities, ecotourism can also disrupt indigenous people and their social structures. Indeed, it is easier said than done to bring the benefits of tourism back to local people without disrupting their way of life. To protect the tourist industry, for example, regulations are sometimes made that destroy local way of life. With their livelihood threatened and often with no skills to work with in the tourism industry, local people can be left with no alternative means of livelihood. Many original inhabitants are often driven out of their area and outsiders move in to try to profit from tourism.

Q Which of the following is the best title for the passage?

(a) Benefits of ecotourism
(b) The trend towards ecotourism
(c) Ecotourism subject to controversy
(d) Compensation for the aboriginal population

37 Some reports show that indoor air is two to five times more harmful than outdoor air. To our astonishment, the air in office buildings, schools, and even homes is not safe to breathe in. Because of indoor air pollution, many people are suffering from headaches, sore throats, or respiratory diseases such as asthma. Then, how can we deal with this situation to make closed environments more secure and harmless? One way is to install good ventilation systems in buildings. It is indispensable for a building to have ventilation because it dilutes contaminants by allowing clean and fresh air in; thus, creating a safer and healthier environment.

Q What is the passage mainly about?

(a) Sources of indoor air pollution
(b) The necessity of ventilation use
(c) Symptoms of indoor air pollution
(d) Ways of reducing indoor air pollution

38 For people suffering from eating disorders, there is a large gap between the way they see themselves and how they actually look. People with anorexia or bulimia frequently have an extreme fear of getting fat or think that they're fat when they aren't. Eating disorders also can be triggered by emotional problems or psychiatric disorders, such as anxiety disorder and obsessive-compulsive disorder. Some research shows that media images contribute to the increase in the incidence of eating disorders. Most women in advertising, movies, TV, and sports programs are very thin, and this may lead girls to think that the ideal of beauty is thinness.

Q What is the main topic of the passage?

(a) Lookism in the mass media
(b) The causes of eating disorders
(c) Individuals prone to eating disorders
(d) Correlation between stress and eating habits

39 Kimchi, a spicy flavored Korean cabbage, is well known as a well-being food. According to studies, the ingredients of Kimchi, such as cabbage, garlic, and red pepper, not only prevent cancer, but also develop immunity to it. Regular intake of cabbage creates less of a chance of getting large intestine cancer, and the garlic restrains gastric cancer. In addition, Kimchi contains abundant vitamins. For example, red pepper contains 37 times more vitamin C than apples, and 7 times more than tangerines. Besides vitamin C, red pepper also has plenty of vitamin A.

Q What is the main topic of the passage?

(a) The benefits of Kimchi
(b) How to make Kimchi
(c) Food that helps prevent cancer
(d) The special ingredients of Kimchi

Part III Read the passage. Then identify the option that does NOT belong.

40 We rank all of the law schools available this year, thereby giving you the necessary information to decide which schools you should apply to. (a) The best advice is to visit the law schools you are seriously thinking of attending after you have been accepted. (b) The variability in these rankings should illustrate that it can only work as a guide, and that you should be the final evaluator where you will be. (c) Before applying, we recommend that you personally visit each law school that you are considering. (d) Which school you attend not only impacts where you will spend three enjoyable and educational years, but also where you will settle down.

TEPS TIPS • 'to부정사'와 '전치사 to' + '동명사' 구별

겉보기로는 쉽게 판단이 안 될 수도 있는 'to + 동사원형' 과 '전치사 to + 동명사'를 구별할 때는 to가 전치사인 경우 몇 가지를 기억하는 편이 더 낫다.

1 '전치사 to + 동명사' 관용 표현

object to ~ing ~에 반대하다	be opposed to ~ing ~에 반대하다
be accustomed to ~ing ~에 익숙하다	get(be) used to ~ing ~에 익숙하다
admit (to) ~ing ~을 인정하다	accede to ~ing ~에 동의하다, 응하다
accommodate to ~ing ~에 적응하다	adapt to ~ing ~에 적응하다
contribute to ~ing ~에 공헌하다	be dedicated(devoted) to ~ing ~에 헌신적이다
look forward to ~ing ~를 고대하다	confess to ~ing ~을 고백하다
when it comes to ~ing ~에 관해서는	What do you say (to) ~ing? ~하는 것은 어때?

I used to (jogging, jog) early in the morning, so I am used to (get, getting) up early.

When it comes to (solve, solving) the difficult problems, my sister is better than I.

The robber confessed to (steal, stealing) the jewelry as the witness insisted.

He did not admit to (be, being) a part of this Dead Poets Society.

Don't accede to them (act, acting) like a prima donna.

2 부정 표현 비교

to부정사의 부정은 'not + to 동사원형' 이고, 동명사의 부정은 'not + 동명사' 이다.

They want me (not to have, to not have) vacation during a high-demand season.

The people object (to not having, not to having) a choice in avoiding genetically modified foods.

During holidays, I got used (to not, not to) teaching every day.

오랜만에 만났을 때

How have you been? 잘 지냈어?

It's really been a long time since I saw you last. 정말 오랜만이야.

I haven't seen you for ages. 오랜만이야.

= It's been a while.

= Long time no see.

You haven't changed a bit. 하나도 안 변했구나.

I haven't heard from him in years.
그 아이랑 연락 끊긴 지 오래됐어.

처음 만났을 때, 소개하기

I've been waiting to meet you for long.
오래 전부터 만나뵙고 싶었어요.

Haven't we met before?
우리 전에 만난 적 있지 않아요?

Have you two ever met before?
두 분 서로 만난 적 있으세요?

=Have you two been introduced?

I've heard a lot about you. 말씀 많이 들었어요.

I'm pleased to make your acquaintance.
알게 되어 기쁩니다.

It's a pleasure to meet you. 만나서 반가워요.

작별 인사

I have to get going. 가봐야 해.

See(Talk, Catch) you later. 또 보자.

Take it easy! 조심해서 잘 가.

Take care! 조심해서 잘 가.

Don't be a stranger. 또 놀러 오세요.

We can get together another time.
다음에 또 만나요.

Say hello to ~. = Give ~ my regards.
~에게 안부 전해주세요.

Can't you stay a little longer?
좀 더 있다가 가지 그래?

= Why are you leaving so soon?
왜 이렇게 빨리 가?

Phrasal verbs

come by 획득하다, 방문하다

correspond with ~와 서신 왕래하다

cut in 간섭하다, 끼어들다

dwell in ~에 살다

go well with ~와 어울리다

head out 출발하다, 떠나다

hear from ~로부터 소식을 듣다

hear of ~에 대한 소문을 듣다

keep away from ~을 가까이하지 않다

talk over 이야기를 나누다

Collocations

an unidentified person 신원불명의 사람

apartment complex 아파트 단지

eventful life 파란만장한 인생

generation gap 세대차

gift of the gab 말주변

persistent rumor 계속 떠도는 소문

superiority complex 우월감

wishful thinking 희망 사항

war of nerves 신경전

pep talk 격려의 말

Idioms

a man of his word 약속을 잘 지키는 사람

a pat on the back 칭찬, 격려

all thumbs 서투른

beat around the bush 둘러말하다

butter up 아부하다

come out of nowhere 불쑥 나타나다

dead tired 몹시 피곤한

get off the ground 출발하다

have a ball 즐거운 시간을 보내다

have a big mouth 입이 싸다

Part I   Choose the most appropriate response to the statement.

1   (a)   (b)   (c)   (d)

2   (a)   (b)   (c)   (d)

3   (a)   (b)   (c)   (d)

Part II   Choose the most appropriate response to complete the conversation.

4   (a)   (b)   (c)   (d)

5   (a)   (b)   (c)   (d)

6   (a)   (b)   (c)   (d)

Choose the option that best answers the question.

7 (a)   (b)   (c)   (d)

8 (a)   (b)   (c)   (d)

9 (a)   (b)   (c)   (d)

Part IV   Choose the option that best answers the question.

10 (a)   (b)   (c)   (d)

11 (a)   (b)   (c)   (d)

12 (a)   (b)   (c)   (d)

Part I Choose the best answer for the blank.

13 A: Please make sure you have all of your personal _____ when you leave your seat.
B: Ok, thanks.

(a) belong
(b) belong to
(c) belonged
(d) belongings

14 A: Let's go and see Mr. Anderson.
B: What _____?

(a) from
(b) for
(c) with
(d) to

15 A: Why does he practice English so hard?
B: His first goal is to make _____ understood in English.

(a) him
(b) himself
(c) of him
(d) for him

16 A: I'm sure she _____ upset if I had told her about the accident.
B: I couldn't agree more.

(a) must be
(b) should be
(c) must have been
(d) should have been

Choose the best answer for the blank.

17   The host family prepared lots of food the decorations _____ were sensational.

(a) whose
(b) which
(c) what
(d) of which

18   During _____ make sure to check the lack of iron in your diet.

(a) a pregnancy
(b) pregnancy
(c) pregnancies
(d) the pregnancy

19   A Spanish judge charged two suspects and _____ accused were all sent to the trial.

(a) that
(b) who
(c) those
(d) this

20   There will be a small charge _____ we considered when they deliver the furniture for.

(a) which
(b) what
(c) where
(d) when

Identify the option that contains an awkward expression or an error in grammar.

21 (a) A: Let's go take a look at Noho.
(b) B: Yes, I heard it is a neighborhood full of wonderful buildings.
(c) A: Do you think what are the most notable buildings in Noho?
(d) B: I think one of them is The Merchant's house, a museum which shows the lifestyle in the 19th century.

Identify the option that contains an awkward expression or an error in grammar.

22 (a) China has the largest Refrigerator markets in the world. (b) When consumers purchase refrigerators, their brand and price become increasing important criteria. (c) The Refrigerator industry is consolidated with top 4 players accounting for 70% market share measured by revenue and they compete in prices and qualities. (d) As a result of intensive competition and manufacturing overcapacity, prices are dropping fast.

Choose the best answer for the blank.

23 A: You look tired. Are you okay?

B: Actually I _____ and turned all night.

(a) threw

(b) changed

(c) moved

(d) tossed

24 A: Congratulations on your promotion! But the work would be extremely demanding!

B: Come on! Don't be a _____ blanket!

(a) wet

(b) spoiled

(c) thick

(d) messed

25 A: Excuse me. Where can I _____ my baggage?

B: Which flight were you on?

(a) demand

(b) request

(c) ask

(d) claim

26 A: I think I'm getting overweight these days. I'm thinking about joining the fitness club.

B: You should _____ on your drinking first!

(a) cut down

(b) cut back

(c) cut in

(d) go down

27 A: What's on the front page of the newspaper?

B: Some protesters were arrested for _____ the law.

(a) rebelling
(b) violating
(c) blowing
(d) driving

Choose the best answer for the blank.

28 Those who are convicted of sexual harassment are placed on _____ instead of being sent to prison.

(a) imprisonment
(b) arrest
(c) probation
(d) prohibition

29 The most _____ way to use your computer for a long time is to update your anti-virus programs on a regular basis.

(a) economic
(b) economize
(c) economical
(d) economics

30 The crisis came _____ and nobody knew how to handle it.

(a) from scratch
(b) on the spot
(c) out of the blue
(d) once in a blue moon

31   After the civil war, many people are afraid of the probability of the political _____ .

(a) excitement
(b) turbulence
(c) confusion
(d) violence

32   She made the most fatal mistake ever and she couldn't _____ submitting her resignation.

(a) help
(b) stop
(c) block
(d) hold

Part I Read the passage. Then choose the option that best completes the passage.

33 The Pygmalion effect, also known as The Rosenthal effect, has to do with the phenomena in which some students produce better results than other students simply because _____.
According to a study by U.S. psychologist Robert Rosenthal, the beliefs and expectations of teachers have a great influence on their students' actual performance. That is, if teachers believe that their students are intelligent and capable enough to derive from enhanced performance, then the students indeed do so. It is explained that the students will respond positively to their teachers' high expectations and apply them to their behavior or learning habits by internalizing them.

(a) they are actually superior
(b) they are expected to do so
(c) their characteristics are always positive
(d) they and their teachers have same expectations

34 A recent study says that smells have an influence on dreams. In this study, 15 healthy women participated as volunteers while a rose scent was injected into their nostrils through tubes during their sleep. When the scientists woke them up one minute after injection, they reported that they had had pleasant dreams. On the contrary, when they were given the odor of rotten eggs, they described their dreams negatively. However there are some people who doubt if this result is really true. They point out that the subjects may not actually have dreamed of it, but may have had an illusion instead, considering that

_____.

(a) women are unable to smell while sleeping
(b) there was only short time between the stimulus and the wakening
(c) the scientists injected an aromatic smell before a disgusting smell
(d) the smell was injected mechanically through tubes and not naturally

35 The Empty Nest Syndrome refers to general feelings of loneliness, grief, or despair experienced by parents or guardians when their children leave them to go to college or to get married. Some of them feel that their lives are worthless or meaningless and want to be alone without any social relationships. Others may feel irresistible sadness, or cry excessively. If these feelings become overwhelming, the parent or guardian should undergo treatment. Thus, experts advise _____ while they are still with their children to prevent experiencing these feelings later on.

(a) saving money in the future
(b) preparing for an empty nest
(c) expressing their feelings openly
(d) forcing children not to leave home

Part II Read the passage and the question. Then choose the option that best answers the question.

36 September 25, 2008
To Whom It May Concern:

Harry Ahn taught English at Durham High School from 2005-2007. He did an excellent job of teaching classes in English literature and Composition. He showed a good grasp of the material and was able to develop excellent rapport with his students. Not only did he get along well with his students but also with the faculty.

Harry Ahn would be a tremendous asset for your school and has my highest recommendation. If you have any further questions with regard to his background or qualifications, please do not hesitate to call me.
Sincerely,

Susan Douglas
Vice-Principal

Q What is the purpose of the letter?

(a) To help Harry Ahn obtain the admission to the college
(b) To explain how Harry Ahn goes along with the faculty
(c) To suggest that Harry Ahn would prove to be good employee
(d) To confirm that Harry Ahn is employed by Durham High School

37 A heat island refers to the increased heat caused by the buildings, concrete, asphalt, and the human and industrial activity of cities. The increased heat requires an increase in the demand of energy for cooling purposes, and increases pollution. Several suggestions have been made to reduce the temperature; most prominent are replacing dark surfaces with light reflective surfaces and planting trees. Planting trees not only provides shade but also increases evapotranspiration, which decreases the air temperature.

Q Which is NOT mentioned in the above statement?

(a) What are the ill effects of a heat island?
(b) How can we improve the cooling system in the cities?
(c) What causes the rise of temperature in the urban areas?
(d) What benefits can we expect from planting trees in the urban areas?

38 Welcome to the Library at the Swinburne University! There are two categories of borrowers: University Borrowers include all current students, faculty and staff. Other Borrowers include alumni, retired faculty and staff, who do not have remote access to electronic indexes, databases or journals. A library card must be presented to borrow materials or to get other services the library offers. Reissue of library cards will be restricted to borrowers with fines. The person whose name is on the card is responsible for all library transactions made with the card. In case of the loss or theft of a card, you must report immediately to the Circulation staff in the Library. Borrowers will be held accountable for transactions on their card until such notification is received.

Q Which of the following is correct according to the passage?

(a) Library cards are transferable between current students.
(b) Library cards will not be issued until all the fines have been paid.
(c) A retired staff has the same borrower privileges as a staff in active service.
(d) A borrower will be exempt from responsibility for the use of his lost card.

39 Although Hollywood celebrities spend millions of dollars on his works and most of his works fetch more than the estimated price at auction, even the agent has allegedly never met Banksy, the elusive graffiti artist. Now it seems that the artist will be constrained to forsake the life of a recluse. He was pictured at work for the first time. There have been a few people claiming to have caught Banksy on camera before, but this is believed to be the first image showing the artist at work. A spokeswoman for Banksy said that the artwork was authentic, but refused to confirm whether the man in the photo was the artist.

Q Which of the following is NOT true about Banksy according to the passage?

(a) His works command prices far beyond expectations.
(b) Very few people are known to have met the artist in person.
(c) Many Hollywood celebrities have been cheated into buying his works.
(d) The street artist refuses to get into the public eye as much as possible.

40 April Van Lines believes that understanding your needs is the key to a successful move. With over 80 years' experience, April, a world-leading moving company has what it takes to make your household or corporate move go smoothly. Whether your type of move is locally within the state or out of the state, April's experienced support staff will guide you through every step of the relocation process. When you move with us, you can count on sincere, reliable service, and unrivalled quality. Contact us today for a free moving estimate from our superb moving service.

Q Which of the following mottos is appropriate for this company?

(a) Dream Skyward!
(b) Make It Happen Now!
(c) Moving Your Memories!
(d) To Persevere and To Excel

TEPS TIPS • 문장 구조의 이해: 본동사의 구별 및 부정어구의 도치구문

문장의 기본을 구성하는 것은 하나의 주어 다음에 오는 하나의 본동사이다. 그 외의 동사들은 본동사가 아니기 때문에 to부정사나 동명사, 현재분사 등의 제한된 형태를 가질 수밖에 없다. 또한 부정어구의 도치구문에서 조동사와 본동사의 위치에 주의해야 한다.

1 **본동사의 형태:** 동사의 현재형, 과거형, will+동사원형, 수동태(be+과거분사), 진행형(be+동사의 -ing), 완료형(have+과거분사)이 있다. 다시 말해서, 동사의 -ing 형태나 과거분사형은 혼자서 본동사가 될 수 없다는 것이다.

One of the most important advances in the study of language acquisition (being, was, been) the creation of the database by many linguists. Among them (are, is, being) Chomsky the greatest, and he (insist, insisting, insisted) that children (are born, be born, bearing) with a hard-wired language acquisition device (LAD) in their brains.

2 **부정어구의 도치구문:** never, little, not only, nowhere, hardly, scarecely, rarely, seldom, not until~ 등의 부정어구가 문장 앞에 나올 때는 '부정어구+조동사+주어+동사'의 도치구문이 된다.

Never have I met her before.

Little did I dream that I could meet the movie star.

Not until he was forty did the poet become famous.

On no account must you be absent tomorrow.

길 찾기

I'm lost. 길을 잃었어요.
I'm a stranger here, too. 저도 이곳이 처음이에요.
= I'm new here.
= I've never been here before.
= This is my first time here.
Can you tell me where I can find ~?
　~이 어디 있는지 알려주실래요?
= How can I get to ~? ~까지 어떻게 가야 하나요?
You can't miss it. 쉽게 찾을 수 있을 거에요.
= You will have no problem finding it.

Phrasal verbs

catch up with ~을 따라잡다
familiar with+사물 ~에 익숙한, ~을 잘 아는
get back 돌아오다
keep up with ~와 보조를맞추다
lead to ~에 이르다
get off 내리다 (차, 말 등)
get on 타다
look for 찾다
make for ~으로 향하다
wait for ~을 기다리다

Collocations

a port in any storm 궁여지책
as clear as a bell 대단히 명료한
blind corner 궁지
cold feet 겁먹음
glimmer of the memory 어렴풋한 기억
instinctive response 본능적 반응
speed merchant 속도광
tall story 허풍
twilight of life 말년
makeshift(temporary) measure 미봉책

Idioms

a far cry from ~와 현격히 다른
bark up the wrong tree 헛다리짚다
be in hot water 곤경에 처하여
call it a day 하루 일을 마치다. 퇴근하다
call it quits 일을 멈추다
get the picture 잘 이해하다
grab a bite 간단히 먹다
hit below the belt 비열한 행동을 하다
on the dot 정확히, 제시간에
on the tip of one's tongue 생각이 날듯 말 듯, 말이
　입에서 뱅뱅 돌고 안 나오는

교통 관련 어휘

bumper to bumper 교통이 혼잡한
catch (버스, 비행기 등을) 잡아타다
debris 파편, 잔해
derailment 탈선
disembarkation card 입국 카드
embargo 입출항 금지명령, 수출금지
embark (배나, 비행기에) 태우다, 싣다
lane change 차선 변경
license plates 자동차 번호판
lift-off (우주선 등의) 수직 이륙, 발사
manned 사람을 실은, 유인의
one-way 편도의
propulsion 추진력
puncture 펑크나다
rut 바퀴자국
spot check 불시 검문
step on it 속력을 내다
traffic congestion 교통 체증
wreck 난파

Part I   Choose the most appropriate response to the statement.

1   (a)   (b)   (c)   (d)

2   (a)   (b)   (c)   (d)

3   (a)   (b)   (c)   (d)

Part II   Choose the most appropriate response to complete the conversation.

4   (a)   (b)   (c)   (d)

5   (a)   (b)   (c)   (d)

6   (a)   (b)   (c)   (d)

Choose the option that best answers the question.

7   (a)   (b)   (c)   (d)

8   (a)   (b)   (c)   (d)

9   (a)   (b)   (c)   (d)

Part IV   Choose the option that best answers the question.

10 (a)   (b)   (c)   (d)

11 (a)   (b)   (c)   (d)

12 (a)   (b)   (c)   (d)

Part I Choose the best answer for the blank.

13 A: What should I bring to a potluck?
B: Why don't _____ some prepared fruit trays or vegetables.

(a) for you to bring
(b) you bringing
(c) you bring
(d) you to bring

14 A: There _____ a police box on the corner.
B: Right, a bar and a liquor shop were, too.

(a) used to be
(b) would be
(c) should be
(d) must be

15 A: What happened? You look like you are in a lot of pain.
B: Don't touch me, my legs are _____.

(a) numb to
(b) numbing to
(c) numbed
(d) to numb

16 A: Do you have any smoking sections in the building?
B: Sorry, _____ in the dormitory.

(a) we're not supposed to smoke
(b) we're supposed to smoke
(c) it seems to smoke
(d) it seems not to be smoking

Choose the best answer for the blank.

17 _____ the reason, the old man answered he would get the top alone.

(a) When asking
(b) When asked
(c) Having asked
(d) Asking

18 The writer who wrote the novel has very delicate manners, _____ a graceful appearance.

(a) balancing
(b) balanced
(c) balanced with
(d) balancing with

19 Molecular cloning refers to the procedure of isolating a defined DNA sequence and obtaining multiple copies of _____.

(a) one
(b) ones
(c) it
(d) them

20 _____ behalf of the president who attended a fringe meeting, he delivered an address at the conference.

(a) In
(b) Of
(c) On
(d) With

Identify the option that contains an awkward expression or an error in grammar.

21 (a) A: Hello, can I speak to a personnel director?
    (b) B: Yes, this is she speaking, ma'am.
    (c) A: I heard you recruited staff on a regular basis.
    (d) B: You're right, we are now looking for a sales executive of online marketing.

Identify the option that contains an awkward expression or an error in grammar.

22 (a) After working for 5 years, he published Johnson's Dictionary of the English Language in 1755. (b) It had a far-reaching impact on Modern English which has been described as "one of the greatest single achievement of scholarship". (c) It brought Johnson popularity and success until the Oxford English Dictionary was published 150 years later. (d) It was viewed as the pre-eminent British dictionary.

Choose the best answer for the blank.

23 A: Have you seen my MP3 player? I can't find it anywhere!

   B: No. That's why I always put things within my arms _____.

   (a) close
   (b) by
   (c) reach
   (d) contact

24 A: I can't believe he's only 15 years old.

   B: My son is _____ compared to other kids of his age.

   (a) precocious
   (b) pretended
   (c) preliminary
   (d) preventable

25. A: Don't you think politicians are wasting public money for nothing?

   B: You're right. I want them to stop spending money on _____ projects.

   (a) serious
   (b) frivolous
   (c) important
   (d) fastidious

26 A: How often do you exercise?

   B: I _____ every day to keep fit.

   (a) go out
   (b) warm up
   (c) work out
   (d) walk out

27 A: We still lag behind other competitors.

B: I agree with you. We need to _____ a great idea.

(a) take into account
(b) draw back
(c) make out
(d) come up with

Choose the best answer for the blank.

28 The new government is giving price stability a top _____ because the low income earners are currently suffering from soaring prices.

(a) priority
(b) necessity
(c) importance
(d) probability

29 He was _____ to a local hospital as soon as he was shot in the head but he died of excessive bleeding.

(a) operated
(b) transferred
(c) transformed
(d) placed

30 It was so dark that the old man _____ over a rock and fell down.

(a) stumped
(b) kicked
(c) stumbled
(d) twisted

31 As a wad of _____ bill was found, the police announced that they would start an investigation as early as the end of this month.

(a) pirate
(b) confidential
(c) certificate
(d) counterfeit

32 When you cut your finger and it keeps bleeding, you should _____ a flow of blood first.

(a) staunch
(b) hold
(c) restrain
(d) prevent

Part I   Read the passage. Then choose the option that best completes the passage.

33   You've all skinned a knee or scraped an elbow at one time or another. After the bleeding stops, you've probably noticed a crusty covering, or scab, that forms over the wound. Once you scrape the skin, special cell fragments called platelets spring into action. Platelets adhere to the cut, forming a clot which keeps more blood from flowing out. The clot contains thread-like stuff called fibrin that helps hold the clot together. Have you ever thought of that scab as a picturesque landscape, a beautiful mountain, or even the Mona Lisa. Probably not. But in its own way, the scab is a masterpiece—an essential part of you body's _____.

(a) fine art
(b) self remedy
(c) martial art
(d) healing art

34   Today, more and more companies are working twenty-four hours a day, seven days a week. Many of them being international trading companies, they often contact with companies in other time zones. Companies must stay open at all times in order to serve and sell products to its global customers. In the past, other people employed as fire-fighters, nurses, or policemen, had work schedules such as 11:00 p.m. to 7:00 a.m., or 3:00 p.m. to 11:00 p.m. However, nowadays the employees of these 24/7 companies have these shifts as well. Influenced by this change, _____.

(a) there are more people who want to work overtime to get a high salary
(b) people prefer some jobs which they can decide their work schedules
(c) local businesses such as supermarkets don't close even late at night
(d) the international trading companies don't want to contact with ones far from their countries

35 The earth balances the radiative equilibrium by emitting thermal infrared radiation after absorbing it from the sun. Various greenhouse gases in the atmosphere don't absorb light of short wavelengths, which comes from the sun, but absorb light of long wavelengths, which the earth gives off, and leave it in the atmosphere. In other words, the greenhouse effect is caused by the build-up of greenhouse gases, which permits light from the sun's rays to warm up the earth, but prevents loss of the heat. Therefore, if the atmosphere didn't exist on Earth, _____. Calculated by this theory, the earth's surface temperature would drop to about -20 Centigrade.

(a) the earth would emit as much thermal infrared radiation as the sun does
(b) the greenhouse effect would be much worse than what we could imagine
(c) the thermal infrared radiation emitted to the earth's surface would fade away
(d) the sun would emit light of long wavelength as well as short wavelength

Part II Read the passage and the question. Then choose the option that best answers the question.

36 The word "kidult," a coined word of "kid" and "adult," refers to an adult who prefers items that are considered for younger generation and enjoys being part of the activities traditionally designed for children. While many adults live up to the social expectation, an increasing minority live on their childhood memories, looking for ways to find consolation and drive away daily stress. A study indicates that this new social trend is a result of people's desire to flee from the reality full of adult responsibilities. Instead, they choose to live in a fantasy world that is free of keen competition and age stereotypes. Some sociologists ascribe this phenomenon to the self-centered lifestyle of modern people, who are focused on their beliefs rather than on what others think about them.

Q Which of the following is NOT the cause of the kidult phenomenon?

(a) Selfishness or focusing on self too much
(b) A refusal to conform to accepted standards
(c) Tendency to have an extended adolescence
(d) Avoidance of taking on adult responsibilities

37 I've lived in many big ugly cities most of my life but I have to say Seoul is one of the ugliest capital cities in the world. I'm not comparing Seoul with European repositories of architecture such as Paris or Rome. Aesthetically Seoul has the cards stacked up against Beijing, Tokyo and some other Asian capitals. This is mainly due to the apartment complexes that are put up like tombstones. Moreover Seoul is busy razing the labyrinths of old houses and putting up apartment blocks in that area, leaving the city without any indigenous architects. Seoul seems unaware that alternative housing to those matchbox-like apartment blocks exists.

Q What is the main idea of the passage?

(a) The city developers come under suspicion of bribery.
(b) The identical apartment blocks make Seoul an exotic spot.
(c) Those all-look-alike apartment buildings mar the beauty of the city.
(d) Seoul should be a model for other Asian cities in its real estate development.

38 According to researchers who have studied how to save energy in the kitchen, washing dishes by hand uses 37 percent more water than using a dishwasher. However, there is a way to save water when you wash dishes by hand. If you wash dishes in one sink with soapy water first, then rinse them in another sink with the faucet closed, you'll use less than half the amount of water you would have used with a dish washer. Moreover, you can also save energy by using a microwave not a stove when you need to reheat or defrost small amounts of food. In the case of large amounts of food, however, a stove is more efficient than a microwave.

Q What is the main idea of the passage?

(a) Using machine requires much energy all the time.
(b) There are various ways to save energy in the kitchen.
(c) It is very dangerous to use an electric machine in the kitchen.
(d) Women who spend more time in the kitchen have to play a major role in saving energy.

39 'Culture shock' is a term used to describe periods of frustration, anxiety, melancholy, and loneliness which someone experiences when he or she lives in a foreign country. It is caused by unfamiliarity with the new surroundings and the inability to communicate with local people. Before feeling disillusionment with the new country, it is very important for newcomers who suffer from culture shock to realize that it is one of the four stages of cultural adjustment. The four stages of cultural adjustment are excitement, culture shock, recovery, and stability.

Q What is the main idea of the passage?

(a) People should try not to suffer from culture shock if possible.
(b) People don't have to experience all of the cultural adjustment stages.
(c) Local people have responsibilities to help newcomers not to feel culture shock.
(d) Culture shock should be considered as a natural process experienced in a new country.

Part III Read the passage. Then identify the option that does NOT belong.

40 In the Postwar years, Hemingway lived in Paris and became a member of expatriate Americans. (a) However, he used his experiences as a reporter during the Spanish Civil War and wrote his most ambitious novel, For Whom the Bell Tolls. (b) His straightforward prose and his predilection for understatement are particularly valuable in his short stories. (c) Among his later works, another outstanding is the short novel, The Old Man and the Sea, the story of an old fisherman's long and lonely struggle with a fish and the sea, and victory in defeat. (d) He also liked to portray soldiers and hunters whose courage and honesty are set against the vicious modern society, and who in this confrontation lose hope and faith.

TEPS TIPS ● 불완전 동사가 있는 문장의 이해: 형용사와 부사 비교

형용사는 보어로서 불완전한 자동사와 함께 쓰여서 문장을 완성해주고, 부사는 주로 형용사나 동사를 꾸며주면서 부가적인 설명을 할 뿐, 문장의 주요한 구성요소로서 역할을 하지 않는다는 것이 가장 큰 차이점이다.

1 불완전 동사의 예
be, remain, become, get, seem, look, sound, grow, feel 등이 있다.

She felt very (happy, happily).

The movie made me (sad, sadly)

2 완전 동사와 불완전 동사의 비교
문장이 완벽하다면 부사를 더 가미해서 의미를 풍요롭고 분명하게 하면 되고, 문장이 자동사로 끝난 상태라 보충어가 필요하다면 형용사를 써야 한다.

Terrorism won't be defeated until our determination is as complete as theirs, our defence of freedom as (absolutely, absolute) as their fanaticism.

➡ be동사가 불완전 동사이기 때문에 형용사 complete가 와서 문장이 완성되었다.

The Emperor ruled his Church as (absolute, absolutely) as his army.

➡ 동사 rule은 보어가 없어도 문장이 완벽하기 때문에 부사 absolutely가 와서 문장의 의미를 분명하게 했다.

약속 정하기

When is the most convenient time for you?
  언제가 편하세요?
Do you have time right now? 지금 시간 있어요?
Will you be free this weekend?
  이번 주말에 시간 있어요?
I can make it this evening.
  오늘 저녁에 갈 수 있어요.
I'm sorry, but I can't make it.
  죄송하지만 못 가겠네요.
Would you please give me a rain check?
  다음에 할 수 있을까요?

파티, 초대

We're going to throw a party.
  우리가 파티를 열려고 해.
Will you come over my place tomorrow?
  내일 우리 집에 올래?
Just bring yourself. 그냥 몸만 오세요.
Thank you for having me. 초대해 주셔서 감사해요.
Make yourself at home. 편하게 계세요.
I had a ball. 굉장히 즐거웠어요.
I'd like to treat you to dinner. / I'd like to buy
  you dinner. 저녁 대접하고 싶어요.
Can I have some more? 좀 더 먹어도 되요?

Phrasal verbs

butt in 참견하다
call off 취소하다
fill sb in 정보를 주다
get away 가 버리다
let on (비밀 등을) 누설하다
look forward to ~을 고대하다, 기대하다
manage to 가까스로 ~하다
show up 나타나다
take place 일어나다, 개최하다
turn up 나타나다, 발견되다

Collocations

a snake in the glass 음흉한 사람
chance meeting 우연한 만남
discordant sounds 불협화음
heavy/hard drinker 술이 센 사람
hen party 여자들만의 파티
stag party 남자들만의 파티
storm in a teacup 공연한 소동
textbook example 교과서적인 예
tip of the iceberg 빙산의 일각
vicious circle 악순환

Idioms

a close call 위기일발, 구사일생
a mixed blessing 희비가 엇갈리는 일
a pain in the neck 눈의 가시, 골치 아픈 일
a tall order 어려운 주문이나 요구
all ears 열심히 듣는
around the corner (시간적) 바로 코앞에
be fed up with 질리다
bring home the bacon 생활비를 벌다
catch one's eye 관심을 끌다
come in handy 유용하다

사회 관련 어휘

authorities 당국
autonomy 자치
consensus 합의
dispute 논쟁, 분쟁
forge 위조하다, 날조하다
equilibrium 균형, 평형
exploitation 착취
facilities 편리함
functionalism 기능주의
fund 자금, 기금
imbalance 불균형의, 어울리지 않는
objectivity 객관성

Part I   Choose the most appropriate response to the statement.

1 (a)   (b)   (c)   (d)

2 (a)   (b)   (c)   (d)

3 (a)   (b)   (c)   (d)

Part II   Choose the most appropriate response to complete the conversation.

4 (a)   (b)   (c)   (d)

5 (a)   (b)   (c)   (d)

6 (a)   (b)   (c)   (d)

Choose the option that best answers the question.

7   (a)   (b)   (c)   (d)

8   (a)   (b)   (c)   (d)

9   (a)   (b)   (c)   (d)

Choose the option that best answers the question.

10 (a)   (b)   (c)   (d)

11 (a)   (b)   (c)   (d)

12 (a)   (b)   (c)   (d)

Choose the best answer for the blank.

13 A: What would you do if you _____ in her shoes?
B: Well, I would definitely not sign the contract.

(a) are
(b) will be
(c) were
(d) was

14 A: _____ it takes to get there?
B: About one and a half hours.

(a) Do you think how long
(b) How long you think
(c) How do you think long
(d) How long do you think

15 A: How about the bank robbery you mentioned last time?
B: The witness insisted that the man _____.

(a) wear a black mask
(b) should wear a black mask
(c) wore a black mask
(d) wearing a black mask

16 A: Thank you for inviting us to this gorgeous dinner.
B: Help yourself _____ all food.

(a) to
(b) at
(c) as
(d) for

Choose the best answer for the blank.

17 Opened in 1930, Koala Park in New South Wales was the first private koala sanctuary and _____ the late Noel Burnet.

(a) founded on
(b) was founded by
(c) which was founded on
(d) founding by

18 It's the time when _____ on the road and the traffic is really bad.

(a) the most cars are there
(b) there are the most cars
(c) there is the most cars
(d) the most cars is there

19 The image charges were taken into account using a fast multiple method modification _____ to the geometry of the system.

(a) adapted specially
(b) special adapt
(c) specially adapt
(d) special adaptation

20 There was even a scheme to have an East Bristol Radial Road, _____ the houses in Fisher Road.

(a) which have built behind
(b) that would have built behind
(c) which would have been built behind
(d) that would have been built behind

Identify the option that contains an awkward expression or an error in grammar.

21 (a) A: Dick, you know what?
       I went to a film festival over the weekend.
   (b) B: Wow, did you enjoy all the wonderful movies?
   (c) A: Yes, especially, I could meet many celebrities.
   (d) B: I wish I were there.

Identify the option that contains an awkward expression or an error in grammar.

22 (a) One of the features symbolized the Turkish way of life is the Turkish Baths, Hamam which is healthy and refreshing. (b) There have been many places in Turkey where they show daily and historical life. (c) They emphasized on cleanliness because of Islam. (d) So, many public bath houses have been built everywhere since Medieval times, and they retain an architectural and historical importance.

Choose the best answer for the blank.

23 A: Hey! What are you doing here?

B: I'm _____ to meet my mother here, but she would be a bit late.

(a) supposed

(b) meant

(c) guessed

(d) promised

24 A: Have you heard Michael was expelled from his school?

B: Yes. He was _____ out of school for taking an illegal drug.

(a) got

(b) pitched

(c) kicked

(d) fired

25 A: When should I submit my resume?

B: Please _____ it in when you come for an interview.

(a) offer

(b) propose

(c) introduce

(d) turn

26 A: What's your attitude towards layoffs in the company? I think it's an unavoidable situation.

B: I don't think so. It is a _____ measure, I think.

(a) difficult

(b) natural

(c) harsh

(d) fair

27 A: Can I use your phone, please? Mine isn't working.

B: Be my _____.

(a) guest

(b) visitor

(c) treat

(d) hand

Choose the best answer for the blank.

28 People had hoped it would keep raining across the country, enough to relieve the drought, but just _____ rain sprinkled the area.

(a) heavy

(b) torrential

(c) regular

(d) sporadic

29 Keep your _____ in case you want to return or exchange the items you bought.

(a) recipes

(b) recipients

(c) receipts

(d) receivers

30 When the products that you've ordered are out of _____, we notify you via text message.

(a) goods

(b) products

(c) selling

(d) stock

31 Since they started selling items at _____ prices, the number of customers decreased because they couldn't get any discounts.

(a) fixed
(b) limit
(c) bottom
(d) negotiable

32 You should not leave the clothes in the dryer for too long, or they will start to _____ .

(a) decrease
(b) small
(c) shrink
(d) shrivel

Part I Read the passage. Then choose the option that best completes the passage.

33 Ramadan, a Muslim religious observance, is a "month of blessing" marked by fasting, self-sacrifice and prayers. During Ramadan, the ninth month of Islamic calendar, the fast is observed every day while the sun is up. Muslims around the world get up before true dawn to eat Suhoor, the pre-dawn meal and have to stop eating and drinking until the fourth prayer of the day, Maghrib (sunset), is due. _____. Hunger and thirst remind Muslims of the suffering of the poor. Fasting is also a chance to practice self-discipline and to purify body and mind.

(a) Fasting serves many purposes
(b) Muslims must feed one poor person each day
(c) The poor and chronically ill are exempt from fasting
(d) The most prominent event of this month is the fasting

34 Modigliani _____. While his life was spinning out of control through drugs, alcohol and declining health leading to his premature death, his paintings were becoming ever more calm and eternal. Modigliani's talent as an artist had been obscured by his flamboyant life. However, as he entered the last phase of his life, especially in his final three years—from 1971 to 1920, Modigliani's works became more cohesive than at any point in his career. It is the singular style of Modigliani's portraits of this period that continues to exert a powerful resonance today. While his legend as the quintessential bohemian will always live on, it is ultimately the art that transcends the personality.

(a) presents a curious paradox
(b) was prodigal with his artistic talent
(c) is known to have led a scandalous life
(d) is one of the most celebrated, yet misunderstood artists

35 The hedgehog's dilemma, or sometimes the porcupine dilemma, refers to the notion that people cannot get intimacy without inflicting psychological pain on each other. This concept originates from Schopenhauer's parable that describes a group of hedgehogs striving to keep the optimal distance where they may feel warm enough without hurting one another with their spines. They usually abandon warmth not to be hurt. It suggests that despite the intention of a close relationship, human intimacy itself causes individuals to erect his spines in self defense. As a result, a person suffering from the hedgehog dilemma _____, due to fear of psychological discomfort.

(a) usually turns to religious society
(b) develops multiple personality disorder
(c) struggles not to be out of touch with people
(d) will usually avoid becoming involved with someone

36 The Golden Globes are American awards which honor both motion pictures and TV programs with the best performances and are presented by Hollywood Foreign Press Association (HFPA). The First Golden Globes were awarded in 1944 and they have since been held annually. They are usually considered as the third most prestigious awards for movies and television, after the Academy Awards (for film) and Emmy Awards (for television). Although they are gaining respectability as an honor in their own right, the Golden Globes _____ because the Golden Globe winners often overlap with the Oscar winners.

(a) have determined and announced the Oscar nominees
(b) have brought greater prestige to the Academy Awards
(c) have come to be regarded a harbinger of the Oscar winners
(d) have made outstanding contributions to the entertainment industry

Read the passage and the question. Then choose the option that best answers the question.

37 Celadon is the most prized ceramic from the Goryeo Dynasty. Celadon is famous for its unique color called as Bi-Saek, which is a bluish or a jade green color. The color of celadon depends on whether or not oxygen exists when a celadon is fired and how much iron is contained in the clay and glaze. To make the Bi-Saek color, a craftsman fires a celadon twice. First, it is fired at 700~800°C and then again after varnishing the glaze, which contains three percentage of iron, at 1,280°C. Bi-Saek is the sole characteristic of Korean celadon, and is very difficult to imitate the color even now with modernized technology.

Q Which of the following is correct about the Bi-Saek color?

(a) The amount of iron plays a key role in deciding the color.
(b) To make the Bi-Saek color, there is no fixed temperature.
(c) How to make the Bi-Saek color was imported from China.
(d) People finally discovered how to make the Bi-Saek color easily.

38 At the International Astronomical Union (IAU) meeting in Prague in 2006, IAU members gathered to decide on a new definition for the word "planet." Celestial bodies can be called a planet only if they satisfy specific criteria. According to the new definition, a planet has to be an object that orbits the sun. It also has to be large enough to have become almost perfectly rounded because of the force of its own gravity, and dominate its neighborhood. Thus, Pluto was demoted from a planet to a dwarf planet because Charon, Pluto's moon, is only a bit smaller than Pluto, so they look like orbiting the sun together.

Q Which is NOT true according to the passage?

(a) Pluto was downgraded because it doesn't dominate Charon.
(b) If a planet is very small, its gravity would not be strong enough to make it round.
(c) According to the new definition, Charon got upgraded to a planet instead of Pluto.
(d) The role of IAU members is definitely important to decide on the astronomical issues.

39 St. Patrick is famous for eliminating snakes which symbolized a pagan. After his death, the Irish considered him as a saint who guarded their country and began to celebrate the day which was thought to be the date of his death. On St. Patrick's Day, people wear green, dissolve green colors into rivers, eat Irish food, and participate in parades. Since the first St. Patrick's Day Parade, which was held in New York on March 17th in 1766, it has been widely celebrated by many people in various parts of the world even though it is not considered an official holiday except for in Ireland.

Q Which of the following is correct according to the passage?

(a) St. Patrick might be dead on March 17.
(b) Only Irish people have festivals on St. Patrick's Day.
(c) Many countries are making St. Patrick's Day an official holiday.
(d) The first St. Patrick's Day Parade was held in Patrick's hometown.

40 Dear Mr. Jones,

I'm writing to tell you that I have received an opportunity to improve my career at NYS Inc. I have accepted a proposal to work for that company as a chief secretary. In accordance with the company policy, I submit this letter in advance. I think you can find a qualified person for my position within 15 days. I'll be looking forward to a positive answer from you. I would like you to know that I will cherish the memories that I have shared with you and my co-workers here.

Sincerely,
Anna Smith

Q What is the purpose of the letter?

(a) To apply for a secretary of NYS Inc.
(b) To express her gratitude to the company
(c) To inform the company of her resignation
(d) To ask the company to change her position

TEPS TIPS • 능동태와 수동태

주어와 동사의 관계를 나타내는 능동태와 수동태를 잘 표현하기 위해서는 정확한 해석이 기본이다. 그러나 외관상 감을 잡을 수 있는 경우도 있다.

1 **외관상 구별할 수 있는 방법**: 수동태는 뒤에 목적어가 오지 않는다.

The awareness of music therapy have been broadened within the public policy arena.

The costs and product qualities are reduced by introducing new technology.

2 목적어가 2개인 경우인 4형식은 수동태 문장에서도 동사 뒤에 목적어가 남아 있을 수 있다.

We were more intimidated when the strange wrapped present was sent us then.

3 **자동사는 수동태가 없다**: 타동사로 착각하기 쉬운 자동사

remain, occur, belong to, consist of , sit, rise, disappear, happen, appear

The chemical steps (were happen, happened) while nobody was in the laboratory.

A typical meal (is consisted of, consists of) a main dish of boiled rice and side dishes of various kinds such as kimchi.

4 **지각동사, 사역동사가 있는 5형식문장의 수동태**: 주어＋지각동사(사역동사)＋목적어＋동사원형
➡ 지각동사나 사역동사가 수동태로 바뀔 때는 원형이 to 부정사로 바뀐다.

I just made him (go , to go) through the woods in a hurry.

➡ He was just made (to go, go) through the woods in a hurry.

고용, 인사 관련

I was wondering if you had any openings. 혹시 사람을 뽑고 있나요?
I got a pay raise. 급여가 올랐다.
I got a promotion. 승진을 했다.
I got transferred to LA. LA로 발령이 났다.
I got fired. 해고 당했다.
=I got dismissed.
=I got laid off.
=They let me go.
=I got a pink slip.

휴가

I want to take a few days off.
　며칠 동안 휴가를 내고 싶어요.
Can I take a sick leave? 병가를 낼 수 있을까요?
I called in sick. 나는 아파서 못나간다고 전화했다.

Phrasal verbs

abstain from ~을 그만두다
apply for ~을 지원하다
come up with (아이디어 등을) 생각해내다
deal with (문제 등을) 다루다, 처리하다
get along 전진하다, 성공하다
look up (사전, 책 등에서) ~을 찾아보다
make up 꾸며내다, 화해하다, 화장하다
turn in 제출하다, 잠자리에 들다
work out (해결책 등을) 생각해내다
work out 운동하다

Collocations

claim one's baggage 수하물을 찾다
violate[break] the law 법을 어기다
harsh measure 가혹한 처사
wedding reception 결혼 피로연
contagious disease 전염병

overwhelming majority 압도적 다수
petty crime 경범죄
entertain questions 질문을 받다
cast a vote 투표를 하다
rat race 치열한 경쟁 사회

Idioms

behind bars 감옥에 갇힌
cost sb an arm and a leg 굉장히 비싸다
face the music 비난을 받아들이다
feel small 기가 죽다
follow suit 선례에 따르다
Hang in there! 견뎌내라!
have an ear for ~소질이 있다
hit bottom 최저치를 기록하다
hit the nail on the head 핵심을 찌르다
turn a deaf ear to 못들은 척 하다

정치 관련 어휘

administration 행정
agenda 의제, 의사일정
anarchy 무정부상태
autocracy 독재정치
ballot-box 투표함
by-election 보궐선거
cabinet 내각
candidate 후보자, 지원자
canvass 주문[권유]하러 돌아다니다
chauvinism 국수주의
communism 공산주의
defection 탈퇴, 탈당
delegate 대표자
deputy 대리인
filibuster 의사진행 방해자
hard-liner 강경파
hegemony 패권, 지배권
imperialism 제국주의
inauguration 취임, 개시

LISTENING COMPREHENSION

Part I   Choose the most appropriate response to the statement.

1   (a)   (b)   (c)   (d)

2   (a)   (b)   (c)   (d)

3   (a)   (b)   (c)   (d)

Part II   Choose the most appropriate response to complete the conversation.

4   (a)   (b)   (c)   (d)

5   (a)   (b)   (c)   (d)

6   (a)   (b)   (c)   (d)

Choose the option that best answers the question.

7   (a)   (b)   (c)   (d)

8   (a)   (b)   (c)   (d)

9   (a)   (b)   (c)   (d)

Choose the option that best answers the question.

10 (a)   (b)   (c)   (d)

11 (a)   (b)   (c)   (d)

12 (a)   (b)   (c)   (d)

Part I

Choose the best answer for the blank.

13 A: What do I have to do to be a nice roommate?
    B: You can do _____.

(a) you do
(b) that you please
(c) as you please
(d) as you pleasing

14 A: When I stayed in Vancouver with my children, we _____
       Science Museums.
    B: Wow. I must have visited there too when I was there.

(a) was visiting
(b) are visiting
(c) used to visit
(d) would like to visit

15 A: Have you heard our school debate team winning the grand prize?
    B: Yes, I can't express _____.

(a) how I am pleased
(b) how pleased am I
(c) how pleasing I am
(d) how pleased I am

16 A: On the way home my car suddenly stopped.
    B: You'd better _____.

(a) get it to fix
(b) get it fixed
(c) it get fixed
(d) get to fix it

Choose the best answer for the blank.

17 A superstition is _____ between certain actions or behaviors, and other actions.

(a) irrational belief about the relation
(b) an irrational belief about relation
(c) irrational belief about the relation
(d) an irrational belief about the relation

18 Korea and the USA _____ about the future of six-party talks, so both sides have expressed willingness to be flexible in negotiations.

(a) are remained optimistic
(b) are remained optimistically
(c) remain optimistic
(d) remain optimistically

19 He probably meant to indicate that you should participate in the course he recommended in the answer _____.

(a) which you refer
(b) when you refer
(c) to that you refer
(d) to which you refer

20 To decide which atoms can be related to the appropriate method of hybrid calculation, a molecule has been divided up _____ three arbitrary layers.

(a) into
(b) as
(c) with
(d) upon

Identify the option that contains an awkward expression or an error in grammar.

21   (a) A: Did you complete the legal papers?
     (b) B: Yes, but I have to check more judical cases.
     (c) A: My case is also tough enough to rise lots of cross examinations.
     (d) B: I love what I am but, nothing seems easy.

Identify the option that contains an awkward expression or an error in grammar.

22   (a) It's said that domestic dogs are descended from the wolf and have been living in association with people. (b) Genetic evidence suggests that Native Americans and Europeans domesticate dogs independently, and later North American dogs were almost completely replaced by dogs that European brought. (c) Before Europeans arrived in America, dogs were used for their fur. (d) They were bred for wool like sheep for making blankets.

Choose the best answer for the blank.

23 A: For the first time in 10 years, I'm going to run my own restaurant!

B: Congratulations! You _____ it. You really worked hard.

(a) qualified

(b) available

(c) worth

(d) deserve

24 A: Is the post office far from here?

B: Not really. It's within walking _____.

(a) way

(b) road

(c) distance

(d) length

25 A: I can't help it. He's quite stubborn about this matter.

B: Leave it to me. I'll _____ him into changing his mind.

(a) tell

(b) speak

(c) talk

(d) address

26 A: Rachel! Long time no see!

B: Hi! I haven't seen you _____. How have you been?

(a) under age

(b) in ages

(c) for since

(d) after all

27 A: Thanks for inviting me. By the way, where's Linda?

B: Oh my god! I forgot to invite her. It just _____ my mind!

(a) slipped
(b) slid
(c) forgot
(d) jumped

Choose the best answer for the blank.

28. The president started to _____ the sales manager about decreasing sales at the moment.

(a) scold
(b) reprimand
(c) punish
(d) tease

29 If your _____ skin easily becomes red and itchy, use cosmetics made of natural ingredients.

(a) sensitive
(b) sensible
(c) sensory
(d) sensual

30 After playing basketball, he started to feel thirsty. But there was nowhere to _____ his thirst in the area.

(a) sip
(b) drink
(c) alleviate
(d) quench

31 The local people objected to building the waste processing _____ in their residential area.

(a) service

(b) amenity

(c) facility

(d) team

32 Many patients waiting for _____ die every day because of the shortage of donated organs.

(a) implants

(b) transplants

(c) transmitters

(d) operations

Part I Read the passage. Then choose the option that best completes the passage.

33 When a school implements an Anti-Bullying campaign, students hold the key to success mainly because they usually know who the bullies and the victims are long before teachers and parents do. A majority of students strongly believe in justice and therefore welcome Anti-Bullying policies that ensure a safe school. However, students are more likely to participate in an Anti-Bullying campaign when they feel secure that reporting bullying will not cause them to lose status in their peer group. _____ in order for the students not to be accused of snitching.

(a) Custody can not be ignored
(b) Remission should be vouched
(c) Impartiality must be predetermined
(d) Confidentiality must be guaranteed

34 During the process of women's suffrage movements, many campaigners agreed that women should be allowed to vote. However, these campaigners still had disagreements about why women should be granted suffrage rights. Some of them thought that women voters would have an enlightening effect on politics and influence laws which impacted on their home and family because a woman's place was in her home. They believed that women were naturally kinder, more caring, and more sympathetic than men. _____ , the other campaigners thought of women's suffrage as a way of compensating for the votes of weaker members of society.

(a) Therefore
(b) As a result
(c) On the other hand
(d) As a matter of fact

35 School phobia is a kind of social anxiety disorder that describes an overwhelming fear of going to school. School phobic children may become physically ill at the thought of being in class and sometimes suffer from severe panic attacks. They should not be mistaken for those who play truant at one time or another. If school refusal continues, discussion with school personnel will be needed to form a unified home and school approach. _____, chronic school phobias can cause the decline in academic performance and failure in peer relationships, possibly leading to adult anxiety disorders.

(a) Otherwise
(b) Likewise
(c) Meanwhile
(d) Therefore

Read the passage and the question. Then choose the option that best answers the question.

36 The Web site www.goodparent.com provides some examples of traits of oldest, middle and youngest children. Parents should know about these characteristics and encourage children to develop desirable characteristics no matter their birth order. Firstborns are usually responsible, and sometimes substitute parent for younger siblings. If in a dysfunctional family, they may feel too much burden on themselves. Middle children are usually good negotiators. They may feel squeezed out and unloved and feel out of place in the family. Last borns are usually outgoing and creative. However, they tend to have few expectations of themselves because their parents may have lower expectations for their youngest after having raised several children already.

Q What can be inferred from the passage?

(a) Birth order stereotypes can bring more harm than good.
(b) Firstborns should take more responsibility than other siblings do.
(c) Children should be given opportunities according to their birth order
(d) Parents need to encourage the middle child to have a sense of belonging.

37 The Digital Home D146, marketing globally, makes its debut this week. It is designed to support up to 16 channels of real-time recording and provide the most flexible operation to allow home users to use it with ease. Users can set up a weekly recording schedule at their own will, and decide which hours of the day they want to record. It can also be installed in various locations in the house. Home users can monitor all cameras at one time and see any suspected images without wasting time if any motions are detected. It is characterized by the leading technology device that enables to restart its task after interruption of electric power or system crash.

Q What is the Digital Home D146?

(a) camcorder
(b) video camera
(c) digital camera
(d) surveillance system

38 Monarchs are large and colorful butterflies that live in various countries such as America, Australia, and Western Europe. The average wingspan of a monarch is almost four inches and the wings are bright orange with decorative black veins and white dots along the edge. A monarch's vivid coloring plays a role in warning predators that they are poisonous. However, even though an animal eats a monarch, it doesn't actually die, it's only sick enough to avoid the butterflies in the future.

Q What can be inferred from the passage?

(a) A monarch is the largest butterfly.
(b) Monarchs live throughout the world.
(c) A monarch's toxins are not fatal but harmful.
(d) A monarch is noticeable even at night due to its colors.

39 The subprime mortgage crisis is a current problem which became more manifest these days. The US mortgages have three levels shch as Prime, Alternative-A, and Subprime. Of the three, Subprime is considered the lowest mortgage loan. It is applied to people who have unstable credit histories like bankruptcies, payment delinquencies, and charge-offs so they hold a mortgage with a high interest rate. The subprime mortgage crisis began as the decrease of lending standards, the increase in loan incentives and the high expectation of housing prices encouraged people to borrow money easily and refinance as well. However, when the interest rates started to rise and the real estate price dropped, borrowers faced totally different situations.

Q What can NOT be inferred as a cause of subprime mortgage crisis?

(a) the excessive individual debt levels
(b) the downturn in the housing market
(c) the risky lending and borrowing policy
(d) the incomplete network of investment banks

Part III   Read the passage. Then identify the option that does NOT belong.

40 Food poisoning is common, but sometimes fatal. (a) Typical symptoms are nausea and diarrhea that occur abruptly within 48 hours after eating a contaminated food. (b) Depending on the poison, fever and bloody stools, dehydration, and nervous system damage may follow. (c) The symptoms, called an outbreak, may affect one person or a group of people who ate the same food. (d) Additionally, there are possible new global threats to the world's food supply through terrorist actions using food toxins.

TEPS TIPS • 동사의 시제 일치

시제일치는 주절 동사의 시제에 따라 종속절의 동사가 제한을 받는 것을 말하는데, 원칙은 주절의 동사가 현재일 경우는 종속절의 시제에 영향을 미치지 않으나, 과거형일 때는 현재나 현재관련 시제가 오지 않는 다는 것이다. 그러나 법칙에 몇 가지 예외가 있다. 즉, 주절의 시제가 과거라도 종속절이 가정법이거나 종속절의 시제를 항상 현재로 쓰는 불변의 진리가 올 경우 등이다.

1 주절의 시제에 영향을 받지 않는 경우

My science teacher said that the sun (rises , rose) in the east.

Not many people seemed to know that the average person (breathes, breathed) 21,600 times a day.

My father and mother said that if I put my mind to it, I can do anything.

2 주장, 제안, 요구, 명령, 권유동사 + that 주어 (should) 동사원형

demand, suppose, suggest + that 주어 (should) 동사원형

종속절에 앞으로 해야 할 당위성을 나타낼 때 should +동사원형을 쓰는데, should를 생략할 수 있으므로 원형만 남아서 실제 주절과 시제가 일치되지 않는다.

그러나 조심해야 할 것은 종속절의 의미가 당위성을 나타내는 것이 아니라면, 원래대로 시제를 주절과 일치시키면 된다.

It is demanded that potable water (had, should have) a quality to meet rather rigid standards.

He suggested that geometric assumptions (are, be) inappropriate because the data may violate the metric theories.

cf) The advocates insisted that it (made, make) no sense to analyze the data before checking its quality.

시험

I have my final in 2 weeks.
2주 후에 기말 고사가 있어.

I passed the exam. 시험에 합격했어.

I passed the test with flying colors.
좋은 성적으로 시험에 합격했어.

What grade did you get on the test?
시험 몇 점 받았어?

What's the minimum G.P.A. requirement for graduation?
졸업하려면 최소 평점이 얼마나 되야 합니까?

I crammed for the exam.
나는 벼락치기로 공부했다.

I did well on the exam. 시험을 잘 봤어.

= I aced the exam.

I flunked the exam. 시험을 망쳤어.

= I bombed the test.

= I messed up.

= I screwed up.

전공

What was your major? 전공이 무엇이었습니까?

= What did you major in?

= What subject did you specialize in?

What was your graduation thesis on?
졸업 논문 주제는 무엇이었습니까?

Phrasal verbs

answer to ~에 부합하다, ~에 답하다.

apply to 적용되다 (=concern, fit)

attribute to ~을 ~탓으로 돌리다.

bring up 교육시키다. 기르다.

call down 꾸짖다.

figure out 이해하다.

mark down 점수를 깎다, 값을 내리다

turn down 거절하다

hold back ~을 억제하다, 자제하다

stick to ~을 고수하다, 지키다

Collocations

bilateral trade 상호 균형 무역

degenerative diseases 퇴행성 질환

redeeming feature 단점을 보충하는 장점

sandwich course 이론과 실습을 병행한 강좌

severe/fierce competition 치열한 경쟁

insatiable appetite 엄청난 식욕

lost cause 가망 없는 것

golden opportunity 황금 같은 기회

inferiority complex 열등감

stifle creativity 창의력을 저해하다

Idioms

kick the bucket 죽다

lend someone a hand ~를 도와주다

once in a blue moon 매우 드물게

one-track mind 편협한 사고방식

pull an all-nighter 밤새워 공부(일)하다

rack one's brains 머리를 쥐어 짜내다

Speak of the devil 호랑이도 제 말하면 온다

spill the beans 비밀을 누설하다

under the weather 몸이 좋지 않은

up in the air 미결의, 정해지지 않은

전공명

biology 생물학	sociology 사회학
psychology 심리학	anthropology 인류학
archeology 고고학	geology 지질학
meteorology 기상학	politics 정치학
economics 경제학	electronics 전자공학
mathematics 수학	linguistics 언어학
engineering 공학	education 교육
agriculture 농학	literature 문학
law 법학	botany 식물학
journalism 신문학	geography 지리학
philosophy 철학	chemistry 화학
accounting 회계	architecture 건축학
astronomy 천문학	

Part I Choose the most appropriate response to the statement.

1   (a)   (b)   (c)   (d)

2   (a)   (b)   (c)   (d)

3   (a)   (b)   (c)   (d)

Part II Choose the most appropriate response to complete the conversation.

4   (a)   (b)   (c)   (d)

5   (a)   (b)   (c)   (d)

6   (a)   (b)   (c)   (d)

Choose the option that best answers the question.

7 (a)   (b)   (c)   (d)

8 (a)   (b)   (c)   (d)

9 (a)   (b)   (c)   (d)

Choose the option that best answers the question.

10 (a)   (b)   (c)   (d)

11 (a)   (b)   (c)   (d)

12 (a)   (b)   (c)   (d)

Choose the best answer for the blank.

13 A: Somebody already checked out the book the teacher recommends, where can I borrow it?

B: I bought one, so if you want, I will _____.

(a) lend it you

(b) lend it for you

(c) lend it to you

(d) get it for you

14 A: How many joined the exhibition?

B: Not so many, just _____ visited our booth.

(a) less

(b) a few

(c) few

(d) more

15 A: I don't understand why parents let the children run around?

B: _____.

(a) So am I

(b) So do I

(c) Me neither

(d) Me either

16 A: How long do we have to go to the palace?

B: _____.

(a) Here I am

(b) Here we are

(c) We are here

(d) Here you are

Choose the best answer for the blank.

17 _____ than the Boeing 747, the airbus, the European manufacturer said, has been slow to react to the company.

(a) Having started the project latter
(b) Having started the project later
(c) Started the project the latter
(d) Starting the project the latter

18 The child whistled for the help and narrowly escaped _____ when being robbed in the street.

(a) to kidnap
(b) being kidnapped
(c) to be kidnapped
(d) have kidnapped

19 Before adopting a pet, _____ , and you'll choose an animal that will fit into your lifestyle.

(a) having some research
(b) doing some research
(c) to do some research
(d) do some research

20 He denied that the result of the match was creating a more cut-throat environment _____ players didn't desire.

(a) in which
(b) for which
(c) what
(d) when

Identify the option that contains an awkward expression or an error in grammar.

21　(a) A: Have you done with this project?

　　(b) B: No. I don't understand why we do this useless project.

　　(c) A: Me, either, however, whether we like it or not, we have to finish it by 5

　　(d) B: That makes me really crazy.

Identify the option that contains an awkward expression or an error in grammar.

22　(a) And yet, during the group's heyday, the group never made big in the States. (b) The group scored a number one hit on Billboard's Top 40 singles chart. (c) But the group's hit singles never quite translated into substantial album sales, and the four individual members were remained fairly anonymous, never turning into household names. (d) Compared to the group's success in Europe and Australia, the impact in the United States was fairly modest.

Choose the best answer for the blank.

23 A: Should I bring you something for your party?

B: Just _____ yourself.

(a) be
(b) make
(c) bring
(d) stay

24 A: Do you want to catch a midnight movie?

B: I'm sorry. I'm a bit tired. I'm just going to _____.

(a) turn in
(b) turn up
(c) go in
(d) lie in

25 A: Why are you taking only 12 credits?

B: The _____ has risen up too much.

(a) fare
(b) charge
(c) tuition
(d) bill

26 A: Excuse me. Are you with me?

B: Sure. I'm all _____.

(a) ears
(b) ear
(c) thumbs
(d) eyes

27 A: What are you going to do for the guests after exchanging gifts?

B: We're going to serve light _____ and snacks.

(a) refreshments
(b) recreation
(c) entertainments
(d) discussion

Choose the best answer for the blank.

28 People were very frightened about the possible spread of a _____ disease called SARS.

(a) mild
(b) chronic
(c) deficiency
(d) contagious

29 Agricultural biotech _____ argue that farmers can benefit from genetically modified foods, at this time of global food shortages, and extreme weather.

(a) protectors
(b) proportions
(c) prosecutions
(d) proponents

30 During _____ the third party talk to both sides in a controversy to make a decision impartially.

(a) aristocracy
(b) arbitration
(c) meditation
(d) argumentation

31 The two leaders who couldn't bridge the differences have failed to
_____ after all.

(a) reciprocate

(b) reconcile

(c) reinforce

(d) refurbish

32 The finance Ministry announced that its budget remained in
_____ this year and it decided to cut taxes.

(a) superstition

(b) surface

(c) subdivision

(d) surplus

Read the passage. Then choose the option that best completes the passage.

33 The term "dysfunctional family" usually describes a condition where a continuum of conflict, misbehavior and even abuse on the part of individual members exist in a family. However, it is not so easy to identify or define what dysfunctional means because it ranges from the damaging, but socially accepted misbehavior that routinely happens in many families to severely abusive situations in which physical and/or sexual abuse occurs. In order to define a dysfunctional family, one must first know _____.
Most families go through some periods of time when functioning is impaired—slightly or harshly. Healthy families regain their normal functioning after the crisis passes. On the contrary, problems tend to be chronic in dysfunctional families.

(a) that perfection is unattainable
(b) why a dysfunctional family stays that way
(c) how impeccable healthy families are
(d) what functional or healthy families are

34 October 19, 1987, is known as Black Monday, the day when the Dow Jones Industrial Average(DJIA) plunged by 508 points, losing 22.6% of its total value. As a consequence of the unprecedented decline, Hong Kong and Australia markets had fallen 45.8% and 41.8%, respectively, by the end of that October. Today's more globalized world economy has a much higher risk of a chain of economic disasters. While the catastrophic crash in 1987 had impacts outside the United States, another U.S. Black Monday now would bring on

_____.

(a) a powerful bull market
(b) widespread pessimism
(c) a global Black Tuesday
(d) global economic equilibrium

35 Various reasons are considered for choosing vegetarianism but ethical reasons that the rearing and killing of other animals for the sole purpose of eating is inherently wrong are viewed the most important of all. It has also been suggested that although consumption of meat should be accepted as an individual's choice of food, the methods by which animals are killed in the factory farming industry should be more humane. However, _____. The entire life of a 'food animal' is an abject one of artificial breeding, cruel castration and/or hormone stimulation, feeding of an abnormal diet, and very restricted mobility. To accept all this and only oppose the heartless cruelty of the last few seconds of its life is "complacency itself."

(a) many slaughter factories have been modernized
(b) the vegetarian lifestyle has become more widespread
(c) the conception of "humane animal slaughter" is refutable
(d) arguments that have nothing to do with animal rights exist

---

Part II Read the passage and the question. Then choose the option that best answers the question.

36 A copycat suicide, sometimes known as a Werther effect, is defined as a duplication of another suicide that is publicized through the accounts or depictions of the original suicide on television and in other media. Reporting suicide methods, romanticizing the suicide, particularly about celebrities, and glorifying the deceased all lead to increases in the suicide rate. Moreover, although studies show a high incidence of psychiatric disorders, reports tend to ignore the impact of them. Reports that deal with this factor and provide help-line contact numbers and advice for people with suicidal feelings can reduce copycat suicides.

Q What is the main idea of the passage?

(a) Reporting of suicide should be totally banned.
(b) There should be a concerted effort to reduce suicide.
(c) The Werther effect has been amplified through the Internet.
(d) Covering suicide, media professionals should be offered guidelines.

37 An inferiority complex is a feeling that one is inferior to others in some way. While an ordinary feeling of inferiority can motivate individuals to achieve more, an inferiority complex is an abnormal state of discouragement, often driving afflicted individuals to self-estrangement. Many suggestions have been made for those who feel inferior to others ; writing down good qualities or plus points, changing self-image, attempts at achieving and becoming superior will, the usage of affirmations, etc. However, all of these only act as a makeshift to an already existing inferiority complex. What use is there of just repeating 10 times "I am a unique creation of God," "I have many good qualities."

Q   What is the main idea of this passage?

(a) One needs to identify our unique quality and develop it.
(b) Auto suggestive therapy helps one to regain confidence.
(c) It takes more than affirmations to overcome inferiority complex.
(d) Affirmations help one get out of the clutches of inferiority complex.

38 There are some people who try to explain Lookism, a form of discrimination or prejudice against others based on their appearance, with Darwin's Survival of the Fittest Principle. If "fittest" means more beautiful, more attractive or healthier, then only more beautiful people should remain. However, when we take into consideration that the majority of the people are physically ordinary, Lookism cannot be accepted naturally. A study from Texas and Michigan Universities reports that good-looking workers are paid 10 more percent. This phenomenon takes place in school, in court, and—believe it or not—at home. If you take Lookism for granted, you can become a victim of it. Now, visit our website, and take part in the discussion about Lookism.

Q   What is the purpose of this passage?

(a) To define Lookism more precisely in various perspectives
(b) To convince people of Lookism and introduce a site against it
(c) To warn people how widely Lookism has spread in a modern society
(d) To explain the relationship between Lookism and Survival of Fittest Principle

39 Visit the legacy of three generations of wine-making excellence, Joseph's Estate Winery in Niagara-on-the-Lake. This soaring, light-filled cathedral of wine, surrounded by vines, is an unmatched winery experience. Let our guest relations team arrange your visit for you, including tours of our underground barrel aging cellar and lush, sprawling vineyard, special wine tasting and seminars, and reservations in our critically-acclaimed restaurant. Don't miss the chance to get a taste of true Canadian wine. You'll find that no detail is overlooked in our pursuit of wine-making excellence.

Q What is the purpose of this advertisement?

(a) To visit the Niagara
(b) To join a wine tasting trip
(c) To invest in wine-making industry
(d) To make wine-making process known

40 As one of the many injured Iraq war veterans, I dare to say that I did my best to protect my country. Once again, I'm going to do my best as a sprinter on behalf of my country at the Paralympics. However, I cannot help but wonder what the results would be like if Paralympic athletes had been fully trained for the last four years. The Olympic Committee provides smaller amounts of training stipends and awards less medal bonuses to Paralympians than Olympians because the Paralympics don't generate as much profits as the Olympics. However, remember that we have to compete with athletes from other countries like Canada and Britain which support their disabled athletes fully.

Q What is the main idea of the passage?

(a) The support and benefits for Paralympic athletes should be improved.
(b) Paralympians should be treated like Olympians equally in every aspect.
(c) Paralympians who are Iraq war veterans deserve more salary and bonus.
(d) Paralympics must be considered as a major sports event like the Olympics.

TEPS TIPS • 목적어로 쓰이는 동명사와 to부정사 비교

두 가지 목적어의 형태가 갖는 가장 큰 차이는 동명사는 주로 과거에 한 일을 나타내며, to부정사는 앞으로 할 일에 대해 나타낸다. 일반적으로 본동사의 특징에 따라 각각 동명사나 to부정사를 목적어로 가지는데, 동명사를 목적어로 취하는 대표 동사들을 기억하는 것이 쉽다.

1 동명사를 목적어로 취하는 동사: 제안, 중지, 부정적인 의미 (m e g a p f e s)

mind / enjoy / give up / avoid / postpone / finish / escape / stop
suggest / recommend / consider / quit / discontinue / dislike / deny

2 동명사와 to 부정사를 모두 목적어로 취하는 동사: 계속해서 시작하고, 싫어하거나, 좋아한다

continue / begin / start / love / like/ prefer / hate

3 두 가지가 모두 가능하지만 뜻이 달라지는 경우

try	try to부정사 열심히 노력하다
	try 동명사 시험 삼아 해보다
remember(forget)	remember(forget)+to부정사 ~할 것을 기억하다(아직 안 한 일)
	remember(forget)+동명사 ~한 것을 기억하다(이미 한 일)
regret	regret + to부정사 ~하게 되어 유감이다
	regret + 동명사 ~한 것을 후회 한다
stop	stop + to부정사 ~하기 위해 멈추다
	stop + 동명사 ~한 것을 그만두다
need(want)	need + to부정사 ~할 필요가 있다
	need+ 동명사 ~가 필요하다(수동의 의미)

The environmental plan needs amending.

➡ The environmental plan needs to be amended.

TEPS TIPS • 어휘·표현 정리

식당, 술집(1)

May I take your order? 주문하시겠어요?
= Are you ready to order?
= What will it be?
What would you like? 무엇을 드시겠어요?
I'd like to see the menu, please.
　　메뉴 좀 보여주세요.
= May I have a menu, please?
= Will you show me the menu, please?
For here or to go?
　　여기서 드시겠어요, 아니면 포장해 가시겠어요?
How many in your party? 일행이 몇 분이세요?
Are you expecting company? 일행이 있으십니까?
= Are you waiting for anyone?
= Is anyone joining you?
This is on the house.
　　이것은 서비스로 드리는 거예요.

Phrasal verbs

account for ~을 설명하다
attend on (upon) 시중들다
call for 요구하다
familiar to+사람 잘 알려져 있는
give in 양보하다, 항복하다
lay out 펼치다, 진열하다, 전개하다
pass out 분배하다
pay off 완불(完拂)하다
pick out 선택하다, 고르다
wait on 시중들다

Collocations

bear fruit 과실을 맺다
fill an order 주문받다
make a fuss 소란 피우다
throw a part 파티를 열다
set a priority 우선 순위를 정하다
satisfy/appease hunger 허기를 채우다

quench/slake thirst 갈증을 풀다
smell a rat 낌새를 채다
morning sickness 입덧
break one's fast 금식을 깨다, 아침을 먹다

Idioms

a drop in the bucket 극히 소량
a sweet tooth 단 음식을 몹시 좋아함
as easy as pie 매우 쉬운
by word of mouth 구전으로
have the time of your life 즐거운 시간을 보내다
hold one's tongue 잠자코 있다
in season 제철을 만난, 한창인
No laughing matter 웃을 일이 아니다
packed on like sardines 콩나물시루 같은
pull one's leg ~에게 농담하다, ~을 놀리다

음식 관련 어휘

appetizer 전채 요리
beverage 음료
chef 주방장
cuisine 요리
dessert 디저트
flavor 맛
main course 주요리
recipe 요리법
vegetarian 채식주의자
refreshments 간식거리
picky eater 입맛이 까다로운 사람
expiration date 유통기한
leftover 먹다 남은 음식
take-out(carry-out) food 포장해서 가져가는 음식
flat (맥주, 탄산음료 등이) 김이 빠진

Part I   Choose the most appropriate response to the statement.

1   (a)   (b)   (c)   (d)

2   (a)   (b)   (c)   (d)

3   (a)   (b)   (c)   (d)

Part II   Choose the most appropriate response to complete the conversation.

4   (a)   (b)   (c)   (d)

5   (a)   (b)   (c)   (d)

6   (a)   (b)   (c)   (d)

Part III Choose the option that best answers the question.

7 (a)   (b)   (c)   (d)

8 (a)   (b)   (c)   (d)

9 (a)   (b)   (c)   (d)

Part IV Choose the option that best answers the question.

10 (a)   (b)   (c)   (d)

11 (a)   (b)   (c)   (d)

12 (a)   (b)   (c)   (d)

Part I   Choose the best answer for the blank.

13   A: How was the movie last night?
   B: Not so bad, but _____.

   (a) too boring
   (b) too bored
   (c) a little bored
   (d) a little boring

14   A: Where should I keep this box?
   B: The box _____ in the refrigerator after opening.

   (a) need to place
   (b) must be placed
   (c) must place
   (d) placing

15   A: What do I have to prepare for dinner?
   B: I will be home late today, so you'll _____.

   (a) have fixed dinner
   (b) don't have to have dinner
   (c) need fixing dinner.
   (d) need to fix yourself dinner

16   A: After completing the survey, where can I return it?
   B: We appreciate _____ the time to fill out our survey.

   (a) your taking
   (b) for you to take
   (c) to take you
   (d) of you to take

Choose the best answer for the blank.

17 _____ the major artists noticed the Korean animation industry undergoing a transition.

(a) At the 1990s
(b) During the 1990s
(c) For 1990s
(d) While the 1990s

18 We have provided sample correspondence _____ their representatives to solve the environmental problems.

(a) for citizens to encourage
(b) of citizens to encourage
(c) citizens to encourage
(d) citizens to encouraging

19 _____ major in this subject, I have broadened my knowledge of Genetic Engineering.

(a) I decided to
(b) I have decided to
(c) I deciding for
(d) Deciding to

20 The World Union wouldn't have promoted human development through the technology _____ .

(a) without the web site
(b) with the web site
(c) were it not for the web site
(d) if it were not for the web site

Identify the option that contains an awkward expression or an error in grammar.

21 (a) A: When is your annual exhibition? Did you invite all guests?
   (b) B: Not, yet. Why?
   (c) A: Can I bring my co-worker, who's really interested in the calligraphy.
   (d) B: Whoever may come, he will welcome.

Part IV

Identify the option that contains an awkward expression or an error in grammar.

22 (a) Given the sermon here, we should try and keep our mouth shut, should we not? (b) Keeping this adage in mind can help us committing a faux pas. (c) It is best to understand that our natural roles in our society were not the same, but were complementary. (d) And, the last one to remember is that we should be more modest in our beliefs.

Part I Choose the best answer for the blank.

23 A: What took you so long?
B: I got a _____ tire on the way here.

(a) worn
(b) flat
(c) spare
(d) hole

24 A: I bought this skirt for half-price.
B: That was a real _____ .

(a) purchase
(b) robbery
(c) customer
(d) bargain

25 A: The manager had no _____ but to quit. But I don't want to.
B: Don't worry. Things are going to be all right.

(a) alternative
(b) free
(c) feeling
(d) option

26 A: Hey! What brings you here?
B: Wow. What a surprise to _____ across each other here!

(a) come
(b) get
(c) take
(d) see

27 A: I can't even lift a finger. My entire body aches.

B: Don't make a _____ ! You're grown up.

(a) worry

(b) fuss

(c) fun

(d) mistake

Part II   Choose the best answer for the blank.

28 The Mexican government decided to intervene in the currency market to halt dollar's _____ which made the peso lose value against the dollar.

(a) depreciation

(b) decrease

(c) appreciation

(d) applause

29 It is favorable to affix a budget upfront before reserving anything for the wedding _____.

(a) reception

(b) receipt

(c) recession

(d) resolution

30 Once he was a very famous actor worldwide, but now he looks a far _____ from when he was in his prime.

(a) way

(b) tear

(c) cry

(d) weep

31 With Christmas just around the _____ the shops throughout the country have begun their annual Christmas sales.

(a) door
(b) corner
(c) start
(d) step

32 You need to be _____ to people when you use your cell phone around them because using your cell phone can be disturbing to others in public places, such as buses or movie theaters.

(a) considerable
(b) considerate
(c) constant
(d) concise

Read the passage. Then choose the option that best completes the passage.

33 Imagine hushed, serene, starry nights & beautiful scenery by day, and this is what we have for you. Situated on 80 acres in the hamlet of Ashburn, our home was built in the Victorian style in 1852. We invite you to 'Step Back In Time' and relax in our beautifully restored Victorian style house. Offering a truly unique getaway, whether you like to take a long walks or just relax, this is the place to be. All Deluxe Rooms offer a private entrance, ensuite bathroom, sitting area, courtesy fridge, coffee maker and more. A full country breakfast awaits you. Come for a quiet getaway and visit our many local attractions. This is _____ that you're looking for!

(a) the hotel
(b) the museum
(c) the amusement park
(d) the bed and breakfast

34 It's hard to believe there was a time when _____.
One heroic young woman proved it could make the difference between life and death. During the Crimean War in 1854, Florence Nightingale found a medical nightmare where patients were dying as much from dirt and disease as from battle wounds. She demanded fresh bedding, clean water, and better food. Watching her tirelessly walking her nightly rounds, they called their angel of mercy "the lady with the lamp." During her lifetime, she was hailed as a world-class expert on hospital treatment and transformed nursing into a lifesaving, life-giving profession.

(a) women were not allowed to engage in nursing
(b) medical services were not easy for the military to get
(c) nursing was looked down on as an unimportant occupation
(d) there was no difference between nursing and medical care

35 _____ often emboldens Internet trolls to attack a blogger with threats or insults. There has been a constant demand for an online discussion aimed at opposing abusive online behavior and developing a blogger's code of conduct. The more popularity blogging is gaining, the stronger the possibility of attacks or threats against the blogger is growing. Malicious online comments, often without any apparent reason, devastate the victims and in a worst-case scenario may drive them to kill themselves.

(a) Supporters of free speech
(b) Anonymity on the Internet
(c) Ethical standards of their own
(d) Vulnerability to verbal attacks

Part II   Read the passage and the question. Then choose the option that best answers the question.

36   According to the Department of Health and Human Services, the number of allegations of misconduct by U.S. researchers rose to record highs last year—50 percent higher than 2007 and the highest since 1990 when a program to deal with scientific misconduct was established. Of the 23 cases closed last year, eight individuals were found guilty of research misconduct. Unfortunately, however, it is suggested that this is but a tip of the iceberg—a small fraction of the prevailing scientific misconduct such as fabrication, falsification and plagiarism.

Q   What is the best title for the passage?

(a) Faked research results on rise
(b) Instances of unethical experimentation
(c) Guidelines for handing allegations of misconduct
(d) Researches motivated by desire for personal advancement

37 The BlackBerry is a wireless handheld device developed by the Canadian company Research In Motion (RIM), which supports push e-mail, mobile telephone, text messaging and other wireless information services. RIM decided on the name "BlackBerry" only after considering all the passable names suggested by Lexicon Branding Inc.. One of the naming experts thought the miniature buttons on the device looked like the tiny seeds in a strawberry but straw sounded too slow. Someone else suggested BlackBerry and RIM applauded it.

Q What is the main topic of the passage?

(a) Success of RIM's pilot device
(b) Name origin of the BlackBerry
(c) New slang brought by the BlackBerry
(d) Brand naming in the world of marketing

38 Giant anteaters spend most of their time foraging for their food – ants and termites—with their excellent sense of smell. They are also known for eating other soft-bodied insects like grubs which don't have heavy jaws or chemical defenses. Once they have found their prey, they use their strong forelegs and sharp claws to rip the prey's nests open and utilize their long snout functioning as a vacuum and their sticky tongue to suck in ants or termites from their shelters.

Q What is the passage mainly about?

(a) An anteater's voracious appetite
(b) The reason why an anteater is called this name
(c) Kinds of insects that an anteater likes or dislikes
(d) An anteater's peculiarities for finding and eating its prey

39 The Boeing 787 Dreamliner, an aircraft currently being developed by the Boeing Company, is famous for using the most advanced technology and as a super efficient airplane. The most remarkable characteristic of the Boeing 787 Dreamliner is that its fuselage is primarily made of carbon fiber composite material so its durability will be improved and it will produce less refuse and waste, being manufactured as a one-piece. In terms of fuel efficiency, it is considered supreme because it will use twenty percent less fuel than today's similar sized airliners. Moreover, thanks to the superior engines which GE and Rolls-Royce has developed, it is expected that engine thrust and fuel efficiency will be increased, while the noise of the jet decreased.

Q What is the best title for the passage?

(a) Boeing 787 Dreamliner, the Most Popular Airplane
(b) The Unparalleled Features of the Boeing 787 Dreamliner
(c) The Boeing Company does business with GE and Rolls-Royce
(d) The Boeing 787 Dreamliner as an Environmental Friendly Aircraft

Part III Read the passage. Then identify the option that does NOT belong.

40 To get a job you really crave for, it is very important to make sure that you are qualified and well prepared. (a) Also, it is crucial that you make a good first impression to the interviewers. (b) Be well groomed, which means your hair should be clean and styled conservatively based on a company's atmosphere and you should not wear excessive make-up, jewelry, or perfume. (c) Dress yourself appropriately according to the position you are looking for, not to mention that your garments must be immaculate. (d) Ask intelligent questions about the position with a clear voice, and the interviewers will respond to you favorably.

TEPS TIPS • 가정법

가정법은 텝스에서 항상 빠지지 않고 나오고 있는 문법사항으로, 앞뒤 관계를 찾는 문제인데, 가정법 형태에 대한 단순한 암기로도 득점이 가능한 간단한 유형에 속한다.

1

가정법 과거: 현재와 반대되는 사실을 가정할 때 〈만약 ~한다면, ~ 할 텐데〉

If 주어+동사의 과거형~, 주어 would/should/could/might+동사원형

2

가정법 과거완료: 과거와 반대되는 사실을 가정할 때 〈만약 ~했다면, ~ 했을 텐데〉

If 주어+had + 동사의 과거분사형~, 주어 would/should/could/might+have+동사의 과거분사

3

혼합 가정법: if절에는 과거의 사실을 가정해보고, 주절에는 현재 사실을 가정할 때

If 주어+had + 동사의 과거분사형~, 주어 would/should/could/might+동사원형

If I had been more diligent when I was young, I (would have been, would be) a nicer person now.

4

If 생략: 동사와 주어가 도치된다.

If you had followed my advice, you would not have failed.

= (Had you, You had) followed my advice, you would not have failed.

5

~ as if ~: 〈마치 ~인 것처럼〉으로 가정법 과거와 과거완료형 모두 가능

The experts talk as if they finished the research.

The experts talk as if they had finished the research last month.

6

But for + 명사 / Without + 명사: 〈 ~가 없다면〉으로 가정법 과거, 과거완료 모두 가능

Without your data, we could not meet the deadline.

Without your help, my dream could not have come true.

식당, 술집(2)

Let's go Dutch. 더치페이 하자.
= Let's split the bill.
Let's go fifty fifty. 반반씩 내자.
= Let's go halves.
I'll pick up the tab. 내가 계산할게.
= I'll foot the bill.
= Let me treat you.
= Let me take care of the bill.
= Let me settle the bill today.
This is my round. 이번에는 내가 낼게.
The next round is on me. 다음에는 내가 살게.
How would you like your steak, sir(ma'am)?
　스테이크 어떻게 해드릴까요?
Let's eat out. 외식하자.
Let's grab a bite. 간단히 뭐 좀 먹자.
Let's have our lunch delivered. 점심 시켜먹자.
Do you want to go for a drink? 술 한잔 하러 갈래?
I'd like to reserve a table for three tonight.
How do you like your coffee?
　커피는 어떻게 드릴까요?
- Just plan. Black, please. 블랙으로 주세요.
- With cream and sugar. 크림과 설탕을 넣어주세요.
- Decaf, please. 카페인 없는 커피로 주세요.
Can you wrap this up for me?
　이것 좀 포장해 주실래요?
= Doggy bag, please.

Phrasal verbs

care for(to) 좋아하다, 돌보다
black out 필름이 끊기다
pass out 필름이 끊기다
carry out 수행하다
deal in 장사하다
happen to 우연히 ~하다
leave out 생략하다
live on 계속 살다, ~을 먹고 살다
rail against ~에 대해 불평하다

make use of ~을 잘 이용하다

Collocations

Dutch courage 술김에 내는 용기
prime time 전성기
shot in the arm 활력소
play for time 시간을 벌려고 꾸물거리다
draw a blank 허탕치다
side effects 부작용
skeleton staff 최소의 인원
apple of discord 분쟁의 씨
as pale as a ghost 얼굴이 새파래진
fly in the ointment 옥의 티

Idioms

a piece of cake 쉬운 일
black sheep 집안의 말썽쟁이, 가문의 수치
cool as a cucumber 침착한, 냉정한
crocodile tears 거짓 눈물
cutting-edge 최신의
eat one's hat 손에 장을 지지다
from scratch 아무것도 없이, 처음부터
get the upper hand 우위를 얻다
in a fog 오리무중인
in the black 흑자인, 이득을 보는

음주 관련 어휘

toast 축배, 건배
bottle beer 병맥주
draft beer 생맥주
sober 술이 취하지 않은
hangover 숙취
liquor 증류주
dilute 희석시키다

Part I Choose the most appropriate response to the statement.

1 (a) (b) (c) (d)

2 (a) (b) (c) (d)

3 (a) (b) (c) (d)

Part II Choose the most appropriate response to complete the conversation.

4 (a) (b) (c) (d)

5 (a) (b) (c) (d)

6 (a) (b) (c) (d)

Choose the option that best answers the question.

7   (a)   (b)   (c)   (d)

8   (a)   (b)   (c)   (d)

9   (a)   (b)   (c)   (d)

Choose the option that best answers the question.

10 (a)   (b)   (c)   (d)

11 (a)   (b)   (c)   (d)

12 (a)   (b)   (c)   (d)

Choose the best answer for the blank.

13 A: What do you usually do on Saturdays?
B: _____ of wildlife.

(a) Usually take pictures
(b) Taking picture
(c) I usually take pictures
(d) Taking to pictures

14 A: What time are you supposed to leave?
B: Don't worry, I still _____.

(a) have more hours
(b) have much time
(c) having more time
(d) will have time

15 A: I really feel drowsy.
B: Shall I _____ some coffee or tea?

(a) get to you
(b) get you
(c) getting you
(d) to get you

16 A: How come _____ again?
B: I don't know why. He also didn't answer the phone.

(a) does he late
(b) does he come late
(c) is he late
(d) he is late

Choose the best answer for the blank.

17 An individual detained doesn't have to be suspected of belonging to an organized crime or of _____ terrorist activities.

(a) involved in
(b) being involved in
(c) having involved in
(d) involving in

18 The Chinese government restricted exports of fireworks to a limited number of ports so that _____ shipments was reported in China.

(a) a definite drop of firework
(b) definite a drop of firework
(c) definite drop of firework
(d) drop of definite firework

19 You can return _____ within the warranty period if the item needs to be checked.

(a) defective item
(b) a defective item
(c) to the defective item
(d) of defective item

20 The number of unemployed persons _____ by 4 million and the unemployment rate has risen this year due to the economic slumps.

(a) having increased
(b) have increased
(c) has increased
(d) has been increasing

Identify the option that contains an awkward expression or an error in grammar.

21 (a) A: What did they agree among the Convention?
    (b) B: Most of them said actions would be taken at the national level.
    (c) A: I couldn't agree anymore. Something efficient is needed right now.
    (d) B: I think the officials discuss about it soon.

Identify the option that contains an awkward expression or an error in grammar.

22 (a) There are many causes of gangrene which are the death of tissue, usually resulted from a loss of blood supply. (b) Poorly-managed diabetes can cause this chronic disease, especially for smokers.
    (c) Many people do not know that gangrene can be closely related to smokers and those who are diabetic, and that means treatment for life.
    (d) So, it is highly recommended to know that it affects a small area of skin, but can also affect even a substantial portion of a limb.

Choose the best answer for the blank.

23 A: All the hospitals are close up!
    B: It's because the doctors have been on a _____ since
       yesterday.

    (a) strike
    (b) picnic
    (c) trip
    (d) vacation

24 A: Why did she pass away suddenly?
    B: I heard that she developed _____ after surgery.

    (a) complicity
    (b) complications
    (c) compliments
    (d) compounds

25 A: I have no idea what this word means.
    B: How do you spell it? I'll _____ it up in the dictionary.

    (a) find
    (b) look
    (c) figure
    (d) solve

26 A: Why are you falling behind the others?
    B: I _____ out of breath when I walk a little bit.

    (a) put
    (b) come
    (c) fall
    (d) get

27 A: Have you heard she moved into an imposing mansion?

B: Yes. People say that she made a _____ in the stock market.

(a) treasure

(b) success

(c) fortune

(d) luck

Part II   Choose the best answer for the blank.

28 The _____ control system is needed in order to control air quality and keep the concentrations of pollutants at a low level.

(a) emission

(b) immersion

(c) environment

(d) circumstance

29 The housing market in the U.S. remains to be _____ due to high interest rates and a lack of properties which contributes to a decrease in new homes sale.

(a) dragging

(b) weak

(c) sluggish

(d) decreased

30 The inexperienced new team won the championship this year and it turned out to be a big mistake to _____ their strength.

(a) undermine

(b) underestimate

(c) undergo

(d) undertake

31 There are still many risks in the uncertain market such as weak stock prices and _____ in the exchange rate.

(a) balances
(b) fluctuations
(c) changes
(d) stability

32 He is very _____ at making a quick decision by ignoring facts that are contrary to his point of view.

(a) adoptive
(b) adept
(c) adapt
(d) adaptive

Read the passage. Then choose the option that best completes the passage.

33 The cornerstone of effective relationships is _____.
It was a tribal custom of Native Americans to nurture listening by the use of a 'talking stick'. During councils of war, important discussions, negotiations or debates, the person holding the talking stick was allowed to speak without interruptions for an unlimited time, but before the opponent was given an opportunity to talk, he had to be able to repeating everything the holder of the stick had said, to the satisfaction of the first speaker. Only when the person in possession of the talking stick was satisfied that his opponent fully comprehended his point would he pass the stick on to that person.

(a) the ability to repeat
(b) in not losing patience
(c) found in the art of listening
(d) taking turns when speaking in a group

34 Chronic Fatigue Syndrome (CFS) is a complicated disorder characterized by extreme fatigue that often won't pass off after rest and rather lasts a long time. It also may be worsened by even slight exertion. People with CFS exhibit symptoms like headaches, sore throat, sleep problems, unexplained muscle pains, or loss of memory. CFS is one of the most mysterious chronic illnesses that are complex and difficult to diagnose because there is no clear cause and cure for CFS. That's why some people have trouble recognizing CFS as a disease, but it is very important to remember that _____.

(a) it is not that serious if you don't really recognize it as a disease
(b) medicines can reduce the symptoms of it and cure the entire syndrome
(c) people healthy and full of energy may not experience it in their 40s and 50s
(d) your fatigue is factual and that you can improve it by working with your doctor

35 The Halo Effect is defined as a cognitive bias about a person's one desirable trait extending to influence the global evaluations of that person. In a study published in 1920, E. L. Thorndike asked army officers to rate their soldiers with regard to intelligence, constitution, leadership, and character and found that there was a high cross-correlation. That is, when a person is assumed to have one outstanding trait, that person is likely to be recognized to possess many other attractive traits as well. This halo effect is fascinating and useful in the business and political world. For example, politicians try to appear affectionate and friendly as much as possible because people tend to believe that _____.

(a) if they look good, their policies are good, too
(b) their appearances are not closely related to their policies
(c) appearances are the most valuable in the modern society
(d) one politician's policy is not much better than that of another

Part II Read the passage and the question. Then choose the option that best answers the question.

36 Bob Marley is the most renowned and revered performer of reggae music, credited for spreading its spirit and gospel to the four corners of the globe. The tiny Third World of Jamaica produced a legendary artist whose work not just displayed the stylistic spectrum of modern Jamaican music from ska to rocksteady—but raised the music to a social force with universal appeal. The severe impoverishment as well as political discontentment with the Jamaican government would cause this foremost emissary of reggae to disseminate calls for political uprising in his lyrics. In addition, Marley's declamatory voice was the best suited messenger.

Q Which of the following is true according to the passage?

(a) Jamaica was in a time of economical transition.
(b) Marley's music advocated for Jamaican government.
(c) Bob Marley urged people to rise and fight for their right.
(d) Public expression of a private truth is peculiar to Marley's music.

37 The novel and sophisticated masterpiece, Citizen Kane (1941) was directed by and starred by Orson Welles, who is acknowledged as one of the great geniuses of film. In a poll, Citizen Kane was voted for greatest film ever made and recommended as a "must-see." Every aspect of this film marked an advance in the development of cinematic technique, with the discontinuous narration through flashbacks, the inventive use of shadows and camera angles in cinematography, and the innovative use of sound technique linked to a complex montage sequence. The techniques created by Orson Welles are still in use today.

Q Which is NOT truthful in accordance with the passage?

(a) Orson Welles is considered as a pioneer in the history of film.
(b) Citizen Kane is a highly-rated film and a landmark of cinema history.
(c) Citizen Kane is famous for its many remarkable scenes and cinematic techniques.
(d) The techniques are so progressive that they are difficult to be used in modern films.

38 Milk-alkali syndrome, also called Burnett's syndrome, is caused by the ingestion of large amounts of calcium and absorbable alkali. Theoretically, oral intake of more than 2 grams of calcium with absorbable alkali results in hypercalcemia but it depends on individual variability. If unrecognized and untreated, chronic milk-alkali syndrome can lead to metastatic calcification and renal failure. With the development of nonabsorbable alkali, milk-alkali syndrome became a rare cause of hypercalcemia. The increasing use of calcium carbonate for dyspepsia and as calcium supplementation, however, causes milk-alkali syndrome to recur in the last few years.

Q Which of the following is NOT mentioned about milk-alkali syndrome in the above statement?

(a) incidence
(b) symptoms
(c) risk factors
(d) causes of resurgence

39 Tsunamis, often incorrectly called "tidal waves," are ocean waves produced by sudden motion on the ocean floor. Among the several ways tsunamis are made, an earthquake is the most primary factor. However, there is a condition to meet in order to generate tsunamis: it must take place underneath or near the ocean and be large enough like an earthquake of magnitude beyond 7.5. Tsunamis generated by regional upheaval or subsidence of the ocean floor during an earthquake can pass through long distances and destroy places where the epicenter is thousands of miles away. Tsunamis are also caused by underwater landslides which produce local tsunamis, uncommonly by submarine volcanic eruptions.

Q Which is true according to the passage?

(a) Tsunamis are known as tidal waves in the geological field.
(b) Tsunamis caused by submarine landslides are the most destructive.
(c) The farther the epicenter is from the ocean, the more powerful tsunamis are.
(d) Uplift or subsidence in the sea floor during an earthquake causes powerful tsunamis.

Part III   Read the passage. Then identify the option that does NOT belong.

40 Acupuncture, a traditional Chinese medical technique, has a long history and is offered as a "complementary" therapy by many traditional doctors. (a) Even so, it was not until recently that acupuncture needles were classified as medical devices for general use by trained professionals. (b) For quite a long time, acupuncture needles had been classified as Class III medical devices, meaning their safety and usefulness was uncertain. (c) Due to that "experimental" status, many insurance companies had agreed to cover acupuncture. (d) This new designation implies more empirical studies using needles as well as more practice of acupuncture.

TEPS TIPS • 분사

분사는 동사가 명사를 수식하는 형용사 역할을 하는 것으로 현재분사와 과거분사의 두 종류가 있다. 현재분사는 진행형에서 알 수 있듯이 꾸밈을 받는 명사와 분사의 관계가 능동의 관계이며, 과거분사는 수동태의 경우처럼 명사와 분사와의 관계가 수동이어야 한다.

1 **현재 분사와 과거분사 구별:** 수식받는 명사가 직접 행동을 하는 경우 현재분사를, 수동으로 행동이 될 때는 과거분사를 사용, 정확한 해석으로 문장 내 의미를 파악할 수 있다.

▶ **사역동사(지각동사) + 사람/사물 + 원형(능동으로 행동할 때)**
사역동사(지각동사) + 사람/사물 + 과거분사(수동으로 행동할 때)

2 **분사구문:** 부사절과 주절로 이뤄진 문장 중 부사절을 –ing나 과거분사로 시작하는 부사구로 만드는 것인데, 뒤나 앞에 오는 주절과의 관계에 따라 시간, 조건, 이유, 양보 상황 등을 나타낼 수 있다. 분사구문의 주어는 통상적으로 주절의 주어와 같을 때 생략하지만 다를 경우에는 생략할 수 없음을 잘 기억해야 한다.

3 **분사도 시제와 태를 나타낼 수 있다:** 본동사와 시제 차이가 날 때는 완료형 분사(having p.p.)로 나타내고, 수동을 나타낼 때는 수동형 분사(being p.p.)를 사용한다.

단순형: 주절과 종속절의 시제가 같을 때
완료형: 주절과 종속절의 시제가 다를 때

Staying with my aunt, my aunt used to cook some Italian pizza as soon as I had come home. (X)

I staying with my aunt, my aunt used to cook some Italian pizza as soon as I had come home.

Having experienced many cases, the detective found out that every person has a distinctive set of finger prints.

4 **분사구문의 부정:** Not(Never) ~ing

Not knowing what we should do, we decided to participate in the missionary trip.

방 예약

I'd like to make a reservation for two nights.
이틀 동안 묵을 방을 예약하고 싶은데요.

Sorry, we're booked up.
죄송하지만 예약이 다 끝났습니다.

Can you put me on the waiting list?
대기자 명단에 올려주실래요?

Do you have a vacancy? 빈 방 있습니까?

I have a reservation under the name of Maria
Thomson. Maria Thomson으로 예약했는데요.

What's the rate per night? 1박에 얼마입니까?

Can you give me a wakeup call at seven?
7시에 모닝콜 좀 해주시겠어요?

사진

I'd like to get the film developed.
사진을 현상해 주세요.

I want to get this picture enlarged (blown up).
이 사진을 확대해주세요.

Phrasal verbs

consist of ~로 구성되다
do without ~없이 지내다.
get rid of 제거하다
give up 포기하다, 항복(降伏)하다
go out 나가다
hand out 나누어 주다
look over ~를 훑어보다, 검사하다, 묵과하다
make up for ~을 보상하다
pack up 짐을 꾸리다, 포장하다
put up at ~에 숙박하다. (=stop at)

Collocations

a price range 가격대
a leap in the dark 무모한 짓
as old as the hills 매우 오래된

price fluctuation 가격 변동
foregone conclusion 뻔한 결론
full-fledged member 어엿한 회원
inordinate/exorbitant demand 과도한 요구
jet lag (비행기 여행으로 인한) 시차증
nursery rhyme 동요
vicious circle 악순환

Idioms

a case in point 비근하며 단적인 예
a walk in the park 매우 쉬운 일, 거저먹기
an act of God 불가항력적인 일
at one's service 바라는 대로, 마음대로
be up and running 사용 가능한
call the shots 명령을 내리다
check out 확인하다, 검토하다
drag one's feet 필요 이상으로 지연하다
drop sb a line 간단히 편지 쓰다
hit the road 길을 떠나다

예술 관련 어휘

antique 옛날의
appreciation (예술품의) 평가, 이해
arrange (타동사) 정돈하다, 배열하다
artificial 인공의, 모조의
avant-garde 전위적인, 전위예술가
denotation 의미, 외연
dim 어둠침침한, 어둑한
motif 주제
obscure 어두컴컴한, 불명료한
opaque 불투명한
performance 연극 공연
transparent 투명한
vandal 예술품 파괴자

Part I Choose the most appropriate response to the statement.

1 (a) (b) (c) (d)

2 (a) (b) (c) (d)

3 (a) (b) (c) (d)

Part II Choose the most appropriate response to complete the conversation.

4 (a) (b) (c) (d)

5 (a) (b) (c) (d)

6 (a) (b) (c) (d)

Choose the option that best answers the question.

7 (a) (b) (c) (d)

8 (a) (b) (c) (d)

9 (a) (b) (c) (d)

Choose the option that best answers the question.

10 (a) (b) (c) (d)

11 (a) (b) (c) (d)

12 (a) (b) (c) (d)

Choose the best answer for the blank.

13   A: Wow, I hardly recognize you. What happened?
   B: Well, I lost some weight because _____ for two hours every morning.

   (a) I went and jogging
   (b) I have been jogging
   (c) I go to jogging
   (d) I went to jogging

14   A: Do you remember _____ ?
   B: Of course, well, what do you mean?

   (a) that you of favor me
   (b) that owe favor you
   (c) favor you to owe me
   (d) that favor you owe me

15   A: Please take care of my cat during my absence.
   B: You know I _____ cats.

   (a) have allergic to
   (b) have allergic for
   (c) am allergic to
   (d) am allergic for

16   A: I'd like to order a pizza. Can I get a free Coke?
   B: Yes, _____ ?

   (a) how you like the crust
   (b) how would you like the crust
   (c) what you like the crust
   (d) what would you like the crust

Choose the best answer for the blank.

17 _____ of the ancient Central and Eastern Europe.

(a) Lying all the capitals behind that line
(b) Lie all the capitals behind that line
(c) Behind that line lie all the capitals
(d) Behind that line all the capitals lie

18 Physical attraction is one thing, love is quite _____.

(a) one another
(b) another
(c) others
(d) the other

19 Researchers of consumer protection suggested that the government
_____ all imported food to improve the eatables' quality.

(a) had investigated
(b) have investigated
(c) investigated
(d) investigate

20 Above and beyond the increases I had earlier requested for space
activities, providing _____ the national goals.

(a) which are funds needed meets
(b) the funds which are needed meets
(c) the funds which are needed to meet
(d) the funds which are needed meet

Identify the option that contains an awkward expression or an error in grammar.

21 (a) A: What's the topic of today's presentation?
(b) B: First of all, I'd like to talk about the ecotourism.
(c) A: Oh, it sounds excited. When does yours start?
(d) B: Around the second session.

Identify the option that contains an awkward expression or an error in grammar.

22 (a) Women's success is attributable to couple of things. (b) One is the support they get from the societies, parents, or sometimes from national or international organizations for women emancipation.
(c) They also have much more accesses to reading materials than men.
(d) Indeed, their excellence proves that harsh environments also influence women to try their best.

Part I   Choose the best answer for the blank.

23   A: How do you like this picture?

B: I like that kind of _____ feeling of a cloudy day.

(a) heavy

(b) energetic

(c) somber

(d) bright

24   A: Why has she brought her son here?

B: You're right. He's a _____ in the neck!

(a) thorn

(b) pain

(c) dirt

(d) bone

25   A: Tell me who are on the list of layoffs this time.

B: Okay. _____ it to yourself.

(a) do

(b) take

(c) get

(d) keep

26   A: How is their after-sales service?

B: It's pretty good. A one-year _____ comes with the product.

(a) customer

(b) warranty

(c) security

(d) contract

27 A: What are you thinking of now? You almost hit the wall!

B: Sorry. I forgot to check the _____ view mirror.

(a) back

(b) end

(c) rear

(d) hind

Part II Choose the best answer for the blank.

28 As more and more students gain access to the Internet, teachers have been grappling with ways to make it more difficult for them to _____ whole papers.

(a) post

(b) plagiarize

(c) plague

(d) navigate

29 Many universities are trying to offer online classes worldwide and Internet access is becoming _____ for college classes.

(a) prestigious

(b) premature

(c) prerequisite

(d) preliminary

30 Although they struggled to block the passage of the bill, it was finally passed by the _____ majority.

(a) overwhelming

(b) narrow

(c) relative

(d) slender

31 Our survey indicates that the sky is _____ about 42% of the time while clear and dry days occur about 31%.

(a) unclouded
(b) overshadowed
(c) overcast
(d) fair

32 If you forgot your password, you can _____ it by providing your email address.

(a) demand
(b) enter
(c) give
(d) retrieve

Read the passage. Then choose the option that best completes the passage.

33 Oprah Winfrey, one of the most successful and influential women in America, suffered from many hardships during her childhood. She was born to unmarried teenage parents and raised by her grandmother. When she was nine, she was raped by a cousin and was once molested by relatives. To make matters worse, she became pregnant and gave birth to a stillborn baby at age 14. She was so rebellious and sexually promiscuous that her life couldn't help being devastated. However, she changed when she was sent to live with her father. Her father helped her turn her life around and settle down _____. She had to read a book every week and write a report on the book, memorize five new words every day, and she was given even curfew.

(a) by forgiving her past
(b) by hiring an experienced tutor
(c) with his strict rules and discipline
(d) with a cordial welcome to his house

34 A constellation is a group of stars that form a visible figure in the sky. People used constellations to divide up the sky into more controllable bits by drawing imaginary lines between the stars to create pictures of people and animals. In the beginning, the purpose of the constellations was to help people _____. For example, if farmers, who were considered to invent constellations to use in their agriculture, knew the names of stars, they could easily tell the season and decide when to plant or harvest crops. This is because some constellations were only visible during certain seasons, due to the revolution of the earth.

(a) produce abundant harvest
(b) remember which stars are which
(c) have exuberant imagination on the universe
(d) see distant stars clearly in the very dark night

35 A hair falls out after growing for 2 to 6 years at an average rate of approximately 0.5 inches a month and resting for a while. There are some cases that the hair may fall out during the growing phase or the resting phase. One of the reasons for a sudden diffuse hair loss is the medication taken during cancer treatment, but fortunately the hair grows again when the medical treatment is over. Unlike hair loss based on disease or delivery, hair loss resulting from common reasons such as age, hormones, or heredity is permanent. _____, this general baldness can't be restored completely as long as the bald don't undergo an operation for hair transplants.

(a) Therefore
(b) Apart from
(c) In comparison
(d) In other words

36 Most people can become excellent wine connoisseurs with a little practice and by following some general guidelines. There are three steps in tasting wine: Look, Smell, and Taste. First, pour as much as one third of the wine into a clear glass, hold it in front of a white piece of paper or neutral settings with plenty of light, and tilt it against the white background to observe the clarity of the wine and the intensity of its color. We can tell much about the wine by studying its appearance. For example, white wines which range from colorless to a deep gold color darken with age, while red wines whose colors are various from pink to black lighten with age, so the paler the rim of the red wine appears, _____.

(a) the younger the wine is
(b) the sweeter the wine tastes
(c) the longer the wine has been aged
(d) the warmer the climate of origin was

Read the passage and the question. Then choose the option that best answers the question.

37 Journalist Mark Bowden gives a strikingly detailed account of the 1993 nightmarish operation in Mogadishu that left 18 American soldiers dead and many more wounded. Bowden does not devote much time to the context. Instead of rationalizing the fiercest close combat that Americans have engaged in since the Vietnam War, Bowden presents snapshots of the anarchy at the heart of combat. He makes full use of the Pentagon's wide-ranging paper trail which includes official reports, investigations, and even radio transcripts to describe the combat with great accuracy.

Q What kind of writing is the passage?

(a) A book review
(b) A movie critique
(c) A product analysis
(d) An in-depth article

38 A 54-year-old participant, Sally, felt stressed out because she was looking after for others all the time. Participating in the stress management program, Sally analyzed what gave her the most happiness and came to the conclusion that a Friday morning bridge game was one of them. One Friday, Sally was preparing to host the card game, when her daughter called to ask if Sally could take care of her son. She wanted neither to cancel the card game nor to refuse to help her daughter with financial difficulties. Instead of being compelled to say yes, Sally asked her daughter to take her son to the day care center and offered to loan her the money. The situation was resolved to everyone's satisfaction.

Q Which of the following strategies has Sally applied to cope with stress?

(a) Ventilation
(b) Assertiveness
(c) Positive Thinking
(d) Diversion and Distraction

39 Omega-3 fatty acids are essential nutrients for health, protecting people from heart disease and stroke. Even though omega-3 fatty acids have many health benefits, we should listen to the doctors and follow their directions since high intakes of omega-3 fatty acids can cause excessive bleeding. A common amount of omega-3 fatty acids in fish oil capsules is 0.18 grams of EPA and 0.12 grams of DHA. According to the recommendations of the American Heart Association, adults with coronary heart disease (CHD) need to consume about 1 gram of EPA and DHA, while patients with high cholesterol levels need 2–4 grams of EPA and DHA per day.

Q According to this passage, how many capsules can patients with CHD take a day?

(a) to one tablet
(b) about 3–4 tablets
(c) over 5 tablets
(d) about 6–7 tablets

40 This research was performed to show not only that stress influences illness but also that different people have different reactions to environmental stress. Although it deals with the influence of stress in specific illnesses, its results apply to the individuals without a disease. Another finding of this research shows that numerous, minor factors are more negative to an outcome than major stressors. Major life events are significant factors in the course of a disease, but daily hassles, which occur on a daily basis, may be more hazardous, and have a more profound effect on exacerbation or onset of disease.

Q Which of the following would affect a patient most according to the passage?

(a) death of a parent
(b) a suit for divorce
(c) increasing workload
(d) sibling's cancer bout

10 | Actual Test

TEPS TIPS • 조동사의 완료형(조동사 + have p.p.)

과거에 일어난 일을 표현할 때 사용하는 특수한 용법으로 출제율이 매우 높다. 가장 혼동하기 쉬운 표현은 must+have+p.p.(~이었음에 틀림없다)와 should+have+p.p.(~했어야 했는데 하지 않았다) 인데, 의미를 명확히 함으로써 혼동하지 않도록 주의한다.

1 cannot+have+p.p.: ~이었을 리가 없다

It can't have been easy to make a movie shot using that money.

2 may+have+p.p.: ~했을 것이다

The rule may have been constituted when the government had started.

3 must+have+p.p.: ~이었음에 틀림없다

Before meeting him, I thought the story must have been true.

4 should+have+p.p.: ~했어야 했는데 …하지 않았다

Here's a list of 13 celebrities who should have attended the conference.

5 should not+have+p.p.: ~하지 말았어야 했는데 했다

I should not have let her go there.

항공권 예약

This flight is bound for Hong Kong.
이 비행기는 홍콩행입니다.

I'd like to book a flight to 목적지 on 날짜.
~에 ~행 비행기를 예약하고 싶습니다.

I'd like a one-way(single) ticket.
편도 티켓으로 주세요.

I'd like a round-trip(return) ticket.
왕복 티켓으로 주세요.

How long is the layover at this airport?
이 공항에서 얼마 동안 기다려야 하나요?

탑승, 비행기내 표현

May I see your boarding pass?
탑승권을 보여주세요.

Do you have any baggage to check in?
부칠 짐이 있으신가요?

No, I'll carry this on board.
아니오, 기내에 가지고 들어갈 거에요.

Do you have any seating preference?
원하는 좌석 있으세요?

This is your captain speaking.
저는 이 비행기의 기장입니다.

We are due to take off in five minute.
이 비행기는 5분 후에 이륙할 예정입니다.

Extinguish all cigarettes. 담배는 모두 꺼 주세요.

Fasten(Buckle) your seat belt.
안전벨트를 착용해주세요.

Phrasal verbs

abide by ~을 지키다
break into 침입하다
clear up 날씨가 개다, 좋아지다
correspond to 일치하다
drag something on 질질 끌다
go over 반복하다, 검사하다
hold up 지연시키다, ~을 지지하다
liable for ~에 책임 있는
look into ~을 조사하다

Collocations

a borderline case 애매한 경우
a pillar of society 사회의 기둥
as bold as brass 철면피인
black sheep 천덕꾸러기
bolt from the blue 청천 벽력
centrifugal force 원심력
far-sighted decision 장기적인 안목에 의한 결정
first-hand report 직접 보고
red tape 관료적 형식주의

Idioms

a dime a dozen 싸구려, 흔해 빠진
a tempest in a teapot 사소한 일로 벌어진 소란
all for it 전적으로 동감하는
bite the bullet (고통이나 불행을) 참고 견디다
black out 기절하다, 정전되다
get a standing ovation 우레와 같은 갈채를 받다
by the skin of one's teeth 간신히, 아슬아슬하게
come of age 성년이 되다
cut short 단축하다, 생략하다, 갑자기 끝내다
dress sb down 야단치다

도로 관련 어휘

alley 골목
avenue 거리
blind alley 막다른 골목
bypass 순환도로
crosscut(=short cut) 지름길
crosswalk 횡단보도
detour 우회하다
devious 꾸불꾸불한
lane 좁은 시골길
pike 유료도로, 통행요금

Part I Choose the most appropriate response to the statement.

1 (a) (b) (c) (d)

2 (a) (b) (c) (d)

3 (a) (b) (c) (d)

Part II Choose the most appropriate response to complete the conversation.

4 (a) (b) (c) (d)

5 (a) (b) (c) (d)

6 (a) (b) (c) (d)

Choose the option that best answers the question.

7   (a)   (b)   (c)   (d)

8   (a)   (b)   (c)   (d)

9   (a)   (b)   (c)   (d)

Choose the option that best answers the question.

10 (a)   (b)   (c)   (d)

11 (a)   (b)   (c)   (d)

12 (a)   (b)   (c)   (d)

Choose the best answer for the blank.

13 A: Have you finished packing?

B: Sure, but please remind me _____ before leaving.

(a) checking the electrics

(b) to check the electrics

(c) of check the electrics

(d) to checking the electrics

14 A: How about your mom? Is she OK?

B: She _____, but she needs to see the doctor.

(a) looks like better

(b) looks much well

(c) looks much better

(d) looking more better

15 A: What are special things about your products?

B: We are using organic vegetables _____ pesticide or herbicide.

(a) grow at the farm without

(b) growing at the farm with

(c) grown at the farm without

(d) growing at the farm without

16 A: Before surgery, I need to check. How often do you drink?

B: Occasionally, I _____.

(a) am drinking heavily

(b) am not heavy drinker

(c) am not a heavy drinking

(d) am not a heavy drinker

Choose the best answer for the blank.

17 This nuclear star cluster may _____ young stars and be central hot stars sitting at the center of the Milky Way.

(a) be consisted of
(b) consist of
(c) consisting of
(d) consisted of

18 The statement describes and analyzes the main arguments of Latin American countries _____ the labor issues in the world trade.

(a) regarding
(b) regarded
(c) to regard of
(d) regard of

19 After changing the election rules, they swept the council elections, _____ could never have happened under the old rules.

(a) in which
(b) that
(c) which
(d) in that

20 High schools _____ German and French language courses are disappearing because new exams don't evaluate foreign languages.

(a) offers
(b) offer
(c) being offered
(d) offering

Identify the option that contains an awkward expression or an error in grammar.

21 (a) A: I'm wondering if you don't mind answering some questions about your article.
(b) B: Sure, just feel free to ask if you require further information.
(c) A: According to yours, the economic situation gets better soon. Is it possible?
(d) B: Certainly, we've researched for several months.

Part IV

Identify the option that contains an awkward expression or an error in grammar.

22 (a) Drivers of hybrid cars are more and more interested in converting its vehicles from gasoline to electric power. (b) While drivers of conventional vehicles complain about higher fuel prices, many early drivers are investing big bucks to make their cars green. (c) The new vehicles are changed through plug-in conversions and by adding more powerful batteries. (d) This conversion allows us to get energy through an electric outlet, so you just charge your car during the night.

Choose the best answer for the blank.

23 A: He keeps changing lanes without turning on the _____.
B: Right. He's really getting on my nerves.

(a) sign
(b) mark
(c) turn signal
(d) light

24 A: Do you think your kid is an outgoing person?
B: I don't think so. He seems to be _____ to being alone.

(a) habitual
(b) likely
(c) accustomed
(d) forced

25 A: How's your new job going?
B: Most of the work I do is _____ and boring.

(a) exciting
(b) tedious
(c) stifling
(d) favorable

26 A: Are you getting along with your new manager?
B: Yes. He is much more humane than his _____.

(a) colleague
(b) boss
(c) competitor
(d) predecessor

27 A: Is your wife still angry with you?

B: Yes. But I want to _____ with her.

(a) make up
(b) catch up
(c) come up
(d) hang up

Part II   Choose the best answer for the blank.

28 It is expected to reach a high _____ rate for the Friday of this week because public schools would be on vacation next Monday.

(a) accident
(b) dropout
(c) absentee
(d) admission

29 Police authorities announced new measures to eradicate _____ crime such as vandalism, graffiti and public urination.

(a) juvenile
(b) daring
(c) copycat
(d) petty

30 The Secretary of Defense stated outright that the government was not going to _____ to the terrorists' demands.

(a) give up
(b) give in
(c) pay off
(d) make up

31 At the beginning of the presentation, the presenter usually indicates whether he or she will _____ questions during the presentation or hold questions until the end of the presentation.

(a) address
(b) raise
(c) entertain
(d) pose

32 Experts mostly agree that education based on rote memorization _____ creativity in children.

(a) energize
(b) stifle
(c) foster
(d) enhance

Part I Read the passage. Then choose the option that best completes the passage.

33 A Dictionary of the English Language, published by Samuel Johnson in 1755, was evaluated as a highly influential and comprehensive dictionary in the history of the English language. It contained the definitions of over 40,000 words with quotes and sentence examples to illustrate the sense and usage of those words. Surprisingly its quotation sources varied from literature to science, medical science, and theology, etc. Occasionally, he seemed to _____.
For example, when he defined a patron as "a wretch who supports with indolence, and is paid with flattery," he must have kept Lord Chesterfield in mind. We could also get a glimpse of his thoughts through his description of the word sonnet, which is "not very suitable to the English language."

(a) quote many experts' works for better reputation
(b) use personal views to color the definitions of words
(c) cite previous dictionaries for more precise definitions
(d) borrow other scholars' opinions to make the dictionary look plausible

34 For the most part, sharks are not detrimental and interested in humans at all, but there are certain conditions that make sharks aggressive. Sharks have an acute sense of smell so strong odors such as the smell of blood incites their offensive behavior. Other smells such as urine and vomit in the water can also stimulate sharks like blood. Moreover, sharks can be affected by the struggles of an injured animal or human, underwater explosions, or even fish trying to escape from a fish line and change suddenly because _____.

(a) these kind of situations irritate sharks
(b) sound as well as smell may guide them to their prey
(c) their sense of hearing is keener than their sense of smell
(d) they are very sensitive to any unusual vibrations in the ocean

35 The term "unschooling" refers to alternative educational practices to conventional schooling by its rejecting the use of a fixed curriculum and other features of traditional schooling. In actual fact, unschoolers disapprove of the inefficiency of "factory-like" school. However, although they typically allow children to learn "naturally" according to their needs and developmental stages, unschoolers allow them to learn "unnaturally"—in traditional way—not when they have reached a certain age but when it makes sense to them to do so. _____ it isn't unusual to find unschoolers who are barely seven-years-old studying astronomy or who are twelve-years-old and just learning to read.

(a) Yet
(b) Otherwise
(c) Therefore
(d) Nevertheless

Part II Read the passage and the question. Then choose the option that best answers the question.

36 As the world's and Singapore's population ages, silver industry rises as a booming industry. Global companies have been fixing their eyes on Asia which is ageing rapidly, especially Singapore as the touchstone for this industry. Its multi-ethnic ageing population, strength in logistics, finance and technology, and senior citizens with strong spending power as well as an unquenchable appetite for new mid-life challenges make Singapore an experimental test-bed for a glittering silver market.

Q What is the strong point of Singapore as the mecca of silver industry?

(a) racial homogeneousness
(b) elder-friendly social system
(c) the state religion of Singapore
(d) financially secure enterprising seniors

37 Hawk-Eye is a computer system used to display the actual path of the ball as a graphic image in cricket, tennis and other sports. In tennis, there had been erroneous calls in a very crucial match so the players complained at times and the chair umpire was dismissed from a tournament. Passing the rigid International Tennis Federation testing measures, Hawk-Eye has been used to assist the umpire in line decisions. Hawk-Eye helps to decide whether balls are in or out of the border line by providing information about the ball's track with at least four high speed video cameras located in different positions in the court within a few minutes.

Q What can be inferred from the passage?

(a) The umpire will disappear rapidly in a tennis court because of Hawk-Eye.
(b) Hawk-Eye is so expensive that it is difficult to be adopted in other sports.
(c) Hawk-Eye makes tennis players' complaints about the umpire's decision decreased.
(d) Television viewers need to be trained to understand the Hawk-Eye's graphic images.

38 The Myers-Briggs Type Indicator (MBTI) assessment, the world's most widely used psychometric questionnaire, was developed to measure psychological preferences in how people perceive the world and make decisions. It is assumed that individuals are either born with, or develop, certain preferred ways of thinking and acting. The test categorizes these psychological preferences into four opposite pairs, or "dichotomies," the permutations of which result in the 16 personality types. Different preferences lead to different communication styles, which can hamper mutual understanding. However, such communication barriers can be removed with mutual respect and understanding of diversity.

Q What can be inferred as the best application of the MBTI in actual life?

(a) supporting better teamwork in a group
(b) supporting more ethical decision making
(c) developing a psychometric questionnaire
(d) changing a left-hander into a right-hander

39 Avian influenza is a flu infection caused by viruses adapted to birds. The viruses can infect not only birds but also human beings through virus mutation, which is a big concern because humans aren't immune against it. Even though all of the viruses are not fatal to human beings, one of subtypes called avian influenza A (H5N1) has caused worldwide epidemics. Symptoms of avian influenza are very similar to those of a typical human flu, which might range from cough, sore throat, high fever, runny nose, diarrhea to severe respiratory diseases. To prevent avian influenza, travelers should be careful in visiting the avian flu outbreak areas. Farmers or people who work with poultry who might be infected should wear protective clothing and masks.

Q What can be inferred from this passage?

(a) Avian influenza A hasn't caused flu pandemics yet.
(b) There are no people who have died of avian influenza.
(c) It is very difficult for H5N1 to spread from one person to another.
(d) Avian influenza infection in humans results from contact with infected poultry.

Part III   Read the passage. Then identify the option that does NOT belong.

40 Astronaut training courses, which are very intensive and rigorous, take place at the John Space Center (JSC) in Houston. (a) During the astronauts' first year of candidacy, they learn about shuttle systems, basic science and technology such as mathematics, physics, computer science, astronomy and meteorology. (b) To become a pilot astronaut, a bachelor's degree in engineering, mathematics or physics and the experience of flying a jet aircraft for 1,000 hours are prerequisite. (c)Another component of astronaut training, the simulation of weightlessness, takes place both in aircraft and in huge water tanks, and this teaches how to perform more complex tasks as well as routine ones. (d) After this first step, they receive another year of advanced training in the Shuttle Mission Simulator where they are taught specific skills during a mission.

TEPS TIPS ● 관계대명사와 관계부사

관계대명사와 관계부사의 가장 큰 차이점을 들자면 관계대명사는 문장의 필수요소(주어, 보어, 목적어)로 쓰이는데, 관계부사는 주요한 요소가 아니라 보충어구로 들어가기 때문에 각각을 제외한 문장의 완성도가 다르다는 것이다.

This is the museum which he mentioned last class. (which는 mention의 목적어)
This is the museum where he visited last summer.

---

1 that을 써야 하는 경우: 선행사에 all, any, the only, the first(최상급), the same 등이 올 때, 선행사가 사람과 동물일 때, 선행사가 의문사절일 때, 관계부사 대용으로 주로 쓰인다.

This generosity, the first (which, that) he showed within years, touches his family.

2 that을 쓸 수 없는 경우: 전치사의 목적어인 경우나 계속적 용법에서는 that을 쓸 수 없다.

3 관계부사는 이미 '전치사＋관계대명사' 이기 때문에 관계부사와 전치사는 같이 오지 않는다.

4 앞 문장 전체를 받을 수 있는 것은 관계대명사 which이다.

The story tells trust on people, (that, which) makes modern people moved.

5 관계대명사가 주격일 때 관계대명사는 선행사와 동일한 대상이기 때문에 그 수는 선행사와 일치한다.

They have an impact on the statistics (where, which) was not anticipated before then.

6 what은 선행사를 포함한 관계대명사이므로 선행사가 없다. what절이 주절일 때는 단수 취급한다.

What the Internet means to me (is, are) that I'm alive in different time zones.

공항 관련 표현

What is your purpose of your visit?
방문 목적이 무엇입니까?

– I'm on business. 사업차 왔습니다.

– I'm visiting my relatives. 친척 방문차 왔어요.

How long do you plan on staying?
얼마나 계실 예정입니까?

Do you have anything to declare?
신고할 물건이 있습니까?

– Nothing to declare. 없습니다.

I need to examine the contents of your purse.
가방 속의 내용물을 살펴봐야겠습니다.

Please place your suitcases on the table.
테이블 위에 짐을 놓아 주세요.

If you have more than ten thousand dollars,
you should declare it.
1만 달러 이상 소지하신 경우에는 신고해야 합니다.

Where is the baggage claim area? 수하물 찾는
곳이 어디지요?

Phrasal verbs

abound in ~이 많다

agree to + 사물 동의하다

agree with + 사람 동의하다. 적합하다

attend to ~에 주의하다

break out 갑자기 일어나다

do away with ~을 제거하다

give away 남에게 주어버리다. 분배하다

go away 떠나다. (문제 등이) 사라지다

long for 갈망하다

look out 주의하다

Collocations

a good buy 싸게 잘 산 물건

a castle in the air 사상누각

blessing in disguise 전화위복

centripetal force 구심력

credit sale 신용 판매

defamation of character 명예 훼손

double-edged remark 복선이 깔린 발언

flash in the pan 용두사미

going concern 순조로운 기업

illiteracy rate 문맹률

Idioms

an eager beaver 열심히 일하는 사람

bite off more than one can chew
지나친 욕심을 부리다

butterflies in one's stomach 가슴이 조마조마한

down the drain 낭비된, 허사가 된, 수포로 돌아간

edge out 근소한 차이로 이기다

follow in one's footsteps
~의 자취를 따르다, ~의 전례를 따르다

get off the hook 곤경에서 빠져 나오다

give the green light 허가하다. 청신호를 보내다

hit the ceiling/roof 머리끝까지 화가 나다

in full swing 한창 진행 중인

경제 관련 어휘

acquire 인수하다

anti-trust law 독과점 반대법

bankruptcy 도산

bear market 주가가 약세인 시장

board meeting 이사회

budget 예산

bull market 주가가 강세인 시장

capitalism 자본주의

collective behavior 집단 행동

conglomerate 대기업

GDP(= Gross Domestic Product) 국내 총생산

GNP(= Gross National Product) 국민 총생산

Part I Choose the most appropriate response to the statement.

1 (a) (b) (c) (d)

2 (a) (b) (c) (d)

3 (a) (b) (c) (d)

Part II Choose the most appropriate response to complete the conversation.

4 (a) (b) (c) (d)

5 (a) (b) (c) (d)

6 (a) (b) (c) (d)

Choose the option that best answers the question.

7 (a)   (b)   (c)   (d)

8 (a)   (b)   (c)   (d)

9 (a)   (b)   (c)   (d)

Choose the option that best answers the question.

10 (a)   (b)   (c)   (d)

11 (a)   (b)   (c)   (d)

12 (a)   (b)   (c)   (d)

Choose the best answer for the blank.

13 A: How long does it take to get to the National Zoo?

B: It _____ 10 minutes by car.

(a) takes me

(b) take

(c) takes

(d) to take

14 A: What does NASA stand for?

B: It _____ National Aeronautics and Space Administration.

(a) is acronym for

(b) is an acronym of

(c) is acronym for

(d) is an acronym for

15 A: Have you heard the news about soaring foreign currency exchange rates?

B: How come _____?

(a) it happened

(b) did it happen

(c) does it happen

(d) happens it

16 A: What's the matter with him? He's hardly absent from school.

B: He went to _____.

(a) the funeral his best friend

(b) the funeral of his best friend

(c) the his funeral best friend

(d) his the funeral of best friend

Choose the best answer for the blank.

17 Had it not been for international aid, the country _____ starving people.

(a) wouldn't have saved
(b) would be
(c) would save
(d) will have saved

18 Her short answer is subtle _____.

(a) but realistic
(b) nor realistic
(c) so realistic
(d) not realistic

19 He has to wait until the ship _____ to pick up the damaged life boat.

(a) will return
(b) returns
(c) was returned
(d) being returning

20 _____ is far from being numinous or, even worse, ridiculous.

(a) What implied here is
(b) Here is implied what
(c) What implied here
(d) What is implied here

Identify the option that contains an awkward expression or an error in grammar.

21 (a) A: My car suddenly broke down. What can I do?
   (b) B: Don't worry, just call the insurance company.
   (c) A: But, I have to pick up my mother-in-law at the airport, too.
   (d) B: Why don't you ask me to help?

Identify the option that contains an awkward expression or an error in grammar.

22 (a) Music Therapy is a recognized health care profession using music and music activities in treatment programs. (b) It addresses the physical, emotional, social and cognitive challenges faced by children and adults with diverse illnesses and special needs. (c) There are many associations established to insure professional services or providing qualified therapists in the United States. (d) They have broadened the awareness of music therapy within the public policy arena.

Choose the best answer for the blank.

23 A: She made a big mistake while preparing this project.

B: Let's _____ that this time. She just joined the company.

(a) oversee

(b) overcome

(c) overlook

(d) overtake

24 A: Who did you vote for this time?

B: I didn't _____ a vote.

(a) do

(b) make

(c) carry

(d) cast

25 A: Can you come down a little? It's too expensive.

B: Sorry. This product is already _____.

(a) sold out

(b) got off

(c) marked down

(d) dealt with

26 A: I'm sorry. These books are overdue.

B: There is a late _____ for overdue books.

(a) fee

(b) fare

(c) money

(d) bill

27 A: How do you guys know him?
B: He was a _____ friend of ours.

(a) related
(b) respective
(c) mutual
(d) coincident

Part II Choose the best answer for the blank.

28 Aside from a degree, you need a teaching _____ to teach students in public schools.

(a) document
(b) certificate
(c) warrant
(d) material

29 People are _____ against the high prices of the mobile phone rates but the mobile operators said that it does not have any plan to cut the rates.

(a) railing
(b) blocking
(c) brushing
(d) discriminating

30 The economic situation has been _____ due to sharp rises in oil prices and the won's fluctuating exchange rate.

(a) deviating
(b) deteriorating
(c) deferring
(d) depleting

31 The talks were held for discussions of measures to relieve tensions between the two nations and to promote _____ trades.

(a) fair
(b) illicit
(c) domestic
(d) bilateral

32 _____ diseases such as arthritis gradually get worse as time passes and cannot be stopped.

(a) Tropical
(b) Degenerative
(c) Contagious
(d) Hereditary

Part I Read the passage. Then choose the option that best completes the passage.

33 Architecture is a major factors influencing the buildings and is involved in shaping the environment. As a three dimensional genre of art, architecture is awakening our sense of meaning in relation to our surroundings. The way architecture is perceived is similar the way sculptures, another three dimensional genre of art, are perceived. The buildings we may encounter everyday make different imaginations and visualizations according to the angle of our view. In other words, a building can be observed differently as we watch the building in different places and heights. Since the building is, at most cases, located outdoors, it can be seen differently _____.

(a) as the statue is corroded
(b) as our way of seeing differs
(c) as the weather and the season changes
(d) as the color and material varies

34 The Curse of the Billy Goat refers to a superstition commonly used to explain the World Series drought that the Chicago Cubs Major League Baseball team has been suffering from since their last appearance in the 1945 World Series. It is supposed that the Billy Goat Curse was placed on the Cubs in 1945 when a tavern owner named Billy Sianis and his pet goat were ejected from Wrigley Field because of the goat's objectionable odor. The enraged man yelled that there would never again be a World Series game played at Wrigley Field as he was being led out and since that day this urban legend has been _____ of the Chicago Cubs.

(a) a rationale of the failure
(b) an evidence that a team has few chances to win
(c) a scapegoat for the losing streak
(d) a historical background recorded in the League

35 The Great Wall, as one of the world's architectural wonders and cultural symbol, attracts many visitors from all over the world every year. Despite its historic value, the China Great Wall Academy reports that less than 30 percent of the Wall remains in good condition due to _____. Since it was exposed to wind, rain, snow and other natural calamities for thousands of years, many sections of the Wall have been havocked. It also suffers from human sabotage. There are some tourists who deface the bricks from the Great Wall and even move them. People foolishly take bricks, earth and stones from the wall to construct roads, reservoirs, and houses.

(a) various environmental reasons
(b) the forces of nature and human's destruction
(c) the deliberate damages by the hand of mankind
(d) serious natural disasters and people's indifference

Part II Read the passage and the question. Then choose the option that best answers the question.

36 Europeans embrace the purity of Canadian Inuit artists who subscribe to an eclectic inspiration that is based on their traditional hunting and fishing practices as well as legends and mythologies to explain their relationship with their environment. Unlike Alaska and Greenland where white man has been presented for a few hundred to one thousand years, white man's decorative art has never had a chance to take foothold in the isolated Canadian Arctic. A former documentary film maker, Raymond Brousseau points out, "You cannot commission a piece from a Canadian Inuit artist. Instead, you have to wait and see what the artist has created."

Q What is the best title for the passage?

(a) Pristine Inuit art
(b) Preservation of Inuit art
(c) An Inuit art lover's passion
(d) Noncommercial Inuit artists

37 Naturalization is the process by which a citizen of a foreign country or nation is bestowed U.S. Citizenship, fulfilling the requirements established by Congress. First, naturalization applicants must be legal permanent residents, who will be asked to produce their green card as proof of their status. They must demonstrate the knowledge of the fundamentals of U.S. history and the principles of the U.S. Constitution as well as the ability to speak, read, write and understand words used in everyday life. They also must be of "good moral character," that is, they are permanently prohibited from naturalization if they have been convinced of murder or an aggravated felony.

Q What is the passage mainly about?

(a) The requirements for being applicants
(b) The process of U.S. Citizenship application
(c) The U.S. Citizenship information and application guide
(d) The general requirements for administrative naturalization

38 It is well known that the distribution of world population is uneven. Areas of high population density tend to comprise a large land area and a moderate climate. Africa is the second largest continent in the world and has around one-eighth of the total population of the world, thus its population distribution is fairly low. Desert areas such as Sahara, Kalahari, and Namib are nearly inhabitable. Other semi-arid land, mountains and dense rain forests also is meagerly inhabited. Most of the densely populated areas are located around the lakes or in the river basins, and along the coasts. In those areas, water is supplied, soil is fertile and farming is possible.

Q What is the topic of the passage?

(a) The distribution of world's population
(b) The natural environment of the Africa
(c) The population distribution of Africa
(d) The densely populated areas of the world

39 Abortion rights advocates often assert "a woman's right to choose" in her life. They believe that it is a woman's right to decide to terminate her pregnancy. However, who can say that a woman has a right to choose murder? If a fetus were a human being, it goes without saying that the woman would be a murderer. Even though the status of an embryo in the first trimester has been argued to determine whether the embryo is a person or not, to our surprise, the answer is very simple. The fact that the embryo is a potential human and we call it "an unborn child" already proves that the embryo is a precious creature. Women can't easily choose abortion if they realize that their future lovely child is breathing in their womb.

Q What is the main idea of the passage?

(a) Abortion should be legalized in some cases.
(b) Abortion should be strongly prohibited in all circumstances.
(c) An embryo should be reconsidered by anti-abortion activists.
(d) Women should not have an abortion in that an embryo is a person.

Part III   Read the passage. Then identify the option that does NOT belong.

40 In literary criticism, "stream of consciousness" is a method for representing the continuous flow of a fictional character's innumerable thoughts, impressions, and feelings. (a) First used in psychology but later transferred to literature, it was developed by some writers such as Dorothy Richardson, James Joyce. (b) The most important stylistic forms are "narrated stream of consciousness" and "interior monologue", often incorrectly used as a synonym for stream of consciousness writing. (c) The stream of consciousness is related to the theme itself but the interior monologue refers to the technique for presenting it. (d) The interior monologue presents the character's thoughts or silent speeches directly, while the stream of consciousness technique mixes them with his or her impressions and perceptions, sometimes defying the linguistic norms.

12 | Actual Test

1

to: 방향, 도착, 일치, 조화

five to nine. 9시 5분전

drink a toast to the new project. 새 프로젝트를 위해 건배

When it comes to ~ing ~에 관해서는

devote (contribute, dedicated) to ~ing ~에 공헌하다

be(get) used to ~ing/ be accustomed to ~ing ~에 익숙하다/익숙해지다

look forward to ~ing ~를 고대하다   **object to ~ing** ~를 반대하다

2

out: 벗어나고 사라지는 것을 의미

run out of time 시간이 없다   **out of order** 고장 나다

slod out 매진되다   **go over it again** 다시 검토하자

3

off: 작동하지 않거나 떨어져 나가는 의미

off the record 비공식   **turn off** 꺼버리다

drive off 운전해 떠나다   **be off** 휴무

4

for: 목적이나, 대상, ~를 위하여

Go for it. 잘해보세요   **What are friends for?** 친구라는 게 뭐니?

5

on: 표면에 닿거나 밀접한 관련이 있을 때

What's on your mind? 무슨 생각을 하는 거니?

get on one's nerves 신경을 거스르다

6

기타

How are you getting along? 어떻게 지내십니까?

He knows his way around. 그 사람 세상 물정에 훤해

I'm through with you. 너와 끝장이야

under the weather 저기압   **make up** 화해하다

의사/병원

Do you have an appointment? 예약하셨어요?

There could be a delay.
좀 기다리셔야 할 수도 있어요.

I made an appointment to see a doctor.
진료 예약했는데요.

The doctor gave me his diagnosis.
의사가 처방을 해주었다.

You should get a thorough medical checkup.
정밀검사를 받아보시는 것이 좋겠습니다.

You need to turn up your humidifier.
가습기를 틀어야 합니다.

Let me take your temperature. 체온을 재 볼게요.

약/회복

Take this to the pharmacy and have it filled.
이것을 약국에 가져가서 약을 지으세요.

How often should I take this medicine?
이 약을 얼마 간격으로 복용해야 합니까?

The pain is almost gone now. I am feeling much better. 지금은 통증이 거의 가셨다. 훨씬 몸이 좋아졌다.

Phrasal verbs

go after ~를 쫓다. 바라다

break down 분해하다

come about 일어나다

come to 회복하다

depend on(upon) 의지하다, 믿다

get over 회복하다, 극복하다

look after ~를 돌보다

put up with 참다, ~을 견디다

recover from 회복하다

rely on (upon) 믿다, 의존하다

Collocations

a tower of strength 커다란 의지가 되는 사람

as deaf as a post 아주 귀가 먼

carcinogenic substances 발암성 물질

charity fund 자선 기금

genetic engineering 유전 공학

hereditary disease 유전병

incipient symptom 초기 증상

life expectancy 예상 수명

maternity leave 출산 휴가

Idioms

blow one's top 화가 머리끝까지 나다

catch one off guard 방심한 틈을 타 놀라게 하다

down on all fours 네 발로 기어서

fair and square 믿기 어려운, 황당한

for a song 헐값으로

good-for-nothing 쓸모없는

hot under the collar 몹시 화남

be in the same boat 같은 배를 타다, 운명을 같이하다

leaf the hard way 아주 힘들게 배우다

look for a needle in a haystack 풀밭에서 바늘 찾기

부상, 질병 관련 어휘

amnesia 기억상실증

bruise 타박상

chronic 만성의

constipation 변비

contagious 전염성의

cramp 쥐

diabetes 당뇨

diarrhea 설사

fracture 골절

heart attack 심장마비

indigestion 소화불량

sprain 염좌

stroke 뇌졸중

LISTENING COMPREHENSION

Part I   Choose the most appropriate response to the statement.

1   (a)   (b)   (c)   (d)

2   (a)   (b)   (c)   (d)

3   (a)   (b)   (c)   (d)

Part II   Choose the most appropriate response to complete the conversation.

4   (a)   (b)   (c)   (d)

5   (a)   (b)   (c)   (d)

6   (a)   (b)   (c)   (d)

Choose the option that best answers the question.

7   (a)   (b)   (c)   (d)

8   (a)   (b)   (c)   (d)

9   (a)   (b)   (c)   (d)

Choose the option that best answers the question.

10 (a)   (b)   (c)   (d)

11 (a)   (b)   (c)   (d)

12 (a)   (b)   (c)   (d)

Choose the best answer for the blank.

13   A: Don't forget to check the switch after using the drier.
   B: OK, I will make sure _____ .

   (a) to turn off
   (b) to turn off it
   (c) to turn it off
   (d) turn it off

14   A: Have you ever thought about the earth in the 22nd century?
   B: I think the world will _____ robots.

   (a) be controlling by
   (b) be controlled by
   (c) control
   (d) controlling

15   A: When did the last train leave?
   B: I don't know. When I arrived, it _____ .

   (a) already left
   (b) already had left.
   (c) have already left.
   (d) had already left.

16   A: May I use the lavatory now?
   B: No, sir. It's dangerous to use it _____ .

   (a) during a turbulence
   (b) during turbulence
   (c) while turbulence
   (d) being turbulence

Choose the best answer for the blank.

17 They finally _____ when she showed the result of the survey.

    (a) found to succeed a way

    (b) way to found succeed

    (c) found the way to succeed

    (d) find the way to succeed

18 Even the best laid plans do not always _____ secret.

    (a) be remained

    (b) remains

    (c) remain

    (d) remaining

19 _____ "Never judge from appearances.", we would remember the lesson of the other proverb, "Appearances are deceptive."

    (a) Given the perspective of

    (b) The perspective given

    (c) Giving the perspective

    (d) Given the perspective

20 _____ a longer bath makes your skin weak and unhealthy.

    (a) Take

    (b) Taking

    (c) Having taken

    (d) To taking

Identify the option that contains an awkward expression or an error in grammar.

21   (a) A: Did you finish packed your stuff?
     (b) B: Not, yet. I have to buy some dried sea weed.
     (c) A: Are you allowed to bring food to America?
     (d) B: Sure, we can bring some dried food.

Identify the option that contains an awkward expression or an error in grammar.

22   (a) Poe, who wrote macabre tales like psychological thrillers, was to work for several publications as both editor and contributor. (b) His career as an editor coincided with his growth as a writer. (c) While worked at a "Gentleman's Magazine," Poe's work continued to flourish. (d) At this time in his career he still was not secure financially, but his work was being recognized and praised, which helped greatly in furthering his reputation.

Choose the best answer for the blank.

23 A: This project is going nowhere. What should I do?

B: Your efforts will _____ fruit sometime.

(a) grow
(b) bear
(c) pick
(d) show

24 A: I have a paper cut.

B: _____ this ointment on it.

(a) Affix
(b) Place
(c) Apply
(d) Utilize

25 A: Mom, buy me this game console.

B: How old are you? Please _____ your age.

(a) reach
(b) look
(c) show
(d) act

26 A: I can't go to her party because I have to go on a business trip.

B: In that case, we have no choice but to _____ the invitation.

(a) send out
(b) turn in
(c) turn down
(d) put in

27 A: He's going too far. Why don't you give him any advice?

B: He already turned a _____ ear to my advice.

(a) big
(b) deaf
(c) thick
(d) light

Part II Choose the best answer for the blank.

28 I was so fascinated by Mona Lisa's _____ smile that I can't even move a little.

(a) infectious
(b) bitter
(c) enigmatic
(d) forced

29 A recent survey revealed that many people tend to _____ the seriousness of flu by believing that flu is the same as having a bad cold.

(a) undergo
(b) undermine
(c) underestimate
(d) undertake

30 Young generations got into the hard rock and roll in 1980's, the _____ of what could be called heavy metal these days.

(a) forerunner
(b) foreboder
(c) rocker
(d) messenger

31 She was put in the detention center but all her supporters did the best to _____ the seriousness of the charges against her.

(a) grasp
(b) realize
(c) decrease
(d) extenuate

32 Many female workers have testified that they also suffered sexual _____ in the male-dominated workplace.

(a) provocation
(b) harassment
(c) irritation
(d) disturbance

Read the passage. Then choose the option that best completes the passage.

33 Obesity has become a big problem in our modern society. It causes related diseases such as diabetes and heart attacks. Recently, experts have shown that those who were obese in childhood grow up into obese adults. Also, they are far more likely to suffer from cardiac disease and cancer in later years. Even worse, overweight kids seem to become a target for bullying at school. The experts suggested that, in order to avoid overweight and obesity in childhood, kids should eat healthy and work out regularly. Since more and more kids are reported as being obese, it is important to educate them

_____.

(a) to lose weight through a low-calorie diet and exercise
(b) to stop smoking in public places
(c) to find solutions for diabetes and heart attack
(d) to solve the problems in our society

34 Pablo Picasso was a modern artist who dominated Western art in the 20th century. Before his 50th birthday, he had made a great reputation for himself. No painter before him had such a large audience in his own lifetime. He and his work were always in the middle of never-ending analysis, gossip, adoration and rumor. He was a sarcastic, cynical man, sometimes mean to his children, often revolting to his women. He had scorn for women artists. His famous remark about women being " _____ " has left him obnoxious to feminists, but his charm was so irresistible that women chose to assume either role eagerly.

(a) artists or patrons
(b) blabbers or naggers
(c) helpers or onlookers
(d) goddesses or doormats

35 Summer Hill School is a British boarding school founded in 1921 by Alexander Sutherland Neil with the belief that children learn best _____. There is a wide choice of subjects and all lessons are optional—no compulsion to attend. In addition to deciding what to do with their own time, children can take part in the self-governing community at which rules affecting their everyday lives are set or unresolved conflicts are adequately managed. Children are completely free from any pressure to conform to adult ideas of growing up and adults are there not to teach them what they should do but to help them do what they want to do.

(a) under parental guidance
(b) without any expectation
(c) with freedom from coercion
(d) when given proper discipline

Part II   Read the passage and the question. Then choose the option that best answers the question.

36 Cats are amazing subjects to sketch, with their elegant lines and graceful movements. However, it's quite hard to capture cat's movement in detail because they move so quickly! Your eyes need to be quick and your hands need to be even quicker. Before you begin your sketching, you need to decide what to draw and what to exclude. You need to make a quick and firm decision since you have limited time. Don't worry too much about detail. You may want to buy a felt-tip artist's pen because they are soft and perfect for fast sketching.

Q What is the topic of the passage?

(a) How to take a picture of moving cats
(b) What to prepare to sketch cats
(c) How cats move quickly with elegance
(d) Why people want to draw cats

37 Many studies show that the global market for biodiesel is on the edge for explosive growth in the next decade. Currently 80% of global biodiesel consumption and production is done by European countries, but the U.S. is now boosting production at a faster pace than Europe. With the progress of major projects for lower-cost feedstocks from renewable diesel including tallow, used vegetable oil and waste recycling, it is possible biodiesel could represent as much as 20% of all on-road diesel used in the BRICs and Europe by the year 2020. Government promotion of research & development in new biodiesel feedstocks such as algae biodiesel will ensure increased investment.

Q What is the main idea of the passage?

(a) Environment-conscious fuels should be created.
(b) Cars using biodiesel fume out much less exhaust gas.
(c) The prospect for biodiesel market is relatively bright.
(d) The government should enact investor-friendly tax incentives.

38 Anger is not a feeling that you must not feel or express but is a normal and natural reaction to criticism, threat, or frustration if it's neither excessive nor uncontrollable. The important aspect related to the feelings of anger is how to control the emotion when you are in the throes of it and how to express anger in a healthy way. This fall, we are going to provide focused sessions which include psychological therapeutic techniques and exercises for those who may have felt unable to cope with anger by themselves. In this course, you will learn and practice empathy, forgiveness, assertive communication techniques, stress management skills, and cognitive behavioral therapy. For more information, contact us any time.

Q What is the purpose of this passage?

(a) To introduce the anger management program
(b) To inform the curriculum in the fall semester
(c) To clear up the misunderstanding about anger
(d) To present how to deal with anger constructively

39 The Boston Red Sox baseball team had won five World Series by 1918 from its inception in 1903. One of the stars of this team was a young left-handed pitcher named George H. Ruth, also known as Babe Ruth or The Bambino. In 1920, however, the Red Sox owner underestimated Babe Ruth and sold him to the New York Yankees at a giveaway price. After this trade, while Boston hadn't won the World Series for 86 years, the once-wretched Yankees became one of the most successful baseball franchises owing to Ruth's remarkable plays as a hitter. Many began to ascribe the failure of the Boston to "the curse of the Bambino," but the curse finally ended in 2004 when they swept the St. Louis Cardinals.

Q Which is truthful in accordance with the passage?

(a) The curse of the Bambino had not been removed to 2004.
(b) The New York Yankees has never been worse than the Boston Red Sox.
(c) The Boston traded Ruth with the Yankees, receiving little money from it.
(d) Babe Ruth was an excellent pitcher who led his team to win the World Series.

40 On October 4, 1957 the Soviet Union succeeded in launching the world's first man made satellite, Sputnik. It caused not only excitement and wonder but also massive political resonance because the United States had believed itself to be the world leader in the western world as well as in space technology. The Soviet Union had demonstrated that it was far ahead of its western rivals, taking the leadership crown from the United States. However, although it took years before the crown could be reclaimed, the news of Sputnik ignited overall social reform including a full-scale revamping of the US high-school science curriculum.

Q Which of the following is true about Sputnik according to the passage?

(a) It made little impact on international relations.
(b) It spurred the Soviet Union to develop another satellite.
(c) It devastated the science education of the United States.
(d) It caused grave concern about the United States social system.

TEPS

ACTUAL TEST 100

LISTENING COMPREHENSION

Part I   Choose the most appropriate response to the statement.

1   (a)   (b)   (c)   (d)

2   (a)   (b)   (c)   (d)

3   (a)   (b)   (c)   (d)

4   (a)   (b)   (c)   (d)

5   (a)   (b)   (c)   (d)

6   (a)   (b)   (c)   (d)

7   (a)   (b)   (c)   (d)

Part II   Choose the most appropriate response to complete the conversation.

8   (a)   (b)   (c)   (d)

9   (a)   (b)   (c)   (d)

10   (a)   (b)   (c)   (d)

11   (a)   (b)   (c)   (d)

12   (a)   (b)   (c)   (d)

13 (a)   (b)   (c)   (d)

14 (a)   (b)   (c)   (d)

15 (a)   (b)   (c)   (d)

Part III   Choose the option that best answers the question.

16 (a)   (b)   (c)   (d)

17 (a)   (b)   (c)   (d)

18 (a)   (b)   (c)   (d)

19 (a)   (b)   (c)   (d)

20 (a)   (b)   (c)   (d)

21 (a)   (b)   (c)   (d)

22 (a)   (b)   (c)   (d)

Choose the option that best answers the question.

23 (a) (b) (c) (d)

24 (a) (b) (c) (d)

25 (a) (b) (c) (d)

26 (a) (b) (c) (d)

27 (a) (b) (c) (d)

28 (a) (b) (c) (d)

29 (a) (b) (c) (d)

30 (a) (b) (c) (d)

Part I Choose the best answer for the blank.

31 A: How often does the shuttle come?

B: _____ until midnight.

(a) Every two an hour

(b) Every an half hour

(c) Any half an hour

(d) Every half an hour

32 A: Guess what? Sally is being promoted soon.

B: Wow, she _____.

(a) deserved the reward

(b) deserving the reward

(c) is deserve the reward

(d) deserves the reward

33 A: What time do I have to submit this report?

B: _____ this afternoon.

(a) Until 5 o'clock

(b) To 5 o'clock

(c) By 5 o'clock

(d) For 5 o'clock

34 A: Wow, so many things have changed.

B: Yes, there _____ a flea market here.

(a) used to be

(b) would be

(c) might used to be

(d) could have used

35 A: Listen, honey, somebody is yelling again.

B: I don't understand _____ other's privacy.

(a) why doesn't she respect
(b) why she doesn't respect
(c) why she won't respect
(d) why won't she respect

36 A: Why do you have such a long face?

B: I got a bad score on the final English test, and _____ feel blue.

(a) a score made me
(b) made me the score
(c) made a score made for me
(d) the score made me

37 A: How may I help you, ma'am?

B: Could I have _____ cup of tea?

(a) other
(b) some
(c) another
(d) others

38 A: Has she completed the whole course?

B: Yes, _____, she ran the whole distance.

(a) a woman as she was
(b) as a woman she was
(c) woman as she was
(d) woman as she was a

39 A: Is your mom at home? I heard she went traveling abroad.

B: No, _____ last week, she will return home tomorrow.

(a) she left
(b) leaving
(c) left
(d) had left

40 A: How was the movie last night?

B: Amazing! You _____ us.

(a) have joined
(b) must have joined
(c) could have joined
(d) should have joined

Part II Choose the best answer for the blank.

41 There are barely any dialogues _____ for the last ten minutes of the film.

(a) spoke
(b) speak
(c) spoken
(d) speaking

42 When they gathered that night to observe the Passover Meal, _____ the significance of what was about to happen.

(a) they hardly could understand
(b) hardly they understood
(c) hardly they could understand
(d) hardly could they understand

43 _____ rust eats iron, so care eats the heart.

(a) Though
(b) As
(c) Like
(d) Despite

44 We always look to see _____ who needs help.

(a) there is anybody
(b) if there is anybody
(c) if anybody is
(d) if anybody is there

45 _____, he wasn't surprised when he saw the initial images of a desolated earth.

(a) Being forewarned
(b) Be forewarned
(c) To be forewarned
(d) Be forewarning

46 That's why your hair looks greasy and _____.

(a) loosing hair easily
(b) loose hair easily
(c) you loose hair easily
(d) you to loose hair easily

47 Learn the ways of _____ and look better so that you control the whole organization.

(a) making you to feel calm
(b) making yourself feel calm
(c) making you felt calm
(d) making yourself felt calm

48 The skin of your palm is more sensitive than _____.

(a) that of your face
(b) those of your face
(c) your face's skin
(d) your face

49 Be reliable, trustworthy, and confidential _____.

(a) of all circumstance
(b) in circumstances
(c) all circumstance
(d) in all circumstances

50 It's _____ their wishes because of the school's policies.

    (a) students undesirable to disregard

    (b) undesirable for students to disregard

    (c) undesirable of students to disregard

    (d) disregard undesirable for students

Part III Identify the option that contains an awkward expression or an error in grammar.

51 (a) A: Don't forget to bring the computer and documents on the table.

    (b) B: OK, what else do I have to check?

    (c) A: Nothing else, just bring it

    (d) B: That's a relief, I have too many things to remember.

52 (a) A: Haven't you ever visited the Natural History Museum?

    (b) B: I did once, but I couldn't look around much.

    (c) A: Poor, Jenny. I went there with my mother and she explained all sections.

    (d) B: It sounds wonderful.

Part IV Identify the option that contains an awkward expression or an error in grammar.

53 (a) A half-dozen robots are working on the surface or in orbit around Mars, discovering that traces of water exist. (b) They even make us think about possibilities of some microbial or other early life forms on the Planet! (c) Thanks to Cassini, we are discovering lakes on Titan, the only place outside Earth which liquid exists on the surface of a world. (d) We're even contemplating the possibility of life in such exotic worlds.

54 (a) What if physiologists were only interested in what made humans dissimilar to other animals? (b) If they were, they would only study bipedalism or a few other characters. (c) They would not study the inner parts such as hearts, lungs, livers, or bones. (d) Similarly; evolutionary psychologists might be interested in the functional structure of individual cognition if or not we share this structure with other animals.

55 (a) Not only do almost students think other foreign languages are complicated, but they also find few opportunities to verbalize.
(b) They simply think German and French are not practical.
(c) However, learning foreign languages is not studying only language but different cultures. (d) So, to avoid unbalance in foreign language learning, teachers should help students gain interest in European language learning.

Choose the best answer for the blank.

56 A: My boss drives me crazy!
B: Same here. I'm really _____ up with this job.

(a) tired
(b) kept
(c) fed
(d) got

57 A: Sorry. I can't tell you anything.
B: Don't _____. Just spit it out!

(a) hold back
(b) butter up
(c) hold still
(d) give up

58 A: What would you like to have for dinner?
B: How about _____ foods like Indian or Thai foods?

(a) appetizing
(b) light
(c) plain
(d) exotic

59 A: Have you heard the rumors that the two companies will merge?
B: I think it is just a _____.

(a) consequence
(b) controversy
(c) features
(d) conjecture

60 A: I like this apartment, but I'm slightly short of money.

B: Why don't you take out a _____ in that case?

(a) loan
(b) decision
(c) rent
(d) purse

61 A: I can't stand him any longer. I hate the way he speaks.

B: I agree. He's kind of arrogant and _____.

(a) apparent
(b) astute
(c) pompous
(d) dexterous

62 A: The subway has finished for today.

B: Don't worry. You can _____ a bus at this time.

(a) travel
(b) wait
(c) catch
(d) run

63 A: Could you _____ this check, please?

B: How would you like it?

(a) honor
(b) endorse
(c) cash
(d) issue

64 A: I broke a glass when I washed dishes.

B: You're so _____!

(a) exhausted
(b) clumsy
(c) fastidious
(d) impartial

65 A: Aren't you here with your girlfriend?
    B: No, I'm not. I _____ up with her last week.

(a) met
(b) got
(c) split
(d) fought

66 A: Do you know what she's like? I think she enjoys being around
    people.
    B: Yes. She's outgoing and _____.

(a) impulsive
(b) gregarious
(c) insolent
(d) lenient

67 A: What made you call this late at night?
    B: I'm sorry to _____ you, but this is urgent.

(a) excuse
(b) worry
(c) upset
(d) disturb

| Part II | Choose the best answer for the blank. |

68 Shakespeare is considered to be a writer of _____ genius in the
    history of English literature.

(a) transcendent
(b) transparent
(c) transitional
(d) transient

69 Jake was going through financial difficulties but he was a man of _____ spirit to overcome the crisis.

(a) guiding
(b) community
(c) indomitable
(d) rebellious

70 I wasn't able to adapt myself to the new environment because people seemed to be nice to me but in a _____ way.

(a) superlative
(b) surplus
(c) superb
(d) superficial

71 There was a three car rear end collision on the highway and one of the injured people is needed an urgent blood _____ due to a significant blood loss.

(a) infusion
(b) profusion
(c) transfusion
(d) fusion

72 British airports are planning to _____ the ban on liquids being carried in hand luggage as soon as the new scanners are proved to be successful to detect harmful liquids.

(a) place
(b) lift
(c) put
(d) impose

73 It was obvious that his _____ appetite for power would draw ruin upon himself but he couldn't help it.

(a) insatiable
(b) healthy
(c) satisfied
(d) bearable

74 Most financial consultants advise people to minimize tax _____ and maximize income in order to increase their assets.

(a) evasion
(b) liabilities
(c) shelter
(d) return

75 The company was reported to be fined for _____ industrial waste into the river, which invoked strong opposition among the residents.

(a) disregarding
(b) disintegrating
(c) disclosing
(d) discharging

76 A majority of U.S. citizens consider the policies against Afghanistan a _____ cause, which shows they have deep public skepticism about the war on terror.

(a) worthy
(b) ultimate
(c) wasted
(d) lost

77 The audience _____ in laughter when the actor fell on the stage while singing a love song with a serious look.

(a) disrupted
(b) erupted
(c) bankrupted
(d) interrupted

78 The company filed a lawsuit against internet users claiming that it's intellectual _____ rights were infringed.

(a) defect
(b) property
(c) power
(d) capacity

79 Most reviewers say this game is very difficult and challenging because the plot is very complicated and tricky, but the _____ feature of this game is the cheap price.

(a) notorious
(b) main
(c) optional
(d) redeeming

80 Taking out an online membership, you can gain access to the National Center for missing people which provides photographs of missing people, and _____ people.

(a) disabled
(b) unidentified
(c) ordinary
(d) boat

Part I   Read the passage. Then choose the option that best completes the passage.

81   In Korea, home baking has become a popular hobby among the people who want to make their own cakes and cookies at home. You could express your affection or make a great present for your family or friends with home made snacks. It is definitely fun and far simpler than you expected. You may want to have a big and beautiful oven first. Those are indeed great for baking, yet _____ that you could simply start with. They are also easy to operate. Then you'll need a hand mixer that you could use to mingle the baking ingredients easily. Mixing bowls, measuring cup sets, and flexible turners are the basic supplies you should include in your shopping list.

(a) there also are fabulous websites
(b) there also are ovens for experts
(c) there also are books that have baking tips
(d) there also are reasonably-priced small ovens

82   The main purpose of advertising is to inform potential customers about a product or service or to create favorable awareness for the product or service. To attract the customers, appealing techniques are used. The most common appealing techniques employed in the media can be divided into two categories: factual appeal and emotional appeal. While the factual appeal focuses on the superiority of the product supplying information, the emotional appeal spotlights on the potential satisfaction of the consumer. The satisfaction is rather personal, in other words, the emotional appeal is designed to stimulate consumer's desires _____.

(a) to be socially acceptable and personally attractive
(b) to increase competitive power and productivity
(c) to inform about the product or service
(d) to appeal as many people as possible

83 Gothic architecture flourished throughout Europe during its prosperous and late medieval period, developing from Romanesque architecture and succeeded by Renaissance architecture. The Gothic style was expressed not only in the great churches and cathedrals but also in many castles and palaces. It was characterized by verticality and huge dimensions of the structure with pointed arches, ribbed vaults, flying buttresses, and slender pillars. It also emphasized on large stained glass windows, allowing more light to enter inside. These features of Gothic architecture were intended _____ : the glory of God versus the insignificance of the man.

(a) to compare God with man
(b) to pass a theological message
(c) to persuade people to convert to Christianity
(d) to focus on the excellence of Gothic architecture

84 Used to be an entertainment of the Roman Emperors, lotteries were approved by the colonial legislatures as an important way of raising funds for public purposes such as church erection or quay construction in the American colonies. In the 19th century, lotteries were prohibited by a law because of the frequent deceit. From the 20th century, lotteries began to be administered by local states to raise revenues without increasing taxes, and were granted the epithets of "tax on stupidity," and "voluntary tax." Since poor people were most likely to buy them, lotteries were used as revenue-raising devices, attracting those consumers who _____ .

(a) had ever won the lottery
(b) couldn't afford to pay taxes
(c) were interested in the public benefit
(d) failed to see the lottery was a bad deal

85 Fiber helps you to maintain your healthy diet as well as to keep in shape. After taken, it goes through your digestive tract since it is indigestible. When it is excreted from the body, the foods left in your internal organs are expelled with it before they turn putrid and become toxic. Through this process, fiber decreases cholesterol level, prevents diabetes and some cancers. When you increase fiber in your diet, you can lessen the amount of food you consume. As fiber in your stomach absorbs water, you can have a feeling of satisfaction easily. If you want to watch your weight, you should _____.

(a) manage your time efficiently
(b) include adequate amounts of fiber in your meals
(c) stop eating fast food and junk food
(d) take pure water as much as you can

86 How many cups of coffee you drink a day? Are you easily tempted by caffe-lattes with fabulous whipped cream and caramel topping? If you drink more than 5 cups of coffee a day, you should cut down on the amount of coffee you take. Coffee can be helpful to keep your brain alert and increase your energy level. However, you may have headaches and sleeplessness after taking too much coffee. Also, your body can be dehydrated because coffee dries up moistures in your body. Why don't you _____?

(a) take some pills to lessen your headaches
(b) add some whipped cream to your coffee
(c) try to drink water or other teas instead of coffee
(d) have a surgery to reduce the size of your stomach

87 The main purpose of the juvenile court system lies in rehabilitation, as opposed to punishment, to enhance the chances of the youth becoming a socially well-adjusted citizen. As for the juvenile crimes, there are frequent occasions when the offender himself is likely to be a victim—a victim of poverty, parental neglect, and all kinds of abuse. Therefore a cautious attitude should be assumed with the juvenile delinquencies. Nevertheless, the juvenile crime, particularly crimes of violence is on dramatic rise. It makes no difference to the victim whether the person who pulled the trigger on the gun is under the age of 18 or not. _____.

(a) Juvenile punishments should exclude incarceration
(b) Mere probation is only a slap on the wrist to violent crime
(c) Any offender has the right to hire a juvenile defense attorney
(d) We should protect juvenile delinquents regardless of their age

88 It is widely known that global warming is fatal to the future of our planet. We are _____. Sea levels are rising as the glaciers and sea ice is melting as the earth is heated. The rise of sea levels is being accelerated because oceans absorb more heat than land. The change in heat and water evaporation causes hurricanes, tornadoes and other storms. So, what can we do? In order to reduce the amount of green house gases that can be made from pollution, we could re-cycle plastic bottles, cups and tin cans. Re-using of plastic shopping bags instead of getting new ones is helpful, too.

(a) making plans to stop global warming like following
(b) witnessing the evidences like the following
(c) in need of developing technologies like following
(d) facing problems of poverty like following

Read the passage and the question. Then choose the option that best answers the question.

89 The prestige of the Nobel Prize stems from its long, thorough, and rigorous nomination and selection process. The respective Nobel Committees asks thousands of previous Nobel Laureates, university professors, scholars in the relevant fields and the committee members themselves to nominate candidates, who aren't even told they have been nominated for the prize. Self and posthumous nominations are disqualified and about two hundred preliminary candidates are selected for the coming year's prizes. Then with experts' help, each committee scrutinizes and selects prize winners through voting.

Q Which of the following is true about the Nobel Prize?

(a) The names of the nominees are publicly announced.
(b) Deceased people can't be nominated in the Nobel Prize.
(c) The winner of Nobel Prize should be decided by a unanimous vote.
(d) One authoritative committee is in charge of the nomination and selection process.

90 The term 'Korean wave' (Hallyu) was coined by journalists in Beijing as the popularity of TV dramas and goods of Korea drastically grew up in China in the late 1990s. Since then, the term has been used to refer to the surge of popularity of Korean pop culture in other countries, especially in Asia. The audiences from China to the Japan got hooked on Korean TV dramas such as 'Winter Sonata' and 'Autumn in my Heart'. Actors who played the main roles in those dramas are now among the highest-paid actors in Asia. A multi-entertainer Rain has made his way from a Korean wave star to a promising actor in Hollywood.

Q What is mainly discussed in the paragraph?

(a) The origin of the term 'Korean wave'
(b) The popularity of Korean goods in China
(c) A perspective on the Korean Wave
(d) The audiences of Korean TV dramas

91 To our customers:

Thank you for taking your time to answer to our survey. The purpose of this survey is to search for the way we could serve you and better meet your needs. This survey is conducted by T&K Co., which is an outstanding consulting firm specializing in customer service. Beside these questionnaires for you, they will interview some of our selected employees about our service to get more meaningful results. We deeply thank you for your time and effort in doing this, and firmly believe that your time and effort will help us to provide you the best service.

Q Which of the following is correct according to the paragraph?

(a) This survey is for the employees of T&K Co.
(b) The purpose of the survey is to improve customer service.
(c) Some selected customers will be interviewed.
(d) T&K Co. provides the customer with consulting.

92 DNA is an abbreviated form of Deoxyribonucleic Acid. It carries the genetic code that makes each person unique. It is often shown in movies and TV shows that a sample of DNA found at the crime scene is used for detection. It is compared with another sample taken from a suspect. If the match is positive, the detection is successful. DNA samples taken from different crime scenes can be linked and collected at the National DNA Database. The National DNA Database is used by every police force in the US to compare other samples taken from scenes of crime.

Q Which of the following is the best title of the passage?

(a) The Use of DNA for Crime Detection
(b) The Definition of DNA
(c) The National DNA Database
(d) The Comparison of DNA Samples

93 As a leading source of news, TNS has provided critical information to media outlets, businesses, organizations and governments for a quarter of a century. We bring the essential news stories from around the world and cover a wide scope of news events. We try to maintain a balanced approach to reporting by talented journalists and a dedicated staff. The international edition of our website provides you the precise information and exclusive analysis on global issues in a constantly updated fashion. Our headquarters is located in Atlanta, Georgia, and we have bureaus worldwide. If you have comments on our articles or questions about how to use our website, please click here.

Q Which of the following is NOT true about TNS?

(a) It was established more than 20 years ago.
(b) It has an international website.
(c) It is a local broadcasting company.
(d) It produces news stories worldwide.

94 Erick Forman, a 23-year old Starbucks barista, was four hours into his shift when he was approached by Caroline Kaker, the chain's Bloomington-based district manager. She pulled him aside and broke the news that Starbucks gave him the ax. Forman was taken aback. Sure, two weeks earlier, he had shown up a half-hour late and was issued a written warning. But that wasn't why Forman was dismissed today. Some employees are given half a dozen or more warnings before receiving a final one. Management decided to get rid of him after learning that Forman had discussed the warning with co-workers. In fact there was another topic Forman had discussed with peers, one not explicitly mentioned in the notice of discharge; unionizing.

Q Which of the following is the decisive reason for Forman's layoff?

(a) Chatting while on duty
(b) Incompetence as a barista
(c) Frequent absence from work
(d) Involvement in an organization

95 Vincent van Gogh created over 30 self-portraits during his life time. It seems that he depicted his face as it appeared in the mirror. The main reason he painted his own portrait was that he couldn't pay models to pose for portraits. Also, there were not many people who commissioned him to do portraits. However, for him, painting self-portrait was not only a way of making money and exploring a variety of painting styles and techniques but also a great vehicle to introspection. His self-portraits tell us a lot about his development as both an artist and an individual.

Q Which of the following is true, according to the passage?

(a) Gogh painted self-portraits though he could hire models for portraits.
(b) The right side in his self-portrait is the left side of his face in reality.
(c) Most of his self-portraits were painted with the same styles.
(d) Painting self-portraits was an important method of making money.

96 Learned helplessness is a mental state in which a human being does not remove himself from stressful, dangerous or even harmful situations, even if they are "escapable," presumably through having learned that situational control is generally out of his hands. Many studies show that it can be minimized by "immunization" focused on increasing one's awareness of previous positive experiences. One of the causes for learned helplessness is emotional abuse, which can range from verbal abuse to more subtle tactics like repeated denial of emotional needs. As things happens in brain washing, emotional abuse wears away at the victim's self-esteem.

Q What can be inferred about emotional abuse according to the passage?

(a) Emotional abusers have low self-esteem, too.
(b) It is difficult to detect because it is domestic violence.
(c) Legal intervention is required to protect the victim from further harm.
(d) Recall of successful experiences helps the victim regain his self-confidence.

97 Emergency situations can occur all of a sudden and they usually require fast and appropriate action. Hospitals use emergency codes to inform their staff about various emergency situations quickly and precisely. The use of codes is also aimed to avoid possible misunderstandings. The codes are often displayed by color, and different color codes represent different events at different hospitals. For example, Code White is used to indicate a pediatric medical emergency in New Jersey, U.S., and a violent patient in Canada.

Q   What does Code White imply in Canada?

(a) a pediatric medical emergency
(b) a patient who needs resuscitation
(c) a violent patient
(d) a staff's misunderstanding

98 In contrast to the worldwide reputation of the Academy Awards, it is reproached by many critics due to its racist and sexist disposition. Until 2008, neither black nor female directors have ever received an Academy Award for Best Achievement in Directing, except for only one black director, John Singleton, who was ever nominated in 1992. Since Sidney Poitier won a Best Performance by an Actor in a Leading Role in 1963, there had been no African American winners for this part up to year 2002.

Q   Which is most likely to follow this passage?

(a) Criticism of the Academy Awards' biased view
(b) Examples of prejudice against women in the Academy Awards
(c) Story on an African American director who first won Best Director
(d) Documents for how black people have struggled for winning the awards

Read the passage. Then identify the option that does NOT belong.

99 Flexible thought is one of the most important characteristics we are required to achieve to manage one's business successfully. (a) Nowadays, an idea of flexible working hours comes into the spotlight and gets positive evaluations. (b) Flexible working hours have been in place for years in some fields, such as computer-related companies and publishing companies. (c) For the last three years, researches have reported that more and more employers and workers are considering flexible working hours as an innovative way of increasing productivity and competitive power. (d) Moreover, in last month's survey, two-thirds of employees are either compassionate or very obstructive of flexible working hours.

100 Red and Blue Oceans are a metaphor for the market space. (a) A strategy formed within a definite economic structure, controlled by demand and availability of resources, is termed Red Ocean Strategy, which represents all of the existing industries in a market place—the known market space. (b) As the market space gets jammed with companies trying to outperform their contenders, cutthroat competition made the market blood-red. (c) In contrast, Blue Ocean Strategy makes the competition irrelevant by capturing or creating new demand rather than grabbing for it. (d) Blue Ocean Strategy is symbolic of the vast potential of uncontested market space.

Actual Test 01

청해				
1	ⓐ	ⓑ	ⓒ	ⓓ
2	ⓐ	ⓑ	ⓒ	ⓓ
3	ⓐ	ⓑ	ⓒ	ⓓ
4	ⓐ	ⓑ	ⓒ	ⓓ
5	ⓐ	ⓑ	ⓒ	ⓓ
6	ⓐ	ⓑ	ⓒ	ⓓ
7	ⓐ	ⓑ	ⓒ	ⓓ
8	ⓐ	ⓑ	ⓒ	ⓓ
9	ⓐ	ⓑ	ⓒ	ⓓ
10	ⓐ	ⓑ	ⓒ	ⓓ
11	ⓐ	ⓑ	ⓒ	ⓓ
12	ⓐ	ⓑ	ⓒ	ⓓ

문법				
13	ⓐ	ⓑ	ⓒ	ⓓ
14	ⓐ	ⓑ	ⓒ	ⓓ
15	ⓐ	ⓑ	ⓒ	ⓓ
16	ⓐ	ⓑ	ⓒ	ⓓ
17	ⓐ	ⓑ	ⓒ	ⓓ
18	ⓐ	ⓑ	ⓒ	ⓓ
19	ⓐ	ⓑ	ⓒ	ⓓ
20	ⓐ	ⓑ	ⓒ	ⓓ

21	ⓐ	ⓑ	ⓒ	ⓓ
22	ⓐ	ⓑ	ⓒ	ⓓ

어휘				
23	ⓐ	ⓑ	ⓒ	ⓓ
24	ⓐ	ⓑ	ⓒ	ⓓ
25	ⓐ	ⓑ	ⓒ	ⓓ
26	ⓐ	ⓑ	ⓒ	ⓓ
27	ⓐ	ⓑ	ⓒ	ⓓ
28	ⓐ	ⓑ	ⓒ	ⓓ
29	ⓐ	ⓑ	ⓒ	ⓓ
30	ⓐ	ⓑ	ⓒ	ⓓ
31	ⓐ	ⓑ	ⓒ	ⓓ
32	ⓐ	ⓑ	ⓒ	ⓓ

독해				
33	ⓐ	ⓑ	ⓒ	ⓓ
34	ⓐ	ⓑ	ⓒ	ⓓ
35	ⓐ	ⓑ	ⓒ	ⓓ
36	ⓐ	ⓑ	ⓒ	ⓓ
37	ⓐ	ⓑ	ⓒ	ⓓ
38	ⓐ	ⓑ	ⓒ	ⓓ
39	ⓐ	ⓑ	ⓒ	ⓓ
40	ⓐ	ⓑ	ⓒ	ⓓ

Actual Test 02

청해				
1	ⓐ	ⓑ	ⓒ	ⓓ
2	ⓐ	ⓑ	ⓒ	ⓓ
3	ⓐ	ⓑ	ⓒ	ⓓ
4	ⓐ	ⓑ	ⓒ	ⓓ
5	ⓐ	ⓑ	ⓒ	ⓓ
6	ⓐ	ⓑ	ⓒ	ⓓ
7	ⓐ	ⓑ	ⓒ	ⓓ
8	ⓐ	ⓑ	ⓒ	ⓓ
9	ⓐ	ⓑ	ⓒ	ⓓ
10	ⓐ	ⓑ	ⓒ	ⓓ
11	ⓐ	ⓑ	ⓒ	ⓓ
12	ⓐ	ⓑ	ⓒ	ⓓ

문법				
13	ⓐ	ⓑ	ⓒ	ⓓ
14	ⓐ	ⓑ	ⓒ	ⓓ
15	ⓐ	ⓑ	ⓒ	ⓓ
16	ⓐ	ⓑ	ⓒ	ⓓ
17	ⓐ	ⓑ	ⓒ	ⓓ
18	ⓐ	ⓑ	ⓒ	ⓓ
19	ⓐ	ⓑ	ⓒ	ⓓ
20	ⓐ	ⓑ	ⓒ	ⓓ

21	ⓐ	ⓑ	ⓒ	ⓓ
22	ⓐ	ⓑ	ⓒ	ⓓ

어휘				
23	ⓐ	ⓑ	ⓒ	ⓓ
24	ⓐ	ⓑ	ⓒ	ⓓ
25	ⓐ	ⓑ	ⓒ	ⓓ
26	ⓐ	ⓑ	ⓒ	ⓓ
27	ⓐ	ⓑ	ⓒ	ⓓ
28	ⓐ	ⓑ	ⓒ	ⓓ
29	ⓐ	ⓑ	ⓒ	ⓓ
30	ⓐ	ⓑ	ⓒ	ⓓ
31	ⓐ	ⓑ	ⓒ	ⓓ
32	ⓐ	ⓑ	ⓒ	ⓓ

독해				
33	ⓐ	ⓑ	ⓒ	ⓓ
34	ⓐ	ⓑ	ⓒ	ⓓ
35	ⓐ	ⓑ	ⓒ	ⓓ
36	ⓐ	ⓑ	ⓒ	ⓓ
37	ⓐ	ⓑ	ⓒ	ⓓ
38	ⓐ	ⓑ	ⓒ	ⓓ
39	ⓐ	ⓑ	ⓒ	ⓓ
40	ⓐ	ⓑ	ⓒ	ⓓ

Actual Test 03

청해				
1	ⓐ	ⓑ	ⓒ	ⓓ
2	ⓐ	ⓑ	ⓒ	ⓓ
3	ⓐ	ⓑ	ⓒ	ⓓ
4	ⓐ	ⓑ	ⓒ	ⓓ
5	ⓐ	ⓑ	ⓒ	ⓓ
6	ⓐ	ⓑ	ⓒ	ⓓ
7	ⓐ	ⓑ	ⓒ	ⓓ
8	ⓐ	ⓑ	ⓒ	ⓓ
9	ⓐ	ⓑ	ⓒ	ⓓ
10	ⓐ	ⓑ	ⓒ	ⓓ
11	ⓐ	ⓑ	ⓒ	ⓓ
12	ⓐ	ⓑ	ⓒ	ⓓ

문법				
13	ⓐ	ⓑ	ⓒ	ⓓ
14	ⓐ	ⓑ	ⓒ	ⓓ
15	ⓐ	ⓑ	ⓒ	ⓓ
16	ⓐ	ⓑ	ⓒ	ⓓ
17	ⓐ	ⓑ	ⓒ	ⓓ
18	ⓐ	ⓑ	ⓒ	ⓓ
19	ⓐ	ⓑ	ⓒ	ⓓ
20	ⓐ	ⓑ	ⓒ	ⓓ

21	ⓐ	ⓑ	ⓒ	ⓓ
22	ⓐ	ⓑ	ⓒ	ⓓ

어휘				
23	ⓐ	ⓑ	ⓒ	ⓓ
24	ⓐ	ⓑ	ⓒ	ⓓ
25	ⓐ	ⓑ	ⓒ	ⓓ
26	ⓐ	ⓑ	ⓒ	ⓓ
27	ⓐ	ⓑ	ⓒ	ⓓ
28	ⓐ	ⓑ	ⓒ	ⓓ
29	ⓐ	ⓑ	ⓒ	ⓓ
30	ⓐ	ⓑ	ⓒ	ⓓ
31	ⓐ	ⓑ	ⓒ	ⓓ
32	ⓐ	ⓑ	ⓒ	ⓓ

독해				
33	ⓐ	ⓑ	ⓒ	ⓓ
34	ⓐ	ⓑ	ⓒ	ⓓ
35	ⓐ	ⓑ	ⓒ	ⓓ
36	ⓐ	ⓑ	ⓒ	ⓓ
37	ⓐ	ⓑ	ⓒ	ⓓ
38	ⓐ	ⓑ	ⓒ	ⓓ
39	ⓐ	ⓑ	ⓒ	ⓓ
40	ⓐ	ⓑ	ⓒ	ⓓ

Actual Test 04

청해				
1	ⓐ	ⓑ	ⓒ	ⓓ
2	ⓐ	ⓑ	ⓒ	ⓓ
3	ⓐ	ⓑ	ⓒ	ⓓ
4	ⓐ	ⓑ	ⓒ	ⓓ
5	ⓐ	ⓑ	ⓒ	ⓓ
6	ⓐ	ⓑ	ⓒ	ⓓ
7	ⓐ	ⓑ	ⓒ	ⓓ
8	ⓐ	ⓑ	ⓒ	ⓓ
9	ⓐ	ⓑ	ⓒ	ⓓ
10	ⓐ	ⓑ	ⓒ	ⓓ
11	ⓐ	ⓑ	ⓒ	ⓓ
12	ⓐ	ⓑ	ⓒ	ⓓ

문법				
13	ⓐ	ⓑ	ⓒ	ⓓ
14	ⓐ	ⓑ	ⓒ	ⓓ
15	ⓐ	ⓑ	ⓒ	ⓓ
16	ⓐ	ⓑ	ⓒ	ⓓ
17	ⓐ	ⓑ	ⓒ	ⓓ
18	ⓐ	ⓑ	ⓒ	ⓓ
19	ⓐ	ⓑ	ⓒ	ⓓ
20	ⓐ	ⓑ	ⓒ	ⓓ

21	ⓐ	ⓑ	ⓒ	ⓓ
22	ⓐ	ⓑ	ⓒ	ⓓ

어휘				
23	ⓐ	ⓑ	ⓒ	ⓓ
24	ⓐ	ⓑ	ⓒ	ⓓ
25	ⓐ	ⓑ	ⓒ	ⓓ
26	ⓐ	ⓑ	ⓒ	ⓓ
27	ⓐ	ⓑ	ⓒ	ⓓ
28	ⓐ	ⓑ	ⓒ	ⓓ
29	ⓐ	ⓑ	ⓒ	ⓓ
30	ⓐ	ⓑ	ⓒ	ⓓ
31	ⓐ	ⓑ	ⓒ	ⓓ
32	ⓐ	ⓑ	ⓒ	ⓓ

독해				
33	ⓐ	ⓑ	ⓒ	ⓓ
34	ⓐ	ⓑ	ⓒ	ⓓ
35	ⓐ	ⓑ	ⓒ	ⓓ
36	ⓐ	ⓑ	ⓒ	ⓓ
37	ⓐ	ⓑ	ⓒ	ⓓ
38	ⓐ	ⓑ	ⓒ	ⓓ
39	ⓐ	ⓑ	ⓒ	ⓓ
40	ⓐ	ⓑ	ⓒ	ⓓ

Actual Test 05

청해

1	ⓐ	ⓑ	ⓒ	ⓓ
2	ⓐ	ⓑ	ⓒ	ⓓ
3	ⓐ	ⓑ	ⓒ	ⓓ
4	ⓐ	ⓑ	ⓒ	ⓓ
5	ⓐ	ⓑ	ⓒ	ⓓ
6	ⓐ	ⓑ	ⓒ	ⓓ
7	ⓐ	ⓑ	ⓒ	ⓓ
8	ⓐ	ⓑ	ⓒ	ⓓ
9	ⓐ	ⓑ	ⓒ	ⓓ
10	ⓐ	ⓑ	ⓒ	ⓓ
11	ⓐ	ⓑ	ⓒ	ⓓ
12	ⓐ	ⓑ	ⓒ	ⓓ

문법

13	ⓐ	ⓑ	ⓒ	ⓓ
14	ⓐ	ⓑ	ⓒ	ⓓ
15	ⓐ	ⓑ	ⓒ	ⓓ
16	ⓐ	ⓑ	ⓒ	ⓓ
17	ⓐ	ⓑ	ⓒ	ⓓ
18	ⓐ	ⓑ	ⓒ	ⓓ
19	ⓐ	ⓑ	ⓒ	ⓓ
20	ⓐ	ⓑ	ⓒ	ⓓ

| 21 | ⓐ | ⓑ | ⓒ | ⓓ |
| 22 | ⓐ | ⓑ | ⓒ | ⓓ |

어휘

23	ⓐ	ⓑ	ⓒ	ⓓ
24	ⓐ	ⓑ	ⓒ	ⓓ
25	ⓐ	ⓑ	ⓒ	ⓓ
26	ⓐ	ⓑ	ⓒ	ⓓ
27	ⓐ	ⓑ	ⓒ	ⓓ
28	ⓐ	ⓑ	ⓒ	ⓓ
29	ⓐ	ⓑ	ⓒ	ⓓ
30	ⓐ	ⓑ	ⓒ	ⓓ
31	ⓐ	ⓑ	ⓒ	ⓓ
32	ⓐ	ⓑ	ⓒ	ⓓ

독해

33	ⓐ	ⓑ	ⓒ	ⓓ
34	ⓐ	ⓑ	ⓒ	ⓓ
35	ⓐ	ⓑ	ⓒ	ⓓ
36	ⓐ	ⓑ	ⓒ	ⓓ
37	ⓐ	ⓑ	ⓒ	ⓓ
38	ⓐ	ⓑ	ⓒ	ⓓ
39	ⓐ	ⓑ	ⓒ	ⓓ
40	ⓐ	ⓑ	ⓒ	ⓓ

Actual Test 06

청해

1	ⓐ	ⓑ	ⓒ	ⓓ
2	ⓐ	ⓑ	ⓒ	ⓓ
3	ⓐ	ⓑ	ⓒ	ⓓ
4	ⓐ	ⓑ	ⓒ	ⓓ
5	ⓐ	ⓑ	ⓒ	ⓓ
6	ⓐ	ⓑ	ⓒ	ⓓ
7	ⓐ	ⓑ	ⓒ	ⓓ
8	ⓐ	ⓑ	ⓒ	ⓓ
9	ⓐ	ⓑ	ⓒ	ⓓ
10	ⓐ	ⓑ	ⓒ	ⓓ
11	ⓐ	ⓑ	ⓒ	ⓓ
12	ⓐ	ⓑ	ⓒ	ⓓ

문법

13	ⓐ	ⓑ	ⓒ	ⓓ
14	ⓐ	ⓑ	ⓒ	ⓓ
15	ⓐ	ⓑ	ⓒ	ⓓ
16	ⓐ	ⓑ	ⓒ	ⓓ
17	ⓐ	ⓑ	ⓒ	ⓓ
18	ⓐ	ⓑ	ⓒ	ⓓ
19	ⓐ	ⓑ	ⓒ	ⓓ
20	ⓐ	ⓑ	ⓒ	ⓓ

| 21 | ⓐ | ⓑ | ⓒ | ⓓ |
| 22 | ⓐ | ⓑ | ⓒ | ⓓ |

어휘

23	ⓐ	ⓑ	ⓒ	ⓓ
24	ⓐ	ⓑ	ⓒ	ⓓ
25	ⓐ	ⓑ	ⓒ	ⓓ
26	ⓐ	ⓑ	ⓒ	ⓓ
27	ⓐ	ⓑ	ⓒ	ⓓ
28	ⓐ	ⓑ	ⓒ	ⓓ
29	ⓐ	ⓑ	ⓒ	ⓓ
30	ⓐ	ⓑ	ⓒ	ⓓ
31	ⓐ	ⓑ	ⓒ	ⓓ
32	ⓐ	ⓑ	ⓒ	ⓓ

독해

33	ⓐ	ⓑ	ⓒ	ⓓ
34	ⓐ	ⓑ	ⓒ	ⓓ
35	ⓐ	ⓑ	ⓒ	ⓓ
36	ⓐ	ⓑ	ⓒ	ⓓ
37	ⓐ	ⓑ	ⓒ	ⓓ
38	ⓐ	ⓑ	ⓒ	ⓓ
39	ⓐ	ⓑ	ⓒ	ⓓ
40	ⓐ	ⓑ	ⓒ	ⓓ

Actual Test 07

청해

1	ⓐ	ⓑ	ⓒ	ⓓ
2	ⓐ	ⓑ	ⓒ	ⓓ
3	ⓐ	ⓑ	ⓒ	ⓓ
4	ⓐ	ⓑ	ⓒ	ⓓ
5	ⓐ	ⓑ	ⓒ	ⓓ
6	ⓐ	ⓑ	ⓒ	ⓓ
7	ⓐ	ⓑ	ⓒ	ⓓ
8	ⓐ	ⓑ	ⓒ	ⓓ
9	ⓐ	ⓑ	ⓒ	ⓓ
10	ⓐ	ⓑ	ⓒ	ⓓ
11	ⓐ	ⓑ	ⓒ	ⓓ
12	ⓐ	ⓑ	ⓒ	ⓓ

문법

13	ⓐ	ⓑ	ⓒ	ⓓ
14	ⓐ	ⓑ	ⓒ	ⓓ
15	ⓐ	ⓑ	ⓒ	ⓓ
16	ⓐ	ⓑ	ⓒ	ⓓ
17	ⓐ	ⓑ	ⓒ	ⓓ
18	ⓐ	ⓑ	ⓒ	ⓓ
19	ⓐ	ⓑ	ⓒ	ⓓ
20	ⓐ	ⓑ	ⓒ	ⓓ

| 21 | ⓐ | ⓑ | ⓒ | ⓓ |
| 22 | ⓐ | ⓑ | ⓒ | ⓓ |

어휘

23	ⓐ	ⓑ	ⓒ	ⓓ
24	ⓐ	ⓑ	ⓒ	ⓓ
25	ⓐ	ⓑ	ⓒ	ⓓ
26	ⓐ	ⓑ	ⓒ	ⓓ
27	ⓐ	ⓑ	ⓒ	ⓓ
28	ⓐ	ⓑ	ⓒ	ⓓ
29	ⓐ	ⓑ	ⓒ	ⓓ
30	ⓐ	ⓑ	ⓒ	ⓓ
31	ⓐ	ⓑ	ⓒ	ⓓ
32	ⓐ	ⓑ	ⓒ	ⓓ

독해

33	ⓐ	ⓑ	ⓒ	ⓓ
34	ⓐ	ⓑ	ⓒ	ⓓ
35	ⓐ	ⓑ	ⓒ	ⓓ
36	ⓐ	ⓑ	ⓒ	ⓓ
37	ⓐ	ⓑ	ⓒ	ⓓ
38	ⓐ	ⓑ	ⓒ	ⓓ
39	ⓐ	ⓑ	ⓒ	ⓓ
40	ⓐ	ⓑ	ⓒ	ⓓ

Actual Test 08

청해

1	ⓐ	ⓑ	ⓒ	ⓓ
2	ⓐ	ⓑ	ⓒ	ⓓ
3	ⓐ	ⓑ	ⓒ	ⓓ
4	ⓐ	ⓑ	ⓒ	ⓓ
5	ⓐ	ⓑ	ⓒ	ⓓ
6	ⓐ	ⓑ	ⓒ	ⓓ
7	ⓐ	ⓑ	ⓒ	ⓓ
8	ⓐ	ⓑ	ⓒ	ⓓ
9	ⓐ	ⓑ	ⓒ	ⓓ
10	ⓐ	ⓑ	ⓒ	ⓓ
11	ⓐ	ⓑ	ⓒ	ⓓ
12	ⓐ	ⓑ	ⓒ	ⓓ

문법

13	ⓐ	ⓑ	ⓒ	ⓓ
14	ⓐ	ⓑ	ⓒ	ⓓ
15	ⓐ	ⓑ	ⓒ	ⓓ
16	ⓐ	ⓑ	ⓒ	ⓓ
17	ⓐ	ⓑ	ⓒ	ⓓ
18	ⓐ	ⓑ	ⓒ	ⓓ
19	ⓐ	ⓑ	ⓒ	ⓓ
20	ⓐ	ⓑ	ⓒ	ⓓ

| 21 | ⓐ | ⓑ | ⓒ | ⓓ |
| 22 | ⓐ | ⓑ | ⓒ | ⓓ |

어휘

23	ⓐ	ⓑ	ⓒ	ⓓ
24	ⓐ	ⓑ	ⓒ	ⓓ
25	ⓐ	ⓑ	ⓒ	ⓓ
26	ⓐ	ⓑ	ⓒ	ⓓ
27	ⓐ	ⓑ	ⓒ	ⓓ
28	ⓐ	ⓑ	ⓒ	ⓓ
29	ⓐ	ⓑ	ⓒ	ⓓ
30	ⓐ	ⓑ	ⓒ	ⓓ
31	ⓐ	ⓑ	ⓒ	ⓓ
32	ⓐ	ⓑ	ⓒ	ⓓ

독해

33	ⓐ	ⓑ	ⓒ	ⓓ
34	ⓐ	ⓑ	ⓒ	ⓓ
35	ⓐ	ⓑ	ⓒ	ⓓ
36	ⓐ	ⓑ	ⓒ	ⓓ
37	ⓐ	ⓑ	ⓒ	ⓓ
38	ⓐ	ⓑ	ⓒ	ⓓ
39	ⓐ	ⓑ	ⓒ	ⓓ
40	ⓐ	ⓑ	ⓒ	ⓓ

Actual Test 09

청해

	a	b	c	d
1	ⓐ	ⓑ	ⓒ	ⓓ
2	ⓐ	ⓑ	ⓒ	ⓓ
3	ⓐ	ⓑ	ⓒ	ⓓ
4	ⓐ	ⓑ	ⓒ	ⓓ
5	ⓐ	ⓑ	ⓒ	ⓓ
6	ⓐ	ⓑ	ⓒ	ⓓ
7	ⓐ	ⓑ	ⓒ	ⓓ
8	ⓐ	ⓑ	ⓒ	ⓓ
9	ⓐ	ⓑ	ⓒ	ⓓ
10	ⓐ	ⓑ	ⓒ	ⓓ
11	ⓐ	ⓑ	ⓒ	ⓓ
12	ⓐ	ⓑ	ⓒ	ⓓ

문법

	a	b	c	d
13	ⓐ	ⓑ	ⓒ	ⓓ
14	ⓐ	ⓑ	ⓒ	ⓓ
15	ⓐ	ⓑ	ⓒ	ⓓ
16	ⓐ	ⓑ	ⓒ	ⓓ
17	ⓐ	ⓑ	ⓒ	ⓓ
18	ⓐ	ⓑ	ⓒ	ⓓ
19	ⓐ	ⓑ	ⓒ	ⓓ
20	ⓐ	ⓑ	ⓒ	ⓓ

	a	b	c	d
21	ⓐ	ⓑ	ⓒ	ⓓ
22	ⓐ	ⓑ	ⓒ	ⓓ

어휘

	a	b	c	d
23	ⓐ	ⓑ	ⓒ	ⓓ
24	ⓐ	ⓑ	ⓒ	ⓓ
25	ⓐ	ⓑ	ⓒ	ⓓ
26	ⓐ	ⓑ	ⓒ	ⓓ
27	ⓐ	ⓑ	ⓒ	ⓓ
28	ⓐ	ⓑ	ⓒ	ⓓ
29	ⓐ	ⓑ	ⓒ	ⓓ
30	ⓐ	ⓑ	ⓒ	ⓓ
31	ⓐ	ⓑ	ⓒ	ⓓ
32	ⓐ	ⓑ	ⓒ	ⓓ

독해

	a	b	c	d
33	ⓐ	ⓑ	ⓒ	ⓓ
34	ⓐ	ⓑ	ⓒ	ⓓ
35	ⓐ	ⓑ	ⓒ	ⓓ
36	ⓐ	ⓑ	ⓒ	ⓓ
37	ⓐ	ⓑ	ⓒ	ⓓ
38	ⓐ	ⓑ	ⓒ	ⓓ
39	ⓐ	ⓑ	ⓒ	ⓓ
40	ⓐ	ⓑ	ⓒ	ⓓ

Actual Test 10

청해

	a	b	c	d
1	ⓐ	ⓑ	ⓒ	ⓓ
2	ⓐ	ⓑ	ⓒ	ⓓ
3	ⓐ	ⓑ	ⓒ	ⓓ
4	ⓐ	ⓑ	ⓒ	ⓓ
5	ⓐ	ⓑ	ⓒ	ⓓ
6	ⓐ	ⓑ	ⓒ	ⓓ
7	ⓐ	ⓑ	ⓒ	ⓓ
8	ⓐ	ⓑ	ⓒ	ⓓ
9	ⓐ	ⓑ	ⓒ	ⓓ
10	ⓐ	ⓑ	ⓒ	ⓓ
11	ⓐ	ⓑ	ⓒ	ⓓ
12	ⓐ	ⓑ	ⓒ	ⓓ

문법

	a	b	c	d
13	ⓐ	ⓑ	ⓒ	ⓓ
14	ⓐ	ⓑ	ⓒ	ⓓ
15	ⓐ	ⓑ	ⓒ	ⓓ
16	ⓐ	ⓑ	ⓒ	ⓓ
17	ⓐ	ⓑ	ⓒ	ⓓ
18	ⓐ	ⓑ	ⓒ	ⓓ
19	ⓐ	ⓑ	ⓒ	ⓓ
20	ⓐ	ⓑ	ⓒ	ⓓ

	a	b	c	d
21	ⓐ	ⓑ	ⓒ	ⓓ
22	ⓐ	ⓑ	ⓒ	ⓓ

어휘

	a	b	c	d
23	ⓐ	ⓑ	ⓒ	ⓓ
24	ⓐ	ⓑ	ⓒ	ⓓ
25	ⓐ	ⓑ	ⓒ	ⓓ
26	ⓐ	ⓑ	ⓒ	ⓓ
27	ⓐ	ⓑ	ⓒ	ⓓ
28	ⓐ	ⓑ	ⓒ	ⓓ
29	ⓐ	ⓑ	ⓒ	ⓓ
30	ⓐ	ⓑ	ⓒ	ⓓ
31	ⓐ	ⓑ	ⓒ	ⓓ
32	ⓐ	ⓑ	ⓒ	ⓓ

독해

	a	b	c	d
33	ⓐ	ⓑ	ⓒ	ⓓ
34	ⓐ	ⓑ	ⓒ	ⓓ
35	ⓐ	ⓑ	ⓒ	ⓓ
36	ⓐ	ⓑ	ⓒ	ⓓ
37	ⓐ	ⓑ	ⓒ	ⓓ
38	ⓐ	ⓑ	ⓒ	ⓓ
39	ⓐ	ⓑ	ⓒ	ⓓ
40	ⓐ	ⓑ	ⓒ	ⓓ

Actual Test 11

청해

	a	b	c	d
1	ⓐ	ⓑ	ⓒ	ⓓ
2	ⓐ	ⓑ	ⓒ	ⓓ
3	ⓐ	ⓑ	ⓒ	ⓓ
4	ⓐ	ⓑ	ⓒ	ⓓ
5	ⓐ	ⓑ	ⓒ	ⓓ
6	ⓐ	ⓑ	ⓒ	ⓓ
7	ⓐ	ⓑ	ⓒ	ⓓ
8	ⓐ	ⓑ	ⓒ	ⓓ
9	ⓐ	ⓑ	ⓒ	ⓓ
10	ⓐ	ⓑ	ⓒ	ⓓ
11	ⓐ	ⓑ	ⓒ	ⓓ
12	ⓐ	ⓑ	ⓒ	ⓓ

문법

	a	b	c	d
13	ⓐ	ⓑ	ⓒ	ⓓ
14	ⓐ	ⓑ	ⓒ	ⓓ
15	ⓐ	ⓑ	ⓒ	ⓓ
16	ⓐ	ⓑ	ⓒ	ⓓ
17	ⓐ	ⓑ	ⓒ	ⓓ
18	ⓐ	ⓑ	ⓒ	ⓓ
19	ⓐ	ⓑ	ⓒ	ⓓ
20	ⓐ	ⓑ	ⓒ	ⓓ

	a	b	c	d
21	ⓐ	ⓑ	ⓒ	ⓓ
22	ⓐ	ⓑ	ⓒ	ⓓ

어휘

	a	b	c	d
23	ⓐ	ⓑ	ⓒ	ⓓ
24	ⓐ	ⓑ	ⓒ	ⓓ
25	ⓐ	ⓑ	ⓒ	ⓓ
26	ⓐ	ⓑ	ⓒ	ⓓ
27	ⓐ	ⓑ	ⓒ	ⓓ
28	ⓐ	ⓑ	ⓒ	ⓓ
29	ⓐ	ⓑ	ⓒ	ⓓ
30	ⓐ	ⓑ	ⓒ	ⓓ
31	ⓐ	ⓑ	ⓒ	ⓓ
32	ⓐ	ⓑ	ⓒ	ⓓ

독해

	a	b	c	d
33	ⓐ	ⓑ	ⓒ	ⓓ
34	ⓐ	ⓑ	ⓒ	ⓓ
35	ⓐ	ⓑ	ⓒ	ⓓ
36	ⓐ	ⓑ	ⓒ	ⓓ
37	ⓐ	ⓑ	ⓒ	ⓓ
38	ⓐ	ⓑ	ⓒ	ⓓ
39	ⓐ	ⓑ	ⓒ	ⓓ
40	ⓐ	ⓑ	ⓒ	ⓓ

Actual Test 12

청해

	a	b	c	d
1	ⓐ	ⓑ	ⓒ	ⓓ
2	ⓐ	ⓑ	ⓒ	ⓓ
3	ⓐ	ⓑ	ⓒ	ⓓ
4	ⓐ	ⓑ	ⓒ	ⓓ
5	ⓐ	ⓑ	ⓒ	ⓓ
6	ⓐ	ⓑ	ⓒ	ⓓ
7	ⓐ	ⓑ	ⓒ	ⓓ
8	ⓐ	ⓑ	ⓒ	ⓓ
9	ⓐ	ⓑ	ⓒ	ⓓ
10	ⓐ	ⓑ	ⓒ	ⓓ
11	ⓐ	ⓑ	ⓒ	ⓓ
12	ⓐ	ⓑ	ⓒ	ⓓ

문법

	a	b	c	d
13	ⓐ	ⓑ	ⓒ	ⓓ
14	ⓐ	ⓑ	ⓒ	ⓓ
15	ⓐ	ⓑ	ⓒ	ⓓ
16	ⓐ	ⓑ	ⓒ	ⓓ
17	ⓐ	ⓑ	ⓒ	ⓓ
18	ⓐ	ⓑ	ⓒ	ⓓ
19	ⓐ	ⓑ	ⓒ	ⓓ
20	ⓐ	ⓑ	ⓒ	ⓓ

	a	b	c	d
21	ⓐ	ⓑ	ⓒ	ⓓ
22	ⓐ	ⓑ	ⓒ	ⓓ

어휘

	a	b	c	d
23	ⓐ	ⓑ	ⓒ	ⓓ
24	ⓐ	ⓑ	ⓒ	ⓓ
25	ⓐ	ⓑ	ⓒ	ⓓ
26	ⓐ	ⓑ	ⓒ	ⓓ
27	ⓐ	ⓑ	ⓒ	ⓓ
28	ⓐ	ⓑ	ⓒ	ⓓ
29	ⓐ	ⓑ	ⓒ	ⓓ
30	ⓐ	ⓑ	ⓒ	ⓓ
31	ⓐ	ⓑ	ⓒ	ⓓ
32	ⓐ	ⓑ	ⓒ	ⓓ

독해

	a	b	c	d
33	ⓐ	ⓑ	ⓒ	ⓓ
34	ⓐ	ⓑ	ⓒ	ⓓ
35	ⓐ	ⓑ	ⓒ	ⓓ
36	ⓐ	ⓑ	ⓒ	ⓓ
37	ⓐ	ⓑ	ⓒ	ⓓ
38	ⓐ	ⓑ	ⓒ	ⓓ
39	ⓐ	ⓑ	ⓒ	ⓓ
40	ⓐ	ⓑ	ⓒ	ⓓ

Actual Test 100

청해				
1	ⓐ	ⓑ	ⓒ	ⓓ
2	ⓐ	ⓑ	ⓒ	ⓓ
3	ⓐ	ⓑ	ⓒ	ⓓ
4	ⓐ	ⓑ	ⓒ	ⓓ
5	ⓐ	ⓑ	ⓒ	ⓓ
6	ⓐ	ⓑ	ⓒ	ⓓ
7	ⓐ	ⓑ	ⓒ	ⓓ
8	ⓐ	ⓑ	ⓒ	ⓓ
9	ⓐ	ⓑ	ⓒ	ⓓ
10	ⓐ	ⓑ	ⓒ	ⓓ
11	ⓐ	ⓑ	ⓒ	ⓓ
12	ⓐ	ⓑ	ⓒ	ⓓ
13	ⓐ	ⓑ	ⓒ	ⓓ
14	ⓐ	ⓑ	ⓒ	ⓓ
15	ⓐ	ⓑ	ⓒ	ⓓ
16	ⓐ	ⓑ	ⓒ	ⓓ
17	ⓐ	ⓑ	ⓒ	ⓓ
18	ⓐ	ⓑ	ⓒ	ⓓ
19	ⓐ	ⓑ	ⓒ	ⓓ
20	ⓐ	ⓑ	ⓒ	ⓓ
21	ⓐ	ⓑ	ⓒ	ⓓ
22	ⓐ	ⓑ	ⓒ	ⓓ
23	ⓐ	ⓑ	ⓒ	ⓓ
24	ⓐ	ⓑ	ⓒ	ⓓ
25	ⓐ	ⓑ	ⓒ	ⓓ
26	ⓐ	ⓑ	ⓒ	ⓓ
27	ⓐ	ⓑ	ⓒ	ⓓ
28	ⓐ	ⓑ	ⓒ	ⓓ
29	ⓐ	ⓑ	ⓒ	ⓓ
30	ⓐ	ⓑ	ⓒ	ⓓ

문법				
31	ⓐ	ⓑ	ⓒ	ⓓ
32	ⓐ	ⓑ	ⓒ	ⓓ
33	ⓐ	ⓑ	ⓒ	ⓓ
34	ⓐ	ⓑ	ⓒ	ⓓ
35	ⓐ	ⓑ	ⓒ	ⓓ
36	ⓐ	ⓑ	ⓒ	ⓓ
37	ⓐ	ⓑ	ⓒ	ⓓ
38	ⓐ	ⓑ	ⓒ	ⓓ
39	ⓐ	ⓑ	ⓒ	ⓓ
40	ⓐ	ⓑ	ⓒ	ⓓ
41	ⓐ	ⓑ	ⓒ	ⓓ
42	ⓐ	ⓑ	ⓒ	ⓓ
43	ⓐ	ⓑ	ⓒ	ⓓ
44	ⓐ	ⓑ	ⓒ	ⓓ
45	ⓐ	ⓑ	ⓒ	ⓓ
46	ⓐ	ⓑ	ⓒ	ⓓ
47	ⓐ	ⓑ	ⓒ	ⓓ
48	ⓐ	ⓑ	ⓒ	ⓓ
49	ⓐ	ⓑ	ⓒ	ⓓ
50	ⓐ	ⓑ	ⓒ	ⓓ
51	ⓐ	ⓑ	ⓒ	ⓓ
52	ⓐ	ⓑ	ⓒ	ⓓ
53	ⓐ	ⓑ	ⓒ	ⓓ
54	ⓐ	ⓑ	ⓒ	ⓓ
55	ⓐ	ⓑ	ⓒ	ⓓ

어휘				
56	ⓐ	ⓑ	ⓒ	ⓓ
57	ⓐ	ⓑ	ⓒ	ⓓ
58	ⓐ	ⓑ	ⓒ	ⓓ
59	ⓐ	ⓑ	ⓒ	ⓓ
60	ⓐ	ⓑ	ⓒ	ⓓ
61	ⓐ	ⓑ	ⓒ	ⓓ
62	ⓐ	ⓑ	ⓒ	ⓓ
63	ⓐ	ⓑ	ⓒ	ⓓ
64	ⓐ	ⓑ	ⓒ	ⓓ
65	ⓐ	ⓑ	ⓒ	ⓓ
66	ⓐ	ⓑ	ⓒ	ⓓ
67	ⓐ	ⓑ	ⓒ	ⓓ
68	ⓐ	ⓑ	ⓒ	ⓓ
69	ⓐ	ⓑ	ⓒ	ⓓ
70	ⓐ	ⓑ	ⓒ	ⓓ
71	ⓐ	ⓑ	ⓒ	ⓓ
72	ⓐ	ⓑ	ⓒ	ⓓ
73	ⓐ	ⓑ	ⓒ	ⓓ
74	ⓐ	ⓑ	ⓒ	ⓓ
75	ⓐ	ⓑ	ⓒ	ⓓ
76	ⓐ	ⓑ	ⓒ	ⓓ
77	ⓐ	ⓑ	ⓒ	ⓓ
78	ⓐ	ⓑ	ⓒ	ⓓ
79	ⓐ	ⓑ	ⓒ	ⓓ
80	ⓐ	ⓑ	ⓒ	ⓓ

독해				
81	ⓐ	ⓑ	ⓒ	ⓓ
82	ⓐ	ⓑ	ⓒ	ⓓ
83	ⓐ	ⓑ	ⓒ	ⓓ
84	ⓐ	ⓑ	ⓒ	ⓓ
85	ⓐ	ⓑ	ⓒ	ⓓ
86	ⓐ	ⓑ	ⓒ	ⓓ
87	ⓐ	ⓑ	ⓒ	ⓓ
88	ⓐ	ⓑ	ⓒ	ⓓ
89	ⓐ	ⓑ	ⓒ	ⓓ
90	ⓐ	ⓑ	ⓒ	ⓓ
91	ⓐ	ⓑ	ⓒ	ⓓ
92	ⓐ	ⓑ	ⓒ	ⓓ
93	ⓐ	ⓑ	ⓒ	ⓓ
94	ⓐ	ⓑ	ⓒ	ⓓ
95	ⓐ	ⓑ	ⓒ	ⓓ
96	ⓐ	ⓑ	ⓒ	ⓓ
97	ⓐ	ⓑ	ⓒ	ⓓ
98	ⓐ	ⓑ	ⓒ	ⓓ
99	ⓐ	ⓑ	ⓒ	ⓓ
100	ⓐ	ⓑ	ⓒ	ⓓ

Actual Test 정답

Test 01

1 (d)	**2** (b)	**3** (b)	**4** (b)	**5** (c)	**6** (c)	**7** (c)	**8** (a)
9 (b)	**10** (c)	**11** (d)	**12** (c)	**13** (c)	**14** (d)	**15** (c)	**16** (a)
17 (c)	**18** (c)	**19** (a)	**20** (d)	**21** (b)	**22** (b)	**23** (b)	**24** (b)
25 (c)	**26** (a)	**27** (d)	**28** (c)	**29** (b)	**30** (a)	**31** (d)	**32** (a)
33 (d)	**34** (c)	**35** (b)	**36** (c)	**37** (d)	**38** (b)	**39** (a)	**40** (a)

Test 02

1 (b)	**2** (d)	**3** (c)	**4** (c)	**5** (b)	**6** (d)	**7** (a)	**8** (b)
9 (b)	**10** (a)	**11** (c)	**12** (d)	**13** (d)	**14** (b)	**15** (b)	**16** (c)
17 (d)	**18** (d)	**19** (c)	**20** (a)	**21** (c)	**22** (b)	**23** (d)	**24** (a)
25 (d)	**26** (a)	**27** (b)	**28** (c)	**29** (c)	**30** (c)	**31** (b)	**32** (a)
33 (b)	**34** (b)	**35** (b)	**36** (c)	**37** (b)	**38** (b)	**39** (c)	**40** (c)

Test 03

1 (b)	**2** (a)	**3** (c)	**4** (b)	**5** (c)	**6** (c)	**7** (d)	**8** (b)
9 (c)	**10** (b)	**11** (a)	**12** (b)	**13** (c)	**14** (a)	**15** (c)	**16** (a)
17 (b)	**18** (c)	**19** (c)	**20** (c)	**21** (c)	**22** (b)	**23** (c)	**24** (a)
25 (b)	**26** (c)	**27** (d)	**28** (a)	**29** (b)	**30** (c)	**31** (d)	**32** (a)
33 (d)	**34** (c)	**35** (a)	**36** (c)	**37** (c)	**38** (b)	**39** (d)	**40** (b)

Test 04

1 (d)	**2** (b)	**3** (d)	**4** (b)	**5** b)	**6** (b)	**7** (c)	**8** (c)
9 (a)	**10** (b)	**11** (b)	**12** (d)	**13** (c)	**14** (d)	**15** (c)	**16** (a)
17 (b)	**18** (a)	**19** (a)	**20** (c)	**21** (d)	**22** (a)	**23** (a)	**24** (c)
25 (d)	**26** (c)	**27** (a)	**28** (d)	**29** (c)	**30** (d)	**31** (a)	**32** (c)
33 (a)	**34** (a)	**35** (d)	**36** (c)	**37** (a)	**38** (c)	**39** (a)	**40** (c)

Test 05

1 (c)	**2** (b)	**3** (b)	**4** (d)	**5** (b)	**6** (c)	**7** (a)	**8** (b)
9 (b)	**10** (b)	**11** (d)	**12** (c)	**13** (c)	**14** (c)	**15** (d)	**16** (b)
17 (d)	**18** (c)	**19** (d)	**20** (a)	**21** (c)	**22** (c)	**23** (d)	**24** (c)
25 (c)	**26** (b)	**27** (a)	**28** (b)	**29** (a)	**30** (d)	**31** (c)	**32** (b)
33 (d)	**34** (c)	**35** (a)	**36** (d)	**37** (d)	**38** (c)	**39** (d)	**40** (d)

Test 06

1 (d)	**2** (d)	**3** (c)	**4** (a)	**5** (d)	**6** (a)	**7** (d)	**8** (b)
9 (d)	**10** (d)	**11** (c)	**12** (c)	**13** (c)	**14** (b)	**15** (c)	**16** (b)
17 (a)	**18** (b)	**19** (d)	**20** (b)	**21** (c)	**22** (c)	**23** (c)	**24** (a)
25 (c)	**26** (a)	**27** (a)	**28** (d)	**29** (d)	**30** (b)	**31** (b)	**32** (d)
33 (d)	**34** (c)	**35** (c)	**36** (d)	**37** (c)	**38** (b)	**39** (b)	**40** (a)

Test 07

1 (a)	**2** (b)	**3** (c)	**4** (b)	**5** (a)	**6** (d)	**7** (b)	**8** (c)
9 (d)	**10** (d)	**11** (a)	**12** (c)	**13** (d)	**14** (b)	**15** (d)	**16** (a)
17 (b)	**18** (a)	**19** (d)	**20** (a)	**21** (d)	**22** (b)	**23** (b)	**24** (d)
25 (d)	**26** (a)	**27** (b)	**28** (c)	**29** (a)	**30** (c)	**31** (b)	**32** (b)
33 (d)	**34** (c)	**35** (b)	**36** (a)	**37** (b)	**38** (d)	**39** (b)	**40** (d)

Test 08

1 (a)	**2** (c)	**3** (b)	**4** (d)	**5** (b)	**6** (c)	**7** (c)	**8** (c)
9 (c)	**10** (c)	**11** (a)	**12** (b)	**13** (c)	**14** (b)	**15** (b)	**16** (d)
17 (b)	**18** (a)	**19** (b)	**20** (c)	**21** (d)	**22** (a)	**23** (a)	**24** (b)
25 (b)	**26** (d)	**27** (c)	**28** (a)	**29** (c)	**30** (b)	**31** (b)	**32** (b)
33 (c)	**34** (d)	**35** (a)	**36** (c)	**37** (d)	**38** (b)	**39** (d)	**40** (c)

Test 09	1 (c)	2 (a)	3 (c)	4 (a)	5 (c)	6 (d)	7 (c)	8 (c)
	9 (a)	10 (b)	11 (d)	12 (d)	13 (b)	14 (d)	15 (c)	16 (b)
	17 (c)	18 (b)	19 (d)	20 (b)	21 (c)	22 (b)	23 (c)	24 (b)
	25 (d)	26 (b)	27 (c)	28 (b)	29 (c)	30 (a)	31 (c)	32 (d)
	33 (c)	34 (b)	35 (a)	36 (c)	37 (a)	38 (b)	39 (b)	40 (c)

Test 10	1 (d)	2 (b)	3 (d)	4 (a)	5 (c)	6 (d)	7 (c)	8 (a)
	9 (b)	10 (b)	11 (c)	12 (d)	13 (b)	14 (c)	15 (c)	16 (d)
	17 (b)	18 (a)	19 (c)	20 (d)	21 (b)	22 (a)	23 (c)	24 (c)
	25 (b)	26 (d)	27 (a)	28 (c)	29 (d)	30 (b)	31 (c)	32 (b)
	33 (b)	34 (d)	35 (c)	36 (d)	37 (c)	38 (a)	39 (d)	40 (b)

Test 11	1 (b)	2 (d)	3 (a)	4 (b)	5 (d)	6 (b)	7 (c)	8 (c)
	9 (d)	10 (b)	11 (c)	12 (d)	13 (c)	14 (d)	15 (a)	16 (b)
	17 (a)	18 (a)	19 (b)	20 (d)	21 (d)	22 (c)	23 (c)	24 (d)
	25 (c)	26 (a)	27 (c)	28 (b)	29 (a)	30 (b)	31 (d)	32 (b)
	33 (c)	34 (c)	35 (b)	36 (a)	37 (d)	38 (c)	39 (d)	40 (a)

Test 12	1 (c)	2 (a)	3 (d)	4 (c)	5 (d)	6 (b)	7 (b)	8 (c)
	9 (d)	10 (b)	11 (b)	12 (c)	13 (c)	14 (b)	15 (d)	16 (b)
	17 (c)	18 (c)	19 (a)	20 (b)	21 (a)	22 (c)	23 (b)	24 (c)
	25 (d)	26 (c)	27 (b)	28 (c)	29 (c)	30 (a)	31 (d)	32 (b)
	33 (a)	34 (d)	35 (c)	36 (b)	37 (c)	38 (a)	39 (c)	40 (d)

1 (a)	**2** (a)	**3** (c)	**4** (b)	**5** (d)	**6** (d)	**7** (b)	**8** (a)
9 (d)	**10** (c)	**11** (d)	**12** (a)	**13** (b)	**14** (c)	**15** (b)	**16** (d)
17 (c)	**18** (d)	**19** (c)	**20** (b)	**21** (c)	**22** (d)	**23** (d)	**24** (c)
25 (d)	**26** (c)	**27** (c)	**28** (b)	**29** (b)	**30** (a)	**31** (d)	**32** (d)
33 (c)	**34** (a)	**35** (b)	**36** (d)	**37** (c)	**38** (c)	**39** (b)	**40** (d)
41 (c)	**42** (d)	**43** (b)	**44** (b)	**45** (a)	**46** (c)	**47** (b)	**48** (a)
49 (d)	**50** (b)	**51** (c)	**52** (b)	**53** (c)	**54** (d)	**55** (a)	**56** (c)
57 (a)	**58** (d)	**59** (d)	**60** (a)	**61** (c)	**62** (c)	**63** (c)	**64** (b)
65 (c)	**66** (b)	**67** (d)	**68** (a)	**69** (c)	**70** (d)	**71** (c)	**72** (b)
73 (a)	**74** (b)	**75** (d)	**76** (d)	**77** (b)	**78** (b)	**79** (d)	**80** (b)
81 (d)	**82** (a)	**83** (b)	**84** (d)	**85** (b)	**86** (c)	**87** (b)	**88** (b)
89 (b)	**90** (c)	**91** (b)	**92** (a)	**93** (c)	**94** (d)	**95** (b)	**96** (d)
97 (c)	**98** (b)	**99** (d)	**100** (b)				

까다로운 우리 입맛에 딱 맞는
최고의 교재가 왔다!

리딩 파워를 제대로 높여주는 한국형 원서

- Reading EDGE는 문법, 어휘, 문장의 기본이 확실한 품격 있는 영어로 구성
- 학생들의 지적호기심을 자극할 만한 흥미로운 지문 수록
- 수입원서의 2% 부족을 채운 한국형 원서. 다양한 문제 구성으로 한국형 테스트에 최적화
- 21세기 정보화 시대를 위한 파워풀한 훈련서. 장문 독해로 가다듬은 실력은 곧바로 속독 능력을 향상

Highly Advanced Reading Curriculum
Reading EDGE

E-Field Academy 지음
국배판(210×297) | 각권 **220**면 내외
부록 : 해설집 · 전 지문 음원 제공(다운로드)
각권 값 **13,500**원

까다로운 우리 입맛에 딱 맞는
최고의 교재가 왔다!

Reading EDGE와 주제를 공유, 읽고 듣는 연계학습으로 최상의 시너지 효과

- 수능 유형 및 출제 빈도 등을 철저히 분석, 치밀한 기획으로 탄생한 Edge 시리즈의 청취교재
- 각 Unit마다 Listening 주제 5개씩 총 50개의 다양한 주제
- 각 Unit마다 Famous Poems, Speech, Word Check 수록 (1 · 2권)
- 모든 Listening에 대한 Dictation 학습 가능
- 다양한 주제에 대한 심화학습으로 탄탄한 배경지식 구축(1 · 2권)

Highly Advanced Listening Curriculum
Listening EDGE

E-Field Academy 지음 | **국배판**(210×297)
1 · 2권 각권 **140**면 내외 | 값 **10,000**원
3 · 4권 각권 **250**면 내외 | 값 **15,000**원
부록 : 해설집 | Cassete Tape 교재 별매

위아
텝스

강의와 자습을 위한 최적의 구성
시간과 점수를 동시에 잡는 맞춤형 TEPS 실전서

위아텝스
실전모의고사 700+

해설

TEPS

3 텝스 중급을 위한 내공 쌓기
Intermediate

We're
위아북스

위아텝스
실전모의고사
해설집

700+ **3** **Intermediate**

EMD MEDIA 지음

위아북스

LISTENING COMPREHENSION · P.20

1 **M** How soon will the train leave?
  W _____

(a) He lives in Toronto.
(b) The train is delayed.
(c) Every twenty minutes.
(d) In a few minutes.

M: 기차가 언제 출발하나요?
W: 곧 출발합니다.

○ 기차가 언제 출발하는지 남자가 묻고 있다. (a)는 leave와 발음이 비슷한 live를 이용하여 혼동을 주기 위한 문장이다. (b)는 기차가 연착되었다는 말이므로 정답이 아니고 (c)의 경우 매 20분마다 출발한다는 뜻으로 이 대답은 how often ~?의 질문에 더 적절한 대답이라고 할 수 있다.

How soon...? 얼마나 빨리~? leave ~을 떠나다 delay ~을 지연시키다

2 **M** How are you?
  W _____

(a) I guess I'd better go.
(b) I've been better.
(c) It was great.
(d) That's terrible.

M: 좀 어때?
W: 나아졌어.

○ 몸 상태가 어떤지 묻는 질문에 대한 답변을 찾아야 한다. (a)는 헤어질 때 '이만 가봐야겠어.' 라는 뜻으로 쓰인 표현으로 적절치 않으며 (b)는 좀 나아졌다는 뜻이므로 정답이 된다. (c)는 좋았다는 뜻이고 (d)는 끔찍하다는 뜻이다.

had better ~하는 편이 낫다 terrible 끔찍한

3 **M** I'm sorry, but we're all booked up.
  W _____

(a) Could you tell me the time?
(b) Could you put me on the waiting list?
(c) I ordered two books 3 days ago.
(d) Don't worry about that.

M: 죄송하지만 예약이 모두 끝났는데요.
W: 대기자 명단에 올려주시겠어요?

○ book은 명사로는 '책' 이라는 뜻이고 동사로 쓰이면 '(좌석, 표 등)을 예약하다, 예매하다' 라는 뜻이다. 남자가 '예약이 다 끝났다' 고 했으므로 그에 어울리는 대답은 (b)가 된다. (a)는 시간을 묻는 질문이고 (c)는 book이 가진 여러 가지 뜻을 이용해 혼동을 주기 위한 보기이다. (d)는 '그것은 걱정하지 마.' 라는 뜻이다.

be booked up 예약이 끝나다 put sb on the waiting list ~을 대기자 명단에 올리다 order ~을 주문하다

4 M Hello, Amanda. This is Mr. Johnson.
   W I'm sorry, I can hardly hear you.
   M I think we have a bad connection.
   W _____

(a) I'll transfer you.
(b) Could you speak up, please?
(c) Let me tell you.
(d) Who do you want to speak with?

M: 안녕하세요. 아만다. 존슨입니다.
W: 죄송합니다만 잘 안 들리네요.
M: 전화 연결 상태가 안 좋은 것 같네요.
W: 크게 말씀해주시겠어요?

◑ 전화 대화 상황이다. 마지막 남자의 대사에서 전화 연결 상태가 좋지 않다고 했으므로 (b) 목소리를 크게 해달라는 표현이 정답이 된다. (a)는 '전화를 돌려드릴게요.' 라는 뜻이고 (c)는 '내가 이야기해 줄게.' (d)는 '누구를 찾으세요?' 라는 뜻으로 (a), (d) 모두 전화상에서 들을 수 있는 표현이지만 모두 통화가 잘 이루어진 상태에서 나올 수 있는 표현이므로 정답이 될 수 없다.

hardly 거의 ~아니다 have a bad connection (전화가) 연결 상태가 안 좋다 transfer ~을 옮기다, 이동시키다, (전화를) 돌려주다, 연결시키다 speak up 큰 소리로 말하다

---

5 M Hi. What a surprise to see you here.
   W Oh, hi. How have you been?
   M Great. How about you?
   W _____

(a) Much better than yesterday.
(b) I've heard a lot about you.
(c) Same as usual.
(d) It's very kind of you.

M: 안녕. 여기서 보다니 놀랍다.
W: 어, 안녕. 잘 지냈어?
M: 잘 지냈어. 너는 어때?
W: 늘 똑같지 뭐.

◑ 뜻밖에 만나게 된 남자와 여자가 안부를 주고받는 상황이다. 여자가 남자의 안부를 묻고 또 다시 남자가 여자의 안부를 묻고 있다. (a)는 어제는 몸이 좋지 않았다가 오늘은 훨씬 나아졌다는 뜻이므로 예상치 못한 만남의 상황에는 어울리지 않는다. (b)는 처음 만났을 때 '말씀 많이 들었어요.' 라는 뜻으로 쓰이는 표현이다. (d)는 '매우 친절하시네요.' 라는 뜻으로 누군가로부터 도움을 받았을 때 쓸 수 있는 표현이다. (c)의 경우 '늘 비슷하지 뭐.' 라는 뜻으로 안부에 대해 적절한 대답이 될 수 있다.

surprise 놀람 How about...? ~은 어때?

---

6 M Excuse me. I think you're in my seat.
   W What?
   M H-5 is my seat.
   W _____

(a) Don't get me wrong.
(b) Fasten your seat belt, please.
(c) Let me check my ticket.
(d) You can't miss it.

M: 실례합니다. 제 자리에 앉아 계신 것 같은데요.
W: 네?
M: H-5는 제 자리에요.
W: 제 티켓을 확인해 볼게요.

◑ 극장이나 공연장 등 좌석이 정해진 곳에서 일어날 수 있는 상황이다. 남자의 마지막 대사에서 H-5가 자기 자리라고 했으므로 가장 적절한 여자의 응답은 (c)가 될 수 있다. (a)는 오해하지 말라는 뜻으로 상황과 맞지 않고, (b)는 seat을 반복하여 혼동을 주기 위한 보기로서 비행기 등에서 안전벨트를 매라는 뜻이며 (d)는 길을 가르쳐줄 때 쓸 수 있는 표현으로서, '쉽게 찾으실 수 있을 겁니다.' 라는 뜻이다.

get sb wrong ~을 오해하다 seat belt 안전벨트 miss ~을 놓치다, 빠뜨리다

7

M What's the problem? When I turn on the faucet, it's just drip and drip.

W It's been going on like that for two days in a row. I guess the pipes are frozen because of the cold weather.

M Really?

W I couldn't take a shower yesterday because the water went off.

M Did you tell the manager about it?

W I haven't been able to reach him.

Q What are the man and woman talking about?

(a) How to reach her manager
(b) The cold weather
(c) The dripping tap
(d) When to move out

M: 문제가 뭐지? 수도꼭지를 틀면 물이 뚝뚝 떨어져.

W: 이틀째 그 상태야. 날씨가 추워서 파이프가 언 것 같아.

M: 정말?

W: 물이 끊겨서 어제는 샤워도 못했어.

M: 관리인에게 말했어?

W: 연락도 안 되고 있어.

○ 추운 날씨 때문에 수도관이 얼어서 물이 잘 나오지 않는 상황이다. 따라서 정답은 (c) 물이 뚝뚝 떨어지는 수도꼭지가 된다. (a)의 관리인에게 연락하는 방법이나 (b)의 추운 날씨는 언급이 되긴 했지만 주요 포인트가 아니므로 정답이 될 수 없다.

turn on (수도, 가스 등을) 틀다 **faucet** 수도꼭지 **drip** (액체가) 뚝뚝 떨어지다 **in a row** 잇따라, 연속해서 **take a shower** 샤워하다

8

M Why are you so late for the meeting this morning? Did you oversleep?

W No. I couldn't find my car keys.

M What happened?

W I locked them in the car.

M How did you open the door, then?

W I called my boyfriend. I gave him a spare key.

M How fortunate.

Q Why is the woman late for the meeting?

(a) She left the keys in the car.
(b) Her boyfriend lost her keys.
(c) The alarm clock didn't go off.
(d) Her car wouldn't start.

M: 오늘 아침 회의에 왜 그렇게 늦은 거야? 늦잠 잤어?

W: 아니, 아무리 찾아도 차 열쇠가 없는 거야.

M: 무슨 일이 있었던 건데?

W: 차 안에 열쇠를 두고 잠갔지 뭐야.

M: 그럼 문을 어떻게 열었어?

W: 남자 친구에게 전화했지. 예비키를 줬었거든.

M: 다행이네.

○ 회의에 늦은 이유를 묻고 있다. 여자가 차 열쇠를 차 안에 두고 잠갔다는 표현을 통해 정답이 (a) 차안에 열쇠를 두었다임을 알 수 있다. (c)는 남자의 늦잠을 잤느냐는 물음에 알람시계로 혼동을 주기 위한 함정이며, 결국 차를 열게 되었으므로 (d)는 정답이 될 수 없다.

oversleep 늦잠자다 **spare** 예비의, 여분의 **go off** (경보, 알람 등이) 울리다

9

M What can I do for you?

W I think there's something wrong with my test scores in linguistics.

M Can I have your name and student I.D. number?

W My name is Ellen Kim and my student I.D. number is 20048257.

M Just a minute, please. Well, you missed classes three times, so you were marked down.

W But I was sick. It was an excused absence.

M Did you turn in the doctor's note at that time?

W Of course.

M: 무슨 일로 오셨어요?

W: 제 언어학 시험 점수가 잘못된 것 같아서요.

M: 이름하고 학번 좀 알려주실래요?

W: 제 이름은 엘렌 김이고 학번은 20048257이에요.

M: 잠깐 기다리세요. 수업을 세 번 빠져서 감점이 되셨네요.

W: 하지만 아팠어요. 말씀도 드렸었어요.

M: 그 때 진단서도 제출했나요?

W: 물론이죠.

○ 대화의 주제를 묻고 있다. 여자가 남자에게 언어학 시험 점수가 잘못되었다고 하면서 점수를 다시 확인하고 있으므로 정답은 (b)가 된다. 학번을 언급했으나 학생증을 발급받는 것은 아니므로 (a)는 정답이 아니고 전공 변경에 대한 언급이 없었으므로 (d) 역시 정답이 아니다.

Q What is the topic of the conversation?

(a) Getting a student I.D. card reissued
(b) Checking test grades
(c) Complaining about malfunctions in a computer system.
(d) Changing a major into linguistics

linguistics 언어학 student I.D. number 학번 mark down 값을 내리다, 점수를 깎다 excused absence 사유가 있는 결석 turn in ~을 제출하다 doctor's note 진단서 malfunction (기계의) 오작동

---

10 Healthy diets and physical activity on a regular basis are major factors in the maintenance of good health throughout a person's life. You can put it into action in everyday life with a little bit of effort. For example, if it's only a short walk, go there on foot. And you can also use stairs instead of using elevators. You can stay healthy with usual activities with brief and of low intensity.

Q What is the main topic of the passage?

(a) The most effective way to go on a diet
(b) A possibility of danger related with using elevators
(c) How to keep healthy in our daily lives
(d) The powerful effect of vigorous exercises

건강한 식단과 정기적인 운동은 평생 동안 건강 유지의 주요한 요소가 된다. 약간의 노력만으로 일상생활에서 실행에 옮길 수 있다. 예를 들어, 짧은 거리라면 걸어서 가라. 그리고 엘리베이터를 이용하는 대신에 계단을 이용할 수도 있다. 간단하면서 강도가 낮은 일상적인 활동으로 건강을 유지할 수 있다.

○ 주제를 찾는 문제이다. 일상생활에서 간단히 할 수 있는 활동만으로도 건강을 유지할 수 있다는 내용의 (c)가 정답이 된다. 다이어트에 대한 내용은 언급되지 않았으며 엘리베이터의 위험성도 전혀 위 내용과 관계가 없다. (d)는 정답과 정반대 이야기이다.

on a regular basis 정기적으로 maintenance 유지 put sth into action ~을 실행에 옮기다 intensity 강도, 세기, 크기 go on a diet 다이어트를 하다 vigorous 힘찬, 활기찬, 강력한

---

11 York Minster is not only a wonderful building, it is also a living and diverse community. Whether you come here as a tourist or a pilgrim, we hope that, as you walk around, you will understand why the cathedral has inspired people of every generation since its completion. York Minster is the largest medieval gothic cathedral in Northern Europe. Not all cathedrals are minsters: not all minsters are cathedrals—but York Minster is both.

Q What will the speaker probably talk about next?

(a) The speaker will discuss why York Minster is very popular.
(b) The speaker will discuss why all minsters are not cathedrals.
(c) The speaker will talk about the similarity of cathedrals and minsters.
(d) The speaker will talk about the difference between cathedrals and minsters.

요크 사원은 멋진 건물일 뿐만 아니라 활기 있고 다채로운 사회입니다. 이곳에 관광객으로 오시든 순례자로 오시든 주변을 둘러보면서 이 성당이 완성된 이후에 모든 세대의 사람들에게 영감을 준 이유를 이해하기를 바랍니다. 요크 사원은 북유럽에서 가장 큰 중세 고딕 대성당입니다. 모든 대성당이 사원은 아닙니다. 모든 사원들이 대성당은 아닙니다. 하지만 요크 사원은 이 모두에 해당됩니다.

○ 다음에 이어질 내용에 대해 묻고 있다. 마지막 부분에 주목하면 답을 쉽게 찾을 수 있다. 모든 대성당이 사원이 아니고 모든 사원이 대성당이 아니라고 하면서 요크 사원은 대성당이면서 사원이라는 이야기를 하고 있다. 따라서 대성당과 사원의 차이점에 대한 이야기가 나올 것임을 유추할 수 있으므로 정답은 (d)가 된다.

minster 수도원 성당 (cf. cathedral 주교좌 성당) diverse 다양한 pilgrim 순례자 inspire (감정, 사상 등을) 불어넣다, 고취시키다 medieval 중세의

12 Ladies and gentlemen, this is your captain speaking. We are going through air turbulence at the moment. Please return to your seat and fasten your seat belt. And stay in your seats while the fasten seat belt lights are on.

Q What is this announcement for?

(a) To let passengers know about the flight delay

(b) To let passengers know about the flight cancellations

(c) To give passengers a caution in case of turbulence

(d) To explain how to deal with emergency situations

승객 여러분, 저는 이 비행기의 기장입니다. 현재 우리 비행기는 난기류를 통과하고 있습니다. 자리로 돌아가서 안전벨트를 매 주시기 바랍니다. 안전벨트 등이 켜져 있는 동안은 자리에서 일어나지 마시기 바랍니다.

○ 안내 방송의 목적에 대해 묻고 있다. air turbulence라는 단어와 안전벨트를 매라는 등의 내용을 통해 난기류에 대비해 승객들에게 주의를 주기 위한 방송이라는 것을 알 수 있으므로 정답은 (c)가 된다.

turbulence 난기류 fasten ~을 단단히 고정시키다, 매다

GRAMMAR • P.22

13 A Would you mind _____ on the air conditioner? It's really hot here.
B Certainly not.

(a) turn
(b) to turn
(c) turning
(d) turned

A: 에어컨 좀 틀어도 될까? 여긴 너무 더워.
B: 물론이지.

○ mind는 '~하는 것을 꺼리다'의 뜻을 가진 동사로, 목적어로 동명사를 취하므로 (c)turning이 적절하다. 또한 대답은 부정형으로 해야 긍정의 뜻이 된다.

certainly 절대, 확실히

---

14 A Can you show me _____?
B Sure, wait a minute, sir.

(a) other
(b) others
(c) one another
(d) another

A: 다른 것 좀 보여주시겠어요?
B: 물론이죠. 잠시만 기다리세요.

○ 일반적으로 옷가게를 배경으로 하는 발화문이다. B가 A에게 보여 준 것 말고 다른 것, 즉 정해지지 않은 어떤 하나를 지칭할 때 another를 쓴다.

---

15 A The fence needs _____.
B Yes, it does.

(a) to paint
(b) paint
(c) painting
(d) painted

A: 울타리를 좀 칠해야겠어.
B: 응, 그런 것 같아.

○ need는 타동사로 '(사람이나 물건이)~되어야 할 필요가 있다'는 뜻이다. 행위의 목적어로 쓰인 대상은 주어에 표시되어 있으므로 이 문장에서는 목적어가 없다. 따라서 주어의 입장에서 수동의 의미를 가지게 된다. 이런 경우 need의 목적격 보어로는 동사의 -ing형이 필요하다.

16 A How did you finally finish your course? I find this course really hard to pass.

B I think the time _____ is a big deal.

(a) arrangement
(b) to arrange
(c) arrange
(d) arranged

A: 너 어떻게 이 과목을 마침내 통과했니? 이 과목은 이수하기가 정말 어려워.

B: 내 생각엔 시간 조정이 가장 중요한 일인 것 같아.

◐ 동사 is의 주어가 되어야 하는데, the time과 결합하여 시간 조정이라는 의미가 성립해야 하므로 (a)arrangement가 가장 알맞다.

finally 마침내, 결국 course 교육 과정, 학과 과목

---

17 Give the presents to _____ takes good care of children.

(a) whom
(b) whomever
(c) whoever
(d) whatever

아이들을 잘 돌보는 사람 누구에게나 선물을 주세요.

◐ 해석상 '아이들을 잘 돌보는 누구에게나' 라는 표현이 필요하고, 뒤 문장의 주어가 필요하므로 (c)whoever가 적절하다.

---

18 The UN urged North Korea to _____ disclose its nuclear weapon programs and proliferation activities within 24 hours.

(a) complete
(b) completed
(c) completely
(d) completion

UN은 북한이 핵무기 개발과 확산 프로그램을 24시간 이내에 완전히 공개할 것을 촉구했다.

◐ 문장의 동사 disclose를 수식해주는 부사가 필요하다.

proliferation 급증, 확산

---

19 Once, people would buy _____ bread for a whole family.

(a) a loaf of
(b) a liter of
(c) a pair of
(d) an amount of

한때는, 사람들이 가족 전체를 위해서 빵을 한 덩어리씩 사고는 했다.

◐ 빵을 세는 단위는 loaf(덩어리)이다.

---

20 _____ the bottom of the castle when her colleague gave her a great push.

(a) Hardly she had reached
(b) She hardly had reached
(c) Had she hardly reached
(d) Hardly had she reached

동료가 그녀를 세게 밀었을 때, 그녀는 거의 그 성의 바닥에 닿을 뻔했다.

◐ 빈도부사는 조동사 · be동사의 뒤, 일반동사의 앞이므로 원래의 문장은 'She had hardly reached the ~' 이다. 'hardly' 를 문장 앞으로 도치시키면 '부정어+had+주어+reached' 로 어순이 바뀐다.

21 (a) A: What's the hurry, Michael?
   (b) B: I have doctor's appointment, but it totally slipped my mind.
   (c) A: Take your time.
   (d) B: Sorry, I don't have enough, I'm supposed to be there by five.

A: 뭐가 그렇게 바쁘니, 마이클?
B: 주치의와 약속이 있는데, 완전히 잊어버렸어.
A: 여유를 좀 가져.
B: 미안해. 시간이 별로 없어. 거기에 5시까지 가기로 되어 있어.

○ (b)의 have와 doctor's appointment 사이에 관사 'a'가 삽입되어야 한다. I have a doctor's appointment, but it totally slipped my mind.

slip one's mind 잊어버리다

---

22 (a) There are many reasons to visit Scotland any time of the year. (b) Especially Edinburgh boasts great architecture which it is blending the old and the new. (c) Other Victorian buildings help you visualize that you are in the dramatic and historical period. (d) It is recommended that visitors had better make arrangements at the places where they want to go ahead of time.

연중 어느 때라도 스코틀랜드를 방문하는 데에는 많은 이유가 있다. 특히, Edinburgh는 신구가 잘 조합된 훌륭한 건축물들을 자랑한다. 다른 빅토리아 시대의 건물들은 당신이 극적이고 역사적인 유적지에 있다는 것을 시각화하는 데 도움을 줄 것이다. 관광객들은 방문할 장소에 대해 순서를 정해 준비를 하는 것이 좋다.

○ (b)에서, 관계대명사 which 다음에 주어가 중복 등장하였으므로 it을 빼 주어야 한다. (b) Especially Edinburgh boasts great architecture which is blending the old and the new.

boast 뽐내다 Victorian 빅토리아 여왕 시대의 visualize 시각화하다

VOCABULARY • P.25

23 A Hey, Richard. Well, I was wondering if...
   B Don't _____ around the bush. Just tell me.

(a) hit
(b) beat
(c) hang
(d) tap

A: 안녕, 리차드. 저기 궁금한 게 있는데...
B: 빙빙 돌리지 말고 그냥 말해.

○ 이디엄 beat around the bush는 빙빙 돌려 이야기하는 것을 말한다. 이디엄을 알고 있지 않으면 풀기 힘든 문제이므로 이디엄이 나올 때마다 잘 익혀두는 것이 중요하다.

beat around the bush 빙빙 돌려 이야기하다, 변죽을 울리다

---

24 A When is your baby due?
   B It was last week. My baby is one week _____.

(a) expired
(b) overdue
(c) hold
(d) overlaid

A: 출산 예정일이 언제죠?
B: 지난주였어요. 우리 아기는 예정일이 한 주 지났어요.

○ 예정일이 지난주였다고 했으므로 한 주 늦춰졌다는 뜻으로 overdue가 정답이다.

baby due 출산 예정일 overdue 기한이 지난 expired 만료된

25 **A** I kept calling you last night. But I couldn't _____.

B I was very busy all day.

(a) get in
(b) get on
(c) get through
(d) get over

A: 어젯밤에 계속 전화했었어. 하지만 연결이 안 되더라고.
B: 하루 종일 바빴어.

○ B가 하루 종일 바빴다고 했으므로 전화 연결이 안 되었다는 것을 알 수 있다. 보기 가운데 '전화 연결이 되다' 라는 뜻은 get through 이다.

get in (안으로) 들어가다, (차에) 타다 **get on** ~에 타다, ~을 입다, 신다 **get through** 전화가 연결이 되다 **get over** (곤란을) 극복하다, (병을) 회복하다

---

26 **A** Thanks for dinner. Next time lunch is on me.

B All right. Next time you'll _____.

(a) treat
(b) take
(c) hold
(d) welcome

A: 저녁 고마워. 다음엔 점심 내가 살게.
B: 좋아. 다음번엔 네가 사.

○ 다음에 점심을 산다고 하자 B가 동의했으므로 정답은 다른 사람에게 식사 등을 대접한다고 할 때 쓰는 treat이 된다.

treat (남에게) 한턱 내다, 대접하다

---

27 **A** Let's _____ it a day!

B Are you leaving already? I've got tons of work to do.

(a) finish
(b) end
(c) say
(d) call

A: 그만 끝냅시다!
B: 벌써 가시게요? 저는 할 일이 많이 남았어요.

○ 관용 표현을 알아야 풀 수 있는 문제이다. B가 벌써 퇴근할 것이냐고 물었으므로 A는 일을 끝내고 돌아가는 뜻의 문장임을 알 수 있다. finish는 뜻으로 보면 맞을 것 같지만 call it a day라는 관용표현이 있으므로 정답은 call이 된다.

Let's call it a day! 그만 끝내자, 퇴근하자

---

28 He was in his first term in _____ when the scandal broke.

(a) official
(b) years
(c) office
(d) position

그 스캔들이 터졌을 때 그는 첫 임기 중에 있었다.

○ office는 '사무실' 이라는 뜻 이외에 '관직, 공직' 등의 뜻이 있다. one's term in office라는 표현은 관용적으로 '~의 임기' 라는 뜻으로 쓰인다.

one's term in office 재임기간

---

29 For low-income parents, getting child care _____ are inevitable.

(a) scholarship
(b) subsidies
(c) investment
(d) sponsorship

저소득층 부모들에게 육아 보조금을 받는 것은 불가피하다.

○ 육아와 관련해서 받을 수 있는 것은 보조금이다. 육아와 관련해서 장학금이나 후원을 받는 다는 것은 어색한 표현이므로 scholarship 이나 sponsorship은 답이 될 수 없다.

low-income 저소득의 **subsidy** 보조금, 교부금 **inevitable** 불가피한 **scholarship** 장학금 **sponsorship** 후원

30 Compared to young people, old people are rather _____ to the flu.

(a) vulnerable
(b) worse
(c) harmed
(d) allergic

젊은 사람들에 비해서 나이든 사람들은 독감에 다소 취약하다.

○ 젊은이들에 비해 노인들이 독감에 잘 걸린다는 표현이 나오는 것이 자연스럽다. harm은 '해를 입히다 '는 표현으로 어울리지 않고 allergic은 알레르기가 있다는 뜻으로 독감과는 어울리지 않는다. 정답은 '저항력이 없는', '취약한' 의 뜻을 가진 vulnerable이다.

vulnerable 취약한, 저항력이 없는 allergic 알레르기가 있는

---

31 Within 15 business days from the date you _____ the complaint, you will be known whether action will be taken.

(a) formed
(b) received
(c) sued
(d) filed

불만 사항을 제출한 지 영업일로 15일 이내에 조치가 취해질지 말지에 대해 알려드릴 것입니다.

○ file은 '서류를 철하다, 정리하다' 라는 뜻 외에 '신청, 항의 따위를 제출하다' 라는 의미가 있다. 여기서는 '불만 사항을 제출하다' 라는 의미가 적절하므로 file이 들어가야 한다. sue의 경우 '소송을 제기하다' 라는 뜻의 단어로서 목적어로 complaint를 취하지 않는다.

business day 영업일 take action 조치를 취하다

---

32 The president had been under investigation for _____ but he cleared himself of all charges within a week.

(a) embezzlement
(b) embodiment
(c) robbery
(d) burglary

그 사장은 횡령 혐의로 조사를 받고 있었지만 일주일 이내로 스스로 모든 혐의를 벗었다.

○ 사장이 조사를 받고 있었다는 것으로 미루어 보아 강도를 뜻하는 robbery나 burglary는 문맥상 적절치 않다. embodiment는 전혀 문맥과 상관없는 단어이고 embezzlement는 '횡령' 을 의미하는 단어로서 정답으로 적절하다.

under investigation 조사를 받고 있는 embezzlement 횡령, 착복 clear of all charges 모든 혐의를 벗다 embodiment 구체화, 구현 robbery 강도, 약탈 burglary 강도질

33 Many people who are not attracted to traditional team sports think that traditional team sports have lots of rules, competition, and coaching. For this reason, more and more people — especially young people — tend to be more excited with _____ extreme sports. There are no such things like winning or losing, and little organizations like teams or leagues in extreme sports. Each person who really loves adventure and seeks it out competes against himself and pushes himself to his own limits.

(a) personal and traditional
(b) competitive and stressful
(c) independent and conventional
(d) individual and unconventional

전통적인 팀스포츠에 매력을 느끼지 못하는 많은 사람들은 거기에 규칙과 경쟁 그리고 경기지도가 많다고 생각한다. 이러한 이유로, 점점 더 많은 사람들 – 특히 젊은이들 – 이 개인적이고 틀에 박히지 않은 익스트림 스포츠에 더 흥분하는 경향이 있다. 익스트림 스포츠에는 승패와 같은 것도 없고 팀이나 경기 연맹과 같은 조직도 거의 없다. 진정으로 모험을 즐기고 찾는 사람이 그 자신과 경쟁하며 자신의 한계까지 그 자신을 몰아가는 것이다.

🔵 전통적인 스포츠의 특징과 반대되는 익스트림 스포츠의 특징을 찾는 문제이다. 단락의 앞부분에 전통적인 팀 스포츠에는 규칙과 경쟁, 지도가 많다고 얘기한 반면, 뒷부분에서는 익스트림 스포츠에 승패나 조직 따위가 없다고 말했기 때문에 익스트림 스포츠가 개인적이면서 틀에 박히지 않은 자유로운 스포츠임을 알 수 있다. 따라서 전통적인 팀 스포츠의 특징에 속하는 traditional, competitive, stressful, conventional과 같은 단어가 들어 있는 선택지 (a)(b)(c)는 오답이 된다.

traditional 전통적인 **competition** 경쟁 **tend to** ~하는 경향이 있다 **unconventional** 틀에 박히지 않은, 자유로운 **extreme sports** 익스트림 스포츠, 극한 스포츠 **organization** 조직 **seek out** ~을 찾아내다, ~을 주의 깊게 찾다 **compete** 경쟁하다 **independent** 남에게 의존하지 않는

---

34 When a non-native English speaking student writes an essay for English speaking readers, organization of ideas is problematical because different cultural backgrounds call for different organizational patterns. Typical readers of English expect the development of ideas to be in a straight line which includes introductions, main ideas, topic sentences, supporting details, conclusions, etc. An Asian writer, however, will often develop ideas in a spiral pattern which means using a variety of facts related to a topic before arriving at the conclusion. It is such an indirect pattern that native English readers often fail to get his or her main point. Although it is not an easy task, it is essential to _____ especially if one wants to be read.

(a) adapt to Asian culture
(b) develop ideas in order of time
(c) meet those cultural expectations
(d) stick to his or her own writing pattern

비영어권 학생이 영어권 독자를 위해 에세이를 쓸 경우, 생각의 정리가 문제가 되는데 이는 문화적 배경이 다를 경우 다른 패턴이 요구되기 때문이다. 전형적인 영어권 독자는 도입, 주제, 주제문, 주제문을 뒷받침하는 내용, 결론 등으로 이어지는 직선적인 형태로 사고가 전개되는 것을 기대한다. 그러나 아시아권의 필자는 결론에 다다르기 전에 논제와 관련되는 가지각색의 사실들을 열거하는 나선형의 패턴으로 사고를 전개하는 경향이 있다. 이는 너무나 간접적인 패턴이라서 영어권 독자들은 종종 작가의 논점을 파악하는 데 실패하게 된다. 쉬운 일은 아니지만, 정말 자신의 글이 읽혀지기를 원한다면 이런 문화적 기대를 충족시키는 것이 필수적이다.

🔵 문화적 배경에 따라 사고를 조직화하는 패턴이 다르다는 것이 주된 내용이므로 문화적 기대를 충족시키는 것, (c)가 정답이다. (a)와 (d)처럼 자신의 문화적 배경이나, 글을 쓰는 패턴을 고수하면 영어권 독자가 주제를 파악하기 힘들다고 했다. 또 시간 순서대로 전개하는 것은 언급되지 않았으므로 (b)도 답이 될 수 없다.

organization 조직(화), 구성 **problematical** 문제가 되는, 문제의 **call for** ~을 요구하다, ~를 필요로 하다 **spiral** 나선형의 **a variety of** 가지각색의, 갖가지의 **such ~ that ...** 매우 ~해서 ...하다 **essential** 필수적인

35 Michael Phelps, who won eight gold medals in the 2008 Olympics, is known for struggling with ADHD (Attention Deficit Hyperactivity Disorder) as a child. His mother, Deborah Phelps, recalls that he never sat still, was always asking zillions of questions and jumping from one thing to another. Finally, his doctor, Charles Wax, diagnosed his case as ADHD and prescribed a stimulant medication for Phelps when he was 9 years old. Although the medication was somewhat helpful at school, swimming was what truly helped him cope with ADHD. It played an important role in helping him _____.

(a) win the gold medals
(b) focus and calm down
(c) overact and exaggerate
(d) hide his medical history

2008년 올림픽에서 여덟 개의 금메달을 따낸 Michael Phelps는 어렸을 때 주의력결핍 과잉행동장애(ADHD)를 앓은 것으로 알려져 있다. 그의 엄마인 Deborah Phelps는 그가 절대로 가만히 앉아 있었던 적이 없고, 항상 수많은 질문들을 해대며 여기저기를 뛰어다녔다고 회상한다. 결국, 그가 아홉 살이었을 때, 그의 의사인 Charles Wax는 그의 병을 주의력결핍 과잉행동장애로 진단하고 자극제를 처방해 주었다. 이 약물치료가 학교에서는 약간 도움이 됐을지라도, 정말 그가 ADHD를 극복하도록 도와준 것은 바로 수영이었다. 수영은 그가 집중하고 진정하도록 하는 데 중요한 역할을 했다.

🡒 어린 시절 주의력결핍 과잉행동장애를 앓은 수영 금메달리스트 Michael Phelps가 수영을 통해서 변화할 수 있었다는 내용의 글이다. 어렸을 때에는 항상 산만하고 말이 많던 Phelps가 수영을 하고 난 뒤, 집중을 잘 하고 침착해 졌다는 내용이 와야 하므로 (b)가 정답이 된다.

be known for ~로(때문에) 유명하다, 알려지다 struggle with ~와 싸우다 recall 상기하다, 생각해 내다 zillion 터무니없이 큰 수 diagnose A as B A를 B로 진단하다 prescribe 처방하다, 지시하다 stimulant (의학) 흥분성의 medication 약물(치료) cope with ~를 대처하다, 극복하다 play an important role in ~에 중요한 역할을 하다

---

36 Although it is based on the underlying principle of minimizing adverse affects on the environment and local communities, ecotourism can also disrupt indigenous people and their social structures. Indeed, it is easier said than done to bring the benefits of tourism back to local people without disrupting their way of life. To protect the tourist industry, for example, regulations are sometimes made that destroy local way of life. With their livelihood threatened and often with no skills to work with in the tourism industry, local people can be left with no alternative means of livelihood. Many original inhabitants are often driven out of their area and outsiders move in to try to profit from tourism.

Q Which of the following is the best title for the passage?

(a) Benefits of ecotourism
(b) The trend towards ecotourism
(c) Ecotourism subject to controversy
(d) Compensation for the aboriginal population

환경과 지역사회에 대한 역효과를 최소화한다는 기본 원칙에 기초를 두고 있기는 하지만, 친환경여행 역시도 토착민들과 그들의 사회적 구조에 혼란을 일으킬 수 있다. 실제로 지역민들의 생활방식에 혼란을 주지 않고 그들에게 관광사업의 이익을 돌려준다는 것은 말처럼 쉬운 것이 아니다. 예를 들어, 관광산업을 보호하기 위하여 때때로 그 지역의 생활방식을 파괴하는 규제가 만들어지기도 한다. 생계를 위협받고, 관광산업에 참여할 만한 기술도 없는 경우가 많은 지역주민들에겐 다른 어떤 생계의 수단도 남아있지 않게 된다. 많은 원주민들은 종종 자신의 구역에서 쫓겨나고, 관광 이익을 얻기 위해 외부인들이 유입된다.

🡒 여행이 초래하는 환경과 지역사회에 대한 역효과 최소화라는 기본 취지에도 불구하고, 친환경여행이 가져올 수 있는 폐단에 대한 언급이 주를 이루고 있으므로 논란의 여지가 있다는 의미의 (c)가 정답이다. 지역민들에게 관광산업의 이익을 돌려준다는 것이 말하기는 쉬우나 실현하기는 어렵다고 표현했으므로 (a)는 답이 될 수 없으며, (b)는 언급된 바 없고, 토착민들에 대한 보상이 필요하다는 것이 아니라 친환경여행 자체가 내포한 문제점에 대해 피력한 글이므로 (d)는 정답이 될 수 없다.

underlying 근원을 이루는, 기초적인 adverse 거스르는, 반대의 ecotourism 친환경여행, 자연 환경을 해치지 않는 범위 내에서 행해지는 관광 여행 disrupt 혼란스럽게 하다, 분열시키다 indigenous 토착의, 지역 고유의 indeed 실제로, 정말로, 대단히 alternative 대신의 inhabitant 주민, 거주자

37 Some reports show that indoor air is two to five times more harmful than outdoor air. To our astonishment, the air in office buildings, schools, and even homes is not safe to breathe in. Because of indoor air pollution, many people are suffering from headaches, sore throats, or respiratory diseases such as asthma. Then, how can we deal with this situation to make closed environments more secure and harmless? One way is to install good ventilation systems in buildings. It is indispensable for a building to have ventilation because it dilutes contaminants by allowing clean and fresh air in; thus, creating a safer and healthier environment.

Q What is the passage mainly about?

(a) Sources of indoor air pollution
(b) The necessity of ventilation use
(c) Symptoms of indoor air pollution
(d) Ways of reducing indoor air pollution

몇몇 보고서에 의하면 실내공기가 실외공기보다 2배에서 5배 정도 더 해롭다고 한다. 놀랍게도 사무실, 학교, 심지어는 가정의 공기조차도 들이쉬기에 안전하지 않다는 것이다. 실내공기의 오염 때문에 많은 사람들은 두통, 인후염, 천식 같은 호흡기 질환을 앓고 있다. 그렇다면 밀폐된 환경을 더 안전하고 무해하게 만들기 위해 우리는 이런 상황에 어떻게 대처해야 되는가? 한 가지 방법은 건물에 좋은 환기장치를 설치하는 것이다. 환기장치들은 깨끗하고 신선한 공기를 유입시켜 오염물질을 희석시킴으로써 더 안전하고 건강한 환경을 만들어 내기 때문에, 건물에는 반드시 환기장치가 있어야 한다.

🔵 전반부에 실내공기 오염이 심각하다는 내용과 그에 따른 증상이 나와 있지만 이것이 주된 내용은 아니므로 (a)나 (c) 모두 정답은 아니다. 중반 이후에 실내공기 오염을 줄이기 위한 방법, 즉 환기장치 설치를 제시하고 있으므로 정답은 (d)가 된다.

indoor 실내의 (cf. outdoor 실외의) harmful 해로운 (cf. harmless 무해한) to one's astonishment 놀랍게도 breathe in 숨을 들이쉬다 air pollution 공기 오염 suffer from ~ 때문에 고생하다, ~병을 앓다 sore throat 인후염 respiratory disease 호흡기 질환 asthma 천식 deal with ~을 다루다, 처리하다, 상대하다 environment 환경 install ~을 설치하다 ventilation 통풍(장치), 환기(장치) indispensable 불가결의, 긴요한

---

38 For people suffering from eating disorders, there is a large gap between the way they see themselves and how they actually look. People with anorexia or bulimia frequently have an extreme fear of getting fat or think that they're fat when they aren't. Eating disorders also can be triggered by emotional problems or psychiatric disorders, such as anxiety disorder and obsessive-compulsive disorder. Some research shows that media images contribute to the increase in the incidence of eating disorders. Most women in advertising, movies, TV, and sports programs are very thin, and this may lead girls to think that the ideal of beauty is thinness.

Q What is the main topic of the passage?

(a) Lookism in the mass media
(b) The causes of eating disorders
(c) Individuals prone to eating disorders
(d) Correlation between stress and eating habits

섭식장애를 겪는 사람들에게는 그들이 자신을 보는 방식과 실제 그들의 외모 사이에 큰 격차가 존재한다. 거식증이나 폭식증을 가진 사람들은 살이 찌는 것에 대한 극도의 두려움을 지니고 있으며, 자신이 뚱뚱하지 않은데도 그렇다고 생각하는 일이 자주 있다. 또한 섭식장애는 정서적인 문제나 불안장애나 강박증과 같은 정신적인 장애에 의해서 촉발되기도 한다. 몇몇 연구에 따르면 대중매체의 이미지가 섭식장애의 발병률을 높이는 원인이 된다고 한다. 광고, 영화, TV, 스포츠 프로그램 속의 여성들 대부분은 매우 말랐는데 이것은 어린 소녀들이 미의 기준이 날씬함이라고 생각하도록 이끌 수도 있다.

🔵 거식증이나 폭식증과 같은 섭식장애의 원인을 잘못된 자아상이나, 정신적 문제 등 개인적인 차원과 대중매체의 이미지가 미의 기준을 왜곡시키는 사회적 차원에서 살펴보는 글이므로 정답은 (b)이다. 대중매체가 언급되기는 하였으나 외모 지상주의의 문제라기보다는 미의 기준이 날씬함으로 획일화되는 현상을 지적한 것이므로 (a)는 답이 될 수 없으며, 정서적으로 문제가 있는 사람이 섭식장애에 걸리기 쉬운 것은 사실이나 이는 전체적인 주제가 아니라 원인의 일부이므로 (c)는 답이 될 수 없고, (d)는 언급되지 않았다.

anorexia 거식증 bulimia 폭식증 obsessive-compulsive disorder 강박신경증 contribute to ~에 기여하다, ~의 원인이 되다 incidence 발생, 발생률, 빈도

39 Kimchi, a spicy flavored Korean cabbage, is well known as a well-being food. According to studies, the ingredients of Kimchi, such as cabbage, garlic, and red pepper, not only prevent cancer, but also develop immunity to it. Regular intake of cabbage creates less of a chance of getting large intestine cancer, and the garlic restrains gastric cancer. In addition, Kimchi contains abundant vitamins. For example, red pepper contains 37 times more vitamin C than apples, and 7 times more than tangerines. Besides vitamin C, red pepper also has plenty of vitamin A.

Q What is the main topic of the passage?

(a) The benefits of Kimchi
(b) How to make Kimchi
(c) Food that helps prevent cancer
(d) The special ingredients of Kimchi

매운 맛이 나는 배추인 김치는 웰빙 음식으로 잘 알려져 있다. 연구에 따르면, 배추나 마늘, 고추와 같은 김치의 재료가 암을 예방할 뿐만 아니라 암에 대한 면역성도 키워준다고 한다. 배추를 규칙적으로 섭취하면 대장암에 걸릴 확률이 줄어들고, 마늘은 위암에 걸리지 않게 해 준다. 게다가, 김치에는 비타민이 풍부하다. 예를 들어, 고추에는 사과보다 비타민 C가 37배 더 많이 들어있고, 귤보다는 7배가 더 들어있다. 고추에는 비타민 C 외에 비타민 A도 풍부하다.

○ 김치를 먹으면 얻을 수 있는 이익 중에 암 예방과 풍부한 비타민의 섭취가 예로 나와 있다. 따라서 김치를 (c)암 예방에 도움을 주는 음식으로만 표현한 것은 너무 범위가 좁고 (d)처럼 김치의 특별한 재료로만 표현한 것도 글의 내용을 모두 포함하는 것은 아니다. 결국, 김치의 특별한 재료를 통해 어떤 이익을 얻을 수 있는가를 설명하고 있다.

flavor 맛을 내다 cabbage 양배추 ingredient 재료 immunity 면역(성) not only A but also B A뿐만 아니라 B도 intake 섭취 large intestine 대장 restrain 제지하다, 못하게 하다 gastric 위(胃)의 in addition 게다가 tangerine 귤

---

40 We rank all of the law schools available this year, thereby giving you the necessary information to decide which schools you should apply to. (a) The best advice is to visit the law schools you are seriously thinking of attending after you have been accepted. (b) The variability in these rankings should illustrate that it can only work as a guide, and that you should be the final evaluator where you will be. (c) Before applying, we recommend that you personally visit each law school that you are considering. (d) Which school you attend not only impacts where you will spend three enjoyable and educational years, but also where you will settle down.

올해 모든 법학대학원 순위를 결정했다. 그래서 당신이 지원하기위해 필요한 정보를 줄 수 있다. (a)가장 권장하는 것은 당신이 신중히 고려하고 있는 학교를 합격 후 방문하는 것이다. (b) 이 순위의 변화 가능성은 이것이 오직 가이드라인으로 적용가능하다는 것을 보여주며 당신이 가야할 곳의 최종 결정자는 당신이다. (c)지원하기 전 당신이 생각하는 각 학교를 직접 방문하길 바란다. (d) 당신이 수업을 듣게 될 학교는 당신이 즐겁게 3년 동안 학업을 즐길 수 있는 곳일 뿐 아니라 앞으로 당신이 정착할 수 있는 곳이기도 하다.

○ 전반적 내용이 법학대학원에 대한 가이드라인을 제공하며 지원자가 지원하기 전 고려해야 할 내용이다. 그러나 (a)는 합격 후 방문을 권장하는 것으로 내용이 약간 멀다.

thereby 그것에 대해, 그것으로 variability 변화성, 변이성 illustrate 설명하다, 예증하다 impact 영향을 주다

LISTENING COMPREHENSION • P.34

1 M May I speak to Steve?
W _____

(a) It is no concern of yours.
(b) He's just stepped out.
(c) I wonder if I could use your phone.
(d) You can't get through.

M: 스티브씨 좀 바꿔 주시겠어요?
W: 방금 나가셨는데요.

🔹 전화상의 대화이다. 스티브씨를 바꿔달라는 남자의 말에 적절한 대답을 찾아야 한다. (a)는 '네가 상관할 바 아니다.' 라는 뜻으로 정답과는 거리가 멀고, (b)는 그 분이 자리에 없다는 뜻으로 상황에 적절한 대답이 된다. (c)는 전화기를 빌릴 때 쓸 수 있는 표현이며 (d)는 전화 연결이 안된다는 뜻인데, get through에는 '~을 지나가다, 통과하다,' '잘 해내다' 등등 다양한 뜻이 있다.

concern 관심사, (개인의) 볼일, 용무 step out 나가다. (자리를) 비우다 get through (전화가) 연결되다, 연락이 되다

2 M Where should I put this table?
W _____

(a) Let's put it this way.
(b) Don't put me on.
(c) You went too far.
(d) Please, put it next to the couch.

M: 이 탁자를 어디에 놓을까요?
W: 소파 옆에 놓아주세요.

🔹 put은 다의어로서 이를 이용한 문제이다. 남자가 사용한 put의 뜻은 '~을 놓다, 두다' 이다. (a)의 경우 put이 '~을 표현하다' 의 의미로서 '이렇게 말해 보자.' 의 뜻이고, (b)의 경우 '비행기 띄우지 마.' 라는 뜻으로 반대 표현으로는 'Don't put me down.' 즉, '날 깔보지 마.' 가 있다. (c)의 경우는 '네가 지나쳤어.' 라는 뜻으로 정답이 아니며 (d)에서의 'put' 이 '~을 놓다, 두다' 의 뜻으로 쓰인 것이므로 정답이 된다.

put ~을 놓다, 두다, ~을 표현하다 go too far 지나치다, 너무하다 next to ~의 옆에

3 M Do you have this in another color?
W _____

(a) It looks very good on you.
(b) You look great in red.
(c) This comes in red, white, and blue.
(d) It doesn't match your skirt.

M: 이거 다른 색깔로 있나요?
W: 빨간색, 하얀색, 파란색이 있어요.

🔹 상점에서 물건을 고르는 상황으로 남자가 물건을 고르고 다른 색이 있냐고 묻는 질문이다. (a)는 고른 물건이 잘 어울린다는 뜻으로 정답이 아니고 (b)는 질문의 'color' 라는 단어를 이용하여 혼동을 주기 위한 보기로 '빨간색이 잘 어울리시네요.' 라는 뜻이므로 역시 정답이 될 수 없다. (d)는 고른 물건이 치마와 어울리지 않는다는 내용으로 문제의 상황과는 거리가 멀다. 따라서 정답은 (c)가 된다.

look good on ~에게 잘 어울리다 match ~와 어울리다, 조화되다

15

4 **M** You're all dressed up today! You look different.
    W Do you like this dress on me?
    M You look good. What's the occasion?
    W _____

(a) This is a special case.
(b) It is a present for my brother's birthday.
(c) I've been invited to a dance party.
(d) My friend threw a party yesterday.

M: 오늘 옷을 잘 차려 입었네! 달라 보인다.
W: 이 옷 나한테 잘 어울려?
M: 잘 어울린다. 무슨 일이야?
W: 댄스파티에 초대받았어.

○ 무슨 특별한 일이 있는지 물어볼 때에 쓰는 표현이 'What's the occasion?'이다. 여자가 옷을 왜 그렇게 빼입었는지 물었으므로 정답으로는 (c)가 가장 적절하다. (a)는 '이것은 특별한 경우야' 라는 뜻이고 (b)는 '그것은 내 남동생 생일 선물이야.' 라는 뜻이며 (d)는 '내 친구가 어제 파티를 열었었어.' 라는 뜻으로 과거의 일을 이야기 하고 있기 때문에 정답이 될 수 없다.

be dressed up 옷을 잘 차려입다 **throw a party** 파티를 열다

---

5 **M** Christine, do you think we can meet tomorrow?
    W I'd love to but I already have plans.
    M Are you sure? I have two tickets to a concert, so…
    W _____

(a) I couldn't make it.
(b) Maybe it can wait.
(c) Please don't hang up.
(d) I missed the chance.

M: 크리스틴, 내일 만날 수 있을까?
W: 그러고 싶은데 이미 계획이 있어.
M: 확실해? 내게 콘서트 티켓이 두 장이 있는데, 그렇다면…
W: 그렇게 급한 일은 아닐 거야.

○ 내일 계획이 있어서 안 되겠다는 듯이 이야기하다가 남자가 콘서트 티켓 두 장이 있다고 말하자 여자의 반응이 달라진다. 즉 '그렇게 급한 일은 아니니 취소할 수도 있다' 는 뉘앙스의 대답인 (b)가 정답이 된다. 'Something can wait.' 는 어떠한 일이 급하지 않다고 할 때, 'Something can't wait.' 는 어떠한 일이 급하여 미룰 수 없을 때 쓸 수 있는 표현이다. (a)는 '가지 못했다' 는 뜻이고 (c)는 '전화를 끊지 마세요' 라는 뜻이며 (d)는 '기회를 놓쳤어' 라는 뜻이다.

hang up (전화를) 끊다 **chance** 기회

---

6 **W** What time will you get back home?
    M I'm not sure. I'm too busy to talk at the moment.
    W You haven't forgotten our anniversary today, right?
    M _____

(a) I got caught in a traffic jam.
(b) Don't worry. I'll have a day off.
(c) No, where did you get it?
(d) Give me a break. I'm tied up here.

W: 집에 몇 시에 들어올 거야?
M: 잘 모르겠어. 너무 바빠서 지금은 통화 못 해.
W: 오늘 우리 기념일인 거 잊지 않았지?
M: 한 번 봐줘. 바빠서 꼼짝할 수 없어.

○ 남편과 아내의 전화대화 상황으로 여자는 집에, 남자는 회사에서 바쁘게 일하고 있는 상황임을 짐작할 수 있다. 지금은 바빠서 이야기 할 수 없다는 남자의 말에 여자는 오늘이 기념일이라고 상기시키고 있다. 이에 적절한 대답으로는 (d)가 가장 적절하다. (a)는 교통 체증에 걸렸다는 뜻으로 문맥상 매끄럽지 않으며 (b)는 걱정하지 말라며 하루 쉴 거라는 뜻으로 현재 남자가 회사에 있는 상황에서는 어울리지 않으며, (c)는 '그거 어디서 구했어?' 라는 뜻으로 위 상황과는 관계가 없다.

too~ to… 너무 ~해서 …할 수 없다 **anniversary** 기념일 **traffic jam** 교통 체증 **have a day off** 하루 쉬다, 하루 휴가 내다 **tied up** 바빠서 꼼짝 못하는

7

M May I see your passport?

W Here you are.

M What is the purpose of your visit?

W I'm here on business.

M How long will you be staying in England?

W For 2 weeks.

M Do you have return tickets?

W Yes. And I made a reservation at a hotel.

Q What is she doing according to the conversation?

(a) She's going through immigration.
(b) She's checking into a hotel.
(c) She's booking her flight.
(d) She's talking to her secretary.

M: 여권 좀 보여주시겠어요?

W: 여기요.

M: 방문 목적이 무엇입니까?

W: 사업차 왔습니다.

M: 영국에는 얼마나 오래 머무르실 예정입니까?

W: 2주 동안이요.

M: 왕복표는 있으신가요?

W: 네, 그리고 호텔에 예약도 되어있습니다.

○ 여자가 무엇을 하고 있는지 묻고 있다. 여권, 방문 목적, 얼마나 머무를 것인지 등의 내용으로 보아 입국 심사를 하고 있음을 짐작할 수 있다. 따라서 정답은 (a)가 된다.

on business 사업차 return ticket 왕복표 immigration 이민국, 입국 심사 check into (호텔에) 체크인하다 secretary 비서

8

M I don't feel well today.

W What's the matter?

M I think I have an upset stomach.

W Why don't you take a day off and just stay home?

M But I have an important meeting at work today.

W Can't you put off the meeting and rest a little?

Q What does the woman want him to do?

(a) She wants him to go see a doctor.
(b) She wants him not to go to work today.
(c) She wants him to cancel the meeting.
(d) She wants him to calm down.

M: 오늘 몸이 안 좋아.

W: 왜 그러는데요?

M: 배탈이 난 것 같아.

W: 하루 휴가 내고 그냥 집에 있는 게 어때요?

M: 하지만 오늘 회사에서 중요한 회의가 있어.

W: 회의 연기하고 조금 쉴 수 없어요?

○ 여자가 남자에게 바라는 것을 묻는 문제이다. 남자가 배탈이 났지만 회사에서 중요한 회의가 있다고 했고, 여자는 회의를 연기하고 집에서 쉬라고 하고 있으므로 정답은 남자가 출근하지 않기를 바란다는 (b)가 된다. 병원에 가거나 회의를 취소하거나 진정하라는 등의 내용은 정답과 거리가 멀다.

upset stomach 배탈 put off ~을 뒤로 미루다, 연기하다 calm down 진정하다

9

M How would you like your hair done?

W I haven't decided yet. What is the hottest hair style these days?

M Nowadays short black hair is hot. Why don't you get a haircut?

W But it takes a long time for hair to grow. I tend to be tired of the same style.

M Well, then how about getting a hair perm? It will make you look more feminine.

W Do you have any stylebooks?

M: 머리를 어떻게 해드릴까요?

W: 아직 결정을 못했어요. 요즘 최신 유행하는 스타일이 뭐에요?

M: 요즘에는 짧고 검은색 단발머리가 유행이에요. 머리를 잘라 보시는 것은 어떠세요?

W: 그렇지만 기르는 데 시간이 많이 걸리잖아요. 제가 똑같은 스타일은 금방 싫증을 내는 편이거든요.

M: 그럼 파마를 해보시는 건 어떠세요? 좀 더 여성스러워 보일 거에요.

W: 스타일북 좀 볼 수 있을까요?

Q What is correct according to the conversation?

(a) She's decided to get a hair cut.
(b) She's thinking of getting a hair perm.
(c) She's going to get her hair dyed.
(d) She doesn't like her hair style at the moment.

○ 대화를 듣고 옳은 내용을 고르는 문제이다. 머리를 자르면 기르는 데 시간이 오래 걸린다고 했으므로 (a)는 정답이 될 수 없다. 파마를 해 보면 어떻겠냐는 남자의 제안에 스타일북을 보여 달라고 했으므로 (b)는 정답이 될 수 있다. 염색에 대한 언급은 없었으므로 (c)는 정답이 아니고, 이 대화만으로는 (d)가 정답인지 알 수 없다.

get a haircut 머리를 자르다   be tired of ~에 싫증이 나다
feminine 여성스러운 dye ~을 염색하다

---

10 Teaching assistants and teachers have very different roles, but both are on the same team and dedicated to giving our children the best start in life. But if the employers get their way, teaching assistants face the penalty of a much worse pension scheme. Under the employers' proposals they will have to work longer, pay a higher rate of pension contributions, and have no protections. And it's not only teaching assistants. Everyone in the Local Government Pension Scheme is facing an unfair and uncertain future. Police staff, voluntary sector, higher and further education, council workers and millions of others are affected.

Q What is the main idea of the public advertisement?

(a) Pensions? it's time to play fair.
(b) Teachers should pay more pensions.
(c) Teaching assistants should be protected from teachers.
(d) The employers are facing the penalty of pension scheme.

조교와 교사는 매우 다른 역할을 담당하고 있지만 모두 같은 팀이며 우리 아이들이 인생에서 최상의 출발을 할 수 있도록 헌신합니다. 하지만 고용주들이 원하는 대로 한다면, 조교들은 훨씬 열악한 연금 제도의 불이익에 직면하고 있습니다. 고용주들의 제안 하에서 더 오랜 시간 일해야 하며, 더 많은 연금 보험료를 내야하며, 그리고 보호를 받지 못합니다. 그것은 조교들만의 문제가 아닙니다. 지방 정부 연금제도에 있어서 모든 사람들은 불공정하고 불확실한 미래에 직면하고 있습니다. 경찰, 사회복지 분야, 고등교육 및 평생교육, 지방의회 근무자들, 그리고 다른 수백만의 사람들이 영향을 받고 있습니다.

○ 광고의 핵심은 불공평하게 적용되고 있는 연금에 대한 지적이다. 따라서 (a)가 정답이라고 할 수 있다. 불공평한 연금에 대한 한 예로서 조교에 대한 이야기가 나온 것이므로 (b)나 (c)는 중심 내용이라고 할 수 없다.

teaching assistant 조교 dedicate ~을 바치다, ~에 전념하다
penalty 불이익, 손실 pension scheme 연금 제도
pension contributions 연금 보험료

---

11 Walk around the house and clean up the odds and ends before prospective buyers arrive. When they arrive, try to make them feel at ease. Kindly introduce you and your family that they may encounter. Then let them tour and answer all their questions. Make sure you always observe any stranger who enters your place, but be careful not to appear to be watching their every move. It is good to mention the good points of your home, but do not "hard sell" them. The purchaser will wonder if there is some problems with the property.

집을 사고자 하는 사람들이 도착하기 전에 집 주위를 둘러보면서 잡동사니를 치우세요. 사람들이 도착하면 편안하게 둘러볼 수 있도록 하세요. 친절하게 자신과 집을 둘러보는 중에 마주칠 수 있는 가족들을 소개하세요. 그리고 나서 집을 구경시켜주시고 모든 질문에 대답을 합니다. 집에 들어오는 모든 낯선 사람들을 항상 경계해야 하지만 일거수일투족을 감시하지 않도록 주의하세요. 집의 장점을 언급하는 것은 좋지만 너무 끈질기게 선전하려고 하지 마세요. 이 경우 구매자가 집에 어떤 문제가 있는지 궁금해 할지도 모르니까요.

○ 집의 구매자가 아닌 판매자의 입장에서 주의해야 할 점들을 이야기하고 있다. 따라서 정답은 (c)가 된다. (a)는 구매자의 입장에서 이야기하는 것이므로 정답이 아니고 (b)와 (d)는 내용과 거리가 멀다.

Q What is the speaker's main purpose?

    (a) To give information about how to find a good house

    (b) To give advice about how to keep the house clean.

    (c) To give some useful information to sell the house

    (d) To give advice about finding out the defects in the house.

odds and ends 잡동사니 **prospective** 장래의, 가망이 있는 **feel at ease** 안심하다, 마음 놓다 **encounter** ~와 우연히 만나다 **observe** 관찰하다 **hard sell** 강제로 팔다, 끈질기게 선전하다 **property** 재산, 자산 **defect** 결함

---

12 From September 2008, new legislation designed for the purpose of protecting animals will be put into effect in Switzerland. According to the new law, dog owners will have to take courses and pass exams if they want to keep their pets. And social animals like guinea pigs will have to be bought in groups of more than two. Private dog-training companies and veterinarians have welcomed this measure since 2005. And they will obtain the authorization to provide the exams after going through a certification process by the government.

Q According to the news, which is correct?

    (a) There was no legislation related with having pets before.

    (b) The dog owners are forced to train their dogs from September 2008.

    (c) You can't buy more than two guinea pigs.

    (d) Veterinarians need a certification to provide the exams.

2008년 9월부터 동물 보호의 목적으로 제정된 새로운 법률이 스위스에서 실시됩니다. 새로운 법에 따르면 개를 가진 소유자들은 강좌를 듣고 시험에 합격해야 계속해서 애완견을 키울 수 있습니다. 그리고 기니피그와 같은 사회적 동물들은 2마리 이상 구매해야만 합니다. 개인 애견 훈련업체들과 수의사들은 2005년부터 이 조처를 환영해왔습니다. 그리고 그들은 정부의 인증 절차를 밟은 뒤에 시험 출제 허가를 얻게 됩니다.

○ 애완동물에 관한 새로운 법에 대한 이야기이지만 이전에 관련법이 있었는지는 알 수 없으므로 (a)는 정답이라고 할 수 없다. 또한 애견을 훈련시키는 것이 아니라 애견 소유자들이 강좌를 직접 듣고 시험을 치르는 것이므로 (b) 역시 답이 아니다. 기니피그의 경우 사회적 동물이므로 반드시 2마리 이상 구매해야 한다고 했으므로 (c)도 정답이 아니고 수의사가 시험 출제를 하기 위해서는 자격증이 필요하다는 (d)가 정답이 된다.

legislation 법률, 법규 **put into effect** (법 등을) 실시하다 **veterinarian** 수의사 **authorization** 허가 **certification process** 인증 절차

GRAMMAR • P.36

13 A Please make sure you have all of your personal _____ when you leave your seat.

    B Ok, thanks.

    (a) belong

    (b) belong to

    (c) belonged

    (d) belongings

A: 좌석을 떠날 때 개인 소지품들을 반드시 확인해 주세요.
B: 네, 고마워요.

○ 빈 칸에는 의미상 '소지품'이라는 명사가 와야 한다. 적당한 것은 (d)belongings이다.

personal 개인의, 자신의

14 **A** Let's go and see Mr. Anderson.

  B What _____?

  (a) from
  (b) for
  (c) with
  (d) to

A: 우리 Anderson씨를 만나러 가자.

B: 왜?

○ '무엇을 위해서' 혹은 '무엇 때문에' 라고 묻고 있는 상황이므로 전치사 for가 와야 한다.

---

15 **A** Why does he practice English so hard?

  B His first goal is to make _____ understood in English.

  (a) him
  (b) himself
  (c) of him
  (d) for him

A: 그는 왜 그렇게 영어 공부를 열심히 할까?

B: 그의 첫 목표는 영어로 자신을 잘 표현하는 것이야.

○ 'make 재귀대명사 understood in English' 는 영어로 자신의 의견을 전달하는 것을 의미하는데, 주어 자신이 다시 목적어로 자신을 필요로 하고 있으므로 목적어로 재귀대명사인 himself가 적절하다.

---

16 **A** I'm sure she _____ upset if I had told her about the accident.

  B I couldn't agree more.

  (a) must be
  (b) should be
  (c) must have been
  (d) should have been

A: 내가 만약 그 사고에 대해 말했다면 분명 그녀는 화를 냈을 거야.

B: 네 말이 맞아.

○ 과거에 '분명히 ~했을 것이다' 라고 말하고 있으므로 (c)must have been이 맞는 답이다. (d)should have been은 '~했어야 했는데' 의 뜻으로 과거에 하지 못한 일에 대한 유감을 나타내는 표현이다.

---

17 The host family prepared lots of food the decorations _____ were sensational.

  (a) whose
  (b) which
  (c) what
  (d) of which

주인 가족이 장식이 훌륭했던 음식들을 많이 준비했다.

○ 관계대명사 소유격에 대한 문제로서 the decorations of which가 적절하다.

---

18 During _____ make sure to check the lack of iron in your diet.

  (a) a pregnancy
  (b) pregnancy
  (c) pregnancies
  (d) the pregnancy

임신 기간 중에는 식단에서 철분 부족을 꼭 체크해야 한다.

○ during의 뒤에는 특정 기간을 나타내는 명사가 와야 하므로, 적절한 답은 (d)the pregnancy이다.

19 A Spanish judge charged two suspects and _____ accused were all sent to the trial.

(a) that
(b) who
(c) those
(d) this

스페인인 법관은 두 용의자를 기소했고, 그들은 모두 재판에 보내졌다.

❍ and 뒤에 나오는 원래 문장은 'those who were accused were~' 이다. those 뒤의 주격 관계대명사와 be동사가 함께 생략되었다고 볼 수 있다.

---

20 There will be a small charge _____ we considered they deliver the furniture for.

(a) which
(b) what
(c) where
(d) when

그들이 가구를 배송해준 데 대한 약간의 요금이 부과될 것이다.

❍ 문장 끝에 전치사 for가 있으므로 빈 칸에는 관계대명사 which가 오는 것이 적절하다.

---

21 (a) A: Let's go take a look at Noho.
(b) B: Yes, I heard it is a neighborhood full of wonderful buildings.
(c) A: Do you think what are the most notable buildings in Noho?
(d) B: I think one of them is The Merchant's house, a museum which shows the lifestyle in the 19th century.

A: 우리 Noho를 좀 둘러보자.
B: 그래, Noho 주변에 멋진 건물들이 많다고 들었어.
A: Noho에서 가장 중요한 건물들이 뭐라고 생각하니?
B: 내 생각에 그 중의 하나는 19세기의 생활 방식을 잘 보여주는 박물관인 Merchant's house 인 것 같아.

❍ (c)에서 간접의문문의 어순에 문제가 있다. do you think는 의문사를 문장 앞으로 빼서 '의문사(보어)+(do you think)+주어+동사' 로 바꾸어야 한다.

---

22 (a) China has the largest Refrigerator markets in the world. (b) When consumers purchase refrigerators, their brand and price become increasing important criteria. (c) The Refrigerator industry is consolidated with top 4 players accounting for 70% market share measured by revenue and they compete in prices and qualities. (d) As a result of intensive competition and manufacturing overcapacity, prices are dropping fast.

중국은 전 세계적으로 가장 큰 냉장고 시장을 가지고 있다. 소비자들이 냉장고를 살 때, 그들의 상표와 가격이 점점 중요한 기준이 되고 있다. 냉장고 산업은 상위 4개 브랜드로 통합되어 그들이 시장 수익을 70% 점유하고 있으며 각자 가격과 품질 면에서 경쟁하고 있다. 극심한 경쟁과 과잉생산의 결과로 가격이 빠르게 낮아지고 있다.

❍ (b)에서, 그들의 상표와 가격이 계속해서 중요한 기준이 되고 있다는 뜻이므로 increasing의 부사형인 increasingly 가 알맞다.

consumer 소비자 criteria 기준, 특징 consolidate 통합하다, 합병 정리하다 revenue 수익

23 A You look tired. Are you okay?
B Actually I _____ and turned all night.

(a) threw
(b) changed
(c) moved
(d) tossed

A: 피곤해 보인다. 괜찮아?
B: 사실 밤새 뒤척였어.

🔵 toss and turn이라는 표현도 자주 접할 수 있는 표현이다. 몸을 뒤척인다는 뜻으로 잠을 이루지 못했다는 뜻이다. 이렇게 굳어진 표현은 다른 단어로 대체될 수 없다. 따라서 정답은 tossed가 된다.

toss and turn 몸을 뒤척이다

---

24 A Congratulations on your promotion! But the work would be extremely demanding!
B Come on! Don't be a _____ blanket!

(a) wet
(b) spoiled
(c) thick
(d) messed

A: 승진 축하해! 하지만 일이 만만치 않을 거야!
B: 제발! 분위기 좀 깨지 마라!

🔵 wet blanket은 이디엄으로 흥을 깨는 사람, 찬물을 끼얹는 사람을 뜻한다. 따라서 정답은 wet이 된다.

demanding (일이) 힘든, 고된 wet blanket 트집쟁이, 흥을 깨는 사람

---

25 A Excuse me. Where can I _____ my baggage?
B Which flight were you on?

(a) demand
(b) request
(c) ask
(d) claim

A: 실례합니다. 수하물은 어디서 찾을 수 있나요?
B: 어떤 비행기를 타고 오셨는데요?

🔵 연어를 잘 알아두어야 한다. 공항에서 일어날 수 있는 상황으로 claim baggage는 '수하물을 찾다' 라는 표현이다.

claim baggage 수하물을 찾다 request ~을 요구하다

---

26 A I think I'm getting overweight these days. I'm thinking about joining the fitness club.
B You should _____ on your drinking first!

(a) cut down
(b) cut back
(c) cut in
(d) go down

A: 요즘 살이 찌는 것 같아. 헬스클럽에 등록할까 생각 중이야.
B: 먼저 술부터 줄이는 게 좋을걸!

🔵 살을 빼기 위해서는 운동보다 술을 줄이는 것이 좋겠다고 말하고 있다. '술, 지방, 비용 등을 줄이다' 라고 할 때에는 cut down on 이라는 표현을 쓴다.

cut back 삭감하다, 감축하다 cut in 끼어들다, 가로막다 go down 침몰하다, 지다, 떨어지다

27
A What's on the front page of the newspaper?
B Some protesters were arrested for _____ the law.

(a) rebelling
(b) violating
(c) blowing
(d) driving

A: 신문 1면에 뭐가 났어?
B: 일부 항의자들이 법을 어겨서 체포되었대.

➲ 체포되었다는 것으로 보아 법을 어겼음을 알 수 있다. '법을 어긴다'는 표현으로는 violate the law를 쓴다.

be arrested for ~으로 체포되다 violate the law 법을 어기다 rebel 반란을 일으키다

---

28 Those who are convicted of sexual harassment are placed on _____ instead of being sent to prison.

(a) imprisonment
(b) arrest
(c) probation
(d) prohibition

성희롱으로 기소된 사람들은 감옥에 가는 대신에 보호관찰을 받는다.

감옥에 가는 대신이라고 했으므로 '감옥에 보낸다'는 뜻의 imprisonment는 답이 될 수 없다. place sb on probation은 '~을 보호관찰 하에 둔다'는 뜻으로 문맥상 가장 적절한 답이 된다.

be convicted of ~로 기소되다 sexual harassment 성희롱 place sb on probation ~을 보호관찰 아래 두다 imprisonment 투옥, 유치 prohibition 금지

---

29 The most _____ way to use your computer for a long time is to update your anti-virus programs on a regular basis.

(a) economic
(b) economize
(c) economical
(d) economics

컴퓨터를 오랫동안 사용하는 가장 경제적인 방법은 정기적으로 바이러스 백신을 업데이트하는 것이다.

➲ 형태가 비슷한 어휘를 통해 혼동을 주기 위한 문제이다. 먼저 economic은 '경제의'라는 뜻이고, economize는 '경제적으로 쓰다, 절약하다'라는 뜻의 동사로서 빈 칸에 들어갈 품사는 형용사이므로 답이 될 수 없다. economical은 '경제적인, 절약이 되는'의 뜻으로 컴퓨터를 오래 쓴다는 내용과 어울리고 품사도 맞으므로 정답이 된다. 마지막 economics는 '경제학'을 뜻한다.

on a regular basis 정기적으로

---

30 The crisis came _____ and nobody knew how to handle it.

(a) from scratch
(b) on the spot
(c) out of the blue
(d) once in a blue moon

위기가 갑자기 닥쳤고 아무도 어떻게 해결해야 할지 몰랐다.

➲ 아무도 위기에 어떻게 대처해야 할지 몰랐다면 위기는 '불시에, 예측할 수 없을 만큼 갑자기' 닥쳐야 한다. 이를 뜻하는 표현은 out of the blue이다.

out of the blue 뜻밖에, 불시에 from scratch 처음부터 on the spot 현장에서 once in a blue moon 아주 드물게

---

31 After the civil war, many people are afraid of the probability of the political _____.

(a) excitement
(b) turbulence
(c) confusion
(d) violence

내전 이후에 많은 사람들은 정치적 동요의 가능성을 두려워한다.

➲ 내전 이후라고 했으므로 정치적 동요가 오는 것이 문맥상 자연스럽다. turbulence는 때때로 폭력을 동반하기도 하는 동요나 소란을 뜻한다.

be afraid of ~을 두려워하다 probability 가능성 turbulence 동요, 소란, 난기류 excitement 흥분

32 She made the most fatal mistake ever and she couldn't _____ submitting her resignation.

(a) help
(b) stop
(c) block
(d) hold

그녀는 지금까지 중 가장 치명적인 실수를 했기 때문에 사직서를 제출하지 않을 수 없었다.

○ 치명적인 실수를 했다는 점으로 미루어 보아 사직서를 제출할 수밖에 없다는 내용이 오는 것이 자연스럽다. help는 '돕다' 라는 뜻 말고도 cannot과 함께 쓰여서 '어쩔 도리가 없다' 라는 의미로 쓰인다.

fatal 치명적인 cannot help ~ing ~하지 않을 수 없다 resignation 사표, 사직서

READING COMPREHENSION • P.42

33 The Pygmalion effect, also known as The Rosenthal effect, has to do with the phenomena in which some students produce better results than other students simply because _____.
According to a study by U.S. psychologist Robert Rosenthal, the beliefs and expectations of teachers have a great influence on their students' actual performance. That is, if teachers believe that their students are intelligent and capable enough to derive from enhanced performance, then the students indeed do so. It is explained that the students will respond positively to their teachers' high expectations and apply them to their behavior or learning habits by internalizing them.

(a) they are actually superior
(b) they are expected to do so
(c) their characteristics are always positive
(d) they and their teachers have same expectations

Rosenthal 효과로도 알려져 있는 피그말리온 효과는 어떤 학생들이 더 나은 결과를 낼 것으로 기대되기 때문에 실제로 다른 학생들보다 더 나은 결과를 산출해 내는 현상과 관계가 있다. 미국의 심리학자 Robert Rosenthal의 한 연구에 따르면, 교사의 믿음과 기대가 학생들의 실제 수행에 지대한 영향을 미친다고 한다. 다시 말해, 교사가 자신의 학생들이 더 향상된 성과를 이끌어낼 만큼 충분히 지적이고 능력이 있다고 믿으면, 학생들은 실제로 그렇게 한다는 것이다. 학생들은 교사의 높은 기대에 긍정적으로 반응하며 그 기대를 내재화함으로써 자신의 행동과 학습 습관에 적용하기 때문으로 설명된다.

○ 교사의 기대에 부응하여 학생들의 실제 성적 및 수행능력도 향상된다는 내용의 글이다. 따라서 학생들이 우수한 성과를 내는 것은 그 학생들이 실제로 더 우수하기 때문이라든가(a), 항상 긍정적인 성격 때문이라든가(c), 그들과 교사가 같은 기대를 하기 때문(d)이 아니라 단지 그들이 우수한 성과를 낼 것으로 기대되기 때문(b)이다.

be known as ~로 알려져 있다. have to do with ~와 관계가 있다. phenomena phenomenon(현상)의 복수 according to ~에 의하면 psychologist 심리학자 expectation 기대 have an influence on ~에 영향을 미치다 that is 즉, 다시 말해서 derive (이익, 즐거움 등을) 끌어내다, 얻다 enhance (질, 능력 등을) 높이다, 강화하다 apply A to B A를 B에 적용하다 internalize 내면화하다, 자기 것으로 하다

24

34 A recent study says that smells have an influence on dreams. In this study, 15 healthy women participated as volunteers while a rose scent was injected into their nostrils through tubes during their sleep. When the scientists woke them up one minute after injection, they reported that they had had pleasant dreams. On the contrary, when they were given the odor of rotten eggs, they described their dreams negatively. However there are some people who doubt if this result is really true. They point out that the subjects may not actually have dreamed of it, but may have had an illusion instead, considering that _____.

(a) women are unable to smell while sleeping

(b) there was only short time between the stimulus and the wakening

(c) the scientists injected an aromatic smell before a disgusting smell

(d) the smell was injected mechanically through tubes and not naturally

최근의 한 연구에 따르면 냄새가 꿈에 영향을 미친다고 한다. 이 연구에는 15명의 건강한 여성들이 자원해서 참여했는데, 이들이 자는 동안에 장미향을 튜브를 통해서 콧속으로 주입시켰다. 장미향을 주입시킨 후 1분이 지나서 과학자들이 그 여자들을 깨웠을 때, 그들은 유쾌한 꿈을 꾸었다고 보고했다. 그와는 반대로, 그들에게 썩은 달걀 냄새를 주입시켰을 때, 그들은 그들의 꿈을 부정적으로 묘사했다. 하지만, 이 결과가 정말 사실인지를 의심하는 사람들이 있다. 그들은 자극을 주고 깨우는 것 사이에 시간이 너무 짧았다는 것을 고려해 볼 때, 피실험자들이 실제로 그러한 꿈을 꾼 것이 아니라 착각을 했을지도 모른다고 지적한다.

◐ 냄새가 꿈에 영향을 미친다는 연구 결과에 의구심을 나타내는 내용이다. 정답은 When the scientists woke them up one minute after injection 구절을 보아 (b)로 유추할 수 있는데, 이것은 피실험자들을 너무 빨리 깨웠기 때문에 그들이 깊은 잠에 빠져서 꿈을 꾼 것이 아니라 남아 있는 향기로 인해 영향을 받았을 수도 있다고 생각하기 때문이다.

participate 참여하다 volunteer 지원자 scent 향기 inject 주입하다 injection 주입 nostril 콧구멍 on the contrary 그와는 반대로 odor 냄새, 악취 rotten 썩은 subject 피실험자 illusion 환각, 착각, 오해

---

35 The Empty Nest Syndrome refers to general feelings of loneliness, grief, or despair experienced by parents or guardians when their children leave them to go to college or to get married. Some of them feel that their lives are worthless or meaningless and want to be alone without any social relationships. Others may feel irresistible sadness, or cry excessively. If these feelings become overwhelming, the parent or guardian should undergo treatment. Thus, experts advise _____ while they are still with their children to prevent experiencing these feelings later on.

(a) saving money in the future

(b) preparing for an empty nest

(c) expressing their feelings openly

(d) forcing children not to leave home

빈둥지증후군은 부모나 보호자가 아이들이 대학에 가거나 결혼을 해서 그들을 떠나게 될 때 경험하는 외로움이나 슬픔, 절망과 같은 일반적인 감정과 관련이 있다. 그들 중 몇몇은 그들의 인생이 가치가 없거나 무의미하다고 느끼며 어떤 사회적 교류(관계) 없이 혼자 있고 싶어 한다. 또 다른 사람들은 억제할 수 없는 슬픔을 느끼거나 지나치게 울기도 한다. 이러한 감정들이 지나쳐서 본인도 어쩔 수 없게 되면, 그 부모나 보호자는 치료를 받아야 한다. 그러므로 전문가들은 나중에 이러한 감정을 느끼는 것을 막기 위해서 아이들과 함께 있는 동안 "빈 둥지"를 준비하라고 조언한다.

◐ 빈둥지 증후군은 미리 대처하지 않으면 치료를 받아야 할 정도로 심각할 수 있기 때문에 아이들과 함께 있을 때부터 준비하라는 내용이다. 빈 칸의 내용을 유추할 수 있도록 마지막 문장에 빈 둥지 증후군을 미리 대처할 수 있는 방법들이 몇 가지 소개되어 있다. 따라서 (a)미래를 위해 돈을 저축한다든가, (c)감정을 솔직히 표현한다거나, (d)아이들을 떠나지 못하게 하는 것은 전문가의 조언이 될 수 없다.

grief 슬픔 despair 절망 guardian 보호자 worthless 가치 없는 meaningless 무의미한 irresistible 억제할 수 없는 excessively 지나치게 overwhelming 저항할 수 없는 undergo (검열, 수술 등을) 받다

36 September 25, 2008

To Whom It May Concern:

Harry Ahn taught English at Durham High School from 2005-2007. He did an excellent job of teaching classes in English literature and Composition. He showed a good grasp of the material and was able to develop excellent rapport with his students. Not only did he get along well with his students but also with the faculty.

Harry Ahn would be a tremendous asset for your school and has my highest recommendation. If you have any further questions with regard to his background or qualifications, please do not hesitate to call me.

Sincerely,
Susan Douglas
Vice-Principal

Q What is the purpose of the letter?

(a) To help Harry Ahn obtain the admission to the college
(b) To explain how Harry Ahn goes along with the faculty
(c) To suggest that Harry Ahn would prove to be a good employee
(d) To confirm that Harry Ahn is employed by Durham High School

2008년 9월 25일
관계자분께

해리 안은 2005년부터 2007년까지 Durham 고등학교에서 영어를 담당했습니다. 그는 영문학과 작문 과목에 탁월한 수업을 진행하였습니다. 자료에 대한 이해도도 뛰어났으며, 학생들과의 신뢰관계를 구축하는 능력도 훌륭했습니다. 학생들과 잘 지낼 뿐만 아니라 교직원들과의 관계도 좋았습니다.

해리 안은 귀 학교에 훌륭한 인적 자원이 될 것이며, 저는 적극 추천합니다. 그의 배경이나 자격에 대해 궁금한 점이 있으시면 언제든지 주저 마시고 저에게 전화 주시기 바랍니다.

수잔 더글라스
교감

○ 해리 안을 위한 취업 추천서이므로 답은 (c)이다. 대학교 입학 추천서가 아니므로 (a)는 답이 아니며, 그가 교직원과 화합하며 잘 지낸 것은 사실이나 이 추천서의 목적은 아니므로 (b)도 답이 될 수 없다. 해리 안이 Durham 고등학교에 취업되었음을 확인해주는 편지도 아니므로 (d)도 답이 아니다.

grasp 이해력, 이해 rapport 신뢰관계, 소통 faculty 교직원 asset 자산, 재산 hesitate 주저하다, 망설이다

37 A heat island refers to the increased heat caused by the buildings, concrete, asphalt, and the human and industrial activity of cities. The increased heat requires an increase in the demand of energy for cooling purposes, and increases pollution. Several suggestions have been made to reduce the temperature; most prominent are replacing dark surfaces with light reflective surfaces and planting trees. Planting trees not only provides shade but also increases evapotranspiration, which decreases the air temperature.

열섬은 도시 지역의 빌딩, 콘크리트, 아스팔트, 인간의 활동이나 산업활동 때문에 증가한 열기를 지칭한다. 도시의 증가된 열기는 냉방에 필요한 에너지 수요를 증대시키며, 오염을 증가하게 한다. 온도를 낮추기 위한 몇 가지 방법이 제안되었다. 가장 눈에 띄는 것은 어두운 색의 표면을 밝고 반사하는 표면으로 대체하는 것과 나무를 심는 것이다. 나무를 심는 것은 단순히 그늘을 제공하는 것뿐만 아니라 증발산을 증대시켜서 대기의 온도를 낮추게 한다.

○ 불쾌지수를 높이고, 냉방수요를 증대시켜서, 결국 환경오염을 심화시키게 된다는 열섬이 초래하는 문제점이 지적되었고, 건물이나 콘크리트, 산업활동 등 열섬을 야기하는 원인이 언급되었으며, 그늘을 제공하고 대기의 온도를 낮추는 나무심기의 장점이 서술되어 있다. 도시의 냉방시스템을 개선하는 방법에 대해서는 언급된 바 없으므로 정답은 (b)이다.

Q Which is NOT mentioned in the above statement?

(a) What are the ill effects of a heat island?
(b) How can we improve the cooling system in the cities?
(c) What causes the rise of temperature in the urban areas?
(d) What benefits can we expect from planting trees in the urban areas?

heat island 열섬 《주변보다 온도가 높은 도시[공업 지대] (상공의 대기)》 prominent 현저한, 두드러진, 탁월한 replace A with B A를 B로 바꾸다, 대체하다 excess 초과, 과다, 과잉 evapotranspiration 증발산

---

38 Welcome to the Library at the Swinburne University! There are two categories of borrowers: University Borrowers include all current students, faculty and staff. Other Borrowers include alumni, retired faculty and staff, who do not have remote access to electronic indexes, databases or journals. A library card must be presented to borrow materials or to get other services the library offers. Reissue of library cards will be restricted to borrowers with fines. The person whose name is on the card is responsible for all library transactions made with the card. In case of the loss or theft of a card, you must report immediately to the Circulation staff in the Library. Borrowers will be held accountable for transactions on their card until such notification is received.

Q Which of the following is correct according to the passage?

(a) Library cards are transferable between current students.
(b) Library cards will not be issued again until all the fines have been paid.
(c) A retired staff has the same borrower privileges as a staff in active service.
(d) A borrower will be exempt from responsibility for the use of his lost library card.

Swinburne 대학 도서관 방문을 환영합니다. 도서 대출자는 두 가지 범주로 구분됩니다. 대학관련자 대출자에는 모든 재학생, 교직원과 직원이 포함됩니다. 기타 대출자에는 졸업생과 퇴임한 교직원과 직원이 해당되는데, 이 경우 전자 색인이나, 자료, 정기간행물 등에 대한 원격접근은 불가합니다. 자료를 대출하거나, 도서관이 제공하는 기타 모든 서비스를 이용하기 위해서는 도서관 카드를 제시해야 합니다. 벌금이 밀려있는 학생에게는 도서관 카드의 재발급이 제한되며, 카드에 이름이 명시된 분은 해당카드로 이루어진 모든 도서관 업무에 대해 책임을 지게 됩니다. 카드를 분실했거나 도난당하신 경우, 즉시 도서관 대출부 직원에게 신고하셔야 합니다. 신고가 접수된 시점까지의 도서관 업무에 대해서는 해당카드의 대출자에게 책임이 있습니다.

◯ 도서관 카드가 재학생 간에 양도 가능하다는 것은 언급된 바 없으므로 (a)는 답이 아니며, 퇴임한 직원은 원격접근이 제한되므로 (c)도 옳지 않다. 카드 분실자는 신고한 이후부터의 책임이 면제되는 것이므로 (d)도 답이 아니다. 벌금이 있으면 재발급이 되지 않으므로 모든 벌금을 납부해야 카드를 다시 발급받을 수 있다는 (b)가 정답이다.

alumni 졸업생, 동창생 remote access 원격접근 reissue 재발행, 재발급 fine 벌금 transaction 처리, 취급, 거래 circulation 대출, 순환 accountable for~ ~에 대해 책임이 있는

39 Although Hollywood celebrities spend millions of dollars on his works and most of his works fetch more than the estimated price at auction, even the agent has allegedly never met Banksy, the elusive graffiti artist. Now it seems that the artist will be constrained to forsake the life of a recluse. He was pictured at work for the first time. There have been a few people claiming to have caught Banksy on camera before, but this is believed to be the first image showing the artist at work. A spokeswoman for Banksy said that the artwork was authentic, but refused to confirm whether the man in the photo was the artist.

Q Which of the following is NOT true about Banksy according to the passage?

(a) His works command prices far beyond expectations.
(b) few people are known to have met the artist in person.
(c) Many Hollywood celebrities have been cheated into buying his works.
(d) The street artist refuses to get into the public eye as much as possible.

헐리우드 유명 인사들이 그의 작품을 수백만 달러에 사들이고, 대부분의 작품이 경매에서 예상가격을 훨씬 상회하는 가격에 낙찰이 되고 있어도, 사람들 눈을 피해 다니는 그래피티 예술가인 Banksy를 그의 대리인조차도 본 적이 없다고 전해진다. 그러나 이제 이 예술가도 어쩔 수 없이 은둔자의 삶을 포기해야 할 것 같다. 그가 최초로 작업하는 모습이 사진에 찍힌 것이다. 이전에도 Banksy를 카메라로 포착했다고 주장하는 사람들이 몇몇 있었지만, 작업 중인 그 예술가를 보여주는 이미지는 이것이 최초로 여겨진다. Banksy의 대변인은 작품은 진품이 맞는다고 말했으나, 사진 속 인물이 그 예술가임을 확인해주는 것은 거부했다.

🔵 그래피티 예술가인 Banksy는 작품의 인기가 많아서 경매에서도 높은 가격에 팔리고 있지만, 최대한 사람들의 시야를 피해 다니기 때문에 은둔자의 이미지를 가지고 있는데, 얼마 전 작업 중인 모습이 포착되었다는 내용이다. 헐리우드 유명 인사들이 속아서 그의 작품을 사게 된 것은 아니므로 (c)가 정답이다.

fetch (물건이) …에 팔리다 allegedly 전해진 바에 따르면, 이른바 elusive (교묘히) 피하는, 잡히지 않는 be constrained to~ 어쩔 수 없이 ~하다 forsake 져버리다, 포기하다 recluse 은둔자, 세상을 버린 사람 claim 주장하다 authentic 진정한, 진짜의 confirm 확인하다

---

40 April Van Lines believes that understanding your needs is the key to a successful move. With over 80 years' experience, April, a world-leading moving company has what it takes to make your household or corporate move go smoothly. Whether your type of move is locally within the state or out of the state, April's experienced support staff will guide you through every step of the relocation process. When you move with us, you can count on sincere, reliable service, and unrivalled quality. Contact us today for a free moving estimate from our superb moving service.

Q Which of the following mottos is appropriate for this company?

(a) Dream Skyward!
(b) Make It Happen Now!
(c) Moving Your Memories!
(d) To Persevere and To Excel

April Van Lines는 여러분의 필요를 이해하는 것이 성공적인 이사를 결정하는 열쇠라고 믿습니다. 80년 이상의 경험을 지닌 세계적인 이사 회사인, April은 가정집 이사든, 회사 이사든 순조롭게 진행될 수 있도록 하기 위한 모든 것을 갖추고 있습니다. 여러분의 이사가 국내이사든지, 국외이사든지 상관없이, April의 경험 많은 지원팀이 이사과정의 모든 단계마다 지원할 것입니다. 우리와 이사를 하시면, 진심 어린, 믿을 만한 서비스와 비할 데 없이 좋은 품질의 이사를 기대하실 수 있습니다. 최상의 이사 서비스에 대한 무료 견적을 원하시면 오늘 연락하세요.

🔵 이사 회사의 광고이므로 회사의 사훈으로 가장 알맞은 것은 (c) 추억도 옮겨드립니다! 이다. (a)는 항공회사의 사훈, (b)는 창업회사 등 각종 회사, (d)는 학교의 교훈으로 적합하다.

household 가족, 가사 relocation 재배치 count on 의존하다, 기대다, 믿다 unrivalled 경쟁자가 없는, 비할 데 없는 superb 최고의, 최상의

LISTENING COMPREHENSION · P.48

1 M I feel like throwing up.
    W _____

(a) What's eating you?
(b) Let's go to the bathroom.
(c) I don't get it.
(d) Will you keep it down?

M: 토할 것 같아.
W: 화장실로 가자.

🔹 '토하다' 라는 뜻으로는 vomit, throw up 등이 있다. 토할 것 같다는 남자의 말에 적절한 여자의 응답은 (b)가 된다. (a)는 '무슨 고민(걱정거리) 있어?' 라는 뜻으로 eat이 '음식을 먹다' 라는 뜻으로 쓰인 것이 아님을 주의하자. (c)는 '이해가 안 된다.' 라는 뜻이고, (d)는 '좀 조용히 해줄래?' 라는 뜻으로 정답과는 거리가 멀다.

throw up (음식을) 토하다 **keep down** (소리를) 낮추다, 조용히 하다

---

2 M We're going to the movies this
       Saturday. Do you want to come?
    W _____

(a) I'm afraid I can't make it.
(b) I'll keep that in mind.
(c) Come over anytime.
(d) Hang in there!

M: 이번 주 토요일에 영화 보러 갈 건데 같이 갈래?
W: 나는 못갈 것 같아.

🔹 영화 보러 가자는 남자의 제안에 적절한 응답으로 (a)가 정답이 된다. make it은 '(시간에 맞게) 가다', '성공하다, 해내다' 등의 뜻으로 구어체에서 많이 쓰는 표현이므로 꼭 알아두자. (b)는 꼭 명심하겠다는 뜻이며 (c)는 언제든 놀러오라는 뜻으로 문제에서 'come' 이 나와 이것으로 혼동을 주기 위한 함정이다. (d)는 힘내라고 격려할 때 쓸 수 있는 표현이다.

go to the movies 영화 보러 가다 **make it** (시간에) 대다, 성공하다. 해내다 **keep sth in mind** ~을 명심하다 **hang in there** 버티다, 견디다

---

3 M Excuse me. Could you keep an eye on
       my bag for a minute?
    W _____

(a) My eyes are getting worse.
(b) Don't stare at me.
(c) Sure, no problem.
(d) Plastic, or paper bag?

M: 실례합니다. 잠깐만 제 가방 좀 봐주시겠어요?
W: 네, 걱정 마세요.

🔹 잠깐 어딜 다녀올 동안 가방을 봐 달라고 부탁을 하는 상황이다. (a)의 경우 문제의 'eye' 를 반복하여 혼동을 주고 있지만 시력이 나빠지고 있다는 뜻으로 상황과 맞지 않다. (b)는 '날 노려보지 마.' 라는 뜻으로 역시 답과는 거리가 멀다. (c)는 부탁이나 제안에 대해 수락하는 표현으로 정답이 되며, (d)는 상점에서 물건을 비닐봉지에 넣어줄지, 종이 가방에 넣어줄지를 묻는 표현으로 문제의 'bag' 이라는 단어로 함정을 준 것이므로 주의하자.

keep an eye on sth ~을 감시하다, 지켜보다 **stare at** ~을 응시하다, 쳐다보다 **plastic bag** 비닐 봉지

4
M Excuse me. Do you need any help?
W Yes. I think I'm lost. I don't know where I am.
M Let me see the map. Where are you headed for?
W _____

(a) The bank is around the corner.
(b) I'm going to the post office.
(c) I'm in a hurry.
(d) I begin to feel light-headed.

M: 실례합니다. 도움이 필요하세요?
W: 네, 길을 잃은 것 같아요. 제가 어디 있는 건지 모르겠어요.
M: 지도 좀 볼게요. 어디로 가시는데요?
W: 우체국에 가고 있어요.

🔵 길을 잃고 헤매고 있는 여자에게 남자가 도움을 주고 있는 상황이다. 남자의 마지막 대사에서 어디로 가냐고 묻고 있으므로 여자는 목적지를 이야기하는 것이 적절하다. 따라서 정답은 (b)가 된다. (a)는 여자가 길을 모르는 상황이므로 적절치 않으며, (c)는 바쁘다는 뜻으로 역시 문맥상 적절치 않다. (d)는 현기증이 나기 시작했다는 뜻으로 상황에 맞지 않는다.

head for ~로 향하다, ~로 가다 **around the corner** 모퉁이를 돌면 **light-headed** 현기증이 나는, 어지러운

5
M I'm going to take my girlfriend to dinner tonight.
W So, where are you planning to go?
M I'm thinking of going to the seafood restaurant. Do you think I need to make reservations?
W _____

(a) I'll show you the way.
(b) I have a lot of reservations about the plan.
(c) I think so. They're usually crowded.
(d) That looks like wishful thinking.

M: 오늘 밤 내 여자 친구 저녁 사주려고 해.
W: 그래서 어디로 갈려고?
M: 해산물 전문 식당으로 갈 예정이야. 예약을 해야 할까?
W: 그러는 게 좋을 거야. 대개 사람이 많잖아.

🔵 남자의 마지막 대사에 주목하자. 해산물 식당에 갈 것인데 예약을 해야 할지 말지에 대해 여자에게 의견을 묻고 있다. (a)는 길을 가르쳐준다는 뜻으로 상황에 어울리지 않고 (b)는 그 계획에 대해 의혹이 많다는 뜻으로 여기서 reservation은 의심, 의혹을 뜻한다. (c)는 보통 사람이 많으므로 예약하는 것이 좋겠다는 뜻으로 정답이며, (d)는 희망 사항처럼 보인다는 뜻으로 문맥과 어울리지 않는다.

reservation 예약, 마음의 의혹, 의심 **crowded** 혼잡한, 붐비는 **wishful thinking** 희망적 기대

6
M It's freezing here.
W You seem to be very sensitive to cold.
M You're right. Do you mind if I close the window?
W _____

(a) Yes. I have cold feet.
(b) Please keep that in mind.
(c) Of course not.
(d) That's okay.

M: 여기 너무 춥다.
W: 너는 추위에 매우 민감한 것 같아.
M: 맞아. 창문 좀 닫아도 될까?
W: 물론이지.

🔵 창문을 닫아도 되느냐는 남자의 물음에 적절한 대답으로 (c)가 정답이 된다. (a)는 겁이 난다는 뜻이며, cold를 이용하여 혼동을 주기 위한 함정이다. (b)는 그것을 명심하겠다는 뜻으로 정답과 거리가 멀고 (d)는 괜찮다는 뜻이다.

sensitive to ~에 민감한 **cold feet** 겁, 주눅, 공포심

7
M Why the long face? Is anything the matter?

W I had a fight with my boyfriend. He's always telling me what to do.

M But you guys have been going out for almost three years. Put yourself in his shoes. Then you'd feel different.

W It's easy for you to say. I can't stand him anymore. He easily loses his temper.

M So, what are you going to do then?

W I don't know. I'm just thinking of breaking up with him.

M Just think about it one last time.

Q Why does the woman feel blue?

(a) She broke up with her boyfriend.

(b) She was stood up again.

(c) She doesn't like a friend of his.

(d) She isn't getting along with her boyfriend.

M: 왜 그렇게 우울한 얼굴을 하고 있어? 무슨 일 있어?

W: 남자 친구랑 싸웠어. 그 애는 항상 내게 이래라 저래라 해.

M: 그렇지만 너희 둘 사귄 지 거의 3년이 다 됐잖아. 남자친구 입장에서 생각해봐. 그럼 다른 생각이 들 거야.

W: 말이 쉽지. 더 이상 못 참겠어. 쉽게 흥분한다니깐.

M: 그래서 어쩔 작정인데?

W: 모르겠어. 헤어질까 생각 중이야.

M: 마지막으로 한 번만 더 생각해봐.

◐ 질문의 feel blue를 알지 못하면 문제를 풀 수 없다. feel blue는 기분이 우울하다는 의미로 여자가 기분이 우울한 이유를 찾아야 한다. 아직 헤어진 것이 아니므로 (a)는 정답이 될 수 없고 (b)는 바람 맞았다는 뜻인데, 언급된 적이 없다. (c)도 역시 남자 친구의 친구들에 대한 언급이 없었으므로 정답이 아니고, 여자가 남자 친구와 잘 지내지 못하고 있다고 하는 (d)가 정답이 된다.

feel blue 기분이 울적하다 long face 시무룩한 얼굴 go out (이성과) 사귀다 put oneself in a person's shoes 남의 입장에서 생각하다 lose temper 흥분하다, 화를 내다 break up with ~와 헤어지다 stand up ~을 바람맞히다 get along with ~와 잘 지내다

8
M How did the interview go?

W I don't know. I was very nervous at first but the interviewers were kind of nice.

M Were there any tricky questions?

W Some of them were kind of difficult to answer, but I think I did handle it well.

M That sounds promising.

W Well, it remains to be seen.

Q What is correct according to the dialogue?

(a) She made a mistake during the interview.

(b) She got an acceptance letter from the company.

(c) There were some difficult questions during the interview.

(d) She promised to go to the interview.

M: 면접 어땠어?

W: 잘 모르겠어. 처음에는 무척 긴장했었는데 면접관들이 잘 대해 주는 편이었어.

M: 까다로운 질문들은 없었어?

W: 몇몇 질문들은 대답하기 어려웠지만 잘 넘긴 것 같아.

M: 그거 희망적인데.

W: 글쎄. 두고 봐야지.

◐ 면접 도중에 까다로운 질문들이 있었지만 잘 넘겼다고 했으므로 (a)는 정답이 아니고 아직 결과를 모르는 상황이므로 (b) 역시 정답이 될 수 없다. 앞서 말한 대로 면접 중에 어려운 질문이 몇 가지 있었으므로 (c)가 정답이 되며 (d)는 promising이라는 단어로 혼동을 주기위해 promised를 썼으나 면접에 가기로 약속했다는 내용은 관계가 없으므로 정답이 아니다.

tricky 까다로운 handle (문제 등을) 다루다, 처리하다 promising 전망이 좋은, 기대되는 acceptance letter 합격 통지서

9

M Don't you think they are totally out of their minds? I can't believe how they did such a horrible thing with the food.

W You're right. That was very shocking news. I almost threw up after I heard the news.

M They have no conscience at all.

W One of the companies mentioned for using harmful substances in food was my favorite brand.

M Really? You must have been angry.

W Yes. I think the government must try to set stricter regulations about food safety.

M I agree with you. The importance of food safety cannot be overemphasized.

Q What do the speakers agree on?

(a) Government should take responsibility for the incident.

(b) Government intervention is needed about food matter.

(c) The companies breaking the law should pay a fine.

(d) Government should emphasize the importance of food safety.

M: 그들이 완전히 정신이 나간 것 아니니? 어떻게 음식을 가지고 그렇게 끔찍한 짓을 할 수 있는지 믿을 수 없어.

W: 맞아. 정말 충격적인 뉴스였어. 그 뉴스를 듣고 토할 뻔했다니까.

M: 그 사람들 양심이라곤 없어.

W: 음식에 유해 물질을 사용했다고 언급된 회사들 중 한 곳은 내가 좋아하는 브랜드였어.

M: 정말? 너 정말 화났겠다.

W: 응. 정부가 식품 안전을 위해 좀 더 엄격한 규정을 만들어야 한다고 생각해.

M: 네 말이 맞아. 식품 안전의 중요성은 아무리 강조해도 지나치지 않지.

○ 마지막 부분이 핵심이 된다. 여자가 식품 안전에 대한 보다 엄격한 규정을 정부가 마련해야 한다고 했고 이에 남자가 동의하고 있다. (a)의 경우 이 사건에 대한 정부의 책임을 이야기하고 있지만 대화에서는 언급되지 않았다. (b)의 경우 정부의 조정이 필요하다는 내용이므로 정답이 된다. (c)의 경우 법을 어긴 회사에 대한 조처는 언급되지 않았다. (d)의 경우 식품 안전의 중요성에 대한 이야기는 나왔으나 그것을 정부가 강조해야 한다는 이야기는 아니었으므로 정답이 될 수 없다.

out of one's mind 제 정신이 아니다 conscience 양심 overemphasize ~을 지나치게 강조하다 take responsibility 책임을 지다 intervention 중재, 조정 break the law 법을 어기다 pay a fine 벌금을 물다

---

10 In today's class, I aim to give an account of the social and political development of England since the opening of the century. I do not attempt any detailed history of the events during that time. And indeed my intention is rather to draw a general picture than to give you a chronicle and a record. I'm also going to describe each remarkable political and social development, and to group the philanthropists of every order by whom each development was assisted in its progress.

Q According to the lecture, which is correct?

(a) The lecturer is going to talk about England in detail.

(b) The lecturer is trying to talk about general things about England.

(c) The lecturer is planning to give a chronicle of the period.

(d) The lecturer is going to focus on the philanthropists.

오늘 강의에서는 세기가 시작된 이후로 영국의 사회적, 정치적 발달에 대해 설명하려고 합니다. 그 시대에 일어났던 사건들의 자세한 역사를 다루지는 않으려고 합니다. 그리고 실제 저의 의도는 연대기와 기록에 대한 설명보다는 전반적인 그림을 그리는 것입니다. 저는 또한 각각의 눈부신 정치적, 사회적 발전을 묘사하고 발전 과정에 도움을 주었던 박애주의자들을 순서대로 묶어서 이야기할 것입니다.

○ 중간쯤에 보면 자세한 역사를 다루는 것이 아니라 전반적인 그림을 그리고자 한다는 강연자의 의도가 나타나있으므로 정답은 (b)가 된다. (a)는 정답과 반대되는 이야기이고, 연대기에 대해서는 다루지 않겠다고 했으므로 (c)는 정답이 아니며, 박애주의자에 관한 이야기는 강연의 일부일 뿐이므로 (d) 역시 정답이라고 할 수 없다.

give an account of ~에 대한 설명을 하다 chronicle 연대기 remarkable 두드러진, 현저한 philanthropist 박애주의자

11 Police in Huntsville, Alabama, say they have a very complex situation on their hands after an employee shot and killed 3 co-workers in a manufacturing plant. Correspondent Paul Powers reports investigators say the suspect's body was discovered in the stolen car near the police headquarters. And it's not clear whether the suspect shot himself or was shot by police. As it turned out, there was an exchange of gunfire for about 5 minutes.

Q Which can be inferred from the news?

(a) The suspect is a worker in a manufacturing plant.
(b) The police shot the suspect on the spot.
(c) Paul Powers was in charge of the investigation.
(d) There was a big fire in manufacturing plant.

알라바마의 헌츠빌 경찰에 따르면 제조 공장에서 한 근로자가 3명의 동료를 총으로 살해한 이후에 경찰은 매우 복잡한 상황에 놓이게 되었다고 합니다. 폴 파워스 기자의 보고에 따르면 용의자의 시신이 경찰 본부 근처 도난 차량에서 발견되었다고 수사관들이 밝혔다고 합니다. 그리고 용의자가 자살을 했는지 경찰에 의해 사살 당했는지는 아직 명확하지 않다고 합니다. 밝혀진 바에 의하면 약 5분 동안 총격전이 있었다고 합니다.

○ 뉴스 초반에 employee라는 단어와 co-worker라는 단어가 나왔으므로 용의자는 제조 공장 근로자임을 짐작할 수 있으므로 정답은 (a)가 된다. 경찰이 현장에서 용의자를 사살했는지는 분명치 않다고 했으므로 (b)는 정답이 될 수 없고, 폴 파워스는 수사관이 아닌 기자이며 공장에 화재가 있었다는 내용은 없었으므로 (c)와 (d) 모두 정답이 아니다.

manufacturing plant 제조 공장 correspondent 특파원, 기자 suspect 용의자 investigator 수사관, 조사원 on the spot 현장에서

---

12 Today, we're going to make chunky peanut butter using this brand-new blender. It takes about ten minutes to prepare. First let me tell you the ingredients and utensils for today's cooking. You need unsalted roasted peanuts, peanut oil, bowl, mixing spoon and definitely this blender. Now, are you ready to start? Well, take about one forth cup of peanuts and set them aside. And then mix the rest with the peanut oil. Process the mixture until it becomes smooth. And pour the mixture into the peanuts you had set aside and stir. Last, store your chunky peanut butter in a sealed container in the fridge for about two hours.

Q Where can you possibly see the program?

(a) In the entertainment show
(b) In the home shopping channel
(c) In the talk show
(d) In the educational channel

오늘 우리는 새로 나온 믹서기를 이용해서 덩어리가 있는 땅콩버터를 만들 것입니다. 준비하는 데 약 10분의 시간이 걸립니다. 우선 오늘의 요리에 필요한 재료와 기구를 말씀드릴게요. 소금이 들어있지 않은 구운 땅콩, 땅콩 오일, 그릇, 젓는 스푼 그리고 당연히 이 믹서기가 필요합니다. 이제 시작할 준비가 되셨나요? 자, 땅콩 4분의 1 컵을 퍼서 따로 챙겨 놓으세요. 그리고 나서 나머지 땅콩을 땅콩 오일과 섞으세요. 그리고 섞은 것이 부드러워질 때까지 믹서기를 돌리세요. 그리고 섞은 것을 아까 따로 챙겨 놓았던 땅콩에 붓고 저으세요. 마지막으로 완성된 땅콩버터를 밀폐 용기에 넣어 냉장고에 약 두 시간 동안 보관하시면 됩니다.

○ 이와 같은 프로그램을 어디서 볼 수 있는지 묻고 있다. 요리 채널이 가장 적합하겠지만 보기에 없으므로 가장 근접한 답을 찾아야 한다. 오락 쇼, 토크 쇼, 교육 채널보다는 홈쇼핑 채널이 정답으로 적합하다. 땅콩버터를 만들면서 계속 믹서기를 강조하고 있기 때문에 (b)가 정답이라고 할 수 있다.

chunky 덩어리가 진 brand-new 새로운, 신품의 blender 믹서기 ingredient 재료, 성분 utensil 도구, 기구, 용구 set aside 따로 챙겨두다, 옆에 치워 두다 stir ~을 휘젓다, 뒤섞다

13 A What should I bring to a potluck?
B Why don't _____ some prepared fruit trays or vegetables.

(a) for you to bring
(b) you bringing
(c) you bring
(d) you to bring

A: 파티에 뭘 가져오지?
B: 과일이나 채소 한 접시는 어때?

○ 'Why don't you~' 는 '~하는 게 어때'의 뜻으로 상대에게 제안이나 권유할 때 쓰는 표현이다. why don't 다음으로는 주어와 동사원형이 오게 되므로 (c)you bring이 맞는 답이다.

potluck 각자 음식을 조금씩 가지고 오는 미국식 파티 **tray** 쟁반, 접시 한 그릇 분량

---

14 A There _____ a police box on the corner.
B Right, a bar and a liquor shop were, too.

(a) used to be
(b) would be
(c) should be
(d) must be

A: 저 모퉁이에 파출소가 있었는데.
B: 맞아, 그리고 술집이랑 주류상도 있었어.

○ 'used to 동사원형' 이 상태 동사로 쓰이면 '과거에는 그랬는데 지금은 그렇지 않다'는 의미를 가지게 된다.

liquor shop 주류 전문상점 **police box** 파출소

---

15 A What happened? You look like you are in a lot of pain.
B Don't touch me, my legs are _____.

(a) numb to
(b) numbing to
(c) numbed
(d) to numb

A: 무슨 일이야? 너 매우 고통스럽게 보여.
B: 건드리지 마, 발이 저려.

○ numb은 타동사이므로 전치사가 필요치 않고, be동사 뒤의 자리에는 동사의 p.p형인 (c)numbed가 와야 한다.

numb 저리게 하다, 마비시키다

---

16 A Do you have any smoking sections in the building?
B Sorry, _____ in the dormitory.

(a) we're not supposed to smoke
(b) we're supposed to smoke
(c) it seems to smoke
(d) it seems not to be smoking

A: 이 건물에는 흡연 구역이 있나요?
B: 죄송합니다만, 우리 기숙사 건물에서는 흡연이 금지되어 있습니다.

○ 'be supposed to 동사원형'은 '~하기로 되어 있다'는 뜻의 표현으로 위 대화에서는 부정어 not과 함께 쓰여 '흡연이 금지되어 있다'는 문장이 되어야 하므로 (a)가 적절하다.

smoking section 흡연 구역 **dormitory** 기숙사

17 _____ the reason, the old man answered he would get the top alone.

(a) When asking
(b) When asked
(c) Having asked
(d) Asking

이유에 대해 질문을 받았을 때, 그 노인은 그가 정상에 혼자 오르려고 했다고 답했다.

○ 문장의 주어와 ask와의 관계가 수동의 관계, 즉 the old man이 질문을 받는 상황이므로 (b)가 가장 적절하다.

---

18 The writer who wrote the novel has very delicate manners, _____ a graceful appearance.

(a) balancing
(b) balanced
(c) balanced with
(d) balancing with

그 소설을 쓴 작가는 우아한 외모에 어울리는 고상한 태도를 지니고 있었다.

○ 분사구문으로, 그 작가의 태도가 우아한 외모에 잘 어울린다는 뜻이므로 (c)가 적절하다.

---

19 Molecular cloning refers to the procedure of isolating a defined DNA sequence and obtaining multiple copies of _____ .

(a) one
(b) ones
(c) it
(d) them

분자 클로닝이란 특정한 DNA 배열을 분리하고, 그것으로부터 다양한 복제본을 얻어내는 처리과정을 의미한다.

○ a defined DNA sequence를 지칭하는 대명사를 찾는 문제로, 답은(c)it 이다.

---

20 _____ behalf of the president who attended a fringe meeting, he delivered an address at the conference.

(a) In
(b) Of
(c) On
(d) With

부수 회의에 참석한 사장을 대신하여, 그가 회의에서 연설을 했다.

○ '~를 대신하여' 라는 표현이므로 (c)On 이 적절하다.

on behalf of ~를 대신하여, ~을 대표하여 fringe 가장자리, 주변

---

21 (a) A : Hello, can I speak to a personnel director?
(b) B : Yes, this is she speaking, ma'am.
(c) A : I heard you recruited staff on a regular basis.
(d) B : You're right, we are now looking for a sales executive of online marketing.

A: 여보세요. 인사 담당자와 통화할 수 있을까요?
B: 네, 제가 인사 담당입니다.
A: 그쪽에서 신입 사원을 정규 모집한다고 들었는데요.
B: 맞습니다. 우리 회사는 온라인 마케팅 담당 관리자를 구하고 있습니다.

○ (c)에서 hear(지각동사)+목적어+동사원형의 형태를 써야 하므로 recruited를 recruit으로 고쳐야 한다.

recruit 신입 사원을 모집하다 on a regular basis 정기적으로 executive 임원, 관리직

22 (a) After working for 5 years, he published Johnson's Dictionary of the English Language in 1755. (b) It had a far-reaching impact on Modern English which has been described as "one of the greatest single achievement of scholarship".(c) It brought Johnson popularity and success until the Oxford English Dictionary was published 150 years later. (d) It was viewed as the preeminent British dictionary.

5년여의 작업 끝에, 그는 1755년에 Johnson's 영어 사전을 출간했다. 이는 학문상 가장 위대한 개인 업적 중 하나로 평가되며 근대 영어에 굉장한 영향을 끼쳤다. 150년 후 옥스퍼드 영어 사전이 발간되기까지, 존슨은 성공과 명성을 누렸다. 그 사전은 걸출한 영국 영어 사전으로 평가받았다.

❍ 'one of~' 는 복수형 명사와 함께 쓰여 '~한 것들 중 하나' 를 의미하는 표현이다. 따라서 (b)에서 achievement를 복수형으로 바꾸어야 한다.

impact 영향

VOCABULARY • P.53

23 **A** Have you seen my MP3 player? I can't find it anywhere!
   B No. That's why I always put things within my arm's _____.

(a) close
(b) by
(c) reach
(d) contact

A: 내 MP3 플레이어 봤어? 찾아봐도 없어!
B: 아니. 그래서 내가 항상 물건들을 손이 닿는 곳에 두는 거야.

❍ MP3를 잃어버렸다고 했을 때 적절한 B의 반응은 물건을 항상 가까운 곳에 두라는 것이다. '손이 닿는 곳에', 즉 '가까운 곳에' 를 뜻하는 표현은 within one's arm's reach이다.

within one's arm's reach ~의 손이 닿는 곳에

---

24 **A** I can't believe he's only 15 years old.
   B My son is _____ compared to other kids of his age.

(a) precocious
(b) pretended
(c) preliminary
(d) preventable

A: 그 애가 겨우 15세 밖에 안 된다니 믿겨지지 않는다.
B: 우리 아들이 동갑내기 친구들에 비해서 조숙해.

❍ 보기가 모두 pre로 시작하고 있어서 헷갈릴 수 있다. 문제에서 '아이가 겨우 15세' 라는 것과 '다른 동갑내기와 비교했을 때' 라는 말이 나오는 것으로 보아 빈 칸에는 '조숙하다, 성숙하다' 라는 의미의 단어가 나오는 것이 자연스럽다.

precocious 조숙한, 어른스러운 compared to ~에 비하면 preliminary 예비의, 준비의 preventable 예방할 수 있는, 피할 수 있는

---

25 **A** Don't you think politicians are wasting public money for nothing?
   B You're right. I want them to stop spending money on _____ projects.

(a) serious
(b) frivolous
(c) important
(d) fastidious

A: 정치인들이 공금을 헛되이 낭비하고 있는 것 같지 않아?
B: 네 말이 맞아. 사소한 프로젝트에 돈 좀 그만 썼으면 좋겠어.

❍ 정치인들이 공금을 낭비한다는 말이 나왔으므로 심각하고 중요한 사안이 아닌 사소한 프로젝트에 돈을 지출하지 않았으면 좋겠다는 대답이 적절하다. 따라서 정답은 frivolous가 된다.

for nothing 무료로, 공짜로, 헛되이, 무익하게 frivolous 사소한, 보잘것없는 fastidious 까다로운, 말이 많은, 엄격한

26 A How often do you exercise?

B I _____ every day to keep fit.

(a) go out
(b) warm up
(c) work out
(d) walk out

A: 운동은 얼마나 자주 하니?
B: 건강 유지를 위해 매일 운동 해.

⊙ exercise와 같은 뜻을 찾아야 한다. warm up의 경우 운동 전에 하는 스트레칭 등의 가벼운 준비 운동을 말하므로 정답이라 할 수 없고, work out은 '문제를 풀다, 계산하다' 라는 의미는 물론 '운동하다' 라는 의미도 있으므로 정답이 된다.

work out(=exercise) 운동하다 keep fit 건강을 유지하다 warm up 준비 운동을 하다 walk out 급히 떠나다, 파업하다

---

27 A We still lag behind other competitors.

B I agree with you. We need to _____ a great idea.

(a) take into account
(b) draw back
(c) make out
(d) come up with

A: 우리는 여전히 다른 경쟁자들보다 뒤처져 있어요.
B: 맞습니다. 좋은 아이디어를 생각해 낼 필요가 있어요.

⊙ 빈 칸 뒤의 a great idea와 잘 어울리는 표현을 찾아야 한다. come up with는 생각이나 아이디어를 내놓는 것을 의미하므로 정답이 된다.

lag behind 뒤처지다 competitor 경쟁자 come up with ~을 생각해내다 take into account ~을 고려하다, 계산에 넣다 draw back 물러서다 make out 잘 해내다, 그럭저럭 해 나가다

---

28 The new government is giving price stability a top _____ because the low income earners are currently suffering from soaring prices.

(a) priority
(b) necessity
(c) importance
(d) probability

새 정부는 저소득자들이 현재 치솟는 물가로 인해 고통받고 있기 때문에 물가 안정을 최고 우선순위에 두고 있다.

⊙ 치솟는 물가로 고통받고 있으므로 물가 안정을 가장 시급한 현안으로 삼아야 한다는 내용이 오는 것이 자연스럽다. priority는 top과 함께 쓰여서 '최우선사항' 이라는 의미로 많이 쓰인다.

price stability 물가 안정 priority 우선사항, 긴급한 일 soaring 치솟는, 상승하는 necessity 필수품

---

29 He was _____ to a local hospital as soon as he was shot in the head but he died of excessive bleeding.

(a) operated
(b) transferred
(c) transformed
(d) placed

그는 머리에 총을 맞고 바로 지역 병원으로 이송되었으나 과다 출혈로 사망했다.

⊙ 사고가 난 이후에 병원으로 이송한다는 이야기가 나오는 것이 자연스럽다. 이러한 의미로 쓰이는 것은 transfer이고 transform은 형태가 비슷하지만 '변형시키다' 라는 뜻의 다른 단어이다.

transfer ~을 이동시키다, 나르다 excessive bleeding 과다 출혈 operate 작용하다, 수술하다 transform 바꾸다, 변형시키다

30 It was so dark that the old man
_____ over a rock and fell down.

(a) stumped
(b) kicked
(c) stumbled
(d) twisted

너무 어두워서 그 노인은 바위에 걸려 넘어졌다.

⟳ 너무 어두웠다고 했으므로 바위에 걸려 넘어지는 상황이 자연스럽다. kick은 채인다기 보다는 발로 차는 것이므로 맞지 않는다. 무엇인가에 걸려 비틀거리는 상황은 stumble이 적절하다

stumble (~에 걸려) 넘어질 듯 비틀거리다 stump ~을 바싹 베다 twist ~을 꼬다. 짜다

---

31 As a wad of _____ bill was found,
the police announced that they would start
an investigation as early as the end of this
month.

(a) pirate
(b) confidential
(c) certificate
(d) counterfeit

위조지폐 한 다발이 발견되자 경찰은 이르면 이달 말에 조사를 시작할 것이라고 발표했다.

⟳ bill과 어울리는 연어를 찾아야 한다. 경찰이 지폐에 대해서 조사를 한다는 내용으로 보아 위조지폐가 발견된 것임을 알 수 있다. 따라서 이러한 의미를 갖는 counterfeit이 정답이 된다.

a wad of bill 지폐 한 뭉치 counterfeit 위조의 pirate 해적, 약탈자 confidential 기밀의, 은밀한 certificate 증명서, 자격증

---

32 When you cut your finger and it keeps
bleeding, you should _____ a flow
of blood first.

(a) staunch
(b) hold
(c) restrain
(d) prevent

손가락을 베여서 계속 피가 나면 우선 지혈을 해야 한다.

⟳ flow of blood는 흐르는 피를 의미하는 것이므로 이것을 지혈한다는 뜻의 단어를 찾아야 한다. 모두 막는다는 뜻이 있지만 특히 지혈을 한다는 의미로는 staunch가 쓰인다.

bleed 출혈하다 staunch 지혈하다 restrain 억누르다, 억제하다

33 You've all skinned a knee or scraped an elbow at one time or another. After the bleeding stops, you've probably noticed a crusty covering, or scab, that forms over the wound. Once you scrape the skin, special cell fragments called platelets spring into action. Platelets adhere to the cut, forming a clot which keeps more blood from flowing out. The clot contains thread-like stuff called fibrin that helps hold the clot together. Have you ever thought of that scab as a picturesque landscape, a beautiful mountain, or even the Mona Lisa? Probably not. But in its own way, the scab is a masterpiece—an essential part of you body's _____.

(a) fine art
(b) self remedy
(c) martial art
(d) healing art

여러분은 한두 번쯤 무릎이 까지거나, 팔꿈치를 긁힌 적이 있다. 출혈이 멈추고 나면, 상처 위에 생기는 딱딱한 껍질인 딱지를 볼 수 있다. 살갗이 긁히면 혈소판이라는 특별한 세포 조직이 활동을 개시한다. 혈소판은 상처에 달라붙어, 더 이상의 피가 흘러나오지 못하도록 피딱지를 형성한다. 피딱지에는 결합을 도와주는 섬유소란 이름의 실처럼 생긴 물질이 포함되어 있다. 여러분은 딱지를 그림처럼 아름다운 풍경이나 아름다운 산 심지어 모나리자 같다고 생각해본 적이 있는가? 아마도 아닐 것이다. 하지만, 그 자체로 보면 딱지는 훌륭한 작품이다. — 신체 치유 예술의 필수적인 부분으로서 말이다.

⊙ 흔하게 보는 딱지이지만 알고 보면 인체가 <u>스스로를 보호하고 치유하기 위한 유기적 과정</u>이 포함되어 있다는 것이므로 정답은 (d)이다. (a) 미술, (b) 자가 치료, (c) 무술은 모두 정답과 관련이 없다.

skin 껍질을 벗기다 **scrape** 스쳐서 상처를 내다, 긁어내다 **crusty** 껍질이 딱딱하고 두꺼운 **scab** (헌데, 상처의) 딱지 **platelet** 혈소판 **spring into action** 즉각 행동을 개시하다 **adhere to~** ~에 달라붙다 **clot** (피 등의) 엉긴 덩어리 **fibrin** 섬유소 **picturesque** 그림 같은, 아름다운 **in one's own way** 나름대로, 상당히

34 Today, more and more companies are working twenty-four hours a day, seven days a week. Many of them being international trading companies, they often contact with companies in other time zones. Companies must stay open at all times in order to serve and sell products to its global customers. In the past, other people employed as fire-fighters, nurses, or policemen, had work schedules such as 11:00 p.m. to 7:00 a.m., or 3:00 p.m. to 11:00 p.m. However, nowadays the employees of these 24/7 companies have these shifts as well. Influenced by this change, _____.

(a) there are more people who want to work overtime to get a high salary
(b) people prefer some jobs which they can decide their work schedules
(c) local businesses such as supermarkets don't close even late at night
(d) the international trading companies don't want to contact with ones far from their countries

오늘날 점점 더 많은 회사들이 하루 24시간, 일주일에 7일을 일하고 있다. 많은 회사들이 국제 무역 회사이기 때문에, 그 회사들은 종종 다른 시간대에 있는 회사들과 접촉하기도 한다. 회사들은 전 세계에 있는 고객들을 응대하고 그들에게 물건을 팔기 위해서 항상 문을 열어 두어야 한다. 과거에는 소방관이나 간호사, 경찰관과 같은 사람들이 밤 11시에서 아침 7시까지, 또는 오후 3시에서 저녁 11시까지 일하는 작업 스케줄을 가졌다. 그러나 요즈음에는 24시간 7일 일하는 회사의 직원들 또한 이러한 교대근무를 한다. 이러한 변화에 영향을 받아서, 수퍼마켓과 같은 지역 사업체들도 밤 늦게까지 문을 닫지 않는다.

⊙ 오늘날 많은 회사들이 하루 24시간, 일주일에 7일을 일함으로써, 과거에는 특정 직업의 사람들만 밤에도 일을 하였으나 요즈음에는 밤에 일하는 사람들이 많아지고 있다는 내용이다. 빈 칸에는 이러한 변화의 영향으로 나타난 결과를 찾아야 하므로 그러한 회사 때문에 지역의 사업장들도 함께 늦게까지 일하게 되었다(c)는 내용이 가장 적합하다. (a)와 (b)는 그럴 듯하지만 본문의 어디에도 이러한 내용을 유추할 수 있는 단서가 없다.

more and more 점점 더 많은 **time zone** 시간대 **shift** 교대(근무) **employee** 고용인, 종업원

35 The earth balances the radiative equilibrium by emitting thermal infrared radiation after absorbing it from the sun. Various greenhouse gases in the atmosphere don't absorb light of short wavelengths, which comes from the sun, but absorb light of long wavelengths, which the earth gives off, and leave it in the atmosphere. In other words, the greenhouse effect is caused by the build-up of greenhouse gases, which permits light from the sun's rays to warm up the earth, but prevents loss of the heat. Therefore, if the atmosphere didn't exist on Earth, _____.
Calculated by this theory, the earth's surface temperature would drop to about −20 Centigrade.

(a) the earth would emit as much thermal infrared radiation as the sun does
(b) the greenhouse effect would be much worse than what we could imagine
(c) the thermal infrared radiation emitted to the earth's surface would fade away
(d) the sun would emit light of long wavelength as well as light of short wavelength

지구는 태양으로부터 흡수한 뜨거운 적외선 복사열을 방출함으로써 복사평형을 이룬다. 대기 중에 있는 다양한 온실가스들은 태양으로부터 오는 단파의 광선은 흡수하지 않는 반면, 지구가 방출하는 장파의 광선은 흡수하여 대기에 남겨둔다. 말하자면, 온실효과는 온실가스의 축적에서 기인하는 것이다. 왜냐하면 온실가스들이 태양광선이 지구의 온도를 높이는 것은 그대로 두면서 지구 복사열의 손실은 막기 때문이다. 그러므로 만약 지구에 대기가 존재하지 않는다면, 태양이 방출하는 적외선만큼 지구도 그대로 적외선을 방출할 것이다. 이 이론에 따라 추산해 보면, 지구 표면의 온도는 대략 섭씨 영하 20도까지 떨어질 것이다.

○ 대기 중에 있는 온실가스로 인해 지구가 흡수한 적외선 복사열을 전부 방출하지 못하기 때문에 온실효과가 발생하고 현재 지구의 온도가 유지된다. 따라서 지구에 대기가 없다면 태양이 방출하는 적외선의 양과 지구가 방출하는 적외선의 양이 같아지고 온실효과가 일어날 수 없기 때문에 지구의 표면온도는 현저히 떨어질 것이라는 내용이다.

balance ~의 균형(평형)을 잡다(맞추다) radiative 방사성의, 방열하는 equilibrium 평형(상태), 균형 emit (빛, 열기, 향기 등을) 방사하다(=give off), 내뿜다 thermal 열의; 뜨거운 infrared 적외선(의) radiation 방사, 복사; 복사에너지; 방사능 absorb 흡수하다 greenhouse gas 온실가스 atmosphere 대기권 short wavelength 단파 long wavelength 장파 give off (증기, 빛, 냄새 따위를) 내다, 풍기다 build-up 축적, 증강 calculate 계산하다, 산정하다, 추산하다

36 The word "kidult," a coined word of "kid" and "adult," refers to an adult who prefers items that are considered for younger generation and enjoys being part of the activities traditionally designed for children. While many adults live up to the social expectation, an increasing minority live on their childhood memories, looking for ways to find consolation and drive away daily stress. A study indicates that this new social trend is a result of people's desire to flee from the reality full of adult responsibilities. Instead, they choose to live in a fantasy world that is free of keen competition and age stereotypes. Some sociologists ascribe this phenomenon to the self-centered lifestyle of modern people, who are focused on their beliefs rather than on what others think about them.

'kid(어린이)' 와 'adult(성인)' 을 조합해서 만든 신조어인 kidult(어린이 같은 어른)는 어린 세대들을 위한 것이라 여겨지는 품목을 선호하거나 전통적으로 어린이들을 위해 고안된 활동에 참가하는 것을 즐기는 성인을 지칭한다. 많은 성인들이 사회적인 기대에 맞추어 생활하는 반면에 점점 더 많은 소수가 유년의 기억에 기대어 위안을 삼고, 일상의 스트레스를 해소할 방법을 찾고 있다. 한 연구는 이런 새로운 사회적 추세는 성인의 책임감으로 가득한 현실에서 도피하고자 하는 사람들의 욕구에서 비롯된다는 점을 시사한다. (그런 현실) 대신에 치열한 경쟁과 나이에 따른 고정관념이 없는 환상의 세계에서 사는 것을 선택하는 것이다. 몇몇 사회학자들은 이 현상이 다른 사람이 어떻게 생각하느냐보다는 자기 자신의 신념에 집중하는 현대인들의 자기중심적 생활방식에 원인을 돌린다.

○ 글에서 언급된 kidult 현상의 원인은 현대인의 자기중심적 생활방식, 나이에 따른 고정관념에 맞추기를 거부하는 것, 성인으로서의 책임감 등이므로 (c) 사춘기를 늘이고자 하는 경향은 정답이 아니다.

Q Which of the following is NOT the cause of the kidult phenomenon?

(a) Selfishness or focusing on self too much
(b) A refusal to conform to accepted standards
(c) Tendency to have an extended adolescence
(d) Avoidance of taking on adult responsibilities

coined word 신조어 live up to ~에 맞는 생활을 하다, ~에 부끄럽지 않게 행동하다 consolation 위로, 위안 drive away 몰아내다, 쫓아내다 indicate 가리키다, 지적하다, 나타내다 keen 치열한 stereotype 고정관념 ascribe A to B A의 원인을 B에 돌리다 phenomenon 현상

---

37 I've lived in many big ugly cities most of my life but I have to say Seoul is one of the ugliest capital cities in the world. I'm not comparing Seoul with European repositories of architecture such as Paris or Rome. Aesthetically Seoul has the cards stacked up against Beijing, Tokyo and some other Asian capitals. This is mainly due to the apartment complexes that are put up like tombstones. Moreover Seoul is busy razing the labyrinths of old houses and putting up apartment blocks in that area, leaving the city without any indigenous architects. Seoul seems unaware that alternative housing to those matchbox-like apartment blocks exists.

Q What is the main idea of the passage?

(a) The city developers come under suspicion of bribery.
(b) The identical apartment blocks make Seoul an exotic spot.
(c) Those all-look-alike apartment buildings mar the beauty of the city.
(d) Seoul should be a model for other Asian cities in its real estate development.

나는 인생의 대부분을 많은 보기 흉한 대도시에서 살아왔지만, 서울이 세계에서 가장 보기 흉한 수도라고 말할 수밖에 없다. 나는 서울을 파리나 로마와 같은 유럽의 건축의 보고와 비교하는 것이 아니다. 미적으로 볼 때, 서울은 북경, 도쿄 그리고 그 밖의 아시아 수도에 훨씬 열등하다. 이는 주로 마치 묘비마냥 늘어서 있는 아파트 단지들 때문이다. 게다가 서울은 미로처럼 복잡하게 늘어선 오래된 건축물들을 남김없이 무너뜨리고, 그 곳에 아파트 단지들을 세워놓기 바빠서, 결국 그 도시 고유의 건축물은 하나도 남지 않은 곳으로 만들어버린다. 서울시는 그 성냥갑처럼 생긴 아파트 단지 말고 다른 대안의 주거형태가 존재한다는 것을 모르는 듯하다.

○ 서울의 똑같이 생긴 아파트 단지들이 도시 미관을 해친다는 내용이므로 (c)가 정답이다. (a)과 (d)는 언급된 바 없고, (b)는 아파트 단지 때문에 서울이 이국적 장소가 된다는 긍정적인 내용이므로 정답이 될 수 없다.

repository 저장소, 보고 aesthetically 심미적으로, 예술적으로 have the cards stacked up against~ ~에 매우 불리하다, 열등하다 due to~ ~때문에 raze (도시 · 집 등을) 남김없이 파괴하다, 무너뜨리다 labyrinth 미로, (건물 등의) 복잡한 거리 tombstone 묘석, 묘비 indigenous 토착의, (그 지역) 고유의 bribery 뇌물 행위 mar 외관을 망치다, 훼손하다

38 According to researchers who have studied how to save energy in the kitchen, washing dishes by hand uses 37 percent more water than using a dishwasher. However, there is a way to save water when you wash dishes by hand. If you wash dishes in one sink with soapy water first, then rinse them in another sink with the faucet closed, you'll use less than half the amount of water you would have used with a dishwasher. Moreover, you can also save energy by using a microwave not a stove when you need to reheat or defrost small amounts of food. In the case of large amounts of food, however, a stove is more efficient than a microwave.

Q What is the main idea of the passage?

(a) Using machine requires much energy all the time.

(b) There are various ways to save energy in the kitchen.

(c) It is very dangerous to use an electric machine in the kitchen.

(d) Women who spend more time in the kitchen have to play a major role in saving energy.

부엌에서 에너지를 절약할 수 있는 방법을 연구해 온 사람들에 따르면, 손으로 설거지를 하면 식기세척기를 사용할 때보다 물을 37퍼센트 더 사용한다고 한다. 그러나 직접 설거지를 할 때에도 물을 아끼는 방법이 있다. 먼저 싱크대 한 곳에서 비눗물로 그릇을 닦고 난 다음, 수도꼭지를 잠근 채 다른 싱크대에서 그릇을 헹구면 식기세척기를 사용할 때 쓰는 양의 절반 이하로 물을 사용하게 될 것이다. 게다가 적은 양의 음식을 다시 데우거나 녹일 필요가 있을 때 화덕이 아니라 전자레인지를 사용하면 에너지를 또한 절약할 수 있다. 하지만 많은 양의 음식일 경우에는 전자레인지보다 화덕이 더 효율적이다.

● 설거지를 하는 방법에 따라서, 재가열하거나 녹이는 음식의 양에 따라서 에너지를 절약할 수 있는 방법이 다양하다는 내용이므로 (b)가 정답이 된다. (a)는 기계를 사용하는 것이 항상 에너지를 더 많이 사용하는 것은 아니므로 틀린 내용이고, (c)와 (d)는 본문에 언급되지 않고 있다.

dishwasher 식기세척기 soapy water 비눗물 rinse 헹구다 faucet 수도꼭지 microwave 전자레인지 stove 요리용 화덕, 화로 reheat 다시 가열하다 defrost (냉동식품을) 녹이다 an electric machine 전기기계

39 'Culture shock' is a term used to describe periods of frustration, anxiety, melancholy, and loneliness which someone experiences when he or she lives in a foreign country. It is caused by unfamiliarity with the new surroundings and the inability to communicate with local people. Before feeling disillusionment with the new country, it is very important for newcomers who suffer from culture shock to realize that it is one of the four stages of cultural adjustment. The four stages of cultural adjustment are excitement, culture shock, recovery, and stability.

Q   What is the main idea of the passage?

(a) People should try not to suffer from culture shock if possible.
(b) People don't have to experience all of the cultural adjustment stages.
(c) Local people have responsibilities to help newcomers not to feel culture shock.
(d) Culture shock should be considered as a natural process experienced in a new country.

'문화충격' 이란 어떤 사람이 외국에서 살 때 좌절, 근심, 우울, 그리고 외로움을 느끼는 기간을 나타낼 때 사용되는 용어이다. 이것은 새로운 환경에 낯설고 지역주민들과 의사소통을 할 수 없기 때문에 일어난다. 문화충격으로 고생하는 이주자들이 새로운 나라에 환멸을 느끼기 전에, 문화충격은 문화적응의 4단계 중 하나라는 것을 인식하는 것이 매우 중요하다. 문화적응의 4단계는 흥분, 문화충격, 회복, 그리고 안정이다.

◐ 문화충격은 문화적응의 4단계 중 한 단계로서 새로운 나라에서 겪게 되는 자연스러운 과정으로 인식되어야 한다는 내용의 (d)가 정답이 된다. 이것은 문화적응의 각 단계별 특징을 설명하기 전에 나와 있는 문장 – it is very important for newcomers who suffer from culture shock to realize that it is one of the four stages of cultural adjustment – 이 결정적인 힌트가 된다. 따라서 (a)가능하면 문화충격을 겪지 않도록 노력해야 한다든가, (b)문화적응의 모든 단계를 다 경험할 필요가 없다든가, (c)새로 온 사람들이 문화충격을 느끼지 않도록 지역주민들이 도울 책임이 있다는 내용은 글의 요지가 될 수 없다.

frustration 좌절 melancholy 우울 unfamiliarity 생소함 surrounding 환경, 상황 inability 무능 disillusionment 환멸 newcomer 새로 온 사람들 suffer from ~로 괴로워하다, 고생하다 adjustment 적응 stability 안정

---

40 In the Postwar years, Hemingway lived in Paris and became a member of expatriate Americans. (a) However, he used his experiences as a reporter during the Spanish Civil War and wrote his most ambitious novel, For Whom the Bell Tolls. (b) His straightforward prose and his predilection for understatement are particularly valuable in his short stories. (c) Among his later works, another outstanding short novel is, The Old Man and the Sea, the story of an old fisherman's long and lonely struggle with a fish and the sea, and victory in defeat. (d) He also liked to portray soldiers and hunters whose courage and honesty are set against the vicious modern society, and who in this confrontation lose hope and faith.

전후 헤밍웨이는 파리에 살았고 미국 추방자들의 모임의 구성원이 되었다. (a)그러나 그는 스페인 내전에서 종군기자의 경험을 살려서 그의 야심찬 소설인 '누구를 위하여 종은 울리나'를 썼다.(b) 그의 직설적 산문이나 간략한 표현의 애용은 그의 단편소설에서 두드러진 특징이다. (c) 그의 후반기 소설 중 또 다른 눈에 띄는 단편소설은 나이든 어부의 물고기와 바다와의 외롭고 긴 투쟁을 결국 승리로 이끈 이야기인 '노인과 바다'이다. (d) 그는 또한 타락한 세상과 투쟁하고, 그런 대립 중에 희망을 잃는 군인이나 사냥꾼을 묘사하는 것을 좋아했다.

◐ (b)의 내용은 헤밍웨이 소설 문체의 전반적 특징으로 (a) (c)사이에 약간 거리가 먼 내용으로 들어가 있다. 또한 문제의 힌트는 (c)의 another novel과 (d)의 He also~의 내용으로 글 (c)와 (d)가 (a) 내용의 연장임을 보여준다.

expatriate 국외 추방자, 추방하다 straightforward 정직한, 솔직한, 간단한 predilection 편애, 애용 understatement 간략한 표현 portray 묘사하다, 묘사 vicious 사악한, 타락한 confrontation 대면, 대결

1 **M** The toilet bowl is clogged again.
　　W _____

(a) It will be the day.
(b) I had a ball.
(c) Where is the rest room?
(d) I'll call a plumber.

M: 변기가 또 막혔어.
W: 배관공에게 전화할게.

○ 변기가 또 막혔다는 남자의 질문에 적절한 응답으로는 배관공에게 전화하겠다고 말하는 (d)가 된다. (a)는 '설마, 그럴 리가' '그런 일은 있을 수 없다' 라는 뜻이며, (b)는 '즐거운 시간을 보냈다' 는 뜻으로 파티나 행사를 다녀온 이후에 쓸 수 있는 표현이다. (c)는 '화장실이 어디에요?' 라는 뜻으로 toilet bowl이라는 단어 때문에 (c)를 정답으로 고르지 않도록 주의하자.

toilet bowl 변기 **clog** ~을 막다 **have a ball** 즐거운 시간을 보내다 **plumber** 배관공

---

2 **M** Is that clear to you?
　　W _____

(a) It is not that clean.
(b) I'm sorry. Please be more specific.
(c) Yes. It is a breeze.
(d) Don't pick on me.

M: 무슨 말인지 알겠어?
W: 미안. 좀 더 자세히 이야기해 줘.

○ clear는 날씨가 맑고 청명할 때, 안색이 밝고 투명할 때, 목소리가 청아할 때뿐만 아니라 어떠한 사실이나 설명이 명백하고 분명할 때에도 쓰이는 다의어이다. (a)의 경우 그리 깨끗하지 않다는 뜻으로 clear와 clean을 혼동하지 않도록 주의하자. specific은 '구체적인, 자세한' 의 뜻이 있어서 이해하지 못했으니 좀 더 구체적으로 말해달라는 뜻이므로 정답이며 (c)는 '식은 죽 먹기' 라는 뜻의 이디엄이다. (d)는 '나를 괴롭히지 마, 못살게 굴지 마' 라는 뜻이다.

specific 특정한, 구체적인, 자세한 **It's a breeze** 식은 죽 먹기 **pick on** ~을 괴롭히다, 못살게 굴다

---

3 **W** How come you're so late?
　　M _____

(a) I can relate to that.
(b) I couldn't sleep a wink.
(c) I was beside myself.
(d) Sorry, something's come up at work.

W: 왜 이렇게 늦었어?
M: 미안. 회사에서 일이 생겨서.

○ 왜 이렇게 늦었느냐는 여자의 질문에 적절한 대답을 고르는 것으로 (a)는 '공감이 된다. 이해가 된다' 는 뜻으로 정답과는 거리가 멀고, (b)는 '한숨도 자지 못했다' 는 뜻이며 (c)는 '이성을 잃었다, 흥분했다' 는 뜻으로 상황과 맞지 않고 (d)는 '갑자기 회사에 무슨 일이 생겼다' 는 뜻으로 왜 늦었는지에 대한 질문에 가장 적절한 대답이 된다.

How come...? 왜...? **relate** ~을 관련짓다, 관계하다 **not sleep a wink** 한숨도 못자다 **beside oneself** 이성을 잃고

4

M What time does your flight arrive?

W 11:30 P.M. But I don't know how to get to the hotel.

M I know what you mean. It's too late.

W _____

(a) I think I'll have jet lag for a while.

(b) Speaking of that, can you please pick me up at the airport?

(c) I hope not so.

(d) Can you come home an hour earlier?

M: 몇 시 비행기로 오세요?

W: 밤 11시 30분이요. 그런데 호텔에 어떻게 가야할 지 모르겠어요.

M: 무슨 말인지 알겠네요. 너무 시간이 늦어서.

W: 말이 나와서 그런데, 공항에 마중 나오실 수 있나요?

○ 비행기 도착시간이 너무 늦다는 남자의 말에 여자가 할 수 있는 응답으로는 (b) 공항에 마중 나올 수 있느냐는 질문이 적절하다. (a)는 잠시 동안 시차증에 시달릴 것 같다는 뜻으로 남자의 마지막 대사와 잘 연결되지 않고 (c)는 그러지 않기를 바란다는 말로 역시 적절치 않으며, (d)는 한 시간 일찍 집에 올 수 있냐는 물음으로 late와 연관시켜 earlier를 씀으로써 혼동을 주려는 보기이다.

jet lag 시차증 for a while 잠시 동안 speaking of that 말이 나온 김에 pick sb up ~을 마중 나가다

5

M Excuse me.

W What can I help?

M Could you break a hundred?

W _____

(a) How much do I owe you?

(b) How would you like it?

(c) It is broken.

(d) Everything has a price.

M: 실례합니다.

W: 무엇을 도와드릴까요?

M: 100달러를 잔돈으로 바꿔줄 수 있나요?

W: 어떻게 바꿔드릴까요?

○ 100달러 지폐를 잔돈으로 바꾸려고 하는 남자의 물음에 여자의 적절한 응답을 찾아야 한다. (a)는 물건을 사거나 서비스를 이용하고 나서 얼마인지 물을 때 많이 쓰는 표현이며 (b)는 돈을 얼마짜리로 바꿀 것인지를 묻는 질문이므로 정답이 된다. (c)는 break를 이용한 함정으로 '그것은 깨졌다'라는 뜻이므로 관계가 없으며 (d)는 모든 일에는 대가가 따른다는 뜻이므로 역시 정답과는 거리가 멀다.

break (단위가 큰돈을) 쪼개다, 바꾸다 owe ~에게 빚지고 있다 broken 깨진, 부서진 Everything has a price. 모든 일에는 대가가 따른다.

6

M What took you so long?

W I'm sorry to have kept you waiting. There was an accident on the way here.

M What? Are you okay?

W _____

(a) Don't mention it.

(b) Yes. It was just a fender-bender.

(c) That's too bad.

(d) Couldn't be better.

M: 왜 이렇게 늦었어?

W: 기다리게 해서 미안해. 여기 오는 길에 사고가 있었어.

M: 뭐라고? 괜찮아?

W: 응. 그냥 가벼운 접촉사고였어.

○ 여자가 사고 때문에 늦었다고 하자 남자가 여자의 상태를 묻고 있다. (a)는 고맙다는 인사에 대한 대답으로 'You're welcome.'과 같은 뜻이다. (b)는 가벼운 접촉사고였다는 뜻으로 많이 다치지 않았다는 뉘앙스가 있으므로 정답이 된다. (c)는 너무 안됐다는 뜻으로 여자의 대사로는 적절치 않다. (d)는 이보다 더 좋을 수 없다는 뜻으로 안부 인사에 대해 아주 잘 지내고 있다는 의미로 쓰인다.

Don't mention it. (감사에 대한 대답으로) 천만에요. fender-bender 접촉사고

7

M You ran through a red light. I'm going to give you a ticket.

W Come on. Please give me a break. I'll be more careful next time.

M Can I have your driver's license, please?

W I don't have it with me. I left my purse behind.

M Then tell me your resident registration number.

W Are you really going to give me a ticket? Please let me go this time. It won't happen again.

M I'm sorry but I can't help it.

Q What's going to happen next?

(a) She'll go home to take her purse.
(b) She'll call her husband to ask for help.
(c) She'll get a ticket for running a light.
(d) She'll get a refund for the tickets.

M: 정지신호를 위반하셨습니다. 딱지를 끊겠습니다.

W: 제발요. 한 번 봐주세요. 다음번에는 조심할게요.

M: 운전면허증 좀 보여주시겠어요?

W: 안 가져왔는데요. 지갑을 놓고 왔어요.

M: 그러면 주민등록번호를 말씀해주세요.

W: 정말 딱지 끊으시게요? 제발 이번만 보내주세요. 다신 안 그럴게요.

M: 죄송합니다만 어쩔 수가 없네요.

○ 다음에 일어날 상황을 묻고 있다. 여자가 신호 위반 후에 경찰에게 봐달라고 조르고 있지만 경찰은 끝내 안 된다고 하고 있다 따라서 (a) 지갑을 가지러 간다, (b) 남편에게 전화를 걸어 도움을 구한다는 상황에 맞지 않으므로 정답이 될 수 없다. 따라서 (c) 신호 위반 딱지를 발부받는가가 정답이 되고 (d)의 경우 ticket의 다른 의미, 즉 공연 티켓 등과 같은 것을 환불받는다는 뜻으로 혼동을 주기 위한 함정이다.

run through a red light 신호를 위반하다 driver's license 운전면허증 leave sth behind ~을 놓고 오다 resident registration number 주민등록번호

8

M How is your new roommate?
W She drives me crazy.
M What's the matter?
W She's always making loud noises at midnight. And she picks a fight whenever I do something.
M Why don't you have a heart to heart with her?
W I already tried, but it didn't work.
M Why don't you complain to the manager in that case?
W I think I will.

Q What can you infer from the dialogue?

(a) She works together with her new roommate.
(b) She's going to change her roommate.
(c) He advises her to talk to the manager.
(d) He will be her new roommate.

M: 새로운 룸메이트는 어때?

W: 그 애 때문에 미치겠어.

M: 무슨 문젠데?

W: 한밤중에 만날 시끄럽게 굴어. 그리고 내가 뭘 하려고만 하면 시비를 걸어.

M: 그 애와 툭 터놓고 이야기해보지 그래?

W: 이미 시도는 해 봤어. 하지만 소용이 없었어.

M: 그러면 매니저에게 하소연해 봐.

W: 그래야 할 것 같아.

○ 여자의 새로운 룸메이트에 대해 이야기하고 있다. 새로운 룸메이트와 함께 일하고 있는지는 이 대화만으로는 알 수 없으므로 (a)는 정답이 될 수 없다. 마지막에 남자가 매니저에게 이야기해 보라고 했고 여자가 그래야겠다고 했으나 룸메이트를 바꿀 것인지는 알 수 없으므로 (b) 역시 정답이라고 하기 힘들다. 남자의 마지막 대사를 통해 (c)가 답이 될 수 있다는 것을 알 수 있고 (d)는 남자가 여자의 새 룸메이트가 된다는 이야기는 언급된 적이 없으므로 정답이 아니다.

drive sb crazy ~을 미치게 하다 pick a fight 시비를 걸다 have a heart to heart with sb ~와 툭 터놓고 이야기하다

9 M Hello. I'm calling about your ad in paper. I'm interested in the one bedroom apartment. Is it still available?

W Yes. The monthly rent is $400 and a $300 security deposit is required.

M Well, the price is okay. How about the location? I need to move to the one near the subway or bus stop.

W Don't worry. It takes only 5 minutes to the subway station on foot.

M That's perfect. Can I move in sometime around next month?

W That's possible.

M May I come over tomorrow to take a look?

Q What can you infer from the dialogue?

(a) He will meet the woman tomorrow.
(b) He will buy the apartment next month.
(c) He will make a contract tomorrow.
(d) He will move out of the apartment next month.

M: 안녕하세요. 신문 광고 보고 전화 드립니다. 침실 하나짜리 아파트에 관심이 있는데요. 아직도 유효한가요?

W: 네, 한 달 임대료가 400 달러이구요, 보증금이 300달러입니다.

M: 가격은 괜찮네요. 위치는 어떻습니까? 지하철이나 버스 정류장 가까운 곳으로 이사 가야 하거든요.

W: 걱정하지 마세요. 도보로 지하철역까지 5분밖에 걸리지 않아요.

M: 아주 좋네요. 다음 달쯤에 이사 들어갈 수 있나요?

W: 가능합니다.

M: 집을 보러 내일 들러도 되나요?

○ 남자의 마지막 대사를 주목하자. 집에 대한 설명을 들은 후 한 번 살펴보기 위해 들른다고 했으므로 남자는 여자를 내일 만나게 될 것이다. 따라서 정답은 (a)이다. 다음 달에 이사를 갈 예정이지 산다고 하지 않았으므로 (b)는 정답이 아니고, 내일 계약을 할지는 미정이므로 (c) 역시 정답이라 할 수 없다.

be interested in ~에 관심이 있다. available 이용 가능한, 유효한 security deposit 보증금 on foot 걸어서 contract 계약

---

10 More than 50 police emergency phones are located around campus. Without dialing, the caller can immediately contact with the University Police. The location of the caller is automatically recorded and response is immediate. University Police may also be reached by calling 268-2723, or dialing 8-2723 on any phone around campus. In response to your call, the dispatcher will send police where you are as soon as possible.

Q Which of the following is correct?

(a) There are 15 emergency phones around campus.
(b) The caller doesn't need to dial to contact with the University Police.
(c) The caller can reach the University Police on a few designated phones.
(d) The caller has to press the red button to record the location.

캠퍼스 안에 50대 이상의 경찰 긴급전화가 비치되어 있습니다. 다이얼을 누르지 않고도 발신자가 즉시 대학 경찰과 연락을 할 수 있습니다. 발신자의 위치는 자동적으로 기록되며 즉각 응답을 받을 수 있습니다. 또한 캠퍼스의 모든 전화기를 이용하여 268-2723으로 전화를 하거나 8-2723번으로 걸면 대학 경찰과 연락할 수 있습니다. 전화를 받는 즉시 급파원이 가능한 빨리 발신자가 있는 위치로 경찰을 보낼 것입니다.

○ (a)에서는 50과 15의 발음상의 비슷한 점을 이용하여 혼동을 주고 있다. (b)는 두 번째 문장에서 without dialing이라고 했으므로 정답이며, 캠퍼스 내의 어떤 전화기로도 대학 경찰과 연락할 수 있다고 했으므로 (c)는 정답이 아니다. 위치는 자동으로 기록된다고 했으므로 (d) 역시 정답이 아니다.

automatically 자동적으로 dispatcher (응급차, 요원들을 보내는) 급파원 designated 지정된

11 Everyday we wash our hair with shampoo. However, excessive washing of hair can be damaging, so it should be done appropriately. Shampoo cleans the scalp and hair strands by removing dandruff. If you wash your hair daily, be sure the shampoo contains vitamins and minerals and is designed for your type of hair. Using the following five techniques can help keep your hair healthy and clean.

Q What is likely to follow this passage?

(a) How to remove dandruff
(b) Some useful techniques to keep healthy hair
(c) Why you shouldn't wash your hair daily
(d) How to choose the shampoo right for your type of hair

우리는 매일 샴푸로 머리를 감습니다. 그러나 머리를 과도하게 감으면 손상이 갈 수 있기 때문에 적정선을 유지해야 합니다. 샴푸는 비듬을 없애줌으로써 두피와 머리카락을 깨끗하게 해줍니다. 머리를 매일 감으면, 샴푸에 비타민과 미네랄이 들어있는지, 자신의 머리 타입에 맞게 만들어진 것인지 확인해야 합니다. 다음 다섯 가지 테크닉으로 당신의 머리를 건강하고 깨끗하게 유지할 수 있습니다.

○ 다음에 이어질 내용을 묻고 있으므로 마지막 부분에 주의해서 들어야 한다. 머리카락을 건강하고 깨끗하게 유지할 수 있는 테크닉 다섯 가지에 대한 언급이 있었으므로 정답은 (b)가 된다.

excessive 과도한, 지나친 scalp 두피 dandruff 비듬

---

12 Some researchers have suggested that power unfairness cannot explain about all gender-related differences in speech. Dean and Ross note that some difficulties in cross-gender communication parallel difficulties in cross-cultural communication. The basic idea is that interlocutors have good intentions but do not always operate on the same presuppositions. As an example, they cite the use of minimal responses, which women generally use more than men. They claim that women interpret minimal responses as an indication that the interlocutor is listening. On the other hand, men interpret them as an indication of agreement.

Q What can be inferred from the result of the research?

(a) Women think men are listening with everything they say.
(b) Men think women are listening with everything they say.
(c) There are more difficulties in cross-gender communication than in cross-cultural communication.
(d) There is an unintentional misunderstanding between the men and the women.

몇몇 연구자들은 언어 능력에 있어서 힘의 불균형이 성별과 관련된 모든 차이점의 이유가 될 수 없다고 제시했다. 딘과 로스는 성별에 따른 의사소통의 어려움이 다문화간 의사소통의 어려움과 유사하다고 말한다. 기본 생각은 대화자들이 좋은 의도를 가지고 있어도 항상 같은 가정대로 움직이지 않는다는 것이다. 한 예로서 그들은 최소반응 사용을 인용하는데, 이것은 일반적으로 여성들이 남성들보다 더 많이 사용한다. 그들은 여성들이 최소반응을 대화자가 경청하고 있다는 표시로 해석한다고 주장한다. 반면 남성들은 최소반응을 동의의 표시로 해석한다.

○ 주요 핵심 내용은 남자와 여자가 서로 최소반응을 다르게 해석한다는 것이다. 이것은 의도와 상관없이 의사소통에 있어서 성별 차이에 따른 오해가 발생할 수 있다는 뜻이므로 정답은 (d)가 된다.

gender-related 성별과 관련한 parallel ~에 필적하다, ~와 유사하다 interlocutor 대화자, 대담자 presupposition 추측, 가정, 전제 조건 interpret 해석하다, 판단하다 indication 표시, 징후 unintentional 고의가 아닌

13 A What would you do if you _____ in her shoes?

    B Well, I would definitely not sign the contract.

(a) are
(b) will be
(c) were
(d) was

A: 만약 네가 그녀의 입장이라면 어떻게 하겠니?
B: 글쎄, 나라면 절대 그 계약서에 서명하지 않겠어.

🔵 'be in one's shoes' 는 '〜의 입장이 되다' 라는 뜻의 표현이고, 위 대화 속 문장에서는 if 가정법과 함께 쓰였다. 따라서 be동사의 가정문에서의 형태인 'were'가 적절하다.

definitely 절대로 **contract** 계약

---

14 A _____ it takes to get there?

    B About one and a half hours.

(a) Do you think how long
(b) How long you think
(c) How do you think long
(d) How long do you think

A: 거기까지 가는 데 시간이 얼마나 걸릴 것 같아요?
B: 한 시간 반이요.

🔵 의미상 '얼마나 시간이 걸릴 것 같은가?' 를 묻는 표현이 빈 칸에 와야 하는데, 'do you think' 는 통상적으로 의문사를 앞으로 끌어내서 표현하기 때문에 How+형용사+조동사+주어+동사' 의 어순을 따른다. 따라서 (d)가 맞다.

---

15 A How about the bank robbery you mentioned last time?

    B The witness insisted that the man _____.

(a) wear a black mask
(b) should wear a black mask
(c) wore a black mask
(d) wearing a black mask

A: 전에 언급했던 은행 강도사건은 어떻게 됐습니까?
B: 목격자는 그가 검은 복면을 썼다고 주장했어요.

🔵 주절에 insist가 있다고 해도 종속절의 내용이 당위성이 아니라 일반적인 사실을 나타내고 있으므로 that 절의 시제를 주절과 일치시킨다. 그래서 (c)가 맞다.

robbery 강도사건 **mention** 언급하다 **witness** 목격자

---

16 A Thank you for inviting us to this gorgeous dinner.

    B Help yourself _____ all food.

(a) to
(b) at
(c) as
(d) for

A: 이렇게 훌륭한 만찬에 초대해주셔서 감사합니다.
B: 마음껏 음식을 드세요.

🔵 'help oneself to (음식)' 은 '〜를 마음껏 드세요' 라는 뜻의 표현이다.

gorgeous 훌륭한, 멋진

---

17 Opened in 1930, Koala Park in New South Wales was the first private koala sanctuary and _____ the late Noel Burnet.

(a) founded on
(b) was founded by
(c) which was founded on
(d) founding by

1930년에 개장한 뉴사우스 웨일즈의 코알라 파크는 최초의 사유(私有) 코알라 은신처인데, 고 Noel Burnet에 의해 지어졌다.

🔵 Koala Park가 고(故) Noel Burnet에 의해 지어졌다는 문장이므로 (b)was founded by 가 알맞다.

late 최근에 죽은, 고(故) **sanctuary** 피신처, 은신처

18 It's the time when _____ on the road and the traffic is really bad.

   (a) the most cars are there
   (b) there are the most cars
   (c) there is the most cars
   (d) the most cars is there

지금이 가장 많은 차가 거리에 나오고 교통이 제일 안 좋을 때이다.

◑ 제한적 용법으로 쓰인 관계부사 when 다음에는 주어와 동사가 순서대로 와야 한다. 따라서 (a)가 가장 적절하다.

---

19 The image charges were taken into account using a fast multiple method modification _____ to the geometry of the system.

   (a) adapted specially
   (b) special adapt
   (c) specially adapt
   (d) special adaptation

그 영상에 관한 일은 시스템의 구조에 특별히 적합한, 신속하고 다양한 조절 방법에 의해 참작되었다.

◑ 바로 앞에 나오는 modification에 대한 수식어구가 필요하다. 또한 문장 뒷부분이 '특별히 시스템의 구조에 맞춰진'으로 해석되므로 동사의 수동형을 취하고 specially(부사)가 이를 수식하는 형태의 답안인 (a)가 가장 적절하다.

take ~ into account 고려하다, 참작하다 multiple 다양한 modification 조절 geometry 기하학, 구조

---

20 There was even a scheme to have an East Bristol Radial Road, _____ the houses in Fisher Road.

   (a) which have built behind
   (b) that would have built behind
   (c) which would have been built behind
   (d) that would have been built behind

Fisher Road의 집 뒤에 만들어지려던 East Bristol 방사상 도로의 설계안이 있었다.

◑ 'Fisher Road 에 있는 집 뒤에 지어지려고 했던~'의 뜻으로 해석하는 것이 가장 적절하다. 빈 칸 앞에 콤마 다음에는 계속적 용법에 사용되는 관계대명사 which가 쓰였고 의미상으로도 가장 적절한 (c)가 답이다.

scheme 설계 radial 방사상

---

21 (a) A : Dick, you know what? I went to a film festival over the weekend.
   (b) B : Wow, did you enjoy all the wonderful movies?
   (c) A : Yes, especially, I could meet many celebrities.
   (d) B : I wish I were there.

A: Dick, 그거 알아? 나 주말 동안 영화제에 갔었어.
B: 와, 훌륭한 영화들을 많이 즐기고 왔니?
A: 특히, 많은 유명 인사들을 만나볼 수 있었어.
B: 내가 거기 있었더라면 좋았을 걸.

◑ (d)에서, 과거의 사실에 대한 반대 내용(소망)을 표현한 가정법이므로 가정법 과거 표현인 were가 아닌 과거완료 형태 had been there가 옳다.

celebrity 유명인, 연예인

22 (a) One of the features symbolized the Turkish way of life is the Turkish Baths, Hamam which is healthy and refreshing. (b) There have been many places in Turkey where they show daily and historical life. (c) They emphasized on cleanliness because of Islam. (d) So, many public bath houses have been built everywhere since Medieval times, and they retain an architectural and historical importance.

터키의 생활 방식을 잘 상징하는 것 중 하나는 건강에 좋고 산뜻한 터키탕, 하맘이다. 터키에는 그들의 일상과 역사적인 삶을 보여주는 많은 장소들이 있다. 그들은 이슬람 문화 때문에 청결을 강조했다. 따라서 많은 공공 목욕탕들이 중세 이후로 곳곳에 지어져왔고, 그것들은 역사적이고 건축학적인 중요성을 간직하고 있다.

○ (a)에서 One of the features를 꾸미는 부분이 '터키의 생활 방식을 상징하는~' 으로 해석되므로 과거분사 symbolized는 적절하지 않고, 능동의 의미인 현재분사 symbolizing으로 바뀌어야 한다.

emphasize 강조하다

VOCABULARY • P.67

23 A Hey! What are you doing here?
  B I'm _____ to meet my mother here, but she would be a bit late.

(a) supposed
(b) meant
(c) guessed
(d) promised

A: 야! 여기서 뭐 하고 있어?
B: 여기서 엄마를 만나기로 했는데, 조금 늦으신대.

○ 상황으로 미루어보아 B가 엄마와 만나기로 약속이 되어 있음을 알 수 있다. be supposed to는 '~하기로 되어 있다 '는 뜻으로 빈 칸에 적절한 단어는 supposed가 된다. promise의 경우 다짐을 뜻하는 약속으로서 누군가와 가볍게 만날 약속을 한다든지 하는 상황과는 어울리지 않는다.

be supposed to ~하기로 되어 있다

---

24 A Have you heard Michael was expelled from his school?
  B Yes. He was _____ out of school for taking an illegal drug.

(a) got
(b) pitched
(c) kicked
(d) fired

A: 마이클이 학교에서 퇴학당했다는 이야기 들었어?
B: 응. 불법 마약을 복용해서 학교에서 퇴학당했대.

○ 마이클이 학교에서 퇴학당했다고 했고 B는 퇴학당한 이유를 말하고 있다. expel과 비슷한 뜻으로 쓰이는 표현을 찾아야 하는데 kick out이 바로 '~을 내쫓다' 라는 뜻으로 쓰인다.

expel ~을 내쫓다, 퇴학시키다 **kick sb out of...** ~을 ...에서 내쫓다

---

25 A When should I submit my resume?
  B Please _____ it in when you come for an interview.

(a) offer
(b) propose
(c) introduce
(d) turn

A: 언제 이력서를 제출하면 됩니까?
B: 면접 보러 오실 때 제출해 주세요.

○ submit과 같은 뜻으로 쓰이는 표현을 찾아야 한다. submit은 '~을 제출하다 '라는 뜻으로 'turn in' 도 역시 같은 뜻으로 쓰인다.

submit ~을 제출하다 **turn sth in** ~을 제출하다, 잠자리에 들다

26 **A** What's your attitude towards layoffs in the company? I think it's an unavoidable situation.

B I don't think so. It is a _____ measure, I think.

(a) difficult
(b) natural
(c) harsh
(d) fair

A: 회사의 해고 조치에 대한 당신의 태도는 무엇입니까? 저는 피할 수 없는 상황이라고 생각해요.
B: 저는 생각이 다릅니다. 너무 가혹한 조치라고 생각해요.

⟳ A는 해고가 어쩔 수 없는 상황이라고 하지만 B는 이에 대해 다른 의견을 가지고 있다. 따라서 가혹하다거나 너무하다는 뜻의 단어가 와야 하는데 보기 중 가장 적절한 답은 harsh라고 할 수 있다.

layoff 해고 **unavoidable** 피할 수 없는 **harsh** 가혹한, 무자비한 **fair** 공정한

---

27 **A** Can I use your phone, please? Mine isn't working.

B Be my _____.

(a) guest
(b) visitor
(c) treat
(d) hand

A: 네 전화기 좀 써도 될까? 내 전화기가 작동이 안 되네.
B: 그렇게 해.

⟳ 물건을 빌릴 때 개의치 말고 마음껏 쓰라고 할 때에는 Be my guest라는 표현을 쓴다. 관용적으로 굳어진 표현이므로 표현 자체로 알아두는 것이 중요하다.

Be my guest 그렇게 하세요. 마음껏 쓰세요.

---

28 People had hoped it would keep raining across the country, enough to relieve the drought, but just _____ rain sprinkled the area.

(a) heavy
(b) torrential
(c) regular
(d) sporadic

사람들은 가뭄을 해소할 만큼 충분한 비가 전국적으로 오길 바랐지만 단지 산발적인 비가 그 지역에 흩뿌렸다.

⟳ but을 기준으로 앞뒤가 반대의 내용이 되어야 한다. 앞에서 가뭄을 해소할 만큼 충분한 비가 오기를 바랐다는 내용이 나왔고 이후에 but이라는 접속사가 나왔으므로 충분한 비가 오지 않았다는 내용이 와야 한다. 따라서 정답은 '산발적'이라는 뜻을 가진 sporadic이 된다.

relieve ~을 경감하다. 덜다 **drought** 가뭄 **sporadic** 때때로 일어나는, 산발성의 **sprinkle** 흩뿌리다 **torrential** 억수 같은, 맹렬한

---

29 Keep your _____ in case you want to return or exchange the items you bought.

(a) recipes
(b) recipients
(c) receipts
(d) receivers

구매한 물건을 환불하거나 교환하고 싶을 때를 대비해서 영수증을 보관하세요.

⟳ 물건을 환불하거나 교환할 때 필요한 것이므로 영수증을 뜻하는 receipt가 정답이 된다. 나머지 보기들은 형태상 비슷한 단어들을 통해 혼동을 주기 위한 것이다.

receipt 영수증 **recipe** 조리법, 처방전 **recipient** 수취인, 수령인 **receiver** 수취인, 수령인

30 When the products that you've ordered are out of _____, we notify you via text message.

(a) goods
(b) products
(c) selling
(d) stock

주문하신 상품들이 재고가 없을 경우에 문자 메시지로 알려드립니다.

◑ '재고가 없다' 라고 할 때에는 out of stock이라는 표현을 쓴다. goods나 products 모두 상품을 뜻하지만 out of 와 함께 잘 쓰이지 않는다.

out of stock 품절되어 notify 통지하다, 알리다 via ~을 통해서, 경유해서

---

31 Since they started selling items at _____ prices, the number of customers decreased because they couldn't get any discounts.

(a) fixed
(b) limit
(c) bottom
(d) negotiable

그들이 상품을 고정 가격에 판매하기 시작한 이후로 고객의 숫자가 감소했는데, 그 이유는 고객들이 할인을 받을 수 없기 때문이다.

◑ 할인을 받을 수 없다고 했으므로 '고정된 가격' 이 오는 것이 자연스럽다. 따라서 정답은 fixed이다. bottom prices나 negotiable prices의 경우 고객의 숫자가 감소할 리가 없으므로 문맥상 어울리지 않는다.

fixed price 정가, 고정 가격 negotiable 협의할 수 있는

---

32 You should not leave the clothes in the dryer for too long, or they will start to _____ .

(a) decrease
(b) small
(c) shrink
(d) shrivel

건조기에 빨래를 너무 오래 두지 않아야 한다. 그렇지 않으면 옷이 수축될 수 있다.

◑ 빨래를 건조기에 오래 넣어둘 경우 줄어든다는 표현이 오는 것이 자연스럽다. decrease의 경우 수치, 가치 등이 하락할 때 쓰이므로 빨래가 줄어든다고 할 때에는 어색한 표현이 된다. 옷이 줄어든다고 할 때에는 shrink를 쓰는 것이 가장 적절하다.

dryer 건조기 shrink 줄어들다, 수축하다 shrivel 시들다, 말라죽다

33 Ramadan, a Muslim religious observance, is a "month of blessing" marked by fasting, self-sacrifice and prayers. During Ramadan, the ninth month of Islamic calendar, the fast is observed every day while the sun is up. Muslims around the world get up before true dawn to eat Suhoor, the pre-dawn meal and have to stop eating and drinking until the fourth prayer of the day, Maghrib (sunset), is due. _____. Hunger and thirst remind Muslims of the suffering of the poor. Fasting is also a chance to practice self-discipline and to purify body and mind.

(a) Fasting serves many purposes
(b) Muslims must feed one poor person each day
(c) The poor and chronically ill are exempt from fasting
(d) The most prominent event of this month is the fasting

이슬람의 종교의식인 라마단은 단식, 자기희생 그리고 기도로 특징 되는 "축복의 달"이다. 이슬람력의 아홉 번째 달인 라마단 기간 동안 매일 해가 떠 있는 동안은 단식이 지켜진다. 전세계의 이슬람교도들 은 정확하게 동트기 전에 일어나서 동트기 전 식사인 Suhoor를 먹 고, 그날의 네 번째 기도인 Maghrib(일몰이라는 뜻)을 드려야 할 시 간까지 먹거나 마시는 것을 금해야 한다. 단식은 여러 가지 목적에 도움이 된다. 허기나 갈증은 이슬람교도들에게 가난한 이들의 고통 을 상기시킨다. 또한 단식은 자기수양을 훈련하고 몸과 마음을 정화 시키는 기회가 되기도 한다.

○ (d)와 같이 이슬람의 종교의식인 라마단의 가장 큰 특징인 단식에 대해 주로 언급하고 있지만, 글의 흐름상 단식이 가난한 이들의 고통 을 상기시켜주거나, 몸과 마음을 정화하고 자기 수양의 기회가 되기 도 한다는 등의 단식의 목적이나 효과 등이 이어지므로 정답은 (a)이 다. (b)와 (c)에 대한 내용은 언급되지 않았다.

Muslim 이슬람교도, 이슬람의 **religious observance** 종교 의식 **mark** 특징짓다, 눈에 뜨이게 하다, 나타내다 **fasting** 단식, 금식 **due** 당연히 치러야 할 **self-discipline** 자기수양(훈련), 자제

---

34 Modigliani _____. While his life was spinning out of control through drugs, alcohol and declining health leading to his premature death, his paintings were becoming ever more calm and eternal. Modigliani's talent as an artist had been obscured by his flamboyant life. However, as he entered the last phase of his life, especially in his final three years—from 1917 to 1920, Modigliani's works became more cohesive than at any point in his career. It is the singular style of Modigliani's portraits of this period that continues to exert a powerful resonance today. While his legend as the quintessential bohemian will always live on, it is ultimately the art that transcends the personality.

(a) presents a curious paradox
(b) was prodigal with his artistic talent
(c) is known to have led a scandalous life
(d) one of the most celebrated, yet misunderstood artists

모딜리아니는 기이한 모순을 보여준다. 그의 인생은 마약과 술로 점 점 통제할 수 없게 되고, 나날이 약해지는 건강으로 결국 요절에 이 르게 되었지만, 그의 그림은 더욱더 차분해지고 불멸의 것이 되어갔 다. 모딜리아니의 화가로서의 재능은 그의 거칠 것 없이 살아온 인 생에 가려져 왔었다. 그러나 그가 인생의 말미에 접어들면서, 특히 1917년부터 1920년까지 마지막 3년 동안, 모딜리아니의 작품은 그 의 경력에 있어 어느 시점보다도 더욱 응집력 있는 그림이 되었다. 오늘날까지 계속해서 강력한 반향을 일으키는 것은 바로 이 시기에 그린 그의 독특한 스타일의 초상화이다. 전형적인 보헤미안으로서 의 그의 전설은 앞으로도 계속 되겠지만, 결국 인격을 초월하는 것 은 예술인 것이다.

○ 보헤미안으로서 절제하지 않고 방탕한 생활을 하던 모딜리아니가 한 인간으로서는 점점 몰락해 갈수록, 예술적으로는 더욱더 완성도 높 은 그림을 그리게 되었다는 대조적인 사실을 통해 그의 인생을 조명하 고 있다. 따라서 기이한 역설을 보여준다는 (a)가 정답이다. (b)는 언 급되지 않았으며, (c)와 (d)는 글의 내용의 흐름상 적절하지 않다.

spin out of control 통제할 수 없게 되다 **premature** 시기상 조의, 너무 이른 **eternal** 영원의, 불멸의 **obscure** 가리다, 덮어 감추다 **flamboyant** 화려한, 대담한, 눈부신 **phase** 단계, 시기 **cohesive** 응집력 있는 **resonance** 반향, 여운 **quintessential** 전형적인, 본질적인 **transcend** 초월하다, 능 가하다

35 The hedgehog's dilemma, or sometimes the porcupine dilemma, refers to the notion that people cannot get intimacy without inflicting psychological pain on each other. This concept originates from Schopenhauer's parable that describes a group of hedgehogs striving to keep the optimal distance where they may feel warm enough without hurting one another with their spines. They usually abandon warmth not to be hurt. It suggests that despite the intention of a close relationship, human intimacy itself causes individuals to erect his spines in self defense. As a result, a person suffering from the hedgehog dilemma _____, due to fear of psychological discomfort.

(a) usually turns to religious society
(b) develops multiple personality disorder
(c) struggles not to be out of touch with people
(d) will usually avoid becoming involved with someone

때로는 호저 딜레마라고도 불리는 고슴도치 딜레마는 사람들이 가까워지면 반드시 서로에게 심리적인 고통을 주게 된다는 생각을 말한다. 그 개념은 고슴도치 무리들이 그들의 가시로 서로를 다치게 하지 않으면서도 따뜻함을 느끼는 최적의 거리를 유지하려고 애쓰는 것을 묘사한 쇼펜하우어의 우화에서 유래되었다. 고슴도치들은 보통 다치지 않기 위해 온기를 포기한다. 그것은 친밀한 관계를 갖고자 하는 의도에도 불구하고 인간의 친교는 개인으로 하여금 자기 방어적으로 자신의 가시를 세우게 한다는 것을 시사한다. 결과적으로 고슴도치 딜레마를 겪는 사람은 심리적인 불편함을 두려워하기 때문에 대개 누군가와 얽히는 것을 포기하게 된다.

◑ 고슴도치 딜레마를 겪는 사람은 서로의 거리가 가까워질수록 자기 방어의 가시를 세우게 되어 결국은 서로에게 가하게 되는 심리적인 고통이나 불편함을 두려워하게 되므로, 타인과의 관계를 포기하게 된다고 추론할 수 있다. (a)와 (b)는 언급되지 않았으며 (c)는 사람들과 멀어지지 않으려고 발버둥 친다는 의미가 되므로 답이 될 수 없다.

hedgehog 고슴도치 porcupine 호저 refer to ~을 나타내다, 표시하다 notion 관념, 생각 intimacy 친교, 친밀함 inflict (벌, 고통 등을) 주다, 가하다 parable 우화 strive to 노력하다, 애쓰다 optimal 최적의, 최상의 spine 바늘, 가시 intention 의향, 의도, 목적 erect 곤두세우다, 일으키다

---

36 The Golden Globes are American awards which honor both motion pictures and TV programs with the best performances and are presented by Hollywood Foreign Press Association (HFPA). The First Golden Globes were awarded in 1944 and they have since been held annually. They are usually considered as the third most prestigious awards for movies and television, after the Academy Awards (for film) and Emmy Awards (for television). Although they are gaining respectability as an honor in their own right, the Golden Globes _____ because the Golden Globe winners often overlap with the Oscar winners.

(a) have determined and announced the Oscar nominees
(b) have brought greater prestige to the Academy Awards
(c) have come to be regarded a harbinger of the Oscar winners
(d) have made outstanding contributions to the entertainment industry

골든글러브는 가장 훌륭한 성과를 낸 영화와 TV 프로그램에 영예를 주는 미국의 상으로, 할리우드 외신 기자협회(HFPA)에서 수여한다. 최초의 골든글러브는 1944년에 수여되었는데, 그 이후로 매년 개최되고 있다. 그 상은 보통 (영화를 위한) 아카데미상과 (TV를 위한) 에미상 다음으로 세 번째로 권위 있는 영화와 TV를 위한 상으로 여겨진다. 골든글러브가 그 자체로도 명예가 되는 존경을 받고 있긴 하지만, 골든글러브 수상자가 아카데미 오스카 수상자와 자주 일치하기 때문에 오스카 수상자를 예고해주는 것으로 여겨지게 되었다.

◑ 미국 영상산업의 3대 주요 상인 아카데미상, 에미상, 골든글러브상의 관계에서 골든글러브 수상자와 오스카 수상자가 자주 겹친다는 내용으로 보아 골든글러브 수상자를 보면 오스카 수상자를 점칠 수 있다고 추론할 수 있으므로 정답은 (c)이다. (a), (b), (d)는 언급되지 않은 내용이다.

award 상, 수여하다 annually 매년 prestigious 명망 있는, 일류의, 훌륭한 in one's own right 자기의 명의로, 자기의 권리로 overlap 겹치다, 일치하다 harbinger 선구자, 조짐, 전조; 미리 알리다

37 Celadon is the most prized ceramic from the Goryeo Dynasty. Celadon is famous for its unique color called as Bi-Saek, which is a bluish or a jade green color. The color of celadon depends on whether or not oxygen exists when a celadon is fired and how much iron is contained in the clay and glaze. To make the Bi-Saek color, a craftsman fires a celadon twice. First, it is fired at 700~800°C and then again after varnishing the glaze, which contains three percentage of iron, at 1,280°C. Bi-Saek is the sole characteristic of Korean celadon, and is very difficult to imitate even now with modernized technology.

Q Which of the following is correct about the Bi-Saek color?

(a) The amount of iron plays a key role in deciding the color.
(b) To make the Bi-Saek color, there is no fixed temperature.
(c) How to make the Bi-Saek color was imported from China.
(d) People finally discovered how to make the Bi-Saek color easily.

청자는 가장 높은 평가를 받는 고려왕조 시대의 도기이다. 청자는 비색이라고 불리는 독특한 푸르스름한 옥빛으로 유명하다. 청자의 색은 그것을 구울 당시의 산소의 존재 여부와 진흙과 유약에 함유된 철의 양에 의해 결정된다. 비색을 만들기 위해 장인은 청자를 두 번 굽는다. 처음에 섭씨 700도 내지 800도에서 한 번 구운 다음, 철을 3퍼센트 함유하고 있는 유약을 덧발라 섭씨 1,280도에서 다시 한 번 굽는다. 비색은 한국 청자의 유일한 특색으로서, 지금의 현대화된 기술로도 모방하기가 힘들다.

🔵 본문에 산소의 유무와 철 함유량이 청자의 색을 결정한다고 했으므로 (a)가 정답이 된다. (b)는 비색을 만들기 위해서, 처음에는 700-800℃, 두 번째는 1,280℃에서 구워야 한다고 했으므로 정해진 온도가 있고, (c)는 비색이 고려청자의 유일한 특색으로 중국자기와 구별된다고 했으므로 중국에서 유입되었다고 볼 수 없다. 그리고 (d)는 현대기술로도 비색을 흉내낼 수 없다고 했으므로 쉽게 비색을 낼 수 있는 방법을 찾았다는 것은 오답이 된다.

celadon 청자 prize 높이 평가하다 ceramic 도기 be famous for ~로 유명하다 unique 하나밖에 없는, 독특한 bluish 푸른빛을 띤 jade green 옥색의 depend on ~에 달려 있다, ~에 좌우되다 oxygen 산소 fire ~에 불을 붙이다, ~을 굽다 iron 철 clay 점토, 찰흙 glaze 유약, 덧칠 craftsman 장인, 공예가 varnish ~에 니스를 칠하다, ~에 광을 내다 sole 유일한, 독점적인 characteristic 특질, 특색 imitate ~을 모방하다, ~을 모조하다 modernize 현대화하다

38 At the International Astronomical Union (IAU) meeting in Prague in 2006, IAU members gathered to decide on a new definition for the word "planet." Celestial bodies can be called a planet only if they satisfy specific criteria. According to the new definition, a planet has to be an object that orbits the sun. It also has to be large enough to have become almost perfectly rounded because of the force of its own gravity, and dominate its neighborhood. Thus, Pluto was demoted from a planet to a dwarf planet because Charon, Pluto's moon, is only a bit smaller than Pluto, so they look like orbiting the sun together.

2006년 프라하에서 열린 국제천문연맹(IAU) 회의에서, IAU 회원들은 한자리에 모여 "행성"이라는 단어의 새로운 정의를 내렸다. 천체들은 일정한 요건을 만족시킬 때에만 행성이라고 불릴 수 있다. 새 정의에 따르면 행성은 태양의 주위를 공전해야 한다. 또한 자신의 중력으로 인해 거의 완전하게 구형을 유지할 수 있을 만큼 충분히 커야 하며, 주변에 있는 천체들보다 우세해야 한다. 그래서 명왕성은 행성에서 왜성으로 강등되었는데, 왜냐하면 명왕성의 달인 Charon이 명왕성보다 약간 작을 뿐이어서, 둘이 함께 태양 주위를 돌고 있는 것처럼 보이기 때문이다.

🔵 행성에 대한 새로운 정의와 이에 따라 명왕성이 왜 강등되었느냐에 관한 글인데, 명왕성의 달인 Charon이 명왕성 대신에 행성으로 격상되었다는 내용은 없으므로 (c)가 정답이 된다. 명왕성은 Charon보다 그리 크지 않아 Charon을 지배한다고 볼 수 없어서 강등되었기에 (a)는 옳은 내용이 되고, (b)도 행성이 작으면 중력이 약하여 행성이 둥글게 될 수 없으므로 옳은 내용이 된다. 또한 (d)는 IAU 회원들이 모여서 행성의 정의를 내리고 행성의 범주를 정하는 것으로 보아 천문학과 관련된 이슈들을 결정하는 데 중요한 역할을 한다고 볼 수 있다.

Q Which is NOT true according to the passage?

(a) Pluto was downgraded because it doesn't dominate Charon.

(b) If a planet is very small, its gravity would not be strong enough to make it round.

(c) According to the new definition, Charon got upgraded to a planet instead of Pluto.

(d) The role of IAU members is definitely important to decide on the astronomical issues.

International Astronomical Union 국제천문연맹 Prague 프라하 (체코공화국의 수도) definition 정의 planet 행성 celestial body 천체 only if 오직 ~인 경우에만 satisfy ~을 만족시키다 specific 특유한, 특정한, 일정한 criteria 기준 according to ~에 따르면, ~에 따라서 orbit 궤도, ~의 주위를 궤도를 그리며 돌다 gravity 중력 dominate ~을 지배하다, ~보다 우세하다 neighborhood 이웃, 근처, 지구 Pluto 명왕성 demote ~의 지위(계급)를 떨어뜨리다, 강등시키다 dwarf planet 왜성(=dwarf star)

---

39 St. Patrick is famous for eliminating snakes which symbolized a pagan. After his death, the Irish considered him as a saint who guarded their country and began to celebrate the day which was thought to be the date of his death. On St. Patrick's Day, people wear green, dissolve green colors into rivers, eat Irish food, and participate in parades. Since the first St. Patrick's Day Parade, which was held in New York on March 17th in 1766, it has been widely celebrated by many people in various parts of the world even though it is not considered an official holiday except for in Ireland.

Q Which of the following is correct according to the passage?

(a) St. Patrick might be dead on March 17.

(b) Only Irish people have festivals on St. Patrick's Day.

(c) Many countries are making St. Patrick's Day an official holiday.

(d) The first St. Patrick's Day Parade was held in Patrick's hometown.

성 패트릭은 이교도를 상징하는 뱀을 제거한 것으로 유명하다. 그의 사후에, 아일랜드 국민들은 그를 조국을 수호한 성인으로 여겨 그의 사망일로 생각되는 날을 기념하기 시작했다. 성 패트릭의 날에 사람들은 녹색 옷을 입고, 녹색 물감을 강에 풀며, 아일랜드 음식을 먹고 시가행진에 참여한다. 비록 이 날을 국경일로 여기는 나라는 아일랜드밖에 없지만, 1766년 3월 17일 뉴욕에서 처음 열린 성 패트릭의 날 행렬 이래로, 세계 각지에 있는 많은 사람들은 성 패트릭의 날을 기념해오고 있다.

◑ 성 패트릭 날의 유래와 관습 등에 대해 설명하는 글이다. 성 패트릭의 사망일로 추정되는 날을 기념하기 시작했다고 했는데, 뉴욕에서는 1766년 3월 17일에 처음으로 행사가 열렸으므로 3월 17일을 사망일로 생각하는 내용의 (a)가 정답이 된다. 성 패트릭의 날은 아일랜드 외의 여러 나라에서 기념되지만 국경일은 아니므로 (b), (c)는 옳지 않고, 성 패트릭은 아일랜드 출신이므로 (d)도 정답이 될 수 없다.

be famous for ~으로 유명하다 eliminate ~을 제거하다, 몰아내다, 무시하다 symbolize ~을 상징하다, 나타내다 pagan 이교도, 우상숭배자 consider A as B A를 B로 생각하다, 간주하다 saint 성인 celebrate ~을 경축하다, 찬양하다 be thought to be ~라고 여겨지다, 생각되다 dissolve ~을 녹이다, 해산시키다 participate in ~에 참가하다, 관여하다 hold (모임 등을)열다, (식을)올리다, 거행하다 even though 비록 ~할지라도 official 공무상의, 공식의 except for ~을 제외하면, ~가 없었더라면

40 Dear Mr. Jones,

I'm writing to tell you that I have received an opportunity to improve my career at NYS Inc. I have accepted a proposal to work for that company as a chief secretary. In accordance with the company policy, I submit this letter in advance. I think you can find a qualified person for my position within 15 days. I'll be looking forward to a positive answer from you. I would like you to know that I will cherish the memories that I have shared with you and my co-workers here.

Sincerely,
Anna Smith

Q What is the purpose of the lefler?

(a) To apply for a secretary of NYS Inc.
(b) To express her gratitude to the company
(c) To inform the company of her resignation
(d) To ask the company to change her position

친애하는 Jones씨

제가 NYS 주식회사에서 제 경력을 향상시킬 수 있는 기회를 얻었다는 것을 말씀드리기 위해서 이 편지를 씁니다. 저는 수석비서관으로서 그 회사에서 일하겠냐는 제안을 받아들였습니다. 회사의 방침에 따라 이 편지를 미리 제출합니다. 제 생각에는 15일 이내에 제 자리의 적임자를 찾을 수 있을 것 같습니다. 긍정적인 답변을 해 주실 것으로 기대하고 있겠습니다. 제가 여기에서 그동안 당신과 동료들과 함께 나눈 기억들을 소중히 간직할 것을 알아주셨으면 합니다.

Anna Smith 올림

○ 본인의 회사에 자신이 NYS 주식회사의 수석비서로 가게 되었다는 것을 알리기 위해서 쓴 편지로서 (c)가 정답이 된다.

opportunity 기회 improve 향상시키다 accept 받아들이다 proposal 제안 secretary 비서 in accordance with ~에 따라서 submit 제출하다 in advance 미리 qualified 적격의 look forward to ~을 고대하다 cherish 고이 간직하다 co-worker 동료 sincerely 편지 끝에 쓰는 말 gratitude 감사 resignation 사임, 사표

1 M How would you like your hair cut?
W _____

(a) It serves you right.
(b) Just stay put.
(c) Just a trim, please.
(d) I'm sorry I'm new here.

M: 머리를 어떻게 잘라드릴까요?
W: 살짝 다듬어 주세요.

○ 미용실에서 들을 수 있는 헤어디자이너와 손님 사이의 대화이다. (a)는 '꼴 좋다, 그래도 싸다' 라는 뜻으로 상황과 거리가 멀고 (b)는 '꼼짝 말고 있어라' 라는 뜻으로 역시 정답이 아니다. (c)는 머리를 살짝만 다듬어 달라고 할 때 쓸 수 있는 표현으로 정답이 된다. (d)는 누군가 길을 물어볼 때 '저도 여기 처음이에요' 라는 뜻으로 쓰인다.

serve sb right ~에게 마땅한 대우를 하다. ~에게 당연한 결과다 trim ~을 다듬다. 정돈하다

2 M How is the weather over there?
W _____

(a) It was cold and dry.
(b) It looks like rain.
(c) The weather is beyond our control.
(d) I'm under the weather.

M: 거기 날씨는 어때?
W: 비가 올 것 같아.

○ 날씨를 묻는 남자의 질문에 적절한 여자의 응답을 고르는 문제이다. 남자는 현재 날씨를 묻고 있으므로 과거형으로 쓰인 (a)는 정답이 될 수 없다. cold와 dry만을 듣고 정답으로 고르지 않도록 주의해야 한다. (b)는 비가 올 것 같다는 뜻으로 상황에 적절한 정답이 되며 (c)는 날씨는 우리 힘으로 어쩔 수 없다는 뜻이며 (d)는 '몸이 안 좋다' 는 뜻으로 날씨와는 무관한 대답이다.

look like ~일 것 같다. ~처럼 보이다 beyond one's control ~의 통제 밖이다 under the weather 몸 상태가 좋지 않아

3 M How do you like working for a bank?
W _____

(a) I go to work everyday.
(b) I find it very difficult.
(c) I couldn't agree more.
(d) Enough is enough.

M: 은행에서 일하는 거 어때?
W: 정말 어려운 것 같아.

○ 은행에서 일하는 게 어떠냐는 남자의 질문에 (a)에서는 work라는 단어를 반복하면서 혼동을 주고 있다. 매일 출근한다는 대답으로 정답이 아니며 (b)는 어렵다는 뜻으로 정답으로 적절하다. (c)는 '찬성이다, 동감이다' 라는 뜻이고 (d)는 '충분하다, 그쯤 해 두어라' 는 뜻으로 상황과 맞지 않는다.

work for ~에서 일하다 go to work 출근하다 Enough is enough. 그쯤 해 둬. 그만하면 충분해.

4 **M** How was the movie?

W I really enjoyed it. It was the best I've ever seen. How about you?

M I especially liked the twist at the ending. It was fantastic.

W _____

(a) Take it easy!

(b) Suit yourself.

(c) Be my guest.

(d) You can say that again.

M: 영화 어땠어?

W: 정말 좋았어. 내가 본 영화 중에 최고였어. 너는 어땠어?

M: 난 특히 결말 부분의 반전이 좋았어. 환상적이더라.

W: 두말하면 잔소리지.

🔵 영화를 함께 본 후 소감에 대해 이야기하고 있다. 여자도 영화를 재미있게 봤고, 남자도 역시 반전이 재미있었다고 했으므로 동의의 표현인 (d)가 정답이 된다. (a)는 여러 상황에서 쓰일 수 있는데, 쉬엄쉬엄 하라는 의미, 헤어질 때 조심해서 잘 가라는 의미, 긴장하지 말고 편히 생각하라는 의미 등으로 쓰인다. (b)는 좋을 대로 하라는 의미이고 (c) 역시 마음대로 하라는 뜻으로 쓰는 표현이다.

twist 꼬기, 비틀기, 반전, 전환

• 동의를 나타내는 표현: **You're telling me. / You said it.**

---

5 **M** I'd like to book a table for 6 at 7 o'clock tonight.

W Sorry, sir. We're fully booked for 7 o'clock. But you can make a reservation for 8 o'clock.

M Okay. Please make it 8 o'clock.

W _____

(a) Let me treat you tonight.

(b) Could you leave your name and number, please?

(c) You're too fussy about food.

(d) It is out of the question.

M: 오늘 저녁 7시에 6명 식사 예약하고 싶은데요.

W: 죄송합니다만 7시는 예약이 꽉 찼습니다. 하지만 8시에는 예약이 가능하신데요.

M: 알겠습니다. 8시로 하지요.

W: 이름과 전화 번호 알려주시겠습니까?

🔵 식당 예약 상황이다. 남자가 7시 예약을 하려고 했으나 여자가 예약이 꽉 찼다고 하면서 8시는 가능하다고 했고, 이에 남자가 수긍을 했으므로 이후에는 예약이 진행되는 내용이 나와야 한다. 따라서 정답은 (b)로서 이름과 전화번호를 묻는 표현이 나오는 것이 자연스럽다. (a)는 오늘밤 자기가 대접하겠다는 뜻으로 식당 직원과 손님과의 대화로는 적절치 않고, (c)는 식성이 너무 까다롭다는 뜻으로 음식과 관련하여 혼동을 주려 했으나 역시 문맥과 어울리지 않으며 (d)는 '그것은 불가능하다'는 뜻이 된다.

book a table (식사) 자리를 예약하다 **treat** 한 턱 내다, 대접하다 **fussy** 까다로운 **out of the question** 불가능한, 말도 안 되는

---

6 **M** What's wrong with your car?

W I don't know. My car won't start.

M Did you check to see if you have fuel in the tank?

W _____

(a) Yes. But I couldn't recognize it.

(b) Yes. They released a new model.

(c) Yes, I did. By the way, can you give me a ride to work?

(d) Yes. I think air pollution is a big problem.

M: 차에 무슨 문제 있어?

W: 모르겠어. 차가 시동이 안 걸려.

M: 기름은 있는지 확인했어?

W: 했어. 근데 회사까지 좀 태워줄래?

🔵 여자의 차가 시동이 걸리지 않자 남자가 기름은 있는지 확인해 보았냐고 물었다. 이에 적절한 답은 (c)이다. 확인했다고 말하는 것으로 보아 연료 문제가 아님을 알 수 있고, 뒤이어 회사에 태워다 달라는 부탁의 말이 오는 것이 자연스럽다. (a)는 알아보지 못했다는 뜻으로 문맥과 상관이 없고, (b)는 새 모델을 출시했다는 뜻으로 차와 관련된 내용으로 혼란을 준 것이며 (d)는 대기 오염이 문제라는 뜻으로 대화 상황과 전혀 관련이 없다.

recognize ~을 알아보다, 분간하다 **release** ~을 발표하다, 공개하다 **give sb a ride** ~을 태워다 주다

7

M Do you know what Samantha's phone number is?

W Oh, Samantha's phone number? Hold on, please. Her number is stored on my cell phone.

M What's her number?

W Oh, god. I left it at home. Hmmm... I can't think of it right off hand.

M Come on. Try to remember. This is urgent.

W Well, why don't you call Mike? I'm sure he knows her phone number.

M I've tried, but no one answered!

Q What can you infer from the dialogue?

(a) Mike knows Samantha well.
(b) The man lost her cell phone.
(c) The man has something to ask her.
(d) The man will call Mike.

M: 사만다의 전화 번호 알고 있어?

W: 사만다 전화 번호? 잠깐만. 번호가 내 휴대폰에 저장되어 있어.

M: 번호가 뭐야?

W: 어머나. 전화기를 집에 두고 왔어. 음... 번호가 지금 당장 생각이 안나네.

M: 제발. 노력해봐. 급한 일이야.

W: 마이크에게 전화해보는 게 어때? 마이크는 알 거야.

M: 해 봤어. 근데 전화를 안받아.

○ 여자의 마지막 말에서 마이크가 사만다의 전화번호를 알고 있을 거라고 했으므로 마이크와 사만다는 잘 아는 사이임을 짐작할 수 있다. 따라서 (a)가 정답이 된다. (b)나 (c)는 이 상황에서는 어울리지 않고, 남자의 마지막 대사에서 이미 마이크에게 전화했다는 것을 알 수 있으므로 (d)는 정답이 될 수 없다.

off hand 즉시, 그 자리에서

8

M What are you doing?

W I have so many pimples on my face. They make me look ugly.

M But don't squeeze or touch the pimples with your fingers. It will make the pimples worse.

W Then, what should I do?

M Why don't you go see a doctor?

W I tried but it didn't work.

M How about using natural soap or cosmetics? My sister uses them. If you want, I can ask her where you can buy them for you.

Q What does the man advise her to do?

(a) He advises her to squeeze the pimples.
(b) He recommends using natural cosmetics.
(c) He advises her to consult his sister.
(d) He advises her to take a day off.

M: 뭐 하고 있어?

W: 얼굴에 여드름이 너무 많이 났어. 얼굴이 추해 보여.

M: 하지만 손가락으로 여드름을 짜거나 만지지 마. 그러면 여드름이 더 심해질 거야.

W: 그럼 어떻게 해야 돼?

M: 병원에 가보지 그래?

W: 갔었는데 별로 효과가 없었어.

M: 천연 비누나 화장품을 써보는 건 어때? 내 여동생이 그런 걸 쓰거든. 동생에게 어디서 살 수 있는지 물어봐줄게.

○ 남자가 여자에게 어떠한 충고를 주고 있는지 고르는 문제이다. 여드름을 손으로 짜지 말라고 했으므로 (a)는 정답이 아니며, 남자의 마지막 말에서 천연 화장품을 써보라고 했으므로 (b)가 정답이 된다. 남자의 여동생에게 천연 화장품을 어디서 사야 하는지 물어본다고 했지 여동생과 상담해보라는 이야기는 아니었으므로 (c) 역시 정답이 아니다. (d)는 언급된 적이 없다.

pimple 여드름 squeeze ~을 짜다

61

9

M What do you think the chances of getting a raise are?

W Chances are slim!

M Why do you think so? You've never gotten a raise since you changed jobs?

W Never. I'll be fortunate if they don't cut my salary. The company's financial situation is not good right now. They can't afford to give a raise.

M That's too bad. Did you ever think of working somewhere else again?

W Yeah. In fact, I have an interview next Tuesday.

M Good luck.

Q What is the conversation about?

(a) Changing jobs
(b) A possible pay raise
(c) Some cutbacks in the company
(d) Getting a promotion

M: 급여가 오를 가능성이 얼마나 된다고 생각해?

W: 거의 희박하지

M: 왜 그렇게 생각해? 직장을 옮긴 이후로 월급이 오른 적이 없었어?

W: 절대. 급여가 깎이지 않는 것만으로도 다행일 거야. 회사의 재정 상태가 현재 좋지 않거든. 급여를 올려줄 여유가 없어.

M: 안됐다. 회사를 다시 옮길 생각은 없어?

W: 있어. 사실 다음 주 화요일에 면접 봐.

M: 행운을 빌어.

○ 대화의 주제에 대해 묻고 있다. 회사의 인원 감축이나 승진에 대한 이야기는 없었으므로 (c), (d)는 정답이 아니며 직장을 옮기는 것에 대한 이야기는 마지막에 잠깐 언급되었으므로 주제라고 하긴 어려우므로 (a)도 정답이 아니다. 급여 인상 가능성에 대한 이야기가 주가 되었으므로 정답은 (b)이다.

get a raise 급여가 오르다 Chances are slim. 가능성이 희박하다 can afford to ~을 살 여유(형편)가 되다 promotion 승진, 판매 촉진

10 The European Union Chamber of Commerce in Korea is holding its monthly meeting next Thursday. This month's speaker is the chairman of Korea Fair Trade Commission, Mr. Park. The luncheon begins at noon and runs until 1:50 p.m. Admission is 50,000 won. It will be held in the Royal Room of the Grand Hotel, Seoul, on the third floor. Visit www.euc.org for more information or call (02) 456-9912.

Q Which is correct according to the announcement?

(a) The meeting will be held next Saturday.
(b) The luncheon will be held on the third floor.
(c) The luncheon starts at noon and runs until 1:15 p.m.
(d) If you want to know more information you must call or send a mail.

주한 유럽연합상공회의소가 다음주 화요일 월례 회의를 주최합니다. 이번 달 연사는 한국 공정거래위원회 회장이신 박 회장님이십니다. 오찬은 정오에 시작해서 오후 1시 50분까지 이어집니다. 입장료는 5만원입니다. 본 행사는 서울에 위치한 그랜드 호텔 3층에 있는 로열 룸에서 열립니다. 더 자세한 정보를 원하시면 www.euc.org를 방문하시거나 (02) 456-9912로 전화해주세요.

○ 모임 날짜는 다음주 화요일이므로 (a)는 정답이 아니고, 오찬은 1시 15분이 아니라 1시 50분까지 열린다고 했으므로 (c) 역시 정답이 아니다. 숫자의 발음에 주의해서 잘 들을 필요가 있다. 더 자세한 정보는 홈페이지를 방문하거나 전화를 하라고 했으므로 (d)도 정답이 아니다. 오찬은 3층 로열 룸에서 열린다고 했으므로 정답은 (b)가 된다.

hold (모임, 행사 등을) 열다, 개최하다 luncheon 오찬 admission 입장, 입회

11 Welcome to our game show, SEIZE THE CHANCE. We have today's contestant, Alley Johns here in the studio. She has just entered our bonus round. Congratulations, Alley! She is trying to win our grand prize, $20,000 in cash and a five-day vacation to France with an all expenses paid. Okay, Alley. In order to win the grand prize, you must answer all five of the bonus questions correctly. All of the questions are true or false. Are you ready to go?

Q Which is correct about the game show?

(a) The show host is Alley Johns.
(b) The contestant is taking part in over the phone.
(c) The contestant won $20,000 in cash.
(d) The contestant has yet to start the bonus round.

게임 쇼, SEIZE THE CHANCE에 오신 것을 환영합니다. 오늘 참가자인 앨리 존스 씨가 여기 스튜디오에 나와 계십니다. 앨리 존스 씨는 방금 보너스 라운드에 진출하셨습니다. 축하드립니다. 앨리 씨! 앨리 씨는 1등을 위해 나와 계신데요. 1등을 하게 되면 2만 달러의 현금과 프랑스 5일 여행을 무료로 갈 수 있는 여행권을 드립니다. 자, 앨리 씨. 1등을 하기 위해서는 보너스 질문 5 문제를 모두 맞혀야 합니다. 모든 질문은 O, X 퀴즈입니다. 준비되셨나요?

○ 보너스 라운드에 진출한 참가자에게 방식을 설명해주고 있다. 따라서 아직 보너스 라운드가 시작된 것은 아니므로 정답은 (d)가 된다. (a) 앨리 존스는 진행자가 아닌 참가자의 이름이며, (b) 직접 스튜디오에 나와서 참여한다고 언급되었으며 (c) 아직 보너스 라운드를 시작한 것이 아니므로 2만 달러를 받지 못했다.

contestant 출전자, 경쟁자 in cash 현금으로 take part in ~에 참가하다 over the phone 전화로 has yet to 아직 ~하고 있지 않다. 아직 ~해야 한다

12 Smoking cigarettes can be an expensive habit. People who smoke one pack of cigarettes per day spend $3 a day on their expensive habit. At the end of one year, these smokers will have spent at least $1,095. But the price of cigarettes is not the only expense cigarette smokers meet with. As cigarette smoke has an offensive smell that infiltrates clothing, blankets, and furniture covered with cloth, smokers must have clean these items more often than non-smokers do.

Q Which can be inferred from the article?

(a) Smoking a pack of cigarette is a bad habit.
(b) Smoking a pack of cigarette is an expensive habit.
(c) Expense of smoking cigarettes includes the cleaning expenses.
(d) Expense of smoking cigarettes is more expensive than the cleaning expense.

흡연은 비싼 습관이 될 수 있다. 하루에 담배 한 갑을 피는 사람들은 비싼 습관에 하루에 3달러를 소비한다. 연말이 되면 이 흡연자들은 적어도 1095달러를 쓰는 셈이 된다. 하지만 담배 가격이 전부는 아니다. 담배 연기는 천으로 덮인 가구, 담요, 의복에 침투하는 악취를 가지고 있어서 흡연자들은 비흡연자들보다 더 자주 이런 물건들을 세탁해야 한다.

○ 흡연이 비싼 습관이라고 하는 이유는 담배 가격뿐만이 아니라 악취로 인한 세탁 비용까지 포함시켜야 한다는 내용을 이야기하고 있다. 따라서 정답은 (c)가 된다. 담배 가격과 세탁 비용은 비교하지 않았으므로 (d)는 정답이 아니다.

offensive smell 악취 infiltrate ~에 침투하다, 스며들다

13 A What do I have to do to be a nice roommate?

B You can do _____.

(a) you do
(b) that you please
(c) as you please
(d) as you pleasing

A: 좋은 룸메이트가 되려면 어떻게 해야 할까?
B: 네가 좋을 대로 해.

◑ 내용상 '네가 좋을 대로 하라'는 표현이 필요한데, 'as'는 접속사로, '~대로'라는 뜻이 있다. 접속사인 'as' 뒤에는 주어와 동사가 와야 하므로 (c)가 가장 알맞다.

---

14 A When I stayed in Vancouver with my children, we _____ Science Museums.

B Wow. I must have visited there too when I was there.

(a) was visiting
(b) are visiting
(c) used to visit
(d) would like to visit

A: 내가 아이들과 함께 밴쿠버에 살았을 때, 우린 종종 과학 박물관을 가곤 했어.
B: 와. 나도 거기 있었을 때 그 곳을 분명 갔던 것 같아.

◑ 과거의 습관적인 일에 대해 말할 때 'used to 동사원형' 표현을 쓴다.

---

15 A Have you heard our school debate team winning the grand prize?

B Yes, I can't express _____.

(a) how I am pleased
(b) how pleased am I
(c) how pleasing I am
(d) how pleased I am

A: 우리 학교 토론 팀이 대상을 받았다는 소식 들었어?
B: 응. 내가 얼마나 기쁜지 말로 표현할 수가 없어.

◑ '얼마나 내가 기쁜지'라는 표현이 와야 하므로, (d)가 적절한 표현이다.

---

16 A On the way home my car suddenly stopped.

B You'd better _____.

(a) get it to fix
(b) get it fixed
(c) it get fixed
(d) get to fix it

A: 집에 오는 길에 갑자기 내 차가 멈췄어.
B: 수리해야 할 것 같은데.

◑ 주어와 목적어(it)의 관계가 수동이므로 'get+목적어' 다음에는 동사의 p.p형태가 와야 한다.

17 A superstition is _____ between certain actions or behaviors, and other actions.

(a) irrational belief about the relation
(b) an irrational belief about relation
(c) irrational belief about the relation
(d) an irrational belief about the relation

미신은 특정한 동작이나 행동과 다른 행동의 관계에 대한 불합리한 믿음이다.

◯ belief는 가산 명사이기 때문에 부정관사가 필요하고, relation은 특정한 관계를 나타내므로 정관사를 동반한다.

superstition 미신 irrational 불합리한

---

18 Korea and the USA _____ about the future of six-party talks, so both sides have expressed willingness to be flexible in negotiations.

(a) are remained optimistic
(b) are remained optimistically
(c) remain optimistic
(d) remain optimistically

한국과 미국은 차기 6자 회담에 대해 긍정적인 자세를 가지고 있고, 따라서 양측은 협상에 유연하겠다는 의사를 기꺼이 표명했다.

◯ '~인 채로 남아있다' 는 뜻의 자동사 remain은 보어가 필요한 단어이다. 따라서 부사가 아닌 형용사 optimistic을 가진 (c)가 답이다.

six-party talks 6자회담 willingness 자진 negotiation 협상

---

19 He probably meant to indicate that you should participate in the course he recommended in the answer _____.

(a) which you refer
(b) when you refer
(c) to that you refer
(d) to which you refer

너의 질문에 대한 대답으로, 그는 아마 네가 그가 추천한 과정에 참가해야 한다는 말이었을 거야.

◯ '네가 물었던 것에 대해' 라는 의미가 빈 칸에 와야 한다.

indicate 은연중 나타내다 participate 참가하다
recommend 추천하다

---

20 To decide which atoms can be related to the appropriate method of hybrid calculation, a molecule has been divided up _____ three arbitrary layers.

(a) into
(b) as
(c) with
(d) upon

어떤 원자가 혼성 실험에 적합한 방법에 관련되는지 결정하기 위해서는 하나의 분자가 임의적인 세 개의 층으로 분류되어야 한다.

◯ '~개로 나누어지다' 의 의미로 전치사 into가 필요하다.

atom 원자 appropriate 적절한 hybrid 잡종, 혼성물
molecule 분자 arbitrary 임의성, 자의성 layer 층

---

21 (a) A: Did you complete the legal papers?
(b) B: Yes, but I have to check more judical cases.
(c) A: My case is also tough enough to rise lots of cross examinations.
(d) B: I love what I am but, nothing seems easy.

A: 법률 문서는 다 만들었니?
B: 응, 하지만 법적 사례들을 더 검토해보아야 해.
A: 내 경우도 수많은 반대 심문을 부를 만큼 어려워.
B: 난 내가 하는 일이 좋지만, 쉬운 게 아무것도 없는 듯해.

◯ (c)에서, rise 다음에 바로 목적어가 등장하므로 자동사 rise가 아닌 타동사 arise를 써야 한다.

legal 법률상의 tough 힘든, 고된 examination 심문, 검사, 심사

22 (a) It's said that domestic dogs are descended from the wolf and have been living in association with people.
(b) Genetic evidence suggests that Native Americans and Europeans domesticate dogs independently, and later North American dogs were almost completely replaced by dogs that European brought.
(c) Before Europeans arrived in America, dogs were used for their fur. (d) They were bred for wool like sheep for making blankets.

가축용 개는 늑대의 후손이며 사람들과 함께 어울려 살아왔다는 말이 있다. 유전학적으로, 미국 원주민들과 유럽인들이 개를 독립적으로 길들였고, 그 후 북미의 개들이 거의 완전히 유럽인들이 들여온 개들로 대체되었다는 증거가 있다. 유럽인들이 미 대륙에 오기 전에는 개들은 그들의 털옷을 만들기 위해 이용되었다. 개들은 담요를 만들 양모를 제공하는 양처럼 길러졌다.

🔘 (c)에서, '유럽인들이 미 대륙에 오기 전에는 개는 털옷을 만들기 위해 이용되었다' 이므로 dogs had been used for their fur로 시제를 대과거로 맞춰주어야 한다.

domesticate 길들이다 descend 후손 replace 대신하다, 대체하다 fur 모피 blanket 담요

VOCABULARY • P.81

23 A For the first time in 10 years, I'm going to run my own restaurant!
B Congratulations! You _____ it. You really worked hard.

(a) qualified
(b) available
(c) worth
(d) deserve

A: 십 년 만에 처음으로 내 명의의 식당을 운영하게 되었어.
B: 축하해. 그럴 만한 자격이 있어. 정말 열심히 했잖아.

🔘 빈 칸 뒤에 나온 문장을 보면 열심히 일했다고 했으므로 '그럴만한 자격이 있다' 라는 내용의 deserve가 나오는 것이 자연스럽다. qualified의 경우 형용사이므로 동사 자리에는 적절치 않다.

run ~을 경영하다, 관리하다 deserve ~할 자격이 있다 qualified 자격이 있는 available 이용 가능한

24 A Is the post office far from here?
B Not really. It's within walking _____.

(a) way
(b) road
(c) distance
(d) length

A: 우체국이 여기에서 먼가요?
B: 아니오. 걸어서 갈 수 있는 거리에 있어요.

🔘 우체국이 머냐는 질문에 멀지 않다고 했으므로 걸어갈 수 있는 거리에 있다는 표현이 적절하므로 보기 중에서 distance가 정답이 된다.

walking distance 걸어서 갈 수 있는 거리

25 A I can't help it. He's quite stubborn about this matter.
B Leave it to me. I'll _____ him into changing his mind.

(a) tell
(b) speak
(c) talk
(d) address

A: 어쩔 수 없어. 그는 이 문제에 대해 꽤 완고해.
B: 내게 맡겨. 내가 그를 설득해서 마음을 바꾸도록 해볼게.

🔘 완고한 사람을 설득해서 마음을 바꾸도록 하겠다는 내용이므로 이에 해당하는 구동사를 찾아야 한다. 빈 칸에 talk를 써서 talk sb into 의 형태로 쓰면 이러한 의미가 된다.

talk sb into 남을 설득하여 ~하도록 시키다

26 A Rachel! Long time no see!

B Hi! I haven't seen you _____.
How have you been?

(a) under age
(b) in ages
(c) for since
(d) after all

A: 레이첼! 오랜만이야!

B: 안녕! 오랜만에 본다. 어떻게 지냈어?

○ 오랜만에 만나 인사를 나누는 상황이다. 관용 표현으로 I haven't seen you in ages 라고 하면 오랫동안 보지 못했다는 뜻이 된다.

Long time no see. (간만에 만났을 때) 오랜만이야. after all 결국

---

27 A Thanks for inviting me. By the way, where's Linda?

B Oh my god! I forgot to invite her. It just _____ my mind!

(a) slipped
(b) slid
(c) forgot
(d) jumped

A: 초대해 주셔서 감사합니다. 그런데 린다는 어디 있죠?

B: 어머나. 린다를 초대한다는 걸 잊었어요. 제가 깜빡했네요.

○ 관용 표현을 알아두어야 한다. slip one's mind는 '잊어버리다, 생각이 나지 않다' 라는 뜻으로 위 상황에 적절한 표현이다.

slip one's mind 잊어버리다, 생각이 나지 않다

---

28 The president started to _____ the sales manager about decreasing sales at the moment.

(a) scold
(b) reprimand
(c) punish
(d) tease

사장은 현재 판매가 감소하는 것에 대해 영업 부장을 질책하기 시작했다.

○ 판매가 감소했다는 내용으로 보아 책임자를 질책한다는 내용이 나와야 자연스럽다. scold나 punish는 주로 아이들을 꾸짖을 때 쓰는 표현으로 이러한 상황에는 어울리지 않는다. tease는 괴롭히고 못살게 군다는 표현으로 역시 문맥과 어울리지 않는다. 따라서 '질책하다, 문책하다' 라는 뜻의 reprimand가 가장 적절하다.

reprimand 질책하다, 문책하다 scold ~을 꾸짖다 punish ~을 벌주다 tease ~을 괴롭히다

---

29 If your _____ skin easily becomes red and itchy, use cosmetics made of natural ingredients.

(a) sensitive
(b) sensible
(c) sensory
(d) sensual

민감한 피부가 쉽게 붉어지고 가려움증이 있다면 천연 성분으로 만든 화장품을 사용해 보세요.

○ 쉽게 붉어지고 가려워진다는 내용으로 보아 피부가 '민감하다' 라는 표현이 나와야 한다. 보기 모두 형태가 비슷하여 혼동될 수 있으므로 뜻을 확실히 알아 두어야 한다. '민감한' 이라는 뜻의 단어는 sensitive이다.

sensitive 민감한 sensible 현명한 sensory 감각의, 지각의 sensual 관능적인

30 After playing basketball, he started to feel thirsty. But there was nowhere to _____ his thirst in the area.

(a) sip
(b) drink
(c) alleviate
(d) quench

농구를 한 후에, 그는 갈증을 느끼기 시작했다. 하지만 그 지역에서는 갈증을 풀 만한 곳이 없었다.

➡ '갈증을 풀다' 라는 표현으로는 quench라는 동사를 쓴다. quench와 thirst는 잘 어울려 함께 쓰이는 단어이다. thirst와 다른 보기의 단어들은 함께 쓰면 어색한 표현이 된다.

sip ~을 홀짝이다, ~을 조금씩 마시다 **alleviate** 고통을 완화시키다 **quench** (갈증을) 풀다

---

31 The local people objected to building the waste processing _____ in their residential area.

(a) service
(b) amenity
(c) facility
(d) team

현지인들은 그들의 거주 지역에 쓰레기 처리 시설을 세우는 것을 반대했다.

➡ 주민들이 쓰레기 처리 시설을 반대한다는 내용이다. waste processing과 잘 어울릴 만한 명사를 찾아야 하는데, 앞서 build라는 단어가 나왔으므로 건물의 형태가 와야 한다. 따라서 정답은 시설을 뜻하는 facility가 된다.

object to ~에 반대하다 **residential area** 거주 지역 **facility** 편의시설, 설비 **amenity** 쾌적함, 오락 시설

---

32 Many patients waiting for _____ die everyday because of the shortage of donated organs.

(a) implants
(b) transplants
(c) transmitters
(d) operations

이식 수술을 기다리는 많은 환자들은 기증된 장기가 부족하여 매일 죽어간다.

➡ 장기 기증 숫자가 부족하여 환자들이 죽어간다는 내용으로 기증된 장기는 환자들에게 '이식' 이 되어야 한다. implant의 경우 인공 기관, 치아 등을 몸에 이식하는 것이므로 이 문맥과는 어울리지 않고 transplant가 심장이나 다른 장기를 이식한다고 할 때 쓰이는 단어이므로 정답이 된다.

donate ~을 기증하다 **organ** 장기 **implant** (피부, 인공 기관 등의) 이식 **transplant** 이식 **transmitter** 전달자, 양도자 **operation** 수술

33 When a school implements an Anti-Bullying campaign, students hold the key to success mainly because they usually know who the bullies and the victims are long before teachers and parents do. A majority of students strongly believe in justice and therefore welcome Anti-Bullying policies that ensure a safe school. However, students are more likely to participate in an Anti-Bullying campaign when they feel secure that reporting bullying will not cause them to lose status in their peer group. _____ in order for the students not to be accused of snitching.

(a) Custody can not be ignored
(b) Remission should be vouched
(c) Impartiality must be predetermined
(d) Confidentiality must be guaranteed

학교에서 폭력방지 캠페인을 실시하는 경우, 성공 여부의 열쇠는 학생들이 쥐고 있는데, 왜냐하면 학생들이야말로 누가 가해자이고 피해자인지를 부모나 교사가 괴롭힘을 눈치채기 훨씬 이전부터 알고 있는 경우가 많기 때문이다. 다수의 학생들은 정의에 대한 믿음이 강하므로, 안전한 학교를 만들려는 폭력방지 캠페인 정책을 반긴다. 그러나 학생들이 폭력신고가 또래집단에서 자리를 잃게 하는 일이 없을 것이라고 확신할 수 있을 때 폭력방지 캠페인에 적극 참여하게 될 것이다. 학생들이 밀고자라는 비난을 받지 않기 위해선 비밀이 보장되어야 한다.

⭕ 성공적인 학교폭력방지 캠페인은 학생들의 참여에 의해서만이 가능한데, 이것이 가능하기 위해서는 폭력을 신고하는 일로 밀고자라는 비난을 받아 또래집단에서 소외되는 것에 대한 두려움을 해소시켜야 한다는 뜻이므로 (d) 비밀이 보장되어야 한다가 정답이다.

implement 실시하다, 실행하다 bully (약자를) 괴롭히는 사람, 괴롭히다 majority 다수 secure 확신하는 snitch 밀고하다, 고자질하다

34 During the process of women's suffrage movements, many campaigners agreed that women should be allowed to vote. However, these campaigners still had disagreements about why women should be granted suffrage rights. Some of them thought that women voters would have an enlightening effect on politics and influence laws which impacted on their home and family because a woman's place was in her home. They believed that women were naturally kinder, more caring, and more sympathetic than men. _____, the other campaigners argued thought of women's suffrage as a way of compensating for the votes of weaker members of society.

(a) Therefore
(b) As a result
(c) On the other hand
(d) As a matter of fact

여성들의 참정권을 확보하기 위한 운동이 진행되는 동안, 많은 운동가들은 여성도 투표할 수 있어야 한다는데 동의했다. 그러나 여성들에게 선거권을 부여해야 되는 이유에 대해서는 여전히 견해가 달랐다. 몇몇 사람들은 여성 유권자들이 정치에 계몽적인 영향을 끼칠 것이며 그들이 가정에 속해 있기 때문에 가정과 가족에 강한 영향을 미치는 법에도 영향을 끼칠 것으로 생각했다. 그들은 여성들이 천성적으로 남자들보다 더 친절하고 더 다정다감하며 더 동정심이 많다고 믿었던 것이다. 한편, 다른 운동가들은 여성의 선거권을 사회 약자들의 참정권을 보상해주는 방법으로 보았다.

⭕ 여성에게 참정권을 주어야 한다는 운동가들 중에서도 여성만의 특성을 부각시켜 선거권을 주어야 한다고 주장하는 사람들과 여성과 남성을 동등한 입장에서 보면서 선거권을 주어야 한다고 주장하는 사람들로 나뉘었다는 내용이다. 두 주장이 서로 다르기 때문에, 전자의 주장은 이런 반면, 후자의 주장은 이러하다는 내용이 들어가므로 (c)가 정답이 된다.

women's suffrage movement 여성 참정권(선거권) 운동 campaigner (사회, 정치 따위의) 운동가 vote 투표하다, 투표, 참정권 disagreement 불일치, 논쟁 suffrage right 참정권, 선거권 enlightening 계몽적인, 계발적인, 명백하게 하는 have an effect on ~에 영향을 미치다 politics 정치, 정치학 influence ~에 영향을 미치다 impact on ~에 강한 영향을 주다 caring 돌보아 주는, 뒷바라지 하는 sympathetic 동정적인, 인정 있는 think of A as B A를 B라고 보다, 생각하다 compensate for ~을 보충하다, 보상하다

35 School phobia is a kind of social anxiety disorder that describes an overwhelming fear of going to school. School phobic children may become physically ill at the thought of being in class and sometimes suffer from severe panic attacks. They should not be mistaken for those who play truant at one time or another. If school refusal continues, discussion with school personnel will be needed to form a unified home and school approach. _____, chronic school phobias can cause the decline in academic performance and failure in peer relationships, possibly leading to adult anxiety disorders.

(a) Otherwise
(b) Likewise
(c) Meanwhile
(d) Therefore

학교공포증은 일종의 사회적 불안장애로서 학교를 다니는 것에 대한 극도의 두려움을 말한다. 학교공포증을 앓는 아이들은 수업 시간을 생각하는 것만으로도 몸이 아플 수도 있고 때로는 심각한 공황 발작으로 고통받기도 한다. 그들은 이따금 학교를 무단결석하는 학생들과 혼동되어서는 안 된다. 등교거부가 계속되면, 가정과 학교가 연대하여 문제에 접근하기 위해 학교 당국과 논의가 필요하다. 그렇지 않으면 만성적인 학교공포증은 학업성적이 떨어지거나 또래집단에 속하지 못하게 되는 일이 발생할 수 있으며, 성인 불안장애로 이어질 가능성이 높다.

◉ 학교공포증이 지속될 경우, 가정과 학교가 연계하여 문제 해결에 나서야 하는데, 그렇지 않고 만성적이 될 경우 야기되는 문제점이 이어지므로 (a)가 정답이다.

phobia 공포증, (병적인) 혐오 **disorder** 장애, 병 **play truant** 학교를 무단결석하다, 시간을 빼먹다 **at one time or another** 때때로 **personnel** (관청, 회사 등의) (전)직원, (총)인원 **chronic** 만성의, 고질의

---

36 The Web site www.goodparent.com provides some examples of traits of oldest, middle and youngest children. Parents should know about these characteristics and encourage children to develop desirable characteristics no matter their birth order. Firstborns are usually responsible, and sometimes substitute parent for younger siblings. If in a dysfunctional family, they may feel too much burden on themselves. Middle children are usually good negotiators. They may feel squeezed out and unloved and feel out of place in the family. Last borns are usually outgoing and creative. However, they tend to have few expectations of themselves because their parents may have lower expectations for their youngest after having raised several children already.

Q What can be inferred from the passage?

(a) Birth order stereotypes can bring more harm than good.
(b) Firstborns should take more responsibility than other siblings do.
(c) Children should be given opportunities according to their birth order
(d) Parents need to encourage the middle child to have a sense of belonging.

웹사이트 www.goodparent.com에서는 맏이, 중간, 막내인 아이들의 특성의 예를 제공하고 있다. 부모들은 이 특성들을 알아둬서, 아이들이 출생 순서에 상관없이 바람직한 특성을 개발할 수 있도록 격려해야 한다. 맏이들은 대개 책임감이 강하고 때로 어린 동생들에게 부모의 대리인 역할을 하기도 한다. 만약 문제가정이라면 맏이들은 너무 많은 부담감을 느낄 수도 있다. 중간에 끼인 아이들은 대개 협상에 능하다. 그들은 소외감을 느끼거나 사랑 받지 못한다고 느낄 수도 있으며 가족에 자신이 어울리지 않는다고 느끼기도 한다. 막내들은 보통 외향적이고 창의적이다. 그러나 부모들이 이미 몇 명의 자녀를 양육해보았기 때문에 막내들에게는 낮은 기대치를 가질 수도 있어서 막내들은 자신에 대해 별 기대를 갖지 않는 경향이 있다.

◉ 출생순서에 따라 형성되는 특성들이 있지만, 이를 잘 활용하여 부모가 격려를 통해 자녀가 선천적으로 부족한 특성을 후천적으로 개발하도록 할 수 있다는 내용이다. 중간에 끼인 아이들은 소외감을 느끼거나, 가족과 어울리지 않는다고 느끼기 쉬우므로 소속감을 가지도록 격려해야 하므로 정답은 (d)이다. 이를 통해 긍정적인 영향을 미칠 수도 있으므로 (a)는 답이 될 수 없고, 맏이가 다른 형제보다 많은 책임을 져야 한다는 것은 언급되지 않았으므로 (b)도 답이 될 수 없으며, 출생순서에 따라 기회가 주어져야 한다는 것은 글의 주제와 상반되므로 (c)도 답이 될 수 없다.

trait 특징, 특색 **birth order** 출생순서 **substitute** 대리의, 대용의 **sibling** 형제, 자매 **dysfunctional family** 역기능[문제]가정 **negotiator** 협상가 **squeeze out** 짜내다, (사람을) 밀어내다, 소외시키다 **out of place** 어울리지 않는, 제자리가 아닌

37 The Digital Home D146, marketing globally, makes its debut this week. It is designed to support up to 16 channels of real-time recording and provide the most flexible operation to allow home users to use it with ease. Users can set up a weekly recording schedule at their own will, and decide which hours of the day they want to record. It can also be installed in various locations in the house. Home users can monitor all cameras at one time and see any suspected images without wasting time if any motions are detected. It is characterized by the leading technology device that enables to restart its task after interruption of electric power or system crash.

Q What is the Digital Home D146?

(a) camcorder
(b) video camera
(c) digital camera
(d) surveillance system

세계적으로 홍보해오고 있는 Digital Home D146이 이번 주에 첫 선을 보인다. 이 장치는 최대 16채널까지 실시간 녹화를 할 수 있고, 매우 유연한 조작으로 가정에서의 이용자들이 쉽게 사용할 수 있도록 설계되었다. 이용자들은 원하는 대로 일주일간의 녹화 계획을 미리 짤 수도 있고, 녹화하고 싶은 시간을 정할 수도 있다. 또한 이것은 집안 다양한 장소에 설치될 수 있다. 이용자들은 모든 카메라를 동시에 감시할 수 있으며, 어떤 움직임이라도 감지되면 즉시 의심이 가는 영상을 볼 수 있다. 정전이나 시스템의 고장 이후 작업을 다시 시작할 수 있도록 해 주는 첨단 기술 장치도 이 제품의 특징이다.

🔵 집안 곳곳에 설치되어 원하는 시간에 녹화를 하고 뭔가 의심이 가는 영상이 발견되면 즉시 그 장면을 볼 수 있다는 것은 감시카메라 (d)의 특징이다.

make one's debut 첫 무대를 밟다, 데뷔하다 design A to V A가 ~하도록 의도하다, 계획하다 support ~을 지탱하다, 지지하다, (컴퓨터 본체가 관련된 기구, 기능을) 지원하다 up to (시간, 공간적으로) 최고 ~에 이르기까지 real-time 실시간의 flexible 유연성이 있는, 적응성이 있는, 융통성이 있는 operation 작업, 효력, 조작, 운영, 수술, 군사작전 allow A to V A가 ~하도록 허락하다 with ease 쉽게 (=easily) set up ~을 세우다, 짜 맞추다 at one's own will ~의 뜻대로, 마음 내키는 대로 install ~을 설치하다 suspect ~이 아닌가 의심하다, (위험, 음모 따위를) 어렴풋이 느끼다 detect (나쁜 것 따위를) 발견하다, 간파하다 ; ~을 탐지하다 characterize ~의 특색을 이루다. ~을 특징 지우다 device 고안, 장치 interruption 방해, 중지, 정전 electric 전기의 crash 충돌, (비행기의) 추락. (컴퓨터 시스템의) 고장

38 Monarchs are large and colorful butterflies that live in various countries such as America, Australia, and Western Europe. The average wingspan of a monarch is almost four inches and the wings are bright orange with decorative black veins and white dots along the edge. A monarch's vivid coloring plays a role in warning predators that they are poisonous. However, even though an animal eats a monarch, it doesn't actually die, it's only sick enough to avoid the butterflies in the future.

Q What can be inferred from the passage?

(a) A monarch is the largest butterfly.
(b) Monarchs live throughout the world.
(c) A monarch's toxins are not fatal but harmful.
(d) A monarch is noticeable even at night due to its colors.

제주왕나비는 미국과 호주, 서유럽과 같은 다양한 나라들에 서식하는 크고 색깔이 화려한 나비이다. 제주왕나비의 평균 날개폭은 거의 4인치나 되고 날개는 밝은 오렌지색인데 검은 시맥과 가장자리에 있는 흰 점들로 장식되어 있다. 제주왕나비의 선명한 색깔은 자신이 유독하다는 것을 천적에게 경고하는 역할을 한다. 그러나 비록 어떤 동물이 제주왕나비를 먹을지라도 그 동물은 실제로는 죽지 않고 단지 앞으로 그 나비를 피할 만큼만 아프게 된다.

🔵 마지막 문장이 문제를 푸는 단서가 된다. 제주왕나비가 자신의 색깔을 통해 독성이 있다는 것을 천적에게 알릴지라도 사실, 제주왕나비를 먹게 되면 죽지는 않고 아프기만 하다는 것으로 보아 제주왕나비의 독소는 치명적이지 않다는 것을 알 수 있다. (a)제주왕나비가 크기는 하지만 가장 큰 나비인지는 알 수 없으며 (b)여러 나라에 살지만 전 세계에 걸쳐서 산다고도 말할 수 없고 (d)본문에는 제주왕나비의 색깔이 밝다고는 나와 있지만 밤에 보일 정도로 밝은지는 알 수가 없다.

monarch butterfly 제주왕나비 wingspan 날개폭 decorative 장식의 vein 시맥(翅脈) edge 끝, 가장자리 vivid 선명한 predator 포식동물, 천적 poisonous 유독한 toxin 독소 fatal 치명적인

39 The subprime mortgage crisis is a current problem which became more manifest these days. The US mortgages have three levels such as Prime, Alternative-A, and Subprime. Of the three, Subprime is considered the lowest mortgage loan. It is applied to people who have unstable credit histories such as bankruptcies, payment delinquencies, and charge-offs so they hold a mortgage with a high interest rate. The subprime mortgage crisis began as the decrease of lending standards, the increase in loan incentives and the high expectation of housing prices encouraged people to borrow money easily and refinance as well. However, when the interest rates started to rise and the real estate price dropped, borrowers faced totally different situations.

Q What can't be inferred as a cause of subprime mortgage crisis?

(a) the excessive individual debt levels
(b) the downturn in the housing market
(c) the risky lending and borrowing policy
(d) the incomplete network of investment banks

subprime mortgage 사태는 요즘 더욱 분명해진 문제이다. 미국의 담보대출은 prime, alternative-a, subprime 이렇게 세 가지 등급으로 나누어진다. 세 가지 중에서 subprime은 가장 낮은 등급의 주택담보 대출로 여겨진다. subprime은 파산이나 채무불이행, 불량채권 상각 등의 불안정한 신용 전력이 있는 사람들에게 적용되는데, 이런 사람들은 높은 이자율의 부담을 안고 집을 저당잡힌다. subprime mortgage 사태는 대출기준은 낮아지고, 대출의 유인요소는 많아지며, 주택가격의 상승에 대한 기대가 커져 subprime 등급에 있는 사람들로 하여금 쉽게 돈을 빌리고, 빚을 갚을 수 있다고 부추겨서 시작되었다. 그러나 이자율이 오르고 부동산 가격은 떨어지기 시작하자 차용인들은 완전히 다른 상황에 직면하게 되었다.

○ subprime mortgage 사태가 왜 일어났는가를 설명하고 있는 글이다. subprime 등급에 있는 사람들이 이자율이 높아지니까 빚이 지나치게 많아지게 되었고(a), 부동산 가격이 떨어지자 주택시장이 침체기에 빠졌으며(b), 신용등급이 좋지 않은 사람들에게 돈을 빌려주고 받은 위험한 정책(c)으로 인해 subprime mortgage 사태가 일어났다는 것이다. 하지만, 투자은행간의 네트워크가 불안정했다(d)는 내용은 언급되어 있지 않다.

mortgage 저당, 저당권, 융자 subprime mortgage 저소득층을 대상으로 하는 주택담보 대출 current 통용되고 있는, 현행의 manifest 명백한 consider A (as) B A를 B로 생각하다, 간주하다 loan 대부(금), 대여, 차관 apply A to B A를 B에 적용하다, 응용하다 unstable 불안정한 bankruptcy 파산, 도산 payment 지불, 납부 delinquency 의무불이행, 연체, (청소년) 비행 charge-off (불량채권 따위의) 상각 interest rate 이자율 incentive 격려, 자극, 유인, 동기 expectation 예상, 기대, 가능성, 확률 housing 주택, 주택공급 encourage A to V A가 ~하도록 용기를 돋우다, 장려하다 refinance 재정을 다시 세우다, 빚을 갚고 또 빚을 내다 real estate 부동산

---

40 Food poisoning is common, but sometimes fatal. (a) Typical symptoms are nausea and diarrhea that occur abruptly within 48 hours after eating a contaminated food. (b) Depending on the poison, fever and bloody stools, dehydration, and nervous system damage may follow. (c) The symptoms, called an outbreak, may affect one person or a group of people who ate the same food. (d) Additionally, there are possible new global threats to the world's food supply through terrorist actions using food toxins.

식중독은 흔하지만 치명적일 수 있다. (a)전형적 증상은 오염된 음식을 먹은 후 48시간 이내에 곧 나타나며 메스꺼움이나 설사의 증상을 보인다. (b) 독성의 증상에 따라 열, 혈변, 탈수, 신경의 손상 등이 올 수 있다. (c)증상, 즉 발병은 같은 음식을 먹은 한 사람이나 단체에 모두 영향을 줄 수 있다. (d) 또한 음식물 독을 이용한 테러리스트들의 행동으로 인해 세계 식량공급에 새로운 위험을 줄 수 있다.

○ 전체 문장은 식중독에 대한 설명인데 반해 마지막 (d)는 테러리스트들의 공격을 우려한다는 내용으로 전반적인 내용에 벗어난다.

fatal 치명적인, 생명에 관련된 nausea 구토, 메스꺼움 diarrhea 설사 abruptly 갑자기, 퉁명스럽게 contaminate 오염시키다, 더럽히다 toxin 독소

LISTENING COMPREHENSION · P.90

1　**M**　Can you give me a hand?
　　W　_____

(a) Get a grip on yourself.
(b) Yes. It's handmade.
(c) No, I don't have it.
(d) By all means.

M: 나 좀 도와줄 수 있어?
W: 그럼요.

⮕ give sb a hand라는 표현을 알아야 풀 수 있는 문제이다. 직역하면 '손을 주다' 인데, '도와주다, 손을 빌려주다' 라는 뜻이다. (b)에서 hand가 나온다고 하여 섣불리 고르지 않도록 한다. handmade는 '수제품' 이라는 뜻으로 문맥과 상관이 없는 보기이다. by all means 는 어떠한 제안에 대해 승낙을 할 때 쓸 수 있는 표현으로 활용도가 높으므로 꼭 기억해두도록 하자.

give sb a hand ~을 돕다 get a grip on oneself 자제하다 by all means (승낙할 때) 그럼요, 기꺼이

2　**M**　Are you being helped?
　　W　_____

(a) I couldn't help it.
(b) Yes. I helped him.
(c) Don't worry. I found it.
(d) No, thank you. I'm just browsing.

M: 도와드리고 있는 점원이 있나요?
W: 아니요, 됐습니다. 그냥 구경하고 있어요.

⮕ 상점이나 식당 등에서 혹시 점원의 도움을 받고 있는지 물어볼 때 Are you being helped?라는 표현을 쓴다. (a)와 (b)는 help를 이용하여 혼동을 주기 위함이며 문맥과는 상관이 없으므로 정답이 아니다. (d)의 경우 '그냥 혼자 둘러보겠다.' 는 의미로 'I'm just browsing.' 이라는 표현을 쓴다. 이와 같은 표현으로는 'I'm just looking around.' 가 있다.

can't help 어쩔 도리가 없다 I'm just browsing. (상점에서) 그냥 둘러보는 중이에요.

3　**M**　How many are there in your party?
　　W　_____

(a) It was a great party.
(b) It'll take a few minutes.
(c) There are three of us.
(d) Usually ten people attend.

M: 일행이 몇 분이십니까?
W: 저희 세 명이요.

⮕ party는 여러 가지 뜻을 가진 다의어이다. 흔히 우리가 알고 있는 '파티' 라는 뜻 외에 일행, 단체라는 뜻도 있고, 정당이나 당파를 뜻하기도 한다. 문제에 나온 표현은 식당에서 점원이 할 수 있는 표현으로 여기서 party는 '일행' 을 의미한다. (a)는 party가 문제와는 다른 의미인 즐기는 파티를 의미하므로 정답이 될 수 없다. (d)는 보통 열 명이 참석한다는 뜻으로 어떠한 모임의 인원수를 말하는 것인데, 사람의 숫자가 나와 혼동될 수는 있지만 상황에 맞지 않으므로 정답이 아니다.

party 파티, 일행, 단체, 정당 attend ~에 참석하다, 출석하다

4
M Please give this report to Lisa.
W Well, she's not here.
M Where is she? Is she late again?
W _____

(a) She called in sick.
(b) She lives off campus
(c) She is going into labor
(d) She didn't sleep a wink.

M: 이 보고서 좀 리사에게 전해줘.
W: 근데, 리사 여기 없는데.
M: 어디 있는데? 또 지각이야?
W: 아프다고 전화 왔어.

◐ 회사에서 일어날 수 있는 상황이다. 리사가 자리에 없다고 했으므로 그 이유로 적절한 것을 찾아야 한다. 가장 적합한 답은 (a)로 '아파서 결근한다고 전화를 했다' 이다.

call in sick 전화로 병가를 내다 off campus 캠퍼스 밖의 go into labor 산고를 겪다, 산기가 있다 not sleep a wink 한숨도 못자다

5
M What's the matter? You look so down.
W I blew the test.
M I'm sorry. Isn't there another chance?
W _____

(a) I think you put on make-up too much.
(b) It's none of your business.
(c) It's not a big deal.
(d) I can take a make-up test.

M: 무슨 일이야? 기분이 가라앉아 보여.
W: 시험을 망쳤어.
M: 안됐다. 만회할 기회는 없는 거야?
W: 재시험을 치를 수 있어.

◐ 남자의 마지막 대사에 주목하자. 또 다른 기회가 없다고 했으므로 정답은 (d) '재시험을 치를 수 있다' 가 정답이 된다. make up은 화장한다는 의미 외에 보충한다는 뜻이 있으므로 문맥을 통해 어떤 의미로 쓰인 것인지 잘 파악해야 한다. 안됐다고 위로하는 친구에게 (b)와 같은 대답은 어울리지 않는다.

blow a test 시험을 망치다 make-up test 재시험 put on make-up 화장을 하다 It's none of your business. 상관하지 말아라 It's not a big deal. 별일 아니다.

6
M I like your jacket.
W Thanks. I bought it at the department store.
M It really goes with that skirt. I think you have an eye for fashion.
W _____

(a) I'm flattered.
(b) I'm an eyesore.
(c) Hem up, please.
(d) I'm green with envy.

M: 재킷 멋지네요.
W: 고마워요. 백화점에서 샀어요.
M: 그 치마와 정말 잘 어울리는데요. 패션 감각이 있으신 것 같아요.
W: 과찬이세요.

◐ 남자가 여자의 패션 감각에 대해 칭찬을 하고 있으므로 칭찬에 대한 겸손한 표현인 (a) '과찬이시네요' 가 정답이 된다. eye라는 단어가 나왔기 때문에 섣불리 (b)를 정답으로 고르지 않도록 한다. eyesore는 전혀 반대의 뜻을 가지고 있기 때문이다. (c)는 단을 줄여 달라는 표현으로 세탁소에 옷을 맡길 때 쓸 수 있는 표현이다.

department store 백화점 go with ~와 잘 어울리다, 조화되다 have an eye for ~에 대한 안목이 있다 I'm flattered. 과찬이십니다. eyesore 눈에 거슬리는 것, 보기 흉한 것 hem ~의 가장자리를 감치다, 옷단을 대다 green with envy 질투하는, 시샘하는

7
M Hi. Welcome to Ann's Hamburger. Are you ready to order?

W Yes. I'd like a hamburger with some mustard and lettuce and a glass of water.

M Will this be for here or to go?

W To go.

M Would you care for anything else like a side order of onion rings?

W No, thank you. Onion rings usually don't agree with me.

M Okay. Your total comes to six ninety.

Q What is correct according to the conversation?

(a) The woman ordered a hamburger and a side dish.

(b) The woman wants to have a hamburger delivered.

(c) The restaurant ran out of onion rings.

(d) The woman doesn't like onion rings.

M: 안녕하세요, 앤 햄버거에 오신 것을 환영합니다. 주문하시겠어요?

W: 네, 머스터드소스와 양배추를 곁들인 햄버거랑 물 한잔이요.

M: 드시고 가실 건가요 아니면 포장해 가실 건가요?

W: 포장해주세요.

M: 양파 링과 같은 사이드 메뉴는 필요없으십니까?

W: 괜찮습니다. 양파 링은 저랑 안 맞더라고요.

M: 네, 알겠습니다. 전부 6달러 90센트입니다.

◆ 대화와 일치하는 것을 고르는 문제이다. 여자가 주문한 음식은 햄버거와 물 한잔이었고 사이드 메뉴는 주문하지 않았으므로 (a)는 정답이 아니다. 여자가 햄버거를 배달시킨 것이 아니므로 (b)도 정답이 될 수 없다. 양파 링을 점원이 권했으므로 양파 링이 다 떨어졌다는 의미의 (c)는 정답이 아니다. 여자가 양파 링이 자기와 잘 안 맞는다고 했으므로 정답은 (d)가 된다.

deliver ~을 배달하다 run out of ~을 다 써버리다. (물건을) 바닥내다

8
M So, how are you feeling today?

W I was feeling okay on Friday, but I started to feel sick Saturday evening.

M Well, why don't you get some rest?

W No, I can't. I'm scheduled to give a presentation at work on Tuesday. I've got tons of work to do.

M So, did you see a doctor? I think you should take some medicine.

W Yes. The doctor said it's just a bad cold. He gave me some cold medicine to take care of my stuffy nose. But it doesn't seem to help.

M Oh, I'm so sorry.

Q What is correct according to the conversation?

(a) The woman is having a rest due to a cold.

(b) The woman is going to give a presentation.

(c) The woman is getting a checkup in the hospital.

(d) The woman doesn't want to take medicine.

M: 그래서 오늘은 좀 어때?

W: 금요일에는 괜찮았는데 토요일 저녁부터 아프기 시작했어.

M: 그럼 좀 쉬는 게 어때?

W: 그럴 수 없어. 화요일에 회사에서 발표를 하기로 되어있어. 할 일이 산더미 같아.

M: 그래서 병원엔 가봤어? 약을 먹는 게 좋을 것 같은데.

W: 갔었어. 의사 선생님이 심한 감기래. 코감기에 좋은 약을 주셨어. 근데 별로 도움이 안 되는 것 같아.

M: 안됐다.

◆ 대화 내용과 일치하는 문장을 고르는 문제다. 여자가 감기에 걸렸지만 일이 많아서 쉴 수 없다고 했으므로 (a)는 정답이 아니다. 여자가 화요일에 발표를 하기로 되어있다고 했으므로 (b)는 정답이 될 수 있다. 여자가 병원에서 건강 검진을 받는다는 이야기는 언급되지 않았으므로 (c)는 알 수 없다. 병원에서 지은 약이 잘 듣지 않는 것 같다고 했으므로 약을 먹고 있는 중이라는 것을 알 수 있다. 그러므로 (d)는 정답이라고 하기 어렵다.

be scheduled to ~하기로 예정되어 있다 give a presentation 발표를 하다 take medicine 약을 먹다 stuffy nose 코막힘 get a checkup 건강 검진을 받다

9　W　You look so worried. What's the matter?

　　M　Well, I really want to sign up for the literature class, but I just found out that the class was already filled up.

　　W　I guess some people might drop the class and then there will be some openings. You never know.

　　M　I hope so.

　　W　Come on, cheer up. Don't worry.

　　M　Okay. I'll wait and see.

　Q　What are the speakers talking about?

　　(a) About giving a presentation
　　(b) About how to drop the classes
　　(c) About job openings
　　(d) About registering for a class

W: 매우 걱정스러운 얼굴이네. 무슨 일이야?
M: 문학 수업을 신청하고 싶은데, 수업이 이미 꽉 찼다는 걸 방금 알았어.
W: 수강 신청 취소하는 사람들도 있을 것이고, 그러면 자리가 조금 생길 것 같아. 누가 알겠어.
M: 그랬으면 좋겠다.
W: 이 봐, 힘내. 걱정하지 말고.
M: 알았어. 기다려볼게.

◗ 대화 주제에 대해 묻고 있다. 수강 신청에 대해 이야기하고 있으므로 정답은 (d)가 된다. (b)의 경우 수강 신청을 취소하는 방법에 대해서는 전혀 언급이 없었으므로 정답이 될 수 없다.

sign up for ~을 신청하다 (= register for) fill up 가득 채우다 drop the class 수강 신청을 취소하다

10　Don't hesitate any longer in making your dreams come true! People usually tend to put off their goal by making poor excuses for why you aren't able to be in the shape you want. If you arm yourself with this information, you'll get the sexy tight body you want. If you care about your health and your loved ones, this is a must-read program. I strongly suggest this is a manual of how to learn to eat healthy for your specific body type. You can download the package in Adobe PDF format right to your computer after ordering.

　Q　What is being advertised?

　　(a) Dietary supplements
　　(b) Manual for using e-books
　　(c) New computer software
　　(d) Body exercise program

꿈을 현실에서 이루는 것을 더 이상 주저하지 마세요. 사람들은 대개 자신이 왜 원하는 몸매가 될 수 없는지에 대해 궁색한 변명을 하면서 목표를 미루는 경향이 있습니다. 만약 이러한 정보로 무장을 한다면 원하는 섹시하고 타이트한 몸매를 갖게 될 것입니다. 자신과 가족의 건강을 염려한다면 이것은 꼭 읽어야만 하는 프로그램입니다. 저는 이것이 특정 신체 타입에 맞춰 음식을 건강하게 섭취하는 방법에 대한 설명서라고 자신 있게 추천합니다. 주문 후에 패키지를 PDF 파일 형식으로 바로 컴퓨터에 다운받으실 수 있습니다.

◗ 광고 대상에 대한 문제이다. 몇 가지 단어만 잘 들었어도 정답을 쉽게 맞힐 수 있다. 'must-read program', 'manual', 'download the package' 등의 단어로 미루어 보아 섭취하는 식품은 아니며 'eat healthy'라고 했으므로 컴퓨터 소프트웨어에 대한 이야기도 아니다. 주로 건강과 타이트한 몸매에 관하여 반복적으로 언급하고 있으므로 정답은 (d)이다. manual이라는 단어 때문에 (b)를 고르지 않도록 주의하자.

hesitate 주저하다, 망설이다 put off ~을 미루다, 연기하다 make one's excuse 변명하다 dietary supplements 건강보조식품

11 When an urgent situation has arisen, what would you do first? Most people easily get to be in a panic. But if you keep in mind what I'm going to tell you from now on, you'll deal with an emergency well. In emergency situations such as fire, theft, and robbery, all you have to do is just call 9-1-1 and answer the operator's questions! Never be at a loss, just stay calm and speak clearly. And report the problem and situation.

Q What is the speaker talking about?

(a) Why people are at a loss in emergency
(b) How to put out a fire
(c) How to deal with emergency
(d) How to answer the 9-1-1 operator

긴급한 상황이 발생하면 제일 먼저 어떻게 하시겠습니까? 대부분의 사람들은 쉽게 당황합니다. 하지만 지금부터 제가 말씀드리는 것을 명심한다면 긴급한 상황에 잘 대처할 수 있을 것입니다. 화재, 절도, 강도와 같은 긴급 상황에서 가장 중요한 것은 911에 전화를 하여 교환원의 질문에 대답하는 것입니다. 절대 당황하지 마시고 침착함을 유지하면서 분명하게 말씀을 하세요. 그리고 문제와 상황을 신고하세요.

○ 주제에 대해 묻고 있다. (a)에 대한 언급은 없었고, 화재는 긴급 상황의 예로 든 것이므로 (b)는 정답이 아니며 (d)에 대해서도 자세한 언급이 없었다. 전체적으로 긴급 상황에 어떻게 대처해야 하는지에 대해 이야기하고 있으므로 정답은 (c)가 된다.

panic 당황, 공포 keep in mind 명심하다 operator 교환원
be at a loss 당황하다 put out (불 따위를) 끄다

---

12 Hello, everyone. Thank you for tuning into the Heart & Talk Show. I'm your host, Amanda Peterson. Today we'll meet a woman who has difficulty recognizing new faces. She has been suffering from recognizing her colleagues and neighbors which makes her experience social embarrassment. Scientists have been researching about this matter for many years. And they suggest her disability might not be caused by her ability to perceive new faces, but by her inability to encode. She relies on some cues such as hair color, eye glasses, and manner of speaking. Now, are you ready to listen to her story? Please stay tuned. I'll be right back.

Q What is likely to follow this talk?

(a) Interview with audiences
(b) Interview with the scientists
(c) Commercials
(d) Introduction of the guest

안녕하세요, 여러분. Hear & Talk 쇼를 시청해 주셔서 감사합니다. 저는 여러분의 호스트, 아만다 피터슨입니다. 오늘은 새로운 얼굴을 인식하는 데 어려움을 겪고 있는 한 여성을 만나보겠습니다. 그녀는 자신의 동료와 이웃을 알아보는 데 어려움을 겪고 있고, 이로 인해 사회생활에 난처함을 겪고 있습니다. 과학자들은 수년 동안 이 문제에 대해 연구를 해 왔는데요. 그들은 그녀의 문제가 새로운 얼굴을 인식하는 능력에서 비롯된 것이 아니라 암호화할 수 없는 능력에서 비롯되는 것이라고 말합니다. 그녀는 머리 색깔, 안경, 어투와 같은 단서에 의존합니다. 자, 그녀의 이야기를 들을 준비가 되셨습니까? 채널 고정해주세요. 잠시 후에 다시 뵙겠습니다.

○ 이어질 내용에 대해 묻고 있다. 다음에 이어질 내용이므로 마지막 부분을 주의해서 들어야 한다. 채널을 고정해 달라는 이야기와 잠시 뒤에 다시 오겠다는 이야기로 미루어보아 프로그램이 시작하기 전 광고 방송이 나갈 것임을 짐작할 수 있다. 따라서 정답은 (c)가 된다.

recognize ~을 인지하다, 인식하다 colleague 동료
disability 무능력 perceive ~을 지각하다, 인지하다
encode ~을 암호화하다 rely on ~에 의존하다 cue 단서, 실마리 commercial 광고 방송

13 A Somebody already checked out the book the teacher recommends, where can I borrow it?

B I bought one, so if you want, I will _____.

(a) lend it you

(b) lend it for you

(c) lend it to you

(d) get it for you

A: 누군가가 이미 선생님께서 추천하신 책을 대여했어. 어디서 이 책을 빌릴 수 있을까?

B: 나 그 책 샀어, 네가 원한다면 빌려줄게

◯ 'B에게 A를 빌려주다' 라는 의미의 'lend A to B' 가 들어가야 한다.

---

14 A How many joined the exhibition?

B Not so many, just _____ visited our booth.

(a) less

(b) a few

(c) few

(d) more

A: 얼마나 많은 사람들이 전시회에 참가했니?

B: 그렇게 많지는 않아, 우리 전시장에는 몇 안 되는 사람들이 방문했어.

◯ 흐름상 B가 '많지는 않지만 조금 방문한다' 라는 의미이므로, '조금' 이라는 뜻의 a few가 적절하다.

exhibition 전시회, 전시품 few 거의 없는 a few 조금 있는

---

15 A I don't understand why parents let the children run around?

B _____.

(a) So am I

(b) So do I

(c) Me neither

(d) Me either

A: 나는 부모님들이 왜 자식들을 뛰어다니게 내버려 두는지 이해가 안돼.

B: 나도 그래.

◯ 부정에 대한 대답이므로 neither를 써야 한다.

---

16 A How long do we have to go to the palace?

B _____.

(a) Here I am

(b) Here we are

(c) We are here

(d) Here you are

A: 궁전에 도착하려면 얼마나 가야 해?

B: 이제 다 왔어

◯ '이제 다 왔어' 라는 의미를 가진 (b)가 적당하다.

palace 궁궐, 대저택

17 _____ than the Boeing 747, the airbus, the European manufacturer said, has been slow to react to the company.

(a) Having started the project latter
(b) Having started the project later
(c) Started the project the latter
(d) Starting the project the latter

보잉 747보다 더 나중에 그 프로젝트를 시작해서 에어버스는 늦게 반응했다고 유럽의 제조사는 밝혔다.

○ 후발주자의 의미, 즉 더 나중에 시작했다는 의미의 분사구문이므로 (a)가 적절하다.

manufacturer 제조업자 latter 더 나중에 later (시간이) 더 늦게

---

18 The child whistled for the help and narrowly escaped _____ when being robbed in the street.

(a) to kidnap
(b) being kidnapped
(c) to be kidnapped
(d) have kidnapped

그 어린이는 길에서 납치되려 했을 때 도움을 청하는 휘슬을 불고서 겨우 도망쳤다.

○ 'escape v-ing' 가 '~로부터 도망치다' 이고, 납치되다는 kidnap의 수동형을 써야하므로 being kidnapped가 된다.

whistle 휘파람을 불다, 경적을 울리다 kidnap 납치하다

---

19 Before adopting a pet, _____, and you'll choose an animal that will fit into your lifestyle.

(a) having some research
(b) doing some research
(c) to do some research
(d) do some research

애완동물을 입양하기 전에 조사를 해라. 그러면 너의 라이프스타일에 맞는 동물을 선택할 수 있을 것이다.

○ '조사 좀 해봐라' 는 명령문 형태의 문장이 필요하다.

adopt 입양하다

---

20 He denied that the result of the match was creating a more cut-throat environment _____ players didn't desire.

(a) in which
(b) for which
(c) what
(d) when

그는 경기의 결과가 선수들이 원치 않는 더 많은 환경파괴를 만들고 있다는 것을 부인했다.

○ 뒤에 오는 문장의 desire동사에는 for가 필요하므로 for + 관계 대명사 형태가 알맞다.

cut throat 흉악한

---

21 (a) A: Have you done with this project?
(b) B: No. I don't understand why we do this useless project.
(c) A: Me, either, however, whether we like it or not, we have to finish it by 5.
(d) B: That makes me really crazy.

A: 너 그 프로젝트 끝냈니?

B: 아니, 난 왜 우리가 이 쓸모없는 프로젝트를 해야 하는지 이해가 안돼.

A: 나도야. 그런데 우리가 이걸 좋아하든 않든 우리는 5시까지 끝내야 해.

B: 그게 정말 나를 미쳐버리게 한다니까.

○ (c)에서 부정에 대한 대답을 하는 상황이므로 either을 neither로 고쳐야 한다.

useless 쓸모없는 whether~ or not ~ 인지 아닌지

22 (a) And yet, during the group's heyday, the group never made big in the States.
(b) The group scored a number one hit on Billboard's Top 40 singles chart. (c) But the group's hit singles never quite translated into substantial album sales, and the four individual members were remained fairly anonymous, never turning into household names. (d) Compared to the group's success in Europe and Australia, the impact in the United States was fairly modest.

한창때에도 그 그룹은 미국 내에서 큰 성공을 못했었다. 그 그룹은 확실히 빌보드 싱글 차트에서 top 40을 기록했다. 그러나 그 그룹의 히트 싱글판은 실제 앨범 판매에서 큰 히트를 치지 못했으며, 4명의 멤버는 귀에 익은 이름이 아닌 무명으로 남아있다. 유럽과 호주에서의 그룹의 성공과 비교해보면 미국에서의 영향력은 꽤 약했다.

◑ (c)에서 remain은 남아있다라는 의미로 수동 표현을 쓰지 않는다. were remained를 remained로 고쳐야 한다.

heyday 한창때 affairs 일, 관심사 substantial 실제의 anonymous 무명, 익명의 modest 미미한, 겸손한

---

23 **A** Should I bring you something for your party?
B Just _____ yourself.

(a) be
(b) make
(c) bring
(d) stay

A: 파티에 뭐 좀 가지고 갈까?
B: 그냥 몸만 와.

◑ 파티에 초대받은 사람이 뭘 좀 가져가야 되느냐고 묻는 질문에 적절한 대답은 '가져올 것이 없으니 그냥 몸만 오라' 는 것이다. 이에 적합한 표현은 'Just bring yourself.' 이다.

Just bring yourself. 그냥 몸만 오세요, 빈손으로 오세요.

---

24 **A** Do you want to catch a midnight movie?
B I'm sorry. I'm a bit tired. I'm just going to _____.

(a) turn in
(b) turn up
(c) go in
(d) lie in

A: 심야영화 보러 갈래?
B: 미안해. 조금 피곤해서. 그냥 잠이나 잘래.

◑ 영화를 보러 가자는 제안에 피곤하다고 했으므로 잠을 자겠다는 표현인 'turn in' 이 정답이 된다.

catch a movie 영화를 보다 turn in 잠자리에 들다, ~을 제출하다 turn up (사람이 어떠한 장소에) 나타나다, (일, 사건이) 갑자기 생기다 go in ~에 들어가다 lie in ~에 있다(consist in)

---

25 **A** Why are you taking only 12 credits?
B The _____ has risen up too much.

(a) fare
(b) charge
(c) tuition
(d) bill

A: 왜 12학점만 듣니?
B: 등록금이 너무 많이 올랐어.

◑ credit이 힌트가 된다. 학점 이수에 대한 이야기가 나왔으므로 정답은 등록금을 뜻하는 tuition이 된다.

credit (이수 단위) 학점 tuition 등록금 fare (기차, 버스 등의) 요금 charge 요금, 수수료, 비용

26 **A** Excuse me. Are you with me?
 B Sure. I'm all _____.

 (a) ears
 (b) ear
 (c) thumbs
 (d) eyes

A: 미안하지만, 내 말 알아들었어?
B: 그럼. 열심히 듣고 있어.

⟳ 'Are you with me?' 의 뜻을 알아야 풀 수 있는 문제이다. '알아듣다, 이해하다' 라는 뜻으로 이와 비슷한 표현을 찾아야 한다. 'be all ears' 라는 표현은 '열심히 듣다' 라는 표현이므로 정답은 ears가 된다.

be all ears 열심히 듣다, 경청하다

---

27 **A** What are you going to do for the guests after exchanging gifts?
 B We're going to serve light _____ and snacks.

 (a) refreshments
 (b) recreation
 (c) entertainments
 (d) discussion

A: 선물을 교환한 다음에 손님들을 위해 무엇을 할 예정이니?
B: 가벼운 다과와 간식을 제공할거야.

⟳ and 다음에 snacks가 나왔으므로 비슷한 뜻의 단어를 찾아야 한다. refreshments가 가벼운 다과, 간식을 의미하므로 정답은 (a)가 된다.

refreshment 다과, 가벼운 음식 **recreation** 기분 전환, 오락

---

28 People were very frightened about the possible spread of a _____ disease called SARS.

 (a) mild
 (b) chronic
 (c) deficiency
 (d) contagious

사람들은 사스라고 불리는 전염병의 확산 가능성에 대해 매우 두려워했다.

⟳ spread가 힌트가 될 수 있다. 병이 확산되기 위해서는 전염성이 있어야 하므로 정답은 (d)가 된다.

contagious 전염성의, 감염이 되는 **chronic** 만성의

---

29 Agricultural biotech _____ argue that farmers can benefit from genetically modified foods, at this time of global food shortages, and extreme weather.

 (a) protectors
 (b) proportions
 (c) prosecutions
 (d) proponents

농업 생명공학 지지자들은 세계 식량 부족 현상과 극단적인 날씨가 나타나는 이러한 시대에 농부들이 유전자 조작 식품들로부터 이익을 얻을 수 있다고 주장한다.

⟳ that 이하의 내용을 살펴보면 농업 생명공학을 찬성하는 사람들의 주장임을 알 수 있다. 따라서 정답은 (d)가 된다.

agricultural 농업의 **proponent** 제안자, 지지자, 옹호자
genetically modified 유전자 조작의 **shortage** 결핍, 부족
proportion 비, 비율 **prosecution** 기소, 고소

---

30 During _____ the third party talk to both sides in a controversy to make a decision impartially.

 (a) aristocracy
 (b) arbitration
 (c) meditation
 (d) argumentation

중재를 하는 동안 제 삼자는 편견 없이 결정을 내리기 위해 논쟁 중인 양 진영과 대화를 나눈다.

⟳ impartially가 중요한 힌트가 되고 있다. 편견 없는 결정을 내린다고 했으므로 중재에 관한 이야기임을 알 수 있다. 다른 보기의 경우 빈 칸에 넣었을 때 해석이 자연스럽지 못하다.

arbitration 중재, 조정 **impartially** 편견 없이, 공평하게
aristocracy 귀족, 명문 **meditation** 심사숙고, 명상
argumentation 추론, 논증

31 The two leaders who couldn't bridge the differences have failed to _____ after all.

(a) reciprocate
(b) reconcile
(c) reinforce
(d) refurbish

의견 차이를 좁히지 못한 두 지도자는 결국 화해에 실패했다.

○ bridge the differences라는 표현을 알아야 풀 수 있는 문제이다. bridge the differences는 '의견 차이를 좁히다' 라는 뜻으로 의견 차이를 좁히지 못했으므로 화해에 실패했다는 표현이 나오는 것이 자연스럽다.

bridge the differences 의견 차이를 좁히다 **reconcile** ~을 화해시키다, 중재하다 **reciprocate** ~을 갚다, 보답하다 **reinforce** ~을 보강하다 **refurbish** ~을 다시 닦다, 일신하다

---

32 The finance Ministry announced that its budget remained in _____ this year and it decided to cut taxes.

(a) superstition
(b) surface
(c) subdivision
(d) surplus

재정경제부는 올해 예산이 흑자로 남아있어서 세금을 깎겠다고 밝혔다.

○ 세금을 낮춘다고 했으므로 예산이 흑자가 되어야 함을 알 수 있다. 이에 해당하는 영어 단어는 surplus이다.

surplus 나머지, 여분, 과잉 **superstition** 미신 **subdivision** 다시 나누기, 세분

33 The term "dysfunctional family" usually describes a condition where a continuum of conflict, misbehavior and even abuse on the part of individual members exist in a family. However, it is not so easy to identify or define what dysfunctional means because it ranges from the damaging, but socially accepted misbehavior that routinely happens in many families to severely abusive situations in which physical and/or sexual abuse occurs. In order to define a dysfunctional family, one must first know _____.
Most families go through some periods of time when functioning is impaired—slightly or harshly. Healthy families regain their normal functioning after the crisis passes. On the contrary, problems tend to be chronic in dysfunctional families.

(a) that perfection is unattainable
(b) why a dysfunctional family stays that way
(c) how impeccable healthy families are
(d) what functional or healthy families are

'역기능 가정' 이란 용어는 통상 어떤 가정 내에서 갈등이나, 나쁜 행동, 심지어 개별 구성원에게 가해지는 학대가 지속적으로 일어나는 상태를 나타낸다. 그러나 역기능적이란 말이 무엇을 의미하는지 식별하거나 정의하는 일은 쉽지 않은데, 왜냐하면 그것의 범위가 많은 가정에서 일상적으로 일어나는 해롭지만 사회적으로 용인이 되는 나쁜 행동에서부터 신체적이거나(신체적이면서) 성적인 학대까지 일어나는 심각하게 가학적인 상황까지 이르기 때문이다. 역기능 가정을 정의하기 위해서는 우선 순기능의 혹은 건강한 가정이 어떤 것인가를 먼저 알아야 한다. 대부분의 가정은 정상적인 기능이 약간 혹은 심각하게 손상되는 어떤 시기를 겪게 마련이다. 건강한 가정은 위기가 지나고 나면 정상적인 기능을 회복하게 된다. 반면에 역기능 가정에서는 문제점들이 만성적이 되는 경향을 보인다.

○ 역기능 가정을 정의하기 위해서 정상적인 가정과의 대조를 이용하고 있다. 본연의 기능을 하는 대부분의 정상적인 가정은 위기가 지나고 나면 본래의 기능을 회복하지만, 역기능 가정은 회복력이 없다는 점이 이어지므로 정답은 (d)이다. 완벽함이나 결점이 없는 것이 정상 가정의 특성이 아니라, 모든 다른 가정과 마찬가지로 갈등을 겪지만 회복한다는 점을 강조하고 있으므로 (a)와 (c)는 답이 될 수 없다. 역기능 가정의 원인은 언급되지 않았으므로 (b)도 답으로 부적절하다.

dysfunctional family 역기능[문제] 가정 〈중독·폭력 등의 문제 가정〉 **continuum** 연속(체) **conflict** 충돌, 다툼, 갈등 **misbehavior** 나쁜 행실, 못된 짓 **range** ~에 걸치다, 미치다 **routinely** 일상적으로 **impair** 손상시키다, 해치다 **harshly** 가혹하게, 심하게

34 October 19, 1987, is known as Black Monday, the day when the Dow Jones Industrial Average(DJIA) plunged by 508 points, losing 22.6% of its total value. As a consequence of the unprecedented decline, Hong Kong and Australia markets had fallen 45.8% and 41.8%, respectively, by the end of that October. Today's more globalized world economy has a much higher risk of a chain of economic disasters. While the catastrophic crash in 1987 had impacts outside the United States, another U.S. Black Monday now would bring on _____.

(a) a powerful bull market
(b) widespread pessimism
(c) a global Black Tuesday
(d) global economic equilibrium

1987년 10월 19일은 검은 월요일이라고 알려져 있는데, 그날은 다우지수가 508 포인트나 추락하며, 시가총액의 22.6%를 잃은 날이다. 전례 없는 하락의 결과로, 그해 10월 말경에 홍콩과 호주 시장은 각각 45.8%와 41.8% 하락했다. 오늘날의 더욱 세계화된 세계경제는 연쇄적인 경제적 파국의 위험성이 훨씬 더 크다. 1987년의 재앙적인 하락이 미국 밖의 시장에 충격을 주었지만, 또한번의 미국의 검은 월요일은 이제 전 세계적으로 검은 화요일을 초래하게 될 것이다.

◐ 검은 월요일의 유래를 들어 미국의 주식시장이 세계 주식시장에 미치는 파장에 대해서 기술하는 내용이다. 시장이 더욱 세계화되어 만약 미국에 다시 검은 월요일의 파국이 발생하면 세계시장은 다음 날, 즉 화요일에 바로 반응할 것이라는 내용이다.

plunge 떨어지다, 추락하다 unprecedented 전례가 없는, 전에 없던 respectively 각각, 제각각 catastrophic 파멸의, 비극적인 bull market (증권) 강세 시장 (cf. bear market 약세 시장) equilibrium 평형상태, 균형

---

35 Various reasons are considered for choosing vegetarianism but ethical reasons that the rearing and killing of other animals for the sole purpose of eating is inherently wrong are viewed the most important of all. It has also been suggested that although consumption of meat should be accepted as an individual's choice of food, the methods by which animals are killed in the factory farming industry should be more humane. However, _____.
The entire life of a 'food animal' is an abject one of artificial breeding, cruel castration and/or hormone stimulation, feeding of an abnormal diet, and very restricted mobility. To accept all this and only oppose the heartless cruelty of the last few seconds of its life is "complacency itself."

(a) many slaughter factories have been modernized
(b) the vegetarian lifestyle has become more widespread
(c) the conception of "humane animal slaughter" is refutable
(d) arguments that have nothing to do with animal rights exist

채식주의를 선택하는 이유로 여러 가지가 고려되지만 오로지 식용의 목적으로만 다른 동물을 사육하고 죽이는 것이 본질적으로 잘못된 것이라는 윤리적 이유가 가장 중요하게 여겨진다. 또한 육류 섭취는 개인의 음식 선택권으로 받아들여져야 하지만, 공장형 사육 산업에서 가축이 도축되는 방법은 좀 더 인도적이어야 한다는 주장도 제기되어 왔다. 하지만 "인도적인 가축 도살"이라는 개념은 논박의 여지가 있다. '식용가축'의 평생은 인공번식, 잔인한 거세 혹은/그리고 호르몬 자극요법, 비정상적인 사료, 제한된 좁은 움직임의 비참한 삶이다. 이 모든 걸 수용하고, 오로지 죽음 전 마지막 몇 초의 가혹한 잔인함에 대해서만 반대한다는 것은 바로 '자기만족'에 지나지 않는다.

◐ 채식주의 선택의 여러 이유 중 윤리적 이유에 대한 내용이다. 도살 방법의 잔인함에만 반대한다는 것은 가축이 사육당하는 참혹한 실상을 외면하고 명분만 그럴싸한 자기만족에 지나지 않는다는 것으로 미루어보아 "인도적인 도축"에 대한 반박을 하고 있으므로 (c)번이 정답이다. (a)와 (b)는 언급되지 않았으며 (고통 없이 살 수 있는) 동물의 권리와 관련 있는 주장이 담겨 있으므로 (d)도 답이 될 수 없다.

vegetarianism 채식주의 ethical 윤리의, 도덕의 rear 키우다, 사육하다 sole 하나뿐인, 유일한 inherently 본질적으로, 타고나서 consumption 소비, 섭취 humane 인도적인, 고통을 주지않는 abject 비참한 breeding 번식, 생식 castration 거세 complacency 자기만족, 충족감

36 A copycat suicide, sometimes known as a Werther effect, is defined as a duplication of another suicide that is publicized through the accounts or depictions of the original suicide on television and in other media. Reporting suicide methods, romanticizing the suicide, particularly about celebrities, and glorifying the deceased all lead to increases in the suicide rate. Moreover, although studies show a high incidence of psychiatric disorders, reports tend to ignore the impact of them. Reports that deal with this factor and provide help-line contact numbers and advice for people with suicidal feelings can reduce copycat suicides.

Q What is the main idea of the passage?

(a) Reporting of suicide should be totally banned.
(b) There should be a concerted effort to reduce suicide.
(c) The Werther effect has been amplified through the Internet.
(d) Covering suicide, media professionals should be offered guidelines.

때로는 베르테르 효과라고 알려져 있는 모방 자살은 텔레비전이나 그밖의 다른 매체의 보도나 묘사를 통해 알려지게 된 자살 사건의 모방으로 정의된다. 자살 방법의 보도나 특히 유명인사의 경우에서 보듯 자살을 낭만적으로 미화하는 것, 그리고 고인을 영웅시하는 것 등은 모두 자살율의 증가를 초래한다. 게다가 각종 연구결과가 정신질환의 높은 증가세를 보여줌에도 불구하고 기사 내용은 그 영향력을 간과하는 경향이 있다. 이런 요인을 다루면서 상담 전화번호와 자살 충동을 느끼는 사람들을 위한 조언을 제공하는 보도가 모방 자살을 줄일 수 있을 것이다.

○ 자살을 다루는 언론의 보도가 모방 자살을 야기시킬 수 있으므로, 정신질환의 측면과 예방책도 함께 제공한다면 모방 자살을 줄일 수 있다는 내용이므로 정답은 (d)이다. 자살 사건의 보도 자체를 금지해야 한다는 주장은 아니므로 (a)는 답이 아니며, 자살을 줄이기 위해 모든 노력을 기울여야 한다는 것은 글의 주제에 비해 너무 일반적이고 광범위한 진술이므로 (b)도 답이 될 수 없다. 인터넷도 매체 중의 하나이므로 이를 통해 베르테르 효과가 더 강해졌을 수 있지만, 글의 주제는 언론의 보도 태도에 관한 것이므로 답에서 제외되어야 한다.

copycat 모방의 Werther effect 베르테르 효과(유명인의 자살을 모방 혹은 동조하는 현상) account 설명, 보고, 기사, 보도 depiction 묘사, 서술 romanticize 낭만적으로 다루다, 쓰다 the deceased 고인, 죽은 사람 lead to 〈어떤 결과에〉 이르다 suicide rate 자살률 help-line 상담전화 서비스 ban 금지하다 concerted effort 혼신의 (온갖) 노력. amplify 〈서술·설명을〉 더 자세히 하다, 부연하다 cover 〈사건 따위〉를 보도(방송)하다, 취재하다.

37 An inferiority complex is a feeling that one is inferior to others in some way. While an ordinary feeling of inferiority can motivate individuals to achieve more, an inferiority complex is an abnormal state of discouragement, often driving afflicted individuals to self-estrangement. Many suggestions have been made for those who feel inferior to others ; writing down good qualities or plus points, changing self-image, attempts at achieving and becoming superior will, the usage of affirmations, etc. However, all of these only act as a makeshift to an already existing inferiority complex. What use is there of just repeating 10 times "I am a unique creation of God," "I have many good qualities."

열등 컴플렉스는 사람이 어떤 측면에서 다른 사람에게 열등하다고 느끼는 감정이다. 보통의 열등감은 개인이 더 많은 것을 성취하도록 동기부여를 할 수도 있으나, 열등 콤플렉스는 비정상적으로 의기소침한 상태를 말하며, 때로 (콤플렉스에) 시달리는 개인을 자기 소외의 상태로까지 몰고간다. 다른 사람에게 열등감을 느끼는 사람들을 위한 많은 제안이 이루어져 왔는데, 예를 들면, 장점이나 강점을 적어보기, 자아상을 바꾸기, 성취해서 우월감을 갖도록 시도하기, 지지하는 진술을 사용하기 등이다. 그러나 이런 모든 것들은 이미 존재하는 열등 콤플렉스에 대한 미봉책에 불과하다. '나는 하느님의 유일한 창조물이다' 라든가, '나는 장점이 많아.'라는 말을 열 번씩 되풀이하는 게 도대체 무슨 소용이 있단 말인가?

○ 글쓴이는 열등감과 열등 콤플렉스를 구별하고, 이제까지 제안된 열등감 극복 방법을 열거하고 있으나 그 효과에 대해 회의적인 입장을 보인다. 따라서 그 방법 중 하나인 지지하는 진술의 사용 이상의 것이 필요하다는 (c)가 정답이다. 사람은 자신의 독창성을 발견하고 개발해야 한다는 내용은 언급된 바 없으므로 (a)는 답이 아니며, 자기암시요법은 일종의 지지하는 진술의 사용으로 볼 수 있으므로 자신감을 회복하는 데 도움이 된다는 것은 글쓴이의 입장과 일치하지 않으므로 (b)도 답이 될 수 없다. 지지하는 진술의 사용이 열등감의 족쇄에서 풀려날 수 있도록 해준다는 것은 글쓴이의 입장과 정반대이므

Q What is the main idea of this passage?

(a) One needs to identify our unique quality and develop it.
(b) Auto suggestive therapy helps one to regain confidence.
(c) It takes more than affirmations to overcome inferiority complex.
(d) Affirmations help one get out of the clutches of inferiority complex.

로 (d)도 답이 아니다.

inferiority 열등감 abnormal 비정상적인 drive··· to~ (강제로) ···가 ~하게 하다 discouragement 의기소침, 실망, 낙담 afflicted 시달리는, 고통받는 self-estrangement 자기소외 affirmation 확언, 단언, 주장 makeshift 임시변통의 것, 대용품, 미봉책. auto-suggestive therapy 자기암시요법 clutch 마수, 지배(력), 손아귀

---

38 There are some people who try to explain Lookism, a form of discrimination or prejudice against others based on their appearance, with Darwin's Survival of the Fittest Principle. If "fittest" means more beautiful, more attractive or healthier, then only more beautiful people should remain. However, when we take into consideration that the majority of the people are physically ordinary, Lookism cannot be accepted naturally. A study from Texas and Michigan Universities reports that good-looking workers are paid 10 more percent. This phenomenon takes place in school, in court, and—believe it or not—at home. If you take Lookism for granted, you can become a victim of it. Now, visit our website, and take part in the discussion about Lookism.

Q What is the purpose of this passage?

(a) To define Lookism more precisely in various perspectives
(b) To convince people of Lookism and introduce a site against it
(c) To warn people how widely Lookism has spread in a modern society
(d) To explain the relationship between Lookism and Survival of Fittest Principle

다른 사람의 외모를 근거로 그 사람을 차별하거나 편견을 가지는 형태인 외모지상(차별)주의를 다윈의 적자생존의 법칙으로 설명하려는 사람들이 있다. "적응성"이 더 아름답거나 더 매력적이고 더 건강한 것을 의미한다면, 더 아름다운 사람들만 남아 있어야 한다. 그러나 대다수 사람들이 육체적으로 평범하다는 것을 고려해 볼 때, 외모지상주의를 당연한 것으로 받아들일 수 없다. Texas와 Michigan 대학의 한 연구에 의하면, 잘생긴 노동자가 10%를 더 받는다고 한다. 이러한 현상은 학교와 법정, 그리고 믿거나 말거나 집에서도 일어난다. 여러분이 외모지상주의를 당연한 것으로 여긴다면, 여러분도 외모지상주의의 희생자가 될 수 있다. 지금, 우리 웹사이트를 방문해서 외모지상주의에 대한 토론에 참여하길 바란다.

◐ 이 글은 외모지상주의에 대해 사람들에게 알리고 그것에 반대하는 사이트를 소개함으로써 참여를 촉구하는 글로서 정답은 (b)가 된다. 글을 끝까지 읽지 않고 성급하게 답을 고르려 한다면 외모지상주의가 현대 사회에 얼마나 널리 퍼져 있는가를 사람들에게 경고하는 글(c)로 오인할 것이다. 외모지상주의를 다양한 관점에서 더 정확하게 정의를 내린다거나(a), 외모지상주의와 적자생존의 법칙 사이의 관계를 설명하는(d) 글은 아니다.

discrimination 차별 prejudice 편견, 선입관 take into consideration ~을 고려하다, 참작하다 majority 대다수 phenomenon 현상 take place 일어나다, 발생하다 take ~ for granted ~를 당연히 여기다 victim 희생(자), 피해자 take part in ~에 참여하다 discussion 토론 perspective 견해, 관점, 사고방식 convince A of B A에게 B를 확신시키다

39 Visit the legacy of three generations of wine-making excellence, Joseph's Estate Winery in Niagara-on-the-Lake. This soaring, light-filled cathedral of wine, surrounded by vines, is an unmatched winery experience. Let our guest relations team arrange your visit for you, including tours of our underground barrel aging cellar and lush, sprawling vineyard, special wine tasting and seminars, and reservations in our critically-acclaimed restaurant. Don't miss the chance to get a taste of true Canadian wine. You'll find that no detail is overlooked in our pursuit of wine-making excellence.

Q What is the purpose of this advertisement?

(a) To visit the Niagara
(b) To join a wine tasting trip
(c) To invest in wine-making industry
(d) To make wine-making process known

3대에 걸친 훌륭한 와인 제조의 전통을 보유한, Niagara-on-the-Lake에 위치한 Joseph 와인 양조장으로 오세요. 포도덩굴로 둘러싸인 이 고풍스럽고 빛이 잘 드는 와인의 전당은 와인 제조에 있어서 상대할 자가 없는 최상의 곳입니다. 우리 방문객 담당 팀이 여러분의 방문을 준비해드릴 것이며, 지하 숙성실과 무성하고 줄기가 뻗어가는 포도밭, 특별 와인 시음회와 세미나, 평론가들의 극찬을 받은 식당의 예약을 포함합니다. 진정한 캐나다산 와인을 맛보실 기회를 놓치지 마십시오. 훌륭한 와인을 향한 저희들의 중단없는 노력에는 어떤 사소한 것도 간과되지 않는다는 걸 발견하시게 될 겁니다.

🔵 와인 양조장 방문을 광고하는 내용이므로 와인 시음 여행에 동참하라는 (b)가 정답이다. 나이아가라 폭포에 방문하라는 내용은 아니므로 (a)는 답이 아니며, 와인 제조 산업에 대한 투자나 와인 제조 기술을 알리는 것이 목적이 아니므로 (c)와 (d)는 답이 될 수 없다.

legacy 조상 전래의 것, 조상 전래의 유물 winery 포도주 양조장 soaring 높이 나는, 치솟는, 고매한 cathedral 대성당 unmatched 비길 데 없는, 무적의 aging 숙성 cellar 지하실, 지하층 lush 무성한, 비옥한, 싱싱한 sprawling 불규칙(무질서)하게 퍼져가는 critically-acclaimed 평론가들이 격찬한 overlook 간과하다, 눈감아주다 pursuit 추구

---

40 As one of the many injured Iraq war veterans, I dare to say that I did my best to protect my country. Once again, I'm going to do my best as a sprinter on behalf of my country at the Paralympics. However, I cannot help but wonder what the results would be like if Paralympic athletes had been fully trained for the last four years. The Olympic Committee provides smaller amounts of training stipends and awards less medal bonuses to Paralympians than Olympians because the Paralympics don't generate as much profits as the Olympics. However, remember that we have to compete with athletes from other countries like Canada and Britain which support their disabled athletes fully.

Q What is the main idea of the passage?

(a) The support and benefits for Paralympic athletes should be improved.
(b) Paralympians should be treated like Olympians equally in every aspect.
(c) Paralympians who are Iraq war veterans deserve more salary and bonus.
(d) Paralympics must be considered as a major sports event like the Olympics.

이라크 전쟁에서 부상당한 많은 퇴역군인 중 한명으로서 나는 감히 조국을 수호하는 데 최선을 다했다고 말한다. 나는 다시 한 번 장애인 올림픽에서 단거리 주자로서 조국을 위해 최선을 다할 것이다. 그러나 나는 장애인 올림픽 운동선수들이 지난 4년 동안 충분한 훈련을 받았다면 그 결과가 어떻게 될지 궁금하지 않을 수가 없다. 올림픽 위원회는 올림픽 출전 선수들 보다 장애인 올림픽 출전 선수들에게 더 적은 양의 훈련비와 메달 보너스를 지급하는데, 그 이유는 장애인 올림픽이 올림픽만큼 많은 이익을 생산해 내지 못하기 때문이다. 그러나 우리가 장애인 선수들을 전적으로 지지해 주는 캐나다와 영국 출신의 선수들과 경쟁해야 한다는 것을 기억하기 바란다.

🔵 이 글은 현재 장애인 올림픽 출전 선수들의 낮은 대우에 대해서 이야기하고 있다. 마지막 문장에서 장애인 선수들의 대우가 좋은 나라들과 비교함으로써 장애인 올림픽 선수들의 이익이 향상되기를 바라고 더 지지해 줄 것을 촉구하는 내용을 암시하고 있으므로 정답은 (a)가 된다. 그러나 (b)처럼 장애인 올림픽 출전 선수들이 올림픽 출전 선수들과 모든 면에 있어서 동등하게 대우를 받아야 한다는 내용은 본문을 통해서 정확하게 이끌어 낼 수 없다. (c)는 이라크 전쟁 퇴역군인 선수들만 더 많은 월급과 보너스를 받을 가치가 있는 것은 아니므로 정답과 멀고, (d)는 장애인 올림픽 자체가 올림픽처럼 중요한 스포츠 행사로 여겨져야 한다는 것도 아니므로 정답이 될 수 없다.

veteran 퇴역군인, 재향군인 sprinter 단거리 경주자 on behalf of ~을 대표하여, ~을 위하여 stipend 봉급 연금 generate 〈결과, 상태, 행동 등을〉일으키다, 초래하다 compete with ~와 겨루다, 경쟁하다 athlete 운동선수 disabled 지체 부자유한

LISTENING COMPREHENSION · P.104

1 **M** Do I know you?

W _____

(a) Yes. I'm in your chemistry class.
(b) Yes. You're well known.
(c) I hope so.
(d) I'm for it.

M: 우리가 어디서 본 적이 있던가?
W: 응. 너와 화학 수업을 같이 들어.

➡ 얼굴은 기억이 나는데 확실치 않을 때 쓸 수 있는 표현이다. 남자가 우리가 서로 아는 사이냐고 물었으므로 정답은 (a)가 된다. (b)의 경우에는 know를 이용하여 혼동을 주기 위한 것이므로 정답이 될 수 없다.

chemistry 화학 **well known** 잘 알려진 **I'm for it.** 그것에 찬성입니다.

2 **M** I brought something for you. I hope you like it.

W _____

(a) Don't let me down.
(b) I really appreciate it.
(c) I made a good guess.
(d) I'll accompany you.

M: 네게 줄 선물을 사왔어. 네 마음에 들었으면 좋겠다.
W: 정말 고마워요.

➡ 선물을 사왔다고 했으므로 감사의 표현이 나오는 것이 자연스럽다. 보기 가운데 감사를 나타내는 표현은 (b)이다. appreciate는 thank you보다 좀 더 격식적인 표현이다. 나머지 보기들은 상황과 맞지 않는 표현들이나 시험에 자주 나오는 표현들이므로 함께 알아두자.

let sb down ~을 실망시키다 **appreciate** ~을 감사하다. (예술 작품 등을) 감상하다 **accompany** ~을 따라가다, 배웅하다

3 **M** When is a convenient time for you?

W _____

(a) It never keeps good time.
(b) It's on me this time.
(c) It's okay whenever.
(d) We're short handed.

M: 언제가 편하세요?
W: 언제든 상관없어요.

➡ 시간 약속을 잡을 때 흔히 들을 수 있는 표현으로 상대방에게 편한 시간을 물을 때 When is the convenient time for you? 라는 표현을 쓸 수 있다. time을 이용하여 혼동을 주기 위해 (a)와 (b)에서 의도적으로 time을 반복하였는데 (a)는 시계의 시간이 잘 맞는다는 뜻이고 (b)는 이번에는 내가 계산하겠다는 뜻이다. (d)는 일손이 모자란다는 뜻으로 문맥과 전혀 상관이 없다. whenever은 '~할 때면 언제든지' 라는 뜻이므로 정답은 (c)가 된다.

convenient 편한 **keep good time** (시계가) 시간이 잘 맞다 **short handed** 일손이 모자라는, 사람이 부족한

4

M I'm going to my hometown this weekend.

W Really? Oh, I really miss your family. They were very nice to me.

M My mother often talks about you.

W _____

(a) Can't complain.

(b) Please give my regards to her.

(c) Let's keep in touch.

(d) What's this regarding?

M: 이번 주에 고향에 갈 예정이야.
W: 정말? 나 정말 네 가족이 그리워. 정말 내게 잘해주셨는데.
M: 우리 엄마도 자주 네 얘기를 하서.
W: 안부 좀 전해줘.

○ 남자의 마지막 대사를 보면 남자의 엄마가 여자에 대해 종종 이야기를 하신다고 했으므로 안부 전해달라는 (b)가 정답이 된다.

complain 불평하다 give one's regard to ~에게 안부를 전해주다 keep in touch ~와 연락을 유지하다 What's this regarding? 무슨 일 때문에 그러시죠?

5

M I'm starving. What time is it?

W It's lunch time. My stomach started growling.

M What do you want to have?

W _____

(a) I can eat a horse.

(b) I'm allergic to banana.

(c) I'm stuffed.

(d) I'm in hot water.

M: 배고파 죽겠다. 몇 시지?
W: 점심시간이야. 배에서 꼬르륵거려.
M: 뭐 먹을까?
W: 배고파서 뭐라도 먹을 수 있을 것 같아.

○ 남자가 무엇을 먹고 싶느냐고 물었으므로 (a) 배고파서 뭐라도 먹을 수 있을 거 같다는 표현이 가장 적절하다. (c) I'm stuffed는 배가 부르다는 뜻으로 대화 상황과 반대되는 내용이므로 정답이 될 수 없다. (d)는 '난처한 상황이다, 곤경에 처해 있다' 라는 뜻이다.

growling 으르렁거리는, 우르르 울리는 be allergic to ~에 알레르기가 있다 I'm stuffed 배가 부르다 in hot water 난처하여, 곤란하여

6

M How was the movie?

W It was great. Especially the leading actor's performance was good.

M Who's starring in the movie?

W _____

(a) He is over the hill.

(b) You are telling me.

(c) She is an eyeful.

(d) It's on the tip of my tongue.

M: 영화 어땠어?
W: 좋았어. 특히 주연 배우의 연기가 훌륭했어.
M: 누가 출연했는데?
W: 입안에서만 뱅뱅 돌고 생각이 안나.

○ 영화에 대한 이야기를 하고 있다. 남자가 여자에게 영화에 누가 출연했느냐고 물었으므로 정답은 (d) 입에서만 뱅뱅 돌고 딱 떠오르지 않는다는 표현이 적절하다. (a)는 사람이 전성기가 지났다는 뜻이고 (b)는 동의할 때 쓰는 표현으로서 비슷한 뜻으로 'You can say that again.' 이 있다.

leading 이끄는, 중요한 over the hill 전성기가 지난, 내리막에 You are telling me. 동감이야, 네 말이 맞아 eyeful 눈을 끄는 사람, 아름다운 여자 It's on the tip of my tongue 입에서만 뱅뱅 돌고 생각이 안나다

7 **W** Excuse me. Can you do me a favor?

M Sure.

W Do you mind taking pictures of us?

M Okay. Is everything set?

W Yes. You can just press the red button here.

M Oh, I see.

W Thank you.

Q Where can you hear this conversation?

(a) At a photo studio

(b) At tourist attractions

(c) At the bus station

(d) At a school

W: 실례합니다. 부탁 한 가지 드려도 될까요?

M: 말씀하세요.

W: 저희 사진 좀 찍어주실래요?

M: 네. 다 세팅 되어 있는 거죠?

W: 네. 여기 빨간 버튼만 누르면 됩니다.

M: 오, 그렇군요.

W: 감사합니다.

○ 여자가 남자에게 사진을 찍어달라고 부탁하고 있다. 이 대화를 들을 수 있는 장소는 (b) 관광지가 적절하다. (a)의 경우 take picture 라는 표현을 이용해서 오답을 유도하기 위한 보기이다.

tourist attractions 관광명소

---

8 **M** How have you been?

W Not bad. How about you?

M Oh, I'm doing okay, but I haven't had time to relax these days.

W What's your major anyway?

M Journalism.

W Well, what do you want to do when you graduate?

M I haven't decided yet, but I think I'd like to work for a broadcasting station. How about you?

W Well, at first I wanted to major in Spanish, but I heard it might be difficult to find a job using the language, so I changed majors to computer science.

Q Why did the woman change her major?

(a) Because her parents wanted to do so.

(b) Because the man advised her to do so.

(c) Because she wanted to have more chances to find a job.

(d) Because she liked to work in computer science field.

M: 어떻게 지냈어?

W: 그럭저럭. 너는 잘 지냈어?

M: 잘은 지내고 있는데 요즘 통 쉬지를 못했어.

W: 근데 네 전공이 뭐지?

M: 저널리즘이야.

W: 졸업하면 뭐 하고 싶어?

M: 아직 결정하지 못했지만, 방송국에서 일하고 싶어. 넌 어때?

W: 처음에는 스페인어를 전공하고 싶었는데, 언어를 이용하는 직업은 구하기 어려울 거라는 이야기를 들어서 컴퓨터공학으로 전공을 바꿨어.

○ 여자가 전공을 바꾼 이유를 묻고 있다. 여자의 마지막 대사에 그 이유가 나타나 있다. 언어를 이용한 직업을 구하기 어려울지 모른다는 이야기를 들었다고 했으므로 구직 기회를 더 많이 갖기 위해 전공을 바꿨다는 것을 짐작할 수 있다. 따라서 정답은 (c)가 된다.

a broadcasting station 방송국 **major in** ~을 전공하다
computer science 컴퓨터공학

9

M Hi! Lina. Come on in.

W Uh, yeah, I was wondering if your apartment was available.

M Yes. I cut back on my working hours to go to school. So I'm a bit tight on money.

W Oh, I see.

M Then, let me show you the place. This is the living room.

W Oh. It is more spacious than I expected. I like it. And what about the kitchen?

M Come this way. Look. It's furnished with all the latest appliances, except...

W Except what?

Q What is the man most likely to say?

(a) The faucet is replaced last week.
(b) The toilet is new.
(c) The rent is pretty high.
(d) The sink has a few leaks.

M: 안녕, 리나! 어서 들어와.

W: 어, 아직 아파트를 구할 수 있나 궁금해서.

M: 응. 학교에 가려고 근무 시간을 줄였거든. 요즘 돈이 좀 달려서.

W: 아, 그렇구나.

M: 그럼 집을 구경시켜줄게. 여기가 거실이야.

W: 예상했던 것보다 넓다. 마음에 들어. 부엌은?

M: 이쪽으로 와. 봐봐. 최신 설비가 모두 갖추어져 있어. 단지...

W: 단지 뭐?

○ 다음에 이어질 남자의 대사로 가장 적절한 것을 묻고 있다. ~만 빼고 최신 설비가 갖추어져 있다고 했으므로 부엌의 안 좋은 점에 대해 말할 것이라는 걸 유추할 수 있다. (a)는 수도를 지난주에 교체했다는 것이고 (b)는 변기가 새 것이라는 의미이다. (c)는 임대료가 꽤 비싸다는 의미인데 지금은 부엌에 관해 이야기하는 중이었으므로 정답이 되기 어렵다. (d)는 싱크대가 약간 샌다는 의미로 부엌에 관한 이야기이면서 안 좋은 점에 대한 것이므로 정답으로 적절하다.

cut back 줄이다, 삭감하다 spacious 넓은 appliance 기계, 용구, 설비 faucet 수도꼭지 leak 새는 곳, 누출

---

10 When you yawn, your body experiences an automatic physiological response that helps to ease an imbalance of carbon dioxide and oxygen in the blood. When too much of carbon dioxide builds up in your blood, you get to let out a yawn because it is waste gas of the body. In addition, a yawn is helpful for other purposes. Don't you feel better after yawning? That's because a yawn relieves tension. And here's another one. When the airplane is descending, you can equalize the pressure in the middle ear by yawning.

Q What is the best title for the passage?

(a) Why carbon dioxide is harmful to the body.
(b) How to build muscles of the body
(c) What circumstances provoke a yawn?
(d) What effects a yawn has on the body.

하품을 할 때, 우리 신체는 혈액 속의 이산화탄소와 산소의 불균형을 완화하는 데 도움을 주는 자동적인 생리학적 반응을 겪는다. 너무 많은 이산화탄소가 혈액 속에 쌓이면 하품을 하게 되는데, 이는 몸에 필요 없는 가스이다. 게다가 하품은 다른 목적에도 유용하다. 하품을 한 뒤에 기분이 나아지는 것을 느끼지 않는가? 그것은 하품이 긴장을 풀어주기 때문이다. 그리고 다른 유용한 점도 있다. 비행기가 하강할 때, 하품을 함으로써 중이의 압력을 일정하게 할 수 있다.

○ 하품에 대한 이야기를 중점적으로 다루고 있으므로 (a)와 (b)는 정답이 아니다. 하품을 유발하는 환경에 대한 것보다는 하품의 효과에 대한 여러 가지 이야기를 하고 있으므로 정답은 (d) 하품이 우리 신체에 끼치는 영향들이 되겠다.

yawn 하품하다 physiological 생리학적인 imbalance 불균형 build up 쌓이다 let out a yawn 하품을 하다 relieve tension 긴장을 완화하다 equalize ~을 일정하게 하다 provoke ~을 일으키다, 생기게 하다

11 When you throw a party by yourself, the most important thing is to plan well in advance. First of all, you should decide what type of party you want to have, and how many people you'll invite to your party. When you invite guests, be careful to make sure there are enough seats for the number of them. If it's going to be an outdoor party, you might be able to ask people to bring their own lawn chairs. If it's an indoor party, you shouldn't invite more than 5 people for a dinner party.

Q What is the purpose of this talk?

(a) Guide to hosting a dinner party
(b) Types of invitation cards
(c) Difference between outdoor and indoor party
(d) Types of dinner party

혼자 파티를 열 때 가장 중요한 것은 미리 준비를 잘 하는 것이다. 우선 어떤 종류의 파티를 열지 결정해야 하고, 파티에 몇 명을 초대할지 결정해야 한다. 손님을 초대할 때에는 손님 숫자에 맞게 자리가 충분한지 확실히 해두어야 한다. 야외 파티라면 사람들에게 야외용 의자를 가져오라고 부탁할 수도 있다. 만약 실내 파티라면 저녁 파티에 초대 손님의 숫자가 5명을 넘지 않는 것이 좋다.

🔵 글의 목적을 묻고 있다. 첫 번째 부분에 힌트가 나와 있다. 혼자 파티를 열 때 중요한 점에 대해 언급하고 있으므로 정답은 (a) 디너파티 주최에 대한 가이드이다. (c) 실외, 실내 파티의 차이점의 경우, 이 글은 차이점이 아니라 상황에 따라 어떻게 대처해야 하는지를 말하고 있으므로 정답이 될 수 없다.

throw a party 파티를 열다 in advance 미리 outdoor 실외의 indoor 실내의

---

12 Do you think that anything labeled as "low fat," or "sugar free" is good for your health? If so, think again! This is the clever marketing strategy of food companies to deceive you. Let me give you the fact about it. Most foods labeled as "low fat" or "sugar free" actually contains artificial sweeteners and some additives, which can cause a hormonal mess in your body. This can store more fat to your body.

Q What is the speaker's attitude?

(a) affirmative
(b) amicable
(c) critical
(d) picky

"저지방," "무설탕"과 같은 표가 붙은 것은 무엇이든 건강에 좋다고 생각하십니까? 그렇다면, 다시 생각해 보세요. 이것은 식품 회사가 당신을 속이기 위한 영석한 마케팅 전략입니다. 제가 이에 관한 사실을 말씀드리겠습니다. "저지방," "무설탕"과 같은 표가 달린 음식들 대부분은 사실상 인공 감미료와 약간의 첨가물을 포함하고 있는데, 이는 신체에 호르몬 이상을 초래할 수 있습니다. 이로써 더 많은 지방이 몸에 축적될 수 있는 것입니다.

🔵 화자의 태도에 대해 묻고 있다. 저지방, 무설탕이라고 내세우는 상품들 대부분이 사실은 인공감미료와 첨가물을 함유하고 있다면서 비판적인 시각으로 이야기하고 있다. 따라서 정답은 (c)가 된다.

deceive ~을 속이다, 현혹하다 artificial sweeteners 인공감미료 additives 첨가물 hormonal mess 호르몬 이상 affirmative 긍정적인 amicable 우호적인, 온화한 picky 까다로운

13 A How was the movie last night?
   B Not so bad, but _____.

   (a) too boring
   (b) too bored
   (c) a little bored
   (d) a little boring

A: 어제 밤에 본 영화 어땠어?
B: 그렇게 나쁘진 않았어, 그런데 좀 지루했어.

○ 해석상 a little이 더 자연스럽고, 주체가 movie 이므로 현재분사 형태를 써야 한다.

---

14 A Where should I keep this box?
   B The box _____ in the refrigerator after opening.

   (a) need to place
   (b) must be placed
   (c) must place
   (d) placing

A: 이 박스를 어디에 보관해야 하죠?
B: 그 박스는 개봉 후에 냉장고에 보관되어야 합니다

○ 주어가 The box 이고 그 박스가 '보관되어야 한다' 가 되어야 하므로 must와 수동형인 be placed가 쓰인다.

refrigerator 냉장고 place 놓다

---

15 A What do I have to prepare for dinner?
   B I will be home late today, so you'll
   _____.

   (a) have fixed dinner
   (b) don't have to have dinner
   (c) need fixing dinner.
   (d) need to fix yourself dinner

A : 저녁으로 무엇을 준비할까?
B: 나 오늘 집에 늦어, 그래서 당신 혼자 저녁 준비해서 먹어.

○ B가 오늘 집에 늦게 온다고 했으므로 A는 혼자 저녁을 준비해야 한다. 그러므로 (d)가 알맞다.

fix (식사, 음식 등을) 준비하다.

---

16 A After completing the survey, where can I return it?
   B We appreciate _____ the time to fill out our survey.

   (a) your taking
   (b) for you to take
   (c) to take you
   (d) of you to take

A: 설문지를 완성한 후, 이것을 어디에 내면 되죠?
B: 설문지에 응해주셔서 감사합니다.

○ appreciate 다음에 목적어는 동명사가 필요하므로 동명사의 의미상의 주어인 소유격+-ing인 your taking이 된다.

take time 시간을 보내다

---

17 _____ the major artists noticed the Korean animation industry undergoing a transition.

   (a) At the 1990s
   (b) During the 1990s
   (c) For 1990s
   (d) While the 1990s

1990년대에 많은 예술가들은 한국의 애니메이션 산업이 과도기를 겪고 있다는 것을 알아차렸다.

○ during 다음에는 때를 나타내는 명사가 오지만, for 다음에는 수사를 동반한 명사가 흔히 온다. 1990s는 1990년대를 나타내므로 during이 적절하다.

undergo 겪다 transition 과도기

18 We have provided sample correspondence _____ their representatives to solve the environmental problems.

(a) for citizens to encourage
(b) of citizens to encourage
(c) citizens to encourage
(d) citizens to encouraging

우리는 시민들이 그들의 대표가 환경 문제를 해결하는데 도와주도록 샘플통신문을 제공해왔다.

○ provide A for B는 'B에게 A를 주다' 라는 의미이므로 (a)가 정답으로 적절하다.

correspondence 대응 repesentatives 대표자

---

19 _____ major in this subject, I have broadened my knowledge of Genetic Engineering.

(a) I decided to
(b) I have decided to
(c) I deciding for
(d) Deciding to

나는 이 주제를 전공하기로 정했기 때문에, 유전자공학에 관한 지식을 더 넓혔다.

○ 분사구문이고 major가 동사이므로 (d)가 적절하다

Genetic Engineering 유전자 공학

---

20 The World Union wouldn't have promoted human development through the technology _____.

(a) without the web site
(b) with the web site
(c) were it not for the web site
(d) if it were not for the web site

세계공동체는 그 웹사이트가 없었더라면 기술을 통한 인간 발전을 증진시키지 못했을 것이다.

○ 앞에 'would have p.p' 형태가 나왔으므로 뒤에는 가정법 과거완료가 와야 한다. 그래서 (c), (d)는 정답이 될 수 없다. '~가 없다면'의 의미인 without이 쓰인 (a)가 적절하다.

union 결합, 합일

---

21 (a) A: When is your annual exhibition? Did you invite all guests?
(b) B: Not, yet. Why?
(c) A: Can I bring my co-worker, who's really interested in the calligraphy.
(d) B: Whoever may come, he will welcome.

A: 정기 전시회는 언제니? 손님들은 많이 초대했어?
B: 아니 아직, 왜?
A: 내 동료를 같이 데려가도 될까? 서예에 정말 흥미를 가지고 있는데.
B: 누구든 환영이야.

○ (d)에서 welcome은 형용사이므로 will 다음에 be가 오거나, 동사로 표현한다면 be welcomed가 와야 한다.

exhibition 전시회 co-worker 회사동료 calligraphy 서예

22 (a) Given the sermon here, we should try and keep our mouth shut, should we not? (b) Keeping this adage in mind can help us committing a faux pas. (c) It is best to understand that our natural roles in our society were not the same, but were complementary. (d) And, the last one to remember is that we should be more modest in our beliefs.

설교를 듣고, 우리는 말없이 일단 실천해 보아야 합니다. 안 그런가요? 이 격언을 마음에 담아두는 것은 우리가 스스로 잘못을 저지르지 않게 하는 데 큰 도움이 됩니다. 사회에서의 우리에게 주어진 역할은 동일하지 않고, 서로 상호 보완적임을 알아야 합니다. 마지막으로 기억해야 할 것은, 우리가 믿음 안에서 겸손해야 한다는 것입니다.

↻ (b)에서, '~를 억제하다' 라는 뜻을 가진 표현은 'keep ~ from~' 이다.

sermon 설교 **adage** 격언 **faux pas** 잘못을 저지르다 **complementary** 상보적인

VOCABULARY • P.109

23 A What took you so long?
 B I got a _____ tire on the way here.
 (a) worn
 (b) flat
 (c) spare
 (d) hole

A: 왜 이렇게 늦었어?
B: 오늘 길에 타이어가 펑크났어.

↻ 늦게 온 이유로 타당한 것은 '타이어가 펑크났다' 는 것이다. 이를 의미하는 표현은 'get a flat tire' 이다.

flat tire 바람 빠진 타이어 **worn** 닳아 해진 **spare tire** 예비 타이어

---

24 A I bought this skirt for half-price.
 B That was a real _____ .

 (a) purchase
 (b) robbery
 (c) customer
 (d) bargain

A: 이 치마를 반값에 샀어.
B: 정말 싸게 샀다.

↻ 치마를 반값에 샀다고 했으므로 싸게 샀다는 내용이 나와야 한다. 관용 표현으로 be a real bargain이라고 하면 '정말 가격이 싸다' 라는 뜻이 된다.

at half-price 반값에 **be a real bargain** 값이 싸다

---

25 A The manager had no _____ but to quit. But I don't want to.
 B Don't worry. Things are going to be all right.

 (a) alternative
 (b) free
 (c) feeling
 (d) option

A: 그 매니저는 그만둘 수밖에 없었어. 그렇지만 나는 그러고 싶지 않아.
B: 걱정하지 마. 모든 게 다 잘 될 거야.

↻ 'have no option but to~, have no choice but to~' 는 '~하는 수밖에 없다, 다른 선택권이 없다' 라는 뜻이다. 매니저가 자의로 그만둔 것이 아니라 어쩔 수 없이 그만둔 것이므로 본인은 그러고 싶지 않았다는 의미가 되어야 자연스럽게 연결이 된다.

have no option but to ~할 수 밖에 없다 **alternative** 양자택일, 대안

26 A Hey! What brings you here?

B Wow. What a surprise to _____ across each other here!

(a) come
(b) get
(c) take
(d) see

A: 야! 여기는 웬일이야?
B: 와, 이런 곳에서 만나다니 놀랍다!

○ What brings you here?은 우연히 만났을 때 할 수 있는 인사 표현이다. '우연히 만나다'에 해당하는 표현으로는 come across, run across, bump into 등이 있다.

come across 우연히 만나다 **get across** (말, 뜻이) 통하다

---

27 A I can't even lift a finger. My entire body aches.

B Don't make a _____ ! You're grown up.

(a) worry
(b) fuss
(c) fun
(d) mistake

A: 손가락 하나도 못 움직이겠어. 온 몸이 쑤셔.
B: 야단법석 좀 부리지마. 너는 어른이야.

○ 대화 상황에 어울리는 표현을 찾아야 한다. 온몸이 쑤셔서 손가락 하나 못 움직이겠다고 하고 있으므로 이에 적절한 반응은 '야단법석 좀 그만 부려라'이다. 이에 해당하는 표현은 'make a fuss'이다.

ache 아프다, 쑤시다 **make a fuss** 소란 피우다, 투덜거리다 **grown up** 성인이 된

---

28 The Mexican government decided to intervene in the currency market to halt dollar's _____ which made the peso lose value against the dollar.

(a) depreciation
(b) decrease
(c) appreciation
(d) applause

멕시코 정부는 달러 대비 페소 가치의 손실을 유발한 달러 절상을 막기 위해 통화 시장에 개입하기로 결정했다.

○ which 이하가 빈 칸에 들어갈 단어를 설명해주고 있다. 달러 대비 페소 가치가 떨어진다고 했으므로 달러의 절상이 오는 것이 자연스럽다. 따라서 정답은 (c)가 된다. 이와 반대의 뜻은 (a) depreciation이다.

intervene 개입하다, 중재하다 **halt** 정지시키다, 멈추게 하다 **appreciation** (화폐가치의) 절상 **depreciation** (화폐가치의) 절하 **applause** 박수갈채, 성원

---

29 It is favorable to affix a budget upfront before reserving anything for the wedding _____ .

(a) reception
(b) receipt
(c) recession
(d) resolution

결혼 피로연을 위해 무엇을 준비하든 그 전에 예산을 먼저 짜 놓는 것이 좋다.

○ wedding과 어울리는 연어를 찾아야 한다. 보통 결혼 피로연을 'wedding reception'이라고 한다. reception과 발음이 비슷한 recession과 혼동하지 않도록 한다. recession은 '퇴거, 후퇴'를 의미한다.

favorable 호의적인, 우호적인 **affix** ~을 첨부하다, (도장을) 찍다 **upfront** 선불의, 맨 앞줄의 **reception** 환영, 접대 **receipt** 영수증 **recession** 퇴거, 후퇴 **resolution** 결의, 결심, 결의안

30 Once he was a very famous actor worldwide, but now he looks a far _____ from when he was in his prime.

(a) way
(b) tear
(c) cry
(d) weep

한때 그는 전 세계적으로 유명한 배우였지만 지금은 전성기 때와는 전혀 다르게 보인다.

❍ a far cry from이라는 표현을 알아야 풀 수 있는 문제이다. 한때 유명했으나 지금은 그렇지 않다는 내용이므로 '전혀 다르다, 판이하다' 라는 뜻의 'a far cry from' 을 써야 한다. weep은 'cry' 와 비슷한 뜻이지만 이와 같은 관용 표현은 다른 단어로 대체될 수 없음을 명심하자.

prime 가장 중요한, 주된 **weep** 슬퍼하다, 한탄하다, 울기 **a far cry from** ~와 아주 동떨어진 것, ~와 전혀 다른 것

31 With Christmas just around the _____ the shops throughout the country have begun their annual Christmas sales.

(a) door
(b) corner
(c) start
(d) step

크리스마스가 바로 앞으로 다가오면서 전국의 상점들은 크리스마스 연례 세일을 시작했다.

❍ (just) around the corner라는 표현을 알아야만 풀 수 있는 문제이다. '바로 코앞에, 임박하여' 라는 뜻으로서 크리스마스가 얼마 남지 않았음을 뜻한다.

annual 1년의, 해마다의

32 You need to be _____ to people when you use your cell phone around them because using your cell phone can be disturbing to others in public places, such as buses or movie theaters.

(a) considerable
(b) considerate
(c) constant
(d) concise

버스나 극장과 같은 공공장소에서 휴대폰을 사용하는 것은 다른 사람들에게 방해가 될 수 있기 때문에 휴대폰을 사용할 때에는 주변사람에게 사려 깊게 행동할 필요가 있다.

❍ 공공장소에서의 휴대폰 사용 예절에 대해 이야기하고 있다. 주변 사람들에게 피해를 주지 말아야 한다는 내용이므로 정답은 '사려 깊다, 신중하다' 의 뜻인 considerate가 정답이 된다. 형태가 비슷한 considerable은 양이 상당하다는 뜻이다.

considerate 사려 깊은, 신중한 **disturbing** 방해가 되는 **considerable** 상당한, 적지 않은 **concise** 간결한, 간명한

33 Imagine hushed, serene, starry nights & beautiful scenery by day, and this is what we have for you. Situated on 80 acres in the hamlet of Ashburn, our home was built in the Victorian style in 1852. We invite you to 'Step Back In Time' and relax in our beautifully restored Victorian style house. Offering a truly unique getaway, whether you like to take a long walks or just relax, this is the place to be. All Deluxe Rooms offer a private entrance, ensuite bathroom, sitting area, courtesy fridge, coffee maker and more. A full country breakfast awaits you. Come for a quiet getaway and visit our many local attractions. This is _____ that you're looking for!

(a) the hotel
(b) the museum
(c) the amusement park
(d) the bed and breakfast

조용하고 고요하며 별이 반짝이는 밤과 아름다운 풍경이 펼쳐지는 낮을 상상하신다면, 이곳이 바로 당신을 위한 곳입니다. Ashburn 마을에 80 에이커에 달하는 곳에 위치한 우리 민박은 1852년에 빅토리아 양식으로 지어졌습니다. 매우 독특한 휴양지인 이곳은 긴 산책을 원하시든, 그저 편하게 쉬기를 원하시든 당신이 필요로 하는 곳입니다. 모든 디럭스 룸에는 개별적인 출입문과 침실에 딸린 화장실, 거실, 서비스 냉장고, 커피메이커 등이 구비되어 있습니다. 넉넉한 시골식 아침 식사가 당신을 기다립니다. 조용한 휴양지로 오셔서 지역의 많은 명소들을 방문하세요. 이곳이 당신이 찾고 계신 아침식사 제공 민박입니다.

◐ 숙박업소를 광고하고 있다. 시골식 아침식사가 제공된다는 문장으로 보아 (a) 호텔은 답이 될 수 없고, (d) 아침식사 제공 민박(B&B) 이 정답이다.

hushed 조용해진, 고요한 serene 고요한, 잔잔한 starry 별이 많은, 별이 총총한 by day 낮에는, 주간에는 hamlet 작은 마을, 촌락 restore 복원하다, 복구하다 getaway 휴양지 en suite bathroom 침실에 딸린 화장실 courtesy 우대의, 서비스의 await 기다리다 attraction 명소, 인기 있는 것(곳) bed and breakfast 아침식사 제공 숙박 (B and B, B&B)

34 It's hard to believe there was a time when _____. One heroic young woman proved it could make the difference between life and death. During the Crimean War in 1854, Florence Nightingale found a medical nightmare where patients were dying as much from dirt and disease as from battle wounds. She demanded fresh bedding, clean water, and better food. Watching her tirelessly walking her nightly rounds, they called their angel of mercy "the lady with the lamp." During her lifetime, she was hailed as a world-class expert on hospital treatment and transformed nursing into a lifesaving, life-giving profession.

(a) women were not allowed to engage in nursing
(b) medical services were not easy for the military to get
(c) nursing was looked down on as an unimportant occupation
(d) there was no difference between nursing and medical care

간호가 하찮은 직업으로 무시되던 시기가 있었다는 것은 믿기 어렵다. 한 영웅적인 젊은 여성이 간호가 삶과 죽음을 가를 수도 있다는 것을 증명해 보였다. 1854년 크림전쟁 동안 Florence Nightingale 은 환자들이 전쟁의 부상으로 죽는 것만큼이나 오염과 질병으로 죽어간다는 끔찍한 의료 상황을 목격했다. 그녀는 청결한 침구, 깨끗한 식수 그리고 나은 음식물 등을 요청했다. 그녀가 지치지도 않고 야간 회진을 도는 것을 보고, 사람들은 그들의 자비로운 천사를 "램프를 든 여인"이라 불렀다. 그녀는 평생 동안 병원의 치료에 대한 세계적인 전문가로 칭송받았으며 간호직을 생명을 구하고, 생명을 불어넣어 주는 전문직으로 변화시켰다.

◐ 간호가 Florence Nightingale의 활동 이후 전문적인 직업으로 가치를 인정받았다는 내용이므로, 이전에는 정반대의 상황이 전개되었다는 것을 알 수 있다. 정답은 (c)이다.

heroic 영웅다운, 훌륭한 wound 부상, 상처 nightly round 야간 회진 hail환호하다, 환호하여 맞이하다 world-class 세계 일류의, 세계적인, 국제급의 transform A into B A를 B로 바꾸다 profession 직업, 전문직

35 _____ often emboldens Internet trolls to attack a blogger with threats or insults. There has been a constant demand for an online discussion aimed at opposing abusive online behavior and developing a blogger's code of conduct. The more popularity blogging is gaining, the stronger the possibility of attacks or threats against the blogger is growing. Malicious online comments, often without any apparent reason, devastate the victims and in a worst-case scenario may drive them to kill themselves.

(a) Supporters of free speech
(b) Anonymity on the Internet
(c) Ethical standards of their own
(d) Vulnerability to verbal attacks

인터넷 상의 익명성은 인터넷 악당들을 더욱 대담하게 만들어서 블로거들을 협박하거나 모욕을 주며 공격하게 한다. 온라인에서의 욕설을 퍼붓는 행동을 저지하고 블로거들의 행동강령을 개발하는 것을 목적으로 하는 온라인 토론회에 대한 요구가 끊임없이 이어져왔다. 블로깅이 더 많은 인기를 얻을수록 블로거들에 대한 공격과 협박의 가능성은 점점 커져간다. 어떤 뚜렷한 이유도 없는 온라인의 악성 글들은 피해자를 황폐하게 만들고, 최악의 경우에는 그들을 자살하게 만들 수 있다.

🔵 인터넷에서 악성 글을 써서 블로거들을 공격하는 인터넷 악당들에 관한 내용이다. 이들을 대담하게 만드는 원인은 바로 정체가 드러나지 않는 익명성이므로 정답은 (b)가 된다. 표현의 자유는 긍정적인 목적에 기여해야 하므로 (a)는 답이 될 수 없으며, (c)의 도덕적 기준 역시 부정적인 결과를 초래하는 것과는 상반되므로 답이 될 수 없다. (d)의 언어적 공격에 대한 취약성은 피해자들에게 해당되는 것이므로 답이 될 수 없다.

embolden ~를 대담하게 하다, 용기를 주다 troll 〈동굴·야산에 사는〉 거인, 장난꾸러기 난쟁이 threat 위협, 협박, 공갈 oppose ~에 반대하다, ~를 저지하다 abusive 입버릇 사나운, 독설의, 함부로 대하는 code of conduct 행동규약 possibility 가능성, 확률 malicious 악의 있는, 심술궂은 apparent 명백한, 분명한 devastate 황폐하게 하다, 철저하게 파괴하다, 압도하다 anonymity 익명(성) vulnerability 상처(비난)받기 쉬움, 취약성

---

36 According to the Department of Health and Human Services, the number of allegations of misconduct by U.S. researchers rose to record highs last year—50 percent higher than 2007 and the highest since 1990 when a program to deal with scientific misconduct was established. Of the 23 cases closed last year, eight individuals were found guilty of research misconduct. Unfortunately, however, it is suggested that this is but a tip of the iceberg—a small fraction of the prevailing scientific misconduct such as fabrication, falsification and plagiarism.

Q What is the best title for the passage?

(a) Faked research results on rise
(b) Instances of unethical experimentation
(c) Guidelines for handing allegations of misconduct
(d) Researches motivated by desire for personal advancement

보건후생부에 따르면 미국 연구원들의 위법행위에 대한 탄원서가 지난해 최고치를 기록했다 – 이는 2007년 보다 50% 높으며, 과학적 위법행위를 다루는 프로그램이 시작된 1990년 이후로 최고치이다. 지난해 종결된 23건 중에서 8명이 연구 위법행위로 유죄임이 드러났다. 그러나 불행히도 이는 빙산의 일각에 불과하다는 점이 제기되고 있다 – 즉 위조, 변조 그리고 표절과 같은 만연하는 과학적 위법행위의 아주 작은 일부분이라는 것이다.

🔵 위조, 변조, 표절 등과 같은 과학 연구의 위법행위가 만연하고 있으며, 이는 점점 증가하는 추세라는 내용이므로 정답은 (a)이다. 비윤리적 실험은 위조나 표절과 같은 위법행위의 범주에 속하는 것은 아니므로 (b)는 답이 될 수 없으며, 위법행위에 대한 탄원을 처리하는 법은 주제와 관련이 없고, 개인적인 출세의 욕망에 대해 언급된 바 없으므로 (c)와 (d)는 답이 될 수 없다.

the Department of Health and Human Services 보건후생부 allegation 주장, 탄원 misconduct 위법행위, 직권남용 record high 최고치 a tip of the iceberg 빙산의 일각 fraction 일부, 작은 부분 prevailing 널리 퍼져 있는, 유행하는, 일반적인 fabrication 위조, 허구 falsification 위조, 변조 plagiarism 표절, 도용 faked 날조된, 모조의, 가짜의 advancement 진보, 전진

37 The BlackBerry is a wireless handheld device developed by the Canadian company Research In Motion (RIM), which supports push e-mail, mobile telephone, text messaging and other wireless information services. RIM decided on the name "BlackBerry" only after considering all the passable names suggested by Lexicon Branding Inc.. One of the naming experts thought the miniature buttons on the device looked like the tiny seeds in a strawberry but straw sounded too slow. Someone else suggested BlackBerry and RIM applauded it.

Q What is the main topic of the passage?

(a) Success of RIM's pilot device
(b) Name origin of the BlackBerry
(c) New slang brought by the BlackBerry
(d) Brand naming in the world of marketing

BlackBerry는 캐나다 회사인 Research In Motion (RIM)에서 개발한 손바닥 크기의 무선 장치이며, 푸시 이메일, 휴대 전화, 문자 메시지 보내기 등 기타 무선 정보 서비스를 제공한다. RIM사는 Lexicon 작명 회사에서 제안한 적당한 많은 이름들을 고려한 후에 BlackBerry로 결정했다. 작명 전문가 중 한 사람이 장치 위의 작은 버튼들이 딸기의 작은 씨앗들처럼 생겼다고 생각했으나 straw는 너무 둔하게 들렸다. 누군가가 검은 딸기(blackberry)를 제안했고 RIM사는 그 이름에 박수를 보냈다.

🔵 BlackBerry라는 무선 장치의 이름이 탄생하게 된 내용이 주를 이루고 있으므로 정답은 (b)이다. (a)와 (c)는 언급된 바 없으며, 마케팅에서의 브랜드 이름짓기는 지문의 내용에 비해 너무 일반적이고 넓은 개념에 해당하므로 (d)도 정답이 될 수 없다.

wireless 무선의 handheld 손에 들고 사용하는, 손안에 드는 크기의 device 장치, 고안물 push e-mail 푸시 이메일(서버 메일 시스템에 의해 수신된 이메일을 휴대 정보 단말기 PDA 랩톱 컴퓨터 기타 휴대기에 자동으로 전송하는 것) passable 적당한 tiny 자그마한, 아주 작은 seed 씨앗, 종자 applaud 박수갈채하다, 성원하다, 찬양하다

---

38 Giant anteaters spend most of their time foraging for their food – ants and termites – with their excellent sense of smell. They are also known for eating other soft-bodied insects like grubs which don't have heavy jaws or chemical defenses. Once they have found their prey, they use their strong forelegs and sharp claws to rip the prey's nests open and utilize their long snout functioning as a vacuum and their sticky tongue to suck in ants or termites from their shelters.

Q What is the passage mainly about?

(a) An anteater's voracious appetite
(b) The reason why an anteater is called this name
(c) Kinds of insects that an anteater likes or dislikes
(d) An anteater's peculiarities for finding and eating its prey

큰개미핥기는 뛰어난 후각을 이용하여 개미와 흰개미 같은 먹이를 찾아다니며 대부분의 시간을 보낸다. 또한 큰개미핥기는 구더기처럼 무거운 턱뼈나 화학적 방어물이 없는 몸이 부드러운 곤충들을 먹는 것으로도 유명하다. 일단 먹이를 발견하면, 큰개미핥기는 강한 앞다리와 날카로운 발톱을 이용하여 먹이가 있는 둥지를 파헤쳐서 열어 젖히고, 진공청소기처럼 작용하는 기다란 코와 끈적끈적한 혀를 이용하여 개미들이 있던 안식처에서 그것들을 핥아먹는다.

🔵 큰개미핥기가 놀라운 후각을 이용하여 먹이를 발견한 후 어떻게 먹이를 먹는지 설명하고 있으므로 정답은 (d)가 된다. 실제로 큰개미핥기의 식욕이 왕성하긴(a) 하지만 본문을 통해서는 알 수 없으며, 큰개미핥기라는 이름으로 불리게 된 이유(b)도 언급되어 있지 않다. 또한 (c)는 본문을 통해 큰개미핥기가 먹는 곤충은 알 수 있지만 싫어하는 곤충은 알 수 없고, 이것이 주된 내용이라고 보기도 어렵기 때문에 정답이 아니다.

forage 마구 뒤지며 찾다 termite 흰개미 grub 땅벌레, 구더기 claw 갈고리 발톱 rip ~을 찢다, 열어젖뜨리다 snout 〈돼지 따위의〉 코, 주둥이 suck ~을 핥다, 핥아먹다 voracious 식욕이 왕성한, 게걸스럽게 먹는 peculiarity 특이한 성질 특징

39 The Boeing 787 Dreamliner, an aircraft currently being developed by the Boeing Company, is famous for using the most advanced technology and as a super efficient airplane. The most remarkable characteristic of the Boeing 787 Dreamliner is that its fuselage is primarily made of carbon fiber composite material so its durability will be improved and it will produce less refuse and waste, being manufactured as a one-piece. In terms of fuel efficiency, it is considered supreme because it will use twenty percent less fuel than today's similar sized airliners. Moreover, thanks to the superior engines which GE and Rolls-Royce has developed, it is expected that engine thrust and fuel efficiency will be increased, while the noise of the jet decreased.

Q What is the best title for the passage?

(a) Boeing 787 Dreamliner, the Most Popular Airplane
(b) The Unparalleled Features of the Boeing 787 Dreamliner
(c) The Boeing Company does business with GE and Rolls-Royce
(d) The Boeing 787 Dreamliner as an Environmental Friendly Aircraft

보잉사가 현재 개발하고 있는 Boeing 787 Dreamliner 항공기는 가장 최신의 기술을 사용하고 있는 것으로 유명한데, 매우 효율적인 비행기로 알려져 있다. Boeing 787 Dreamliner의 가장 주목할 만한 특징은 비행기의 동체가 주로 탄소섬유 합성물질로 만들어져서 내구성이 향상될 것이며, 동체가 하나의 덩어리로 만들어지기 때문에 폐기물이나 쓰레기가 덜 나오게 될 것이라는 점이다. 연료의 효율성 면에서도 최상으로 여겨지는데, 이것은 오늘날 같은 크기의 비행기보다 연료를 20% 정도 덜 사용하기 때문이다. 게다가 GE와 Rolls-Royce사가 개발한 우수한 엔진 덕분에 엔진 추진력과 연료 효율성은 더 증가하는 한편, 비행기의 소음은 감소할 것으로 기대된다.

○ Boeing 787 Dreamliner의 비길 데 없이 우수한 특징들이 소개되어 있으므로 정답은 (b)가 된다. (d)는 Boeing 787 Dreamliner가 연료를 적게 쓰고 쓰레기를 덜 생산하는 점 등으로 미루어보아 환경친화적이라고 할 수 있으나, 이것은 Boeing 787 Dreamliner의 특징들 중 하나이므로 협소한 주제라고 할 수 있다.

currently 최근에 developmental 발달(발전)의 remarkable 놀랄 만한, 주목할 만한 fuselage 〈비행기의〉 동체, 기체 be made of ~로 만들어지다 carbon fiber 탄소 섬유 composite 합성물, 혼성물 durability 내구성 refuse 쓰레기, 찌꺼기 manufacture ~을 제작하다, 생산하다 in terms of ~에 의해서, ~의 견지에서 efficiency 효율성 supreme 최고의, 최상의 thrust 추진력 unparalleled 비길 데 없는, 유례없는

---

40 To get a job you really crave for, it is very important to make sure that you are qualified and well prepared. (a) Also, it is crucial that you make a good first impression to the interviewers. (b) Be well groomed, which means your hair should be clean and styled conservatively based on a company's atmosphere and you should not wear excessive make-up, jewelry, or perfume. (c) Dress yourself appropriately according to the position you are looking for, not to mention that your garments must be immaculate. (d) Ask intelligent questions about the position with a clear voice, and the interviewers will respond to you favorably.

당신이 정말 원하는 직업을 얻기 위해서는 당신이 적임자며 잘 준비되었음을 확신시키는 것이 매우 중요하다. (a) 또한, 면접관에게 첫인상을 좋게 심어주는 것도 아주 중요하다. (b) 단정히 가다듬어 몸단장을 해라. 즉, 머리도 깨끗하고 회사 분위기에 맞춰 보수적으로 꾸며야 하며, 지나친 화장이나, 보석 또는 향수를 사용하지 마라. (c) 당신의 옷이 청결해야 함은 물론이고, 당신이 찾고 있는 직책에 따라 적합한 옷차림을 해라. (d) 분명한 목소리로 그 자리에 대한 지적인 질문들을 해라. 그러면 면접관들이 당신에게 호의적으로 대할 것이다.

○ (a)에서 첫인상이 중요하다고 한 다음, (b)와 (c)에서 첫인상을 좋게 하기 위해 외모를 어떻게 꾸며야 하는지 설명하고 있다. 반면 (d)는 외모에 관한 내용이 아니므로 글의 흐름과 어울리지 않는다.

crave for ~을 갈망(열망)하다 qualified 자격 있는, 적격의 crucial 아주 중대한, 결정적인 groom 〈복장 따위〉를 단정히 가다듬다, 몸단장을 하다 conservatively 보수적으로 not to mention ~은 말할 것도 없고 garment 옷, 의상 immaculate 깨끗한, 청결한 favorably 호의적으로, 호의를 가지고

LISTENING COMPREHENSION · P.118

1 M Do you have anything to declare?
W _____

(a) Nothing to declare.
(b) Take it easy.
(c) I hope it clears up.
(d) That's the spirit.

M: 신고하실 것이 있습니까?
W: 없습니다.

○ 세관 신고를 할 때 많이 들을 수 있는 표현이다. 보통 문제에 나온 단어가 보기에서 반복되면 오답일 경우가 많지만 항상 그런 것은 아니다. 신고할 것이 없을 때에는 간단히 (a)처럼 Nothing to declare 라고 하면 된다. (c)의 경우 declare의 발음과 비슷한 clear을 이용하여 혼동을 주고 있다.

declare ~을 선언하다, 공표하다, (과세품)을 신고하다 take it easy. 잘 가, 쉬엄쉬엄 해 clear up (날씨가) 개다 That's the spirit. 바로 그런 정신이 필요하다

2 M It's 23 dollars all together.
W _____

(a) How much do I owe you?
(b) Could I cash this check, please?
(c) Here you are. You can keep the change.
(d) It's a deal.

M: 모두 합해서 23달러입니다.
W: 여기 있어요. 잔돈은 가지세요.

○ 남자는 점원으로 보인다. 물건이나 서비스를 받고 계산을 하려고 하는 상황이며, 총 23달러라고 했으므로 이와 어울리는 대답을 찾아야 한다. (a)의 경우 얼마냐고 물어보는 상황이므로 이 대화 이전에 나왔어야 한다. (b)의 경우 수표를 바꿔달라는 뜻으로 역시 어딘가 자연스럽지 못하다. (c)의 경우 돈을 내면서 잔돈을 가지라고 하는 것이므로 정답으로 적절하고 (d)는 상대방의 제안을 받아들일 때, '좋아, 그렇게 하자' 라는 수락의 의미로 많이 쓰는 표현이다.

cash ~을 현금화하다 change 잔돈, ~을 바꾸다, 고치다 It's a deal. (어떠한 제안에 대해) 좋아, 합의 봤어!

3 M How come you are so late?
W _____

(a) By bus.
(b) I got caught in traffic.
(c) I was so busy lately.
(d) The line is busy.

M: 왜 이렇게 늦었어?
W: 차가 막혔어.

○ 왜 늦었는지 이유를 묻고 있다. (a)는 어떠한 교통수단을 이용했는지 물었을 때 나올 수 있는 표현이고, (b)의 경우 교통 체증에 걸렸다는 뜻이므로 늦은 이유에 대한 답이 된다. (c)와 (d)는 상황에 맞지 않으므로 정답이 아니다.

how come S+V? 왜? (이유를 묻는 표현으로 뒤에 주어, 동사의 순으로 나옴에 주의하자.) The line is busy. 전화가 통화중이다.

4　M　This soup is so good. You are a great cook.

　W　I'm happy you enjoyed it.

　M　Can I have one more bowl of soup?

　W　_____

(a) Yes, it's pie in the sky.
(b) You are a couch potato.
(c) Sure, this is on me.
(d) Sure, help yourself.

M: 이 수프 정말 맛있네요. 요리를 참 잘하세요.
W: 맛있게 드셨다니 좋네요.
M: 한 그릇 더 먹어도 될까요?
W: 그럼요, 마음껏 드세요.

❍ 남자가 여자의 요리 솜씨를 칭찬하면서 수프 한 그릇을 더 먹어도 되느냐고 요청하고 있다. 이에 대한 적절한 답은 마음껏 더 먹으라는 뜻의 (d)이다. (a), (b)등은 파이나 감자와 같은 음식과 관련된 단어들이 나왔지만 음식과 관련된 의미가 아니므로 주의해야 한다. (c)의 경우 음식을 사 먹고 계산을 내가 하겠다는 의미이므로 정답이 될 수 없다.

pie in the sky 실현 가능성이 적은, 그림의 떡인 **couch potato** 소파에 앉아 TV만 보는 사람 **help yourself** 마음껏 드세요

5　M　Do you know a new boss is coming next week?

　W　Yes, I've just heard.

　M　What about the old project then?

　W　_____

(a) It's out of the questions.
(b) It's still up in the air.
(c) Don't jump to conclusions.
(d) It was a close call.

M: 다음 주에 새로운 사장이 온다는 소식 들었어?
W: 어, 방금 들었어.
M: 그럼 이전 프로젝트는 어떻게 되는 거야?
W: 아직 어떻게 될지 몰라.

❍ 사장이 바뀌면 전부터 진행해오던 프로젝트가 어떻게 되는 것인지 남자가 묻고 있다. (a)는 불가능하다, 말도 안 된다는 뜻으로서 대화문과 관계가 없고, (c)는 성급하게 판단하지 말라는 뜻으로 남자가 어떠한 결론을 내린 것이 아니라 앞으로 어떻게 되는 것인지 궁금하여 질문을 한 것이므로 정답이 될 수 없다. 여기에서는 아직 결정이 나지 않았다고 하는 (b)가 가장 적절한 답이 된다.

up in the air (계획이) 막연한, 미결 상태인 **out of question** 논외인, 불가능한, 말도 안 되는 **jump to a conclusion** 속단하다 **close call** 위기일발, 구사일생

6　M　Hello. Is this T&T office?

　W　Yes. How can I help you?

　M　I'd like to speak with Mr. Smith.

　W　_____

(a) Okay. I'll call you back later.
(b) I have to ring it up.
(c) I'll transfer you to him.
(d) I'm speechless.

M: 안녕하세요. T&T 사무실인가요?
W: 네, 무엇을 도와드릴까요?
M: 스미스 씨와 통화하고 싶은데요.
W: 전화를 돌려드릴게요.

❍ 통화하고 싶은 사람의 이름을 대었으므로 정답은 그 사람에게 연결시켜 주겠다고 하는 (c)가 된다. 전화 대화 상황이므로 전화와 관련된 표현들을 보기에 넣어서 혼동을 주려 하고 있다. (a)의 대답은 스미스 씨 본인이라야 할 수 있는 말이다.

ring up ~에게 전화 걸다, 금전 등록기의 키를 눌러 (어떤 금액)을 나오게 하다 **transfer** (전화를) ~에게 돌리다 **speechless** 말문이 막힌

7

W   Dad. You forgot to give me allowance again!

M   Oh. I'm sorry. How much do I owe you?

W   Just twenty dollars.

M   Twenty dollars? I think I paid you the other day.

W   No. You forgot two times. So it has been piling up.

M   So, what are you going to do with the money?

W   I'm going to use some to buy books and put the rest in savings.

M   Oh, good girl.

Q   According to the dialogue, which is correct?

(a) The man doesn't have money at the moment.

(b) The girl borrowed some money from the man.

(c) The man forgot to give his daughter pocket money.

(d) The man bought his daughter some books.

W: 아빠, 용돈 주는 걸 또 잊으셨어요!

M: 미안하다. 얼마 줘야 하지?

W: 20달러만 주시면 돼요.

M: 20달러? 일전에 줬던 것 같은데.

W: 아니에요. 두 번이나 잊으셨어요. 그래서 밀린 거라고요.

M: 용돈으로 무엇을 할 생각이니?

W: 일부는 책을 사고 나머지는 저축할 거예요.

M: 착하기도 하지.

◑ 대화문과 일치하는 것을 고르는 문제이다. (a)는 언급되지 않았으므로 알 수 없으며, 아빠가 딸에게 용돈 주는 것을 깜빡 잊은 것이므로 (b)는 사실이 아니다. allowance는 용돈이라는 뜻으로 pocket money로 달리 표현할 수 있다. 따라서 정답은 (c)이다. 받은 용돈으로 책을 살 거라고 했으므로 (d)는 정답이 아니다.

allowance(=pocket money) 용돈   the other day 일전에, 며칠 전에   pile up 쌓이다, 축적되다   savings 저금, 저축액

8

M   Where are you dashing off to?

W   I'm heading home.

M   Did you forget to have group study tonight?

W   No. I'm just going to grab something to eat. I'll come back to school by six.

M   Okay. Why don't you buy some snacks for everyone while you're out?

W   Okay.

Q   Where is the conversation most likely to occur?

(a) At a restroom

(b) At a snack bar

(c) At school

(d) At home

M: 어딜 그렇게 급히 가니?

W: 집에 가고 있어.

M: 오늘밤 스터디 모임 있는 거 잊었어?

W: 아니, 그냥 뭐 좀 간단히 먹고 오려고. 6시쯤에 학교로 돌아올 거야.

M: 좋아. 나가는 김에 모두를 위해 간식 좀 사오는 것이 어때?

W: 알았어.

◑ 대화가 일어나는 장소에 대해서 묻고 있다. 여자가 집에 가서 뭐 좀 먹고 다시 학교로 올 것이라 했으므로 장소는 (c) 학교가 정답이다. 집에 다녀오는 길에 간식을 사오라고 한 것 때문에 (b) 스낵바를 고르지 않도록 유의하자.

dash off to ~로 급히 가다   grab 재빨리 먹다, 손에 넣다

9

W How much did you pay for it?

M 250 dollars.

W Are you sure? 250 dollars for such a thing like that? What a rip-off!

M What do you mean?

W It's not worth it. You are not very streetwise.

M Oh, I guess I really got ripped off.

W Where did you get it anyway?

Q Which is correct according to the dialogue?

(a) The man bought something at a discount.

(b) The man bought a used product.

(c) The man bought something at an unreasonable price.

(d) The man sold something to the woman at a high price.

W: 그거 얼마 주고 샀어?

M: 250 달러.

W: 확실해? 그런 물건을 250 달러 주고 샀다고? 완전 바가지다!

M: 무슨 뜻이야?

W: 그럴 가치가 없어. 너는 세상 물정도 참 모른다.

M: 아이고, 정말 바가지 썼나보다.

W: 근데 어디서 산 건데?

🔹 대화문과 일치하는 내용을 고르는 문제이다. 남자가 바가지를 썼다고 했으므로 할인 가격에 샀다고 하는 (a)는 정답이 될 수 없다. 남자가 산 물건이 중고 물품인지 알 수 없으므로 (b)는 정답이 아니다. 터무니없는 가격에 물건을 산 것이므로 (c)가 정답이다. (d)에서 남자가 여자에게 높은 가격에 물건을 팔았다는 내용은 전혀 관계가 없다.

rip-off 착취, 폭리, 바가지 streetwise 세상 물정에 밝은 used product 중고 물품 unreasonable price 터무니없는 가격

---

10 Air France has revoked the plan to lower wages and working hours by 4 percent. Air France said passenger traffic has been increasing since the end of the Gulf War, which resumes previously canceled spring and winter flight programs and can open new flights to some destinations. Air France said, however, there will be no change in other cutbacks including a salary freeze, and limited new hiring. AP News, Jim McGuire.

Q What is correct according to the news report?

(a) Air France decided to lower wages of workers.

(b) Air France halted operations due to the gulf war.

(c) A salary freeze will remain in effect as planned.

(d) Air France plans to increase new hiring.

에어 프랑스는 임금과 근무 시간을 4 % 줄인다는 계획을 철회했습니다. 에어 프랑스 측은 걸프전 종전 이후로 승객 이동량이 증가하고 있고, 이로 인해 이전에 취소했던 봄과 겨울 비행 프로그램을 재개하고 일부 목적지에 새 비행편 개설이 가능할 것이라고 말했습니다. 그러나 임금 동결과 신입사원 고용 제한을 포함한 다른 축소 안에는 변화가 없을 것이라고 말했습니다. AP 뉴스, 짐 맥과이어입니다.

🔹 뉴스 내용과 일치하는 것을 묻고 있다. 보기를 하나하나 살펴보면 첫 부분에서 에어 프랑스가 임금 삭감 계획을 철회했다고 했으므로 (a)는 정답이 될 수 없다. 걸프전 이후로 승객 이동량이 증가했다고 했으므로 걸프전 때문에 운항을 중단했다는 내용의 (b)도 역시 정답이 될 수 없다. 마지막 부분에 임금 동결은 변화가 없을 것이라고 했으므로 계획대로 실시될 것이라는 (c)가 정답이 된다. 그리고 신입사원 고용 역시 늘릴 계획이 없다고 했으므로 (d)역시 정답이 될 수 없다.

revoke 철회하다 passenger traffic 승객 이동량 resume ~을 재개하다 cutback 축소, 삭감 salary freeze 임금 동결

11 However having no deadlines doesn't mean I'm tardy. Actually I like writing at a set time in the morning. This is very helpful for good writing. Why I can be a good writer is that I don't think writing is a chore. The sci-fi author Lois McMaster Bujold said that the speed of writing had doubled compared to when she wrote to specific deadlines. And she added that she had more fun doing that. The secret of my work is that I write when I want to write.

Q What is the speaker talking about?

(a) The writing style of the speaker
(b) The advantage of having deadlines
(c) How to be a fast writer
(d) The number of books the speaker's written

그러나 마감일이 없다는 것이 제가 게으르다는 의미는 아닙니다. 사실 저는 아침에 정해진 시간에 글을 쓰는 것을 좋아합니다. 훌륭한 글쓰기에 이것은 매우 도움이 됩니다. 제가 좋은 작가가 될 수 있는 이유는 글쓰기를 노동이라고 생각하지 않기 때문입니다. 공상과학 소설가인 Lois McMaster Bujold는 특정 마감일에 맞추어서 글을 쓸 때보다 글쓰기 속도가 배가 되었다고 말합니다. 그리고 그녀는 이렇게 하는 것이 더 재미있다고 덧붙였습니다. 내 글쓰기의 비밀은 내가 쓰고 싶을 때 쓰는 것입니다.

◑ 화자가 이야기하고 있는 것은 자신의 글쓰기 스타일이다. 마감일을 정해놓지 않고 쓰고 싶을 때 쓴다고 하면서 다른 작가의 예를 들고 있다. 따라서 정답은 (a)가 된다. (b)의 경우 작가의 글쓰기 스타일과 반대되는 내용이며 (c)나 (d)에 대한 내용은 언급된 바가 없다.

deadline 마감일 tardy 게으른, 굼뜬 compared to ~에 비해서 advantage 이점

---

12 You don't need a magnifying glass to trim your baby's fingernails. If you know a few tips, you can clip your baby's nails without difficulty. First, you need a grooming set designed for infant size. Second, wait until your baby is in deep sleep so that you can clip without your baby squirming around. Third, put slight pressure on the skin under the nail to make it stick out. Fourth, be careful not to leave sharp edges when you clip the nails. Last, clip toenails once a week, but your infant's fingernails may need more frequent clipping.

Q Which of the following is true according to the passage?

(a) Using a magnifying glass is a good way of trimming your baby's nails
(b) It is difficult to clip your baby's nails when your little one's awake.
(c) You should be careful not to make the nail stick out when trimming.
(d) Your baby's toenails grow faster than fingernails.

아기의 손톱을 자르기 위해 확대경은 필요하지 않습니다. 몇 가지 요령을 알면 어려움 없이 아기의 손톱을 자를 수 있습니다. 우선 유아의 사이즈에 맞게 디자인 된 도구가 필요합니다. 두 번째로 아기가 깊이 잠들 때까지 기다려서 아기가 가만히 있을 때 손톱을 자를 수 있도록 합니다. 세 번째로 손톱 아래 피부를 살짝 눌러서 손톱이 드러나도록 합니다. 네 번째로 손톱을 자를 때 끝이 날카롭지 않도록 주의하세요. 마지막으로 발톱은 일주일에 한 번씩 잘라도 되지만 손톱의 경우 더 자주 손질할 필요가 있습니다.

◑ 내용과 일치하는 보기를 찾는 문제이다. 첫 부분에서 확대경이 필요하지 않다고 했으므로 (a)는 정답이 아니다. 아이가 깊이 잠들 때까지 기다린 다음 손톱을 자르라고 했으므로 아기가 깨어있을 때는 손톱을 자르기 어렵다는 의미가 된다. 따라서 정답은 (b)가 된다. 손톱을 자를 때에는 손톱 아래를 살짝 눌러 손톱이 드러나게 하라고 했으므로 이와 정반대의 기술을 한 (c)도 답이 아니다. 마지막 부분에서 발톱은 일주일에 한 번, 손톱은 더 자주 손질하라고 했으므로 손톱이 더 빨리 자란다는 것을 알 수 있다. 따라서 (d)도 정답이 될 수 없다.

magnifying glass 확대경 trim ~을 정돈하다, 손질하다 clip ~을 자르다 groom ~을 다듬다, 손질하다 squirm 몸부림치다, 꿈틀거리다 stick out 돌출하다, 뛰어나오다

13 A What do you usually do on Saturdays?
B _____ of wildlife.

(a) Usually take pictures
(b) Taking picture
(c) I usually take pictures
(d) Taking to pictures

A: 너 토요일에 주로 뭐해?
B: 나 주로 야생동물의 사진을 찍어

○ 주어와 동사가 모두 있는 완벽한 문장인 (c)가 정답이다 (b)는 picture에 관사가 필요하다.

take a picture 사진을 찍다

---

14 A What time are you supposed to leave?
B Don't worry, I still _____.

(a) have more hours
(b) have much time
(c) having more time
(d) will have time

A: 너 몇 시에 떠나야 하니?
B: 걱정 마. 나 아직 시간 많아.

○ I still have much time이 적절하다.

be supposed to ~해야 한다

---

15 A I really feel drowsy.
B Shall I _____ some coffee or tea?

(a) get to you
(b) get you
(c) getting you
(d) to get you

A: 나 정말 졸려.
B: 커피나 차 좀 갖다 줄까요?

○ get은 타동사이므로 목적어 you를 쓰면 된다.

drowsy 졸음이 오는

---

16 A How come _____ again?
B I don't know why. He also didn't answer the phone.

(a) does he late
(b) does he come late
(c) is he late
(d) he is late

A: 그가 왜 또 늦었어?
B: 나도 모르겠어. 그는 전화도 안받아.

○ how come 의문문에서는 how come 다음에 주어＋동사 어순이 오기 때문에 (d)가 적절하다

how come 왜(＝why)

---

17 An individual detained doesn't have to be suspected of belonging to an organized crime or of _____ terrorist activities.

(a) involved in
(b) being involved in
(c) having involved in
(d) involving in

억류된 개인이 범죄조직에 속해있다거나 테러활동에 포함되어 있다는 의심을 받을 필요는 없다.

○ 전치사 뒤이므로 ing형태가 나오고, 테러활동에 '포함되는' 것이므로 수동형이 와야 한다.

detain 구류하다 **suspect** 의심하다

18 The Chinese government restricted exports of fireworks to a limited number of ports so that _____ shipments was reported in China.

(a) a definite drop of firework
(b) definite a drop of firework
(c) definite drop of firework
(d) drop of definite firework

중국 정부가 정해진 항구에서만 폭죽을 수출하도록 제한함으로써 폭죽 선적의 갑작스런 하락이 보도되었다.

○ definite이 drop을 수식하는데, drop에는 부정관사를 붙여서 a definite drop of firework (a)가 적절하다.

restrict 제한하다, 금지하다 firework 불꽃

---

19 You can return _____ within the warranty period if the item needs to be checked.

(a) defective item
(b) a defective item
(c) to the defective item
(d) of defective item

만약 제품을 확인할 필요가 있다면 당신은 그 결함 제품을 보증 기간 안에 반품할 수 있다.

○ return 다음에 목적어가 필요한데, item이 셀 수 있는 명사이므로 관사 a가 필요하다.

warranty 보증, 담보 defective 결함이 있는

---

20 The number of unemployed persons _____ by 4 million and the unemployment rate has risen this year due to the economic slumps.

(a) having increased
(b) have increased
(c) has increased
(d) has been increasing

실업자의 수가 4백만 명까지 증가했고, 올해의 실업률은 경제 부진 때문에 상승했다.

○ the number of는 단수이기 때문에 has increased가 적절하다.

unemployment rate 실업률

---

21 (a) A: What did they agree among the Convention?
(b) B: Most of them said actions would be taken at the national level.
(c) A: I couldn't agree anymore. Something efficient is needed right now.
(d) B: I think the officials discuss about it soon.

A: 그 집회에서 그들은 무엇에 동의했니?
B: 그들 대부분이 활동이 국가적 수준에서 일어나야 한다고 말했어.
A: 맞아. 뭔가 효과적인 것이 당장 필요해
B: 나는 이것에 대에서 임원들이 곧 의논할 거라고 생각해.

○ discuss에는 이미 '~에 대하여 토론하다'로 about의 의미를 포함하고 있는 타동사이기 때문에 about을 쓰지 않는다.

convention 집회 national 국가적인 efficient 효과적인

22 (a) There are many causes of gangrene which are the death of tissue, usually resulted from a loss of blood supply. (b) Poorly-managed diabetes can cause this chronic disease, especially for smokers. (c) Many people do not know that gangrene can be closely related to smokers and those who are diabetic, and that means treatment for life. (d) So, it is highly recommended to know that it affects a small area of skin, but can also affect even a substantial portion of a limb.

주로 혈액 공급 부족의 결과로 나타나며 조직이 죽는 괴저현상에는 많은 원인이 있다. 당뇨병을 잘못 관리하면 특히 흡연자들에게 이 만성 질병이 유발된다. 많은 사람들은 그 괴저현상이 당뇨병 환자와 흡연자들과 밀접한 관련이 있고, 그것은 일생 동안 치료할 필요가 있다는 것을 모른다. 그래서 이것은 피부의 적은 부분에 침범하지만, 사람의 수족의 중요 부분에도 침범할 수 있다는 것을 알아야 할 필요가 있다고 한다.

❍ (a)의 which는 gangrene를 설명하고 있으므로 복수 동사 are가 아니라 단수 동사 is를 써야 한다.

gangrene 괴저 diabetes 당뇨병 chronic 만성의 substantial 많은, 중요한 limb 수족

VOCABULARY • P.123

23 A All the hospitals are close up!
   B It's because the doctors have been on a _____ since yesterday.

   (a) strike
   (b) picnic
   (c) trip
   (d) vacation

A: 병원이 모두 문을 닫았어!
B: 어제부터 의사들이 파업에 들어가서 그래.

❍ 모든 병원이 문을 닫았다고 했으므로 의사들이 파업을 했다고 하는 것이 자연스럽다. '파업을 하다' 라는 표현은 'go on a strike' 를 쓴다.

be on a strike 파업 중이다

---

24 A Why did she pass away suddenly?
   B I heard that she developed _____ after surgery.

   (a) complicity
   (b) complications
   (c) compliments
   (d) compounds

A: 그녀가 왜 갑자기 돌아가신 거예요?
B: 수술 후에 합병증이 생겼다고 들었어요.

❍ 갑자기 돌아가셨고, 수술을 받았다고 했으므로 질병과 관련한 단어가 나오는 것이 자연스럽다. complications는 '합병증'을 뜻하는 단어이므로 빈 칸에 적절하다.

pass away 죽다 complicity 공모, 연루 complications 합병증 compliment 칭찬 compound 혼합물

---

25 A I have no idea what this word means.
   B How do you spell it? I'll _____ it up in the dictionary.

   (a) find
   (b) look
   (c) figure
   (d) solve

A: 이 단어가 무슨 뜻인지 모르겠어.
B: 스펠링이 어떻게 되는데? 내가 사전에서 찾아볼게.

❍ 단어의 뜻을 모른다고 하자 스펠링을 물으면서 사전 이야기를 했으므로 사전을 찾아본다고 하는 것이 자연스럽다. 'look up' 은 어떠한 정보를 찾아본다는 뜻이므로 빈칸에 적절한 단어는 (b) look이다.

look up ~을 찾다, 조사하다

26 A Why are you falling behind the others?
B I _____ out of breath when I walk a little bit.

(a) put
(b) come
(c) fall
(d) get

A: 왜 다른 사람들보다 뒤처지고 있어?
B: 조금만 걸어도 숨이 차.

➡ 숨이 차다고 할 때에는 'get out of breath' 라고 한다. 숨이 가빠서 다른 사람들보다 뒤처지고 있는 상황임을 알 수 있다.

fall behind ~에게 뒤지다 get out of breath 숨이 차다

---

27 A Have you heard she moved into an imposing mansion?
B Yes. People say that she made a _____ in the stock market.

(a) treasure
(b) success
(c) fortune
(d) luck

A: 그녀가 으리으리한 맨션으로 이사 갔다는 이야기 들었어?
B: 응. 사람들이 말하기를 주식으로 큰돈을 벌었대.

➡ imposing mansion이라고 한 것으로 보아 돈을 많이 벌었음을 알 수 있다. '돈을 많이 벌다'에 해당하는 표현은 'make a fortune'이다.

imposing 인상적인, 남의 눈을 끄는 make a fortune 재산을 모으다, 큰돈을 벌다

---

28 The _____ control system is needed in order to control air quality and keep the concentrations of pollutants at a low level.

(a) emission
(b) immersion
(c) environment
(d) circumstance

배출가스 조절 시스템은 대기의 질을 조절하고 오염물질의 밀집을 낮게 유지하기 위해 필요하다.

➡ 대기의 질이나 오염원의 밀집에 대한 이야기가 나왔으므로 오염을 유발하는 것을 조절하는 시스템에 대한 언급이 나와야 한다. 이에 가장 적절한 단어는 emission이다.

emission 방출, 발산 concentration 집중, 밀집 pollutant 오염원, 오염 물질 immersion 담금, 몰두, 투입 circumstance 상황, 환경

---

29 The housing market in the U.S. remains to be _____ due to high interest rates and a lack of properties which contributes to a decrease in new homes sale.

(a) dragging
(b) weak
(c) sluggish
(d) decreased

미국의 주택시장은 새로운 주택 판매의 둔화에 공헌한 높은 이자율과 자산 부족 때문에 부진한 상태로 남아있다.

➡ 주택 시장 상황이 안 좋다는 것을 알 수 있는데, 보기 가운데 이러한 의미를 가진 단어는 sluggish이다.

sluggish 나태한, 불경기인 interest rates 이자율 dragging 느릿느릿한, 동작이 둔한

---

30 The inexperienced new team won the championship this year and it turned out to be a big mistake to _____ their strength.

(a) undermine
(b) underestimate
(c) undergo
(d) undertake

경험이 없는 새로운 팀이 올해 선수권을 거머쥐었는데, 그들의 능력을 과소평가한 것이 큰 실수였음이 드러났다.

➡ 예상치 못했던 팀이 우승했으므로 그들의 능력을 과소평가했다는 내용이 나오는 것이 적절하다. 따라서 정답은 (b)가 된다.

inexperienced 경험이 없는, 미숙한 underestimate 과소평가하다 undermine ~의 밑을 파다, ~의 기초를 위태롭게 하다 undergo ~을 겪다, 경험하다 undertake ~을 맡다, 떠맡다

31 There are still many risks in the uncertain market such as weak stock prices and _____ in the exchange rate.

(a) balances
(b) fluctuations
(c) changes
(d) stability

약세를 보이는 주식 가격과 환율의 변동과 같이 불확실한 시장에는 여전히 많은 위험 요소들이 있다.

🔵 uncertain market에서 나타날 수 있는 예시들로 적당한 것을 찾아야 한다. (a)나 (d)는 불확실한 시장 상황과는 반대되는 내용이므로 정답이 될 수 없다. 그리고 환율이 동요한다고 할 때에는 fluctuation을 쓴다.

fluctuation 변동, 등락 exchange rate 환율 stability 안정, 고정

---

32 He is very _____ at making a quick decision by ignoring facts that are contrary to his point of view.

(a) adoptive
(b) adept
(c) adapt
(d) adaptive

그는 자신의 관점에 상반되는 사실들을 무시함으로써 빠른 결정을 내리는 데 매우 능숙하다.

🔵 be adept at은 '~에 능숙하다, 뛰어나다' 라는 뜻을 가지고 있다. 형태가 비슷한 어휘들을 보기에 제시하였으나 (b)를 제외한 다른 어휘들은 의미상 모두 적절하지 않다.

adept 숙련된, 뛰어난, 정통한 contrary 어긋나는, 상반되는 point of view 관점 adoptive 채용의, 채용하기 쉬운 adapt (환경에) 순응하다, 적응하다 adaptive 적응성의, 순응하다

READING COMPREHENSION · P.126

33 The cornerstone of effective relationships is _____. It was a tribal custom of Native Americans to nurture listening by the use of a 'talking stick'. During councils of war, important discussions, negotiations or debates, the person holding the talking stick was allowed to speak without interruptions for an unlimited time, but before the opponent was given an opportunity to talk, he had to be able to repeating everything the holder of the stick had said, to the satisfaction of the first speaker. Only when the person in possession of the talking stick was satisfied that his opponent fully comprehended his point would he pass the stick on to that person.

(a) the ability to repeat
(b) in not losing patience
(c) found in the art of listening
(d) taking turns when speaking in a group

효과적인 관계의 기본은 경청의 기술에서 볼 수 있다. '말하기 막대'를 사용하여 듣는 능력을 키우는 것은 아메리카 원주민 부족의 관습이었다. 전쟁 회의나, 중요한 토론이나 협상 혹은 논쟁 중에 말하기 막대를 쥐고 있는 사람은 중단 없이 무제한 이야기를 할 수 있었으나, 상대방에게 말할 기회가 주어지기 전에 막대기를 쥐고 있던 사람이 말한 모든 것을 첫 번째 화자가 만족할 만큼 그대로 말할 수 있어야 했다. 말하기 막대를 쥐고 있던 사람이 상대방이 자신의 논지를 완전히 이해했다고 만족해야만 그는 상대방에게 막대기를 넘겼다.

🔵 상대방의 말을 되풀이하는 것이 요점이 아니라 마지막 문장에서 서술되어 있듯이, 상대방의 요점을 완전히 이해한 경우에만 자신도 말할 기회가 주어졌다는 것으로 보아 경청의 기술의 중요성에 대한 것으로 볼 수 있으므로 (c)가 정답이다. 되풀이 말할 수 있는 능력이나, 인내심도 요구되지만 이는 제대로 듣기 위한 방법이므로 (a)와 (b)는 정답이라고 볼 수 없다. 말하기 막대가 순서대로 말하기 위한 용도는 아니므로 (d)도 답이 아니다.

cornerstone 토대, 주춧돌 tribal 부족의, 종족의 nurture 키우다, 발달을 촉진하다 council 회의, 협의회, 심의회 debate 토의, 토론, 논쟁 interruption 중단, 방해 opponent 상대, 적수, 대항자 possession 소유, 소지

34 Chronic Fatigue Syndrome (CFS) is a complicated disorder characterized by extreme fatigue that often won't pass off after rest and rather lasts a long time. It also may be worsened by even slight exertion. People with CFS exhibit symptoms like headaches, sore throat, sleep problems, unexplained muscle pains, or loss of memory. CFS is one of the most mysterious chronic illnesses that are complex and difficult to diagnose because there is no clear cause and cure for CFS. That's why some people have trouble recognizing CFS as a disease, but it is very important to remember that

_____.

(a) it is not that serious if you don't really recognize it as a disease
(b) medicines can reduce the symptoms of it and cure the entire syndrome
(c) people healthy and full of energy may not experience it in their 40s and 50s
(d) your fatigue is factual and that you can improve it by working with your doctor

만성피로증후군(CFS)은 복잡한 병으로 극도로 피곤한 상태가 휴식 후에도 사라지지 않고 도리어 오랫동안 지속되는 특징이 있다. CFS 는 가벼운 활동에 의해서도 악화될지 모른다. CFS를 앓고 있는 사람들은 두통, 인후염, 수면장애, 설명할 수 없는 근육통증 또는 기억력 상실과 같은 증세를 보인다. CFS는 복잡하고 진단내리기 어려운 가장 불가사의한 고질병 중 하나인데 그것은 CFS에 대한 확실한 원인과 치료가 없기 때문이다. 그러한 이유로 어떤 사람들은 CFS를 병으로 진단내리기를 어려워하지만, 여러분의 피로는 실제적인 것이며 의사와 함께 그 병을 개선시킬 수 있다는 것을 기억하는 것이 매우 중요하다.

💠 만성피로증후군의 특징과 증상을 설명하고 있는 글로서 빈 칸의 앞 문장(CFS is one of the~)부터 힌트가 된다. 즉, 만성피로증후군은 명백한 원인과 치료법이 없어서 진단하기 어려운 병이기 때문에 먼저 병으로 인식하고 대처해 나가는 것이 중요하다는 것이다. (a)는 CFS를 병으로 인식하지 않으면 그렇게 심각하지 않다는 내용으로 정답과 상반되는 내용이고, (b)는 약물이 CFS의 증상을 줄이고 병을 치료할 수 있다는 내용으로 본문과 다르다. 건강하고 에너지가 넘치는 사람들은 4,50대에 CFS를 겪지 않을지도 모른다는 내용(c)은 본문을 통해서 알 수 없다.

chronic 〈병이〉 만성의, 고질의 fatigue 피로 disorder 〈가벼운〉 병 pass off 〈아픔, 피로 따위가〉 차츰 사라지다 exertion 〈육체와 정신의〉 격렬한 활동 노력, 애씀 symptom 증상 diagnose A as B A를 B라고 진단하다 have trouble ~ing ~하는데 어려움이 있다 factual 실제의, 사실상의

35 The Halo Effect is defined as a cognitive bias about a person's one desirable trait extending to influence the global evaluations of that person. In a study published in 1920, E. L. Thorndike asked army officers to rate their soldiers with regard to intelligence, constitution, leadership, and character and found that there was a high cross-correlation. That is, when a person is assumed to have one outstanding trait, that person is likely to be recognized to possess many other attractive traits as well. This halo effect is fascinating and useful in the business and political world. For example, politicians try to appear affectionate and friendly as much as possible because people tend to believe that _____.

후광효과는 어떤 사람의 한 가지 바람직한 특징이 그 사람을 전체적으로 평가하는 데까지 영향을 미치는 인지적 편견으로 정의된다. 1920년 한 연구에서, Thorndike는 육군 장교들에게 지성, 체격, 리더십 그리고 성격과 관련하여 병사들을 평가하도록 했는데, 거기에 높은 연관성이 있음을 알아냈다. 즉, 어떤 사람에게 한 가지 뛰어난 특징이 있는 것으로 여겨지면, 그 사람은 또한 다른 많은 매력적인 특징들을 가지고 있는 것으로 여겨지는 것 같았다. 이 후광효과는 사업계와 정치계에서 매혹적이고 유용하다. 예를 들어, 사람들은 정치가들이 훌륭하게 보이면, 그들의 정책 또한 우수하다고 생각하는 경향이 있기 때문에 정치가들은 가능한 한 상냥하고 다정하게 보이려고 노력한다.

💠 후광효과는 한 가지 특징이 다른 특징의 평가를 내릴 때 영향을 미치는 것이기 때문에 그와 관련된 예를 찾으면 된다. 즉, (b)정치가의 모습과 정책과는 밀접한 관련이 없을 지라도 사람들은 (a)처럼 정치가의 모습이 보기 좋으면 정책도 좋을 것이라고 생각한다는 것이다. (c)는 외모가 현대 사회에서 가장 중요한 가치라는 것이고, (d)는 한 정치가의 정책이 다른 정치가의 정책보다 훨씬 낫지는 않다는 것으로 후광효과와 관련이 없다.

(a) if they look good, their policies are good, too

(b) their appearances are not closely related to their policies

(c) appearances are the most valuable in the modern society

(d) one politician's policy is not much better than that of another

define 정의를 내리다 cognitive 인식의, 인지되는 bias 편견 desirable 바람직한, 매력 있는 evaluation 평가 with regard to ~에 관해서 constitution 체격, 체질 correlation 상호관련 assume 가정하다, 추측하다 outstanding 눈에 띄는, 우수한 affectionate 애정이 있는, 상냥한

---

36 Bob Marley is the most renowned and revered performer of reggae music, credited for spreading its spirit and gospel to the four corners of the globe. The tiny Third World of Jamaica produced a legendary artist whose work not just displayed the stylistic spectrum of modern Jamaican music from ska to rocksteady—but raised the music to a social force with universal appeal. The severe impoverishment as well as political discontentment with the Jamaican government would cause this foremost emissary of reggae to disseminate calls for political uprising in his lyrics. In addition, Marley's declamatory voice was the best suited messenger.

Q Which of the following is true according to the passage?

(a) Jamaica was in a time of economical transition.

(b) Marley's music advocated for Jamaican government.

(c) Bob Marley urged people to rise and fight for their right.

(d) Public expression of a private truth is peculiar to Marley's music.

Bob Marley는 레게 음악의 정신과 신념을 지구상 구석구석에 퍼뜨린, 가장 유명하고 존경받는 음악가이다. 자마이카라는 작은 제 3세계 국가가 ska부터 rocksteady에 이르는 현대 자마이카 음악의 스타일의 다양성을 보여줄 뿐만 아니라 음악을 보편적인 호소력을 갖는 사회적 세력으로 격상시킨 이 전설적인 예술가를 배출한 것이다. 자마이카 정부에 대한 정치적인 불만뿐만 아니라 심각한 가난이 이 레게음악의 선구자로 하여금 그의 가사를 통해 정치적인 모반의 필요성을 전파하게 했다. 게다가 Bob Marley의 호소력 있는 목소리는 그에 가장 알맞은 전령이었다.

◐ Bob Marley가 음악을 통해 민중들로 하여금 정치적인 운동에 참여하도록 했다는 내용이므로 정답은 (c)가 된다. 경제적으로 가난함과 과도기는 일치하지 않으므로 (a)는 정답이 아니며, 그가 자마이카 정부를 옹호했다는 것은 글의 내용과 상반되므로 (b)도 답이 될 수 없다. 개인적인 진실을 공적으로 표현하는 것은 Bob Marley 음악의 특징이 아니므로 (d)도 답이 될 수 없다.

renowned 유명한, 저명한 revere 존경하다, 경외하다 credited for ~의 공적이 있는 gospel 복음, 주의, 신조 the four corners of the globe 지구의 구석구석 legendary 전설의, 전설적인, 유명한 spectrum 범위, 스펙트럼 impoverishment 가난, 피폐함 discontentment 불만, 불만족 foremost 맨 앞의, 주요한, 맨 처음의 emissary 사절, 특사, 밀사 disseminate 〈정보·지식·사상 따위〉를 퍼뜨리다, 보급(유포)시키다 call for ~에 대한 요구 uprising 반란, 모반 declamatory 연설투의, 수사적인 suited 알맞은, 어울리는 transition 과도기 advocate for ~를 옹호, 변호, 지지하다 urge … to~ …가 ~하도록 부추기다, 재촉하다 peculiar 고유의, 독특한, 특유의

37 The novel and sophisticated masterpiece, Citizen Kane (1941) was directed by and starred by Orson Welles, who is acknowledged as one of the great geniuses of film. In a poll, Citizen Kane was voted for greatest film ever made and recommended as a "must-see." Every aspect of this film marked an advance in the development of cinematic technique, with the discontinuous narration through flashbacks, the inventive use of shadows and camera angles in cinematography, and the innovative use of sound technique linked to a complex montage sequence. The techniques created by Orson Welles are still in use today.

Q Which is NOT truthful in accordance with the passage?

(a) Orson Welles is considered as a pioneer in the history of film.
(b) Citizen Kane is a highly-rated film and a landmark of cinema history.
(c) Citizen Kane is famous for its many remarkable scenes and cinematic techniques.
(d) The techniques are so progressive that they are difficult to be used in modern films.

참신하고 세련된 걸작인 '시민 케인(1941)'은 영화계의 천재 중 한 명으로 인정받는 Orson Welles가 감독하고 주연을 맡았다. 투표에서 '시민 케인'은 지금까지 만들어진 영화 중에서 가장 훌륭한 영화로 뽑혔으며 "꼭 봐야할 영화"로 추천되었다. 이 영화의 모든 면은 영화기술의 발달과정에서 진보를 이루었다. 플래시백을 통한 불연속적인 내레이션, 영화 촬영 기술에서 그림자와 카메라 앵글의 창의적인 사용, 그리고 복잡한 몽타주 화면과 연결된 혁신적인 음향 기술의 사용을 통해서 말이다. Orson Welles가 만들어 낸 이 기술들은 오늘날에도 여전히 사용되고 있다.

🔵 영화 '시민 케인'의 혁신적인 특징들과 영화사에서의 의의를 소개하고 있는 글이다. 따라서 (a)는 감독이자 배우였던 Orson Welles가 영화계에서 천재로 불리는 것으로 보아 맞는 내용이고, (b)와 (c)도 시민 케인이 놀라운 장면과 영화 기법으로 가장 훌륭한 영화로 인정되고 있기 때문에 맞는 내용이 된다. 하지만 (d)는 영화 기법이 너무 진보적이어서 현대 영화에서는 사용하기 어렵다는 내용으로 마지막 문장과 상반된다.

novel 새로운, 신기한, 참신한 sophisticated 매우 복잡한, 정교한 〈문체 등이〉 세련된, 지나치게 기교적인 masterpiece 명작, 걸작 acknowledge ~을 인정하다, 승인하다 cinematic 영화의, 영화에 관한 discontinuous 불연속의, 중단된 flashback (영화) 플래시백 (회상 따위를 위해 장면이 되돌아가는 일) inventive 발명의, 창의성이 풍부한 cinematography 영화 촬영 기술(기법) innovative 혁신적인 montage (영화, TV) 몽타주 (개개의 아주 짧은 장면을 많이 빨리 연속시켜 종합적인 효과를 노리는 기법) sequence (영화) 일련의 화면, 한 국면 pioneer 개척자, 선구자 landmark 획기적인 사건 progressive 진보적인, 진취적인

38 Milk-alkali syndrome, also called Burnett's syndrome, is caused by the ingestion of large amounts of calcium and absorbable alkali. Theoretically, oral intake of more than 2 grams of calcium with absorbable alkali results in hypercalcemia but it depends on individual variability. If unrecognized and untreated, chronic milk-alkali syndrome can lead to metastatic calcification and renal failure. With the development of nonabsorbable alkali, milk-alkali syndrome became a rare cause of hypercalcemia. The increasing use of calcium carbonate for dyspepsia and as calcium supplementation, however, causes milk-alkali syndrome to recur in the last few years.

종종 버넷씨 증후군이라 불리는, 우유알칼리 증후군은 칼슘과 우리 몸에 흡수될 수 있는 알칼리를 다량으로 섭취해서 생긴다. 이론적으로는, 흡수되는 알칼리와 함께 2 그램 이상의 칼슘을 구강으로 섭취하면 칼슘과다혈증이 생길 수 있지만 그것은 개인에 따라 다르다. 만성적인 우유알칼리 증후군을 알아차리고 치료하지 않으면 전이성 석회화와 신장의 이상으로 이어질 수 있다. 몸에 흡수되지 않는 알칼리의 개발로, 우유알칼리 증후군 때문에 칼슘과다혈증이 생기는 일은 드물어졌다. 그렇지만 소화불량이나 칼슘 보충을 위해 탄산칼슘 섭취량을 늘리게 되면 우유알칼리 증후군이 몇 년 후에 재발할 수도 있다.

🔵 우유알칼리 증후군이 어떤 경우 발병하는지, 어떤 경우 위험해지는지와 재발의 가능성을 높이는 경우에 대해 기술되어 있으나, 우유알칼리 증후군의 증상에 대해서는 언급된 바 없으므로 정답은 (b)이다.

Q Which of the following is NOT mentioned about milk-alkali syndrome in the above statement?

(a) incidence
(b) symptoms
(c) risk factors
(d) causes of resurgence

Milk-alkali syndrome 우유알칼리 증후군 ingestion 섭취, 복용 absorbable 흡수할 수 있는 theoretically 이론상으로 intake 흡입, 흡입(량) hypercalcemia 칼슘과다혈증 variability 변하기 쉬움, 가변성 chronic 만성적인 metastatic 전이하는, 전이성 calcification 석회화, 조직내 석회 침착 renal 신장의, 신장부의 dyspepsia 소화불량 supplementation 보충, 추가, 보충제 recur 다시 일어나다, 재발하다 resurgence 소생, 부활

---

39 Tsunamis, often incorrectly called "tidal waves," are ocean waves produced by sudden motion on the ocean floor. Among the several ways tsunamis are made, an earthquake is the most primary factor. However, there is a condition to meet in order to generate tsunamis: it must take place underneath or near the ocean and be large enough like an earthquake of magnitude beyond 7.5. Tsunamis generated by regional upheaval or subsidence of the ocean floor during an earthquake can pass through long distances and destroy places where the epicenter is thousands of miles away. Tsunamis are also caused by underwater landslides which produce local tsunamis, uncommonly by submarine volcanic eruptions.

Q Which is true according to the passage?

(a) Tsunamis are known as tidal waves in the geological field.
(b) Tsunamis caused by submarine landslides are the most destructive.
(c) The farther the epicenter is from the ocean, the more powerful tsunamis are.
(d) Uplift or subsidence in the sea floor during an earthquake causes powerful tsunamis.

쓰나미는 종종 "해일"로 잘못 불리는 것으로, 해저에서 갑작스러운 움직임이 일어나서 발생하는 파도를 말한다. 쓰나미가 생기는 여러 가지 방법 중에 지진이 가장 주요한 요인이다. 그러나 쓰나미를 일으키기 위해서는 충족시켜야 할 조건이 있다. 즉, 지진은 바다 속이나 근처에서 일어나야 하며 진도 7.5 이상 정도로 거대해야 한다. 지진이 일어나는 동안 해저에서 발생한 국부적인 융기와 침강으로 인해 생긴 쓰나미는 장거리를 지나서 진원지에서 수천 마일 떨어진 곳도 파괴할 수 있다. 쓰나미는 또한 지역적인 쓰나미를 일으키는 해저 산사태에 의해서도 발생할 수 있고, 일반적이지는 않지만 해저화산의 폭발 때문에 일어나기도 한다.

🔵 쓰나미가 일어나는 상황에 대해 설명하는 글이다. 쓰나미는 해일로 잘못 불리고 있다고 했으므로 (a)는 사실이 아니고, 해저 산사태는 지역적인 쓰나미를 일으키므로 (b)도 본문과 일치하지 않는다. (c) 또한 지진이 바다 속이나 근처에서 일어나야 쓰나미를 일으킬 수 있으므로 잘못된 내용이다. (d)처럼 일어난 쓰나미는 장거리를 가서 파괴시키기 때문에 강력하다고 할 수 있으므로 정답이 된다.

tidal waves 해일 primary 주요한, 주된 generate 〈결과, 상태 등을〉 일으키다, 초래하다 magnitude 지진규모 regional 지역의, 지방의, 국부의 upheaval (지질) 융기 (=uplift) subsidence 침강, 함몰 pass through 지나가다, 횡단하다, 통과하다 epicenter (지질) 진앙, 진원지 landslide 산사태, 무너져 내린 토사 submarine 해저의 volcanic 화산(성)의 eruption 〈화산의〉 폭발, 〈용암 따위의〉 분출 geological 지질학(상)의 destructive 파괴적인, 해로운, 파멸을 초래하는

40 Acupuncture, a traditional Chinese medical technique, has a long history and is offered as a "complementary" therapy by many traditional doctors. (a) Even so, it was not until recently that acupuncture needles were classified as medical devices for general use by trained professionals. (b) For quite a long time, acupuncture needles had been classified as Class III medical devices, meaning their safety and usefulness was uncertain. (c) Due to that "experimental" status, many insurance companies had agreed to cover acupuncture. (d) This new designation implies more empirical studies using needles as well as more practice of acupuncture.

중국의 전통적인 의료 기술인 침술은 긴 역사를 지니고 있으며 많은 전통적인 의사들도 보완 요법으로 제안하기도 한다. (a) 그렇긴 하지만 최근에 들어서야 침술에 쓰이는 바늘이 훈련된 전문가에 의해 일반적인 용도로 사용될 수 있는 의료 도구로 분류되었다. (b) 꽤 오랫동안 침은 3급 의료 도구로 분류되어 왔는데, 이는 그 안전성과 효과가 불확실하다는 것을 의미한다. (c) 그러한 실험적인 위치 때문에 많은 보험회사들은 침술을 보험대상으로 포함하는 데 동의해왔다. (d) 이번 지정은 더 많은 침술 의료 행위뿐만 아니라 침을 이용한 더 많은 경험적 연구가 가능하리라는 것을 의미한다.

⭕ 의료 도구로 확실하게 분류되지 못하고, 안정성과 효과에 대해 확신할 수 없는 실험적인 상태이므로 보험회사에서는 보험대상으로 포함하기를 "거부했다"가 내용의 흐름상 자연스러우므로 정답은 (c)이다.

acupuncture 침술(요법) complementary 보완적인, 보충이 되는 due to ~ 때문에 status 지위, 신분, 상태 insurance 보험 cover 〈보험이〉 …에 대해 보상하다. designation 지정, 지명 empirical 경험의, 경험적인 A as well as B B 뿐만 아니라 A도 practice 업무, 행위, 습관, 관례

LISTENING COMPREHENSION · P.132

1 M I'd like to speak to Mr. Thomas.
W _____

(a) Speak your mind.
(b) Nice talking to you.
(c) Who's calling, please?
(d) I'm in charge here.

M: 토마스 씨 좀 바꿔주실래요?
W: 누구시죠?

🔵 전화상에서 들을 수 있는 표현이다. 흔히 ~와 통화할 수 있는지 물어볼 때에는 'May I speak to~' 나 'I'd like to speak to~' 와 같은 표현을 쓴다. (b)는 만나고 헤어질 때 하는 표현으로 상황에 적절치 않다. '전화거는 분이 누구시죠?' 라고 물을 때에는 Who's calling, please?를 쓰면 된다. 따라서 정답은 (c)가 된다.

Speak your mind. (솔직하게) 네 생각을 말해 봐. **in charge** 담당인, 책임지고 있는

2 M What time do you usually get off work?
W _____

(a) I usually get off at 7.
(b) I got off at the wrong stop.
(c) The time is right.
(d) It's my pleasure.

M: 보통 몇 시에 퇴근하세요?
W: 보통 7시에 퇴근합니다.

🔵 퇴근 시간을 묻고 있다. get off의 경우 '출발하다' 의 의미 외에 '차에서 내리다' 라는 뜻이 있다. (b)에서는 get off가 '차에서 내리다' 라는 뜻으로 쓰여 '정거장을 잘못 내렸어요.' 라는 의미이므로 상황과 맞지 않을 뿐더러 시제도 맞지 않다. (c)는 time을 반복하여 혼동을 주기 위한 함정이고 (d)는 감사 인사에 대한 대답으로 'You're welcome.' 과 같은 뜻이다.

get off work 퇴근하다 **get off** (차에서) 내리다, 출발하다 **It's my pleasure.** (감사하다는 표현에 대해) 천만에요.

3 M I'm trying to email Linda. But it keeps on getting returned.
W _____

(a) I'll pick up the tab.
(b) It's up to you.
(c) It might have been blocked by spam filter.
(d) I get a lot of spam mails a day.

M: 린다에게 이메일을 보내려고 하는데 계속 반송이 되네.
W: 스팸 차단 프로그램에 걸려졌을지도 몰라.

🔵 이메일이 자꾸 반송이 된다는 말에 적절한 반응을 찾아야 한다. (c)에서 스팸 차단기에 걸려졌을지 모른다고 함으로써 반송되는 이유에 대해 이야기하고 있으므로 정답이 된다. (d)는 하루에 스팸 메일을 많이 받는다고 함으로써 (c)와 (d)를 혼동하게 하려는 장치인데, 상황에 적절치 않으므로 정답이 될 수 없다.

pick up the tab 비용을 부담하다, 계산하다 **up to** ~에 달려있는, ~의 뜻에 따라 정해지는 **block** ~을 막다 **spam filter** 스팸 차단기

4   **M**   Would you care for some coffee?

    W   Yes. I'd love to.

    M   How would you like it?

    W   _____

(a) I like my coffee weak.

(b) Let's toast.

(c) Well done, please

(d) No, thanks.

M: 커피 좀 드실래요?

W: 네. 주세요.

M: 어떻게 드세요?

W: 연하게 먹어요.

➲ 커피에 대한 이야기이고, 마지막 남자의 대사가 How would you like it?이므로 커피를 마시는 취향을 묻는 질문이다. 따라서 연하게 마신다는 뜻의 (a)가 정답이 된다. 반대로 진하게 마신다고 할 때는 strong을 쓰면 된다. 또 How would you like it?은 스테이크 등에도 쓸 수 있다. (b)는 술자리에서 건배를 들 때 하는 말이다.

care for ~을 좋아하다 **toast** ~을 위해 건배를 제안하다 **well done** (스테이크가) 바짝 구워진

---

5   **M**   I have a severe toothache.

    W   You should go see a dentist immediately.

    M   I was going to the hospital today, but I have no time.

    W   _____

(a) Let's wait and see.

(b) You have to take a few tests.

(c) The sooner, the better.

(d) You'll pay for this.

M: 치통이 심해.

W: 당장 치과에 가는 게 좋아.

M: 오늘 병원에 가려고 했는데 시간이 안 나.

W: 빨리 갈수록 좋을 거야.

➲ 여자의 두 번째 대사를 보면 immediately가 등장한다. 당장 치과에 가라고 했으므로 빠를수록 더 좋다는 뜻의 (c)가 정답이 된다. (a)는 정반대의 표현이므로 정답이 아니고, (d)는 계산한다는 뜻이 아니라 언젠가 대가를 치르게 될 것이라는 뜻이므로 상황과 맞지 않는다.

wait and see 관망하다, 서두르지 않고 지켜보다 **You'll pay for this.** 후회하게 될 것이다. 대가를 치르게 될 것이다.

---

6   **M**   Wow, what's the occasion? Did you go shopping again?

    W   Yes. It was a real bargain.

    M   You're so rich. How about buying me a dinner tonight?

    W   _____

(a) It's out of my price range.

(b) I want to get a refund.

(c) I'm all set.

(d) Now, I'm broke.

M: 와, 어쩐 일이야? 또 쇼핑 갔었어?

W: 응, 정말 싸게 샀어.

M: 너 정말 부자구나. 오늘 저녁 한턱 내지 그래?

W: 이제 나 빈털터리야.

➲ 남자가 여자에게 쇼핑을 또 갔었느냐는 말을 하는 것으로 보아 이전에도 여자가 쇼핑을 갔었음을 알 수 있다. 따라서 저녁을 사달라는 남자의 말에 적절한 여자의 응답은 (d) '이제 빈털터리이다'가 된다. 이미 산 물건에 대한 이야기이므로 (a)는 적절치 않고, 물건을 마음에 들어 하고 있으므로 (b) 역시 정답이 될 수 없다.

be a real bargain 정말 싸다, 싸게 팔다 **price range** 가격대 **get a refund** 환불 받다 **I'm all set.** 준비 다 됐어요.

7

W   What's the matter with your face?
It looks swollen.

M   I had to get cavities filled today.

W   Oh, I see. How was it? Did it hurt?

M   Don't even mention it. It killed me!

W   That's why you have to take good care
of your teeth all the time.

M   I know. You know what? The bill is
going to be humongous!

W   Really? You have a dental insurance,
do you?

M   I do, but it doesn't cover everything.

Q   What are the speakers mainly talking
about?

(a) They are talking about plastic surgery.

(b) They are talking about paying for the
bill.

(c) They are talking about dental
treatment.

(d) They are talking about a dental
insurance.

W: 얼굴이 왜 그래? 부은 것 같아.

M: 충치를 치료했어.

W: 그랬구나. 어땠어? 아팠어?

M: 말도 마. 죽는 줄 알았어!

W: 그래서 항상 치아를 잘 관리해야하는 거야.

M: 알아. 근데 그거 알아? 치료비가 어마어마해!

W: 정말? 의료보험 있지?

M: 그래. 근데 전부 혜택을 받을 수 있는 게 아니야.

○ 대화 주제에 대해 묻고 있다. 남자가 충치 치료를 한 이야기를 하고 있다. 보험에 대해서도 언급이 있긴 했지만 주제라고는 할 수 없다. 따라서 정답은 (c)가 된다.

swollen 부은, 부풀어 오른 cavity 충치 humongous 거대한, 엄청나게 큰 plastic surgery 성형 수술

8

W   Good evening, sir.
How can I help you?

M   Well, we're going to stay here.
What kind of rooms do you have?

W   How many are in your party?

M   Just three of us. Two adults and one
child.

W   We have a room with two double beds.
How many nights do you want to stay?

M   Just one. We're only staying overnight.

Q   Where can you hear this conversation?

(a) At a hospital

(b) At the post office

(c) At a hotel

(d) At an airport

W: 안녕하세요. 무엇을 도와드릴까요?

M: 여기 묵으려고 하는데요. 방은 어떤 종류가 있죠?

W: 일행이 몇 분이신데요?

M: 저희 세 명이요. 성인 두 명하고 아이 한 명이요.

W: 더블 침대 두 개인 방이 있어요. 며칠 묵으실 예정이죠?

M: 하루요. 하루만 묵을 예정입니다.

○ 대화가 일어나는 장소에 대해 묻고 있다. 방의 종류, 일행의 수, 며칠 묵을 것인지에 대해 이야기하고 있으므로 정답은 (c) 호텔이 된다.

stay overnight 일박하다

9
M I heard you're going to New York tonight.

W Yes. I'm supposed to have a party with my friends there.

M In that case, you should leave as early as possible.

W What does it mean?

M It's Christmas tomorrow, so everybody tries to get off work early today so that they can go back home early. Traffic usually becomes bumper to bumper.

W Oh, I didn't know that. Well, I'll leave earlier today then. About 2 PM.

M That would be my advice.

Q Why did the man advised her to leave early?

(a) Because it's Christmas season.
(b) Because it's a long distance.
(c) Because there was a car accident.
(d) Because the weather condition is not good.

M: 오늘밤 뉴욕에 간다고 들었어.

W: 응. 거기서 친구들과 파티를 열기로 했어.

M: 그럼 가능한 빨리 출발하는 게 좋을 거야.

W: 그게 무슨 뜻인데?

M: 내일이 크리스마스잖아. 그래서 모두가 오늘 일찍 퇴근해서 집에 일찍 가려고 할 거야. 교통이 대개 막히게 마련이지.

W: 어머, 몰랐어. 그럼 오늘 더 일찍 출발해야겠다. 오후 두 시쯤.

M: 내 말이 그 말이야.

🔵 남자가 여자에게 일찍 출발하라고 충고한 이유에 대해 묻고 있다. 크리스마스 시즌이므로 교통 체증이 예상된다고 했으므로 정답은 (a)가 된다. 교통에 대해 언급하였기 때문에 (c)를 고르는 오류를 범하지 않도록 한다.

---

bumper to bumper (자동차가) 꽉 들어찬, 꼬리를 문

---

10 Can you imagine the situation in which you can't go anywhere by yourself and have a private life? If you can't look your brother in the face, how would you feel? Here is the tragedy of the twin brothers. They were joined at the skull, but they have separate brains. Now they are willing to take possible risks in the operation. Surgeons say bleeding would be a problem because the twins share only one vein. Many people including the twins' family and relatives wish they would lead separate lives after the operation. Lauren McGinty, NTV News.

Q What is the speaker mainly talking about?

(a) The tragedy of the twins' family
(b) The operation to separate the twins
(c) The cause of the failure in the operation
(d) The risks of the operation

혼자서 아무데도 갈 수 없고 사생활이 없는 상황을 상상할 수 있으십니까? 만약 남동생의 얼굴을 쳐다볼 수 없다면 어떤 느낌일까요? 여기 쌍둥이 형제의 비극이 있습니다. 그들은 머리는 붙어 있지만 뇌는 떨어져 있습니다. 이제 그들은 수술로 인해 야기될 수도 있는 위험을 감당하려고 합니다. 의사들은 쌍둥이 형제에게 혈관이 하나뿐이기 때문에 출혈이 문제가 될 것이라고 말합니다. 형제의 가족과 친척들을 포함한 많은 사람들은 수술 후에 그들이 각자의 삶을 살기를 염원하고 있습니다. NTV 뉴스의 로렌 맥긴티였습니다.

🔵 뉴스의 주제에 대해 묻고 있다. 뉴스의 초점은 뇌가 붙은 쌍둥이 형제의 수술이다. 따라서 정답은 (b)이다. 수술이 아직 실시된 것이 아니므로 (c)는 정답이 될 수 없고, 가족이나 수술의 위험 등은 부분적인 이야기이므로 (a)나 (d) 역시 정답이라고 하기 어렵다.

---

skull 두개골, 머리 operation 수술, 운영, 경영 vein 정맥, 혈관

11 There are many different jobs in the world but not every job is always given full attention. I want to talk about it here. The person in this field is infrequently seen, but always heard. At many athletic contests, the person contributes to the atmosphere for the event. The person should have some public speaking experience, knowledge of the game to be announced, and wit to know when to speak and when not to speak.

Q What is the speaker mainly talking about?

(a) Athletic contests
(b) Tips for public speaking
(c) The basic knowledge of sports
(d) The public address announcer

세상에는 다양한 많은 직업들이 있지만 모든 직업이 항상 완전한 주목을 받는 것은 아닙니다. 저는 여기서 그것에 대해 이야기하고 싶습니다. 이 분야에서 일하는 사람은 거의 보이지 않지만, 항상 들을 수 있습니다. 많은 운동 경기에서 이 사람은 행사의 분위기에 공헌합니다. 이 사람은 대중 앞에서 이야기해본 경험이 있어야 하고, 방송될 경기에 대한 지식이 있어야 하며, 언제 이야기하고 언제 하지 말아야 할지에 대한 재치가 있어야 합니다.

○ 화자가 이야기하고 있는 것은 어떠한 직업에 관한 것이다. 이 직업을 가지고 있는 사람의 특징, 자질에 대해 이야기하고 있다. 이것으로 보아 정답은 (d) 장내 아나운서가 된다.

infrequently 드물게 athletic 운동 경기의, 체육의

---

12 Have you ever experienced a moment it's easier to remember information at the beginning or end of a unit? According to a recent study, the position of information affects recall, which is known as the serial position effect. If you have difficulty in recalling information placed on the middle position, you can make use of this method. That is, you can spend extra time reviewing this information or changing the position of it so it will be easier to remember. It is a way of overcoming this problem.

Q What can be inferred from the passage?

(a) The position of information has nothing to do with recall.
(b) Many people have been suffering from the serial position effect.
(c) The best way of remembering information is transferring it to long-term memory.
(d) If you can't recall middle information, shifting the position of it to the beginning might be helpful.

한 유닛의 맨 처음이나 끝에 있는 정보를 더 기억하기 쉬운 순간을 경험한 적이 있습니까? 최근 연구에 따르면, 정보의 위치가 기억에 영향을 미치는데, 이것은 계열 위치 효과라고 알려져 있습니다. 중간에 위치한 정보를 기억하는데 어려움이 있다면 이 방법을 이용할 수 있습니다. 즉, 여분의 시간을 이 정보를 재검토하는 데 쓰거나 정보의 위치를 바꿈으로써 기억을 더 쉽게 할 수 있습니다. 이것이 문제를 극복하는 한 방법이 됩니다.

○ 추론 문제이다. 중점적으로 다루고 있는 이야기는 정보의 위치에 따라 기억의 정도가 달라질 수 있다는 것이다. 따라서 (a)는 정답이 될 수 없다. (b)는 언급되지 않았으므로 알 수 없다. 장기 기억에 관한 언급 역시 없었으므로 (c)도 역시 알 수 없다. 만약 정보를 기억하기 힘들다면 위치를 바꿔보라는 충고가 있었으므로 (d)는 정답이 된다.

recall 회상, 상기 serial position effect 계열 위치 효과 make use of ~을 이용하다, 활용하다 overcome ~을 극복하다 have nothing to do with ~와 관계가 없다

13 A Wow, I hardly recognize you. What happened?

B Well, I lost some weight because _____ for two hours every morning.

(a) I went and jogging
(b) I have been jogging
(c) I go to jogging
(d) I went to jogging

A: 우와, 나 너 거의 못 알아봤어. 무슨 일 있었어?
B: 나 매일 아침마다 두 시간씩 조깅했더니 살이 좀 빠졌어.

○ 매일 아침 계속해서 조깅을 해서 살을 뺐다는 내용이기 때문에 (b)가 적절하다.

recognize 알아보다 loss weight 살이 빠지다

---

14 A Do you remember _____?

B Of course, well, what do you mean?

(a) that you of favor me
(b) that owe favor you
(c) favor you to owe me
(d) that favor you owe me

A: 너 나한테 갚아야 할 의무가 있는 거 기억해?
B: 당연하지, 근데, 무슨 말이야?

○ favor가 명사로 쓰였으므로 적절한 어순은 (d)이다.

owe 빚지다

---

15 A Please take care of my cat during my absence.

B You know I _____ cats.

(a) have allergic to
(b) have allergic for
(c) am allergic to
(d) am allergic for

A: 나 없는 동안 내 고양이 좀 돌봐줘
B: 나 고양이 알레르기 있는 거 너 알잖아.

○ '~에 알레르기가 있다' 라는 의미로 be allergic to~가 쓰인다

absence 부재 allergic 알레르기

---

16 A I'd like to order a pizza. Can I get a free Coke?

B Yes, _____?

(a) how you like the crust
(b) how would you like the crust
(c) what you like the crust
(d) what would you like the crust

A: 피자를 주문하고 싶은데요, 콜라는 무료인가요?
B: 네, 빵은 어떻게 해드릴까요?

○ crust는 피자의 빵을 말하는 것으로 '피자의 빵은 어떻게 해 드릴까요?' 라는 의미로 (b)가 적절하다.

crust 빵

---

17 _____ of the ancient Central and Eastern Europe.

(a) Lying all the capitals behind that line
(b) Lie all the capitals behind that line
(c) Behind that line lie all the capitals
(d) Behind that line all the capitals lie

고대 중앙과 동부 유럽의 모든 수도들이 그 선을 중심으로 뒤에 놓여 있다.

○ Behind that line이 문장 앞으로 나갔으므로 주어와 동사가 도치되어야 한다. 자동사는 직접 주어 앞으로 나가면서 도치가 일어난다.

ancient 고대의 capital 수도

121

18 Physical attraction is one thing, love is quite _____.

(a) one another
(b) another
(c) others
(d) the other

육체적인 매력과 사랑은 별개의 것이다

🔵 '육체적인 매력과 사랑은 별개의 것이다' 라는 의미로 "~ is one thing, ~ is another" 문장이다.

---

19 Researchers of consumer protection suggested that the government _____ all imported food to improve the eatables' quality.

(a) had investigated
(b) have investigated
(c) investigated
(d) investigate

소비자보호연구원들은 정부가 식료품의 질을 높이기 위해서 모든 수입식품을 검사해야 한다고 제안했다.

🔵 주절의 동사가 suggest이고 종속절이 당위성을 나타낼 때는 should+동사원형이 오는데, should는 생략할 수 있다. 그래서 정답은 (d)이다.

protection 보호 eatables 식료 investigate 조사하다

---

20 Above and beyond the increases I had earlier requested for space activities, providing _____ the national goals.

(a) which are funds needed meets
(b) the funds which are needed meets
(c) the funds which are needed to meet
(d) the funds which are needed meet

내가 우주탐사활동을 위해 제안한 증가분을 넘어서 필요한 자금을 공급하는 것은 국가의 목표를 달성하는 것이다.

🔵 동명사 providing이 주어이기 때문에, the funds which are needed가 의미상 목적어로 쓰였다. 또한 동명사 providing은 단수 취급하므로 동사 meets가 쓰인 (b)가 적절하다.

goal 목적. 목표

---

21 (a) A: What's the topic of today's presentation?
(b) B: First of all, I'd like to talk about the ecotourism.
(c) A: Oh, it sounds excited. When does yours start?
(d) B: Around the second session.

(a) 오늘 발표의 주제가 뭐야?
(b) 먼저 저는 환경지향 관광에 대하여 얘기하고 싶어.
(c) 우와, 재미있겠다. 언제 시작하니?
(d) 두 번째 시간 즈음에 해.

🔵 (c)에서 excite의 주체가 it이므로 현재분사 exciting을 써야 한다.

presentation 발표 ecotourism 환경지향 관광

---

22 (a) Women's success is attributable to couple of things. (b) One is the support they get from the societies, parents, or sometimes from national or international organizations for women emancipation. (c) They also have much more accesses to reading materials than men. (d) Indeed, their excellence proves that harsh environments also influence women to try their best.

여자들의 성공은 몇 가지의 이유 때문이다. 하나는 그들이 사회나 부모, 때론 국가나 국제적인 여성해방조직으로부터 받는 지원 때문이다. 그들은 또한 남성들보다 더 많이 읽을거리와 접할 기회를 갖는다. 실제로, 그들의 우수성은 또한 힘겨운 환경이 여성들로 하여금 최선을 다하도록 영향을 주었다는 것을 입증한다.

🔵 (b)에서, 국내의 그리고 국제적인 여성해방운동 조직을 의미하기 때문에 national 앞에 정관사 the를 써야 한다.

attributable ~의 원인을 돌릴 수 있는 emancipation 해방 excellence 우수성 harsh 거친

23 A How do you like this picture?

B I like that kind of _____ feeling of a cloudy day.

(a) heavy
(b) energetic
(c) somber
(d) bright

A: 이 사진 어때요?

B: 구름 낀 날의 그런 흐릿한 느낌이 마음에 들어요.

⊙ cloudy day와 연관이 되는 단어를 골라야 한다. (b)와 (d)는 구름 낀 날과는 어울리지 않으므로 정답이 아니다. somber는 '흐릿한, 어두운'의 뜻이 있으므로 (c)가 정답이 된다.

somber 흐릿한, 칙칙한, 어두운

---

24 A Why has she brought her son here?

B You're right. He's a _____ in the neck!

(a) thorn
(b) pain
(c) dirt
(d) bone

A: 그녀가 아들을 왜 여기 데려온 거지?

B: 그러게. 그 애는 골칫거리인데 말이야!

⊙ a pain in the neck이라는 이디엄을 알아야 풀 수 있는 문제이다. a pain in the neck은 '눈엣가시, 골칫거리'라는 뜻으로 쓰인다. 우리말을 그대로 번역하여 thorn을 고르지 않도록 주의해야 한다.

a pain in the neck 눈엣가시, 골칫거리 **thorn** (식물의) 가시

---

25 A Tell me who are on the list of layoffs this time.

B Okay. _____ it to yourself.

(a) do
(b) take
(c) get
(d) keep

A: 이번에 정리해고 명단에 누가 있는지 말해줘.

B: 좋아. 대신 너만 알고 있어.

⊙ 해고자 명단을 알려달라는 부탁에 알려주는 대신 비밀을 지키라고 말한다. 'keep it to yourself'는 비밀 이야기를 하면서 '너만 알고 있어라'라고 하는 표현이다.

layoff 해고 **Keep it to yourself.** 너만 알고 있어. 비밀 지켜.

---

26 A How is their after-sales service?

B It's pretty good. A one-year _____ comes with the product.

(a) customer
(b) warranty
(c) security
(d) contract

A: 거기 애프터서비스는 어때?

B: 꽤 좋아. 1년 보증서가 상품과 함께 나와.

⊙ 애프터서비스에 관해 물어보고 있으므로 이와 관련된 단어는 '보증서'가 된다. 따라서 정답은 (b)이다.

after-sales service 애프터서비스 **warranty** 보증(서) **security** 보안, 치안

---

27 A What are you thinking of now? You almost hit the wall!

B Sorry. I forgot to check the _____ view mirror.

(a) back
(b) end
(c) rear
(d) hind

A: 지금 무슨 생각을 하고 있는 거야? 벽에 박을 뻔했잖아!

B: 미안해. 백미러를 확인하는 것을 깜빡했어.

⊙ 보기 모두 '뒤'와 연관된 단어들이다. 하지만 자동차의 백미러를 가리키는 것은 'rear view mirror'이다.

rear view mirror 자동차의 백미러 **hind** 뒤쪽의, 후방의

28 As more and more students gain access to the Internet, teachers have been grappling with ways to make it more difficult for them to _____ whole papers.

(a) post
(b) plagiarize
(c) plague
(d) navigate

점점 더 많은 학생들이 인터넷에 접속하면서 교사들은 전체 리포트를 표절하는 것을 어렵게 하기 위한 방법들을 찾아내기 위해 고심하고 있다.

🔵 whole papers와 자연스럽게 어울리는 표현을 찾아야 한다. 학생과 교사, 인터넷이 언급되었으므로 리포트를 베낀다는 표현이 나오는 것이 자연스럽다. 따라서 정답은 (b)가 된다. (a)의 경우 리포트를 인터넷에 올리는 것을 어렵게 해야 하는 근거가 충분히 제시되지 않았으므로 정답이라고 할 수 없다.

gain access to ~에 접근하다 grapple with ~와 씨름하다, ~에 맞서다 plagiarize 표절하다, 도용하다 plague 전염병, 돌림병 navigate 항해하다

---

29 Many universities are trying to offer online classes worldwide and Internet access is becoming _____ for college classes.

(a) prestigious
(b) premature
(c) prerequisite
(d) preliminary

많은 대학들이 전 세계적으로 온라인 수업을 제공하려고 하고 있고, 인터넷 접속이 대학 수업에 있어서 필수가 되고 있다.

🔵 온라인 수업을 제공하기 위해서는 인터넷 접속이 필요하다. 따라서 필수적이라는 뜻의 'prerequisite'이 정답이 된다. 보기 모두가 pre-로 시작하는 단어로 의미를 혼동하지 않도록 주의하자.

prerequisite 필수적인, 없어서는 안 될 prestigious 유명한, 일류의 premature 시기상조의 preliminary 예비의

---

30 Although they struggled to block the passage of the bill, it was finally passed by the _____ majority.

(a) overwhelming
(b) narrow
(c) relative
(d) slender

그들은 그 법안의 통과를 막으려고 분투했지만 결국 그것은 압도적인 다수에 의해 통과되었다.

🔵 법안 통과 저지에도 불구하고 결국 통과되었다는 것은 다수가 찬성했다는 뜻이다. 따라서 '압도적인 다수'라는 뜻에 해당하는 (a)가 정답이 된다.

passage 통과, 통행 overwhelming majority 압도적 다수 slender 얼마 안 되는, 빈약한

---

31 Our survey indicates that the sky is _____ about 42% of the time while clear and dry days occur about 31%.

(a) unclouded
(b) overshadowed
(c) overcast
(d) fair

우리가 조사한 바에 따르면 42% 정도는 하늘이 흐린 반면 맑고 건조한 날은 31% 정도로 그치고 있다.

🔵 while을 주목할 필요가 있다. while 뒤에 맑고 건조한 날이라고 했으므로 그 앞에는 상반된 내용이 나와야 한다. 따라서 흐리다는 뜻의 overcast가 정답이 된다.

overcast 흐린, 구름으로 덮인 unclouded 구름 없는, 맑은 overshadow 그늘지게 하다 fair 갠, 맑은

32 If you forgot your password, you can _____ it by providing your email address.

(a) demand
(b) enter
(c) give
(d) retrieve

비밀번호를 잊어버렸을 경우 이메일 주소를 입력하면 비밀번호를 다시 알 수 있습니다.

◎ 비밀번호를 잊어버렸을 경우 이메일 주소를 입력하면 비밀번호를 알 수 있다는 내용이 나오는 것이 자연스럽다. 이러한 의미로 쓰이는 표현은 retrieve이다. 비밀번호를 모르는 상황이므로 enter, give 등은 쓸 수 없다.

retrieve 되찾다, 회수하다, 상기하다

READING COMPREHENSION • P.140

33 Oprah Winfrey, one of the most successful and influential women in America, suffered from many hardships during her childhood. She was born to unmarried teenage parents and raised by her grandmother. When she was nine, she was raped by a cousin and was once molested by relatives. To make matters worse, she became pregnant and gave birth to a stillborn baby at age 14. She was so rebellious and sexually promiscuous that her life couldn't help being devastated. However, she changed when she was sent to live with her father. Her father helped her turn her life around and settle down _____. She had to read a book every week and write a report on the book, memorize five new words every day, and she was given even curfew.

(a) by forgiving her past
(b) by hiring an experienced tutor
(c) with his strict rules and discipline
(d) with a cordial welcome to his house

미국에서 가장 성공하고 영향력 있는 여성 중 하나인 Oprah Winfrey는 어린 시절 많은 어려움을 겪었다. 그녀는 결혼하지 않은 십대 부모에게서 태어났고 할머니 밑에서 자랐다. 아홉 살에 사촌에게 강간을 당했고 친척들에게 성희롱을 당한 적도 있었다. 설상가상으로, 그녀는 14살에 임신해서 사산아를 낳기도 했다. 그녀는 너무 반항적이고 성적으로 문란해서 그녀의 삶은 파괴되지 않을 수 없었다. 그러나 그녀는 아버지와 살게 되었을 때 변화했다. 그녀의 아버지는 엄격한 규칙과 규율로 그녀의 삶이 변화되고 정착될 수 있도록 도와주었다. 그녀는 매주 책을 읽고 책에 관한 리포트를 썼으며, 매일 다섯 개의 새로운 단어를 외워야 했고 심지어는 통행금지도 있었다.

◎ Oprah Winfrey의 어린 시절 삶에 관한 이야기로 아버지의 도움으로 그녀의 삶이 변화되었다는 내용이다. 답은 빈 칸 뒤에 나오는 문장, 즉 그녀가 매일, 매주 해야 하는 일들이 나열되어 있는 것으로 보아 아버지가 그녀를 정해진 규칙에 따라 엄격하게 교육시키고 양육했음을 알 수가 있다.

influential 영향력 있는 **hardship** 고난, 역경 **rape** 강간하다 **molest** 〈여자, 어린이를〉 성희롱하다, 강간하다 **to make matters worse** 설상가상으로 **give birth to** 〈아이를〉 낳다 **stillborn** 사산의 **rebellious** 반항하는 **promiscuous** 사람을 가리지 않는, 무차별의 **devastate** 〈사람을〉 망연자실케 하다, 압도하다, 파괴하다 **turn around** 〈의견, 태도를〉 바꾸게 하다 **settle down** 안정하다, 진정되다, 정착하다 **curfew** 통행금지 **cordial** 진심에서 우러나는, 따뜻한

34 A constellation is a group of stars that form a visible figure in the sky. People used constellations to divide up the sky into more controllable bits by drawing imaginary lines between the stars to create pictures of people and animals. In the beginning, the purpose of the constellations was to help people _____. For example, if farmers, who were considered to invent constellations to use in their agriculture, knew the names of stars, they could easily tell the season and decide when to plant or harvest crops. This is because some constellations were only visible during certain seasons, due to the revolution of the earth.

(a) produce abundant harvest
(b) remember which stars are which
(c) have exuberant imagination on the universe
(d) see distant stars clearly in the very dark night

별자리는 하늘에서 눈에 보이는 형상을 만드는 별들의 집합이다. 사람들은 하늘을 더욱 관리 가능한 부분으로 나누기 위해서 별자리를 사용했는데, 이것은 사람이나 동물의 형상을 만드는 별들 사이에 상상의 선을 그어서 만들어졌다. 처음에 별자리는 사람들로 하여금 어느 별이 어느 것인지 기억하도록 돕는 게 목적이었다. 예를 들어, 별자리를 농사지을 때 사용하려고 발명해 낸 것으로 여겨지는 농부들이 별자리의 이름을 알면 쉽게 계절을 구분하고 언제 곡식을 심고 추수할지를 결정할 수 있었다. 이것은 어떤 별자리들은 지구의 공전 때문에 특정한 계절에만 보이기 때문이다.

🔵 별자리를 통해 사람들이 별의 모양과 이름을 기억함으로써 계절의 변화를 알게 되고 농업에 이용할 수 있었다는 내용이므로 정답은 (b)가 된다. (a)는 농업과 관련이 있지만 별자리의 목적이 풍작과 관련된 것은 아니므로 정답이 될 수 없고, 우주에 대한 풍부한 상상력을 갖게 한다거나(c), 어두운 밤에 먼 거리에 있는 별들을 명확하게 보게 한다(d)는 것도 목적과는 거리가 멀다.

constellation 별자리 controllable 관리, 통제할 수 있는 imaginary 상상의 agriculture 농업 visible 눈에 보이는 due to ~때문에 revolution 공전 exuberant 풍부한

---

35 A hair falls out after growing for 2 to 6 years at an average rate of approximately 0.5 inches a month and resting for a while. There are some cases that the hair may fall out during the growing phase or the resting phase. One of the reasons for a sudden diffuse hair loss is the medication taken during cancer treatment, but fortunately the hair grows again when the medical treatment is over. Unlike hair loss based on disease or delivery, hair loss resulting from common reasons such as age, hormones, or heredity is permanent. _____ , this general baldness can't be restored completely as long as the bald don't undergo an operation for hair transplants.

(a) Therefore
(b) Apart from
(c) In comparison
(d) In other words

머리카락은 한 달에 평균적으로 약 0.5인치씩 2년에서 6년 정도 자라고 잠시 정체되어 있다가 빠진다. 어떤 경우에는 머리카락이 자라는 시기나 정체되어 있는 시기에 빠질 수도 있다. 갑작스러운 확산성 탈모를 일으키는 이유들 중 하나는 암 치료시 복용한 약물 때문이지만 다행히 약물치료가 끝나면 머리카락은 다시 자란다. 질병이나 출산으로 인한 탈모와는 달리 나이나 호르몬 또는 유전과 같은 일반적인 이유로 발생하는 탈모는 영구적이다. 그러므로 이런 일반적인 대머리는 머리카락 이식수술을 받지 않는 한 완전히 회복될 수는 없다.

🔵 탈모의 성향과 특징에 관한 글이다. 빈 칸의 앞 문장에서 일반적인 이유 때문에 생긴 탈모는 영구적이라고 했으므로 이식수술을 받지 않으면 대머리를 벗어날 수 없다는 내용이 결과적으로 이어지는 것이 자연스럽다. 따라서 정답은 (a)가 된다.

approximately 대략, 대체로 phase 〈변화, 발달의〉 단계, 시기 diffuse 널리 퍼진, 흩어진 medication 약물 투약 delivery 출산, 분만 heredity 유전 bald 대머리의 (baldness 대머리) restore 〈건강, 원기, 의식 등을〉 회복시키다 undergo 〈검열, 수술을〉 받다 transplant 이식(수술)

36 Most people can become excellent wine connoisseurs with a little practice and by following some general guidelines. There are three steps in tasting wine: Look, Smell, and Taste. First, pour as much as one third of the wine into a clear glass, hold it in front of a white piece of paper or neutral settings with plenty of light, and tilt it against the white background to observe the clarity of the wine and the intensity of its color. We can tell much about the wine by studying its appearance. For example, white wines which range from colorless to a deep gold color darken with age, while red wines whose colors are various from pink to black lighten with age, so the paler the rim of the red wine appears,

_____.

(a) the younger the wine is
(b) the sweeter the wine tastes
(c) the longer the wine has been aged
(d) the warmer the climate of origin was

대부분의 사람들은 조금만 연습하고 몇 가지 일반적인 지침만 따르면 훌륭한 와인 감식가가 될 수 있다. 와인을 시음할 때에는 눈으로 보기, 향 맡기, 맛보기라는 세 단계가 있다. 먼저 와인을 투명한 유리잔에 3분의 1정도 붓고, 흰 종이 앞이나 빛이 많이 들어오는 곳에서 와인 잔을 든다. 그리고 와인의 투명한 정도와 와인 색의 농도를 관찰하기 위해서 잔을 흰 배경에서 기울여본다. 우리는 와인을 겉으로만 봐도 와인에 대해서 많은 것을 알 수 있다. 예를 들어, 무색부터 진한 금색까지 띠는 백포도주는 오래될수록 색이 어두워지는 반면, 분홍색부터 검은색까지 다양한 색을 띠는 적포도주는 오래될수록 색이 옅어진다. 따라서 적포도주의 가장자리 색이 옅으면 옅을수록, 그 와인은 오래되었다는 것이다.

◉ 와인 테이스팅의 3가지 단계 중에서 1단계인 눈으로 보기가 설명되고 있다. 적포도주는 백포도주와 달리 오래될수록 색이 옅어진다고 했으므로 정답은 (c)가 된다. (a)는 정답과 상반된 내용이고, 와인의 색을 봐서 와인이 더 달콤하다든가(b), 와인이 생산된 지역의 기후가 더 따뜻하다(d)는 내용은 알 수 없다.

connoisseur 감정가, 감식가 neutral 중립인 무색의 tilt 기울이다 clarity 〈액체의〉 투명도 intensity 농도 appearance 외관, 겉보기 pale 〈색깔이〉 옅은 rim 가장자리

---

37 Journalist Mark Bowden gives a strikingly detailed account of the 1993 nightmarish operation in Mogadishu that left 18 American soldiers dead and many more wounded. Bowden does not devote much time to the context. Instead of rationalizing the fiercest close combat that Americans have engaged in since the Vietnam War, Bowden presents snapshots of the anarchy at the heart of combat. He makes full use of the Pentagon's wide-ranging paper trail which includes official reports, investigations, and even radio transcripts to describe the combat with great accuracy.

Q What kind of writing is the passage?

(a) A book review
(b) A movie critique
(c) A product analysis
(d) An in-depth article

작가 Mark Bowden은 18명의 미군 병사가 사망하고 훨씬 더 많은 수의 부상자를 남겼던 1993년 Mogadishu의 끔찍했던 작전에 대해 대단히 자세하게 묘사한다. Bowden은 전후관계나 정황에는 많은 시간을 들이지 않는다. 베트남전 이후로 미국이 참여했던 전투 중 가장 참혹한 접전을 그럴 듯하게 묘사하는 대신에 Bowden은 전투 중심부의 혼돈 장면을 연속사진으로 묘사하고 있다. 그는 공식적인 보고, 조사와 심지어 대단히 정확하게 전투를 묘사한 무선통신 기록에 이르기까지 미 국방부의 방대한 서류를 충분히 활용하고 있다.

◉ 작가의 표현 기법의 특징이나, 자료 조사를 어떻게 활용해서 글을 썼는지에 대한 내용이므로 정답은 (a)이다. (b)와 (c)는 관련이 없고, 심층기사라고 하기엔 작가의 표현기법에 치중했으며, 책에 대한 다각도의 분석이 이루어지지 않았으므로 (d)는 답이 될 수 없다.

strikingly 두드러지게, 대단히 nightmarish 악몽 같은, 무서운 operation 군사행동, 작전 rationalize 합리적으로 설명하다, ~에 그럴 듯한 설명을 붙이다 fierce 무시무시한, 잔인한 engage in ~에 종사하다, 참여하다 anarchy 혼란, 무질서 make full use of ~를 충분히 활용하다 paper trail 문서 족적(개인의 과거를 알아보는 실마리가 되는 기록) accuracy 정확도 critique 비평, 논평 in-depth article 심층 기사

38 A 54-year-old participant, Sally, felt stressed out because she was looking after for others all the time. Participating in the stress management program, Sally analyzed what gave her the most happiness and came to the conclusion that a Friday morning bridge game was one of them. One Friday, Sally was preparing to host the card game, when her daughter called to ask if Sally could take care of her son. She wanted neither to cancel the card game nor to refuse to help her daughter with financial difficulties. Instead of being compelled to say yes, Sally asked her daughter to take her son to the day care center and offered to loan her the money. The situation was resolved to everyone's satisfaction.

Q Which of the following strategies has Sally applied to cope with stress?

(a) Ventilation
(b) Assertiveness
(c) Positive Thinking
(d) Diversion and Distraction

54세 참가자인 Sally는 그녀가 항상 다른 사람들을 위해 돌보기만 하기 때문에 스트레스로 지쳐 있었다. 스트레스 관리 프로그램에 참여하면서, Sally는 무엇이 그녀에게 가장 큰 행복감을 주는지 분석해보았고, 금요일 오전 브리지 게임이 그 중 하나라는 결론을 내렸다. 어느 금요일, Sally는 카드 게임을 치를 준비를 하고 있었는데, 그녀의 딸이 전화를 걸어와 Sally가 손자를 돌보아줄 수 있는지를 물었다. 그녀는 카드 게임을 취소하는 것도, 경제적으로 어려움을 겪고 있는 그녀의 딸의 부탁을 거절하는 것도 원치 않았다. 마지못해 승낙을 하는 대신에 그녀는 딸에게 손자를 주간 탁아소에 맡기라고 하고, 그녀에게 돈을 꾸어주겠다고 했다. 상황이 해결되어 모두가 만족했다.

🔵 Sally가 스트레스를 관리하는 방법 중 하나로 터득한 것은 상대를 공격하거나 비난하지 않으면서도 자신의 거부 의사를 전달하는 단호함이므로 (b)가 정답이다. 감정의 분출이나 긍정적인 사고방식은 언급된 바 없으므로 (a)와 (c)는 답이 될 수 없으며, 브리지 게임이 오락에 해당되나, 지문에서 Sally가 적용한 방법은 다른 사람을 위해 거절을 못하고 마지못해 어떤 일을 하는 대신에, 자신의 의사를 자신감 있게 표현하는 것이므로 (d)도 정답으로 적절하지 않다.

participant 참가자 stressed out 스트레스로 지친 host 개최(주최)하다 financial 금전상의, 재정의 be compelled to 억지로 ~하다 resolve 해결하다 ventilation 〈감정의〉 표출, 발로 assertiveness 단호함, 단정적임 diversion and distraction 기분전환과 오락

---

39 Omega-3 fatty acids are essential nutrients for health, protecting people from heart disease and stroke. Even though omega-3 fatty acids have many health benefits, we should listen to the doctors and follow their directions since high intakes of omega-3 fatty acids can cause excessive bleeding. A common amount of omega-3 fatty acids in fish oil capsules is 0.18 grams of EPA and 0.12 grams of DHA. According to the recommendations of the American Heart Association, adults with coronary heart disease (CHD) need to consume about 1 gram of EPA and DHA, while patients with high cholesterol levels need 2–4 grams of EPA and DHA per day.

Q According to this passage, how many capsules can patients with CHD take a day?

(a) to one tablet
(b) about 3–4 tablets
(c) over 5 tablets
(d) about 6–7 tablets

오메가3지방산은 건강에 필수적인 영양분으로 심장병이나 뇌일혈로부터 사람들을 보호해 준다. 오메가3지방산이 건강상 많은 유익이 있을지라도, 많이 섭취하게 되면 과도한 출혈을 일으킬 수 있기 때문에 의사의 말을 듣고 지시를 따라야 한다. 보통 어유캡슐에 들어있는 오메가3지방산은 EPA가 0.18g, DHA가 0.12g 정도 들어있다. 미국심장협회의 권고에 따르면, 관상동맥 질환을 앓고 있는 성인의 경우 하루에 EPA와 DHA를 약 1g 정도 섭취할 필요가 있는 반면, 콜레스테롤이 높은 환자는 2~4g 정도가 필요하다.

🔵 일반적으로 하나의 어유캡슐에 EPA가 0.18g, DHA가 0.12g 들어 있다고 했으므로 둘을 더하면 0.3g이 된다. 관상동맥 질환 환자의 경우 하루에 EPA와 DHA를 합하여 약 1g을 섭취할 수 있으므로 3알(0.9g)~4알(1.2g) 정도 복용할 수 있다.

Omega-3 fatty acid 오메가3지방산 nutrient 영양분(제) stroke 〈병의〉 발작, 뇌일혈 direction (보통 ~s) 지시 사용법, 지침서 intake 섭취, 흡입 excessive 과다한, 과도의 bleeding 출혈 recommendation 충고, 권고 coronary heart disease 관상동맥 질환 consume 소비하다

40 This research was performed to show not only that stress influences illness but also that different people have different reactions to environmental stress. Although it deals with the influence of stress in specific illnesses, its results apply to the individuals without a disease. Another finding of this research shows that numerous, minor factors are more negative to an outcome than major stressors. Major life events are significant factors in the course of a disease, but daily hassles, which occur on a daily basis, may be more hazardous, and have a more profound effect on exacerbation or onset of disease.

Q Which of the followng would affect a patient most according to the passage?

    (a) death of a parent
    (b) a suit for divorce
    (c) increasing workload
    (d) sibling's cancer bout

이 연구는 스트레스가 질병에 영향을 끼칠 뿐만 아니라 사람마다 외부 스트레스에 대한 반응이 다르다는 것을 보여주기 위해 시행되었다. 이 연구가 특정 질병에 미치는 스트레스의 영향력을 다루고 있지만, 그 결과는 질병이 없는 사람에게도 적용된다. 이 연구의 또 다른 발견 중 하나는 수많은 사소한 인자들이 주된 스트레스 인자들보다 결과에 더 부정적이라는 것이다. 병의 진행과정에서 삶의 큰 사건들이 중요한 영향을 끼치는 것은 사실이지만, 매일 매일 일어나는 일상의 골치 아픈 일들이 병의 발병과 악화에 더 중대한 영향을 끼친다.

➡ 스트레스와 질병의 관계에서 삶의 굵직한 사건들보다 매일 매일 일어나는 지속적인 스트레스 인자가 환자에게 더 부정적인 영향을 끼치게 되므로 답은 (c)이다. (a), (b), (d)는 major stressor, 즉 스트레스를 주는 큰 사건에 해당하므로 답이 될 수 없다.

perform 수행하다, 행하다 **reaction** 반응, 반동, 반작용 **numerous** 매우 많은, 무수한 **outcome** 결과, 결론, 성과 **stressor** 스트레스 요인 **significant** 중요한, 중대한, 주목할 만한 **hassle** 골치 아픈 것(일), 혼란, 말다툼 **basis** 기초, 기조, 토대 **hazardous** 위험한, 모험적인, 운에 맡긴 **profound** 깊은, 완전한 **exacerbation** 악화 **onset** 〈병의〉 발병, 공격, 개시 **suit** 소송, 청원, 탄원 **workload** 작업량, 일의 양 **bout** 〈병의〉 발작, 기간

LISTENING COMPREHENSION • P.146

1 M I can't stand it any longer!
　 W _____

(a) I can live with that.
(b) Nice try!
(c) You stood me up again.
(d) Pull yourself together.

M: 더 이상 못 참겠어!
W: 진정해.

○ 남자가 더 이상 못 참겠다고 하며 흥분한 상태이므로 (d) 진정하라는 표현이 정답이 된다. pull oneself together은 진정하라는 뜻과 함께 기운 내라는 의미도 있으므로 함께 알아두자.

stand ~을 참다, 견디다 any longer 더 이상 pull oneself together 기운을 되찾다, 냉정해지다 I can live with that. 그건 받아들일 수 있어. Nice try! 잘했어! 시도가 좋았어! stand sb up ~을 바람맞히다

2 M It's time to go home.
　 W _____

(a) I don't have time.
(b) Okay. Let's wrap things up.
(c) That'll be the day.
(d) No. I'm in a hurry.

M: 집에 갈 시간이다.
W: 알았어. 일을 마무리 짓자.

○ 집에 갈 시간이라고 했으므로 (a)시간이 없다는 표현은 적절치 않으며, (c) 말도 안 된다는 표현 역시 정답이 될 수 없다. (d) 안 돼, 서둘러야 해. 라는 표현도 상황과 맞지 않는다. (b)의 경우 일을 마무리 짓자고 하면서 맞장구를 치고 있으므로 정답이 된다.

wrap up (물건을) 싸다, ~을 매듭짓다 That'll be the day. 어림도 없는 소리다. 설마 말도 안 된다. in a hurry 급히, 서둘러

3 M How often do I have to work overtime?
　 W _____

(a) At 7 o'clock.
(b) At noon.
(c) For about a week.
(d) It depends.

M: 초과 근무는 얼마나 자주 해야 합니까?
W: 상황에 따라 다릅니다.

○ 초과 근무를 몇 번이나 해야 하는지를 묻고 있으므로 시간이 나오면 어색해진다. 따라서 (a), (b)는 정답이 될 수 없다. (c)는 '일주일 동안' 이라는 기간을 이야기했으므로 빈도수를 묻는 문제와는 어울리지 않는다. 여기서는 '상황에 따라 다르다' 는 표현인 (d)가 정답이 된다.

overtime 시간 외 근무 It depends. 상황에 따라 다르다

4
  M Is anything wrong?
  W Don't touch me! I can't move at all.
  M Why? Please stand up.
  W _____

  (a) My leg is asleep.
  (b) I have a fever.
  (c) My arm hurts.
  (d) I got stood up.

M: 뭐 잘못된 거라도 있어?
W: 건드리지 마! 꼼짝도 못 하겠어.
M: 왜? 일어나 봐.
W: 다리에 쥐가 났어.

🔘 여자가 움직일 수 없다는 것이 힌트가 된다. 다리에 쥐가 나서 움직일 수 없는 상황이 문맥상 자연스럽다. 따라서 정답은 (a)가 된다. 그리고 stand up의 경우 '일어나다'의 뜻 말고도 '바람맞히다'라는 뜻이 있으므로 문제에서는 '일어나다'의 뜻으로, 보기 (d)에서는 '바람맞히다'의 뜻으로 사용되었음에 유의해야 한다.

stand up 일어서다, ~을 바람맞히다 **My leg is asleep** 다리에 쥐가 나다

5
  M What time shall we meet?
  W How about three?
  M I'm afraid I can't make it at three. How about six?
  W _____

  (a) It's five past six.
  (b) You're on time.
  (c) I'll fit into your schedule.
  (d) My watch keeps good time.

M: 몇 시에 만날까?
W: 3시 어때?
M: 3시에 갈 수 없을 거 같아. 6시는 어때?
W: 내가 네 스케줄에 맞출게.

🔘 숫자가 많이 나오기 때문에 특히 주의해서 들어야 한다. 약속을 정하고 있는 상황인데 남자가 3시는 불가능하다고 하면서 6시는 어떠냐고 물었다. 이에 적절한 여자의 반응으로는 남자의 스케줄에 맞추겠다고 하는 (c)가 정답이 된다. (a)의 경우 시간을 물었을 때 나올 수 있는 표현이고 (b)는 제시간에 왔다는 뜻으로 상황에 맞지 않는다. (d)는 시계가 잘 맞는다는 뜻으로 보기가 모두 시계나 시간과 관련된 표현이므로 의미를 잘 파악해야 오답을 피할 수 있다.

make it (시간에) 맞게 가다, 성공하다 **on time** 시간에 맞게 **fit into** ~에 꼭 들어맞다

6
  M Can you do me a favor?
  W Sure. What is it?
  M Do you know what's wrong with this report?
  W _____

  (a) The paper got stuck.
  (b) I'll check it in the paper.
  (c) I'm okay. Thank you.
  (d) I just can't pinpoint it.

M: 부탁 좀 해도 될까?
W: 그럼. 뭔데?
M: 이 보고서가 어디가 잘못되었는지 알겠어?
W: 딱 꼬집어 말할 수가 없어.

🔘 남자가 여자에게 보고서의 잘못된 점이 무엇인지 묻고 있다. (a)는 프린터기 등을 사용하면서 종이가 끼었을 때 쓸 수 있는 표현이다. paper를 이용하여 혼동을 주기 위한 함정이다. (b)에서 paper는 신문을 말하는 것으로 신문에서 확인해보겠다는 내용으로 문맥과 관계가 없다. (d)는 정확히 뭐라 꼬집어 말하기 어렵다는 뜻으로 문맥과 자연스럽게 어울리므로 정답이 된다.

pinpoint (원인 등을) 정확히 지적하다 **get stuck** 끼이다, 걸리다

7 **W** Fine Recruitment, how may I help you?
M Oh hello. I saw your advertisement in the paper for a photographer.
W Aha.
M I was wondering whether you would be able to send me an application form, please?
W Certainly, can I have your last name please?
M Okay. My last name is Johns.
W And your first name?
M Brian.
W And your zip code please?

Q What will the man tell the woman next?

(a) His occupation
(b) His phone number
(c) His address
(d) His qualification

W: Fine Recruitment입니다. 무엇을 도와드릴까요?
M: 안녕하세요. 신문에서 사진작가 뽑는 광고를 봤어요.
W: 아, 네.
M: 지원서를 보내주실 수 있는지 궁금해서요.
W: 물론이죠. 성을 알려주시겠어요?
M: 성은 존스입니다.
W: 이름은요?
M: 브라이언이요.
W: 그리고 우편번호도 알려주세요.

남자의 다음 대사를 묻고 있다. 여자의 마지막 말을 유의해서 들었다면 쉽게 맞출 수 있는 문제이다. zip code, 즉 우편번호를 물었으므로 주소를 말할 것이라고 짐작할 수 있다. 따라서 정답은 (c)가 된다.

advertisement 광고 application form 신청서, 지원서 zip code 우편번호(=postcode) occupation 직업 qualification 자질, 적성, 능력

---

8 **W** I haven't seen you these days. How is Jenna?
M We're not seeing each other any more.
W What? Did you guys break up? Why?
M Out of sight, out of mind.
W Oh, I'm sorry. Do you think you guys can get back together?
M I don't know. I think we'd better take a break.

Q What can you infer from this conversation?

(a) The man's girlfriend was apart from him.
(b) The man had a fight with his girlfriend.
(c) The man wants to make up with his girlfriend.
(d) The woman advised the man to take a break.

W: 요새 통 보지 못했네. 제나는 어떻게 지내?
M: 우리 서로 더 이상 안 만나.
W: 뭐라고? 둘이 헤어졌어? 왜?
M: 안 보면 멀어지는 법이지.
W: 안됐다. 다시 만날 가능성은 없어?
M: 잘 모르겠어. 잠시 떨어져 있는 게 좋을 것 같아.

대화를 통해 유추할 수 있는 것이 무엇인지 묻고 있다. 중간에 남자가 보이지 않으면 마음에서도 멀어진다고 했으므로 여자 친구와 떨어져 지냈음을 유추할 수 있다. 따라서 정답은 (a)가 된다. 남자가 여자 친구와 싸웠는지는 나타나 있지 않으므로 (b)는 정답이라 할 수 없고, 여자 친구와 떨어져 있는 게 좋을 것 같다고 했으므로 (c)도 역시 정답이 아니다. 대화에서 여자는 남자에게 어떠한 충고도 하고 있지 않으므로 (d) 역시 정답이 아니다.

break up 헤어지다 Out of sight, out of mind. 눈에서 멀어지면 마음에서도 멀어진다 take a break 휴식을 갖다 apart from ~와 떨어져 있는 make up with ~와 화해하다

9

W Hello, Dr. Kim, my name's Katie Ryan. My roommate, Julie Emerson, wanted me to call you.

M Julie Emerson? Oh, I see. She's taking my class. So what's the problem?

W She submitted a job application last week and the interview was rescheduled for today. She's afraid she won't be able to attend your class this afternoon.

M Okay. It wouldn't be counted as an absence.

W And would it be okay if I gave you her assignment?

M Uh, you can bring it to my office anytime today.

W Would it be possible to come by tomorrow? I have classes all day long today.

M Then leave it with my assistant.

Q What can you infer from the conversation?

(a) Katie Ryan is taking Dr. Kim's class.
(b) Julie is going to miss the class today.
(c) Katie is going to visit him today.
(d) Julie hasn't finished her assignment yet.

W: 안녕하세요, 김 교수님. 저는 케이티 라이언이라고 합니다. 제 룸메이트 줄리 에머슨이 제게 교수님께 전화를 드려달라고 부탁해서요.

M: 줄리 에머슨? 아, 알겠네요. 제 수업을 듣는 학생이에요. 무슨 일 있나요?

W: 줄리가 지난주에 입사 지원서를 냈는데, 면접 일정이 오늘로 다시 잡혀서요. 그래서 오늘 오후에 교수님 수업에 참석할 수 없을 것 같다고요.

M: 알겠어요. 결석 처리는 하지 않을게요.

W: 그리고 제가 줄리의 숙제를 대신 제출해도 될까요?

M: 오늘 언제든 사무실에 와서 제출해도 좋아요.

W: 내일 들러도 될까요? 제가 오늘 하루 종일 수업이 있어서요.

M: 그럼 내 조교에게 맡겨두세요.

🔹 대화문으로부터 추측할 수 있는 내용을 묻고 있다. 김교수의 수업을 듣는 것은 케이티가 아닌 줄리이므로 (a)는 정답이 아니다. 줄리는 면접 때문에 수업을 빠질 것이므로 (b)가 정답이 된다. 케이티는 오늘 하루 종일 수업이 있다고 했으므로 (c)는 정답이 아니고, 줄리의 과제를 케이티가 대신 내 준다고 한 것으로 보아 줄리는 과제를 완성했음을 알 수 있으므로 (d) 역시 정답이 아니다.

job application 입사 지원서 attend ~에 참석하다, 출석하다 absence 결석 come by 잠시 들르다 assignment 과제

---

10 I don't want to say you must give up coffee completely, but I want to say it's not a good idea to stay addicted to it. If you feel you're getting an addiction, please try one of the methods that I mentioned earlier today such as transition to herbal tea or grain coffee. Then you can still enjoy your tea time without the side effects like a drop in intuition, creativity, and something like that. If you find it difficult to stop drinking coffee entirely, this could be a really helpful way.

Q What is likely to be previously mentioned?

(a) The danger of becoming coffee addiction
(b) A substitute for coffee
(c) Side effects of caffeine
(d) The methods of improving creativity

제가 말하고 싶은 것은 커피를 완전히 끊어야 된다는 것이 아니라, 커피에 중독된 상태로 살아가는 것은 좋은 생각이 아니라는 것입니다. 만약 자신이 중독이 되어가고 있다고 느낀다면 오늘 전에 언급했던 방법들, 예를 들어 허브티나 곡물 커피 등으로 바꿔보는 등의 방법 중의 하나를 시도해 보시기 바랍니다. 그러면 직관, 창의성 등의 저하와 같은 부작용 없이 티타임을 즐길 수 있습니다. 커피를 완전히 끊는 것이 어렵다고 느껴지면 이러한 방법이 정말 도움이 될 수 있습니다.

🔹 앞에 나왔던 내용을 고르는 문제다. 중간에 'the methods that I mentioned earlier today'라는 표현이 힌트가 된다. 이렇게 말하면서 예로 든 것이 허브티나 곡물 커피로 바꿔보라는 것이었다. 따라서 정답은 커피의 대용품에 대한 언급이 있었음을 알 수 있으므로 정답은 (b)가 된다.

addiction 중독 transition 이동, 변화 intuition 직관 substitute 대용품, 대용식

11 Nowadays it's getting easier and easier to meet people through online dating and personal sites. There are many web sites in which you can find love with a few clicks of the mouse. While you can meet the right date through them, you should be careful. You should never give out your number or address, initially. Take your time to get to know them, and if you're interested in the person, meet them at a public place with your friends.

Q Which of the following can be inferred from the passage?

(a) Finding the right date through online is not a good way.
(b) If the person interests you, exchange phone numbers instantly.
(c) You shouldn't meet the person you're interested in by yourself.
(d) Some dating web sites have been proved to be inappropriate.

요즘에는 온라인 데이트 사이트와 개인 사이트들을 통해 사람들을 만나는 것이 점점 더 쉬워지고 있다. 마우스를 몇 번만 클릭하면 사랑을 찾을 수 있는 웹사이트들이 많이 있다. 그러한 사이트들을 통해 자기에게 맞는 데이트 상대를 만날 수 있는 반면, 주의가 필요하다. 처음부터 전화번호나 주소를 주면 안 된다. 시간을 갖고 상대방에 대해 알아간 다음에 그 사람에게 관심이 있게 되면 친구들과 함께 공공장소에서 만나는 것이 좋다.

○ 추론 문제이다. 온라인으로 데이트 상대를 고르는 것에 대해 부정적인 것이 아니라 몇 가지 주의 사항에 대해 이야기하고 있으므로 (a)와 (d)는 정답이 아니다. 바로 전화번호를 교환하지 말라고 했으므로 (b)도 정답이 아니다. 관심 있는 사람을 공공장소에서 친구와 함께 만나라고 충고하고 있으므로 정답은 (c)가 된다.

give out ~을 나누어주다 initially 처음에 by oneself 혼자서

---

12 Are you tired of your old appliances or furniture in your house? Do you want to give new life to your house? Here is the best solution to it. We have everything you need here. From dining room tables to video machines, we have a variety of quality appliances and cheap prices. Don't hesitate to catch a chance to give your home a new look and feel. We're located downtown one block west of city hall. We're always welcome everyone.

Q What can be inferred from the advertisement?

(a) You can buy furniture at a discount.
(b) The store opened after remodeling.
(c) You can contact the store through phone call.
(d) The store is near city hall.

집에 있는 낡은 가전제품이나 가구에 싫증이 나셨습니까? 집에 새로운 생명을 불어넣고 싶습니까? 여기 최고의 해결책이 있습니다. 여러분이 필요한 모든 것이 여기 있습니다. 식탁에서부터 비디오 플레이어에 이르기까지 우리는 품질이 우수하고 저렴한 다양한 제품을 갖추고 있습니다. 주저하지 말고 새로운 모습과 느낌으로 집을 바꿀 기회를 잡으십시오. 저희 가게는 시청 서쪽으로 한 블록 떨어진 시내에 위치해 있습니다. 언제나 여러분 모두를 환영합니다.

○ 추론 문제이다. 가구를 할인해 주는지에 대해서는 알 수 없으므로 (a)는 정답이 아니다. 가게가 리모델링을 했는지는 알 수 없으므로 (b)도 정답이 될 수 없다. 전화번호는 언급하지 않았으므로 (c)역시 알 수 없다. 시청에서 한 블록 더 가면 있다고 했으므로 가게는 시청 주변에 있음을 알 수 있으므로 정답은 (d)가 된다.

appliance 기구, 가전제품 catch a chance 기회를 잡다

13 A Have you finished packing?

B Sure, but please remind me _____ before leaving.

(a) checking the electrics
(b) to check the electrics
(c) of check the electrics
(d) to checking the electrics

A: 짐 다 꾸렸어?

B: 물론, 근데 떠나기 전에 전기 좀 확인하도록 알려줘.

○ remind 목적어 to 부정사의 형태를 묻는 문제이다.

pack 싸다, 포장하다 leave 떠나다

---

14 A How about your mom? Is she OK?

B She _____, but she needs to see the doctor.

(a) looks like better
(b) looks much well
(c) looks much better
(d) looking more better

A: 너희 엄마 어떠셔? 괜찮으셔?

B: 훨씬 나아지셨어, 그런데 병원에 가야 돼.

○ looks good(좋아 보인다)의 비교급인 looks better에 much가 붙어서 훨씬 더 좋아 보인다라는 의미로 쓰였다.

---

15 A What are special things about your products?

B We are using organic vegetables _____ pesticide or herbicide.

(a) grow at the farm without
(b) growing at the farm with
(c) grown at the farm without
(d) growing at the farm without

A: 당신의 제품에 특별한 점이 무엇입니까?

B: 우리는 농약이나 살충제 없이 유기농 채소를 사용합니다.

○ 유기농 채소이려면 농약과 살충제는 없어야 하므로 without이 쓰이고 organic vegetables를 수식해주어야 하므로 grown의 형태가 적절하다.

organic vegetables 유기농 채소 pesticide 농약 herbicide 제초제

---

16 A Before surgery, I need to check. How often do you drink?

B Occasionally, I _____.

(a) am drinking heavily
(b) am not heavy drinker
(c) am not a heavy drinking
(d) am not a heavy drinker

A: 수술 전에 확인할 것이 있습니다. 얼마나 자주 음주를 하십니까?

B: 가끔씩이오, 저는 술꾼이 아닙니다.

○ 음주를 가끔씩 한다고 함으로써 술을 자주 하는 편이 아니라는 표현이 적절하다.

(heavy) drinker 술꾼

---

17 This nuclear star cluster may _____ young stars and be central hot stars sitting at the center of the Milky Way.

(a) be consisted of
(b) consist of
(c) consisting of
(d) consisted of

이 핵성단은 어린 별들로 구성되어 있고, 은하수 중심에 자리한 고열의 별들일 것이다.

○ may가 조동사이므로 뒤에는 동사원형이 오고, consist of는 '구성되다'의 뜻으로 수동태 형식을 취하지 않는다.

Milky Way 은하수 consist of 구성되다

18 The statement describes and analyzes the main arguments of Latin American countries _____ the labor issues in the world trade.

(a) regarding
(b) regarded
(c) to regard of
(d) regard of

그 성명은 세계 무역에서 노동력에 관한 라틴 아메리카 국가들의 주요 논쟁을 표현하고 분석한 것이다.

🔵 '~와 관련하여' 의 의미로 regarding이 적절하다.

describe 묘사하다 labor 노동 trade 무역

---

19 After changing the election rules, they swept the council elections, _____ could never have happened under the old rules.

(a) in which
(b) that
(c) which
(d) in that

선거법을 바꾼 후로 그들은 지방의회 선거를 휩쓸었다. 이것은 옛 법체제에서는 절대로 일어날 수 없었던 일이다.

🔵 앞 문장을 모두 받는 관계대명사 which가 적절하다.

election 선거 sweep 휩쓸다,청소하다 council 지방의회

---

20 High schools _____ German and French language courses are disappearing because new exams don't evaluate foreign languages.

(a) offers
(b) offer
(c) being offered
(d) offering

새로운 시험이 외국어를 평가하지 않기 때문에 독일어와 프랑스어 과정을 제공하는 고등학교는 사라지고 있다.

🔵 are가 본동사이므로 offer는 앞의 단어를 수동이나 능동으로 꾸며 주는 분사의 형태로 오는 것이 적절하다. 그러므로 '제공하는' 의 의미로 현재분사 형태가 알맞다.

disappear 사라지다 offer 제공하다

---

21 (a) A: I'm wondering if you don't mind answering some questions about your article.
(b) B: Sure, just feel free to ask if you require further information.
(c) A: According to yours, the economic situation gets better soon. Is it possible?
(d) B: Certainly, we've researched for several months.

A: 당신의 글에 대해서 몇 가지 질문을 해도 될까요?
B: 물론이죠. 더 자세한 것이 필요하면 편하게 물어보세요.
A: 당신 글에 따르자면, 경제상황이 곧 나아질 것이라는데, 그것이 가능하겠어요?
B: 분명해요. 우리는 몇 달 동안 연구했어요.

🔵 (a)에서 mind에 대한 질문은 반대로 대답해야 한다. 즉, '괜찮아'라고 하려면 sure 등 긍정적인 대답 대신 'No I don't mind' 등의 부정어로 대답해야 한다.

article 기사 further 한층 더

22 (a) Drivers of hybrid cars are more and more interested in converting its vehicles from gasoline to electric power. (b) While drivers of conventional vehicles complain about higher fuel prices, many early drivers are investing big bucks to make their cars green. (c) The new vehicles are changed through plug-in conversions and by adding more powerful batteries. (d) This conversion allows us to get energy through an electric outlet, so you just charge your car during the night.

하이브리드 자동차의 운전자들은 점점 더 그들의 자동차를 가솔린 차에서 전력 활용 차로 바꾸는 데 흥미를 두고 있다. 보통 자동차의 운전자들이 그들의 높은 연료비에 불평을 하는 동안 선구자들은 많은 돈을 친환경 자동차를 만드는 데 투자하는 중이다. 새로운 자동차는 충전식으로의 개조와 더 강력한 배터리를 추가함으로써 변화했다. 이러한 개조는 우리가 전기를 통해 동력을 얻을 수 있도록 해준다. 그래서 이제 당신은 밤새 자동차를 충전하기만 하면 된다.

⊙ (a)에서 its는 '그들의 자동차'가 되어야 하므로 their를 쓰는 것이 적절하다.

convert 변환하다 invest 투자하다 charge 충전하다

---

23 A   He keeps changing lanes without turning on the _____.
   B   Right. He's really getting on my nerves.

   (a) sign
   (b) mark
   (c) turn signal
   (d) light

A: 저 남자 방향지시등을 켜지도 않고 계속 차선을 바꾸네.
B: 그러게. 정말 내 신경을 거슬리게 하고 있어.

⊙ 차선을 계속 바꾼다고 했으므로 차선을 바꿀 때 필요한 방향지시등이 정답이 된다. 방향지시등은 indicator라고도 한다.

change lanes 차선을 바꾸다 turn on (전기, TV 등)~을 켜다 get on one's nerves ~의 신경을 거슬리다

---

24 A   Do you think your kid is an outgoing person?
   B   I don't think so. He seems to be _____ to being alone.

   (a) habitual
   (b) likely
   (c) accustomed
   (d) forced

A: 댁의 아이가 사교적이라고 생각합니까?
B: 그런 것 같지 않아요. 혼자 있는 것에 익숙한 것 같아요.

⊙ 아이가 사교적이지 않다고 했으므로 혼자 있는 것을 좋아한다든지, 익숙하다든지 하는 표현이 나와야 한다. 따라서 정답은 (c)가 된다.

outgoing 외향적인, 사교적인 be accustomed to ~에 익숙하다

---

25 A   How's your new job going?
   B   Most of the work I do is _____ and boring.

   (a) exciting
   (b) tedious
   (c) stifling
   (d) favorable

A: 새로운 일은 어때?
B: 내가 하는 일은 대부분 따분하고 지루해.

⊙ and 다음에 boring이라는 단어가 나왔으므로 이와 비슷한 뜻의 단어를 찾아야 한다. (a)와 (d)는 그와 상반된 뜻이므로 정답이 아니다. (b)는 따분하다, 지루하다는 뜻을 가지고 있으므로 정답이 된다.

tedious 따분한, 지루한 stifling 질식할 것 같은, 숨 막히는

26 A Are you getting along with your new manager?

B Yes. He is much more humane than his _____.

(a) colleague

(b) boss

(c) competitor

(d) predecessor

A: 새로운 매니저와는 잘 지내고 있어?

B: 응. 전임자보다는 훨씬 더 인간적이야.

🔵 새로운 매니저와의 관계를 묻고 있음에 주목해야 한다. 새로운 매니저와 그 전임자를 비교하는 상황이 가장 적절하다고 할 수 있으므로 정답은 (d)가 된다.

get along with ~와 사이 좋게 잘 지내다 **humane** 인간적인 **predecessor** 전임자

---

27 A Is your wife still angry with you?

B Yes. But I want to _____ with her.

(a) make up

(b) catch up

(c) come up

(d) hang up

A: 네 아내는 아직 네게 화나 있니?

B: 응. 근데 나는 아내랑 화해하고 싶어.

🔵 아내가 화나 있다는 것은 싸웠다는 의미이므로, 문맥상 화해하고 싶다는 내용이 적절하다. 따라서 정답은 (a)가 된다.

make up with ~와 화해하다 **catch up with** ~을 따라잡다 **come up with** ~을 생각해내다, ~을 제안하다 **hang up with** ~와 어울리다, 사귀다

---

28 It is expected to reach a high _____ rate for the Friday of this week because public schools would be on vacation next Monday.

(a) accident

(b) dropout

(c) absentee

(d) admission

공립학교가 다음주 월요일 방학에 들어가기 때문에 이번주 금요일에 결석률이 높을 것으로 예상된다.

🔵 absentee는 결석자, 결근자를 의미하는 단어이다. 방학에 들어간다는 내용이 나왔으므로 결석률이 높을 것이라는 내용이 문맥상 적절하다. (a)의 사고와는 연관지을 만한 내용이 없으므로 정답이 될 수 없다.

absentee 결석자, 결근자 **dropout** 낙제생, 중도 퇴학생

---

29 Police authorities announced new measures to eradicate _____ crime such as vandalism, graffiti and public urination.

(a) juvenile

(b) daring

(c) copycat

(d) petty

경찰 당국은 공공기물 파괴행위, 그라피티 그리고 노상 방뇨와 같은 경범죄를 근절하기 위한 새 조치들을 발표했다.

🔵 공공기물 파괴나 그라피티(일종의 낙서), 노상 방뇨는 보통 경범죄에 해당하므로 보기 가운데 이러한 의미를 가진 petty를 골라야 한다. serious crime은 petty crime과 반대되는 의미로 중범죄를 의미한다.

eradicate ~을 근절하다, 박멸하다 **petty crime** 경범죄 **vandalism** 공공기물 파괴행위 **public urination** 노상 방뇨

30 The Secretary of Defense stated outright that the government was not going to _____ to the terrorists' demands.

(a) give up
(b) give in
(c) pay off
(d) make up

정부는 테러리스트의 요구에 굴복하지 않을 것이라고 국방장관이 명백히 밝혔다.

○ 문맥상으로 테러리스트의 요구에 굴복하지 않을 것이라는 내용이 나와야 자연스럽다. 이런 의미를 가진 구동사는 (b) give in이다.

outright 솔직한, 명백한, 철저한 give in 굽히다, 양보하다 give up 포기하다 pay off (빚을) 청산하다 make up 화장하다, 벌충하다, 보완하다

---

31 At the beginning of the presentation, the presenter usually indicates whether he or she will _____ questions during the presentation or hold questions until the end of the presentation.

(a) address
(b) raise
(c) entertain
(d) pose

프리젠테이션 초반에 발표자는 대개 프리젠테이션 중간에 질문을 받을지 아니면 프리젠테이션이 끝나고 나서 질문을 받을지 알려준다.

○ 문장 뒷부분을 보면 프리젠테이션이 끝날 때까지 질문을 받지 않는다고 했으므로 그 앞 부분은 프리젠테이션 중간에 질문을 받는다는 내용이 나와야 한다. 보기 가운데 질문을 받는다는 뜻의 단어는 entertain이다.

indicate 가리키다, 표시하다, 보여주다 entertain 즐겁게 해주다, (제의, 질문을) 받아들이다 hold 억누르다, 억제하다, (행사 등을) 개최하다 raise(pose) a question 문제를 제기하다

---

32 Experts mostly agree that education based on rote memorization _____ creativity in children.

(a) energize
(b) stifle
(c) foster
(d) enhance

전문가들은 주입식 교육에 기초한 교육이 아이들의 창의성을 억제한다는 데 대부분 동의한다.

○ '창의성을 말살시키다, 억누르다' 라는 표현은 'stifle creativity' 라고 한다. enhance의 경우 정반대의 뜻을 가지고 있다.

rote memorization 주입식 교육 stifle 숨을 막다, 질식시키다, 억누르다, 억제하다

33 A Dictionary of the English Language, published by Samuel Johnson in 1755, was evaluated as a highly influential and comprehensive dictionary in the history of the English language. It contained the definitions of over 40,000 words with quotes and sentence examples to illustrate the sense and usage of those words. Surprisingly its quotation sources varied from literature to science, medical science, and theology, etc. Occasionally, he seemed to _____.
For example, when he defined a patron as "a wretch who supports with indolence, and is paid with flattery," he must have kept Lord Chesterfield in mind. We could also get a glimpse of his thoughts through his description of the word sonnet, which is "not very suitable to the English language."

(a) quote many experts' works for better reputation
(b) use personal views to color the definitions of words
(c) cite previous dictionaries for more precise definitions
(d) borrow other scholars' opinions to make the dictionary look plausible

1755년 Samuel Johnson이 출판한 영어사전은 영어 역사상 매우 영향력 있고 이해하기 쉬운 사전으로 평가받았다. 그 사전은 4만 개 이상의 단어들의 의미와 어법을 설명하기 위해서 인용문과 예문을 들어 정의를 내렸다. 놀랍게도 그 인용문들의 출처는 문학으로부터 과학, 의학, 신학에 이르기까지 다양했다. 때때로 그는 단어의 정의를 윤색하는 데 개인적인 견해를 사용하기도 했다. 예를 들어, 그가 patron을 "게으르고 아첨을 좋아하는 철면피"로 정의했을 때 그는 틀림없이 Chesterfield 경을 마음속에 담아두었을 것이다. 우리는 또한 그가 sonnet를 "영어에는 어울리지 않는" 것으로 묘사한 것을 통해서도 그의 생각을 엿볼 수 있다.

○ 밑줄 다음에 나오는 두 가지 예가 문제를 푸는 단서가 된다. 두 가지 예의 정의를 보면 Samuel Johnson의 극히 개인적인 견해가 들어가 있으므로 정답은 (b)가 된다. 누구나 패트런이나 소네트를 그런 식으로 정의 내리지는 않기 때문이다. 따라서 더 나은 평판을 위해서 전문가의 작품을 인용했다든가(a), 더 정확한 정의를 내리기 위해서 기존의 사전을 인용했다든가(c), 사전을 그럴 듯하게 보이게 하려고 학자들의 의견을 차용했다(d)는 것은 정답이 될 수 없다.

comprehensive 포괄적인, 이해력 있는 define A as B A를 B로 정의하다 quote 인용하다(=cite) illustrate 〈에 따위를 들어〉설명하다, 예증하다 usage 〈언어의〉용법, 어법 vary 다양하다 literature 문학(작품) theology 신학 patron 〈예술, 사업 따위의〉후원자, 지원자, (로마역사) 평민 보호자로서의 귀족 wretch 비열한 사람, 철면피 indolence 나태, 게으름 flattery 아첨, 아부(의 말) keep ~ in mind ~을 마음에 담아 두다 get a glimpse of ~을 힐끗(얼핏) 보다 description 서술, 묘사 sonnet 소네트(14행시) reputation 평판, 명성 precise 정확한, 명확한 plausible 그럴 듯한

34 For the most part, sharks are not detrimental and interested in humans at all, but there are certain conditions that make sharks aggressive. Sharks have an acute sense of smell so strong odors such as the smell of blood incites their offensive behavior. Other smells such as urine and vomit in the water can also stimulate sharks like blood. Moreover, sharks can be affected by the struggles of an injured animal or human, underwater explosions, or even fish trying to escape from a fish line and change suddenly because
_____.

(a) these kind of situations irritate sharks
(b) sound as well as smell may guide them to their prey
(c) their sense of hearing is keener than their sense of smell
(d) they are very sensitive to any unusual vibrations in the ocean

대부분 상어는 전혀 해롭지도 않고 인간에게 관심도 없지만 상어를 공격적으로 만드는 특별한 환경이 있다. 상어는 후각이 예민해서 피냄새와 같이 강한 냄새는 상어에게 공격적인 행동이 일어나도록 한다. 수중에서 소변이나 구토 냄새를 맡는 것도 피냄새를 맡는 것과 같이 상어에게 자극이 된다. 게다가 상어는 부상당한 동물이나 사람이 몸부림칠 때나 물속에서 폭발이 일어날 때, 물고기가 낚싯줄에서 빠져 나오려고 애쓸 때에도 영향을 받아서 갑자기 변할 수가 있는데, 이것은 상어가 바다에서 평소와는 다른 진동에 매우 민감하기 때문이다.

🔵 상어의 공격성을 유발하는 원인으로 냄새와 진동이 언급되어 있다. 냄새의 예로는 피와 소변, 구토가 나와 있다. 따라서 마지막 문장에서 the struggles of an injured animal or human, underwater explosions, or even fish trying to escape from a fish line이 무엇의 예로 쓰였는가를 생각해 보면 정답을 알 수 있다. 이 예들에서 진동을 느낀다고 보는 것이 더 적합하다.

for the most part 대부분, 거의 detrimental 해로운 aggressive 공격적인(=offensive) acute 예리한, 민감함(=keen) incite 자극하다 urine 오줌, 소변 vomit 구토 struggle 몸부림 노력 injure 상처를 입히다, 부상시키다 explosion 폭발 irritate 짜증나게 하다, 화나게 하다

---

35 The term "unschooling" refers to alternative educational practices to conventional schooling by its rejecting the use of a fixed curriculum and other features of traditional schooling. In actual fact, unschoolers disapprove of the inefficiency of "factory-like" school. However, although they typically allow children to learn "naturally" according to their needs and developmental stages, unschoolers allow them to learn "unnaturally"—in traditional way—not when they have reached a certain age but when it makes sense to them to do so. _____ it isn't unusual to find unschooling students who are barely seven-years-old studying astronomy or who are twelve-years-old and just learning to read.

(a) Yet
(b) Otherwise
(c) Therefore
(d) Nevertheless

'무교수학습법' 이란 용어는 정해진 교육과정의 사용과 그 밖의 전통적인 교육의 특징들을 거부하는 전통적 교육에 대한 대안적인 교육 활동이다. 사실상 무교수학습주의자들은 공장 같은 학교의 비효율성에 반대한다. 그러나 전형적으로 그들은 아이들이 스스로의 필요와 발달단계에 따라 "자연스럽게" 학습하도록 하지만, 무교수학습주의자들도 아이들이 "자연스럽지 않게"-전통적인 방법으로- 학습하도록 할 때가 있는데, 아이들이 특정 연령에 도달할 때가 아니라 아이들이 그렇게 하는 것이 이치에 닿을 때 그렇게 한다. 그러므로 겨우 일곱 살이 된 무교수학습자가 천문학을 공부하고 있거나, 열두 살이 되었는데 이제 막 글 읽기를 시작한 무교수학습자를 발견한다 해도 특이한 일은 아닌 것이다.

🔵 무교수학습법이 특정 연령에 특정 교육과정을 배우도록 하는 전통적인 교육에 반대하지만, 필요에 따라 전통적인 학습법을 따르기도 한다는 내용이며, 천문학을 공부하는 일곱 살과 글 읽기를 막 배우기 시작하는 열두 살 무교수학습자를 예로 들었으므로 정답은 (c)가 된다.

unschooling 무교수학습법 reject 거절하다, 거부하다 fixed 고정된 feature 특징, 특색, 주안점 in actual fact 사실상 disapprove of ~에 찬성하지 않다, 반대의견을 갖다 inefficiency 비능률, 무효과 typically 전형적으로 developmental stage 발달단계 barely 겨우, 간신히, 가까스로 astronomy 천문학

36 As the world's and Singapore's population ages, silver industry rises as a booming industry. Global companies have been fixing their eyes on Asia which is ageing rapidly, especially Singapore as the touchstone for this industry. Its multi-ethnic ageing population, strength in logistics, finance and technology, and senior citizens with strong spending power as well as an unquenchable appetite for new mid-life challenges make Singapore an experimental test-bed for a glittering silver market.

Q What is the strong point of Singapore as the mecca of silver industry?

(a) racial homogeneousness
(b) elder-friendly social system
(c) the state religion of Singapore
(d) financially secure enterprising seniors

전세계와 싱가포르의 인구가 노화함에 따라, 실버산업이 급속하게 성장하는 산업으로 부상하고 있다. 세계적 회사들이 빠르게 노화하고 있는 아시아에 눈독을 들이고 있으며, 특히 싱가포르를 산업의 성공여부를 예측할 수 있는 시금석으로 여기고 있다. 다민족의 노화하는 인구와 기획, 재정, 기술적인 면의 강점 그리고 새로운 중년생활에 도전하겠다는 억누를 수 없는 욕구뿐만 아니라 구매력도 갖춘 장년층들이 싱가포르를 번창하는 실버산업의 시험대로 만들고 있다.

◑ 싱가포르가 실버산업의 시험대가 될 수 있는 요인으로 다민족 노인 국가, 장년층이 구매력, 기획, 재정, 기술적인 면에서 강하다는 점이 언급되어 있으므로 정답은 (d)이다. (a)는 지문의 내용과 상반되며, (b)와 (c)는 언급된 바가 없으므로 답이 될 수 없다.

silver industry 실버산업 booming 인기 상승의, 급속히 발전하는 touchstone 시금석 multi-ethnic 다민족의 logistics 사업의 세부 계획·입안·집행 unquenchable 억누를 수 없는 appetite 욕구 test-bed 시험대 glittering 번쩍이는, 화려한 homogeneous 동종의, 동일 조직의, 동일성의 elder-friendly 노인 우대의

---

37 Hawk-Eye is a computer system used to display the actual path of the ball as a graphic image in cricket, tennis and other sports. In tennis, there had been erroneous calls in a very crucial match so the players complained at times and the chair umpire was dismissed from a tournament. Passing the rigid International Tennis Federation testing measures, Hawk-Eye has been used to assist the umpire in line decisions. Hawk-Eye helps to decide whether balls are in or out of the border line by providing information about the ball's track with at least four high speed video cameras located in different positions in the court within a few minutes.

Q What can be inferred from the passage?

(a) The umpire will disappear rapidly in a tennis court because of Hawk-Eye.
(b) Hawk-Eye is so expensive that it is difficult to be adopted in other sports.
(c) Hawk-Eye makes tennis players' complaints about the umpire's decision decreased.
(d) Television viewers need to be trained to understand the Hawk-Eye's graphic images.

호크아이는 크리켓과 테니스 같은 경기에서 공의 실제 경로를 생성한 영상으로 보여주기 위해 사용되는 컴퓨터 시스템이다. 테니스에서 매우 중요한 경기 때 판정이 잘못 내려져서 선수들이 때때로 불만을 토하고 주심이 경기에서 해고되기도 했었다. 호크아이는 국제테니스연맹의 엄격한 테스트 기준을 통과하여 심판들이 선에 공이 떨어졌는지 판정을 내릴 때 도와주는 역할을 하고 있다. 호크아이는 코트 내 다른 위치에 설치되어 있는 최소한 4대의 고속 비디오카메라가 몇 분 내에 볼의 경로를 알려줌으로써 볼이 경계선 안쪽에 떨어졌는지 바깥쪽에 떨어졌는지를 결정하는 데 도움을 준다.

◑ 호크아이가 도입되기 전에 심판의 판정에 불만이 많았다는 내용으로 보아 호크아이가 사용된 후에는 불만이 줄어들었을 것이기에 정답은 (c)가 된다. 호크아이는 심판의 판정을 돕는 역할을 하는 것으로 이 때문에 심판이 사라지지는(a) 않을 것이고, 크리켓, 테니스 그리고 다른 스포츠에서 이미 사용되고 있기 때문에 (b)도 오답이 된다. 또한 호크아이는 공의 경로를 생성한 화면으로 보여주기 때문에 이것을 보기 위해서 훈련이 필요하지는 않을 것이다(d).

display 보여주다, 진열하다 actual 실제의, 사실상의 erroneous 잘못된, 틀린 call 〈심판의〉 판정 crucial 아주 중대한 at times 때때로 umpire 〈경기의〉 심판원 dismiss 해고하다, 해임하다 rigid 엄격한

38 The Myers-Briggs Type Indicator (MBTI) assessment, the world's most widely used psychometric questionnaire, was developed to measure psychological preferences in how people perceive the world and make decisions. It is assumed that individuals are either born with, or develop, certain preferred ways of thinking and acting. The test categorizes these psychological preferences into four opposite pairs, or "dichotomies," the permutations of which result in the 16 personality types. Different preferences lead to different communication styles, which can hamper mutual understanding. However, such communication barriers can be removed with mutual respect and understanding of diversity.

Q What can be inferred as the best application of the MBTI in actual life?

(a) supporting better teamwork in a group
(b) supporting more ethical decision making
(c) developing a psychometric questionnaire
(d) changing a left-hander into a right-hander

세계에서 가장 널리 사용되는 심리측정 질문지인 Myers-Briggs Type Indicator(MBTI) 검사는 사람들이 세상을 인지하고 결정을 내리는 데 사용하는 심리적인 선호를 측정하기 위해 만들어졌다. 인간은 선호하는 사고방식이나 행동방식을 선천적으로 타고 나거나, 후천적으로 개발한다고 여겨진다. (MBTI) 평가는 이런 심리적 선호를 2분법, 즉 네 쌍의 대조적인 짝으로 분류하는데, 이것들을 조합하면 16가지의 성격 유형이 도출된다. 다른 선호는 다른 의사소통 방식으로 이끄는데, 이것이 서로를 이해하는 것을 방해한다. 그러나 그러한 의사소통 장벽은 상호 존중과 다양성에 대한 이해를 통해 제거될 수 있다.

⊙ MBTI 검사는 인간이 선천적으로 타고나거나 후천적으로 갖게 된 심리적인 선호를 기준으로 성격을 16가지 유형으로 분류하는데, 이러한 다양성을 이해하고 서로를 존중한다면 의사소통을 효율적으로 할 수 있다는 내용이다. 그러므로 실제 생활 속에서 타인의 성격을 이해하고 존중하여 의사소통 능력을 신장시킨다면 서로 조화롭게 공존할 수 있게 되므로 정답은 (a)가 된다. (b)와 (c)는 언급된 바 없으며, (d)처럼 인간이 타고난 것을 바꾸는 것은 차이에 대한 존중이라는 MBTI 검사의 취지와도 맞지 않으므로 답이 될 수 없다.

assessment 평가, 감정 psychometric 정신(심리) 측정(학)의 questionnaire 질문지, 질문표 perceive 지각하다, 인지하다, 알아채다 assume 가정하다, 간주하다, 당연한 일로 생각하다 categorize 분류하다, 범주에 넣다 dichotomy 양분, 둘로 나누기 permutation 순열 hamper 훼방하다, 방해하다 barrier 장애물, 장벽 mutual 상호의, 공동의 diversity 다양성, 차이(점)

39 Avian influenza is a flu infection caused by viruses adapted to birds. The viruses can infect not only birds but also human beings through virus mutation, which is a big concern because humans aren't immune against it. Even though all of the viruses are not fatal to human beings, one of subtypes called avian influenza A (H5N1) has caused worldwide epidemics. Symptoms of avian influenza are very similar to those of a typical human flu, which might range from cough, sore throat, high fever, runny nose, diarrhea to severe respiratory diseases. To prevent avian influenza, travelers should be careful in visiting the avian flu outbreak areas. Farmers or people who work with poultry who might be infected should wear protective clothing and masks.

조류인플루엔자는 새에게 적응된 바이러스에 의해 일어나는 조류 독감 감염이다. 그 바이러스들은 새뿐만 아니라 바이러스 변형을 통해서 인간도 감염시킬 수 있는데, 인간은 그 바이러스에 면역이 없기 때문에 큰 문제가 되고 있다. 모든 바이러스가 인간에게 치명적이지는 않을지라도 조류인플루엔자 A(H5N1)라고 불리는 하나의 특수한 유형은 세계적인 유행병을 일으켰다. 조류인플루엔자의 증상은 전형적인 인간 독감의 증세와 매우 유사해서 기침, 인후염, 고열, 콧물, 설사로부터 심각한 호흡기 질환까지 일으킨다. 조류인플루엔자를 예방하기 위해서 여행객들은 조류인플루엔자가 발생한 지역을 방문할 때 조심해야 한다. 농부나 가금류를 다루는 사람들도 그것들이 감염이 됐을지도 모르기 때문에 방호복과 마스크를 착용해야 한다.

⊙ 마지막 문장이 문제를 푸는 열쇠가 된다. 농부와 가금류를 다루는 사람들이 방호복과 마스크를 써야 한다는 것으로 보아 감염된 가금류와 접촉하면 인간에게도 조류인플루엔자가 감염될 수 있다는 (d)는 유추가 가능하다. (a)는 조류인플루엔자 A가 유행병을 일으켰으므로 본문과 상반되는 내용이고, (b)조류인플루엔자로 죽은 사람이 없다와 (c)조류인플루엔자 A는 사람에서 사람에게로 퍼지기 힘들다는 것은 본문에서 세계적인 유행병을 일으켰다는 내용과 상반된다.

Q What can be inferred from this passage?

(a) Avian influenza A hasn't caused flu pandemics yet.

(b) There are no people who have died of avian influenza.

(c) It is very difficult for H5N1 to spread from one person to another.

(d) Avian influenza infection in humans results from contact with infected poultry.

flu 독감 infection 감염 mutation 변형, 변질 immune 면역 (성)의 fatal 치명적인 subtype 〈일반형에 포함되어 있는〉 특수형 epidemic 유행병 sore throat 인후염 diarrhea 설사 respiratory 호흡(작용)의 outbreak 발생, 발발 poultry 가금류 protective 보호하는 pandemic 전국적(전대륙적, 세계적) 유행병 die of 〈병, 굶주림, 노령으로〉 죽다

---

40 Astronaut training courses, which are very intensive and rigorous, take place at the John Space Center (JSC) in Houston. (a) During the astronauts' first year of candidacy, they learn about shuttle systems, basic science and technology such as mathematics, physics, computer science, astronomy and meteorology. (b) To become a pilot astronaut, a bachelor's degree in engineering, mathematics or physics and the experience of flying a jet aircraft for 1,000 hours are prerequisite. (c) Another component of astronaut training, the simulation of weightlessness, takes place both in aircraft and in huge water tanks, and this teaches how to perform more complex tasks as well as routine ones. (d) After this first step, they receive another year of advanced training in the Shuttle Mission Simulator where they are taught specific skills during a mission.

우주비행사 훈련과정은 매우 집약적이고 엄격한데, Houston에 있는 John Space Center에서 행해진다. (a) 우주비행사 후보자는 첫 해에 우주왕복선의 시스템과 수학, 물리학, 컴퓨터 과학, 천문학, 기상학과 같은 기초 과학과 기술을 배운다. (b) 우주선 조종사가 되기 위해서는 공학이나 수학, 물리학 학위가 있어야 하며 제트 비행기를 1,000시간 비행해 본 경험이 있어야 한다. (c) 우주 비행사 훈련의 또 다른 과정인 무중력상태 시뮬레이션은 항공기에서와 거대한 물탱크에서 모두 시행되며, 이 훈련을 통해 일상적인 임무뿐만 아니라 좀 더 복잡한 임무를 수행할 수 있게 된다. (d) 이 첫 번째 단계 후에, Shuttle Mission Simulator에서 고급 훈련을 한 해 더 받게 되는데, 여기에서는 임무 수행시 필요한 구체적인 기술들을 배우게 된다.

◐ 우주비행사가 되기 위해 받는 훈련을 소개하고 있다. (a)와 (c)는 첫 해에 받는 훈련이고 (d)는 다음 해에 받는 훈련이다. (c)의 Another component of astronaut training을 통해 (c)가 (a)다음에 온다는 것을 알 수 있다. (b)는 비행 우주비행사가 되기 위한 필요한 조건이므로 글의 전체적인 흐름과 관계가 없다.

astronaut 우주비행사 intensive 집중적인, 철저한, 집약적인 rigorous 엄격한, 엄한 candidacy 입후보, 후보자격 astronomy 천문학 meteorology 기상학 bachelor 학사 prerequisite 미리(우선) 필요한 component 구성 요소, 성분 weightlessness 무중력상태

144

LISTENING COMPREHENSION · P.160

1 M Yesterday's hurricane in L.A. was terrible. Did you watch the news?

W _____

(a) No. When exactly was the last time?
(b) No. Can you fill me in on that?
(c) Don't mention it.
(d) Have you got that?

M: L.A.에서 어제 일어난 허리케인은 끔찍했어. 뉴스 봤어?
W: 아니. 그것에 대해 설명해줄래?

🔁 뉴스를 봤느냐는 말에 이어질 대답으로 적절한 것을 골라야 한다. fill in은 남에게 모르는 정보를 자세히 알려주는 것이다. 따라서 뉴스를 보지 못했으므로 그에 대해 내가 모르는 정보를 채워달라는 뜻의 (b)가 정답이 된다. (d)는 그것을 이해했느냐는 뜻이다.

fill in ~을 메우다, ~을 설명하다 **Don't mention it.** (감사 인사에 대해) 천만에요.

---

2 M I can't swim in this deep water. It's too dangerous.

W _____

(a) You're so absent-minded.
(b) There's nothing we can do about it.
(c) I'm ready to take on the world.
(d) Just give it a try.

M: 이렇게 깊은 물에서는 수영을 못 해. 너무 위험해.
W: 그냥 한 번 해봐.

🔁 너무 위험해서 수영을 못하겠다는 말에 적절한 대답을 찾아야 한다. (a)의 경우 정신을 딴 데 두고 있는 것 같다는 뜻으로 문맥과 어울리지 않는다. (b)의 경우 우리가 할 수 있는 것은 아무것도 없다는 뜻으로 역시 응답으로 자연스럽지 못하다. (c)는 건강 상태가 아주 좋다는 뜻으로 I'm physically fit. I'm in great shape. 등과 같은 뜻이다. (d)의 경우 무섭더라고 그냥 한 번 해보라고 설득하는 표현으로 응답으로 적절하다.

absent-minded 넋 놓은 **I'm ready to take on the world.** 건강 상태가 좋다 **give it a try** 시도하다, 한 번 해보다

---

3 M Thank you for inviting me. I hope we can see each other from time to time.

W _____

(a) Let's keep in touch.
(b) Keep your chin up.
(c) Don't put me on.
(d) Just bring yourself.

M: 초대해 주셔서 감사합니다. 가끔씩 서로 만날 수 있기를 바랍니다.
W: 연락하고 지냅시다.

🔁 가끔씩 만나자는 말에 어울리는 응답으로는 연락하고 지내자는 뜻의 (a)가 알맞다. (b)는 힘든 상황에 있는 사람에게 격려의 뜻으로 할 수 있는 표현이며, (c)는 칭찬을 받았을 때 할 수 있는 표현이다. (d)는 파티 등에 사람들을 초대했을 때 아무것도 가져오지 말고 몸만 오라는 뜻의 표현이다.

from time to time 때때로, 이따금 **keep in touch** ~와 연락을 유지하다 **keep one's chin up** 용기를 잃지 않다, 힘 내다 **Don't put me on .** 비행기 태우지 마세요. (= You're flattering me.)

4　W　Lost and Found. May I help you?
　　M　I think I lost my wallet.
　　W　Can you tell me what it looks like?
　　M　_____

(a) I left it on the bus.
(b) It's a black stripped one.
(c) It looks like mine.
(d) It's very kind of you.

W: 분실물 센터입니다. 무엇을 도와드릴까요?
M: 지갑을 잃어버린 것 같아요.
W: 어떻게 생겼는지 말씀해주세요.
M: 검은색 줄무늬가 있는 것이에요.

◐ 여자는 분실물 센터 담당자로 남자에게 지갑의 생김새를 묻고 있으므로 지갑의 생김새를 알려주는 보기를 골라야 한다. 따라서 정답은 (b)가 된다. (a)는 잃어버린 장소를 물어봤을 때 나올 법한 대답이다. (d)는 누군가 지갑을 찾아주었을 때 할 수 있는 표현이다.

lost and found 분실물 센터　striped 줄무늬가 있는

5　W　Why are you so late?
　　M　I'm so sorry. I have an excuse.
　　W　What is it?
　　M　_____

(a) It won't happen again.
(b) Don't mention it.
(c) I'm not sure about it.
(d) My car broke down on the way.

W: 왜 이렇게 늦었어?
M: 정말 미안해. 사정이 있어.
W: 뭔데?
M: 오는 길에 차가 고장났어.

◐ 남자가 늦은 이유에 대한 답이 나와야 한다. (a)는 다시는 이런 일이 없을 것이라는 내용이고 (b)는 감사 인사에 대해 '천만에요' 라는 뜻이고 (c)는 확신이 없다는 뜻으로 모두 관계가 없다. 차가 고장 났다는 내용은 늦은 이유가 될 수 있으므로 (d)가 정답이 된다.

excuse 이유, 핑계, 구실　break down 고장나다

6　W　What's the matter? Your eyes are bloodshot.
　　M　The exam is right around the corner.
　　W　You seem to study very hard.
　　M　_____

(a) I think I failed my exam.
(b) I was up all night cramming for the test.
(c) I don't have time to catch up.
(d) I want my eyes checked.

W: 무슨 일이야? 눈이 빨개.
M: 시험이 바로 코앞이야.
W: 공부 정말 열심히 하는 것 같다.
M: 벼락치기 하느라 밤샜어.

◐ 남자의 눈이 충혈되어 있는데, 그 이유는 시험이 얼마 안 남았다는 것이다. 따라서 시험 공부와 관련된 내용을 찾아야 한다. 아직 시험을 치르지 않았으므로 (a)는 정답이 아니다. (b)는 밤새 벼락치기를 하느라 잠을 안 잤다는내용이므로 남자의 상황과 잘어울린다. 따라서 (b)가 정답이 된다. (c)는 공부 등을 따라잡을 시간이 없다는 뜻이고, (d)는 눈 검사를 한다는 뜻인데, 여자의 첫 대사를 듣고 이것을 정답으로 착각하지 않도록 주의한다.

bloodshot 충혈된, 핏발이 선　cram for ~에 대비해 벼락치기를 하다　catch up ~을 따라잡다. 부족한 것을 채우다

7
M Why don't we buy these pants for dad? They look really cool.
W We bought him clothes last year. We'd better choose another one.
M How about this tie?
W That's not bad. But usually he doesn't like to wear ties.
M There are so many things to choose from. I don't know what to buy.
W How about these sunglasses? Does he have a pair?
M Yes, he does. But I think he'll like these.

Q What is the topic of this conversation?

(a) Preparing surprise party
(b) Going shopping
(c) Picking up a gift
(d) Deciding what to wear

M: 아빠에게 이 바지를 사드리는 것이 어때? 정말 멋진데.
W: 작년에 옷을 사 드렸잖아. 다른 것을 고르는 게 좋을 것 같아.
M: 이 넥타이는 어때?
W: 나쁘지 않네. 하지만 아빠는 넥타이 매는 거 좋아하시지 않아.
M: 종류가 너무 많아서 고르기 힘들다. 어떤 걸 사야 할지 모르겠어.
W: 이 선글라스는 어때? 아빠에게 선글라스가 있나?
M: 응. 하지만 아빠가 이거 좋아하실 것 같아.

◐ 대화의 주제에 대해 묻고 있다. 바지, 타이, 선글라스 등을 언급하면서 아버지의 취향에 대해 이야기하는 것으로 보아 아버지에게 드릴 선물을 고르고 있음을 짐작할 수 있다. 따라서 정답은 (c)가 된다. pick up은 '~을 사다' 라는 뜻이 있는 구동사이다.

wear a tie 넥타이를 매다 pick up ~을 사다

8
W Can I help you?
M I'd like to pick up a car for two days.
W Just a moment, please. We have compact and mid-sized cars you can rent.
M Mid-sized one sounds good to me. What is the rate?
W It'll be 30 dollars per day.
M Okay.
W Can I have your name and credit card number, please?

Q What is happening in this conversation?

(a) The man is trying to buy a new car.
(b) The man is calling in to confirm a reservation
(c) The man is calling in to rent a car.
(d) The man is calling a repairing service.

W: 무엇을 도와드릴까요?
M: 차를 이틀 동안 빌리고 싶은데요.
W: 잠시만 기다려주세요. 소형차와 중형차가 있습니다.
M: 중형차가 좋겠네요. 렌트 비용이 얼마죠?
W: 하루에 30 달러입니다.
M: 알겠습니다.
W: 성함과 신용 카드 번호를 알려주시겠어요?

◐ 대화 상황을 묻고 있다. 차를 렌트 해주는 회사에 전화를 걸어서 차를 빌리는 상황이다. 차의 크기와 비용 등을 묻고 있는 것으로 짐작할 수 있다. 따라서 정답은 (c)가 된다.

compact (차가) 소형의 call in (회사 등에) 전화를 하다

9

W Check to make sure nothing's been left behind.

M Don't worry. It seems like everything is all set.

W How about the airline tickets?

M I have those in my purse.

W Good. And did you get the traveler's checks?

M Sure. And I didn't forget to get credit cards.

W Okay. And don't forget the itinerary.

Q What are the man and woman talking about?

(a) Cashing the traveler's checks
(b) Changing planes
(c) Paying with a credit card
(d) Packing for a trip

W: 뭐 빠뜨린 것이 없는지 확인해라.
M: 걱정하지 마세요. 모든 것이 다 준비된 것 같아요.
W: 항공권은?
M: 가방에 있어요.
W: 좋아. 여행자 수표는 샀니?
M: 그럼요. 그리고 신용 카드도 잊지 않았어요.
W: 그래. 일정표도 잊지 말아라.

○ 무엇에 대해 이야기하고 있는지를 묻고 있다. 여자는 계속해서 무엇을 잊지 않았는지 묻고 있고 남자는 계속 챙겼다고 대답하고 있다. 그리고 항공권, 여행자 수표 등이 언급된 것으로 보아 정답은 (d)가 된다.

traveler's checks 여행자 수표 itinerary 여행 일정표, 여행 안내서

---

10 Italian sunsets are all beautiful but those of Venice are the loveliest of all. Their softness and splendor cannot be described. The last which I saw here, on a night in June, surpassed all others I'd ever seen. The shadows were falling to the eastward. The cares of life seemed to be disappearing down the west. Between us and the setting sun there seemed to fall a shower of powdered gold. The entire city was pervaded by a golden light, which was perfectly transparent.

Q What is the best title for the passage?

(a) The peaceful life in Italy
(b) The beautiful scenery of Venice
(c) The dark side of Venice
(d) The merchant of Venice

이탈리아의 일몰은 모두 아름답지만 베니스의 일몰은 그 중 단연 가장 아름답다. 그 부드러움과 장관은 형언할 수 없다. 내가 이곳에서 본 마지막 일몰은 6월의 어느 날 밤이었는데, 내가 지금까지 본 모든 일몰을 능가했다. 그림자가 동쪽으로 드리워지고 있었다. 삶의 근심들은 서쪽으로 사라지고 있는 것 같았다. 우리와 지는 해 사이에 금가루가 쏟아져 내리는 것 같았다. 전 도시가 완벽하게 투명한 금빛에 둘러싸여 있었다.

○ 이 글에 가장 어울리는 제목을 고르는 문제이다. 베니스의 일몰에 대한 묘사이므로 정답은 (b)이다. 이탈리아의 삶에 대한 이야기는 언급이 없었으므로 (a)는 정답이 아니고, 베니스의 어두운 면에 대해서도 (c) 역시 언급이 없었다. (d)는 베니스의 상인이라는 책 제목이다.

splendor 화려, 장관 surpass ~을 능가하다, 넘다 pervade 널리 퍼지다, 고루 미치다 transparent 투명한, 비치는 merchant 상인

11 You must block out every trace of white light in the dark-room. In any case care should be taken to shut out every trace of light. If your room is just a temporary dark-room by means of blinds or screens, these blinds or screens should be opaque. Perhaps the best way to do this is to have two blinds; one is a red one and the other is a black or green blind which, coming down over the red one, entirely cuts out any trace of light and makes the room absolutely dark.

Q What is the talk mainly about?

(a) Importance of applying sunscreen
(b) How to choose a good blind
(c) The dark-room and its equipment
(d) Danger of light pollution

암실에서는 아주 소량의 백색광도 차단시켜야 한다. 어떤 경우라도 모든 빛 줄기가 차단되도록 신경을 써야 한다. 만약 블라인드나 스크린을 이용한 임시적인 암실이라면, 이 블라인드와 스크린은 불투명해야 한다. 아마도 이렇게 하는 최상의 방법은 블라인드를 두 개 치는 것이다. 하나는 빨간색, 다른 하나는 검은색이나 녹색으로 하여 빨간색 블라인드 위로 내려오게 하는 것인데, 이는 모든 빛을 차단하고 방을 완전히 어둡게 해준다.

❍ 중심 내용에 대해 묻고 있다. 암실에서는 빛을 완벽하게 차단하는 것이 중요하다는 점과 이를 위해서는 어떠한 장치가 필요한가에 대해서 이야기하고 있다. 따라서 정답은 (c)가 된다. (a)의 경우는 자외선 차단제를 바르는 것의 중요성으로서 내용과 상관이 없다.

block out ~을 차단하다 white light 백색광 a trace of 아주 조금의, 소량의 temporary 일시적인 opaque 불투명한 sunscreen 자외선 차단제

12 Did you see red apples on trees with green leaves in your dream? If so, it is considered to be propitious to the dreamer. If you ate them, it's not a good sign unless they are flawless. Ripe apples on a tree denote that the time has arrived for you to realize your hopes. If you have any plans, go fearlessly ahead. Apples on the ground imply that false friends and flatterers are around you and intend to do you harm. Decayed apples indicate hopeless efforts.

Q What is the talk mainly about?

(a) Effect of apples
(b) Superstitions about fruits
(c) Relationship between sleep and dream
(d) Dream interpretation

꿈속에서 푸른 잎이 달린 나무에 빨간 사과를 보았습니까? 만약 그렇다면, 꿈을 꾼 사람에게 길조라고 여겨집니다. 만약 그 사과들을 먹었다면, 사과에 흠집이 없지 않는 한 좋은 징조는 아닙니다. 나무에 달린 익은 사과는 당신이 희망을 실현할 시간이 왔음을 의미합니다. 어떠한 계획이 있다면 두려워하지 말고 추진하세요. 땅 위의 사과들은 거짓 친구들과 아첨꾼들이 당신을 해치기 위해 당신 주변에 있다는 것을 의미합니다. 썩은 사과들은 가망 없는 노력을 나타냅니다.

❍ 중심 내용에 대해 묻고 있다. 어떠한 사과가 꿈에 나왔는지에 따라 다른 해석을 하고 있다. 사과가 반복적으로 등장했지만 중점적인 내용은 그를 바탕으로 한 꿈의 해석이다. 따라서 (a), (b)는 정답이 될 수 없고, (d)가 정답이 된다. 잠에 대한 내용은 언급되지 않았으므로 (c) 역시 정답이 될 수 없다.

propitious 길조의 flawless 결점(흠)이 없는 ripe 익은, 여문 denote 표시하다, 뜻하다, 나타내다 imply 내포하다, 함축하다 flatterer 아첨꾼 decayed 썩은 indicate 나타내다, 암시하다

13 A How long does it take to get to the National Zoo?

B It _____ 10 minutes by car.

(a) takes me
(b) take
(c) takes
(d) to take

A: 국립 동물원까지 얼마나 걸려요?
B: 차 타고 10분 걸려요

○ 주어가 단수이므로 동사에 –s를 붙여야 한다.

---

14 A What does NASA stand for?

B It _____ National Aeronautics and Space Administration.

(a) is acronym of
(b) is an acronym of
(c) is acronym for
(d) is an acronym for

A: NASA가 무엇을 뜻하는 거야?
B: 그건 미국 항공우주국의 약자야

○ 단수명사이므로 앞에 관사 an을 붙인다. acronym은 전치사 for 과 함께 쓰인다.

stand for 뜻하다 acronym 두문자어, 머릿글자어

---

15 A Have you heard the news about soaring foreign currency exchange rates?

B How come _____?

(a) it happened
(b) did it happen
(c) does it happen
(d) happens it

A: 너 급상승하는 외환 환율에 대한 뉴스 들어봤어?
B: 어째서 그런 일이 일어났지?

○ How come~? 의문문은 뒤에 평서문 어순(주어＋동사＋~) 이 오게 된다.

soaring 급상승하는, 치솟는 currency 통화, 화폐

---

16 A What's the matter with him? He's hardly absent from school.

B He went to _____.

(a) the funeral his best friend
(b) the funeral of his best friend
(c) the his funeral best friend
(d) his the funeral of best friend

A: 그에게 무슨 문제가 있니? 그는 거의 결석을 하지 않잖아.
B: 그는 가장 친한 친구의 장례식에 갔어.

○ 어순을 묻는 문제이다. '그의 가장 친한 친구의 장례식' 에 맞는 답 은 (b)이다.

---

17 Had it not been for international aid, the country _____ starving people.

(a) wouldn't have saved
(b) would be
(c) would save
(d) will have saved

국제적인 도움이 없었더라면, 그 나라는 굶주린 사람들을 구할 수 없었을 것이다.

○ 'had it not been for' 는 가정법 과거완료시제 표현인 'If it had not been for' 에서 if가 생략된 표현으로, '~없었다면' 라는 뜻의 표 현이다. 문장이 과거 사실의 반대 내용을 담고 있으므로 (a) wouldn't have saved 가 맞다.

starving 굶주린

18 Her short answer is subtle _____.

    (a) but realistic
    (b) nor realistic
    (c) so realistic
    (d) not realistic

그녀의 짧은 대답은 미묘하지만 현실적이다.

➲ 해석상 '미묘하면서도 현실성 있는'에 부합되려면 (a)but realistic 이 적절하다.

subtle 미묘한

---

19 He has to wait until the ship _____ to pick up the damaged life boat.

    (a) will return
    (b) returns
    (c) was returned
    (d) being returning

그는 그 배가 망가진 구명보트를 구출하러 올 때까지 기다려야만 한다.

➲ 시간과 조건의 부사절에서는 현재 시제가 미래 시제를 대신한다. until, before, after, when, if가 조건 부사절을 이끄는 대표적인 접속사이다.

---

20 _____ is far from being numinous or, even worse, ridiculous.

    (a) What implied here is
    (b) Here is implied what
    (c) What implied here
    (d) What is implied here

여기에 암시된 것은 신비스러운 것과는 거리가 멀며 터무니없기까지 하다.

➲ '암시된 것'으로 해석되므로 의미상 수동의 표현이 필요하다. what은 선행사를 포함하는 관계대명사로, 'the thing that'으로도 바꿔 쓸 수 있다. 가장 적절한 표현은 (d)이다.

numinous 초자연적인, 신비스러운 ridiculous 터무니없는

---

21 (a) A: My car suddenly broke down. What can I do?
    (b) B: Don't worry, just call the insurance company.
    (c) A: But, I have to pick up my mother-in-law at the airport, too.
    (d) B: Why don't you ask me help?

A: 내 차가 갑자기 고장이 났어. 어떡하지?
B: 걱정 마, 일단 보험회사에 전화해봐.
A: 그렇지만 공항에 장모님을 모시러 가야 해.
B: 내가 좀 도와줄까?

➲ (d)의 ask는 목적보어로 to 부정사를 갖는다. 따라서 ask me to help로 바꿔 써야 한다.

mother-in-law 장모

---

22 (a) Music Therapy is a recognized health care profession using music and music activities in treatment programs. (b) It addresses the physical, emotional, social and cognitive challenges faced by children and adults with diverse illnesses and special needs. (c) There are many associations established to insure professional services or providing qualified therapists in the United States. (d) They have broadened the awareness of music therapy within the public policy arena.

음악 요법이란 치료 과정에서 음악이나 음악적인 활동을 사용하는 공인된 건강관리 방법이다. 그것은 다양한 질병이나 특정한 요구에 직면한 어린아이나 성인들의 신체적, 감정적, 사회적 그리고 인지적인 어려움을 말한다. 미국에는 검증된 임상이나 전문적인 서비스를 보장하기 위해 설립된 많은 단체들이 있다. 그들은 공공 정책 분야 안에서 음악 요법의 인식을 넓혀왔다.

➲ (c)에서 insure와 or 뒤에 나오는 providing이 병렬의 관계이고, 전치사 to에 연결되어 있으므로 providing 을 동사 원형인 provide 로 고쳐야 한다.

address 다루다, 처리하다 insure 확신하다, 확실히 하다 broaden 넓히다

23 A She made a big mistake while preparing this project.

B Let's _____ that this time. She just joined the company.

(a) oversee
(b) overcome
(c) overlook
(d) overtake

A: 이 프로젝트를 준비하면서 그녀는 큰 실수를 저질렀어.

B: 이번만 넘어가자. 그녀는 입사한 지 얼마 안됐잖아.

➲ B의 두 번째 문장을 살펴보면 입사한 지 얼마 안되었으므로 실수에 대해 그냥 넘어가자고 하는 내용이 나오는 것이 자연스럽다. 보기는 모두 over로 시작하여 형태가 비슷한 단어들인데 그 중 (c) overlook이 '~을 너그럽게 봐주다, 눈감아주다'의 뜻을 가지고 있다.

oversee 감독하다, 단속하다 overcome 압도하다, 극복하다 overtake 따라잡다, 만회하다

24 A Who did you vote for this time?

B I didn't _____ a vote.

(a) do
(b) make
(c) carry
(d) cast

A: 이번에 누구에게 투표했어?

B: 투표를 하지 않았어.

➲ '투표를 하다'에 해당하는 연어를 알아야 하는 문제이다. 'cast a vote'라고 하면 'cast'가 '던지다'라는 뜻이 있기 때문에 '표를 던지다', 즉 '투표하다'라는 뜻이 된다. 다른 동사들과 a vote를 같이 쓰면 어울리지 않는 어색한 표현이 된다. 참고로 '찬성 투표를 하다'는 'cast a vote for~', '반대 투표를 하다'는 'cast a vote against~'를 쓰면 된다.

cast a vote 투표를 하다

25 A Can you come down a little? It's too expensive.

B Sorry. This product is already _____.

(a) sold out
(b) got off
(c) marked down
(d) dealt with

A: 조금만 깎아주시면 안돼요? 너무 비싸요.

B: 죄송합니다. 이것은 이미 할인이 된 상품이에요.

➲ 물건 가격을 깎아달라는 말에 'Sorry'라고 했으므로 깎아줄 수 없는 이유로 적절한 대답이 나와야 한다. 보기 중 (c)가 '값을 내리다'라는 뜻이 있으므로 이미 할인이 된 상품이라 더 이상 깎아줄 수 없다는 의미가 되어 적절하다.

sell out ~을 다 팔다 get off 차에서 내리다, ~에서 떨어지다 mark down 값을 내리다, 점수를 깎다 deal with ~을 다루다, 처리하다, 해결하다

26 A I'm sorry. These books are overdue.

B There is a late _____ for overdue books.

(a) fee
(b) fare
(c) money
(d) bill

A: 죄송합니다. 이 책이 연체가 되었어요.

B: 연체된 책에 대해서는 연체료가 있습니다.

➲ 책을 연체한 것에 대한 연체료로 적당한 표현은 a late fee이다. fare의 경우 교통수단을 이용할 때 내는 요금에 대해 쓴다.

overdue 늦은, 기한이 지난 fee (의사, 변호사에 대한) 보수, 각종 요금, 납부금 fare (교통 수단 이용의) 요금, 운임 bill 계산서, 지폐

27 A How do you guys know him?

B He was a _____ friend of ours.

(a) related
(b) respective
(c) mutual
(d) coincident

A: 너희는 그를 어떻게 알아?
B: 서로 다 아는 친구야.

🔵 상황으로 보아 여러 명이 '그'를 아는 상태임을 알 수 있다. 이런 의미로는 'mutual'을 쓸 수 있는데 '공통의'라는 뜻이 있어서 'mutual friend'라고 하면 나도, 다른 사람도 각각 서로 알고 있는 친구라는 의미가 된다.

related 관계 있는, 친척인 respective 각각의, 개인의 mutual 상호의, 공통의 coincident 일치하는, 부합하는

---

28 Aside from a degree, you need a teaching _____ to teach students in public schools.

(a) document
(b) certificate
(c) warrant
(d) material

학위 외에도 공립 학교에서 학생들을 가르치기 위해서는 교원 자격증이 필요하다.

🔵 공립 학교에서 학생들을 가르치기 위한 조건으로 적절한 것은 학위와 교원 자격증이다. 자격증에 적합한 어휘는 'certificate'이다.

aside from ~이외에, ~에 덧붙여 degree 학위 certificate 면허증, 자격증 warrant 권한, 인가, 소환장 teaching material 교재

---

29 People are _____ against the high prices of the mobile phone rates but the mobile operators said that it does not have any plan to cut the rates.

(a) railing
(b) blocking
(c) brushing
(d) discriminating

사람들은 높은 휴대폰 사용 요금에 대해 비난하고 있지만 통신사들은 요금 인하 계획이 없다고 말했다.

🔵 'but'으로 두 문장이 연결되어 있으므로 상반된 내용이 되어야 한다. 사람들이 비난을 하고 있으나 요금 인하 계획이 없다고 해야 자연스럽게 연결이 된다. '비난하다'에 해당하는 표현으로는 'rail against'가 있다.

rail against ~에 대해 비난하다 cut rates 요금을 인하하다 brush against ~에 살짝 닿다, 스치다

---

30 The economic situation has been _____ due to sharp rises in oil prices and the won's fluctuating exchange rate.

(a) deviating
(b) deteriorating
(c) deferring
(d) depleting

석유 가격의 급격한 상승과 원화의 동요하는 환율 때문에 경제 상황이 악화되고 있다.

🔵 'due to' 이하의 내용을 살펴보면 석유 가격이 오르고 환율이 동요한다는 내용이므로 경제 상황이 안 좋다는 것을 알 수 있다. 'deteriorate'는 '~을 악화시키다, 저하시키다'라는 뜻이 있으므로 정답으로 적절하다.

due to ~때문에 fluctuating 변동이 있는, 동요하는 exchange rate 환율 deviate (진로, 방향 등이) 빗나가다, 벗어나다 deteriorate 악화시키다, 저하시키다 defer 연기하다, 미루다 deplete 고갈시키다, 소모하다

31 The talks were held for discussions of measures to relieve tensions between the two nations and to promote _____ trade.

(a) fair
(b) illicit
(c) domestic
(d) bilateral

그 회담들은 두 나라 사이의 긴장을 완화하고 양자간 무역을 증진시키기 위한 방법을 토의하기 위해 열렸다.

○ 두 나라 사이의 관계에 대해 이야기하고 있다. 따라서 두 나라 간의 무역을 증진시킨다는 이야기가 나오는 것이 문맥상 적절하므로 정답은 'bilateral' 이 된다. 'fair trade' 는 공정 무역을 말하지만 이를 뒷받침할 만한 근거가 지문상에 나와 있지 않으므로 이것보다는 'bilateral' 이 정답으로 더 적절하다고 할 수 있다.

relieve 완화시키다, 덜다 tension 긴장 illicit 위법의, 불법의 domestic 국내의, 가사의 bilateral 양자간의, 양국간의

---

32 _____ diseases such as arthritis gradually get worse as time passes and cannot be stopped.

(a) Tropical
(b) Degenerative
(c) Contagious
(d) Hereditary

관절염과 같은 퇴행성 질병은 시간이 지나면서 더 악화되고 진행이 멈추지 않는다.

○ 관절염을 예로 들면서 이 질병의 특징을 뒤에 나열하고 있다. 시간이 지나면서 악화되고 진행이 멈추지 않는다는 점으로 미루어보아 '퇴행성 질환' 을 이야기하는 것임을 알 수 있다. 따라서 정답은 (b) degenerative가 된다.

arthritis 관절염 tropical 열대의, 열대성 degenerative 퇴행성의 contagious 전염성의 hereditary 유전성의

READING COMPREHENSION • P.168

33 Architecture is a major factors influencing the buildings and is involved in shaping the environment. As a three dimensional genre of art, architecture is awakening our sense of meaning in relation to our surroundings. The way architecture is perceived is similar the way sculptures, another three dimensional genre of art, are perceived. The buildings we may encounter everyday make different imaginations and visualizations according to the angle of our view. In other words, a building can be observed differently as we watch the building in different places and heights. Since the building is, at most cases, located outdoors, it can be seen differently _____.

(a) as the statue is corroded
(b) as our way of seeing differs
(c) as the weather and the season changes
(d) as the color and material varies

건축물은 건물에 영향을 미치고 환경을 구체화하는 주요 요소이다. 예술의 3차원적인 장르로서 건축물은 우리를 둘러싸고 있는 환경에 연관된 의미에 대한 우리의 감각을 일깨운다. 건축물이 인식되는 방식은 예술의 또 다른 3차원적 장르인 조각상이 인식되는 방식과 유사하다. 우리가 매일 마주치는 건물들은 우리 시각의 견지에 따라 다른 감상과 심상을 만들어 낸다. 다른 말로 하자면, 우리가 한 건물을 다른 장소와 높이에서 바라볼 때 그 건물은 다르게 보여질 수 있는 것이다. 대부분의 경우 그 건물은 야외에 위치해 있기 때문에 기후와 계절이 바뀜에 따라 다르게 보일 수도 있다.

○ 건축물과 조각상은 예술의 3차원적 장르라는 점에서 같으며, 둘 다 보는 위치와 각도에 따라 달리 보인다는 내용의 문단이다. 빈칸 바로 앞에 나오는, 건물들이 대부분의 경우 야외에 위치해 있다는 언급에 주의해서 보아야 한다. 야외라서 다르게 보일 수 있는 요소들을 찾아보면 기후와 계절의 변화가 가장 적절하다.

architecture 건축물, 건축(술) shape 형성하다, 구체화하다 모양, 형상 dimensional 차원의 surrounding 주변, 처지, 환경 주변의 angle 각도, 국면, 양상, 견지 imagination 상상, 감상 visualization 심상, 시각화, 구상화

34 The Curse of the Billy Goat refers to a superstition commonly used to explain the World Series drought that the Chicago Cubs Major League Baseball team has been suffering from since their last appearance in the 1945 World Series. It is supposed that the Billy Goat Curse was placed on the Cubs in 1945 when a tavern owner named Billy Sianis and his pet goat were ejected from Wrigley Field because of the goat's objectionable odor. The enraged man yelled that there would never again be a World Series game played at Wrigley Field as he was being led out and since that day this urban legend has been _____ of the Chicago Cubs.

(a) a rationale of the failure
(b) an evidence that a team has few chances to win
(c) a scapegoat for the losing streak
(d) a historical background recorded in the League

염소의 저주란 시카고 커브스 메이저리그 야구팀이 1945년 월드 시리즈 이후로 월드 시리즈에서 우승하지 못하고 있는 것을 설명할 때 흔히 사용되는 미신을 말한다. 추정되기로는 커브스에 저주가 내려진 것은 1945년 Billy Sianis라는 이름의 선술집 주인과 그의 염소가 염소의 역한 냄새 때문에 Wrigley 구장에서 쫓겨났을 때라고 한다. 분노한 남자가 구장에서 쫓겨나면서 Wrigley 구장에서는 다시는 월드시리즈가 열리지 않으리라 외쳤고, 그날 이후 이 도시의 전설은 시카고 커브스 팀의 연패에 대한 희생양이 되어 왔다.

❍ 염소의 저주가 계속되는 시카고 커브스 팀의 연패에 대한 일종의 책임전가라고 볼 수 있으므로 정답은 (c)이다. 이것은 일종의 미신이므로 실패에 대한 이론적 설명이라고 볼 수 없기 때문에 (a)는 답이 될 수 없다. 역사적 사실이 아닌 구전을 통해 전해오는 허구에 가까운 이야기이므로 (d)도 답으로 적절하지 않다.

curse 저주, 악담 superstition 미신 drought 부족, 결핍, 가뭄 tavern 선술집 eject 쫓아내다, 추방하다, 퇴장시키다 objectionable 불쾌한, 못마땅한, 반대할만한 odor 냄새, 향기, 향내 enraged 격노한, 분노한 yell 큰 소리로 외치다 rationale 근본적 이유, 이론적 설명 scapegoat 속죄양, 희생양, 희생물 streak 연속

35 The Great Wall, as one of the world's architectural wonders and cultural symbol, attracts many visitors from all over the world every year. Despite its historic value, the China Great Wall Academy reports that less than 30 percent of the Wall remains in good condition due to _____. Since it was exposed to wind, rain, snow and other natural calamities for thousands of years, many sections of the Wall have been havocked. It also suffers from human sabotage. There are some tourists who deface the bricks from the Great Wall and even move them. People foolishly take bricks, earth and stones from the wall to construct roads, reservoirs, and houses.

(a) various environmental reasons
(b) the forces of nature and human's destruction
(c) the deliberate damages by the hand of mankind
(d) serious natural disasters and people's indifference

만리장성은 세계의 경이로운 건축물이자 문화유산 중 하나로서 매년 전 세계로부터 많은 관광객들을 끌어들이고 있다. 만리장성의 역사적 가치에도 불구하고, 자연의 힘과 인간의 파괴 때문에 만리장성의 30%도 안 되는 부분만 상태가 양호하다고 중국 만리장성 협회는 전한다. 만리장성은 바람과 비, 눈과 다른 자연재해에 수천 년 동안 노출되었기 때문에 많은 부분이 파괴되었다. 또한 인간의 파괴 때문에도 고통받고 있다. 어떤 여행객들은 벽돌의 외관을 손상시키고 벽돌을 옮겨 놓기도 한다. 사람들은 우습게도 도로와 저수지, 집을 건축하기 위해서 만리장성의 벽돌과 흙, 돌들을 떼어가기도 한다.

❍ 만리장성이 무엇 때문에 파괴되었는지를 설명하는 글이다. 하나는 자연재해 때문이고 다른 하나는 인간의 파괴 때문이므로 정답은 두 가지를 모두 포함하고 있는 (b)가 된다. (d)번의 경우 심각한 자연재해는 맞지만 인간의 무관심보다는 인간의 파괴가 내용에 더 적합하므로 정답에서 제외된다.

architectural 건축의, 건축(학)상의 heritage 유산 historic 역사상 중요한 due to ~때문에 expose 드러내다, 노출시키다 calamity 재해, 재난, 재앙 havoc 파괴하다, 엉망으로 만들다 sabotage 파괴, 방해 deface 표면을 더럽히다, 외관을 손상하다 ridiculously 우습게 reservoir 저수지 deliberate 고의의, 계획적인 disaster 재해, 재앙

36 Europeans embrace the purity of Canadian Inuit artists who subscribe to an eclectic inspiration that is based on their traditional hunting and fishing practices as well as legends and mythologies to explain their relationship with their environment. Unlike Alaska and Greenland where white man has been presented for a few hundred to one thousand years, white man's decorative art has never had a chance to take foothold in the isolated Canadian Arctic. A former documentary film maker, Raymond Brousseau points out, "You cannot commission a piece from a Canadian Inuit artist. Instead, you have to wait and see what the artist has created."

Q What is the best title for the passage?

(a) Pristine Inuit art
(b) Preservation of Inuit art
(c) An Inuit art lover's passion
(d) Noncommercial Inuit artists

유럽인들은 환경과의 관계를 설명해주는 전설이나 신화뿐만 아니라 전통적인 사냥이나 물고기를 잡는 관습에 기초한 영감을 나누어주는 캐나다 이뉴잇족 예술가들의 순수함을 깊이 받아들이고 있다. 수백년에서 천년 동안 백인들에게 알려져온 알래스카나 그린랜드와는 달리, 이 동떨어진 캐나다 북극해는 백인의 장식예술의 영향이 전혀 미치지 않았다. 전직 다큐멘터리 영화 제작자 Raymond Brousseau는 다음과 같이 말한다 "캐나다 이뉴잇족 예술가에게는 돈을 주고 작품 제작을 의뢰할 수 없다. 대신 당신은 그저 예술가가 만들어 내는 것을 기다려서 봐야 한다."

◑ 이뉴잇족 예술의 때묻지 않은 순수함이 주된 내용이므로 정답은 (a)이다. 이뉴잇족 예술의 보호에 대해서는 언급된 바 없으므로 (b)는 답이 될 수 없고, 이뉴잇족 예술 애호가의 열정에 대해서 설명한 것이 아니라 그의 견해가 피력된 것이므로 (c)도 답이 아니며, (d) 상업적이 아닌 예술가는 주제의 일부분이므로 제목으로 부적절하다.

embrace (사상 따위를) 받아들이다, 껴안다, 포옹하다 Inuit 이뉴잇족(캐나다·그린랜드의 에스키모) subscribe to 기부 약속을 하다, 기부를 하다, 출자하다 eclectic (여러 재료·학설 따위에서) 취사선택하여 만들어진, 절충적인 decorative 장식이 되는, 장식용의, 장식예술 (decorative art) foothold 확고한 지위, 거점 commission (일 따위를) 위탁하다, 의뢰하다, 주문하다 pristine 때묻지 않은, 순박한

---

37 Naturalization is the process by which a citizen of a foreign country or nation is bestowed U.S. Citizenship, fulfilling the requirements established by Congress. First, naturalization applicants must be legal permanent residents, who will be asked to produce their green card as proof of their status. They must demonstrate the knowledge of the fundamentals of U.S. history and the principles of the U.S. Constitution as well as the ability to speak, read, write and understand words used in everyday life. They also must be of "good moral character," that is, they are permanently prohibited from naturalization if they have been convinced of murder or an aggravated felony.

Q What is the passage mainly about?

(a) The requirements for being applicants
(b) The process of U.S. Citizenship application
(c) The U.S. Citizenship information and application guide
(d) The general requirements for administrative naturalization

귀화는 외국인이 국회가 정한 필요조건을 이행한 후 미국 시민권을 얻게 되는 과정이다. 먼저 귀화 신청자들은 합법적으로 영구히 거주할 수 있는 사람이어야 하므로 그들의 신분을 증명하기 위해서 영주권을 제시해야 한다. 그들은 일상생활에서 사용되는 단어들을 말하고, 읽고, 쓰고, 이해하는 능력뿐만 아니라 미국 역사에 대한 기초지식과 미국 헌법의 원리에 대한 지식도 증명해야 한다. 그들은 또한 "도덕성 기준"에 적합해야 하는데, 이것은 그들이 살인이나 중 범죄를 범한 경우 영원히 귀화가 금지된다.

◑ 이 글은 귀화에 필요한 조건이 설명되어 있으므로 정답은 (d)가 된다. 귀화는 미국 시민권을 얻는 여러 가지 방법 중 하나이기 때문에 (a)는 포괄적이고, (c)또한 시민권에 대한 정보라든가 안내라는 말이 너무 포괄적이어서 정답이 아니다. (b)는 본문에 미국 시민권 지원을 위한 과정은 소개되어 있지 않아서 정답이 될 수 없다.

naturalization 귀화 bestow 수여하다, 증여하다 requirement 필요조건, 자격 Congress (미) 국회 applicant 지원자, 신청자 resident 거주자, 거류민 produce 〈증거 따위〉를 제시(제출)하다 green card (미 연방 정부가 외국인에게 발행하는) 영주권 status 지위, 신분 demonstrate ~을 논증하다, 증명하다 fundamental 기본(원칙), 기초, 바탕 principle 원리, 법칙 주의, 방침 constitution 헌법, 법령 commit 〈죄, 과실 등〉을 범하다, 저지르다 aggravated 〈부담, 죄 따위〉를 한층 무겁게 하다 felony (법률) 중죄 administrative 행정(통치)상의, 관리상의, 경영상의

38 It is well known that the distribution of world population is uneven. Areas of high population density tend to comprise a large land area and a moderate climate. Africa is the second largest continent in the world and has around one-eighth of the total population of the world, thus its population distribution is fairly low. Desert areas such as Sahara, Kalahari, and Namib are nearly inhabitable. Other semi-arid land, mountains and dense rain forests also is meagerly inhabited. Most of the densely populated areas are located around the lakes or in the river basins, and along the coasts. In those areas, water is supplied, soil is fertile and farming is possible.

Q What is the topic of the passage?

(a) The distribution of world's population
(b) The natural environment of the Africa
(c) The population distribution of Africa
(d) The densely populated areas of the world

세계 인구의 분포가 불균등하다는 것은 잘 알려져 있다. 높은 인구 밀도를 가진 지역은 넓은 대지라든가 온화한 기후를 포함하는 것이 보통이다. 아프리카는 세계에서 두 번째로 큰 대륙인데 세계 인구의 8분의 1만이 살고 있어서 인구 밀도가 상당히 낮다. 사하라나 칼라하리, 나미브와 같은 사막 지역은 거의 사람이 살 수 없다. 다른 반건조 지대와 산맥, 우림 지역 또한 거의 사람이 살 수 없다. 가장 인구가 밀집된 지역들은 호수 주위라든가 하천 바닥, 그리고 해안지역을 따라 위치해 있다. 이들 지역에서는 물이 공급되고 토양이 비옥하며 농경이 가능하다.

○ 세계 인구의 분포와 아프리카의 자연환경에 대해서 부분적으로 다루고 있기는 하지만 그것이 문단 전체의 주제는 될 수 없으므로 (a) 와 (b)는 답이 될 수 없다. 문단 전체를 아우르는 주제는 아프리카의 인구 분포이므로 (c)가 답이다. (d)에 나오는 세계 인구 밀집 지역은 언급되지 않았다.

distribution 분포, 분배, 배포, 배달 density 밀도, 농도, 조밀함 comprise 포함하다. 이루어지다, 구성되다 inhabitable 사람이 살 수 없는 semi-arid 반건조의, 비가 오지 않는 fertile 비옥한, 생산이 가능한

39 Abortion rights advocates often assert "a woman's right to choose" in her life. They believe that it is a woman's right to decide to terminate her pregnancy. However, who can say that a woman has a right to choose murder? If a fetus were a human being, it goes without saying that the woman would be a murderer. Even though the status of an embryo in the first trimester has been argued to determine whether the embryo is a person or not, to our surprise, the answer is very simple. The fact that the embryo is a potential human and we call it "an unborn child" already proves that the embryo is a precious creature. Women can't easily choose abortion if they realize that their future lovely child is breathing in their womb.

낙태 권리를 옹호하는 사람들은 종종 인생에 있어서 "여성의 선택할 권리"를 주장한다. 그들은 여성에게 임신을 끝낼지 결정할 권리가 있다고 생각한다. 그러나 누가 여성에게 살인을 선택할 권리가 있다고 말할 수 있겠는가? 태아가 인간이라면, 그 여자는 살인자가 된다는 것은 말할 필요도 없다. 지금까지 처음 3개월 안의 태아가 인간인지 아닌지를 결정하기 위한 논의가 있어 왔음에도 불구하고, 답은 놀랍게도 간단하다. 태아가 잠정적인 인간이고 우리가 그것을 "아직 태어나지 않은 아이"라고 부른다는 사실은 태아가 하나의 소중한 생명체임을 증명하는 것이다. 여자들이 미래의 사랑스러운 아이가 그들의 자궁 속에서 숨을 쉬고 있다는 것을 깨닫는다면 쉽게 낙태를 선택하지는 못할 것이다.

○ 태아도 인간이라는 태아에 대한 견해를 피력함으로써 낙태를 반대하는 내용의 글이다. 따라서 (c)처럼 낙태 반대 운동가들에 의해서 태아의 상태가 재고되어야 한다는 것은 이 글의 요지가 아니며, (a)처럼 낙태가 어떤 경우에든 합법화되어야 한다는 것도 본문의 내용과 상반된다. (b)는 낙태를 반대하는 입장이긴 하지만 이 글에서는 낙태를 어떤 경우에도 금지해야 한다고 주장하고 있지는 않기 때문에 정답이 아니다.

Q What is the main idea of the passage?

(a) Abortion should be legalized in some cases.

(b) Abortion should be strongly prohibited in all circumstances.

(c) An embryo should be reconsidered by anti-abortion activists.

(d) Women should not have an abortion in that an embryo is a person.

abortion 낙태, 유산 advocate 옹호자, 지지자, 주창자 assert 단언하다, 주장하다 terminate 끝내다, 종결시키다, 마치다 pregnancy 임신 fetus 태아 it goes without saying that~ ~은 말할 나위도 없다 status 지위, 신분 embryo 태아(보통 임신 8주까지) trimester 3개월(간) to one's surprise 놀랍게도 potential 가능성을 가진, 잠재력이 있는 unborn 태내에 있는, 미래의 precious 소중한, 귀중한 creature 피조물, 생물 breathe 숨을 쉬다 womb 자궁 legalize 합법화하다 reconsider 재고하다 activist 행동주의자, 활동가 in that ~라는 점에서

---

40 In literary criticism, "stream of consciousness" is a method for representing the continuous flow of a fictional character's innumerable thoughts, impressions, and feelings. (a) First used in psychology but later transferred to literature, it was developed by some writers such as Dorothy Richardson, James Joyce. (b) The most important stylistic forms are "narrated stream of consciousness" and "interior monologue", often incorrectly used as a synonym for stream of consciousness writing. (c) The stream of consciousness is related to the theme itself but the interior monologue refers to the technique for presenting it. (d) The interior monologue presents the character's thoughts or silent speeches directly, while the stream of consciousness technique mixes them with his or her impressions and perceptions, sometimes defying the linguistic norms.

문학 비평에서 "의식의 흐름"은 소설의 인물에게서 끊임없이 일어나는 수많은 생각과 기분, 느낌들을 표현하는 하나의 방법이다. (a) 그것은 처음에 심리학에서 사용되다가 나중에 문학으로 옮겨온 후에, Dorothy Richardson과 James Joyce와 같은 작가들에 의해서 발전되었다. (b) 가장 중요한 문체상의 형식으로 "서사적인 의식의 흐름"과 "내적 독백"이 있는데, 의식의 흐름 기법과 종종 동의어로 잘못 사용된다. (c) 의식의 흐름은 주제 자체와 관련이 있지만 내적 독백은 그 주제를 진술하는 방법과 관계가 있다. (d) 내적 독백은 인물의 생각이나 속말을 직접적으로 표현하는 반면, 의식의 흐름은 때때로 언어 규범을 무시하면서 인물들의 생각을 느낌이나 지각과 섞어서 표현한다.

◎ 의식의 흐름의 두 가지 형식인 서사적인 의식의 흐름과 내적독백이 무엇인지 설명하고, 이 두 가지를 (b), (c), (d)에서 서로 비교하고 있다. 그러나 (a)는 의식의 흐름 기법에 있어서 초기 사용과 발전시킨 작가들에 관한 내용이므로 글의 흐름과 어울리지 않는다.

literary 문학(상)의 (literature 문학) criticism 비평 stream of consciousness 의식의 흐름 represent 나타내다, 의미하다 continuous 연속의, 계속적인 fictional 소설의, 허구의 innumerable 무수한, 헤아릴 수 없는 psychology 심리학 transfer 옮기다, 이동시키다, 건네다 stylistic 문체(상)의, 어법(상)의 interior monologue 내적 독백 synonym 동의어, 유의어 be related to ~와 관련이 있다. theme 주제 refer to ~와 관계가 있다, 관련되다 적용하다 perception 지각(력); 인식(력) defy 무시하다, 거부하다, 저지하다 linguistic 언어의, 언어학의 norm 규범, 표준, 기준

Actual Test

1 W I've just found that he called me names.

M _____

(a) Don't make trouble for yourself.
(b) Let me sleep on it.
(c) Don't take it too hard.
(d) Let's call it a day.

W: 방금 그가 내 욕을 한다는 것을 알았어.
M: 너무 심각하게 받아들이지 마.

➡ 누가 자신의 욕을 한다고 하는 말에 적절한 응답으로 보기 가운데 가장 적절한 것은 너무 심각하게 받아들이지 마라는 (c)가 된다. (d) 의 경우 하루 일과를 끝내면서 할 수 있는 표현이다.

call a person names ~의 욕을 하다 Don't make trouble for yourself. 사서 고생하지 마세요. Let me sleep on it. 생각할 시간을 좀 주세요. call it a day 하루 일을 끝내다, 마감하다

2 M I'm really nervous. This is my turn. Oh, come on!

W _____

(a) Break a leg!
(b) Let's flip for it.
(c) Chances are good.
(d) It serves you right.

M: 정말 떨린다. 이번이 내 차례야. 어떻게 해!
W: 힘 내!

➡ 발표 등을 앞두고 긴장한 사람에게 할 수 있는 표현으로 적절한 것을 골라야 한다. 격려를 해주는 표현인 (a)가 가장 적절하다. (c)는 가능성이 높다는 뜻으로 문맥에 어울리지 않는다.

Let's flip for it. 동전을 던져서 결정하자. It serves you right. 당해도 싸다. 꼴 좋다

3 W It's very kind of you to help me.

M _____

(a) You deserve it.
(b) That'll do.
(c) I've got to hand this to you.
(d) Think nothing of it.

W: 저를 도와주시다니 정말 친절하시네요.
M: 천만에요.

➡ 도움에 대한 감사 내지는 칭찬에 대해 할 수 있는 표현으로 적절한 것을 골라야 한다. (d)는 감사 표현에 대해 할 수 있는 말로 '별 것 아니다. 아무것도 아닌데 크게 생각하지 말아라.' 의 뜻이다. (a)는 좋은 일에 대해서는 '그럴 만한 자격이 있다' 라는 뜻이고, 그 반대의 상황에서는 '그래도 싸다, 쌤통이다' 와 같은 뜻이다. (b)는 주문을 하거나 물건을 살 때 '그 정도면 됐다.' 라는 뜻으로 쓰인다. (c)에서 'hand' 는 동사로 쓰여 '건네주다' 의 의미이다.

deserve ~할 가치가 있다. 권리가 있다.

4
W Are you being served?
M No. May I see the menu?
W Here you are. What would you like?
M _____

(a) I'd like another serving.
(b) No, thank you. I'm full.
(c) Can we order a little later?
(d) I'd appreciate it.

W: 주문을 담당하는 분이 계신가요?
M: 아니오. 메뉴 좀 보여주실래요?
W: 여기 있습니다. 무엇을 드시겠어요?
M: 조금 있다가 주문해도 될까요?

○ 식당에서 벌어지고 있는 상황이다. 남자가 손님이고 여자가 웨이트리스인데 여자의 마지막 대사를 보면 주문을 받고 있는 중임을 알 수 있다. 이에 적합한 반응으로는 주문할 음식을 말하거나 나중에 주문하겠다는 표현이 올 수 있다. 따라서 정답은 (c)가 된다. (a)는 식사를 한 후에 한 그릇 더 먹고 싶을 때 할 수 있는 표현이며, (b)는 음식을 더 권했을 때, 거절하는 표현이다.

serving 음식 한 그릇, 음료 한 잔 **be full** 배가 부르다 **appreciate** ~을 감사하다

5
W What time is it?
M It's 11:30.
W Oh my god. The last bus has just gone.
M _____

(a) The next round is on me.
(b) The watch doesn't tell the time.
(c) Sorry, but I can't go.
(d) I'm afraid you'd better call a cab.

W: 몇 시지?
M: 11시 30분이야.
W: 어머나. 막차가 방금 갔어.
M: 택시를 부르는 게 좋을 것 같아.

○ 여자가 시간을 묻는 이유는 막차가 지나갔는지 확인하기 위해서이다. 여자의 마지막 대사에서 막차 시간이 지났음을 알 수 있고, 여자의 말에 적절한 남자의 답으로는 택시를 부르는 게 좋겠다는 (d)가 된다. (a)는 술자리에서 2차는 자기가 산다고 할 때 쓸 수 있는 표현이다. (b)는 시계가 가지 않는다는 뜻이고 (c)는 초대와 같은 제안에 갈 수 없다며 거절하는 표현이다.

call a cab 택시를 부르다

6
W Don't forget dinner tonight.
M Can I take a rain check on that?
W Again?
M _____

(a) I'm out of cash.
(b) I'll make it up to you.
(c) Let's eat out tonight.
(d) I seem to be lost.

W: 오늘 저녁 약속 잊지 마.
M: 다음 번으로 미루면 안될까?
W: 또?
M: 다음에 보상할게.

○ 저녁 약속을 또 미루려는 남자가 할 수 있는 말로는 다음에 보상해주겠다는 내용의 (b)이다. (a)는 현금이 떨어졌다는 이야기고, (c)는 외식을 하자는 뜻으로 대화와 반대되는 상황이며 (d)는 길을 잃은 것 같다는 뜻이다.

take a rain check 다음으로 미루다 **out of cash** 현금이 없는 **make up** ~을 보상하다 **eat out** 외식하다

7

M What did you have in mind?

W I'd like to try something different, but I'm not sure what would be good.

M How about having a perm? Or you can just get your hair dyed. I think it would look good on you.

W Do you really think so?

M Yes. I'll show you some pictures of different styles.

W That sounds good.

M Anything you like?

W I like this style.

Q Where is the conversation most likely to occur?

(a) At the photo studio
(b) At the hair salon
(c) At the gym
(d) At the clothing shop

M: 뭐 생각하고 계신 것이라도 있으세요?

W: 뭔가 다른 것을 하고 싶은데요, 무엇이 좋을지 모르겠어요.

M: 퍼머를 해보는 것은 어때요? 아니면 그냥 염색을 해보시는 것도 좋고요. 잘 어울리실 것 같아요.

W: 정말 그렇게 생각하세요?

M: 네. 스타일 사진 몇 장 보여드릴게요.

W: 좋아요.

M: 뭐 마음에 드는 스타일 있어요?

W: 이 스타일이 마음에 들어요.

💬 대화가 일어나는 장소에 대해 묻고 있다. 남자의 두 번째 대사에서 확실히 파악할 수 있다. 퍼머, 염색 등이 언급되었고 잘 어울릴 것 같다고 하는 것으로 보아 미용실에서 일어나는 대화임을 알 수 있으므로 정답은 (b)가 된다. 중간에 사진을 보여준다고 한 것은 헤어 스타일을 볼 수 있는 사진이므로 이것만으로 (a)를 고르지 않도록 주의하자.

8

M Wow, you look so thin! Have you lost weight?

W Yes. I'm on a diet.

M If so, I think it really works. What's your secret?

W I eat fruits and vegetables. I don't eat much red meat.

M I want to lose some weight, but I can't cut out meat and sweets.

W I think you must cut down on your drinking and smoking first.

M I'd rather die first.

Q What are the man and woman talking about?

(a) Healthy eating habits
(b) Cutting out junk foods
(c) Getting in shape
(d) The danger of alcohol and smoking

M: 너 너무 말라 보인다! 살 뺐어?

W: 응, 다이어트 중이야.

M: 그렇다면 정말 효과가 있는 것 같아. 비결이 뭐야?

W: 과일과 야채를 먹어. 붉은 육류는 먹지 않고.

M: 나도 살을 좀 빼고 싶은데 고기랑 단것을 끊을 수가 없어.

W: 내 생각에 술과 담배를 먼저 끊어야 할 것 같아.

M: 먼저 죽는 편이 낫겠다.

💬 대화 주제에 대해 묻고 있다. 여자가 다이어트에 성공한 것을 보고 남자가 그 비밀을 묻고 있다. 따라서 그들은 몸매 유지에 대해 이야기하고 있음을 알 수 있다. 따라서 정답은 (c)가 된다. (a)나 (b)는 다이어트에 성공하기 위한 한 방법에 대한 것이므로 정답이 될 수 없다.

be on a diet 다이어트 중이다 cut out ~을 절제하다, 끊다
cut down on ~을 삼가다, 절제하다

9

W Is this everything for you today?

M Yes. What's the total?

W Your total comes to 12 dollars. Will it be cash or charge?

M Charge. Here you are.

W Okay. Sorry, your card isn't going through. I'll try once again.

M Is there a problem with my card?

W No, it's going through fine this time. Please sign it here.

M Okay.

Q What is the woman's occupation?

(a) Housekeeper

(b) Bank clerk

(c) Hotel staff

(d) Cashier

W: 오늘 사실 것은 이게 다에요?

M: 네, 전부 얼마죠?

W: 전부 12달러입니다. 현금으로 하시겠어요, 카드로 하시겠어요?

M: 카드요. 여기 있습니다.

W: 네. 죄송합니다. 카드가 읽히지 않네요. 다시 한 번 해 볼게요.

M: 제 카드에 문제가 있나요?

W: 아니요. 이번엔 잘 되네요. 여기 사인해주세요.

M: 네.

🔵 여자의 직업에 대해 묻고 있다. 마트나 상점에서 계산을 하는 과정에서 일어날 수 있는 상황이다. 여자가 물건 가격이 총 12달러라고 했고, 남자에게 결제 수단을 물어보았던 점 등으로 미루어보아 여자의 직업은 계산원임을 알 수 있다. 따라서 정답은 (d)이다.

go through ~을 빠져나가다, 통과하다 occupation 직업
cashier 계산원

---

10 Industrialization and development of technology have been affecting marriage ceremonies and rituals around the world. However, remnants of traditional customs still exist in many weddings. In Mexico, the bride and groom exchange wedding rings which the priest blesses, and the groom gives coins to the bride during ceremony. These coins are a symbol of the husband's dedication to his new family. During the ceremony the bride and groom are loosely wrapped with a rope rosary. This symbolizes the couple are bound by love.

Q What is the best title for the talk?

(a) The change of marriage institution

(b) The wedding traditions in Mexico

(c) Convergence of catholic and traditional rites.

(d) Importance of coins in weddings in Mexico

산업화와 기술의 발전은 전 세계의 결혼 예식과 의식에 영향을 주었습니다. 그러나 전통 관습의 자취들이 여전히 많은 결혼예식에 남아 있습니다. 멕시코에서는 신랑과 신부는 사제가 축복하는 결혼 반지를 교환하며 신랑은 예식 중에 신부에게 동전을 줍니다. 이 동전들은 새로운 가족에 대한 남편의 헌신의 상징입니다. 예식 동안 신랑과 신부는 줄로 된 묵주로 느슨하게 묶여집니다. 이것은 부부가 사랑으로 묶여졌음을 상징합니다.

🔵 강연의 제목으로 가장 적합한 것을 묻고 있다. 멕시코의 결혼식에서 볼 수 있는 장면들을 설명하고 있으므로 정답은 (b)가 된다. 신랑과 신부가 동전을 교환한다는 언급은 있었지만 그것이 중점적인 내용이라고는 할 수 없으므로 (d)는 정답이 될 수 없다.

industrialization 산업화 ritual 의식, 예식 remnant 나머지, 잔여, 옛모습, 자취 dedication 봉헌, 헌신 rosary 묵주, 염주
institution 제도, 관례 convergence 집중, 수렴

11 Attention, please. We hope all beach-goers follow the rules for your safety. Children under 10 must be accompanied by an adult. And those who can't swim please make sure that you are putting on a life vest. Even if you can't swim, you have many activities to enjoy with relative safety. Until you become an accomplished swimmer, never go into the sea alone and go beyond the safe swimming zone. Thank you in advance for your cooperation.

Q What is the speaker mainly talking about?

(a) A water safety certificate
(b) Safety regulations in the beach
(c) Water activities for those who can't swim
(d) Annual swimming competition

주목해주시기 바랍니다. 해변으로 가시는 모든 분들께서는 안전을 위한 수칙들을 지켜주시기 바랍니다. 10세 미만의 아이들은 성인을 동반하여야 합니다. 그리고 수영을 못하시는 분들은 구명조끼를 꼭 착용해 주십시오. 수영을 못하더라도 적절히 안전하게 즐길 수 있는 활동들이 많이 있습니다. 수영 실력이 능숙해질 때까지 바다에 혼자 들어가지 마시고, 안전선을 넘어가지 마십시오. 협조해주셔서 감사합니다.

● 주요 내용에 대해 묻고 있다. 해변에 가는 사람들에게 안전을 위해 주의 사항을 알려주고 있으므로 정답은 (b)가 된다. (a), (d)에 대한 내용은 언급이 없었으며 (c)은 잠깐 언급한 내용으로 중심 내용이라고 보기 어렵다. 따라서 (c) 역시 정답이라고 할 수 없다.

accompany ~와 동반하다, 따라가다 life vest 구명조끼 accomplished 뛰어난, 소양이 있는 cooperation 협조

---

12 Let's suppose you got a car. Now what? Well, you might think just fill up the gas tank and go, right? Not exactly. You missed something big. You must buy car insurance. This is most important thing in having a car. If you drive a car without car insurance, it's against the law. And without insurance, just a fender bender could cost you an arm and a leg. Insurance protects you when you have a problem with your car. In the case of an accident, you are covered by insurance.

Q What is the main focus of the talk?

(a) How to avoid a fender bender
(b) How to save money on car repair costs
(c) Why you need car insurance
(d) How to choose the appropriate car insurance

당신이 차를 샀다고 가정해 봅시다. 이제 무엇을 하시겠어요? 자, 당신은 아마 기름을 가득 채우고 달려보자고 생각할지도 모릅니다. 그렇죠? 꼭 그렇지는 않습니다. 무엇인가 큰 것을 빠뜨렸습니다. 자동차 보험에 꼭 가입해야 합니다. 차를 소유하는 데 있어서 이것이 가장 중요한 점입니다. 보험 없이 차를 운전한다면 법에 위배됩니다. 보험 없이 단지 접촉사고를 내더라도 큰 비용이 들어갈 수도 있습니다. 차로 인해 문제가 생겼을 때 보험이 당신을 보호해줍니다. 사고가 난 경우에 보험으로 보호받게 되는 것입니다.

● 중점적으로 다루는 내용을 묻고 있다. 중심 내용은 자동차 보험이 어떠한 점에서 이로운가, 왜 필요한가에 대한 것이다. 따라서 정답은 (c)가 된다. (a)는 fender bender를 반복하여 정답으로 착각하기 쉽지만 보험이 없으면 접촉사고라도 돈이 많이 들 수 있다고 함으로써 보험의 필요성을 강조하는 한 예를 든 것이므로 요점이라고는 할 수 없다.

fill the gas up 기름을 가득 채우다 insurance 보험 fender bender 가벼운 접촉사고 cost an arm and a leg 큰 돈이 들다

13 A Don't forget to check the switch after using the drier.
  B OK, I will make sure _____.

  (a) to turn off
  (b) to turn off it
  (c) to turn it off
  (d) turn it off

A: 드라이기 쓰고 나서 스위치 확인하는 것 잊지 마.
B: 알겠어. 꼭 끌게.

⊃ make sure 는 to와 함께 쓰여 '반드시 ~하다' 의 의미를 가진다. 그리고 2어동사의 목적어로 대명사가 쓰일 때는 대명사가 2어동사 가운데 와야 한다.

make sure to do 반드시~하다.

---

14 A Have you ever thought about the earth in the 22nd century?
  B I think the world will _____ robots.

  (a) be controlling by
  (b) be controlled by
  (c) control
  (d) controlling

A: 22세기의 지구에 대해서 생각해본 적 있어?
B: 나는 세계가 로봇에 의해서 조정될 것이라고 생각해.

⊃ '로봇에 의해서 조정되다' 라는 의미로 수동태가 필요하므로 be p.p 형태인 (b)가 정답이다.

---

15 A When did the last train leave?
  B I don't know. When I arrived, it _____.

  (a) already left
  (b) already had left.
  (c) have already left.
  (d) had already left.

A: 마지막 기차가 언제 떠났어?
B: 모르겠어. 내가 도착했을 때, 그건 벌써 떠났어.

⊃ B가 도착했던 것보다 더 먼저 일어난 일이므로 과거완료인 had p.p 형태를 써야 한다. already의 위치는 조동사 뒤, 일반동사 앞이 적절하다.

leave 떠나다 **arrive** 도착하다

---

16 A May I use the lavatory now?
  B No, sir. It's dangerous to use it _____.

  (a) during a turbulence
  (b) during turbulence
  (c) while turbulence
  (d) being turbulence

A: 화장실(세면실) 좀 지금 사용해도 될까요?
B: 안됩니다. 손님. 지금 난기류 상황이기 때문에 위험합니다.

⊃ '~동안' 이라는 뜻은 같지만, during 다음에는 단어나 구가 오고, while 다음에는 절이 온다. turbulence는 명사이므로 during이 적절한데, turbulence는 불가산 명사이므로 부정관사가 필요하지 않다.

lavatory (비행기)화장실, 세면대 **turbulence** 난기류

17 They finally _____ when she showed the result of the survey.

(a) found to succeed a way
(b) way to found succeed
(c) found the way to succeed
(d) find the way to succeed

그녀가 연구 결과를 보여주었을 때, 그들은 마침내 성공할 방법을 찾게 되었다.

○ 'the way~'는 '~하는 방법'이고, 형용사적 용법의 to부정사가 같이 쓰인 (c)가 알맞다. when 이하의 내용을 보아 시제는 과거이다.

survey 조사, 연구

---

18 Even the best laid plans do not always _____ secret.

(a) be remained
(b) remains
(c) remain
(d) remaining

은밀하게 준비되어진 계획들이라고 해도 항상 비밀인 채로 남아있는 것은 아니다.

○ remain은 자동사로서 '~인 채로 남아있다'는 뜻을 가지고 있다. 주어가 복수이므로 (b)는 될 수 없다.

---

19 _____ "Never judge from appearances.", we would remember the lesson of the other proverb, "Appearances are deceptive."

(a) Given the perspective of
(b) The perspective given
(c) Giving the perspective
(d) Given the perspective

"결코 외형으로 평가하지 말라"는 격언이 주는 사고방식에서, 우리는 "외형은 믿을 수 없다"라는 다른 속담이 주는 교훈을 되새겨 볼 수 있다.

○ '(속담이나 격언) ~에서 주어진 관점에서'의 의미에 가장 알맞은 표현은 (a) Given the perspective of이다.

appearance 외모, 외형 proverb 속담 deceptive 믿을 수 없는, 속이기 쉬운

---

20 _____ a longer bath makes your skin weak and unhealthy.

(a) Take
(b) Taking
(c) Having taken
(d) To taking

목욕을 오래 하는 것은 당신의 피부를 약하게 만든다.

○ 동명사는 '~하는 것'의 의미로, 문장의 주어로 쓰일 수 있다.

---

21 (a) A: Did you finish packed your stuff?
(b) B: Not, yet. I have to buy some dried sea weed.
(c) A: Are you allowed to bring food to America?
(d) B: Sure, we can bring some dried food.

A: 짐 꾸리는 것 다 했어?
B: 아직. 김을 좀 사야 해.
A: 미국에 음식을 가져가는 게 허가되어 있니?
B: 그럼, 말린 음식은 가져갈 수 있어.

○ finish는 목적어로 동명사를 취하기 때문에 (a)에서 packed 대신 packing을 써야 한다.

stuff 짐, 물건

22 (a) Poe, who wrote macabre tales like psychological thrillers, was to work for several publications as both editor and contributor. (b) His career as an editor coincided with his growth as a writer. (c) While worked at a "Gentleman's Magazine," Poe's work continued to flourish. (d) At this time in his career he still was not secure financially, but his work was being recognized and praised, which helped greatly in furthering his reputation.

심리 스릴러와 같은 공포소설을 쓴 작가인 Poe는 몇 개의 출판사에서 편집자이자 투고가로 일하려고 했다. 편집자로서의 그의 경력은 작가로서의 그의 성장과도 부합되었다. "Gentleman's Magazine"에서 일할 때, Poe의 작품 활동은 계속해서 풍성해졌다. 그 때의 그의 직업에서 그는 여전히 재정적으로는 튼튼하지 않았지만, 그의 작품은 인정받고 칭송받기 시작했고, 그 이후의 명성에도 지대한 영향을 주었다.

◐ (c)에서, 접속사 뒤의 주어가 생략되었는데, 그 뒤에 주어가 능동으로 행동하기 때문에 과거분사 worked가 아니라 현재분사 working이 와야 한다.

macabre 무시무시한 contributor 투고가 career 경력, 직업 coincide 동시에 일어나다 flourish 번창하다 reputation 명성

VOCABULARY • P.179

23 A This project is going nowhere. What should I do?
  B Your efforts will _____ fruit sometime.

  (a) grow
  (b) bear
  (c) pick
  (d) show

A: 이 프로젝트는 진전이 없어. 어떻게 해야 하지?
B: 네 노력이 언젠가 결실을 맺을 거야.

◐ 지금은 답답한 상태지만 언젠간 좋은 결과가 있을 것이라는 내용이 되야 한다. 그러한 의미로 'bear fruit' 이라는 표현은 '결실을 맺다' 라는 뜻이다.

bear(produce) fruit 결실을 맺다

24 A I have a paper cut.
  B _____ this ointment on it.

  (a) Affix
  (b) Place
  (c) Apply
  (d) Utilize

A: 종이에 베였어.
B: 이 연고를 상처에 발라.

◐ 종이에 베였다고 했으므로 연고를 바르는 내용이 와야 한다. 'apply' 는 '(약 등을) 바르다, (페인트 등을) 칠하다' 라는 뜻이 있으므로 빈 칸에 적절한 단어는 'apply' 가 된다.

have a paper cut 종이에 베이다 ointment 연고 affix 첨부하다, (도장을) 찍다 apply 바르다, 칠하다 utilize 이용하다

25 A Mom, buy me this game console.
  B How old are you? Please _____ your age.

  (a) reach
  (b) look
  (c) show
  (d) act

A: 엄마, 이 게임기 사주세요.
B: 네가 몇 살이지? 좀 나이에 맞게 행동해라.

◐ 게임기를 사달라고 조르는 아이에게 몇 살이냐고 물어보면서 그 뒤에 자연스럽게 연결될 수 있는 내용은 '나이에 맞게 행동해라' 가 되겠다. 이러한 의미의 표현은 'act one's age' 이다.

game console 게임기 act one's age 나이에 맞게 행동하다

26 A I can't go to her party because I have to go on a business trip.

B In that case, we have no choice but to _____ the invitation.

(a) send out
(b) turn in
(c) turn down
(d) put in

A: 출장을 가야 해서 그녀의 파티에 못가.
B: 그러면 초대를 거절하는 수밖에 없겠네.

◯ 그녀의 파티에 갈 수 없다고 했으므로 초대를 거절할 수밖에 없다는 내용이 와야 한다. '거절하다'의 의미로는 'turn down'이 있다. (a)의 경우 초대장을 보낸다는 의미가 되므로 상황에 맞지 않다.

have no choice but to ~하지 않을 수 없다 send out 보내다, 발송하다 turn in 제출하다, (경찰에) 신고하다 turn down 거절하다, (경기가) 나빠지다 put in 임명하다, 삽입하다, 끼워넣다

---

27 A He's going too far. Why don't you give him any advice?

B He already turned a _____ ear to my advice.

(a) big
(b) deaf
(c) thick
(d) light

A: 그가 너무 지나친 것 같아. 그에게 충고 좀 해주지 그래?
B: 이미 내 충고 따위는 듣지도 않아.

◯ 이디엄을 알아야 풀 수 있는 문제이다. 충고를 해주라는 말에 이미 했으나 듣지 않는다는 내용이 나와야 하므로 이에 해당하는 이디엄인 'turn a deaf ear'가 적당하다.

go too far 도를 지나치다 turn a deaf ear to ~에 귀를 기울이지 않다

---

28 I was so fascinated by Mona Lisa's _____ smile that I can't even move a little.

(a) infectious
(b) bitter
(c) enigmatic
(d) forced

나는 모나리자의 불가사의한 미소에 너무 매료되어서 꼼짝 할 수 조차 없었다.

◯ 모나리자의 미소는 신비스럽고 불가사의한 것으로 잘 알려져 있다. 이에 해당하는 단어로는 'enigmatic'이 있다. 참고로 'infectious smile'은 '전염성이 있는 미소'라는 뜻으로 말은 되지만 모나리자라는 작품의 잘 알려진 특징상 (a)보다는 (c)가 더 적절하다 할 수 있다.

infectious 전염이 되는 bitter 쓴, 괴로운 enigmatic 수수께끼 같은, 불가사의한 forced 가식의, 억지의

---

29 A recent survey revealed that many people tend to _____ the seriousness of flu by believing that flu is the same as having a bad cold.

(a) undergo
(b) undermine
(c) underestimate
(d) undertake

최근 조사에 따르면 많은 사람들이 독감이 감기에 걸리는 것과 같다고 믿음으로써 독감의 심각성을 경시하는 경향이 있음이 밝혀졌다.

◯ 문맥을 살펴보면 독감은 감기와는 다르며 훨씬 심각하다는 뉘앙스를 읽을 수 있다. 따라서 빈 칸에 들어갈 단어는 독감의 심각성을 경시한다는 뜻의 'underestimate'가 가장 적절하다.

undergo 겪다, 경험하다 undermine 밑을 파다 underestimate 과소평가하다, 경시하다 undertake 떠맡다

30 Young generations got into the hard rock and roll in 1980's, the _____ of what could be called heavy metal these days.

(a) forerunner
(b) foreboder
(c) rocker
(d) messenger

젊은 세대들은 1980년대 격한 로큰롤에 빠졌는데, 이는 오늘날 헤비메탈이라 불리는 것의 선조격이다.

○ 로큰롤에 대한 이야기를 하면서 오늘날에는 헤비메탈이라고 부른다고 했으므로 로큰롤이 헤비메탈의 선조격이라 할 수 있다. 따라서 정답은 (a)이다.

get into ~에 빠지다, 열중하다 forerunner 선배, 선조 foreboder 예언자 rocker 록 연주가 messenger 전달자, 예언자

---

31 She was put in the detention center but all her supporters did the best to _____ the seriousness of the charges against her.

(a) grasp
(b) realize
(c) decrease
(d) extenuate

그녀는 구치소에 수감되었지만 그녀를 따르는 모든 지지자들은 그녀의 혐의의 심각성을 완화하기 위해 최선을 다했다.

○ 구치소 수감자의 혐의에 대해 지지자들이 혐의의 심각성을 완화시키려 한다는 내용이 오는 것이 자연스러우므로 정답은 'extenuate'가 된다. 'decrease'는 가치, 양, 수치 등이 내려간다고 할 때 많이 쓰이므로 정답이 될 수 없다.

detention center 구치소 charge 혐의, 고소, 고발 grasp 붙잡다, 파악하다 extenuate (벌을) 가볍게 하다, 완화하다, 정상참작의 여지를 주다

---

32 Many female workers have testified that they also suffered sexual _____ in the male-dominant workplace.

(a) provocation
(b) harassment
(c) irritation
(d) disturbance

많은 여성 근로자들은 또한 남성이 지배적인 직장 내에서 성희롱을 겪었다고 증언했다.

○ 남성 지배적인 직장 내에서 여성이 겪을 수 있는 상황이고 'sexual'이라는 단어가 앞에 있으므로 이와 잘 어울리는 연어로 'harassment'가 정답이 된다.

testify 증언하다 dominant 지배적인, 우세한 provocation 자극, 도발 sexual harassment 성희롱 irritation 화나게 하기 disturbance 소란, 훼방

33 Obesity has become a big problem in our modern society. It causes related diseases such as diabetes and heart attacks. Recently, experts have shown that those who were obese in childhood grow up into obese adults. Also, they are far more likely to suffer from cardiac disease and cancer in later years. Even worse, overweight kids seem to become a target for bullying at school. The experts suggested that, in order to avoid overweight and obesity in childhood, kids should eat healthy and work out regularly. Since more and more kids are reported as being obese, it is important to educate them to _____ _____.

(a) to lose weight through a low-calorie diet and exercise
(b) to stop smoking in public places
(c) to find solutions for diabetes and heart attack
(d) to solve the problems in our society

비만은 우리 현대 사회에서 큰 문제가 되고 있다. 비만은 당뇨와 심장마비와 같은 관련 질병을 유발한다. 최근 전문가들은 유년기에 비만이었던 사람들이 커서도 비만 성인이 된다고 밝혔다. 게다가, 그들은 이후에 심장 질환이나 암으로 고생할 가능성이 크다. 설상가상으로 비만 아동은 학교에서 괴롭힘의 대상이 되는 것으로 보인다. 전문가들은 유년기의 과체중과 비만을 예방하기 위해서 아동들이 건강한 식습관을 유지하고 정기적으로 운동을 해야 한다고 말한다. 점점 더 많은 아동들이 비만인 것으로 보고되고 있기 때문에, 저칼로리 식단과 운동을 통해서 체중을 줄이도록 교육하는 것이 중요하다.

🔵 아동 비만과 그 폐해 및 해결 방법에 대한 글이다. 비만 아동은 비만 성인이 될 가능성이 크고, 또한 각종 질병에 걸릴 위험이 큰 동시에 학교에서 괴롭힘을 당하기도 하기 때문에, 이를 예방하기 위해 건강한 식습관과 정기적인 운동을 해야 한다는 언급이 나오고 있다. 점점 더 많은 아동들이 비만에 걸리고 있으므로 그들에게 교육해야 하는 중요한 점으로 적절한 것은 (a)이다.

obesity 비만, 비대 **heart attack** 심장마비, 심장발작 **cardiac** 심장의, 심장에 관한 **bullying** 괴롭힘, 따돌림 **avoid** 피하다, 회피하다, 막다 **work out** 운동하다

34 Pablo Picasso was a modern artist who dominated Western art in the 20th century. Before his 50th birthday, he had made a great reputation for himself. No painter before him had such a large audience in his own lifetime. He and his work were always in the middle of never-ending analysis, gossip, adoration and rumor. He was a sarcastic, cynical man, sometimes mean to his children, often revolting to his women. He had scorn for women artists. His famous remark about women being "_____" has left him obnoxious to feminists, but his charm was so irresistible that women chose to assume either role eagerly.

(a) artists or patrons
(b) blabbers or naggers
(c) helpers or onlookers
(d) goddesses or doormats

Pablo Picasso는 20세기 서양 미술에 지대한 영향을 끼친 현대 화가이다. 그는 50세가 되기 이전에 대단한 명성을 얻었다. 그 이전의 어떤 화가도 살아있는 동안 그만큼 많은 관람객을 모으지 못했다. 그와 그의 작품은 언제나 끊임없는 분석, 뒷공론, 흠모 그리고 풍문의 한가운데 있었다. 그는 비꼬기를 좋아하며 냉소적인 사람이었으며, 때로는 자신의 아이들에게도 인색했고, 그의 여성에겐 때로 역겨운 사람이기도 했다. 그는 여류화가들을 경멸했다. 여성은 "여신 아니면 흙털개"라는 그의 유명한 발언은 여성주의자들에게는 그를 혐오스러운 존재로 만들었으나, 그의 매력은 거부할 수 없을 만큼 강렬해서 여성들은 둘 중 하나의 역할을 기꺼이 떠맡곤 했다.

🔵 Pablo Picasso의 예술가적 면모보다 한 인간으로서의 면모에 대한 기술이 주를 이룬다. 그의 여성에 대한 태도가 부정적이었음을 알 수 있으며, 그의 발언이 여성주의자들에게 역겨움을 유발했다는 내용으로 보아 (d)가 정답이다.

dominate 지배하다, 큰 영향을 주다 **reputation** 평판, 명성 **heaps of** 많은 **adoration** 흠모, 동경, 열애 **sarcastic** 비꼬는, 풍자적인 **cynical** 냉소적인, 남을 믿지 않는 **mean to** ~에게 인색한 **revolting** 메스껍게 하는, 불쾌감을 느끼게 하는 **scorn** 경멸, 모욕, 깔봄 **remark** 논평, 의견, 언급 **obnoxious** 아주 싫은, 역겨운 **irresistible** 저항할 수 없는 **assume** (태도를) 취하다, (역할을) 떠맡다 **patron** 후원자 **blabber** 밀고자 **nagger** 잔소리꾼 **onlooker** 구경꾼, 방관자 **doormat** 현관 흙털개, 학대받아도 가만히 있는 사람

35 Summer Hill School is a British boarding school founded in 1921 by Alexander Sutherland Neil with the belief that children learn best _____. There is a wide choice of subjects and all lessons are optional—no compulsion to attend. In addition to deciding what to do with their own time, children can take part in the self-governing community at which rules affecting their everyday lives are set or unresolved conflicts are adequately managed. Children are completely free from any pressure to conform to adult ideas of growing up and adults are there not to teach them what they should do but to help them do what they want to do.

(a) under parental guidance
(b) without any expectation
(c) with freedom from coercion
(d) when given proper discipline

서머힐 학교는 1921년 Alexander Sutherland Neil이 아이들은 강압에서 벗어나 자유로울 때 가장 잘 배운다는 믿음으로 세운 영국의 기숙학교이다. 과목의 선택이 폭이 넓으며, 모든 수업은 선택에 따르기 때문에 반드시 출석해야 하는 의무가 아니다. 아이들은 자신의 시간을 어떻게 보내는가를 결정하는 것뿐만 아니라, 자신의 일상생활에 영향을 끼칠 규칙을 정하거나 해결되지 않은 갈등을 적절하게 조절하는 자치 모임에 참여할 수 있다. 아이들은 성장에 대한 어른들의 생각을 따라야 한다는 어떤 압력으로부터도 자유로우며, 어른들은 그들에게 어떻게 하라고 가르치기 위해서가 아니라 아이들이 원하는 것을 하도록 도와주기 위해 존재한다.

🔵 서머힐 학교의 특색 가운데 아이들의 자발적인 의지에 의한 학습과 군림하고 통제하는 성인이 아닌 조력자로서의 성인을 강조하고 있으므로 정답은 (c)가 된다. 부모의 보호 역시 아이가 필요한 경우이므로 (a)는 답이 아니며, (b)는 언급되지 않았으며, 훈육은 서머힐의 교육 이념과는 동떨어지므로 (d)도 답이 될 수 없다.

boarding school 기숙학교 found 설립하다, 세우다 optional 선택제의, 선택자유의 compulsion 강요, 강제 self-governing 자치의 affect 영향을 미치다 unresolved 미해결의, 풀리지 않은 adequately 적당히, 충분히 conform to ~에 따르다, ~을 지키다 coercion 강제, 억압, 강압

---

36 Cats are amazing subjects to sketch, with their elegant lines and graceful movements. However, it's quite hard to capture cat's movement in detail because they move so quickly! Your eyes need to be quick and your hands need to be even quicker. Before you begin your sketching, you need to decide what to draw and what to exclude. You need to make a quick and firm decision since you have limited time. Don't worry too much about detail. You may want to buy a felt-tip artist's pen because they are soft and perfect for fast sketching.

Q What is the topic of the paragraph?

(a) How to take a picture of moving cats
(b) What to prepare to sketch cats
(c) How cats move quickly with elegance
(d) Why people want to draw cats

고양이들은 고상한 선과 우아한 움직임을 가지고 있어서 스케치하기에 아주 좋은 대상이다. 하지만 고양이의 움직임을 세세하게 잡아내기란 꽤 힘든 일인데, 이는 그들이 아주 빠르게 움직이기 때문이다! 당신의 눈은 빨라야 하고 당신의 손은 그보다 더 빨라야 한다. 당신은 스케치를 시작하기 전에 무엇을 그릴 것이며 무엇을 제외할 것인가를 결정해야 한다. 당신의 시간은 제한되어 있기 때문에 당신은 빠르고 단호한 결정을 내려야 한다. 세부적인 사항에 대해서는 너무 걱정하지 마시길. 당신은 부드러워서 속성 스케치에 안성맞춤인 미술가용 검은색 펠트펜이 사고 싶어질 것이다.

🔵 주어진 문단은 고양이를 그리는 데 있어서 준비할 용품과 본격적인 스케치 전에 유의해야 할 사항들에 대해서 말하고 있다. 스케치할 대상과 부분을 취사선택할 때 그 결정이 빠르고 단호해야 한다고 말하고 있다.

subject 대상, 주제, 제재, 피사체 movement 움직임, 동작, 운동 exclude 제외하다, 차단하다, 못 들어오게 하다 felt-tip pen 펠트펜 (펜촉을 펠트천으로 만든 미술용 펜)

37 Many studies show that the global market for biodiesel is on the edge for explosive growth in the next decade. Currently 80% of global biodiesel consumption and production is done by European countries, but the U.S. is now boosting production at a faster pace than Europe. With the progress of major projects for lower-cost feedstocks from renewable diesel including tallow, used vegetable oil and waste recycling, it is possible biodiesel could represent as much as 20% of all on-road diesel used in the BRICs and Europe by the year 2020. Government promotion of research & development in new biodiesel feedstocks such as algae biodiesel will ensure increased investment.

Q What is the main idea of the passage?

(a) Environment-conscious fuels should be created.
(b) Cars using biodiesel fume out much less exhaust gas.
(c) The prospect for biodiesel market is relatively bright.
(d) The government should enact investor-friendly tax incentives.

많은 연구에 따르면 바이오디젤의 세계 시장이 향후 십년내로 폭발적인 성장을 앞두고 있다고 한다. 현재 전 세계 바이오디젤 소비와 생산의 80%는 유럽 국가들에 의해 이루어지고 있지만, 미국이 유럽보다 빠른 속도로 생산을 증대시키고 있다. 수지, 폐식용유, 재활용쓰레기를 포함하는 재생 가능한 디젤로부터 비용이 적게 드는 공급원료를 개발하는 주요 프로젝트가 진행됨에 따라 2020년까지는 바이오디젤이 브릭스와 유럽에서 운행하는 디젤차의 20% 가까이를 충당하는 것도 가능하다. 조류 바이오디젤과 같은 새로운 바이오디젤 공급원료의 연구 개발을 정부가 독려한다면 투자유치도 틀림없이 증가할 것이다.

○ 바이오디젤의 시장 전망이 밝다는 것이 주된 내용이므로 정답은 (c)이다. 환경친화적인 연료의 필요성에 대해서는 언급되지 않았으므로 (a)는 답이 될 수 없고, 바이오디젤을 사용하는 차가 배기가스를 덜 배출한다는 것은 직접적으로 언급되지 않았으므로 (b)도 답이 아니다. 투자유치를 위해 정부가 독려할 것은 연구개발이지 세금의 혜택이 아니므로 (d)는 답이 될 수 없다.

be on the edge of 막 ~하려는 참이다, 막 ~하려 하다 **explosive** 폭발적인 **boost** 밀어올리다, 지지하다 **feedstock** 공급 재료(제조 과정에서 필요로 하는 직접 원료) **tallow** 수지, 쇠기름, 양기름 **ensure** 보증하다, 확실히 하다 **algae** 말, 조류 **fume out** 발산하다, 배출하다 **exhaust gas** 배기가스 **prospect** 전망 **enact** 법률로 만들다, 법제화하다 **BRICs** 브라질(Brazil), 러시아(Russia), 인도(India), 중국(China)의 총칭

---

38 Anger is not a feeling that you must not feel or express but is a normal and natural reaction to criticism, threat, or frustration if it's neither excessive nor uncontrollable. The important aspect related to the feelings of anger is how to control the emotion when you are in the throes of it and how to express anger in a healthy way. This fall, we are going to provide focused sessions which include psychological therapeutic techniques and exercises for those who may have felt unable to cope with anger by themselves. In this course, you will learn and practice empathy, forgiveness, assertive communication techniques, stress management skills, and cognitive behavioral therapy. For more information, contact us any time.

화는 비판이나 협박, 좌절에 대해 여러분이 느끼거나 표현하지 말아야 하는 감정이 아니라 정상적이고 자연스러운 반응입니다. 그 감정이 너무 과도하거나 다루기 힘들 정도가 아니면 말입니다. 화가 날 때 느끼는 감정과 관련하여 중요한 것은 여러분이 한창 화가 날 때에 그 감정을 어떻게 제어할 것이며 어떻게 그 화를 건전한 방법으로 표현할 것인가입니다. 올 가을 우리는 혼자서는 화를 다룰 수 없다고 느꼈을지도 모르는 사람들에게 심리학적 치료 기술과 연습을 포함하는 집중 수업을 제공할 것입니다. 이 과정에서 여러분은 감정이입, 용서, 자기주장적 의사소통 기술, 스트레스 관리 기술 그리고 인지행동 치료에 대해 배우고 연습할 것입니다. 더 많은 정보를 위해서는 언제든지 우리에게 연락하십시오.

○ 화란 무엇인지, 화를 다룰 때 중요한 점은 무엇인지를 언급한 후에 올 가을에 있을 분노조절 프로그램에 대해서 소개하고 있으므로 정답은 (a)가 된다. (c)는 이 글의 첫 문장에서 화에 대한 바른 이해를 시켜주고 있을 뿐 이것이 글의 목적은 아니며, (d)는 본문에 화를 건설적으로 다루는 방법에 대해서는 나와 있지 않으므로 정답이 될 수 없다.

Q What is the purpose of this passage?

(a) To introduce the anger management program

(b) To inform the curriculum in the fall semester

(c) To clear up the misunderstanding about anger

(d) To present how to deal with anger constructively

criticism 비평, 비판 threat 협박, 위협, 공갈 frustration 좌절, 실패 neither A nor B A도 B도 아닌 excessive 과도한, 극단적인 uncontrollable 통제할 수 없는, 제어하기 힘든, 다루기 힘든 aspect 상황, 국면 in the throes of 한창 ~할 때에 provide B for A A에게 B를 제공하다 session 학기 수업(시간) psychological 심리학(상)의 therapeutic 치료(상)의, 치료법의 cope with ~을 대처하다 by oneself 혼자서, 혼자 힘으로 empathy (심리) 감정이입 forgiveness 용서 assertive 단정적인, 단언적인 cognitive 인지의, 인지적인 behavioral 행동의, 행동에 관한 therapy 치료, 요법 curriculum 교 육 과 정 clear up 해 결 하 다 misunderstanding 오해 constructively 건설적으로

---

39 The Boston Red Sox baseball team had won five World Series by 1918 from its inception in 1903. One of the stars of this team was a young left-handed pitcher named George H. Ruth, also known as Babe Ruth or The Bambino. In 1920, however, the Red Sox owner underestimated Babe Ruth and sold him to the New York Yankees at a giveaway price. After this trade, while Boston hadn't won the World Series for 86 years, the once-wretched Yankees became one of the most successful baseball franchises owing to Ruth's remarkable plays as a hitter. Many began to ascribe the failure of the Boston to "the curse of the Bambino," but the curse finally ended in 2004 when they swept the St. Louis Cardinals.

Q Which is truthful in accordance with the passage?

(a) The curse of the Bambino had not been removed to 2004.

(b) The New York Yankees has never been worse than the Boston Red Sox.

(c) Boston traded Ruth with the Yankees, receiving little money from it.

(d) Babe Ruth was an excellent pitcher who led his team to win the World Series.

Boston Red Sox 야구팀은 1903년 창단 이래 1918년까지 월드시리즈에서 다섯 번 우승을 했다. 이 팀의 스타 중 한 명은 George H. Ruth라는 이름의 젊은 왼손잡이 투수로 Babe Ruth 또는 Bambino로도 알려져 있었다. 그러나 1920년에 Red Sox의 구단주는 Babe Ruth를 과소평가하여 헐값으로 New York Yankees에 팔아 넘겼다. 이 거래 후에 Boston은 86년 동안 월드시리즈에서 우승을 못했지만, 한때 형편없었던 Yankees는 타자 Ruth의 놀란 만한 경기 덕택에 가장 성공한 야구 구단이 되었다. 많은 사람들은 Boston의 실패를 "밤비노의 저주" 때문으로 생각하기 시작했으나 그 저주는 2004년에 Boston이 St. Louis Cardinals를 이겼을 때 마침내 끝났다.

➡ (a)는 마지막 문장에서 밤비노의 저주가 2004에 끝났다고 했으므로 틀린 내용이고 (b)는 Yankees가 한때는 형편없었고 Boston이 월드시리즈에서 우승한 적이 있으므로 틀린 내용이다. (d)는 Yankees가 월드시리즈에서 우승할 때 Ruth가 투수가 아니라 타자였으므로 틀린 반면 (c)는 Boston이 Ruth를 Yankees에 적은 돈을 받고 이적시켰으므로 맞는 내용이 된다.

inception 시작, 개시, 발단 underestimate 과소평가하다, 오산하다, 경시하다 at a giveaway price 헐값으로 wretched 서투른, 열등의, 시시한 franchise (야구) 프랜차이즈, 구단 소유권 owing to ~덕택에 remarkable 놀란 만한 ascribe A to B A를 B의 탓으로 돌리다 curse 저주 sweep 〈시합, 승부〉에서 이기다

40 On October 4, 1957 the Soviet Union succeeded in launching the world's first man made satellite, Sputnik. It caused not only excitement and wonder but also massive political resonance because the United States had believed itself to be the world leader in the western world as well as in space technology. The Soviet Union had demonstrated that it was far ahead of its western rivals, taking the leadership crown from the United States. However, although it took years before the crown could be reclaimed, the news of Sputnik ignited overall social reform including a full-scale revamping of the US high-school science curriculum.

Q Which of the following is true about Sputnik according to the passage?

(a) It made little impact on international relations.
(b) It spurred the Soviet Union to develop another satellite.
(c) It devastated the science education of the United States.
(d) It caused grave concern about the United States social system.

1957년 10월 4일, 소련이 세계 최초의 인공위성인 Sputnik호의 발사에 성공했다. 그것은 흥분과 경이로움 뿐만 아니라 거대한 정치적 파장을 불러 일으켰는데, 왜냐하면 미국이 스스로를 우주 과학기술 분야뿐만 아니라 서구세계의 지도자라고 믿어왔기 때문이다. 소련은 자신이 서구 경쟁국가들보다 훨씬 앞서 있다는 것을 증명해 보이며 미국으로부터 지도자로서의 지위를 뺏어버렸다. 그러나 그 지위를 다시 찾기까지 오랜 세월이 걸렸지만, Sputnik 발사 소식은 미국의 고등학교 과학 교육과정의 전면적인 개정을 비롯한 미국 사회의 전면적인 개혁에 불을 붙였다.

✪ 소련의 세계 최초 인공위성 발사가 가져온 영향에 대한 내용이다. 정치적 파장이 막대했으므로 (a)는 지문과 반대되는 내용이며, 소련이 또 하나의 위성을 개발하도록 자극이 되었다는 것은 언급되지 않았으므로 (b)도 답이 될 수 없다. 과학 교육과정을 개정하여 강화한 것이므로 (c)는 지문과 정반대되는 내용으로 답이 아니다. 전면적 사회개혁에 원인을 제공했으므로 정답은 (d)가 된다.

launch 발사하다 satellite 위성 massive 크고 묵직한, 대량의 , 대규모의 resonance 파장, 울림, 여운 demonstrate 증명하다, 시연해보이다 reclaim 되찾다, 재생하다 ignite 불을 붙이다, 점화하다 overall 총체적인, 전체적인 reform 개혁 full-scale 본격적인, 전력을 다하는, 전면적인, 철저한 revamp 개정하다, 개편하다 spur 박차를 가하다, 자극하다, 격려하다

LISTENING COMPREHENSION · P.188

1 W How did the test go?

M _____

(a) It was a piece of cake!
(b) I couldn't sleep a wink.
(c) It was a close call.
(d) Give me a break.

W: 시험 본 것 어떻게 됐어?
M: 식은 죽 먹기였지!

➡ 시험이 어땠느냐고 묻고 있다. 이에 적절한 대답으로는 어려웠다, 쉬웠다, 잘 봤다, 망쳤다 등이 올 수 있다. 보기 가운데 이에 해당하는 것은 (a) '식은 죽 먹기였다' 이다. (b)는 시험 공부 열심히 했느냐는 질문에 적절한 대답이 될 수 있겠다.

a piece of cake 식은 죽 먹기 not sleep a wink 한 숨도 못 자다 close call 위기일발, 구사일생 Give me a break 한 번 봐주세요. 기회를 주세요.

2 M Are you all set for the trip to Paris?

W _____

(a) I need to brush up on my French.
(b) I have to take off now.
(c) I'm tied up at the moment.
(d) It is no picnic.

M: 파리 여행 준비는 다 되었니?
W: 프랑스어를 복습할 필요가 있어.

➡ 파리로 여행을 계획하는 사람에게 준비는 다 했냐고 묻고 있다. 이 질문에 적절한 대답으로는 여행에 대비해 프랑스어를 다시 복습해야겠다고 하는 (a)가 되겠다. (b)는 지금 출발해야 한다는 뜻으로 상황에 적절치 않다.

brush up ~의 공부를 다시 하다 take off 출발하다, 이륙하다 be tied up 바쁜, 얽매인 It is no picnic. 쉬운 일이 아니다. 장난이 아니다.

3 W I heard you're getting a promotion soon.

M _____

(a) I'm in debt up to my ears.
(b) I'm all ears.
(c) That's music to my ears.
(d) I've got an ear for music.

W: 곧 승진하신다는 얘기 들었어요.
M: 기분 좋은 소리네요.

➡ 승진 소식을 알려주는 상대방에게 할 수 있는 표현으로는 '기쁜 소식이다. 듣기 좋은 소식이다' 라는 뜻의 (c)가 가장 적절하다. 보기 모두 'ear' 을 활용한 다양한 이디엄으로 정확한 뜻을 알아두자.

get a promotion 승진하다 music to my ears 기분 좋은 소식, 반가운 소식 I'm in debt up to my ears. 내 코가 석자다. be all ears 열심히 경청하다 have an ear for ~에 안목이 있다, 일가견이 있다

4 **W** How is your new business?
   M _____

   (a) I'm still feeling sick.
   (b) Things are looking up.
   (c) You're telling me.
   (d) Let me get the check.

W: 새로운 사업은 어때요?
M: 상황이 나아지고 있어요.

○ 새로운 사업에 대해 묻고 있다. (a)의 경우 아직 아프다는 뜻으로 응답으로 어색하고, 상황이 나아지고 있다는 뜻의 (b)가 정답이 된다. (c)는 상대의말에 대한 동의의 표현이다.

You're telling me. 동감이다 check 계산서

---

5 **M** Hello. This is me. Sorry, I was too busy to get the phone yesterday.
   W _____

   (a) I'll call you back tomorrow!
   (b) I called in sick yesterday.
   (c) I can't hear you very well.
   (d) Thanks for returning my call.

M: 여보세요. 접니다. 어제 너무 바빠서 전화를 못 받았어요.
W: 전화 다시 주셔서 감사합니다.

○ 상황으로 보아 B가 어제 전화를 했지만 전화를 받지 못한 A가 다음날 전화를 건 상황이다. 따라서 정답으로 적절한 것은 다시 전화를 걸어주어서 고맙다는 뜻의 (d)가 된다. (b)는 아플 때 전화로 병가를 낸다는 의미로 상황과 관계가 없다. (c)는 전화상 목소리가 잘 안 들릴 때 할 수 있는 표현이다.

call in sick 전화로 병가를 알리다 return a call 전화로 답신을 하다

---

6 **M** What do you think it is?
   W _____

   (a) I don't think so.
   (b) It is a good idea.
   (c) It's not a big deal.
   (d) I don't have the slightest idea.

M: 그게 뭐인 것 같아?
W: 전혀 모르겠어.

○ 그것이 무언인 것 같느냐는 물음에 적절한 대답으로 보기 중 (d)가 가장 자연스럽다. 'I don't have the slightest idea.' 는 전혀 생각이 떠오르지 않는다는 뜻이다. 어떠한 의견에 대해 반대 의견을 제시 할 때는 (a)를 쓸 수 있고, 어떠한 의견에 맞장구 칠 때는 (b)를 쓸 수 있다. (c)는 어떠한 일이나 사건에 대해 별일 아니다, 대수롭지 않다는 의미로 쓰는 표현이다.

not a big deal 별것 아닌, 대수롭지 않은

---

7 **W** Which way do you want to go?
   M _____

   (a) I've lost my way.
   (b) It doesn't make any difference.
   (c) I feel the same way.
   (d) Hang in there.

W: 어떤 길로 가고 싶으세요?
M: 어느 쪽으로 가도 상관 없어요.

○ way의 다양한 뜻을 알아야 한다. '길, 도로' 등의 의미와 '방법, 방식' 의 뜻을 가지고 있다. 문제에서는 어느 길로 가고 싶은지 물어보는 의미였고 (c)는 way가 '방법, 방식' 의 뜻으로 쓰여 '동감이다' 라는 뜻이므로 (c)는 정답이 아니다. (a)는 길을 잃었다는 뜻으로 문맥과 관련이 없고, (d)는 격려의 표현이므로 역시 정답이 될 수 없다. (b)는 직역하면 '그것이 어떠한 차이도 만들어내지 못한다.' 는 뜻으로 어느 쪽으로 가든 똑같다는 의미이므로 정답은 (b)가 된다.

lose one's way 길을잃다 make a difference 차이를 낳다, 변화를 가져오다 feel the same way 동감이다 hang in there 버티다, 견디다

8 W You look so tired. Why don't you take a break?

M That's what I want. But I have too much work to do.

W I know, but it's hard to work all day.

M _____

(a) Let's have some coffee then.
(b) It's left my head.
(c) We went for a walk.
(d) You should work overtime.

W: 정말 피곤해 보인다. 좀 쉬지 그래?
M: 내가 원하는 바야. 하지만 할 일이 너무 많아.
W: 알아. 하지만 하루 종일 일하는 것은 힘들어.
M: 그럼 커피 좀 마시자.

○ 피곤해 보이는 남자에게 여자가 하루 종일 일하는 것은 힘들다고 말한다. 이에 남자가 보일 수 있는 반응은 커피를 마시자고 하는 (a)가 가장 적절하다. 여자의 마지막 대사에서 work가 나온 것을 듣고 발음이 비슷한 walk를 사용한 (c)와 잔업을 해야 한다는 (d)를 고르지 않도록 주의하자.

take a break 쉬다, 휴식하다 go for a walk 산책을 나가다 overtime 시간 외의

---

9 W It's really hot here. I can't breathe.

M Really? Actually I'm okay. What's wrong with you?

W I don't know. Can I just open the window and get some air?

M _____

(a) I'm walking on air.
(b) Over here, by the window.
(c) No, thanks.
(d) Suit yourself.

W: 여기 정말 덥다. 숨을 쉴 수 없어.
M: 정말? 실은 난 괜찮은데. 뭐가 문제야?
W: 잘 모르겠어. 그냥 창문 좀 열고 환기 좀 시켜도 될까?
M: 마음대로 해.

○ 여자의 마지막 대사를 주목하자. 창문을 열고 환기를 시켜도 되냐고 묻고 있으므로 괜찮다고 하는 (d)가 정답이 된다. air라는 단어로 혼동을 주기 위해 (a)를 넣었는데 walk on air은 대단히 기쁘다는 뜻이다. 역시 window라는 단어를 반복함으로써 (b)에서도 혼동을 주고 있다. (c)는 무엇인가를 권하는 상황에서 고맙지만 괜찮다며 거절하는 표현이다.

breath 숨을 쉬다 walk on air 들뜨다, 대단히 기쁘다 suit yourself 마음대로 해, 좋을 대로 해

---

10 W Yesterday I almost burned the house down.

M What happened?

W I took a shower with the stove turned on.

M _____

(a) It's just a shower.
(b) My ears are burning.
(c) Such things do happen.
(d) I don't know what you mean.

W: 어제 집을 홀랑 태울 뻔 했어.
M: 무슨 일이 있었는데?
W: 가스를 켜 놓고 샤워를 했어.
M: 그런 일이 종종 일어나긴 하지.

○ 여자가 가스를 켜 놓고 샤워를 했다고 했을 때 남자의 반응으로 적절한 것을 찾아야 한다. (a)에서 shower는 '샤워하다'의 샤워가 아닌 소나기를 뜻한다. 같은 단어를 반복하여 혼동을 주기 위한 보기이며, (b)는 누가 내 욕을 하는 것 같다는 뜻으로 burn이라는 단어로 역시 혼동을 주기 위한 보기이다. (c)는 그런 일은 종종 일어난다는 뜻으로 상황에 적절하므로 정답이 된다.

burn down ~을 몽땅 태우다 take a shower 샤워하다 turn on (가스, 수도, 전기 등을) 틀다 shower 소나기 My ears are burning. (누가 욕하는 것 같이) 귀가 간지럽다

11 **M** Hello. May I speak to Mr. Thomas?

W I'm sorry. He's out to lunch. Would you care to leave a message?

M How soon do you expect him back?

W _____

(a) He'll leave as soon as possible.

(b) I didn't expect you back so soon.

(c) Could you call him back, please?

(d) He should be back before 2 p.m.

M: 안녕하세요. 토마스씨 계신가요?

W: 죄송합니다. 점심 드시러 나가셨어요. 메모 남기시겠어요?

M: 언제쯤 들어오실지 아세요?

W: 2시 전에는 돌아오실 거예요.

○ 전화를 하는 상황으로 토마스씨가 언제쯤 돌아올지 묻고 있으므로 적절한 여자의 대답으로 2시 전에 돌아올 것이라는 (d)가 정답이 된다. 대화에 등장했던 단어들인 leave, expect, back 등으로 혼동을 주고 있는데 (a)는 '남기다' 라는 뜻의 leave가 아니라 '떠나다' 라는 뜻의 leave이며 (b)는 '당신이 그렇게 빨리 돌아올 줄 몰랐다' 는 뜻으로 상황과 맞지 않는다.

leave a message 메모를 남기다 **expect** ~을 예상하다, 기대하다

---

12 **W** Christmas is just around the corner. Do you have any plans?

M I'm taking my girlfriend out to dinner. How about you?

W I don't have time to take a break. I have a pile of work to do.

M _____

(a) All work and no play makes Jack a dull boy.

(b) Did you guys break up?

(c) There are piles of clothes to be washed.

(d) Think nothing of it.

W: 크리스마스가 바로 코앞이다. 무슨 계획 있어?

M: 여자 친구에게 저녁을 사주려고. 너는 어때?

W: 쉴 시간이 없어. 할 일이 쌓여 있거든.

M: 놀지도 않고 일만 하면 바보가 된다는 말이 있잖아.

○ 크리스마스인데도 불구하고 쉬지 못한다는 여자의 말에 적절한 남자의 대답을 골라야 한다. 일만 하지 말고 좀 쉬면서 하라는 내용의 대답이 적절한데 이와 관련된 속담이 (a)이다. 나머지 보기들은 대화 상황과는 어울리지 않는 표현들이다.

All work and no play makes Jack a dull boy. 놀지도 않고 일만 하면 바보가 된다. **break up** 헤어지다 **Think nothing of it.** (감사 인사에 대해) 천만에요, 별 것 아닌데요 뭘.

---

13 **M** Hello. Where to?

W I'm going to the National Gallery.

M Okay. Are you here for sightseeing?

W _____

(a) It's really nice to see you.

(b) No, I work as a curator.

(c) I'm into taking a picture.

(d) Sorry, I can't hear you.

M: 안녕하세요? 어디로 가세요?

W: National Gallery요.

M: 알겠습니다. 관광차 오신 거예요?

W: 아니오. 큐레이터로 일하고 있어요.

○ 택시 안에서 기사와 손님이 나누는 대화이다. 택시 기사가 관광하러 왔느냐는 질문에 여자의 대답으로 적절한 것은 그렇다거나 아니면 일 때문에 왔다는 등의 방문 목적이 나와야 한다. 이에 해당하는 보기는 (b)이다. (a)는 처음 만났을 때 하는 인사, (c)는 사진 찍는 걸 좋아한다는 내용. (d)는 잘 안 들린다는 뜻으로 전화 대화에서 많이 들을 수 있는 표현이다.

sightseeing 관광 **curator** (박물관, 도서관의) 관장, 관리자 **take a picture** 사진을 찍다

14 W Happy birthday.
   M Thank you for coming.
   W I'll light the candles first.
   M _____

   (a) Can you give me a light?
   (b) This is yours.
   (c) I'll make a wish before blowing out them.
   (d) The lights went out all of a sudden.

W: 생일 축하해.
M: 와줘서 고마워.
W: 먼저 내가 촛불을 켤게.
M: 촛불을 끄기 전에 소원을 빌어야겠다.

○ 생일 축하 파티를 하는 상황이다. 여자가 케이크에 촛불을 켠다고 했으므로 이에 적절한 남자의 대답으로는 소원을 빌겠다고 하는 (c)가 된다. (a)는 light가 명사로 쓰여 담뱃불 좀 빌려달라는 뜻이고, (b)는 선물을 줄 때 할 수 있는 표현으로 여자의 대사로 적합하다. (d)는 전기가 갑자기 나갔다는 뜻으로 light를 이용해 혼동을 주기 위한 보기이다.

light 불을 붙이다, 성냥, 담뱃불 **make a wish** 소원을 빌다 **blow out** (불을) 불어서 끄다 **all of a sudden** 갑자기

---

15 W Dad. Can I have some candy?
   M What time is it? I think it's getting close to dinner time.
   W It's five. Just one, please.
   M _____

   (a) No, thank you.
   (b) It will spoil your appetite.
   (c) You're welcome.
   (d) I have something for you.

W: 아빠. 사탕 좀 먹어도 되요?
M: 몇 시지? 저녁 시간이 다 된 것 같은데.
W: 5시요. 하나만요. 제발.
M: 사탕을 먹으면 입맛을 버릴 거야.

○ 사탕을 먹어도 되느냐고 조르는 딸아이에게 저녁 시간이 다 되었다고 했으므로 사탕을 먹으면 입맛을 버리니 먹지 말라는 뉘앙스의 (b)가 정답이 된다. (a)는 고맙지만 사양하겠다는 뜻이고 (c)는 감사 인사에 대해 '천만에요' 라는 뜻, (d) 선물 등을 줄 때 '네게 줄 것이 있어' 라는 뜻이다.

spoil 망치다 **appetite** 식욕

---

16 M What are you going to do tonight? How about going to the library?
   W Come on, dad! We're going out to eat, and then we're going to the movies.
   M What movie are you going to see?
   W It's a romantic comedy. Anyway, don't worry. It's rated PG-13.
   M Hey, I was thinking about seeing a movie down there, too.
   W Oh, please.
   M Okay, then. When will you be back? Be home by 9 o'clock.
   W Dad. The movie starts at 7:30.

   Q What is the man's attitude in this conversation?

   (a) encouraging
   (b) amicable
   (c) sarcastic
   (d) prying

M: 오늘밤 뭐할 거야? 도서관에 가는 게 어때?
W: 제발, 아빠. 우리는 나가서 밥을 먹고 영화를 보러 갈 거에요.
M: 무슨 영화를 볼 건데?
W: 로맨틱 코미디에요. 어쨌든 걱정 마세요. 13세 이상 관람가 영화에요.
M: 어, 나도 거기서 영화를 볼까 생각하고 있었어.
W: 아빠, 제발
M: 알겠다. 그럼. 언제 돌아올 거야? 9시까지 들어와.
W: 아빠. 영화가 7시 30분에 시작해요.

○ 남자의 태도에 대해 묻고 있다. 남자는 여자의 아버지임을 알 수 있고, 딸아이의 사생활에 대해 이것저것 간섭하고 캐묻고 있으므로 이러한 뜻에 해당하는 prying이 정답이다.

go to the movies 영화 보러 가다 **amicable** 우호적인, 원만한 **sarcastic** 풍자적인, 비꼬는 **prying** 꼬치꼬치 캐기 좋아하는

미국 영화등급 체계: G(general audiences) 누구나 입장할 수 있는 영화 PG(parental guidance suggested) 학부모의 지도를 요하는 영화 R(restricted) 17세 이하의 경우 부모나 어른을 동반해야 하는 영화 NC-17 17세 이하 관람불가의 영화

17 M Hurry up! We're going to miss our train.

W I'm almost done. I'm changing my clothes.

M If we miss this train, we'll have to wait for the next one.

W When is the next train?

M I'm not sure, but I think we'll have to wait more than two hours.

Q What is correct according to the conversation?

(a) The speakers bought train tickets in advance.

(b) The woman is waiting for the man to be ready to leave.

(c) The speakers have yet to leave the place.

(d) The woman is complaining to the man.

M: 서둘러! 기차를 놓치겠어.

W: 거의 다 됐어. 옷을 갈아입고 있어.

M: 이 기차를 놓치면 다음 기차를 기다려야 할 거야.

W: 다음 기차는 언제 있는데?

M: 잘 모르겠지만, 두 시간 이상 기다려야 할 거야.

○ 대화와 일치하는 내용을 고르는 문제이다. 기차표를 미리 샀는지에 대한 것은 이 대화만으로는 알 수 없으므로 (a)는 정답이라고 하기 어렵다. 남자가 여자를 기다리고 있는 상황이므로 (b)와 (d)는 정답이 아니다. 아직 출발하지 못한 상황이므로 (c)는 정답이 된다.

miss ~을 놓치다. ~을 그리워하다 **have yet to** 아직 ~하지 않았다

---

18 W Excuse me. Do you know how to get to the nearest subway station?

M Well, there aren't any around here. Where are you going?

W I'm going to City Hall.

M You can catch a bus, but you should transfer.

W Where is the bus stop?

M Go straight along this street and turn left at the blue sign. Do you see it?

W Yes. What number should I take?

M Number 25, and 26. And you should transfer to number 5 at the Central Bank.

Q Which is correct according to the conversation?

(a) The speakers are talking in the bus.

(b) The woman is going to the Central Bank.

(c) The woman took the wrong bus.

(d) The man is giving the woman directions.

W: 실례합니다. 가장 가까운 지하철역에 어떻게 가는지 아세요?

M: 글쎄요. 이 주변엔 하나도 없는데요. 어디로 가시는데요?

W: 시청이요.

M: 버스를 타시면 되는데요. 갈아타셔야 해요.

W: 버스 정류장은 어디죠?

M: 이 길을 따라 곧장 가시다가 파란색 간판이 있는 곳에서 왼쪽으로 꺾으세요. 파란 간판 보이세요?

W: 네. 몇 번을 타야 하나요?

M: 25번과 26번이요. 그리고 중앙은행에서 5번으로 갈아타세요.

○ 대화와 일치하는 것을 고르는 문제이다. 여자가 지하철 역을 묻자 남자는 근처에 없다고 하면서 버스 정류장을 가르쳐주고 있다. 따라서 대화 장소는 버스 안이 아님을 알 수 있으므로 (a)는 정답이 아니다. 여자가 가는 곳은 시청이고 중앙은행에서 버스를 갈아타야 하므로 (b)도 정답이 될 수 없다. 여자가 버스를 잘못 탔다는 (c)는 전혀 무관한 이야기이다. 남자가 여자에게 길을 알려주고 있으므로 (d)가 정답이 된다.

catch a bus 버스를 타다 **transfer** (버스, 전철 등을) 갈아타다 **sign** 간판, 표지 **direction** 방향, 사용법

19 W Hey, Jake. What are you doing this weekend?

M Well, nothing special.

W I'm going to see a movie with Sara. Do you want to come? I got complimentary tickets.

M Which movie is it?

W It's a horror movie and the reviews are quite good.

M Okay, I'm in! I'm not into horror movies, though.

Q Which is true according to the conversation?

(a) The man has something to do this weekend.

(b) The woman wants him to treat her.

(c) The man decided to see the movie.

(d) The man likes to see horror movies.

W: 안녕, 제이크. 이번 주말에 뭐 할 거야?

M: 글쎄. 특별한 계획은 없어.

W: 나는 사라랑 영화 보러 갈 거야. 같이 갈래? 초대권이 있어.

M: 어떤 영화인데?

W: 공포 영화인데 평이 좋아.

M: 그래, 나도 갈래! 공포 영화는 별로 좋아하지 않지만.

○ 대화와 일치하는 내용을 고르는 문제이다. 남자의 첫 대사를 보면 특별한 계획이 없다고 했으므로 (a)는 정답이 아니다. 여자가 초대권이 있다고 했으므로 (b)도 정답이 아니다. 마지막에 남자가 'I'm in'이라고 하면서 같이 가겠다고 했으므로 영화를 보기로 결정했음을 알 수 있으므로 (c)가 정답이 된다. 공포 영화를 좋아하지 않는다고 했기 때문에 (c)를 오답으로 생각할 수 있는데 though는 '그럼에도 불구하고' 라는 뜻이다.

complimentary ticket 우대권, 초대권 be into ~에 열중하다, ~에 빠지다 treat ~을 대접하다 though ~에도 불구하고

---

20 M Could you please arrange a meeting with our clients for this week?

W Absolutely. Which day is best for you?

M Thursday or Friday would be okay.

W You have a full schedule this week. How about next Monday?

M Well, let's make it for next Monday afternoon then.

W I got it.

Q Which is correct according to the conversation?

(a) The man is scheduled to meet his clients this Thursday.

(b) The man has no schedule next Monday.

(c) The woman is complaining about the man's busy schedule.

(d) The man and the woman is talking about the meeting venue

M: 이번 주에 우리 고객과 미팅을 잡아줄래요?

W: 알겠습니다. 언제가 가장 좋으세요?

M: 목요일이나 금요일이 좋겠네요.

W: 이번 주는 일정이 다 잡혀 있습니다. 다음주 월요일은 어떠세요?

M: 그럼 다음주 월요일 오후로 합시다.

W: 알겠습니다.

○ 대화와 일치하는 내용을 묻고 있다. 미팅 일정은 최종적으로 다음 주 월요일로 잡혔다. 따라서 (a)는 정답이 아니다. 다음주 월요일에 미팅 계획을 잡았다고 했으므로 그날은 스케줄이 없다는 것을 알 수 있다. 따라서 (b)는 정답이 된다. 여자는 남자의 비서로 불평을 하고 있는 것이 아니므로 (c)는 정답이 아니고, 회의 장소에 대한 언급은 없었으므로 (d)도 정답이 아니다.

arrange 계획하다, 준비하다 venue (행사, 회의 등의) 장소

21 **M** Dinner is almost ready!

 W Coming! What are you doing? Where's mom?

 M Your mom is not feeling well today. So I prepared dinner for you.

 W Is there anything I can do to help?

 M No. Just go wash your hands first.

 W I will. By the way, what's for dinner?

 M I made curry today.

 Q Which is true according to this conversation?

 (a) The man work as a cook.
 (b) Curry is the woman's favorite food.
 (c) The woman's mom is too sick to cook.
 (d) The man has never cooked before.

M: 저녁 거의 다 됐다!

W: 가요! 뭐하세요? 엄마는 어디 있어요?

M: 엄마는 오늘 몸이 안 좋아. 그래서 아빠가 저녁을 준비했어.

W: 제가 도와드릴 거 있어요?

M: 아니. 그냥 가서 손부터 씻어.

W: 네. 근데 저녁 메뉴는 뭐예요?

M: 오늘 카레를 했어.

○ 대화와 일치하는 내용을 묻고 있다. 남자의 직업이 요리사인지는 알 수 없으므로 (a)는 정답이 아니고, 여자가 카레를 좋아하는지는 언급이 되지 않았으므로 (b) 역시 정답이라 할 수 없다. 여자의 엄마가 몸이 아파 아빠가 대신 저녁을 준비한 것이므로 (c)가 정답이 된다. (d)도 언급되지 않았으므로 알 수 없다.

favorite 아주 좋아하는 too ~ to 너무 ~해서 ~할 수 없다

---

22 **M** Jenny, why did you come in so early? You still have an hour before the class begins.

 W What are you talking about? The class starts at 9:00. Wake up!!

 M The professor said she had something to take care of. So the class starts at 10:00 today.

 W Oh, I didn't know that. I shouldn't have left the classroom early. But why are you here then?

 M Actually I didn't know that, either. I heard it from the assistant.

 W Well, would you care for some coffee?

 Q What can you infer from the dialogue?

 (a) The man is a teaching assistant.
 (b) The woman missed the last class.
 (c) The man doesn't want to attend the class today.
 (d) They are going to kill some time together.

M: 제니, 왜 이렇게 빨리 왔어? 수업이 시작하려면 한 시간이나 남았는데.

W: 무슨 이야기 하는 거야? 수업은 9시에 시작하잖아. 정신 차려!!

M: 교수님이 처리해야 할 일이 있다고 말씀하셨잖아. 그래서 수업은 오늘 10시에 시작해.

W: 어머, 나는 몰랐어. 강의실을 일찍 나가지 말았어야 했는데. 근데 그럼 넌 왜 여기 있니?

M: 사실 나도 몰랐거든. 조교 선생님한테 들었어.

W: 그래, 그럼 커피라도 마실래?

○ 추론 문제이다. 남자는 여자와 같은 수업을 듣는 학생이므로 (a)는 정답이 아니다. 여자는 수업이 끝나고 일찍 강의실을 나간 것이지 수업을 빠진 것이 아니므로 (b)도 정답이 아니다. 남자는 수업 시간보다 일찍 와서 기다리고 있었으므로 (c)도 정답이 아니다. 여자의 마지막 대사를 보면 같이 커피를 마시러 나갈 것임을 알 수 있다. 수업 시간이 한 시간 남았으므로 같이 시간을 때울 것임을 추측할 수 있으므로 정답은 (d)가 된다.

wake up (잠을 깨울 때) 일어나! 정신 차려! assistant 조교, 보조자 attend 출석하다, 참석하다 kill time 시간을 보내다

23 The salmon is a beautiful and amazing fish. They live in the sea but return to fresh water to spawn and then die. They spawn in September and October, when they can be seen passing up the river. They find shallow places to breed. July and August is the best time to catch them. During this period, they come up from the sea and have gained a lot of weight. The rivers in Ireland and Scotland are good places for salmon.

Q Which is correct about the salmon?

(a) The salmon returns to the sea after they spawned.
(b) They swim up the river in June, July and August.
(c) They lay their eggs in the deep places of the river.
(d) The rivers in Ireland and Scotland are abundant in salmon

연어는 아름답고 놀랍다. 연어는 바다에 살지만 민물로 돌아와 알을 낳고 죽는다. 연어는 9월과 10월에 알을 낳는데 이 때 연어가 강을 거슬러 올라가는 모습을 볼 수 있다. 연어는 알을 낳기 위해 얕은 곳을 찾는다. 7, 8월이 연어를 잡기 가장 좋은 시기이다. 이 시기에 연어는 바다에서 올라오는데, 살이 꽉 차올랐다. 아일랜드와 스코틀랜드에 있는 강은 연어를 잡기 좋은 장소들이다.

◐ 연어에 대한 내용 중 옳은 것을 묻고 있다. 알을 낳고 죽는다고 했으므로 (a)는 정답이 아니다. 7, 8월에 연어를 가장 잡기 좋다고 했지만 9월에 강을 거슬러 올라오는 모습을 볼 수 있다고 했으므로 (b)도 정답이 아니다. 알을 낳기 위해 얕은 곳을 찾는다고 했으므로 (c)도 정답이 아니다. 아일랜드와 스코틀랜드에 있는 강들이 연어를 잡기 좋은 장소라고 했으므로 연어가 풍부하다는 것을 알 수 있다. 따라서 정답은 (d)이다.

salmon 연어 spawn 알을 낳다 breed 알을 낳다 lay 알을 낳다 abundant 풍부한

---

24 Do you like your appearance? Do you like to look into a mirror? If not, you don't have to be worried. No problem. Just go to the plastic surgeon. The technology will solve your dilemma. Do you feel bad about your fair complexion? It's not a problem because tanning salons are everywhere. The list goes on and on. These are insecurities that surround us. However, beauty is in the eye of the beholder. Something might be seen attractive to one person. But others might not think so. This is my thought. Every individual has their own unique traits.

Q Which is correct according to the talk?

(a) People who underwent plastic surgery are not content with the results.
(b) Plastic surgery is good for people with no confidence.
(c) We should value our own unique personality.
(d) People who got lasic surgery suffer from complications.

여러분은 자신의 외모가 마음에 듭니까? 거울 보는 것이 좋으신가요? 그렇지 않다면, 걱정하실 필요가 없습니다. 아무 문제가 없습니다. 그냥 성형외과 의사에게 가세요. 기술이 여러분의 딜레마를 해결해줄 것입니다. 흰 피부가 싫습니까? 선탠을 할 수 있는 곳이 어디에나 있기 때문에 문제가 되지 않습니다. 그 밖에도 리스트는 계속 이어집니다. 이것들이 우리를 둘러싼 불안 요소들입니다. 그러나 아름다움은 제 눈에 안경입니다. 어떤 것이 한 사람에게는 매력적으로 보일지 모릅니다. 하지만 다른 사람들에게는 그렇지 않을 수도 있습니다. 이것이 저의 생각입니다. 모든 개인은 자신의 독특한 특색이 있습니다.

◐ 내용과 일치하는 것을 고르는 문제이다. 성형수술을 겪은 사람들이 결과에 만족하지 못한다는 내용은 언급이 없었으므로 (a)는 정답이 아니다. (b) 역시 언급이 없었으므로 정답이 될 수 없다. 마지막 부분에 개인마다 독특한 특색이 있다고 했으므로 이러한 개성을 중시해야 한다는 것을 알 수 있다. 따라서 정답은 (c)이다. 라식 수술에 대해서는 이야기하지 않았으므로 (d)도 정답이 될 수 없다.

appearance 외모, 외관 plastic surgeon 성형외과 의사 fair complexion 흰 피부 insecurity 불안감 trait 특색, 특징 content 만족한 complication 합병증

25 A 20-year-old woman was arrested for failing to pay her library fines. The library had sent two notices as well as making two phone calls to her to retrieve the books she had taken out. But she didn't respond. So the library transferred the case to local police. And the police notified her by mail that she would either have to pay a $250 fine or appear in court. She said she was going to appear in court, but got stuck at work.

Q Which is correct according to the news report?

(a) The woman paid 250 dollars for her library fines.
(b) The library didn't warn the woman about late payment in advance.
(c) The police called the woman that she would have to appear in court.
(d) The woman knew she had to appear in court, but she didn't.

20세 여자가 도서관 벌금을 내지 않아 체포되었습니다. 그 도서관은 그녀가 대출한 책을 회수하기 위해 그녀에게 두 번이나 전화했을 뿐 아니라 두 번의 공지를 보냈습니다. 하지만 그녀는 답변하지 않았습니다. 그래서 도서관 측은 이 사건을 지역 경찰에 넘겼습니다. 그리고 경찰은 메일로 그녀에게 250달러의 벌금을 내거나 법정에 출두해야 한다고 알렸습니다. 그녀는 법정에 출두하려고 했으나 일이 바빠서 꼼짝할 수 없다고 말했습니다.

○ 뉴스의 내용과 일치하는 것을 고르는 내용이다. 여자는 연체료를 내지 않아 체포되었다고 했으므로 (a)는 사실과 다르다. 도서관 측에서는 두 번의 공지를 했다고 했으므로 미리 경고하지 않았다는 내용의 (b)는 정답이 아니다. 경찰은 여자에게 법정에 출두하라고 전화를 한 것이 아니라 메일을 보냈으므로 (c) 역시 정답이 아니다. 그녀는 바빠서 법정에 출두하지 못했다고 했으므로 여자는 출두해야 한다는 사실을 알고 있었으므로 정답은 (d)가 된다.

arrest 체포하다 **fine** 벌금 **notice** 공지 **retrieve** 되찾다, 회수하다 **transfer** 이동시키다, 옮기다 **in advance** 미리

---

26 If you have a dog, it can be difficult to train it to behave. However, behavior training is not that difficult. Make sure that it is what kind of behavior you will allow in the first place. You should let your dog know what's good and bad. Dogs are very sensitive to intonation. So when you train them or teach them a new behavior, try to use a firm voice. If you have any trouble with training your dog nevertheless, you can get help from a dog training guide.

Q What is correct according to the talk?

(a) You must not allow your dog to walk without leash.
(b) The speaker is talking about a pet supplies department.
(c) When you discipline your dog, it is better to use a stern voice.
(d) It is better to train your dog yourself than through the pet training center.

만약 강아지를 키우고 있다면 행동 훈련이 가장 어려울 수 있습니다. 그러나 행동 훈련은 그렇게 어렵지 않습니다. 우선 그것이 해도 되는 행동이라는 것을 확실히 해주세요. 어떤 것이 좋은 행동이고 어떤 것이 나쁜 행동인지 강아지에게 알려주어야 합니다. 개들은 억양에 매우 민감합니다. 그래서 개를 훈련하거나 새로운 행동을 가르칠 때에는 단호한 목소리를 사용하도록 노력해야 합니다. 그럼에도 불구하고 개를 훈련시키는 데 어려움이 있다면 개 훈련 도우미의 도움을 받을 수 있습니다.

○ 내용과 일치하는 것을 고르는 문제이다. 목줄을 매고 안 매고의 문제는 언급하지 않았으므로 (a)는 정답이 아니다. 애완 용품에 대한 언급 역시 없었으므로 (b)도 정답이 아니다. 개를 훈련시킬 때에는 단호한 목소리를 사용하라고 했으므로 (c)가 정답이 된다. 개를 훈련시키는 데 어려움이 있을 경우 훈련 도우미의 도움을 받으라고 했으므로 (d)도 정답이 아니다.

in the first place 우선 **intonation** 억양 **firm** 단호한, 확고한 **leash** (개를 묶는) 가죽 끈 **discipline** 훈련하다 **stern** 엄격한, 단호한

27 I'd say the biggest problem for people who suffer from insomnia is going to bed when they aren't actually sleepy. If you aren't sleepy, just get up and stay up for a while. Don't sleep until your body secretes the hormones that disturb your consciousness. If you go to bed when you feel sleepy and get up at a fixed time, your insomnia will be cured naturally. You can make it a habit to fall asleep right away after a few days of training.

Q What is correct according to the talk?

   (a) Insomnia is a cause of disrupting human hormones.

   (b) There's no way to cure insomnia completely.

   (c) When you feel sleepy, your body releases some hormones.

   (d) You shouldn't struggle to get up at a fixed time to cure insomnia.

가장 큰 문제는 불면증을 겪는 사람들이 진짜 졸리지 않을 때 잠자리에 드는 것이라고 말씀드릴 수 있겠습니다. 졸리지 않다면, 그냥 일어나서 잠시 동안 깨어 있으세요. 몸이 의식을 방해하는 호르몬을 분비할 때까지 잠을 자지 마세요. 졸릴 때 잠자리에 들고 고정된 시간에 일어난다면 불면증은 자연스럽게 치료될 것입니다. 며칠 동안의 훈련 후에 바로 잠자리에 드는 것을 습관화할 수 있습니다.

◐ 내용과 일치하는 것을 고르는 문제이다. 불면증이 호르몬을 파괴하는 원인이라는 언급은 없었으므로 (a)는 정답이 아니다. 불면증은 훈련으로 자연스럽게 치료할 수 있다고 했으므로 (b)도 정답이 아니다. 의식을 방해하는 호르몬이 분비되면 잠자리에 들라고 했으므로 졸릴 때 호르몬이 분비됨을 알 수 있다. 따라서 (c)가 정답이 된다. 불면증을 치료하려면 고정된 시간에 일어나는 것이 좋다고 했으므로 (d)도 정답이 아니다.

insomnia 불면증 stay up 깨어 있다 secrete 분비하다 consciousness 의식 make it a habit to ~하는 것을 습관화하다

---

28 We have many active subscribers and you are always welcome to sign up for our web site. You can use all the contents in the web site for free. Newsletters are sent every other week. And if you want to unsubscribe, just click the cancellation link. Your personal information will be kept confidential. And if you use spam-blocker, please make sure to add the web site address to your email list not to block our newsletter.

Q What is correct according to the talk?

   (a) You can use some information for free in the web site.

   (b) You can get biweekly newsletter after signing up for the site.

   (c) You don't need to enter your personal information to join the site.

   (d) The web site provides spam-blocker service for free.

저희 사이트에는 적극적인 많은 구독자들이 있고 여러분께서도 저희 웹사이트에 가입하시길 언제나 환영합니다. 사이트의 모든 컨텐츠는 무료로 이용하실 수 있습니다. 뉴스레터는 2주에 한 번씩 보내드립니다. 그리고 구독을 중단하고 싶으시다면 취소 버튼을 누르시기만 하면 됩니다. 당신의 개인 정보는 비공개로 유지될 것입니다. 그리고 스팸 차단기를 이용하신다면 저희 뉴스레터를 차단하지 않도록 이메일 리스트에 저희 웹사이트 주소를 등록해 주십시오.

◐ 내용과 일치하는 것을 고르는 문제이다. 웹사이트의 일부 내용이 아닌 모든 내용을 무료로 이용할 수 있다고 했으므로 (a)는 정답이 아니다. 격주로 뉴스레터를 보내준다고 했으므로 (b)가 정답이 된다. 개인 정보는 비공개로 유지된다고 했으므로 가입시 개인 정보를 입력해야 함을 알 수 있다. 따라서 (c)도 정답이 아니다. 스팸 차단기가 뉴스레터를 차단하지 않도록 이메일 주소 목록에 웹사이트 주소를 첨가하라고 주의를 주고 있지만 사이트 자체에서 스팸차단 서비스를 제공한다는 이야기는 없었으므로 (d)도 정답이 될 수 없다.

active 활기 있는, 적극적인, 능동적인 subscriber 구독자 for free 무료로 confidential 은밀한, 비밀의

29 The number of Internet users is increasing drastically. There are many good points about online shopping but online fraud is a cause for concern amongst internet users. Many people sometimes end up with their personal information in the hands of criminals. And a busy Christmas season approaches, online sales are predicted to rise. It means consumers using Internet to shop will have to pay particular attention to avoid online fraud. There are, however, some steps you can take to protect yourself from fraud and shop safely and grab the bargains.

Q What will the speaker likely talk about next?

(a) Good points about using Internet shopping
(b) A few steps for safe online shopping
(c) Types of online fraud and how to deal with it
(d) Leaking of private information through online shopping

인터넷 사용자의 수가 급격히 증가하고 있습니다. 온라인 쇼핑은 장점이 많지만 온라인을 통한 사기는 인터넷 사용자들 사이에 걱정의 원인이 됩니다. 많은 사람들은 가끔 범죄자들의 손에 개인 정보를 넘겨줍니다. 그리고 바쁜 크리스마스 시즌이 다가옴에 따라 온라인 판매가 증가할 것으로 예상됩니다. 이것은 인터넷을 이용하는 소비자들이 온라인 사기를 피하기 위해 각별한 주의를 기울여야 한다는 것을 의미합니다. 그러나 사기꾼으로부터 자신을 보호하고 안전하게 쇼핑하고 싼 물건을 살 수 있는 몇 가지 단계가 있습니다.

🔵 다음에 이어질 내용에 대해 묻고 있다. 마지막 문장에 주의해서 들어야 한다. 안전한 온라인 쇼핑을 위한 몇 가지 단계가 있다고 했으므로 그에 대한 자세한 이야기가 나올 것이라고 추측할 수 있다. 따라서 정답은 (b)가 된다.

drastically 맹렬히, 철저히 **fraud** 사기 **approach** 다가오다, 근접하다 **predict** 예상하다 **leak** 누출, 누설

---

30 Did you know 60% of written English is not phonetic? It makes many learners feel a sense of frustration in pronouncing English words. But it's too early to give up. The Web Text Converter is your answer! It changes English text into readable English. This might be a quick and easy way to improve your accent, pronunciation, and reading skills. Please do not hesitate to choose this product if you want to read and speak English correctly.

Q What can be inferred from the advertisement?

(a) Most of English words are not spoken as they are written.
(b) The Web Text Converter translates English into other languages.
(c) This is an advertisement about English language course.
(d) This is technology for those who can't read English.

문자로 된 영어의 60%가 발음과 다르다는 사실을 아셨나요? 이로 인해 많은 학습자들은 영어 단어를 발음하는 데 있어서 좌절감을 느낍니다. 하지만 포기하기에는 너무 이릅니다. Web Text Converter가 바로 답입니다! 이것은 영어 텍스트를 읽을 수 있는 영어로 바꿔줍니다. 이것은 억양, 발음, 읽기 기술을 향상시키기 위한 빠르고 쉬운 방법이 될지 모릅니다. 영어를 바르게 읽고 말하고 싶다면 주저하지 마시고 이 상품을 선택해주세요.

🔵 광고로부터 추측할 수 있는 것을 고르는 문제이다. 첫 문장에서 문자로 된 영어의 60%가 발음과 다르다고 했으므로 대부분의 영어 단어들이 철자대로 읽히지 않는다는 사실을 추측할 수 있다. 따라서 정답은 (a)가 된다. Web Text Converter의 경우 영어를 읽을 수 있게 바꿔주는 것이므로 다른 언어로 번역해준다는 내용의 (b)는 정답이 아니다. 영어 강좌에 대한 광고가 아니므로 (c)도 정답이 아니다. 영어를 읽지 못하는 사람들을 위한 기술이 아닌 영어를 읽기는 읽되 더 쉽고 빠르게 읽을 수 있도록 도와주는 기술이므로 (d)는 정답이라 할 수 없다.

phonetic 발음에 따른, 발음 그대로의 **frustration** 좌절 **readable** 읽을 수 있는, 읽기 쉬운

31 **A** How often does the shuttle come?

B _____ until midnight.

(a) Every two an hour
(b) Every an half hour
(c) Any half an hour
(d) Every half an hour

A: 셔틀버스가 얼마나 자주 오니?
B: 밤 12시까지 30분마다 와.

○ '~마다' 를 뜻하는 every가 필요하고, '30분' 을 뜻하는 표현은 half an hour 이므로 (d)가 답이다.

midnight 자정

---

32 **A** Guess what? Sally is being promoted soon.

B Wow, she _____.

(a) deserved the reward
(b) deserving the reward
(c) is deserve the reward
(d) deserves the reward

A: 그거 알아? Sally가 곧 승진한대.
B: 와, 그녀는 그런 대접을 받을 만해.

○ '~할 만하다, 자격이 있다' 는 의미의 타동사 deserve가 필요하며, 내용상 현재 시제이다.

promote 승진하다 **deserve** 받을 만하다 **reward** 포상, 보수

---

33 **A** What time do I have to submit this report?

B _____ this afternoon.

(a) Until 5 o'clock
(b) To 5 o'clock
(c) By 5 o'clock
(d) For 5 o'clock

A: 이 보고서 언제까지 제출해야 해?
B: 오늘 오후 5시까지.

○ 기한을 나타낼 때, 일반적으로 '~까지' 의 의미로 by(=not later than)를 쓴다.

submit 제출하다

---

34 **A** Wow, so many things have changed.

B Yes, there _____ a flea market here.

(a) used to be
(b) would be
(c) might used to be
(d) could have used

A: 우와, 많은 게 바뀌었어.
B: 응, 여기 벼룩시장이 열리곤 했었는데.

○ 과거의 일이나 상태를 회상하는 표현으로는 used to가 가장 적절하다. used to는 '~하곤 했었다, ~가 있었다' 는 의미의 조동사이다. (c)는 might라는 조동사가 거듭 쓰였기 때문에 정답이 될 수 없다.

flea market 벼룩시장

---

35 **A** Listen, honey, somebody is yelling again.

B I don't understand _____ other's privacy.

(a) why doesn't she respect
(b) why she doesn't respect
(c) why she won't respect
(d) why won't she respect

A: 들어봐 자기야, 누군가가 또 소리 지르고 있어.
B: 나는 그녀가 왜 다른 사람의 사생활을 존중하지 않는지 이해가 안가.

○ 간접의문문이므로 의문사+주어+동사 순으로 와야 한다. 현재 시제를 써야 하므로 정답은 (b)이다.

yell 소리 지르다 **respect** 존중하다, 존경하다

36 A Why do you have such a long face?
B I got a bad score on the final English test, and _____ feel blue.

(a) a score made me
(b) made me the score
(c) made a score made for me
(d) the score made me

A: 너 표정이 안 좋아 보이는데 무슨 일 있니?
B: 기말 영어시험 성적이 나빠. 그리고 그 성적 때문에 우울해.

◐ '나'를 우울하게 만든 것은 그 성적이므로 주어로 'score'를 써야 한다. 앞에서 score를 한번 언급해 주었으므로 정관사 the를 쓴다.

long face 우울한 얼굴 score 점수, 성적 blue 우울한

---

37 A How may I help you, ma'am?
B Could I have _____ cup of tea?

(a) other
(b) some
(c) another
(d) others

A: 부인, 무엇을 도와드릴까요?
B: 차 한 잔 더 할 수 있을까요?

◐ 상황을 추론해볼 때, B는 이미 차 한 잔을 마시고 한 잔을 더 청하는 상황이므로 another가 가장 적절하다.

---

38 A Has she completed the whole course?
B Yes, _____, she ran the whole distance.

(a) a woman as she was
(b) as a woman she was
(c) woman as she was
(d) woman as she was a

A: 그녀는 전 코스를 완주했니?
B: 응, 여자인데도 그녀는 전체 거리를 달렸어.

◐ 형용사나 혹은 부사/관사가 없는 명사가 앞에 쓰인 접속사 as는 '~이지만'이라는 양보의 뜻을 가진다. (c)가 가장 적절하다.

complete 완성하다 whole 전체의 distance 거리, 장거리

---

39 A Is your mom at home? I heard she went traveling abroad.
B No, _____ last week, she will return home tomorrow.

(a) she left
(b) leaving
(c) left
(d) had left

A: 너희 엄마 집에 계시니? 해외여행 가셨다고 들었는데.
B: 아니, 지난주에 떠나셨는데, 내일 집에 오실 거야.

◐ 분사구문으로, 주어와의 관계가 능동이므로 현재분사를 쓴 (b)가 가장 적절하다.

abroad 해외의 return 돌아오다

---

40 A How was the movie last night?
B Amazing! You _____ us.

(a) have joined
(b) must have joined
(c) could have joined
(d) should have joined

A: 어젯밤에 그 영화 어땠어?
B: 재미있었어! 너도 우리랑 함께 했으면 좋았을 텐데.

◐ 과거에 못 한 일에 대한 유감을 나타내는 표현은 'should have p.p'이다.

41 There are barely any dialogues
_____ for the last ten minutes of the
film.

(a) spoke
(b) speak
(c) spoken
(d) speaking

영화의 마지막 10분 동안 거의 아무 대화도 없었다.

○ 분사를 형용사처럼 쓸 때, 분사가 수식하는 대상과 문장의 의미상의 주어간의 관계가 위 문장처럼 수동인 경우에는 현재분사가 아니라 과거분사를 써야 한다.

barely 거의 ~ 않다

---

42 When they gathered that night to observe
the Passover Meal, _____ the
significance of what was about to happen.

(a) they hardly could understand
(b) hardly they understood
(c) hardly they could understand
(d) hardly could they understand.

그날 밤 최후의 만찬을 거행하기 위하여 모였을 때, 그들은 앞으로 일어날 일에 대한 중요성을 거의 알지 못했다.

○ 원래의 문장 'they could hardly understand' 에서, 부정의 의미를 가진 부사 hardly를 앞에 도치했을 때 나머지 단어들의 어순을 묻는 문제이다.

gather 모이다 observe (의식 등을)거행하다 the Passover Meal 최후의 만찬

---

43 _____ rust eats iron, so care eats
the heart.

(a) Though
(b) As
(c) Like
(d) Despite

녹이 철을 부식하듯이, 지나친 걱정은 마음을 다치게 한다.

○ As ~ , so – 는 '~처럼, – 하다' 의 의미를 가진 접속사로 쓰인다.

rust 녹

---

44 We always look to see _____ who
needs help.

(a) there is anybody
(b) if there is anybody
(c) if anybody is
(d) if anybody is there

우리는 도움이 필요한 누군가가 있는지 항상 살핀다.

○ if ~가 '혹시 ~인지 아닌지' 의 의미를 가지는 간접의문문 표현을 묻는 문제이다.

---

45 _____ , he wasn't surprised when
he saw the initial images of a desolated
earth.

(a) Being forewarned
(b) Be forewarned
(c) To be forewarned
(d) Be forewarning

사전에 통고를 받았기 때문에, 그는 최초의 지구의 황량한 모습을 보고서도 놀라지 않았다.

○ 'Because(=As) he was forewarned' 를 분사구문으로 올바르게 바꾸어 쓴 것을 찾는 문제이다. 수동의 의미는 (being)+동사의 p.p형태로 표현한다.

initial 처음의 desolate 황량한, 쓸쓸한 forewarn 미리 경고하다

46 That's why your hair looks greasy and
_____ .

(a) loosing hair easily
(b) loose hair easily
(c) you loose hair easily
(d) you to loose hair easily

그것이 당신의 머리카락이 기름져 지저분해 보이고, 머리카락이 쉽게 빠지는 이유입니다.

➲ That's why~ 라는 표현에 두 개의 절이 병렬적으로 연결된 문장이다.

greasy 기름진

---

47 Learn the ways of _____ and look better so that you control the whole organization.

(a) making you to feel calm
(b) making yourself feel calm
(c) making you felt calm
(d) making yourself felt calm

자신을 침착하게 만들어 더 낫게 보이는 법을 배워 조직 전체를 통제하도록 해라.

➲ make가 사역동사이므로 목적격보어 자리에 feel이 동사원형 형태로 와야 한다. '너 자신을 침착하게 만드는 방법' 으로 해석되므로 명령문이라 생략된 주어인 you가 다시 자신을 목적어로 갖기 때문에 재귀대명사 yourself를 써야 한다.

---

48 The skin of your palm is more sensitive than _____.

(a) that of your face
(b) those of your face
(c) your face's skin
(d) your face

손바닥의 피부는 얼굴의 그것보다 예민하다.

➲ 원래는 'the skin of your face' 가 맞는 표현이지만, 중복되는 부분을 대명사로 바꾼 표현을 찾는 문제이다. 대명사로 바꿔야 할 부분이 단수이므로 that 이 적절한 표현이다.

palm 손바닥 sensitive 민감한

---

49 Be reliable, trustworthy, and confidential _____.

(a) of all circumstance
(b) in circumstances
(c) all circumstance
(d) in all circumstances

모든 상황에서 믿을 만하고, 신뢰가 가며, 자신 있는 사람이 되어라.

➲ '모든 상황에서' 의 표현을 쓸 때는 전치사 in이 적절하다.

reliable 믿을 수 있는 trustworthy 신뢰할 만한

---

50 It's _____ their wishes because of the school's policies.

(a) students undesirable to disregard
(b) undesirable for students to disregard
(c) undesirable of students to disregard
(d) disregard undesirable for students

학생들이 그들의 소망을 학교 정책 때문에 낮추는 것은 바람직하지 못하다.

➲ 'It~ for~ to~' 구문은 'for 이하의 대상이 to 이하 하는 것이 It 이하 하다' 는 표현이다.

disregard 무시하다

51 (a) A: Don't forget to bring the computer and documents on the table.
(b) B: OK, what else do I have to check?
(c) A: Nothing else, just bring it
(d) B: That's a relief, I have too many things to remember.

A: 탁자 위의 컴퓨터와 서류 가져오는 거 잊지 마.
B: 알았어, 내가 확인할 게 또 있니?
A: 아니, 그냥 그것만 가져와.
B: 안심이다. 기억할 게 너무 많아.

○ 지시 대명사 사용 오류를 찾는 문제이다. (c)번의 it은 them으로 바꿔야 한다.

---

52 (a) A: Haven't you ever visited the Natural History Museum?
(b) B: I did once, but I couldn't look around much.
(c) A: Poor, Jenny. I went there with my mother and she explained all sections.
(d) B: It sounds wonderful.

A: 자연사 박물관에 가본 적이 있니?
B: 한번 가봤어, 근데 충분히 돌아다니질 못했지.
A: 유감이야, Jenny. 난 엄마랑 갔었는데 모든 구역을 다 설명해주셨어.
B: 정말 좋았겠다.

○ A가 Have~? 를 사용해서 질문을 했으므로 B의 대답도 do/did가 아닌 have를 사용해서 해야 한다. I did once를 Once I have로 고친다.

---

53 (a) A half-dozen robots are working on the surface or in orbit around Mars, discovering that traces of water exist. (b) They even make us think about possibilities of some microbial or other early life forms on the Planet! (c) Thanks to Cassini, we are discovering lakes on Titan, the only place outside Earth which liquid exists on the surface of a world. (d) We're even contemplating the possibility of life in such exotic worlds.

여섯 대의 로봇이 물이 존재했던 흔적을 찾으며 화성 표면과 궤도에서 작업하고 있다. 그 로봇들은 행성의 미생물이나 다른 초기의 생명 형태가 존재할 수도 있다는 가능성을 생각하게 해주기도 한다. Cassini호 덕택에 우리는 표면에 물이 있는 유일한 지구 밖 공간인 타이탄에서 호수를 발견했다. 우리는 심지어 다른 외부 세계의 생명체의 존재 가능성에 대해서도 예상하고 있다.

○ (c)의 which liquid exists on the surface of a world.에서 '표면에 물이 있는' 이라는 문장으로 완벽하기 때문에 관계대명사 which 대신 관계부사 where가 오는 것이 적절하다.

surface 표면 orbit 궤도 trace 자취, 발자국 microbial 미생물의 exotic 이국적인, 외래의 Titan 토성의 제 6 위성

---

54 (a) What if physiologists were only interested in what made humans dissimilar to other animals? (b) If they were, they would only study bipedalism or a few other characters. (c) They would not study the inner parts such as hearts, lungs, livers, or bones. (d) Similarly; evolutionary psychologists might be interested in the functional structure of individual cognition if or not we share this structure with other animals.

생리학자들이 오직 인간을 다른 동물들과 구별되게 하는 것에만 관심이 있다면 어떨까? 만약 그렇다면, 그들은 인간의 두 발 보행이나 혹은 다른 몇 개의 특징들만을 연구할 것이다. 그들은 심장, 폐, 간이나 뼈와 같은 내부 구조들에 대해서는 연구하지 않을 것이다. 비슷하게, 진화론적 심리학자들은 인간의 개인 인식의 기능적인 구조를 다른 동물과 공유하든 안하든 그 구조에만 관심을 가질 것이다.

○ 명사절을 이끌어 '~이든 아니든'의 의미로 쓰일 때, if or not을 쓰지 못한다. 따라서 whether or not으로 바꾸어야 한다.

physiologist 생리학자 bipedalism 두 발 보행 evolutionary 진화론적인 cognition 인지, 인식

55 (a) Not only do almost students think other foreign languages are complicated, but they also find few opportunities to verbalize. (b) They simply think German and French are not practical. (c) However, learning foreign languages is not studying only language but different cultures. (d) So, to avoid unbalance in foreign language learning, teachers should help students gain interest in European language learning.

학생들은 외국어가 복잡하다고 생각할 뿐만 아니라 말로 표현할 기회도 적음을 안다. 그들은 단순히 독어와 불어는 실용적이지 않다고 본다. 그러나 외국어를 습득하는 것은 언어만이 아닌 다른 문화도 배우는 것이다. 그러므로 외국어 습득에서 불균형을 피하기 위해서는 학생들이 유럽의 언어를 배우는 데 흥미를 갖도록 교사가 도와야 할 것이다.

⊙ (a)에서 almost는 부사이므로 직접 명사를 수식할 수 없다. almost all(every) 등으로 바꿔 써야 한다.

complicated 복잡한 verbalize 말로 나타내다 practical 실용적인

VOCABULARY • P.197

56 A My boss drives me crazy!
　　B Same here. I'm really _____ up with this job.

(a) tired
(b) kept
(c) fed
(d) got

A: 우리 사장님 때문에 미치겠어!
B: 나도 그래. 이 일이 정말 지겨워.

⊙ 'be fed up with' 는 '~에 싫증나다, 지치다' 의 뜻으로 쓰인다. 상사와 일에 대한 불만을 이야기하고 있으므로 정답은 (c)가 된다.

drive a person crazy ~을 미치게 하다 be fed up with ~에 싫증나다, 지치다

---

57 A Sorry. I can't tell you anything.
　　B Don't _____. Just spit it out!

(a) hold back
(b) butter up
(c) hold still
(d) give up

A: 미안해. 네게 아무것도 말할 수 없어.
B: 억누르지 마. 그냥 시원하게 말해!

⊙ 아무것도 말할 수 없다는 말에 시원하게 내뱉으라고 했으므로 그 전에 올 말은 '감추지 말아라, 억제하지 말아라' 의 의미를 가진 표현이 필요하다. 이에 해당하는 표현은 'hold back' 이다.

hold back 자제하다, 억제하다 spit it out 숨김없이 말하다 butter up 아첨하다 hold still 조용히 하다, 가만히 있다 give up 포기하다

---

58 A What would you like to have for dinner?
　　B How about _____ foods like Indian or Thai?

(a) appetizing
(b) light
(c) plain
(d) exotic

A: 저녁 뭐 먹고 싶어?
B: 인도 음식이나 태국 음식 같은 이국적 음식이 어때?

⊙ 보기 모두 foods와 어울리는 형용사이지만 문맥상 인도음식이나 태국음식을 예로 들었으므로 이와 관련된 'exotic' 이 가장 적절하다.

appetizing 식욕을 돋우는 plain 담백한, 양념을 치지 않은 exotic 이국적인

59 **A** Have you heard the rumors that the two companies will merge?

B I think it is just _____.

(a) consequence
(b) controversy
(c) feature
(d) conjecture

A: 두 회사가 합병한다는 소문 들었어?
B: 그것은 그냥 추측인 것 같아.

○ 'rumors' 라고 했으므로 아직 확인된 사실이 아님을 알 수 있다. 따라서 '추측, 억측' 이라는 뜻의 'conjecture' 가 정답이 된다.

merge 합병하다 **consequence** 결과, 결론 **controversy** 논쟁, 토론 **feature** 특색, 특성 **conjecture** 짐작, 추측

---

60 **A** I like this apartment, but I'm slightly short of money.

B Why don't you take out a _____ in that case?

(a) loan
(b) decision
(c) rent
(d) purse

A: 이 아파트가 마음에 들긴 하지만, 약간 돈이 모자라요.
B: 그럼 대출을 받는 것은 어때요?

○ 아파트를 얻기에는 돈이 약간 부족하다고 했으므로 대출을 받으라는 내용이 들어가면 자연스럽게 연결이 되겠다. '대출을 받다' 라는 의미의 표현으로는 'take out a loan, get a loan, receive a loan' 등이 있다.

be short of ~이 모자라다, 부족하다 **take out a loan** 대출을 받다(=get a loan, receive a loan)

---

61 **A** I can't stand him any longer. I hate the way he speaks.

B I agree. He's kind of arrogant and _____.

(a) apparent
(b) astute
(c) pompous
(d) dexterous

A: 그를 더 이상 못 참겠어. 그가 말하는 방식이 싫어.
B: 맞아. 그는 약간 건방지고 거만해.

○ 그가 말하는 방식이 싫어서 견딜 수 없다는 말에 동의의 뜻을 표하는데 'arrogant' 가 'and' 로 연결되어 있으므로 'arrogant' 와 비슷한 뜻의 어휘를 골라야 한다. 보기 가운데 'pompous' 가 거만하다는 뜻이 있으므로 정답이 된다.

arrogant 건방진, 거만한 **apparent** 분명한, 명백한 **astute** 예리한, 영리한, 빈틈없는 **pompous** 젠 체하는, 거만한 **dexterous** 솜씨 좋은, 손재주 있는

---

62 **A** The subway has finished for today.

B Don't worry. You can _____ a bus at this time.

(a) travel
(b) wait
(c) catch
(d) run

A: 오늘 지하철은 끝났어.
B: 걱정 마. 이 시간에도 버스를 탈 수 있어.

○ 지하철이 끝났으나 걱정하지 말라고 했으므로 버스를 탈 수 있다는 이야기가 나와야 한다. '버스를 타다' 는 뜻의 표현으로는 'catch a bus' 가 있다.

catch a bus 버스를 타다

63 **A** Could you _____ this check, please?

B How would you like it?

(a) honor
(b) endorse
(c) cash
(d) issue

A: 이 수표를 현금으로 바꿔주시겠어요?
B: 어떻게 바꿔드릴까요?

◐ 'How would you like it?' 은 주문을 할 때, 돈을 바꿀 때 쓸 수 있는 표현이다. 'cash a check' 은 수표를 현금화한다는 의미가 있고 현금화할 때 어떤 단위로 바꿔주길 원하는지 묻는 표현으로 'How would you like it?' 을 쓴 것이다.

endorse (어음, 수표 등에) 배서하다 issue 발행하다

---

64 **A** I broke a glass when I washed dishes.

B You're so _____!

(a) exhausted
(b) clumsy
(c) fastidious
(d) impartial

A: 설거지를 하다가 유리컵을 깨뜨렸어요.
B: 넌 너무 덜렁거려!

◐ 설거지를 하면서 컵을 깼기 때문에 서툴고 덜렁댄다는 의미의 'clumsy' 가 정답이 된다.

exhausted 다 써버린, 지친 clumsy 어색한, 서투른, 덜렁대는 fastidious 까다로운, 꼼꼼한, 엄격한 impartial 편견 없는, 공평한

---

65 **A** Aren't you here with your girlfriend?

B No, I'm not. I _____ up with her last week.

(a) met
(b) got
(c) split
(d) fought

A: 여자친구랑 같이 안 왔어?
B: 응. 지난주에 그녀와 헤어졌어.

◐ 여자친구와 같이 오지 못한 이유가 나와야 하므로 헤어졌다는 뜻의 'split up' 이 정답으로 적절하다.

meet up with ~와 우연히 만나다 split up 헤어지다

---

66 **A** Do you know what she's like? I think she enjoys being around people.

B Yes. She's outgoing and _____.

(a) impassive
(b) gregarious
(c) insolent
(d) lenient

A: 그녀가 어떤 사람인지 알아? 사람들과 함께 있는 걸 즐기는 것 같아.
B: 응. 그녀는 외향적이고 사교적이야.

◐ 'outgoing' 과 'and' 로 연결되어 있으므로 이와 비슷한 의미의 어휘가 와야 한다. 보기 가운데 '사교적인' 의 뜻을 가진 어휘는 (b)gregarious이다.

impassive 냉정한, 침착한 gregarious 사교적인 insolent 건방진, 무례한 lenient 인자한, 관대한

---

67 **A** What made you call this late at night?

B I'm sorry to _____ you, but this is urgent.

(a) excuse
(b) worry
(c) upset
(d) disturb

A: 이렇게 밤 늦게 무슨 일로 전화를 했어?
B: 귀찮게 해서 미안한데, 급한 일이야.

◐ 늦은 시간에 전화를 했을 경우 할 수 있는 말로 '귀찮게 하다, 방해하다' 라는 뜻의 'disturb' 가 정답이 된다.

disturb 방해하다, 폐를 끼치다

68 Shakespeare is considered to be a writer of _____ genius in the history of English literature.

(a) transcendent
(b) transparent
(c) transitional
(d) transient

셰익스피어는 영국 문학 역사상 탁월한 천재 작가로 간주된다.

➦ 'genius'와 잘 어울리는 연어를 찾아야 한다. 'transparent'는 '투명한'의 의미로 어울리지 않으며, 'transitional'은 과도기적이라는 뜻으로 역시 빈칸에 들어가기에 부적절하다. 'transient'는 '덧없는, 일시적인'의 뜻으로 역시 정답이 될 수 없다. 'transcendent'의 경우 '탁월한, 비상한'의 뜻으로 'genius'와 함께 쓰면 탁월한 천재(성)를 뜻한다.

transcendent 탁월한, 비상한 **transparent** 비치는, 투명한 **transitional** 과도기적인 **transient** 덧없는, 일시적인, 무상한

---

69 Jake was going through financial difficulties but he was a man of _____ spirit to overcome the crisis.

(a) guiding
(b) community
(c) indomitable
(d) rebellious

제이크는 재정적 어려움을 겪고 있었지만 그는 위기를 이겨낼 만한 불굴의 정신을 가진 남자였다.

➦ 끝부분에 위기를 이겨낸다는 표현이 있으므로 이와 연관된 내용이 나와야 한다. 'indomitable spirit'은 '불굴의 의지'라는 뜻으로 위기를 극복한다는 내용과 자연스럽게 연결이 되므로 정답은 (c)이다.

go through ~을 겪다 **indomitable** 불굴의, 꿋꿋한 **rebellious** 반역하는, 반항하는

---

70 I wasn't able to adapt myself to the new environment because people seemed to be nice to me but in a _____ way.

(a) superlative
(b) surplus
(c) superb
(d) superficial

사람들이 내게 잘 대해주는 듯했지만 겉으로만 그러했기 때문에 나는 새로운 환경에 적응할 수 없었다.

➦ 새로운 환경에 적응할 수 없었던 이유가 'because' 이하 절에 나와 있다. 사람들이 잘 해주긴 하지만 겉으로만 그러했다는 내용이 나오는 것이 문맥에 맞는다고 할 수 있겠다. 이러한 뜻의 어휘는 'superficial'이다. 나머지는 빈 칸에 들어갈 경우 모두 문맥과 어울리지 않는 어색한 표현이 된다.

adapt oneself to (환경에) 적응하다, 순응하다 **superlative** 최상의, 최고의 **surplus** 과잉의, 잉여의 **superb** 아주 훌륭한, 뛰어난 **superficial** 피상적인, 표면상의

---

71 There was a three car rear end collision on the highway and one of the injured people needed an urgent blood _____ due to a significant blood loss.

(a) infusion
(b) profusion
(c) transfusion
(d) fusion

고속도로에서 3중 추돌사고가 있었고 부상자 가운데 한 명은 과다 출혈로 긴급 수혈이 필요하다.

➦ 과다 출혈이 있었다고 했으므로 이와 관련해서 수혈이 필요하다는 이야기가 나오는 것이 자연스럽다. 수혈은 영어로 'transfusion'이라고 한다. 보기 모두 'fusion'이 들어가는 단어로서 혼동을 주고 있다.

three car rear end collision 3중 추돌 사고 **massive** 대량의, 대규모의 **infusion** 주입, 고취 **profusion** 풍부, 다량, 사치 **transfusion** 주입, 수혈 **fusion** 용해, 융합

72 British airports are planning to
_____ the ban on liquids being
carried in hand luggage as soon as the
new scanners are proved to be successful
to detect harmful liquids.

(a) place
(b) lift
(c) put
(d) impose

영국 공항은 새로운 스캐너가 해로운 액체를 감지하는 데 성공적이라고 입증되면 즉시 기내에 휴대 반입하는 술에 대해서는 금지 조치를 해제할 계획이다.

○ 새로운 스캐너가 해로운 물질을 잘 감지하면 그 동안 기내 반입이 금지되었던 술에 대해서 금지를 풀 것이라는 내용이 오는 것이 자연스럽다. 'lift the ban'은 '금지를 해제하다'라는 뜻이다. (a)와 (b), (d)가 빈 칸에 들어가면 반대로 '~을 금지하다'라는 뜻이 된다.

liquid 액체, 술 detect ~을 찾아내다, 탐지하다 impose (세금, 의무 등을)부과하다 lift the ban 금지를 해제하다

73 It was obvious that his _____
appetite for power would draw ruin upon
himself but he couldn't help it.

(a) insatiable
(b) healthy
(c) satisfied
(d) bearable

만족할 줄 모르는 그의 권력욕이 자신을 파멸로 이끌 것이 분명했지만 그 자신도 어쩔 수 없었다.

○ 권력욕이 파멸로 이끈다고 했으므로 'appetite for power'와 어울릴 만한 형용사에는 'insatiable'이 있다. 문맥으로 보아 부정적인 뉘앙스의 단어가 와야 하므로 (b), (c) 등은 어울리지 않는다.

draw ruin upon oneself 자신의 파멸을 초래하다 insatiable 만족할 줄 모르는, 탐욕스러운 bearable 견딜 수 있는, 참을 수 있는

74 Most financial consultants advise people
to minimize tax _____ and
maximize income in order to increase their
assets.

(a) evasion
(b) liabilities
(c) shelter
(d) return

대부분의 재정 컨설턴트들은 사람들에게 자산을 늘리기 위해서는 세금 부담액을 최소화하고 수입을 최대화하라고 조언한다.

○ 자산을 늘리기 위한 방법으로 수입을 최대화하라고 했으므로 세금으로 지출이 되는 부분은 최소화하라는 내용이 나와야 문맥상 매끄럽다. 'tax liability'에서 'liability'는 '책임, 의무'라는 뜻으로 세금 부담을 말한다. 'tax evasion'은 '탈세'를 의미하므로 재정 컨설턴트의 조언으로는 부적합하므로 (a)는 답이 될 수 없다.

evasion (책임, 의무로부터의) 도피, 회피 tax liability 세금 부담액 shelter 피난처, 은신처

75 The company was reported to be fined for
_____ industrial waste into the river,
which evoked strong opposition among
the residents.

(a) disregarding
(b) disintegrating
(c) disclosing
(d) discharging

그 회사는 산업 폐기물을 강에 버린 데 대해 벌금형을 받았다고 전해졌는데, 이는 주민들 사이에 강한 반발을 일으켰다.

○ 산업 폐기물을 강에 '버린다'고 해야 자연스러운 문장이 된다. 이에 해당하는 어휘는 'discharge'이다.

waste 폐기물, 폐수 evoke 일으키다, 자아내다 resident 주민, 거주자 disregard 무시하다, 경시하다 disintegrate 분해하다, 붕괴시키다 disclose 폭로하다, 적발하다 discharge 방출하다, 배출하다

76 A majority of U.S. citizens consider the policies against Afghanistan a _____ cause, which shows they have deep public skepticism about the war on terror.

(a) worthy
(b) ultimate
(c) wasted
(d) lost

미국 시민들의 다수는 아프가니스탄에 대한 정책들이 실패로 끝난 정책이라고 생각하는데, 이는 그들이 테러에 대한 전쟁에 대해 깊은 대중적 회의감을 가지고 있음을 보여준다.

◐ which 이하의 절을 보면 전쟁에 대해 회의감을 갖고 있다고 했으므로 아프가니스탄에 대한 정책을 실패작이라고 생각한다는 내용이 나오는 것이 자연스럽다. 'lost cause' 는 '실패로 끝난 주장, 운동' 의 뜻이 있다.

skepticism 의심, 회의, 회의론 ultimate 최후의, 궁극적인 (ultimate cause 결정적 원인) wasted 황폐한, 소용 없는, 헛된 lost cause 실패로 끝난 주장, 가망성 없는 주장

77 The audience _____ in laughter when the actor fell on the stage while singing a love song with a serious look.

(a) disrupted
(b) erupted
(c) bankrupted
(d) interrupted

관객들은 그 배우가 심각한 표정으로 사랑 노래를 부르다가 무대에서 넘어지자 웃음을 터뜨렸다.

◐ 심각한 노래를 하는 중 무대에서 넘어진 상황이므로 갑자기 웃음이 터지는 상황이 되어야 자연스럽다. 'erupt' 는 원래 '폭발하다' 라는 뜻이 있는데 'erupt in tears, erupt in laugher' 는 '울음을 터뜨리다, 웃음을 터뜨리다' 라는 뜻이 된다.

disrupt 혼란에 빠뜨리다, 중단시키다 erupt 폭발하다, 분화하다 bankrupt 파산하다 interrupt 방해하다, 차단하다

78 The company filed a lawsuit against internet users claiming that its intellectual _____ rights were infringed.

(a) defect
(b) property
(c) power
(d) capacity

그 회사는 회사의 지적 재산권이 침해당했다고 주장하면서 인터넷 사용자들을 상대로 소송을 제기했다.

◐ 문제에서 'rights' 는 권리를 말하는 것으로 이와 잘 어울리는 언어를 찾아야 하는데 'infringe' 라는 단어를 통해 권리는 권리이나 법적으로 침해당할 수 있는 권리가 되어야 함을 알 수 있다. 'intellectual property rights' 는 지적 재산권을 뜻하는 표현으로 'infringe' 라는 동사를 써서 '지적 재산권을 침해하다' 라는 표현으로 쓸 수 있다.

file a lawsuit 소송을 제기하다 claim 주장하다 infringe 어기다, 위반하다 defect 결점, 단점 property 재산, 자산 capacity 수용력, 능력, 역량

79 Most reviewers say this game is very difficult and challenging because the plot is very complicated and tricky, but the _____ feature of this game is the cheap price.

(a) notorious
(b) main
(c) optional
(d) redeeming

평가자들 대부분은 이 게임이 스토리가 매우 복잡하고 까다로워서 매우 어렵고 도전적이지만 이것을 보상해주는 요소는 저렴한 가격이라고 말한다.

◐ 'but' 으로 연결되어 있으므로 상반된 내용이 와야 한다. 앞에서는 이 게임의 단점에 대해 이야기하고 있으므로 이와는 반대의 장점이 와야 하는데 'redeem' 은 '결점을 상쇄하다' 라는 뜻이 있으므로 정답은 (d)가 된다.

complicated 복잡한 notorious 악명 높은 redeem (결점 등을) 벌충하다, 상쇄하다(redeeming feature = 보완 요소, 보상 요소)

80 Taking out an online membership, you can gain access to the National Center for missing people which provides photographs of missing people, and _____ people.

(a) disabled
(b) unidentified
(c) ordinary
(d) boat

온라인 회원에 가입하면 실종자를 위한 국립 센터에 접속할 수 있는데, 여기에는 실종자와 신원 미상인 사람들의 사진을 제공한다.

○ 'and' 로 연결되어 있으므로 'missing people' 과 의미상 연결이 되는 표현을 찾아야 한다. 따라서 신원이 확인되지 않은 신원미상자가 정답이 되는 것이 자연스럽다. 따라서 보기 가운데 이러한 뜻을 가진 'unidentified' 가 정답이 된다.

gain access to ~에 접근하다, ~에 닿다 **disabled** 신체 장애의 **unidentified** 확인할 수 없는, 신원 미상의 **boat people** 표류 난민

READING COMPREHENSION • P.203

81 In Korea, home baking has become a popular hobby among the people who want to make their own cakes and cookies at home. You could express your affection or make a great present for your family or friends with home made snacks. It is definitely fun and far simpler than you expected. You may want to have a big and beautiful oven first. Those are indeed great for baking, yet _____ _____ that you could simply start with. They are also easy to operate. Then you'll need a hand mixer that you could use to mingle the baking ingredients easily. Mixing bowls, measuring cup sets, and flexible turners are the basic supplies you should include in your shopping list.

(a) there also are fabulous websites
(b) there also are ovens for experts
(c) there also are books that have baking tips
(d) there also are reasonably-priced small ovens

한국에서 홈베이킹은 집에서 직접 케이크와 쿠키를 만들기를 원하는 사람들 사이에서 인기 있는 취미가 되고 있다. 당신은 손수 만든 과자로 가족과 친구들에게 당신의 사랑을 표현할 수도 있고, 근사한 선물을 만들어줄 수도 있다. 그것은 분명 즐겁고 당신이 예상한 것보다 훨씬 간단하다. 당신은 먼저 크고 멋진 오븐을 가지고 싶을 것이다. 크고 멋진 오븐이 굽기에는 좋겠지만, 당신이 간단하게 가지고 시작할 수 있는 저렴한 가격의 작은 오븐들도 있다. 그 작은 오븐들은 조작하기도 쉽다. 그 다음으로 당신은 베이킹 재료들을 손쉽게 섞을 수 있는 핸드 믹서가 필요할 것이다. 믹싱볼과 계량컵 그리고 탄력 뒤집게 등은 당신이 쇼핑 리스트에 포함시켜야 할 기본적인 도구들이다.

○ 빈칸 앞에 있는 접속사 yet과 빈칸 뒤에 이어서 나오는 설명들에 주의한다. 앞에서 언급된 크고 멋진 오븐이 물론 좋다는 말에 반대되는 말이 나와야 한다. 그리고 빈칸 뒤에 나오는 쉽게 베이킹을 시작할 수 있고 조작하기도 용이하다는 설명을 만족시키는 답은 (d)이다.

affection 애정, 호의 **definitely** 명확히, 확실히 **indeed** 실로, 대단히, 정말, 당연히 **reasonably-priced** 저렴한 가격의, 적당한 가격의 **operate** 작용하다, 움직이다, 수술하다 **ingredient** 재료, 요소 **measuring cup** 계량컵 **flexible** 탄력적인, 유연한, 구부러지는 **turner** 뒤집는 주걱, 뒤집게 **supply** 준비물, 공급, 공급품

197

82 The main purpose of advertising is to inform potential customers about a product or service or to create favorable awareness for the product or service. To attract the customers, appealing techniques are used. The most common appealing techniques employed in the media can be divided into two categories: factual appeal and emotional appeal. While the factual appeal focuses on the superiority of the product supplying information, the emotional appeal spotlights on the potential satisfaction of the consumer. The satisfaction is rather personal, in other words, the emotional appeal is designed to stimulate consumer's desires _____.

(a) to be socially acceptable and personally attractive
(b) to increase competitive power and productivity
(c) to inform about the product or service
(d) to appeal as many people as possible

광고의 주된 목적은 잠재적인 소비자들에게 제품이나 서비스에 관한 정보를 제공하거나 그 제품 혹은 서비스에 대한 호의적인 인식을 만들어내는 것이다. 소비자들을 끌어당기기 위해서 호소라는 광고 기법이 사용된다. 매체에서 가장 일반적으로 사용되는 호소 기법은 두 가지 범주로 나뉜다: 사실의 호소와 감성의 호소이다. 사실의 호소가 정보를 제공하면서 제품의 우월성에 초점을 맞추는 반면 감성의 호소는 소비자의 잠재적인 만족에 주목한다. 만족은 보다 개인적인 것인데, 다른 말로 하면, 감성의 호소는 사회적으로 인정받고 싶고 개인적으로 매력적이고 싶은 고객의 욕구를 자극하기 위해 고안된다는 것이다.

❏ 빈칸 앞에 쓰여진 말에 유의한다. 사실의 호소와 감성의 호소를 비교하고, 감성의 호소가 소비자의 잠재적인 만족에 주목한다고 말하고 있다. 주어진 보기 중 개인이 사회적으로 인정받기를 원하는 것이나 매력적이고 싶은 것이 앞에서 말한 개인적인 만족이라는 언급과 가장 일맥상통한다고 볼 수 있으므로 정답은 (a)이다.

potential 잠재된, 가능성 있는 awareness 자각, 인식, 깨닫고 있음 attract 유인하다, 끌어당기다, 매혹하다 appeal 호소, 매력, 애원, 간청 category 범주, 카테고리 stimulate 자극하다, 고무하다, 격려하다 acceptable 훌륭한, 만족스러운, 받아들일 수 있는

---

83 Gothic architecture flourished throughout Europe during its prosperous and late medieval period, developing from Romanesque architecture and succeeded by Renaissance architecture. The Gothic style was expressed not only in the great churches and cathedrals but also in many castles and palaces. It was characterized by verticality and huge dimensions of the structure with pointed arches, ribbed vaults, flying buttresses, and slender pillars. It also emphasized on large stained glass windows, allowing more light to enter inside. These features of Gothic architecture were intended _____ _____: the glory of God versus the insignificance of the man.

(a) to compare God with man
(b) to pass a theological message
(c) to persuade people to convert to Christianity
(d) to focus on the excellence of Gothic architecture

고딕 건축은 중세 번영기와 후기 동안 전 유럽에 걸쳐 번창했는데, 로마네스크 건축에서 발전하여 르네상스 건축으로 이어졌다. 고딕 양식은 대교회와 대성당뿐만 아니라 많은 성과 궁전에도 표현되었다. 고딕 양식은 수직성과 거대한 구조의 규모로 특징 지워지는데, 뾰족한 아치와 리브볼트, 플라잉 버트레스와 가느다란 기둥들이 그 특징이다. 또한 스테인드 글라스가 강조되었는데, 이것은 더 많은 빛을 내부로 들어오게 했다. 고딕 건축의 이러한 특징들은 신학적인 메시지를 전달하기 위해서였다. 즉, 신의 영광에 대한 인간의 보잘 것없음을 의미한다.

❏ 고딕 건축은 수직성이 특징이라고 했듯이 뾰족하게 하늘을 향해 솟아있다. 정답은 이러한 특징과 고딕 건축이 중세에 성행했다는 점과 콜론 뒤의 어구를 통해서 종교와 관련이 있음을 알 수 있다. 결정적으로 콜론 뒤의 어구가 a theological message를 설명하고 있으므로 정답은 (b)가 된다.

architecture 건축, 건축물 flourish 번영하다 prosperous 번영하고 있는, 번창하고 있는 medieval 중세의, 중세풍의 succeed 상속하다, 계승하다 cathedral 대성당 verticality 수직(성), 수직 상태 rib 늑골을 붙이다 vault 〈아치형의〉 둥근 천장 buttress 버팀벽 지지물 slender 가느다란, 호리호리한 pillar 기둥 versus 〈소송, 운동경기에서〉 ~대 insignificance 무의미 보잘것없음 theological 신학적인, 신학(상)의 convert 개종시키다

84 Used to be an entertainment of the Roman Emperors, lotteries were approved by the colonial legislatures as an important way of raising funds for public purposes such as church erection or quay construction in the American colonies. In the 19th century, lotteries were prohibited by a law because of the frequent deceit. From the 20th century, lotteries began to be administered by local states to raise revenues without increasing taxes, and were granted the epithets of "tax on stupidity," and "voluntary tax." Since poor people were most likely to buy them, lotteries were used as revenue-raising devices, attracting those consumers who _____.

(a) had ever won the lottery
(b) couldn't afford to pay taxes
(c) were interested in the public benefit
(d) failed to see the lottery was a bad deal

로마 황제의 오락거리로 사용되기도 했던 복권은 미국 식민지 시대에 입법부에 의해 허가되었는데, 이것은 복권이 교회를 건립하거나 부두를 건설하는 것과 같은 공공의 목적으로 사용되는 자금을 조성하는 데 중요한 방법이었기 때문이다. 19세기에는 사기가 빈번했기 때문에 복권이 법으로 금지되었다. 20세기부터는 세금을 올리지 않고 세입을 늘리기 위해서 주에서 복권을 관리하기 시작했으며, "어리석음에 부과된 세금", "자발적인 세금"이라는 별칭을 얻었다. 가난한 사람들이 주로 복권을 샀기 때문에, 복권이 안 좋은 거래라는 것을 보지 못하는 소비자들을 유혹하면서 세입을 늘리는 장치로 이용되었다.

🔵 복권이 세금을 따로 부과하지 않고 세입을 늘리는 방법으로 사용되었다는 글이다. 즉, 사람들이 복권을 사면 세금을 내는 것과 같은데 이것을 눈치채지 못한 사람들이 복권을 샀다는 것이므로 정답은 (d)가 된다. 특히, 가난한 사람들은 세금을 내기가 힘들었을 텐데 결국 복권을 삼으로써 세금을 대신하게 되었다는 것이다.

approve 허가하다, 인가하다 colonial 식민지의, 식민지 시대의 legislature 입법부, 입법기관 erection 건립, 건설, 설립 quay 부두, 선창 prohibit 금하다, 금지하다 because of ~ 때문에 frequent 빈번한, 자주 일어나는 deceit 사기, 기만, 허위 administer 관리하다, 통치하다 revenue 〈국가, 도시의〉 세입 epithet 〈경멸적〉 별명, 별칭 stupidity 어리석음, 멍청함 voluntary 자발적인, 임의의 device 장치, 고안물

---

85 Fiber helps you to maintain your healthy diet as well as to keep in shape. After taken, it goes through your digestive tract since it is indigestible. When it is excreted from the body, the foods left in your internal organs are expelled with it before they turn putrid and become toxic. Through this process, fiber decreases cholesterol level, prevents diabetes and some cancers. When you increase fiber in your diet, you can lessen the amount of food you consume. As fiber in your stomach absorbs water, you can have a feeling of satisfaction easily. If you want to watch your weight, you should _____ _____.

(a) manage your time efficiently
(b) include adequate amounts of fiber in your meals
(c) stop eating fast food and junk food
(d) take pure water as much as you can

섬유소는 당신이 식단을 건강하게 유지하는 것뿐만 아니라 몸매를 유지하는 데도 도움이 된다. 섬유소는 소화되지 않기 때문에 섭취된 후 당신의 소화기관을 통과하게 된다. 섬유소가 당신의 몸으로부터 배출될 때 당신의 내장에 남아 있던 음식물도 부패하거나 그래서 독소가 되기 전에 섬유소와 함께 배출된다. 이 과정을 통해 섬유소는 콜레스테롤 수치를 낮추고, 당뇨병과 일부의 암을 예방한다. 당신이 식단에서 섬유소를 늘리면 당신은 섭취하는 음식의 양을 줄일 수도 있다. 섬유소가 당신의 위에서 물을 흡수하면서 당신은 포만감을 쉽게 느낄 수 있기 때문이다. 당신이 체중조절을 원한다면 식사에 알맞은 양의 섬유소를 꼭 포함시켜야 한다.

🔵 섬유소의 효능에 관한 글이다. 섬유소가 건강 유지뿐 아니라 몸매 유지에도 도움이 되는데, 섬유소가 체내에서 수분을 흡수함으로써 포만감을 주어 섭취하는 음식의 양을 줄여준다는 언급 뒤에 올 수 있는 말을 찾는 것이 문제이므로 그에 적절한 답은 (b)이다.

fiber 섬유소, 섬유질 keep in shape 몸매를 유지하다, 건강을 유지하다 digestive 소화의, 소화력 있는, 소화를 촉진하는 tract 〈신체〉 관, 계, 지역 excrete 배설하다, 분비하다, 방출하다 turn putrid 부패하다 diabetes 당뇨병 consume 섭취하다, 먹다, 소비하다 a feeling of satisfaction 포만감, 만족감 adequate 알맞은, 충분한, 적정한

199

86 How many cups of coffee you drink a day? Are you easily tempted by caffe lattes with fabulous whipped cream and caramel topping? If you drink more than 5 cups of coffee a day, you should cut down on the amount of coffee you take. Coffee can be helpful to keep your brain alert and increase your energy level. However, you may have headaches and sleeplessness after taking too much coffee. Also, your body can be dehydrated because coffee dries up moistures in your body. Why don't you _____?

(a) take some pills to lessen your headaches
(b) add some whipped cream to your coffee
(c) try to drink water or other teas instead of coffee
(d) have a surgery to reduce the size of your stomach

당신은 하루에 커피를 몇 잔이나 드시나요? 끝내주는 휘핑 크림과 카라멜 토핑을 얹은 카페라테에 쉽게 흔들리시나요? 당신이 하루에 커피를 다섯 잔 이상 마신다면, 당신은 섭취하는 커피의 양을 줄여야 합니다. 커피는 당신의 뇌를 깨어 있게 하고, 에너지 레벨을 높이는 데 도움이 됩니다. 하지만 너무 많이 마시게 되면 두통과 불면증이 올 수 있습니다. 또한 커피가 당신의 체내에 있는 수분을 말려버리기 때문에 당신의 몸은 탈수될 수 있습니다. 커피 대신에 물이나 다른 차를 마시도록 노력하는 게 어떨까요?

○ 전반적으로 보아 커피의 부정적인 면에 대해서 서술하고 있다. 커피가 두통과 불면증을 유발할 수 있고, 탈수를 야기할 수 있다는 언급 뒤에 올 수 있는 조언을 찾는 문제이다. 가장 적절한 답은 커피 대신에 물이나 다른 음료를 마셔보라고 말하는 (c)이다.

tempt 유혹하다, 마음을 끌다 **whipped** 거품을 일게 한 **take** 섭취하다. 얻다, 가지다 **alert** 깨어 있는, 각성한 **dehydrate** 탈수하다. 건조시키다

---

87 The main purpose of the juvenile court system lies in rehabilitation, as opposed to punishment, to enhance the chances of the youth becoming a socially well-adjusted citizen. As for the juvenile crimes, there are frequent occasions when the offender himself is likely to be a victim—a victim of poverty, parental neglect, and all kinds of abuse. Therefore a cautious attitude should be assumed with the juvenile delinquencies. Nevertheless, the juvenile crime, particularly crimes of violence is on dramatic rise. It makes no difference to the victim whether the person who pulled the trigger on the gun is under the age of 18 or not. _____
_____.

(a) Juvenile punishments should exclude incarceration
(b) Mere probation is only a slap on the wrist to violent crime
(c) Any offender has the right to hire a juvenile defense attorney
(d) We should protect juvenile delinquents regardless of their age

청소년 법원 시스템의 주된 목적은 처벌에 반대되는 개념인 갱생에 있으며, 이는 젊은 층이 사회적으로 잘 적응된 시민으로 성장할 가능성을 높이기 위함이다. 청소년 범죄에 있어서, 범법자 자신이 동시에 가난이나 부모의 무관심 그리고 여러 종류의 학대의 피해자인 경우가 빈번하다. 따라서 청소년 비행과 관련해서는 신중한 접근이 필요하다. 그럼에도 불구하고 청소년 범죄, 특히 폭력사건이 크게 증가하고 있다. 희생자에게는 방아쇠를 당긴 사람이 18세 이하인지 아닌지는 아무 상관이 없다. 보호관찰은 폭력사건에 솜방망이 처벌에 불과하다.

○ 청소년 범죄를 법적으로 다룰 때, 청소년을 사회에 책임있는 성인으로 복귀시켜야 하고 또한 가난이나 부모의 무관심, 학대 등의 결과로 비행 청소년이 되는 경우가 많으므로 신중한 태도가 필요하다. 그럼에도 불구하고 최근 급격하게 청소년 범죄가 늘어나고 있고, 특히 폭력 범죄의 경우에는 엄중한 처벌이 필요하다는 내용이므로 그것을 뒷받침하는 진술은 (b)이다.

juvenile 청소년의 **rehabilitation** 사회복귀, (범죄자들의) 갱생 **well-adjusted** 잘 적응한. 안정된 **offender** 범죄자, 위반자 **cautious** 조심성 있는, 주의 깊은, 신중한 **juvenile delinquency** 청소년 비행 **trigger** 방아쇠 **incarceration** 투옥. 감금 **probation** 집행유예, 보호관찰 **a slap on the wrist** 솜방망이 처벌 **regardless of** ~에 상관없이

88 It is widely known that global warming is fatal to the future of our planet. We are _____. Sea levels are rising as the glaciers and sea ice is melting as the earth is heated. The rise of sea levels is being accelerated because oceans absorb more heat than land. The change in heat and water evaporation causes hurricanes, tornadoes and other storms. So, what can we do? In order to reduce the amount of green house gases that can be made from pollution, we could re-cycle plastic bottles, cups and tin cans. Re-using of plastic shopping bags instead of getting new ones is helpful, too.

(a) making plans to stop global warming like following

(b) witnessing the evidences like the following

(c) in need of developing technologies like following

(d) facing problems of poverty like following

지구 온난화가 우리 지구의 미래에 치명적인 것이라는 사실은 널리 알려져 있다. 우리는 다음과 같은 증거들을 목격하고 있다. 지구가 뜨거워짐에 따라 빙하와 해빙이 녹으면서 해수면의 높이가 높아지고 있다. 해수위의 상승은 대양이 대륙보다 더 많은 열을 흡수하기 때문에 가속화되고 있다. 열과 물의 증발의 변화는 허리케인, 토네이도 그리고 다른 폭풍우들을 야기한다. 그렇다면, 우리는 무엇을 할 수 있는가? 공해로부터 만들어질 수 있는 온실가스의 양을 줄이기 위해서 우리는 플라스틱 병과 컵 그리고 깡통을 재활용할 수 있다. 플라스틱 봉지를 새 것으로 사지 않고 재사용하는 것 또한 도움이 된다.

◐ 빈칸 뒤에 오는 내용에 주목한다. 빙하와 해빙이 녹으면서 야기되는 해수면의 상승과 각종 자연재해라는 지구 온난화의 치명적인 현상들이 뒤따라오는 것으로 보아 '다음과 같은 증거들을 목격하고 있다'라는 의미를 가진 (b)가 답으로 적절하다.

fatal 치명적인, 운명적인, 숙명의 glacier 빙하 sea ice 해빙 evaporation 증발, 발산 reduce 줄이다, 감소하다, 적게 하다 pollution 오염, 공해, 더러움, 불결

89 The prestige of the Nobel Prize stems from its long, thorough, and rigorous nomination and selection process. The respective Nobel Committees asks thousands of previous Nobel Laureates, university professors, scholars in the relevant fields and the committee members themselves to nominate candidates, who aren't even told they have been nominated for the prize. Self and posthumous nominations are disqualified and about two hundred preliminary candidates are selected for the coming year's prizes. Then with experts' help, each committee scrutinizes and selects prize winners through voting.

노벨상의 명성은 길고도 철저하며 엄격한 후보 추천과 선발의 과정에 기인한다. 각각의 노벨위원회에서는 기존의 노벨 수상자들, 대학 교수들, 관련 분야의 학자들 그리고 위원회 구성원 등 수천 명의 사람들에게 후보를 추천해 달라고 요청하는데, 정작 후보들은 자신이 노벨상에 추천되었는지를 모른다. 자기 추천과 사후 추천은 실격이 되고, 약 이백 명의 예비 후보들이 다음해의 수상 후보로 선발된다. 그리고 나서 전문가의 도움으로, 각 위원회에서는 노벨상 수상자에 대해 면밀히 검토한 후 투표를 통해서 수상자를 선발하게 된다.

◐ 노벨상 수상자의 추천과 선발과정이 간략하게 설명되어 있다. (a)는 후보자 자신도 추천되었는지 모른다고 했으므로 명단이 공개적으로 발표된다는 것은 옳지 않고, (c)는 노벨상 수상자가 투표로 정해지지만 만장일치로 정해진다는 내용은 없으므로 알맞지 않다. (d)는 각각의 노벨상 위원회가 있다고 했으므로 하나의 권위 있는 위원회가 그 과정을 책임지고 있다는 것은 사실이 아니다. 반면 (b)는 사후 추천이 실격이라고 했으므로 내용과 일치한다.

Q Which of the following is true about the Nobel Prize?

(a) The names of the nominees are publicly announced.

(b) Deceased people can't be nominated in the Nobel Prize.

(c) The winner of Nobel Prize should be decided by a unanimous vote.

(d) One authoritative committee is in charge of the nomination and selection process.

prestige 명성, 위신, 신망 stem from ~에서 유래하다, 일어나다 thorough 철저한, 완전한 rigorous 엄격한 엄밀한, 정밀한 nomination 지명, 추천 selection 선택, 선발 respective 각각의, 개개의 Nobel Laureate 노벨 수상자 relevant 〈당면한 문제에〉 관련된 적절한 candidate 후보 posthumous 사후(死後)의, 사후에 생긴 disqualified 자격을 잃은, 실격이 된 preliminary 예비의, 시초의, 발단의 scrutinize 면밀히 검사하다 deceased 죽은, 작고한 unanimous 만장일치의, 이구동성의 authoritative 권위 있는, 믿을 만한 be in charge of ~을 담당하다

---

90 The term 'Korean wave(Hallyu)' was coined by journalists in Beijing as the popularity of TV dramas and goods of Korea drastically grew up in China in the late 1990s. Since then, the term has been used to refer to the surge of popularity of Korean pop culture in other countries, especially in Asia. The audiences from China to the Japan got hooked on Korean TV dramas such as 'Winter Sonata' and 'Autumn in my Heart'. Actors who played the main roles in those dramas are now among the highest-paid actors in Asia. A multi-entertainer Rain has made his way from a Korean wave star to a promising actor in Hollywood.

Q What is mainly discussed in the paragraph?

(a) The origin of the term 'Korean wave'

(b) The popularity of Korean goods in China

(c) A perspective on the Korean Wave

(d) The audiences of Korean TV dramas

한류라는 용어는 1990년대 후반 중국에서 한국산 텔레비전 드라마와 상품들의 인기가 치솟게 되면서 베이징의 언론인들이 만들었다. 이후 그 명칭은 다른 나라에서 특히 아시아에서의 한국 대중문화의 인기의 상승을 지칭하는 데 쓰이고 있다. 중국에서부터 일본까지 관객들은 '겨울 연가'와 '가을 동화'와 같은 한국 텔레비전 드라마에 빠져들었다. 이들 드라마에서 주역을 맡은 한국 남성 연기자들은 현재 아시아에서 가장 많은 출연료를 받는 배우들에 속한다. 멀티 연예인인 비는 한류 스타에서 헐리우드의 유망한 배우로 자신의 길을 추구해왔다.

● 한류라는 용어의 기원(a)이라든가 중국 내에서의 한국 상품의 인기(b), 한국 드라마의 관객(d)과 같은 내용에 관한 언급은 있지만 모두 국지적인 내용으로 답이 될 수는 없다. 문단의 내용을 아우르는 적절한 것은 한류에 대한 개관이라는 내용의 (c)이다.

term 용어, 전문어, 조건, 학기 coin (신어 등을) 만들어 내다, (통화를) 주조하다 drastically 급격하게, 급속히 surge 급상승, (큰 파도) 솟아오르다 get hooked on ~에 빠져들다, 사로잡히다 pursue 추구하다, 좇다 promising 유망한, 창창한

91 To our customers:

Thank you for taking your time to answer to our survey. The purpose of this survey is to search for the way we could serve you and better meet your needs. This survey is conducted by T&K Co., which is an outstanding consulting firm specializing in customer service. Beside these questionnaires for you, they will interview some of our selected employees about our service to get more meaningful results. We deeply thank you for your time and effort in doing this, and firmly believe that your time and effort will help us to provide you the best service.

Q Which of the following is correct according to the paragraph?

(a) This survey is for the employees of T&K Co.

(b) The purpose of the survey is to improve customer service.

(c) Some selected customers will be interviewed.

(d) T&K Co. provides the customer with consulting.

고객님들께:

본 설문에 시간을 내어 응해주셔서 감사드립니다. 이 설문의 목적은 우리가 여러분들을 더욱 잘 모시고 여러분들의 필요를 만족시켜드릴 수 있는 방법을 찾는 것입니다. 이 설문은 고객서비스 분야를 전문으로 하는 독보적인 컨설팅 기업 T&K Co.에 의해 시행되고 있습니다. 좀 더 의미 있는 결과를 얻기 위해 T&K Co.는 여러분에게 이 질문지를 드리는 것 외에도 우리 직원들 중 일부를 엄선하여 인터뷰할 것입니다. 우리는 여러분께서 시간과 노력을 들여 이 설문에 응해주시는 것에 깊은 감사를 드리며, 여러분의 시간과 노력이 우리가 여러분께 최고의 서비스를 제공할 수 있는 데 도움이 될 것이라고 굳게 믿습니다.

○ 'To our customers'라는 도입부로 보아 고객들을 위한 글이므로 (a)는 답이 될 수 없다. 이 설문조사의 목적은 고객서비스를 향상하기 위한 것이라는 언급이 나오므로 답은 (b)이다. 일부의 고객이 아닌 직원들이 인터뷰를 하게 될 것이므로 (c) 또한 답이 될 수 없고, T&K Co.가 컨설팅을 제공하는 것은 맞지만 그 대상이 고객이 아닌 이 글의 화자격인 기업체이므로 (d)는 답이 아니다.

survey 설문조사, 측량, 살펴보다 purpose 목적, 의도, 용도, 취지 conduct 시행하다, 수행하다, 지휘하다 consulting firm 컨설팅 회사 (자문 회사) questionnaire 질문서, 질문사항 meaningful 의미 있는, 의미 심장한

---

92 DNA is an abbreviated form of Deoxyribonucleic Acid. It carries the genetic code that makes each person unique. It is often shown in movies and TV shows that a sample of DNA found at the crime scene is used for detection. It is compared with another sample taken from a suspect. If the match is positive, the detection is successful. DNA samples taken from different crime scenes can be linked and collected at the National DNA Database. The National DNA Database is used by every police force in the US to compare other samples taken from scenes of crime.

Q Which of the following is the best title of the passage?

(a) The Use of DNA for Crime Detection

(b) The Definition of DNA

(c) The National DNA Database

(d) The Comparison of DNA Samples

DNA는 디옥시리보핵산의 축약형이다. 그것은 각 사람을 고유하게 하는 유전자 코드를 가지고 있다. 범죄 현장에서 발견된 DNA 샘플이 수사를 위해 사용되는 것은 영화나 TV 프로그램에서 자주 보여지는 장면이다. 그것은 용의자에게서 추출된 다른 샘플과 비교된다. 그것이 꼭 들어맞게 되면 수사는 성공적인 것이다. 서로 다른 범죄 현장에서 추출된 DNA 샘플들이 연관되어 국가 DNA 데이터베이스에 수집된다. 이 국가 DNA 데이터베이스는 범죄 현장에서 나온 다른 샘플들과 비교하기 위해 미국의 모든 경찰관이 사용할 수 있다.

○ 문단에 가장 어울리는 제목을 찾는 문제이다. DNA의 정의라든가 국가 DNA 데이터베이스가 부분적으로 언급되어 있기는 하지만 제목으로 쓰이기에는 국지적인 내용이므로 (b)와 (c)는 답이 될 수 없다. DNA 샘플의 비교 또한 부분적으로 다루어졌지만 전체를 아우를 수 있는 제목으로는 (a) 범죄수사에서의 DNA의 사용이 알맞다.

abbreviated 단축된, 축약된, 짧게 한 Deoxyribonucleic Acid 디옥시리보핵산 genetic code 유전자 코드 detection 발견, 간파, 탐지, 발각 suspect 용의자 match 필적하는 것, 대등한 것

93 As a leading source of news, TNS has provided critical information to media outlets, businesses, organizations and governments for a quarter of a century. We bring the essential news stories from around the world and cover a wide scope of news events. We try to maintain a balanced approach to reporting by talented journalists and a dedicated staff. The international edition of our website provides you the precise information and exclusive analysis on global issues in a constantly updated fashion. Our headquarters is located in Atlanta, Georgia, and we have bureaus worldwide. If you have comments on our articles or questions about how to use our website, please click here.

Q Which of the following is NOT true about TNS?

(a) It was established more than 20 years ago.
(b) It has an international website.
(c) It is a local broadcasting company.
(d) It produces news stories worldwide.

TNS는 대표적인 뉴스 원천으로서 사반세기 동안 매체 통로와 사업체, 기관, 정부들에 중요 정보를 제공해 왔습니다. 우리는 세계 방방곡곡으로부터 주요 뉴스거리를 전달하며 넓은 폭의 뉴스 사건들을 다루고 있습니다. 우리는 재능 있는 언론인들과 헌신적인 직원들과 함께 뉴스를 전달하는 데 균형 있는 접근방식을 유지하려고 애쓰고 있습니다. 우리 웹사이트의 세계판은 여러분께 글로벌 이슈들에 대한 정확한 정보와 독점적인 분석을 계속 업데이트되는 버전으로 전해 드립니다. 우리 본부는 조지아 주의 애틀란타에 위치해 있으며, 세계 곳곳에 지부가 있습니다. 우리 기사에 대한 의견이 있으시거나 우리 웹사이트 이용에 관한 질문이 있으시면 여기를 클릭하십시오.

○ 본문에서 TNS의 역사가 a quarter of a century(사반세기)라고 했으므로 (a)의 20년 이상이라는 언급과 일치한다. 문단의 마지막 문단으로 보아 이 글이 쓰여져 있는 곳이 TNS의 국제판 웹사이트라는 것을 알 수 있으므로 (b)는 맞는 말이다. 세계 곳곳에 지부가 있다는 언급으로 보아 지방 방송국이 아니므로 (c)는 옳지 않다. 따라서 정답이다. 문단 내용으로 보아 세계적인 뉴스거리를 제공한다고 한 (d) 또한 맞는 말이다.

source 원천, 소스, 근원, 출처　**outlet** 통로, 출구, 배출구, 수단　**quarter** 4분의 1, 25센트(화폐)　**scope** 범위, 여지, 넓이, 폭　**dedicated** 헌신적인, 일신을 바친, 전용의　**exclusive** 독점적인, 배타적인, 한정적인　**headquarters** 본부, 본사

---

94 Erick Forman, a 23-year old Starbucks barista, was four hours into his shift when he was approached by Caroline Kaker, the chain's Bloomington-based district manager. She pulled him aside and broke the news that Starbucks gave him the ax. Forman was taken aback. Sure, two weeks earlier, he had shown up a half-hour late and was issued a written warning. But that wasn't why Forman was dismissed today. Some employees are given half a dozen or more warnings before receiving a final one. Management decided to get rid of him after learning that Forman had discussed the warning with co-workers. In fact there was another topic Forman had discussed with peers, one not explicitly mentioned in the notice of discharge; unionizing.

23세의 Starbucks 바리스타인 Erick Forman이 근무 교대 후 4시간째 일하고 있을 때 Bloomington 구역 매니저인 Caroline Kaker가 다가왔다. 그녀는 그를 구석으로 부르더니, Starbucks사가 그를 해고했다는 소식을 전했다. Forman은 깜짝 놀랐다. 확실히 2주 전에 그가 30분 늦게 출근한 적이 있어서 경고장이 발급된 적이 있긴 하다. 그러나 오늘 Forman이 해고된 이유는 그게 아니었다. 일부 고용인들은 최종 경고장을 받기 전에 6장 이상의 경고장을 받기도 한다. 경영진은 Management이 경고에 대해 동료들과 토론을 벌인 사실을 알고, 그를 해고하기로 결정했다. 사실 해고장에 명시적으로 언급되지 않았지만 Forman이 동료들과 논의한 화제가 하나 더 있었다: 바로 노조에 가입하는 것이다.

○ Erick Forman이 해고된 결정적 원인은 노조 가입을 동료들과 논의한 것이며, 지각과 관련된 경고장은 해고의 빌미에 지나지 않았으므로 정답은 (d)이다. 근무 중 잡담을 나눈 것은 아니므로 (a)는 답이 아니며, 바리스타로서의 능력에 대해서는 언급된 바 없으므로 (b)도 답이 아니다. 직장을 자주 결근한 것이 아니라, 30분 늦게 출근한 적이 1회 있으므로 (c)도 답이 될 수 없다.

Q Which of the following is the decisive reason for Forman's layoff?

(a) Chatting while on duty
(b) Incompetence as a barista
(c) Frequent absence from work
(d) Involvement in an organization

---

95 Vincent van Gogh created over 30 self-portraits during his life time. It seems that he depicted his face as it appeared in the mirror. The main reason he painted his own portrait was that he couldn't pay models to pose for portraits. Also, there were not many people who commissioned him to do portraits. However, for him, painting self-portrait was not only a way of making money and exploring a variety of painting styles and techniques but also a great vehicle to introspection. His self-portraits tell us a lot about his development as both an artist and an individual.

Q Which of the following is true, according to the passage?

(a) Gogh painted self-portraits though he could hire models for portraits.
(b) The right side in his self-portrait is the left side of his face in reality.
(c) Most of his self-portraits were painted with the same styles.
(d) Painting self-portraits was an important method of making money.

Vincent van Gogh는 그의 생애 동안 30여 점의 자화상을 제작했다. 그는 거울에 비친 자신의 얼굴을 그린 것으로 보인다. 그가 자신의 초상화를 그린 주된 이유는 초상화를 위해 포즈를 취해 줄 모델을 고용할 비용이 없었기 때문이다. 또한 그에게 초상화를 의뢰하는 사람들도 많지 않았다. 하지만 그에게 있어 자화상을 그리는 것은 돈을 벌거나 다양한 회화 기법과 작법을 탐구해 보는 것뿐 아니라 자기 성찰을 할 수 있는 좋은 기제였다. 그의 자화상들은 우리에게 그의 예술가로서만이 아니라 한 개인으로서의 발전에 대해서 많은 것을 말해준다.

○ Van Gogh가 자화상을 그리게 된 것은 모델료를 지급할 형편이 못 되었기 때문이라고 했으므로 (a)는 답이 될 수 없다. 그는 자화상을 그리는 과정을 통해 다양한 회화 작법을 탐구해 보았다고 했으므로 (c)또한 답이 될 수 없다. 그가 거울에 비친 자신의 얼굴을 그렸다고 했으므로 그림 속 얼굴의 좌우가 실제와 바뀌어 있다는 (b)는 정답이 된다.

96 Learned helplessness is a mental state in which a human being does not remove himself from stressful, dangerous or even harmful situations, even if they are "escapable," presumably through having learned that situational control is generally out of his hands. Many studies show that it can be minimized by "immunization" focused on increasing one's awareness of previous positive experiences. One of the causes for learned helplessness is emotional abuse, which can range from verbal abuse to more subtle tactics like repeated denial of emotional needs. As things happens in brain washing, emotional abuse wears away at the victim's self-esteem.

Q What can be inferred about emotional abuse according to the passage?

(a) Emotional abusers have low self-esteem, too.
(b) It is difficult to detect because it is domestic violence.
(c) Legal intervention is required to protect the victim from further harm.
(d) Recall of successful experiences helps the victim regain his self-confidence.

학습된 무기력은 상황에 대한 통제가 자신의 능력 밖이라는 것을 경험한 사람이 벗어날 수 있는 상황에서도 스트레스가 많고, 위험하거나 심지어 해로운 상황에서도 물러나려 하지 않는 정신 상태를 말한다. 많은 연구에 따르면 그것은 과거의 긍정적인 경험에 대한 인식을 늘려주는 것에 초점을 맞춘 "면역요법"에 의해 최소화될 수 있다. 학습된 무기력의 원인들 중 하나는 언어적 학대부터 정서적 욕구를 반복해서 거부하는 보다 미묘한 방법에 이르는 정서적 학대이다. 세뇌에서 보듯이, 정서적 학대는 피해자의 자아존중감을 손상시킨다.

○ 학습된 무기력에 대한 치료방법 중 과거의 긍정적 경험의 회상을 통한 인지치료에 대해 설명하고 있으며, 학습된 무기력을 앓고 있는 사람은 자아존중감이 낮으므로 정답은 (d)가 된다. 낮은 자아존중감은 정서적 학대의 가해자의 특징이 아닌 피해자의 특징이므로 (a)는 답이 아니며, (b)와 (c)는 언급된 바 없다.

learned helplessness 학습된 무기력 remove oneself 물러나다, 떠나다 presumably 아마, 추측컨대 out of one's hands 감당할 수 없는 minimize 최소화하다 immunization 면역되게 함, 면제, 예방주사 tactics 책략, 술책, 방책 wear away at ~을 닳아 없어지게 만들다 intervention 중재, 조정, 사이에 끼어들기 recall 회상

---

97 Emergency situations can occur all of a sudden and they usually require fast and appropriate action. Hospitals use emergency codes to inform their staff about various emergency situations quickly and precisely. The use of codes is also aimed to avoid possible misunderstandings. The codes are often displayed by color, and different color codes represent different events at different hospitals. For example, Code White is used to indicate a pediatric medical emergency in New Jersey, U.S., and a violent patient in Canada.

Q What does Code White imply in Canada?

(a) a pediatric medical emergency
(b) a patient who needs resuscitation
(c) a violent patient
(d) a staff's misunderstanding

위급 상황들은 갑자기 발생할 수 있어서 통상적으로 신속하고 적절한 대처가 필요하다. 병원들은 직원들에게 다양한 위급 상황에 대해 빠르고 정확하게 정보를 전달하기 위해 위급 신호를 이용한다. 신호의 사용은 또한 발생 가능한 오해를 피하고자 하는 목적도 있다. 신호는 종종 색으로 표시되는데, 병원마다 서로 다른 사안에 대해 다른 색의 신호들을 사용한다. 예를 들어 흰색 신호가 미국의 뉴저지에서는 소아과 의료적인 응급 상황을, 캐나다에서는 폭력적인 환자를 나타내기 위해 사용되는 식이다.

○ 서로 다른 색의 기호가 병원마다 다른 사안을 나타낸다는 언급 후에 예시된 두 지역 중 하나가 문제로 출제되었다. 흰색 기호는 뉴저지에서는 소아과적인 응급 상황을, 캐나다에서는 폭력적인 환자를 나타낸다.

emergent 응급의, 위기의 appropriate 적절한, 어울리는 충당하다 precisely 정확하게, 정밀하게 misunderstanding 오해, 의견차이 represent 나타내다, 의미하다, 대표하다, 상징하다 pediatric 소아과적인, 소아과의 resuscitation 인공호흡

98 In contrast to the worldwide reputation of the Academy Awards, it is reproached by many critics due to its racist and sexist disposition. Until 2008, neither black nor female directors have ever received an Academy Award for Best Achievement in Directing, except for only one black director, John Singleton, who was ever nominated in 1992. Since Sidney Poitier won a Best Performance by an Actor in a Leading Role in 1963, there had been no African American winners for this part up to year 2002.

Q Which is most likely to follow this passage?

(a) Criticism of the Academy Awards' biased view

(b) Examples of prejudice against women in the Academy Awards

(c) Story on an African American director who first won Best Director

(d) Documents for how black people have struggled for winning the awards

아카데미상은 세계적인 명성과는 대조적으로 인종차별적이고 성차별적인 성향으로 많은 비평가들에게 비난을 받고 있다. 2008년까지 어느 흑인 감독이나 여자 감독도 아카데미 감독상을 수상한 적이 없다. 단지 John Singleton라는 흑인 감독이 1992년에 후보로 추천된 적이 있을 뿐이다. Sidney Poitier가 1963년에 남우주연상을 수상한 이래 2002년까지 남우주연상을 수상한 흑인 배우가 없었다.

◑ 첫 문장에서 아카데미상은 인종차별적이고 성차별적인 성향으로 비난을 받고 있다고 한 뒤, 흑인 감독과 흑인 배우들이 상을 좀처럼 수상하지 못했다는 얘기가 나온다. 따라서 이것은 인종차별의 예가 되므로 이어서 성차별의 예가 나올 것이기에 정답은 (b)가 된다. 이미 아카데미상의 편견에 대해 비판하고 있으므로 (a)는 정답이 아니고, 아직 감독상을 수상한 흑인 감독은 없으므로 (c)도 정답이 될 수 없다. (d)는 흑인들이 상을 받기 위해서 얼마나 애써 왔는지에 관한 기록을 언급하겠다는 건데, 본문에 이를 유추할 만한 단서가 없으므로 정답이 될 수 없다.

in contrast to ~와 대조적으로, ~와 달리 reputation 평판, 명성 reproach 비난하다, 꾸짖다 critic 비평가, 평론가 (criticism 비평, 비판) due to ~때문에 racist 인종 차별의, 인종 차별적인 sexist 성차별적인 disposition 성질, 기질 director (영화의) 감독 Best Achievement in Directing 감독상 except for ~을 제외하고 a Best Performance by an Actor in a Leading Role 남우주연상 up to ~까지 biased 편견을 가진 prejudice 편견, 선입관 struggle for 애쓰다, ~하려고 분투하다

---

99 Flexible thought is one of the most important characteristics we are required to achieve to manage one's business successfully. (a) Nowadays, an idea of flexible working hours comes into the spotlight and gets positive evaluations. (b) Flexible working hours have been in place for years in some fields, such as computer-related companies and publishing companies. (c) For the last three years, researches have reported that more and more employers and workers are considering flexible working hours as an innovative way of increasing productivity and competitive power. (d) Moreover, in last month's survey, two-thirds of employees are either compassionate or very obstructive of flexible working hours.

유연한 사고는 우리가 사업체를 성공적으로 운영하기 위해 필요한 가장 중요한 요소 중 하나이다. 요즘 자유 근무 시간제라는 아이디어가 각광을 받고 있고 긍정적인 평가도 받고 있다. 자유 근무 시간제는 몇 년간 컴퓨터 관련 기업체들이나 출판 기업들과 같은 일부 분야에서 행해졌다. 지난 3년간 학술 연구들이 발표한 바에 따르면 더욱 많은 고용인들과 노동자들이 자유 근무 시간제에 대해 생산성과 경쟁력을 키우는 혁신적인 방법으로 생각하고 있다. 게다가, 지난달에 이루어진 설문조사에서는 피고용인의 3분의2가 자유 근무 시간제에 대해 찬성하거나 아주 반대하고 있다.

◑ 자유 근무 시간제에 대해서 긍정적인 서술을 하고 있는 문단이다. 최근 들어 이 아이디어가 각광 받고 있고 학술 연구들이 생산성과 경쟁력 향상에 도움이 되는 것으로 발표했다는 말에 이어 나오는 접속사 moreover을 주의 깊게 볼 필요가 있다. 앞에서 언급된 내용에 대해 긍정하면서 내용을 덧붙이는 진술이 오는 것이 적절한데, obstructive라는 표현이 내용과 거리가 멀다.

flexible 유연한, 나긋나긋한, 융통성 있는 characteristic 특질, 특색, 특성 manage 운영하다, 다루다, 관리하다 positive 긍정적인, 호의적인 research 학술 연구, 조사, 연구 productivity 생산성 competitive power 경쟁력 obstructive 의사에 반하는

100 Red and Blue Oceans are a metaphor for the market space. (a) A strategy formed within a definite economic structure, controlled by demand and availability of resources, is termed Red Ocean Strategy, which represents all of the existing industries in a market place—the known market space. (b) As the market space gets jammed with companies trying to outperform their contenders, cutthroat competition made the market blood-red. (c) In contrast, Blue Ocean Strategy makes the competition irrelevant by capturing or creating new demand rather than grabbing for it. (d) Blue Ocean Strategy is symbolic of the vast potential of uncontested market space.

레드 오션이나 블루 오션은 시장에 대한 비유이다. 일정한 경제 구조 내에서 형성되고, 자원의 수요와 유효성의 지배를 받는 전략을 레드 오션 전략이라 하는데, 이는 시장에 존재하는 모든 산업을 나타낸다. 즉 이미 알려진 시장을 가리킨다. 시장이 경쟁자들을 능가하려는 회사들로 넘쳐남에 따라 치열한 경쟁이 시장을 핏빛으로 물들였다. 반면에 블루 오션 전략은 수요를 잡으려고 애쓰기보다 새로운 수요를 포착하거나 창출해냄으로써 경쟁 자체를 무의미하게 만든다. 블루 오션은 경쟁 상대가 없는 시장의 무한한 잠재력을 상징한다.

○ red와 blue라는 색을 이용하여, 기존의 경쟁으로 가득 찬 시장에서 경쟁하는 red ocean과 새로운 수요를 창출해 내는 데 경쟁 상대 자체가 없는 새로운 시장인 blue ocean을 대비시켜서 설명하는 지문이다. 그러나 (b)는 치열한 경쟁이 시장을 핏빛으로 물들였다는 내용으로 의미 설명에서 벗어난 부분이 된다.

metaphor 은유, 비유 strategy 전략, 방법 definite 일정한, 한정된 represent 나타내다, 표현하다 jam 쑤셔 넣다, 꽉 채우다 outperform (기계 따위가) ~보다 성능이 뛰어나다 contender 경쟁자, 경쟁 상대 cutthroat 잔인한, 무자비한, 격렬한 irrelevant 부적절한, 엉뚱한, 아무 관련이 없는 grab for ~을 움켜쥐려 하다 vast 광대한, 막대한, 끝없이 넓은 potential 가능성, 잠재력 uncontested 경쟁상대가 없는, 겨룰 사람이 없는, 명백한

T
E
P
S

최소시간 투자로 최대효과를 노려라!

- 청해 · 문법 · 어휘 · 독해 4영역을 최소단위로 반복 연습
- 매회 40문항 30분에 소화하도록 수업 · 강의 · 자습 최적화
- 최근 이슈를 문제화함으로써 가장 유망한 예상문제집으로 구성
- 매회 주요 문법 Tip과 카테고리별 어휘 · 표현 제시
- 적절한 해석, 탄탄한 해설, 자세한 어구풀이로 효율성 강화
- 언제라도 자신의 성적을 예측할 수 있는 최소단위 구성과 채점법

더 이상의 교재는 없다!
독해 실력에 날개를 달아라!

실제 강의 시수에 최적화된 완벽한 구성!
다양한 난이도의 참신한 지문으로 선택의 폭이 넓은 교재!

- 실질적인 지문과 다양한 주제
- 독해력 향상을 위한 9가지 문제 형식
- 독해력과 직결된 9가지 핵심 문법 정리
- 독해력을 위한 8가지 핵심 구조 파악
- 독해 지문을 활용한 영작

상위권을 위한 필독서
AIM HIGH Reading

In-Depth Lab 지음
4×6배판(188×257) | 각권 150면 내외
부록 : 해설집 · 전 지문 음원 제공(다운로드)
각권 값 **8,500원**

Active Curriculum
for Successful Listening

실제 강의에 최적화된 구성, 완벽한 난이도 배치
선생님과 학생들이 원하던 청취교재가 왔다!

- 귀를 뚫어주는 Sound & Sound 학습법 채택, 소리를 듣고 바로 이해
- 모든 문제를 8가지 유형으로 분석, 어떤 문제에도 완벽대응.
- 핵심 정보 메모로 듣기 전에 다음 내용을 떠올리게 하는 Listening Note 학습법
- 철저하게 계산된 주제문과 대화 형태, 지문 길이로 실력별 학습효과 배가
- 중요 구문 Dictation으로 듣지 못했던 문장 다시 한 번 더블 체크

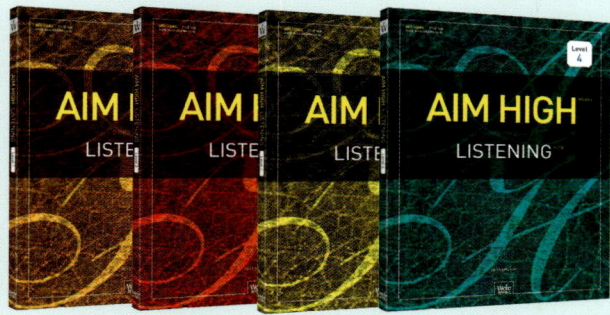

Active Curriculum for Successful Listening
AIM HIGH Listening

In-Depth Lab 지음
국배판(210×297) | 각권 220면 내외
Cassete Tape 교재 별매
각권 값 **12,500원**